AF428427

A MORAL HISTORY OF
WESTERN
SOCIETY

An Historical Review of the
West's Great Political, Social,
Cultural, and Intellectual Legacy

Volume Two

From the Mid-1800s to the Present

Miles Huntley Hodges

ISBN 979-8-9900799-4-6 (Hardback)
ISBN 979-8-9900799-5-3 (Paperback)
ISBN 979-8-9900799-6-0 (Laminate)
ISBN 979-8-9900799-7-7 (eBook)

Library of Congress Control Number: 2023924528

spiritualpilgrim.net

CONTENTS

CHAPTER TWELVE

GLORY

✳ ✳ ✳

THE FRENCH SECOND EMPIRE

Louis Napoleon (Napoleon III). Although Louis Napoleon was the nephew of the great Napoleon Bonaparte, he was very different from him in temperament ... and ability. Yet the name Napoleon was what brought him to his position of French leadership ... and what forced him to move in directions that he was really not able to manage successfully. He did his best when he did little.

Because of the growing disillusionment among the middle and working classes of France with their "citizen king" Louis-Philippe, a highly romanticized cult of Napoleon (and thus things Napoleonic) began to infect France during the 1840s. When Napoleon's son died in 1832 (Napoleon II), the Bonapartists looked to Louis Napoleon to take the lead. Being an individual with a love for the dramatic, Louis Napoleon was more than happy to do so ... in 1836 and then again in 1840 attempting to overthrow the government of Louis-Philippe by military action. Both efforts failed ... resulting in his brief banishment in the first instance and his imprisonment in the second. But while in prison he was active writing political tracts which kept the Bonapartist dream alive. Then in 1846 he escaped prison by disguising himself as a prison worker, fleeing through Belgium to London ... where he waited for a new opportunity to arise.

In 1848, with Louis-Philippe's abdication, that moment had arrived. He moved immediately to France, but let Bonapartists open the doors for him politically ... being elected to multiple seats in the new (Second) Republic's National Assembly. His name was then put forward for the Presidency ... in which he was up against only the conservative candidate, General Cavaignac, who had fired on Paris protesters when Louis-Philippe was first in trouble. By a 5 to 1 margin, the popular vote in December (1848) went to Louis Napoleon as the Republic's new president.

The birth of the Second Empire. But once in office Louis Napoleon began to move on his dream of being head of a restored Empire. The conservative majority in the Assembly (which disliked the populism of Louis Napoleon) did the job for him, passing voting restrictions which in essence took the vote away from a third (the working classes) of the voting population. Napoleon played on the anger of the lower classes by touring the country and holding public meetings among the adoring masses. He then challenged the Assembly to restore the votes to those taken off the roles, which the Assembly refused to do ... giving the appearance of Louis Napoleon as being the true champion of the people.

He was by this time ending his four-year term limit as president and knew it was time to act. On the night of 1-2 December (1851) he had officers arrest a large number of civil and military opponents and awakened France the next morning to the news that the Assembly had been dismissed, universal suffrage restored, and a new constitution was in the making, one which would give the president (himself) virtually all governing powers for a term of ten years.

The reaction to the news in Paris proved to be timid ... though resistance in the French countryside was substantial. Then on December 21, the French voted an overwhelming approval of the new constitution ... and a year later also voted overwhelmingly to re-designate the head of the country as Emperor rather than President. And thus the French Second Empire was born (December 1852), with Louis Napoleon as Emperor Napoleon III.

The glory years. The amazing prosperity that followed in the next years settled the French into a political calm not experienced in a long time. New commercial banks were founded, canals dug, railroads laid out, and steamships added to the French commercial fleet. The emperor and his Spanish wife Eugénie were active in improving and increasing the health, safety, and nurture (hospitals, orphanages, convalescent homes) of the French working class. The Paris capital was rebuilt extensively by Baron Georges-Eugène Haussmann with new and elegant public and private buildings, tree-lined boulevards, parks, bridges, public buses, a new water system, sewers, paved streets, gas street lights, etc. ... turning Paris into the most elegant city in the world.

The Crimean War (1854-1856). Being a Napoleon, of course, the emperor could not avoid even in his own mind being compared to his famous uncle, the fabled general of old. Louis Napoleon felt compelled to measure up somehow. And that meant military action in some form or other.

He soon found his opportunity when Tsar Nicholas began pressuring the Turkish "Sick Man of Europe" (the Ottoman sultan) to have himself named as "Protector" of the Christian subjects and Christian places of pilgrimage inside the Ottoman Empire. Napoleon saw this as a move to replace Catholic supervision with Orthodox supervision ... and the British saw this as simply a ploy of the Russian Tsar to seize land in the Balkan Peninsula ... and even along the Mediterranean coast if possible. Thus both France and Britain (and the smaller Italian Kingdom of Sardinia-Piedmont) moved to support the Turkish sultan against Russian aggression. When the Tsar moved Russian troops into Moldavia and Wallachia, the allies responded with their own counter-move against Russia (March 1854). Actually the Turks on their own managed to turn the Russians back when they attempted to march on Constantinople (Istanbul) ... and it looked as if the matter had resolved itself as a standoff.

But the British were not content to let it end there, and decided to carry the war to the Russians, in particular to Sevastopol in the Crimea where a Russian naval fleet was based. The British wanted to end any possibility that the Russians might get into a position to challenge the British domination of the Eastern Mediterranean ... where British commerce had to pass to reach India and the huge British interests there. Thus the allies combined forces and landed about 60,000 troops in Crimea in order to seize the Russian naval base. But they wasted valuable time getting moving once on land, allowing the Russians to move their own troops into a strong, defensive position. Thus the attack stalled ... and at Balaclava the attack even turned into a grand disaster for them.[*] Then a hard winter – for which the allies were totally unprepared – set in, creating even more anguish and death than had the guns of the Russians.

Fighting resumed the next spring, but it was not until September that the Russian fortress at Sevastopol was finally taken by the allies. Nonetheless the war dragged on through another winter ... until finally in early 1856 the Russians called for a peace settlement. The allies wisely accepted the request, for their own citizens were tiring greatly from a war that seemed to yield nothing but dead and wounded. Thus the powers gathered in March to sign the Treaty of Paris (March 1856).

Overall, the war cleared the Black Sea of a Russian navy ... at least for a while. It undercut the great power status of Russia. It shattered the basic unity that had characterized the Concert of Europe, not only isolating Russia among the Big Five powers of Europe, but also undercutting Austria ... which had failed to come to the aid of its formerly close ally Russia. Smarting from this Austrian betrayal, Russia would return the snub when Austria found itself in trouble, particularly in the face of a rising Prussian power to the north in Germany. Also, although the Ottoman Empire came

---

[*]This was the event that inspired the English Poet Laureate Alfred Lord Tennyson to write his famous poem, "The Charge of the Light Brigade."

out on the "winning" side, it clearly revealed that it did so only because of the support of England and France. Indeed, it highlighted the Ottoman Empire as the "sick man of Europe" ... inviting various ethnic minorities in the Empire to begin to push for their own national autonomy within, even independence from, the Ottoman Empire.

Yet most importantly for Louis Napoleon, it restored France to the status of being the strongest continental power in Europe. It was thus at this point that Emperor Napoleon III reached the height of his popularity at home and glory abroad.

✳ ✳ ✳

THE FOUNDING OF THE ITALIAN NATION-STATE
(THE *RISORGIMENTO*)

Since the fall of the Roman empire, "Italy" was more a geographic designation on a map of Europe than an actual political entity. Italy – like Germany – was made up of a number of small but very independent states ... including the Pope's own Papal States. Being so divided, Italy was thus easy prey for the larger powers of Europe, Spain and France ... joined eventually by Austria.

Italy got caught up in the political turmoil of the French Revolution, especially when in 1796 Napoleon Bonaparte brought his French army into the region and established something of a Republic which briefly included most of Italy ... until a peasant reaction in Napoleon's absence returned Italy to its former status quo (including the restoration of the Papal States and Austria's dominance). But once Napoleon took full power in France he returned to Italy (1800) and brought quickly most of northern Italy again under French control. He established in 1805 the title of "King of Italy" and then had his troops seize the southern Kingdom of Naples (1806), adding it to the Italian kingdom. In 1809 he completed the unification of Italy by seizing Rome and the Papal States. At this point, whether they were for or against Napoleon, Italians clearly understood the importance – and the possibilities – of a unified Italian state.

When Napoleon was finally overthrown in 1815, Italy was divided into nine states ... and efforts were made by Metternich and the "Big Five" of Europe to restore Italy to its pre-Napoleonic social-cultural status. But young Italians had little love for this situation. Secret societies were formed, chief among them the Carbonari, for the purpose of instituting a unified Italian state – by force if necessary. But failed uprisings in 1820 and 1831 brought great discouragement.

Nonetheless they persisted. And by the mid-1800s it appeared that the possibilities of a unified Italian state hinged greatly on the efforts of three key individuals: Giuseppe Mazzini, Count Camillo di Cavour, and Giuseppe Garibaldi (with Victor Emmanuel II also important).

Mazzini.   The young and energetic intellectual Mazzini, with strong republican loyalties, was imprisoned in 1830, escaped, founded from his exile in France an organization called Young Italy (1832) which spread rapidly in membership and reach in Italy. He wrote countless pamphlets brought secretly into Italy, outlining the noble nature of a "Risorgimento" ("resurgence" or "rising again") ... involving the political unification of all Italy. Thus it was that he himself became something of its "soul" in the process.

His cause was naturally opposed by others – those wanting a national monarchy rather than a republic ... and those who wanted an independent but federal Italy of unified states under the authority of the pope. Indeed when the liberal-minded Pius IX took the papal position in 1846 this seemed to be the most likely path that Italian independence would take... until the huge support of many Italians for the ideals of the 1848 revolutions sweeping Europe shocked the pope. As we noted previously, Pius was bitterly opposed to such democratic or republican instincts and turned himself into a full reactionary.

Cavour ... and the Kingdom of Sardinia-Piedmont.   The uprisings of 1848 indeed brought movement, at least briefly, toward the ideals of Mazzini and Young Italy. All through northern Italy the Austrians and their local colleagues were driven from power, and at first the rulers of Tuscany and Naples – and the pope – joined in support of this nationalist movement. But strong disagreements as to what direction Italy was to take next crippled the movement, and Naples and the Papal States pulled out of the movement altogether. This left only the liberal-minded King Charles Albert of the Kingdom of Sardinia-Piedmont to continue the battle as the Austrians and their colleagues regained their positions in northern Italy. By 1849 the Austrians had defeated Charles Albert and his smaller army ... and the effort on behalf of Italian independence seemed to have come to an end. But the Italian hopeful would not forget the sacrificial effort of Sardinia-Piedmont in support of the cause.

A tired Charles Albert turned his throne over to his son, Victor Emmanuel II (1848), who continued his father's liberal policies. Best of all, he had the wisdom in 1852 to pick as his prime minister the highly capable Cavour. Cavour understood that Italy's destiny was closely connected to Sardinia-Piedmont's leadership and immediately set himself to the task of building up the social muscle (industrial, commercial, military) of the kingdom. He also understood the importance of diplomatic connections ... and thus engaged Sardinia-Piedmont fully in the Crimean War as an ally with France and Britain. Cavour even sent his attractive cousin, the Countess Castiglione, to woo (successfully) Napoleon III.

Now, in alliance with France, Cavour was ready to move against Austria in northern and central Italy. He cleverly drew Austria into declaring war (1859) to which France and Sardinia-Piedmont responded by routing the Austrian forces at Magenta and Solferino (June). Then, just as Austria was about to be run out of Italy, Napoleon III, seeing his own armies badly bloodied by the action, decided to conclude his own separate armistice with the Austrian Emperor Franz Joseph, ignoring his promise to Victor Emmanuel to fight until Austria was run out of all of Italy. However, in its treaty with France, Austria ceded much of its holdings in northern Italy to Sardinia-Piedmont ... but was allowed to keep Venice and its large holdings in the northeast.

While this was a cruel blow to Cavour ... it was also a hugely foolish move on Napoleon's part. Napoleon did get the regions of Nice and Savoy added to France (given up by Sardinia-Piedmont as part of the deal). But his actions so strongly in favor of Austria raised questions about his reliability as an ally and as a player in Europe's diplomatic games. It also seemed in the eyes of liberal French to be a betrayal of the hope of a spread of liberal political philosophy to the rest of Europe ... and to Italy in particular. And on the other hand, the alliance with Cavour, and his clear goal of absorbing all of Italy (including the Papal States) into a liberal Italy, alienated Napoleon III from the strongly Catholic instincts of the French countryside. His Italian policy would thus mark the beginning of Napoleon III's political decline.

For Cavour however, things worked out better. Inspired by his actions, a number of Italian states in northern Italy took the initiative themselves in 1860 to oust their Austrian overlords and declare their union with Sardinia-Piedmont.

Garibaldi. At the same time (1860) activity of the same nature was stirring in the south of Italy. At its head was the adventuresome Garibaldi, a long-time rebel in favor of political liberalism, who had escaped to South America after a failed uprising in Genoa in 1830 and there learned the art of guerrilla warfare. He returned in 1847 in time to participate in the 1848 uprising, put down by Napoleon III, which forced him to flee Italy a second time. He made a small fortune in America and returned to live on a small island off the coast of Sardinia in 1854. Then when in 1859 things began moving again in the form of a revived Italian nationalism, he organized in Naples a small army of "Red Shirts" and in 1860 moved them to Sicily and then, accompanied by Victor Emmanuel, to Naples to end the Bourbon Kingdom of the Two Sicilies ... and bring the region into union with Victor Emmanuel's kingdom. In 1861 a new Italian national parliament then met at Turin to organize the new Kingdom of Italy ... and put it to a vote of the Italian people. By an overwhelming majority, the Kingdom and its constitution ... and Victor Emmanuel as its king ... were approved by the people.

This left the question of Venice (still under the Austrians) and the status of Rome and the Latium region unanswered. Wars elsewhere would soon provide the answers. When in 1866 Prussia defeated Austria in a struggle over German leadership, Austria was forced to give Venice (and the entire region of Venetia) over to the new kingdom of Italy as part of the peace agreement. Then when Prussia engaged France in war in 1870, Napoleon III was forced to pull his troops out of Rome, and the Pope lost his military protector. This allowed Victor Emmanuel then to hold an Italian plebiscite on the matter, with a majority of Italians voting in favor of attaching both Rome and Latium to the Italian Kingdom. This then allowed him to seize Rome and make it his new capital city, minus a very small area inside of Rome left to the Papacy – "Vatican City."

Thus it was that the Italian dream had just been fulfilled. The Italians now had their own kingdom, with Rome as its grand capital.

Pius IX (pope 1846-1878) fights back. The huge political loss by Pius of the Papal States to the new Kingdom of Italy turned him from something of a social Liberal to a very conservative – most would even say highly reactionary – Catholic leader. He excommunicated the Italian King Victor Emmanuel and the rest of the Italian political leadership for how they had terminated the Church's ability to carry out its long-standing responsibilities.

But at least the loss freed Pius to turn his attention to strictly religious matters, although he – and the popes that would follow for the next half century – remained deeply opposed politically to the new Italian state ... and would denounce it at every opportunity.

Early on Pius knew how to reach the hearts of Catholics everywhere – whether they be Italian, Spanish, Polish, Irish, German, Austrian, Belgian, French, American etc. – with his efforts in 1848 to elevate, through a papal encyclical, Jesus's mother Mary to the status of being totally sinless, most notably untouched by sexual intercourse,* having brought forward the Christ Child through a process of "immaculate conception." And being thus sin-free (from birth to death) she was herself well-situated to be sought devotedly for divine intercession on behalf of a confessing sinner.

However, this in turn raised the question: does the pope have the

---

*This inevitably raised the old question: who exactly then were the brothers and sisters of Jesus mentioned in Scripture (Mark 3:31-35, Mark 6:3, Galatians 1:19, etc.)?

right to decide such theological matters through the simple means of papal encyclicals – of which Pius had been issuing many? Thus in 1869 a council (the First Vatican Council) was called to decide the matter. And indeed it did. When the Council concluded its work the following year, it had confirmed very strongly the doctrine of "papal infallibility." The pope's words issued *ex cathedra* carried the full weight of Catholic Truth in all matters of faith and morals. Period.

But would this bold step forward of Catholic authority hold back the growing Secular trend clearly overtaking the West?

And what about the rising spirit of nationalism? National loyalties were clearly growing ever-stronger than traditional Christian loyalties. True, Westerners continued to identify themselves as "Christians." But what they truly seemed ready to stand on – and even die for – was their identities as Italians, Spanish, Polish, Irish, etc. Christian loyalties by no means held anywhere near the same position in the hearts of Westerners that rising national loyalties now did.

✳ ✳ ✳

BISMARCK AND THE NEW GERMANY

The *Zollverein*. As Italy had formerly been, Germany had long been more a geographic designation on the map of Europe than a single society. Linguistically the German language (in the form of many quite distinct dialects) had been something of a unifying factor ... thanks in great part to Luther's German Bible. But politically, Germany had long been split into a multitude of competing German states large and small ... some 300 of them! Napoleon had forcibly consolidated this vast number into 39 German states ... a configuration that was retained even after Napoleon's defeat. But that meant that in the early 1800s there were still 39 German states continuing to compete politically and economically, crippling German power.

A move towards union occurred when after the Napoleonic wars Prussia started to liberalize the tariffs among the German states ruled by the Hohenzollern king of Prussia.   But other German states were invited to join Prussia in some kind of expanding customs union. This finally led in 1834 to the creation of a grand customs union or *Zollverein*. Initially the Zollverein included 18 states. Austria was not part of the membership (Austria was unwilling to lower its high protective tariffs ... and Metternich was opposed to such a link with Prussia). But over the years other German states joined ... until by the early 1850s Austria was the only German state outside the Zollverein. Thus Germany was taking shape as a single entity ... at least economically. But such economics easily registered itself politically.

Bismarck vs. the German Liberals. The son of a Prussian Junker (minor nobleman), Otto von Bismarck came to public attention first as a delegate to the Prussian assembly or Diet that the Prussian king Frederick William IV had called in 1847 in response to liberal demands. Bismarck stood out from the Liberals in his strong defense of the sovereign rule of the Hohenzollern ... and in his belief that only the Hohenzollern monarchy had the call to unite all of Germany. In 1851 he was a Prussian representative to the Diet of the Austrian-dominated Germanic Confederation where he showed himself unwilling to bow to the Austrian domination of German politics. To Bismarck, only Prussia had the makings of true German leadership. He made his views well known not only to Austria and the rest of the German world, but also to Frederick William, whom he regularly consulted with in Berlin.

In 1857, when Frederick William was incapacitated by a massive stroke, his brother William (or Wilhelm) took over Prussian rule as Regent. But Wilhelm was of a more liberal mind-set and found Bismarck's politics so challenging to the prevailing liberal political mood that in 1859 he sent Bismarck off to Russia as ambassador. This effectively removed a frustrated Bismarck from the unfolding drama taking place in Italy and central Europe. But Bismarck used his time "on ice" in St. Petersburg to good effect, learning more about the intricacies of European diplomacy ... and building up a relationship with the Russian court that would later serve him well. He would also use that time to develop a close political relationship with Prussian generals Albrecht von Roon (Prussian Minister of War) and Helmut von Moltke (Prussian Military Chief of Staff). Then in 1862 Bismarck was sent to Paris as Prussian Ambassador, using his time there to become acquainted with the personal traits of Napoleon III ... and in a long visit to London, to familiarize himself with Britain's chief politicians, Prime Minister Palmerston, Foreign Secretary Russell and Conservative Party leader Benjamin Disraeli.

The situation in Berlin began to swing in Bismarck's favor when in 1861 Frederick William died and Wilhelm I became fully Prussian king ... and found himself increasingly at odds with the Liberals in the Prussian Diet. A crisis developed in 1862 between Wilhelm and the Diet when the Liberals refused to fund the strengthening of the Prussian army. The situation reached a point where Wilhelm was ready to abdicate, when Bismarck, called to Berlin by Roon, arrived in time to talk him out of it. At this point Wilhelm was ready to entrust the strong-willed Bismarck with the position of president of his ministry (effectively, prime minister or chancellor). Now Bismarck could get to work building his long-sought united Germany under Prussian command. With Roon and Moltke at his side, Bismarck was about to show Europe how the game of politics and diplomacy is supposed to be played.

With respect to the Liberals' unwillingness to provide funding for the military, Bismarck simply ignored the Prussian constitution and continued to collect taxes on the basis of earlier legislation ... infuriating the Liberal Diet, which however seemed to have no answer to the overbearing Bismarck. Bismarck then tightened supervision of the press, causing him even greater unpopularity. But neither Bismarck – nor Wilhelm – were slowed up by popular opposition, even when a new Diet came to office with an even greater Liberal majority.

Ignoring his Liberal opposition, Bismarck had moved to strengthen greatly the Prussian military, explaining that:

> *Germany looks not to the liberalism of Prussia, but to its power.*
> *... The great questions of the time cannot be resolved by speeches*
> *and parliamentary majorities – that was the great mistake of 1848*
> *and 1849 – but by iron* (Eisen) *and blood* (Blut).

For the next four years (1862-1866) he was unquestionably the most hated person in Germany. But that was about to change.

The Schleswig-Holstein question and the Austro-Prussian War (1863-1866). Bismarck was looking for some pretext to put Austria to the test before the watchful eyes of the rest of Germany. In 1863 he found his opportunity when Frederick VII of Denmark died ... and a dispute arose over who should inherit the throne ... and in particular the Danish duchies of German-speaking Holstein and Schleswig (the southern half also with a German-speaking population). When the new Danish king Christian IX moved under a rising spirit of Danish nationalism to fully annex Schleswig, Bismarck reacted to this insult to the equally strong spirit of German nationalism and got Austria to join him (1864) in invading Denmark and forcing Christian to give up both provinces. Now the question remained of who should get which of the two duchies. Ultimately (1865) Austria took Holstein and Prussia took Schleswig.

But, as Bismarck anticipated, Austria began to encourage a German duke to claim the right to rule the duchies ... giving Bismarck the opportunity to depict Austria as trying to stir up liberal troubles in northern Germany. Claiming this to be simply a defensive move, Bismarck ordered his Prussian troops into Austria-occupied Holstein. The Austrians resisted ... and Bismarck (with his carefully cultivated Italian allies moving against Austria in Italy) easily crushed a divided Austrian army at Königgrätz (or Sadowa).

By this time the Germans had been stirred to intense patriotic nationalism (and Bismarck had become Germany's national hero, no longer its most hated citizen!). But Bismarck played a cool hand by refusing to let Prussian troops do any more damage to a crushed Austrian ego. To add further insult to injury, Bismarck was relatively generous to his defeated enemy, increasing greatly Prussia's political stature. In victory Prussia received additional German lands ... but none taken from Austria. Austria was forced only to pay a small indemnity to Prussia and to accord full rights to Prussia in Schleswig-Holstein. However Italy did receive Venetia from Austria as its reward for allying with Prussia in the conflict.

Austria also had to agree to the dissolution of the German Confederation – which Austria had long dominated – its place taken by a new huge North German Confederation – in which clearly Prussia would dominate (Austria was excluded from membership). According to the new constitution, member states would retain full sovereignty in domestic matters. As a federal union it would possess a legislature of an upper house (Bundesrat) representing the various member states and a lower house (Bundestag) representing the German voting public. Also the new North German Confederation would be headed by the Prussian king, who would also be charged with the conduct of the confederation's foreign diplomacy.

The Franco-Prussian War (1870-1871). Now it was time for Bismarck to bring the southern German states (still excluding Austria) into his newly forming Germany. Napoleon III would unwittingly facilitate that move. Napoleon had been expecting to be a Prussian ally in the conflict with Austria. He thus expected in compensation the extension of French territory in the south of Germany all the way to the Rhine River. But the war was over so quickly that he lost out on the payoff. He then complained that at least his neutrality deserved him such a reward. Bismarck tricked him into putting his demand in writing ... and then showed it to the southern German states, infuriating them and driving them into Prussia's arms as protector against such French ambitions. Now all Bismarck needed was an event – a French attack on Germany – to spark just those conditions, and complete the unification of all Germany.

That event was to soon develop around the matter of naming a successor to the Spanish throne after Queen Isabella was deposed by a Spanish revolt in 1868. A Hohenzollern Prussian prince Leopold was one of several possibilities ... causing Napoleon and France deep concern about a Prussian encirclement from the south and the east. When Leopold withdrew his name from the list, it looked as if Bismarck was not going to get the confrontation he was looking for. Napoleon was content to leave matters at that. But his meddlesome wife pushed for a Prussian pledge that no Hohenzollern would ever become a candidate for the Spanish throne. Wilhelm refused the request ... and then sent a telegram from Ems (where Wilhelm was vacationing) to Bismarck briefly explaining the event. Bismarck reworked the telegram a bit, making the French demand appear insulting to German pride ... and Wilhelm's reply insulting to French pride. He then sent the revised Ems telegram for publication in the official newspaper. It had the desired effect of stirring an already sore French national pride into full fury ... leading Napoleon and the French Parliament to declare war in mid-July 1870. But the Germans were now united behind Bismarck and ready to take on their old national foe, Napoleonic France.

Now appeared the huge differences in levels of political skill separating Bismarck and Napoleon III. Napoleon was led by the passions of the French, who believed that their troops would be in Berlin in a matter of mere weeks. Bismarck was the master of German opinion, not its servant. Bismarck had over the years carefully prepared his military for this major superpower confrontation. Napoleon's France was unprepared ... its officers, its equipment, its numbers of trained soldiers. Diplomatically, Bismarck had carefully laid the groundwork so that France would find itself isolated when it looked to former allies for help. The Austrians had been neutralized, not just by the shock of their loss to the Prussians in their recent war but because they were afraid that the Russians, who Bismarck had been cultivating as allies, might join any conflict against them. And Victor Emmanuel's Italy was now clearly a Prussian ally, understanding that with France occupied in a war with Prussia, the Pope would lose French protection ... and thus the Papal States would be ripe for the plucking by the new Kingdom of Italy. In short, Napoleon stood no chance of success in any conflict with Bismarck's Germany.

It did not take long for German superiority to register itself. A French army sent out to hit the Germans was itself hit in a series of battles that within a month had it surrounded (August). A second French army was sent out to relieve the first French army and it too was surrounded ... and destroyed (September 2) at Sedan, including Napoleon III who was captured trying to lead the French attack.

The news of the French defeat at Sedan was the signal for French politicians in Paris to take charge, to declare a provisional government or "Government of National Defense" of a new Third Republic (Napoleon III's Second Empire had simply vanished). Everyone expected the French and Germans at this point to meet for negotiations.

But Bismarck was not finished. He ordered his troops to march on Paris, which was fully surrounded before the end of the month. The French were now up in arms all around the country and the war dragged on. But Paris was soon starving and France was becoming increasingly chaotic. When in early February (1871) it became obvious that Léon Gambetta's French troops would not be able to break the German encirclement of Paris, the provisional government was finally forced to surrender.

Europe was shocked ... having expected the famous French army to make short work of the German army – rather than the opposite. The results for France were disastrous. As part of the terms of peace, France was required to turn over to Germany the border regions of Alsace and Lorraine, pay a large indemnity to Germany, and have the northern half of France occupied by German troops until the indemnity was paid up. To add further insult to France, a month earlier Wilhelm had been crowned the Emperor of the new German (Second) Empire at the Versailles Palace outside of Paris.

✳ ✳ ✳

VICTORIAN ENGLAND (1837-1901)

In 1837 an 18-year-old Victoria succeeded to her uncle William IV's throne as Queen of the United Kingdom of Great Britain and Ireland. Any doubts that she would be able to live up to the heavy duties laid on her by this inheritance were soon dispelled. She was studious in her approach to problems, devoted to the welfare of Great Britain and its people and wise in her choice of counselors. Consequently, she gave her people a long reign devoid of the kinds of turmoil that shook the countries of continental Europe.

Parliamentary leaders. Several major political figures stood out during this long period of British politics. In her early years the person who influenced her most was her German cousin and husband Albert (married in 1840), who shared her interests, her wisdom and her political skills. Also, in cooperation with whichever political party held the majority of seats in Parliament, she worked with a variety of influential prime ministers. In the early days that was principally the Whigs William Lamb, 2nd Viscount Melbourne and Henry John Temple, 3rd Viscount Palmerston ... and the Tory Robert Peel. After Albert's death in 1861 several other figures would play a key role during her reign: the Conservatives Benjamin Disraeli and Robert Cecil, Third Marquess of Salisbury, and the Liberal William Gladstone. Mostly the policies of these men differed only in detail and not in philosophy (though personally Victoria did not much care for Gladstone). Disraeli and Gladstone both worked hard over their long careers to bring British politics closer to the democratic ideal ... and to defeat the other (their personal rivalry was relentless). And both men seemed simply to alternate back and forth, in and out of power, as either Chancellor of the Exchequer (head of the treasury) or Prime Minister, from approximately 1852 to 1880.

With the death of Disraeli in 1881, his place at the head of the

Conservative Party was taken by Salisbury, a member of the House of Lords, who then alternated with Gladstone (who died in 1898) until shortly after Victoria's death in 1901.

The Irish Question. One of the issues greeting Victoria and her advisors or cabinet in her first years was the matter of the Irish. Ireland was fervently Catholic ... England and Scotland equally fervently Protestant. Over the centuries the Irish, used to tribal government, were brought into English feudalism – where the land came under the ownership of English lords, mostly absentee landlords who remained in England while they collected taxes and services from the Irish farmers ... offering the Irish few (if any) benefits in return. The unfairness of all this hit hard in the 1840s when a rapidly expanding Irish population – which lived mostly off a diet of potatoes ... found themselves facing starvation when a potato blight in 1845 destroyed the all-important Irish potato crop. The Irish could have somehow survived the worst of the crisis ... except that 1) the Corn Laws (grain laws) passed in 1815 to protect English farming essentially made the import of foreign grain virtually impossible and 2) Ireland still produced enough food (grain, sheep, cattle, etc.) to have fed (meagerly) the Irish population ... except that English landlords sold the Irish production to foreign purchasers.

The plight of the Irish caused parliament finally to repeal the Corn Laws the next year (1846) ... except the blight again destroyed the potato crop. Food was brought in from India ... though too little to hold off the starvation of the Irish, which was now reaching major proportions. Then in 1847 – and again in 1848 and 1849 – the blight continued. And so did the starvation ... which given the weakened condition of the Irish was now joined by the plague. In those five years over 700,000 Irish died. And an equally huge number escaped death only by emigrating (many to America). Consequently, the crisis left a deep bitterness among the Irish towards their English masters. Secret societies formed with a goal similar to the ones on the European continent: national independence.

It was not until Gladstone took office as British prime minister in 1868 that a serious effort was made to address the Irish question. Gladstone pushed through an act disestablishing the Anglican (Protestant) Church in Ireland, undertook land reform offering greater opportunity for the Irish to secure ownership of their lands, and promising fairer rent payments. Sadly, English landlords would often ignore these reforms. Thus over time a "Home Rule" movement gathered momentum in Ireland ... demanding Irish self-rule in all matters except foreign or imperial policy abroad. But efforts of Gladstone in 1886 and 1893 to push such a policy through parliament were met by defeat. Thus as the 20th century approached, the political situation in Ireland was becoming explosive.

British democratic reform. It is important to note that Great Britain does not have some great single document called a constitution, such as America has possessed since 1787 and such as political reformers on the European continent sought to put in place since the late 1700s. According to constitutional theory in Great Britain, any act of Parliament has constitutional authority. Thus when we talk of reform or development of the British Constitution we are simply describing the history of the various acts of Parliament that have shaped British political society. Actually and most importantly, when the British talk of their constitution they are describing not even just a series of laws passed by Parliament but a larger moral-ethical sense that underlies all British politics. It is this larger moral-ethical sense by which they are "constituted" politically.

The Reform Act of 1832 had cleared up much of the political corruption of the "rotten boroughs" generated by strong demographic changes in a rapidly industrializing Britain and had brought an expansion in the number of citizens entitled to vote. But that expansion reached only to the level of the middle classes ... ignoring the right of political participation of the even more rapidly expanding population of the British rural and urban industrial working class. At first the Chartist movement of the 1840s attempted to bring reforms to a more fully democratic basis. But its seeming connection with the continental events of 1848 merely brought stiff resistance to the movement, and it soon died away. But the Tory or Conservative Prime Minister Disraeli took up the cause in 1867 ... just after the Liberal Gladstone had succeeded the previous year in pushing through the House of Commons a very weak reform measure. Disraeli's Reform Bill extended the vote to all householders and long-term renters (except that it still exempted most miners, whose families occupied company-owned housing, and migratory farm workers).

Actually it was the Liberals who first benefited from this expansion of the electorate. With a majority in the House of Commons in 1868, Gladstone was able to begin to push through a series of pieces of legislation providing for the secret rather than the oral ballot, the expansion of national education (doubling the number of local schools), and the reform of both the civil service and the military (appointment by exam or proven merit ... not just personal connections!). Then in 1874 a national election returned Disraeli and the Conservatives to power ... and Disraeli continued the reform movement, focusing more on the working conditions and hours of the British working classes. In 1880 the national vote turned again in Gladstone's favor, and he was able in 1884 to extend the vote to the agricultural laborer. And the next year his Liberal majority passed an act redesigning the individual constituencies so that they represented more equitably the spread of the British population. And thus it was that by the end of the century Great Britain could claim to be truly a constitutional democracy.

✳ ✳ ✳

TSARIST RUSSIA

Autocracy. The word "autocrat" had originally been merely a Greek or Byzantine title for "emperor."* It conveyed pretty much the same political sense that "divine rights" did among West Europe's kings. Thus the Russian Tsar proudly pronounced himself to be the Russian Autocrat. But it was the actual behavior of the tsars over time that gradually made "autocrat" to mean "despot" or even "cruel dictator," someone possessing unquestioned or total power over his people.

This had not always been the case. The build-up of Tsarist power in Russia occurred in tandem with the development of the rise of monarchical power to the west in Europe ... except that unlike Western kingdoms, there were no other institutions such as the church or the aristocracy offering some kind of check, even though small, on the powers of the king. In Russia, the church did not have a political base outside the reach of the tsar, and the tsar thus controlled the personnel and activities of the church ... which existed mostly to bring the Russian people to faithful support of the autocratic tsar. Russia did have a small class of noblemen but they had no independent power, the tsar being able to appoint them ... but also depose them, not only from his imperial service but from even their lands and titles. There existed few towns and thus hardly anything constituting a Russian middle class.

Serfdom. The economy of Russia was nearly entirely agricultural, with all but five percent of the population making up the peasant class. And even this huge class had its earlier rights completely taken from it over the course of the 1600s and 1700s – as the farmers were increasingly restricted in their ability to move about in the quest for better working conditions, being locked into place by law under landlords given increasingly absolute control over their lives. Thus gradually step by step they were turned into the semi-slave category of "serf" ... at a time when West Europe was moving in the opposite direction, gradually freeing up their serfs and recasting them as free (peasant) farmers.

But the Napoleonic wars made very clear the dangers to Russia created by this archaic social system. There was no question of loyalty of the serfs to their tsar, Alexander I ... though their attitudes to their landlord noblemen was a different matter (revolts were frequent). They worshiped

---

*From the Greek – αυτόυ (auto) meaning "self" and κράτωρ (krator) meaning "ruler" or "governor" – someone given the power to make political decisions independently or by his own authority.

the tsar. But the tsar needed more than worship. He needed a society with a strong industrial economy and a national army of some modern (i.e., educated) sophistication. He had neither.

Nicholas I (1825-1855). Alexander died suddenly in late 1825, just as the spirit of military revolt was gathering momentum. His younger brother Constantine had no desire to become tsar and stepped aside for the even younger brother Nicholas ... upsetting the reformist soldiers who went into full revolt in December at the news, thus the "Decembrist Revolt." Nicholas crushed the Decemberists, setting the stage for the rest of his repressive reign. One of the goals of the Decembrists had been the ending of serfdom ... consequently making the reform of serfdom one of the main objects of Nicholas' wrath for the duration of his reign. Constantly fearing reformist movements, he tightened censorship of the press ... and cut back on national education at both the local and university level, driving Russia even deeper into intellectual darkness.

The backwardness of Russia finally registered itself fully during the Crimean War ... when it seemed that all of Europe was lined up against Nicholas. In short order, not only did his huge military apparatus disintegrate but his civil government itself seemed to collapse in corruption. In the midst of the conflict he died of pneumonia ... though there were rumors of suicide.

Alexander II (1855-1881). Nicholas's son Alexander II quickly reversed course and headed Russia down the path of reform in order to bring the country into the modern era. In 1861 he authorized the emancipation of the serfs, then moved to give Russia a more systematic legal system and a new judicial system to supervise it, encouraged local self-government with his *zemstvo* system, brought educational reform back into play ... and instituted universal military training and service. His goal was completely pragmatic, the strengthening of the social foundations of Russia in the new modern era, and not particularly idealistic, for he proved to be just as repressive as his forebears when it came to organized attempts to oppose his rule. Indeed, when Polish patriots rose up in 1863 against Russian rule, Alexander responded by ending Poland's separate status (Alexander was Polish king as well as Russian tsar) and simply incorporated the Polish territory into Russia. Nonetheless, he was still at work trying to reform Russian politics in order to make it acceptable to reformist interests when he was assassinated (1881).

✻ ✻ ✻

AMERICA SUFFERS A TRAGIC CIVIL WAR ...
YET ALSO EXPERIENCES INDUSTRIAL GREATNESS

The issue of slavery. At the time of the creation of the American Constitution, the issue of slavery and how slaves were to count in deciding representation in the House of Representatives had put a strain on the relations among the new states, divided on this issue within the new union largely on a north-south basis. Southern culture with its semi-feudal instincts had come to depend heavily on slave labor ... but knew somehow it was morally wrong. Optimists claimed that it would simply wither away by itself as an institution over time. Some went so far as simply to free their slaves ... usually as part of their will at death (Washington, for instance; however, because of his huge debts, Jefferson did not). Indeed, one of the last acts of the wartime Continental Congress before it turned power over to the new Federal Congress in 1789 was to designate the territories northwest of the Ohio River over to the French colonial border along the Mississippi River to be forever free of slavery.

But the acquiring of new lands beyond the Mississippi with the Louisiana Purchase from France in 1803 stirred the slavery issue to new life. Southerners, whose cotton farming had exhausted the land, were as interested in the territory west of the Mississippi as were the northern farmers. Southerners fought to keep the new territories open to slavery ... and won the idea in principle with the Missouri Compromise of 1820. Entrance of new territories into the Union as full states would occur in such a way that for every "free" state brought in, the South would be entitled to enter a "slave" state ... thus keeping a balance in numbers of free and slave states in the Senate.

At this point the issue for Southerners was no longer a question of when slavery might be ended (as it had elsewhere in the Western world) but how it might be protected ... and even be justified morally. Biblical testimony at this point was brought in to prove that somehow slavery was even part of God's intentions. The North of course was horrified at this misuse of holy scripture. Thus a deep moral divide, as well as an economic lifestyle divide, deepened further a growing political-cultural split separating the North and the South.

Bleeding Kansas. In 1854 the decision to split the Nebraska territory into two states, Nebraska in the North and Kansas in the South, brought the issue to the boiling point. Nebraska would clearly become a free state. But the idea of then making Kansas a slave state brought such an angry reaction from Northerners that the decision was made to let the people of Kansas decide their status themselves. This was the signal of both sides to send masses of settlers to Kansas to weigh the outcome in their favor ... producing in Kansas itself a scene of bloody violence between armed defenders of one group of settlers against the other. Soon the entire country was caught up emotionally over this bitter issue.

The Lincoln-Douglas debates (1858). The nation watched closely the debates in Illinois between Abraham Lincoln and Stephen Douglas as they competed for a U.S. Senate seat. The leading U.S. Senator of the day, Douglas, pressed for tolerance on the slavery issue; the rising Lincoln was certain that slavery would destroy the Union if it were not abolished. Douglas won the election ... but Lincoln won the heart of the new Republican Party ... which two years later nominated him for the presidential race.

The outbreak of civil war (1861). When Lincoln was indeed elected president in the 1860 national elections, Southern states declared their separation from the Union and the formation of a Confederacy of Southern states. When Lincoln refused to surrender to the Confederacy Federal forts located in the South, the first shots of what would become a very bloody civil war were fired (1861).

Lincoln ... the man. Lincoln was vastly more the man than his Republican Party opponents (at first) believed him to be – supposing him to be just some kind of "country boy." Thankfully for America, Lincoln was a truly great leader, understanding deeply the importance of *long-term grand strategy* – when the political world around him could think only in terms of *immediate tactics*.

Previous presidents had merely kicked down the road the can of the increasingly divisive slavery issue ... for those that came after them to deal with. The political cost of bringing the matter to a solution was just something previous presidents could not stomach. But Lincoln knew God had called him to bring this horrible issue to full resolution ... if the God-ordained Union (which Lincoln talked about frequently) were to be saved.

Indeed, he drew closer and closer to God as the contest dragged on, depending on God's counsel – and most frequently, *God's counsel alone* – in directing what was becoming the bloodiest contest that the country had ever seen (or seen even since then!).

Tragically, not achieving immediate success in their efforts to bring matters to a resolution, the will of those around him (including his wife) to press forward in the face of this challenge faltered badly. Why not just give it up ... and let the South go its way?

The war itself (1861-1865). The war was dragging on year after year, with Lincoln changing commanding generals one after the other because of their rather unexceptional service. Consequently, the North was tiring of the war ... and it took the incredible will of Lincoln not to call it quits and simply let the South slip away.

Very sadly for the multitudes who died or were gravely wounded in military service – with little to show for their supreme sacrifice – it took Lincoln over two years to find military leaders (Ulysses S. Grant and William Tecumseh Sherman) who understood that wars are not won by great battles ... but only by the wearing down of the enemy's resolve to continue. And that, not just a grand battle here and there, would take many battles – and very unpleasant measures – to bring to actual victory.

The war was largely a defensive one for the South, more easily understandable and thus easier to conduct ... thus defensive except in the one instance when Southern General Robert E. Lee invaded the North – but was soundly defeated at the Battle of Gettysburg (July 1963) in Pennsylvania. This Northern victory certainly picked up the wearied spirit of the North ... though not greatly.

"Victory" was not yet in the picture ... until General Grant took over the Northern forces. At this point Lee discovered that he was up against an opponent who, though not a brilliant tactician, was a relentless bulldog that was determined to push the South relentlessly ... to the point of exhaustion. And that point came at Appomattox in April of 1865. The South finally had to bow in total defeat. The Union was saved ... and the issue of slavery was finally resolved.

Lincoln's famous 2nd Inaugural Address (1865). With that victory in the making, Lincoln was faced with the challenge of putting the Union back together as a truly unified community ... bringing former slaves into the full responsibilities of citizenship, and re-integrating into the community those who had fought so hard to preserve that slavery. Lincoln – and the country – would need God's help ... as Lincoln made very clear in his new inaugural address, issued in taking up his second term as U.S. president.

It is well worth quoting ... for he stated very clearly the moral-spiritual challenge facing the nation – the likes of which has not been heard from an American presidential leader ever since ... for it was very much more than just a fine speech. It was a sermon to a hurting nation:

... Neither party expected for the war, the magnitude, or the duration, which it has already attained. Neither anticipated that the cause of the conflict might cease with, or even before, the conflict itself should cease. Each looked for an easier triumph, and a result less fundamental and astounding. Both read the same Bible, and pray to the same God; and each invokes His aid against the other. It may seem strange that any men should dare to ask a just God's assistance in wringing their bread from the sweat of other men's faces; but let us judge not that we be not judged.

The prayers of both could not be answered; that of neither has been answered fully. The Almighty has His own purposes.

He then explained that slavery was one of those offenses against God that God would allow – but only until such time as he was ready to exact his judgment, through the terrible war they had been experiencing.

If we shall suppose that American Slavery is one of those offences which, in the providence of God, must needs come, but which, having continued through His appointed time, He now wills to remove, and that He gives to both North and South, this terrible war, as the woe due to those by whom the offence came, shall we discern therein any departure from those divine attributes which the believers in a Living God always ascribe to Him? Fondly do we hope – fervently do we pray – that this mighty scourge of war may speedily pass away. Yet, if God wills that it continue, until all the wealth piled by the bond man's two hundred and fifty years of unrequited toil shall be sunk, and until every drop of blood drawn with the lash, shall be paid by another drawn with the sword, as was said three thousand years ago, so still it must be said the judgments of the Lord, are true and righteous altogether.

He concluded:

With malice toward none; with charity for all; with a firmness in the right, as God gives us to see the right, let us strive on to finish the work we are in; to bind up the nation's wounds; to care for him who shall have borne the battle, and for his widow, and his orphan – to do all which may achieve and cherish a just, and a lasting peace, among ourselves, and with all nations.

Lincoln is assassinated. Then tragically, Lincoln was shot and killed only a couple of weeks later by a Southerner who thought he was doing the defeated South a great favor in taking down their primary adversary. With that bullet, any thought of a much-needed cultural-moral reconciliation between the North and the South disappeared.

Equally tragically (for both North and South), those that came after Lincoln had neither the moral courage nor the political leverage to move the country forward to Lincoln's plan for restored national unity. Instead,

---

*Lincoln's two famous speeches are carved into the walls of the Lincoln Memorial in Washington, DC – the Gettysburg Address on the South Wall and this 2nd Inaugural Address on the North Wall.

Congress's Radical Republicans undertook self-righteous measures designed to keep former Confederates powerless, measures which merely drove the country more deeply into a political-moral standoff. This would do neither North nor South any good.

Efforts to impeach the new president. In accordance with this new moral self-appointment of the Radicals, impeachment charges were leveled at President Andrew Johnson (the former vice president) in an effort to remove him from power ... because he was considered too soft on the South – when he tried to follow Lincoln's efforts to reunite politically the South with the North, rather than punish the South.

The use of the impeachment instrument was designed for very exceptional circumstances (a president actually committing a serious federal crime) rather than just for political purposes. This was its first use ... though hardly over a criminal matter. This was simply very bad political morality in action. Thankfully, the effort to chase Johnson from office would fall just short of the necessary two-thirds vote of the Senate. But it would leave Johnson powerless as president thereafter.

This powerful political tool would not be put to use again until a century later (the effort to drive Nixon from the White House) ... and then – most tragically – would become part of Congress's political weaponry used quite frequently by the president's political opposition in Congress ... a sign of the moral decline of Washington politics. But more about that later!

The after-effects of the war. However, peace ultimately weakened the resolve of the North to continue to press the South to implement full equality for all of its citizens, Black and White. And in subtle ways the South gradually found ways of putting Southern Blacks back under complete political, economic and cultural restraint ... leaving a huge social problem yet unresolved.

But at this point, the North was busy with its attention focused elsewhere, opening more lands for settlement along the Western frontier and continuing the rapid development in the East of the American industrialization that the war had promoted heavily. The South meanwhile sunk back into its semi-feudal ways, with the old families still dominating life from behind the political scenes and with a resentful population of poor Whites determined to keep Southern Blacks fully oppressed. Thus the opportunity produced by the Civil War to bring the South into harmony with Northern democratic and egalitarian ideals was lost ... for a full century.

But the social scene in the North was not all that serene either. The frontier with the Indians was closing, and there was no more good, cheap land for the expanding Anglo population to move to. The squeeze was on for younger sons to find a way to make their own fortunes, with most of them having to move to the urban-industrial East to find employment in the mines and manufacturing plants, where wages barely covered life's most basic expenses. This occurred at the same time that multitudes of immigrants were leaving Europe behind to come to America in the search for the same manufacturing and mining jobs. Anglo-America balked at how this was changing the country from a largely rural nation to one where urban life was fast taking the social lead ... and with all sorts of inhabitants (and corrupt political bosses and urban governments) that made urban America feel "foreign."

America's rise as an industrial giant. But this was also indicative of the deep changes going on within the American economy. America continued to possess vast wealth in its extensive farmlands and its multitude of small rural towns. And America's huge railroad and shipping infrastructure made for an extremely efficient and powerful market for agricultural goods. But its cities were also amassing great wealth as they turned to the manufacture of a vast array of new machines that greatly energized the American economy, and the mining of iron, coal and even oil to answer the voracious appetites for raw materials of these mammoth manufacturing operations. Indeed, so great was the industrial growth of America during this time that by 1914 and the outbreak of the European "Great War" (World War One), America alone produced one-third of the world's total industrial wealth, more than Britain, Germany and France combined.

The "captains" (some would say "robber barons") of American industry. Behind this growth was not a government (as in Europe, mostly) but a small group of powerful individual capitalists, who developed the ability to gather vast sums of money to undertake industrial investment on a massive scale. Cornelius Vanderbilt grew a business from a small ferry service (from New Jersey to New York City) by the mid-1800s to a massive steamship corporation, and then combined a number of railroad companies operating in the East into the New York Central Railroad.* Competing with him in the 1870s were Jay Gould and James Fisk, attempting a similar hold over much of the East's railroad business. Then there was Andrew Carnegie who came from Scotland to America in 1848 as a youth, taking whatever jobs he could to pay the bills, but advancing himself by teaching himself new skills that caught the attention of American businessmen, which in turn led him into deep investment in the steel business – until he became by the end of the 1800s the owner and director of America's

---

*By this time, he had made himself into the second richest man in American history!

largest steel-producing operation. This in turn was bought out by the most powerful banker in American history, J.P. Morgan, who went on to build a vast financial-industrial empire, that was called on twice (1895 and 1907) by America's presidents to save the country from economic collapse. Then there was indeed the richest man in American history, John D. Rockefeller, who started small in the oil business (originally focused on making the kerosene that would replace the whale oil lamps used in all American homes) that came at one point (the 1870s) to control 90% of America's oil industry, before his business was forced in 1911 by the Supreme Court to break itself into 34 independent and thus competing oil companies – under the impetus of America's "antitrust" crusade that broke out exactly because of Rockefeller's monopolistic position in this vital industry. Nonetheless Rockefeller would remain America's wealthiest man in its history.

THE THIRD REPUBLIC OF FRANCE

With Napoleon III's capture by German troops in the battle of Sedan (September 1870), French government simply melted away. Hearing the news of his capture, a Paris mob descended on the French Assembly demanding the formation of a new republic. It was assumed that this would rally the French and reverse the direction the war was going. But stunningly quickly the German troops were able to march on and surround Paris. Gambetta was able to escape the encirclement (hot air balloon) and organize a new French army. But at Metz another huge French army was forced to surrender ... and Gambetta's forces were unable to break the German encirclement of Paris.

A French Provisional Government was formed in the south of France at Bordeaux to try to carry on French government ... and secure peace terms with Germany. But the delegates that gathered were hotly divided as to what shape the new government should take. Only about a third of the members were in favor of a republic. The others favored the restoration of the monarchy ... but were hotly divided as to whether the new king should be a Bourbon or an Orleanist. Deadlocked over the monarchy issue, the decision was made simply to stay temporarily with the idea of a new republic (the third such republic) ... until the Bourbon-Orleanist dispute could be settled.* For the time being, peace negotiations were opened up

____

*Interestingly, the "temporary" Third Republic would last 70 years, from 1870 all the way up until 1940 ... when Hitler forced France to submit to German authority ... leaving only a smaller "French State" at Vichy to govern the South of France (1940-1944).

with the Germans (concluded, to the great disadvantage of the French, in January 1871), and the new National Assembly immediately moved itself to Versailles, just outside German-encircled Paris.

The Paris Commune (1871). Meanwhile in Paris itself, conditions were breaking down as the population ran out of food and medicine. Anger developed quickly in Paris over the "betrayal" by the new government which had failed them in war and seemed to be ready to impose a monarchy over them in peace. When soldiers were sent into Paris to secure cannon lest they fall into the hands of the Paris mob, they were fiercely resisted ... and the street barricades went up, announcing Paris's refusal to acknowledge the new Versailles government. Instead rebel leaders declared Paris to be an autonomous Commune (late March 1871) ... defended by Paris's own National Guard. France had fallen into civil war.

The next six weeks proved to be bloodier than had been the war against the Germans, as French national troops fought their way into Paris defended by members of the Paris National Guard. The "Bloody Week" of May (21-28) saw much of Paris burned and countless thousands killed in battle ... and even executed in surrender.

Eventually the Commune was suppressed ... with 30,000 people having been killed, countless others wounded and perhaps 50,000 executed or imprisoned ... 7,000 of those exiled to the prison colony of New Caledonia in the Pacific. Thousands of other communards were able to escape from France to Switzerland, Belgium and England.

The struggles of the new Third Republic. Eventually the Third Republic was able to work its way past the divisions among the monarchists to draw up a new constitution (1875) which provided for a national President, a Chamber of Deputies elected by universal manhood suffrage and a Senate whose members were in part appointed for life and the rest selected by various regional electoral colleges. As it turned out, the Chamber was strongly republican in character and the Senate monarchist ... though the Chamber itself was always divided among small political groups of one or another ideological bent or just personal loyalty to some particular political figure. Consequently, French politics during the Third Republic would remain unsteady ... yet be held together at a higher level by a burning sense of French nationalism.

WESTERN IMPERIALISM

Defining "imperialism."   Imperialism, in today's understanding, is to impose a society's will on another society, exploiting the weakness of the subject society to the benefit of the dominant society. Imperialism may take all kind of different shapes. It may be purely economic, controlling the markets, the labor, the material resources of another society. It may be demographic, resettling portions of the population of the dominant society in the lands of the subject society. It may be cultural, "converting" the thinking of the subject society to the thought processes of the dominant society, thus making it easier to control and govern the subject society. It may be purely political, replacing the subject society's leaders with leaders appointed by the dominant society ... and similar to political, it may be administrative, replacing the laws and institutions of the subject society with those of the dominant society. In most cases in history, imperialism conducted by one society over another tends to combine elements of all these types of imperialism.

Imperialism is not a new phenomenon in human history. In fact it seems to be very central to the dynamics of a society in its rise and decline. Accusing a society of practicing imperialism is to accuse it of being aggressively expansive ... rather normal behavior on the part of a society on the rise. A society on the decline tends to detest imperialism in principle ... either because it senses that imperialism of another society is being aimed at it, or because it is hoping to create a moral universal designed to convince the players of the social game to accept a freeze of a particular political status quo that it likes and does not want to lose, but is no longer able or willing to defend by force.

But there are other reasons to find oneself in opposition to imperialism. If pushed too far it becomes burdensomely expensive, that is, draining on the resources of the dominant society. And that has often been the case in history. It worked out this way for England in its efforts to hang on to its American colonies (economic and political relations between the two groups actually improved greatly after England let go of its empire in mid North America). Spain also found that trying to hang on to its colonies in America during the Napoleonic wars was a losing proposition, coming at a time when Spain could ill afford to lose any more power, its decline had reached such a deep level. The Bourbon kings of France had more than once emptied their treasuries playing the imperialism game (which they largely lost anyway in America). Even Napoleon recognized the burden of American empire, being willing to sell the entire Louisiana territory to the young American republic. And so too the Russian tsar sold off his American holdings in Alaska ... for much the same reason.

British India

Yet for the British, being a small island with a rapidly growing population and an even more rapidly growing industrial economy, imperialism was less a choice than a necessity ... not that this was all conducted as official government policy however; much of British imperialism (at least initially) was conducted by private corporate interests, such as the Muscovy Company, the Virginia Company, the Massachusetts Bay Company ... and most importantly, the English East India Company. Yet these companies did have close relations with English royalty, in that they were understood to be vital sources of taxes for the royal treasury. So there was a lot of cooperation between company and crown. For instance, it was the dumping of tea of the English East India Company by angry Massachusetts "patriots" that helped greatly to push the English crown into confrontation with its colonies in America, a confrontation that led to the American War of Independence.

In fact the English East India Company had long been a central piece in the British imperial program ... for better or for worse. Much too often it was for the worse. That was the problem in the confrontation with the American colonies: the profits of the Company were declining and George III had made the move to allow the sale of only the Company's tea in the colonies. This move not only infuriated the colonies, it sparked much debate in parliament about the wisdom of mercantilism (political protectionism such as the case with the English East India Company's new monopoly on tea sold to America) and whether mercantilism or "free trade" actually worked better for Britain in the long run. The argument in favor of free trade (the economics of free competition) was that it encouraged efficiency and lower prices, which actually generated a larger market for manufactured goods. Indeed, the British moved ahead rapidly in the area of free trade, trying to get other countries to get in the free trade game ... where Britain had a decided trading advantage. That was their basic approach in encouraging the 1823 American Monroe Doctrine: rather than enforcing closed markets such as existed in Spanish America (mercantilism), all nations should be open for trade with any other nation (where the British could easily outsell any competitor). It all seemed so "fair." Actually, this economic principle advantaged the British commercial economy tremendously.

But India was a different matter. The English East India Company had undertaken to create alliances with a number of local Indian princes or rajas, English power sought by the rajas and Indian markets for English goods sought by the Company. Initially the arrangement seemed to work well for both English and Indians. However, as the Company grew in wealth and position, it found itself increasingly in a very commanding position at the heart of Indian politics. In subtle ways, by the beginning of the 1800s the Company (referred to now as the British East India Company) found itself in a governing position in large sections of India not very different from that of a traditional Indian imperial government (governing the three constantly expanding presidencies of Bombay, Bengal and Madras). As such, the Company attempted to act the part of the benevolent emperor, improving roads, installing railroads, dams, canals, and reservoirs, instituting legal reforms, ending *suttee* (the "self-inflicted" death of widows at their husbands' funerals), etc. as a way of winning the hearts of the Indians.

But vast cultural differences made the task of uniting the Company's interests with the Indian soul very difficult. The British could not understand that reforming the highly discriminatory caste system did not bring approval but instead confusion and frustration among the Indians. Many of the industrial improvements brought by the English (such as the telegraph) even stirred fears among the Indians that the British had introduced something very sinister among them! Also the move of the Company to take over an Indian state when an Indian prince died without an heir – or even just when the British deemed the prince incompetent – stirred deep bitterness among many Indians.

The Sepoy Mutiny of 1857. Finally there was the matter of the new cartridges shipped from England for use by the sepoy (Indian) troops in the employ of the Company. Rumors spread rapidly that these cartridges had been greased in the fat of pigs and cows, to protect them from the dampness of the sea journey. In the eyes of the Muslim sepoys, pork fat was highly polluting; and in the eyes of the Hindu sepoys, cow fat was in violation of the basic sacredness of all life ... but especially that of the cow, whose life was considered more sacred than human life. When English officers saw this refusal to use these cartridges as simply insubordination – and when it appeared to the sepoys that their British officers were not going to back down – rebellion broke out among the sepoys and spread rapidly across northern India. Not only British officers but civilians, women and children as well as men, were murdered by angry sepoys ... with British troops then responding in kind. The slaughter on both sides was terrible.

The timing for the British was terrible also because most of the British troops were away fighting in the Crimean war. However loyal Indians troops contributed greatly to the British effort to regain control over the situation ... nonetheless taking six months to bring the rebellion to an end. Overall it was all a scandalous, bloody mess.

Victoria, Empress of India. The net result was that in 1858 the British parliament ended the Company's charter and transferred British governance in India to the crown as part of the British Empire (the Indian portion of the Empire known as the British Raj). Under Queen Victoria's instructions, the public works programs begun by the Company in India (particularly transportation and education) were extended greatly, transforming India into a budding industrial society with a growing awareness of modern democratic-national political norms. So devoted was she to the development of India that in 1876 she took upon herself the title "Empress of India."

Nonetheless despite Victoria's (and her successors) positive intentions, Indians were ambivalent about British reforms. On the one hand the British idea of the equality of all citizens within the Empire undermined the caste system, which stood as the foundation of traditional Indian society. On the other hand there was something hypocritical about the ideal of equality in the way Indians felt looked down on by the English, causing irritation especially among the more Westernized Indians who were expecting more egalitarian treatment, but did not find this to be actually the case no matter how hard they tried to be "English."* Much like the case in Ireland, the demand for "Home Rule" (not quite independence but at least a lot of political autonomy within the British Empire) began to grow in India. But, as in Ireland, these would be largely ignored by the British authorities.

The British dominions

Canada. During the 1830s there was a growing demand for political reform all through Europe. This was no less the case for the English and French provinces in Canada. Although they each had their own legislatures, their governors were appointed by the crown – not by the leading local political party. Armed revolt actually broke out in Canada in 1837, causing the colonial office to take the matter of reform seriously enough that in 1846 the Canadian legislatures were finally given control over the appointment of their provincial governors. Then in 1867 the British parliament passed the British North America Act, uniting as a new federation or "Dominion" the English and French provinces of upper and lower Canada, plus Nova Scotia and New Brunswick. The new Dominion was given a federal parliament (with a House of Commons and a Senate) located at Ottawa. Although the Governor-General was appointed by the British crown, the real executive power was vested in the prime minister, who functioned in Canada similar to the prime minister in England.

Australia and New Zealand. Originally a British penal colony (early 1800s), Australia began to receive immigrants on their own initiative, especially after gold was discovered there in 1851. Soon Australia had settled six different states, each with its own British-styled government.

---

*Gandhi was a classic example of an Indian who turned bitterly against things English when, despite his 40+ year effort to measure up as "quite British," felt himself to always be looked down on because of the color of his skin.

But federation on the Canadian model did not move forward as quickly as it had in Canada, and it was not until the end of the 1800s that work got seriously underway on the project, resulting finally in 1900 in the Australian Commonwealth Act. But in Australia, the model followed was not the British parliamentary model, but a federal system closer to the one in the United States, with much autonomy accorded the individual states.

New Zealand was asked to become part of the Australian venture but declined to do so, preferring to maintain its own "national" identity. In 1867, at the same time that Canada was set up as a British dominion, New Zealand was accorded self-government. Finally in 1907, it was accorded dominion status as a distinct nation.

South Africa

The Dutch Cape colony. We have already mentioned how, in the mid-1600s, the Dutch established a colony at the Cape of South Africa, and then expanded that settlement into the South African interior ... then when, in 1779, the Dutch met the first Xhosa tribesmen at the Great Fish River, dividing Western and Eastern South Africa. Here they fought each other to a standstill, making it the eastern boundary of the Cape colony and a western boundary for the Bantu tribesmen.

The British takeover. During the Napoleonic wars of the early 1800s, the British seized the strategic Cape Colony from the Dutch ... and had their ownership confirmed at the Congress of Vienna (1814-1815) in agreeing to pay the Dutch 6 million pounds for the colony. But their English-only language policy plus their abolition of slavery in 1834 upset the Dutch inhabitants so much that they began migrating away from the Cape deeper into the African interior – Cape Dutch population growth also being part of the driving force behind this migration.

The Zulu and the *Boer Voortrekkers*. At the same time an African chieftain, Shaka, had forged a huge Zulu tribe into a fierce fighting force to the northeast of the Cape colony (early 1800s). His warring (the *Mfecane*) was so brutal that he actually slaughtered off or scattered a number of tribes once inhabiting the open highlands northwest of his new Zululand. This then actually enabled the Dutch farmers ("Boers") to move themselves easily into the now relatively depopulated highland region (the upper Veld) during the "Great Trek" away from the English-controlled Cape. Consequently, some ten thousand *voortrekkers* ("advancing migrants" or frontiersmen) would make the journey, eventually establishing two Boer Republics, the Orange Free State, and, further to the northeast, the Transvaal.

But further entry into Zulu territory (south across the Drakensberg Mountains) was very dangerous ... as the Voortrekkers were to discover in 1838 ... when a large group of them (accompanied by other African tribesmen) were slaughtered by the Zulu impi (warriors) of Shaka's brother, Dingane (ruled KwaZulu 1828-1840).

Natal.[*] At the same time, the British had begun to move into the region along the Indian Ocean midway between the tribal regions of the Xhosa in the south and the Zulu in the north. But the Dutch were also migrating into the area and the two groups fell into fighting in 1842. The Boer voortrekkers were driven north back across the Drakensberg mountains ... and thousands of British were subsequently brought in to settle the new British province called "Natal." But with slavery having been abolished in Britain, the British were eventually forced to turn to India to find cheap labor for their sugar farms (the Zulu were scornful of such labor). During the second half of the 1800s over 150 thousand Indians were brought into Natal as indentured workers, making them more numerous than the Europeans living there.

Then the British began to think about creating a southern African federation similar to the one established in Canada. The hope was to bring the Cape, the Dutch Republics, Natal Province and a number of African tribal territories together ... something however to which neither the Boers nor the Zulu were going to be willing to agree. When the British pressed the issue with the Zulu, war broke out. The results were extremely bloody for both sides. But in the end, Zulu power was broken.

The Boer War (1899-1902). But the Boers would be no less resistant to the idea of a British federation or union. When in 1867 diamonds were discovered in the Orange Free State, imperial ambitions of the English at the Cape were ignited. Stoking the fires of English ambition was Cecil Rhodes, who from 1871 to 1888 worked his way from diamond digger to fabulously wealthy diamond monopolist. He then moved into South African politics, which he likewise came to dominate, becoming prime minister of the Cape Colony in 1890.

In the meantime, gold had been discovered further north in the Transvaal in 1885. But this time the Boers were more resistant to the efforts of the English industrialists to exploit the gold ... which laid well below the surface. Boer farmers, no matter how poor, were not interested in going down into the gold mines to work for the English entrepreneurs. Thus in an effort to secure the necessary labor to work the gold mines, European laborers (principally British) were brought into the Transvaal –

---

[*]"Natal" is actually the name for that coastal region assigned by the Portuguese explorer da Gama, when he first sighted it on Christmas Day, 1497.

much to the displeasure of the Boers, who sensed that they were losing political ground to these *uitlanders* (foreigners) ... and did what they could to bring this immigration to a halt.

But Rhodes was not one to have his plans set aside, and plotted a takeover of the Transvaal government by the uitlanders – with a raid on Johannesburg by his friend Dr. Jameson and 500 men. But this ended up disastrously for the English. Now feelings ran hot.

The British colonial secretary Chamberlain then demanded full rights for the uitlanders ... with Transvaal president Kruger answering back with a call for war if the British did not remove their troops from the Transvaal border. The British refused. Thus war was declared (October 1899) by Kruger.

The world watched closely as the war unfolded between the superpower Great Britain and the little but defiant Boer Republics. The British regular armies under Lord Kitchener found the guerrilla tactics of the Boer commandos difficult to counter (shades of the American Revolution!) Thus, to break the spirit of the Boer, he began a shameless scorched earth policy ... plus the confinement of Boer families in "concentration camps" – in which Boer women and children died in massive numbers from hunger and disease.

Much to the shock of the British, who thought that this war would be won quickly and easily, this gruesome war dragged on and on. This in turn generated a growing anti-war opinion in Britain ... and a rising European scorn for Britain's shameful behavior.

Finally however, in May of 1902 the Boers accepted surrender ... and the incorporation of the Orange Free State and the Transvaal within a new South African Union. But this was accompanied by the British promise also of South African self-government – with dominion status – in the near future (actually fulfilled in 1910).

Ultimately, the war had proven very costly in lives and expenditures ... gaining little for the British victors in the process – except a tarnishing of the British image as "enlightened" empire-builders.

The early stages of French imperialism

Algeria.   One of the most extensive moves by the French to extend and incorporate overseas territories into the growing French Empire occurred directly across the Mediterranean from Southern France: Algeria. In 1827 French Bourbon king Charles X turned a minor incident involving the Muslim governor ("dey") of Algiers into an excuse for a blockade of the port of Algiers ... which step by step escalated into all-out war between France and Algiers in 1830. A French army of 34,000 troops invaded Algiers and fairly quickly defeated the dey's army ... and proceeded to commit numerous atrocities against the civilian population afterwards. Then in the midst of the action Charles was deposed and Louis Philippe took his place as French king ... but continued the action in North Africa, extending the war to Oran and Constantine (comprising most of today's Algerian coastlands) by 1847. Conquest was soon followed up by the annexing of the Algerian territories as part of a reviving French empire.

Also, a large number of French (and other Europeans) began to settle the fertile lands of Algeria, for the purpose of cotton farming (subsequently wine production). By 1860, European immigrants to Algeria numbered around 200 thousand. So alarmed were the Algerian Arabs that in 1864 a massive uprising of the Arabs against their French occupiers occurred ... requiring a huge French army and a full year of action to break the power of the rebellion. Napoleon III, attempting to appease the Arab population, promised a number of social and political reforms ... but found his plans upset by a whole range of disasters which hit Algeria (locusts, drought, famines, and disease), plus the resistance of the French colonists opposed to his reforms.

Nonetheless, Algeria began to develop a distinct French-Arab culture of its own out of these tensions. But the plan now was to integrate Algeria fully into French national territory as one of France's departments ... that is, Algeria would no longer be seen as a French colony, but instead would be considered to be an integral part of France itself (like Alaska and Hawaii would become to America).

New Caledonia.   One of the more interesting pieces in France's imperial puzzle was New Caledonia (in the South Pacific just east of Australia and north of New Zealand), which was turned into a penal colony during the second half of the 1800s, receiving 22,000 criminals during that time. Eventually other French would join these individuals, looking to start a new life in this distant colony.

Senegal.   Senegal in West Africa became a key French holding in Africa during the same period. From its coastal capital at Dakar, the French African colony was extended into the African interior, posing itself as a French model of modern social, economic and cultural development. In this it was a key piece in France's "civilizing mission" (*la mission civilisatrice*) which provided moral justification for a rising sense in France of the necessity of French imperialism.

Napoleon III's blunder in Mexico: "Emperor" Maximilian. In 1861, with the United States deeply involved in its own civil war between the

North and the South, Napoleon (along with some support from Great Britain and Spain) decided to invade and seize the government of Mexico ... using the excuse of Mexican President Juarez's suspension of interest payments to European creditors. But once it became clear to his British and Spanish allies that Napoleon's intentions were fully imperialistic and not just debt-collection, they withdrew from the project.

Initially the Mexicans were able to defeat a French army on May 5th 1862 (thus the Cinco de Mayo Mexican national holiday!). But Napoleon brought in more French troops (including the troops of the famous French Foreign Legion) and finally was able to seize Mexico City the next year in June. Juarez and some of his men escaped to Chihuahua, where they continued to operate guerrilla style from there. But with Juarez gone from the capital, a conservative military junta (military council) was set up and, under orders from Napoleon, called on Maximilian of Habsburg (the younger brother of the Austrian Emperor Franz Joseph I) to rule Mexico as its new emperor. Early the following year (1864) the French brought Maximilian to Mexico to be crowned Mexican Emperor.

France now had a puppet emperor that not only gave the French access to Mexico's mineral wealth, it served as a seal on a new French-Austrian friendship ... that both monarchies sensed they needed to counterbalance Prussia's rapid rise to power in Germany. It also put in Mexico a Catholic counterpart to the strong American Protestantism to the north in the United States.

Maximilian tried to win Mexican hearts with rather liberal ideas for an emperor – merely alienating in the process the conservative Mexicans who had been co-sponsors with France in this whole venture. In the meantime Mexican Republicans under Juarez had been gathering strength ... and the following year (1865) were able to gain important victories in battles against Maximilian's forces (despite even his French help). At this point Maximilian took on a more brutal stand in his dealing with the Republicans.

Now with its civil war brought to an end in mid-1865, the United States moved to become more directly involved. American funding and arms began to pour in to support Juarez and his Republican forces. Then in 1866 Napoleon, now preferring good relations with the United States rather than with the Maximilian government, began to withdraw its military support of Maximilian – opening the way for the Republicans to begin to advance on the Mexican capital, taking city by city as they went. By early 1867 Maximilian was forced to attempt flight from the capital, then Mexico itself – getting caught along the way. He was tried and sentenced to death – causing European heads of state to plead for his release. But Juarez wanted the Europeans to get the message that there was to be no more such meddling in Mexican affairs. In June of 1867, Maximilian and two of his generals were executed by a firing squad.

The net effect of this episode was that Napoleon lost more credibility at a time when he could ill afford it, Mexican conservatives were discredited, Juarez once again (the man never seemed to go away) overstayed his welcome among the Mexican people, but died in 1872 amidst another rebellion against his heavy-handed rule ... and life went on as before in Mexico.

Western imperialism in China and East Asia

The First Opium War (1839-1842). Europeans had long had an interest in Chinese goods – silks, tea, porcelain – but had little to sell of serious interest to the Chinese ... until the British East India Company began exporting Indian opium to China, creating an ever-expanding market for their product among a rapidly growing number of Chinese addicts. When in 1839 the Chinese emperor seized a huge amount of this product (over a thousand tons) in an effort to shut down this ruinous commerce, the British struck back and by mid-1842 succeeded in overrunning a number of key Chinese ports, forcing the Qing (or Manchu) Emperor to grant (Treaty of Nanking) the British free trading rights in five Chinese ports, the transfer of Hong Kong Island to the British ... and the rights of Christian missionaries to enter China freely.

The opening of Japan (1853-1854). Meanwhile in nearby Japan, American naval commodore Perry and four ships under his command pushed their way into Tokyo harbor in 1853 ... then returned the next year with an ultimatum demanding the opening of relations with America. After considering the unreadiness of the Japanese to fend off the powerful American artillery, the shogunate (government) accepted the American terms. But this was the signal to the shogunate council to undertake their own military modernization as a counter to this Western intrusion. But these reforms were opposed by a strong traditionalist element in the council that wanted the removal of the shogun (military strongman) and the restoration of the emperor to power instead as the answer to the Western challenge. A number of earthquakes and a tsunami which destroyed thousands of buildings (in a town where the new American consul was to take residence) convinced the traditionalists that the gods were registering their opposition to the modernization of Japan. The Japanese leadership was thus split on the matter.

The Taiping Rebellion (1850-1864) and the Second Opium War (1856-1860). At this point, the Chinese imperial government was fully absorbed in trying to suppress a "Taiping Rebellion" ... an uprising started in 1850 by disillusioned Chinese who considered the humiliated Qing Emperor to have lost the "Mandate of Heaven" and thus needing to be replaced by new leadership. Rebels led by a quasi-Christian Hong Xiuquan (considered himself to be the younger brother of Jesus!) had succeeded in taking control of large parts of China, and for the longest time the imperial army was unsuccessful in its struggle against the Taiping rebels who seized a number of key Chinese cities.

Meanwhile, by the mid-1850s there was growing commercial competition among Western powers to gain an ever-larger position within the Chinese (mostly opium) market. Americans and French merchant companies secured trade concessions ... and as the Nanking Treaty was due to be renewed (after its 12-year term), the British sought to have the British position expanded. Confusion over a pirated ship (the *Arrow*) in 1856 led to fighting between the Chinese and the British ... which itself became complicated with the Sepoy mutiny in India and the Crimean War against Russia going on at the same time.

But finally (December of 1857), with the Crimean War and the Sepoy mutiny out of the way as issues, the British (and the French) were ready to attack the Chinese at Canton. With the Emperor Wenzong deeply distracted with the Taiping Rebellion, Canton was easily captured at the beginning of January of the following year (1858).

Then at this point the new round in the Opium War widened as America and Russia joined the British and the French ... finally forcing the Emperor to grant new treaties (June 1858) recognizing a much-expanded position of the four Western powers in China. The Western powers now ranged more widely around the Chinese coast, attacking and moving inland up Chinese rivers ... but got stopped at the Taku forts outside of the Chinese capital of Beijing. Finally in 1860, they were able to bring down this piece of the Chinese resistance. In September, their forces were able to enter the capital itself ... and then proceed to destroy the palaces of the emperor's Forbidden City.

The result was that the British, French – and Russians – took control of major strategic locations in and around China (the British receiving Kowloon Peninsula opposite Hong Kong, instance, and the Russians receiving vast amounts of Chinese territory in the Chinese north) ... and forced the emperor not only to pay them a huge indemnity but also to allow the opium trade to operate legally in China.

At about the same time however a powerful local leader, Zeng Guofan, stepped forward with his Xiang Army to attack the Taiping rebels. Finally after much bloodshed, in July of 1864 Zeng overran the Taiping position at Nanjing ... but only after the death of the Taiping leader Hong in June.

Remnants of the Taiping fled to the mountains to continue their efforts. But by and large the rebellion was over.

Zeng and his officers were celebrated widely as the saviors of the Qing dynasty. But this pointed importantly to the fact that the emperor was increasingly dependent on his subjects and their leaders to preserve his throne. In a sense the imperial government was giving way to increasing governance nationally and locally by a rising class of local warlords. This did not speak well for imperial China ... being a sign understood by all Chinese confirming the fact that the emperor was losing the Mandate of Heaven.

Korea (1866). In the 1700s, French missionaries in Korea had brought thousands to Catholicism. In 1866 the Korean king ordered the mass execution of French priests operating in Korea ... and some ten thousand Korean converts. The French retaliated ... but for the moment with no success.

Japan and the beginning of the Meiji Restoration (1867-1868). In Japan the young emperor moved to make the emperorship more than just a symbolic position ... pitting himself against the Tokugawa Shogunate which had been governing Japan since the 1600s. The emperor drew on Western support and technology to make his move. But so did the shogun ... thus drawing Westerners deeply into the contest. In the end, critical Western support of the emperor helped him defeat the shogun and his troops ... ending the reign of the shoguns and the restoration of imperial Japan. Under the emperor Meiji, the modernization of Japan would continue, but under the management of the Japanese themselves. The Westerners would participate, but in a more passive fashion than was the case elsewhere in Asia.

French Indochina (1858-1870). In the southeastern corner of Asia where Indian and Chinese cultures met (thus "Indochina"), Napoleon III decided to move on his own to establish French dominance there ... ahead of the possible move of other European powers. The French had held an interest in the area since the 1600s when French priests arrived there to try to bring the region under Catholicism. In 1858, the Vietnamese emperor, sensing the dangers of the Western presence in Asia, attempted to expel the missionaries. But here Napoleon was more successful in opposing the move ... sending a combined French and Spanish-Filipino military force to Vietnam, which overwhelmed the Vietnamese emperor's forces. He thus submitted to the French demand not only for the protection of the Vietnamese Catholics, but the opening of Vietnamese ports to French trading.

Then when French troops were removed to fight in China, the emperor broke the terms of the treaty ... until the French returned in 1862 and demanded even more drastic supervisory rights in Vietnam. In 1864, the area was then simply converted into a new French territory.

Once again, the French saw themselves as advancing under the imperative of their *mission civilisatrice* ... endeavoring to bring superior French culture to the "less advanced" peoples of Asia.

Meanwhile, next door in Cambodia, the Cambodian king involved the French in his struggle against the Thai king, who had formerly placed him in power. Now the Cambodian king was hoping to get French assistance in securing his independence from Thailand. In the end, a diplomatic settlement was achieved which gave Cambodia its "independence" ... at the cost of the loss of part of Laos, which was granted to Thailand in exchange. Nonetheless by doing so, Cambodia now found itself operating completely under French "protection."

Singapore. In 1819 the British signed a treaty with the local sultan allowing them to develop a British East India Company trading post on a large island at the very tip of the Malay peninsula, strategically placed to monitor shipping moving between the Indian Ocean and the South China Sea. Gradually this sparsely inhabited island began to grow in population, heavily Chinese because of all the Chinese workers brought into the settlement to work the rubber plantations developing there. Indeed, by the 1870s Singapore had turned itself into the center of the rubber industry.

The Dutch East Indies. The Portuguese had established commercial relations in the "Spice Islands" of Southeast Asia (roughly today's Indonesia) as early as the late 1400s. The trade was highly profitable ... and soon the Dutch got involved through its United East India Company (the Vereenigde Oostindische Compagnie or VOC), which established in 1619 a commercial base at Batavia (modern Jakarta) on the Island of Java. From there the Dutch constantly widened the sphere of their control ... but lost that position briefly during the Napoleonic Wars at the beginning of the 1800s when Napoleon placed his brother on the Dutch throne and the British reacted by seizing the Dutch holdings in Asia (also Africa). After the war the area was restored to the Dutch (1816), with some exchanges of territorial control with the British, as the British ceded their settlements on the neighboring island of Sumatra to the Dutch in exchange for the Dutch holdings on the Malay peninsula which were turned over to the British.

The Indonesians naturally had their own thoughts about this Western imperialism, and there were a number of uprisings or wars by a number of Muslim sultans against this Dutch intrusion, especially during the last quarter of the 1800s. One by one they were suppressed, although one of these uprisings, the Aceh War, lasted all the way until 1912.

The Boxer Rebellion (1899-1901). Most unsurprisingly, the Western intrusion into China had a huge impact on Chinese society ... part of China deciding that the proper response to the overbearing Western presence was simply to adapt China to Western ways, in the hopes that this might restore China to greatness ... or at least soften the impact of the West's intrusion into China. But other Chinese grew increasingly bitter over this Western intrusion, angry not only at the Westerners overrunning their country ... but even angrier at the Chinese who had somehow accommodated themselves to this Western intrusion.

Unsurprisingly, A Chinese secret society, the Righteous and Harmonious Fists ("Boxers"), had been forming in reaction to this Western intrusion, dedicated to the complete removal of these non-Chinese influences ... and also any of their own people who had allowed themselves to fall under the sway of the Western outsiders. And remove such individuals they did ... most bloodily. And as terrible as the treatment of the Westerners was, the Boxers' treatment of their own Chinese "traitors" was far worse (specifically targeted were thousands of Chinese Christians).

But the Chinese behavior served importantly to unify the Westerners (and also bring Japan into action on the side of the Westerners) as an 8-nation alliance which brought in a combined total of about 20 thousand troops, and fairly quickly but also very bloodily crushed the rebellion.

The Chinese government (actually not part of the uprising) was forced by angry Westerners to agree to pay a huge reparations payment ... which in fact greatly exceeded the Qing's total tax revenues ... for a period of 39 years. At this point the Qing dynasty was virtually finished.

European imperialism in the Middle East

The Suez Canal. In the early 1800s Europeans began to explore the idea of digging a canal in Egypt that would link the Mediterranean to the Red Sea and the Indian Ocean beyond ... a much shorter route than the one reaching Asia in going South around Africa. It was the French who took the initiative to actually begin the project when Ferdinand de Lesseps received from the Egyptian khedive (Muhammad Ali's grandson) in the mid-1850s permission to construct the canal. A commercial company was formed to finance and direct the construction of the canal, and work on the canal began in 1859.

Over the next ten years tens of thousands of Egyptian laborers worked under severe conditions to complete the canal (thousands also dying in the process). The British, afraid that the canal might increase the competition for its favored trading position in the East-West trade, were opposed to the project and did what they could to have it stopped. Nonetheless the work went forward and the canal was opened for business in 1869 ... although the project cost twice the anticipated amount and the Suez Canal Company found itself in deep financial trouble. The result was that in order to avoid bankruptcy, the khedive was forced to sell his shares in the company ... to the British, who bought him out in 1875 (Prime Minister Disraeli pushing hard to seize this opportunity)! This now began the period of active British involvement in the affairs of Egypt. Indeed, in 1882 the British (at the invitation of the Khedive) moved troops into Egypt ... to protect their investment in Egypt from a spreading rebellion among angry Muslim traditionalists organizing up the Nile River in the Sudan.

Syria / Lebanon (1860-1861). When it became apparent that the Ottoman Sultan's forces were unable to stop the murderous violence between Christians and quasi-Muslim Druze that had erupted at the beginning of 1860 in the region of Lebanon – which then spread quickly to the surrounding Syrian region – Napoleon III took the initiative of intervening there on behalf of the Christian community ... again, with the British opposed, because they did not want to see French imperial influence expanded there. French troops sent that summer quickly separated the warring parties. And then Napoleon called an international conference in Paris to work out peace terms. The next summer Napoleon pulled his troops out of the region having achieved peace, a hero in the eyes of his Frenchman. France would henceforth be a serious factor in future developments within the region.

The Balkan peninsula. With the Ottoman Turkish Empire in a clear state of decline, the temptation presented to the major European powers to take whatever control they could in the Balkan region of Southeastern Europe became too great to resist. Especially ambitious in this matter was the Austro-Hungarian Empire,[*] landlocked in central Europe ... and hoping to pick up a coastal position on the Mediterranean in order to position a naval base there of its own. But Russia, itself failing to have any unimpeded access to the Mediterranean, was just as ambitious in this matter.

However, the same Ottoman decline also increased greatly the rising spirit of nationalism of Ottoman Turkey's former subject peoples in that same Balkan region (Greeks, Bulgarians, Romanians, Serbs, etc.).

But remembering the devastation caused by the Napoleonic Wars, and the way those wars led the Europeans to fall into devastating conflict

____

[*]In order to try to gain its status as a great power, following its humiliation by the Prussians and Italians, Habsburg Austria had joined in full and equal partnership with the Hungarians in 1867 ... not just to double the size of a dwindling Austria, but to pacify an increasingly restive nationalism stirring in Hungary.

with each other, the major powers gathered in Berlin in 1878 ... in part to decide how they wanted to quietly divide up the dying Ottoman Empire, theoretically still governing parts of this strategic region. They wanted no wars among themselves to arise from this shift in the European power picture.

They ultimately decided to leave the matter to the newly rising, local interests of the Greeks, Serbs, Bulgarians, etc. ... Christian societies eager to confirm formally their independence from the Ottoman Empire ... even to gain the rights to expand their holdings in the region as free nations.

The Turks were naturally part of these discussions, not really happy to see what was happening to their empire, but not in a position to do much diplomatically on their own behalf.

And so it looked as if the European powers had succeeded in preventing a thorny question close to home (right there in Europe itself) distract them from looking further abroad where much greater imperial challenges awaited them. But all of this still left unanswered the question of how the Serbs, Greeks, Romanians, Bulgarians (and other locals) were going to hold onto that same diplomatic caution ... as each of them began to look for greater national expansion in the surrounding Balkan world. This was going to produce some serious conflicts among these local players. Ultimately this problem would become one monumental in size ... the cause of the startup of World War One in 1914.

The partitioning of Africa (1870s - 1880s)

With the exception of the Dutch (the Cape) and Portuguese (Angola and Mozambique) colonies in southern Africa, Europeans had involved themselves with Sub-Saharan Africa only marginally, setting up trading posts (prior to the early 1800s mostly concerned with the slave trade) and naval refueling posts at various points along the African coastline. What lay beyond coastal Africa remained largely unknown to the Europeans. To them Africa was a "dark" and dangerous continent: unbearable heat, jungle growth, malaria and dangerous tribes made the costs of exploration and settlement appear greater than the possible rewards.

But attitudes on this matter were changing by the mid-1800s. Christian missionaries were beginning to explore the interior, hoping to improve both the spiritual and physical life of Africa. Most prominent among these missionaries was the medical missionary David Livingstone operating under the London Missionary Society. Newspaper accounts of his exploration of the dark continent in an effort to map out the African interior ... but also in the face of constant sickness and physical hardships ... stirred a great interest among Europeans and Americans. Then when

Livingstone disappeared from view, an American journalist, Henry Stanley, decided to go searching for Livingstone. He not only finally discovered the doctor but subsequently in return visits (1878-1885) discovered as well the vast riches of the African interior. In this he was supported by the Belgian king Leopold II who was also interested in the further exploration of this African wealth.   Soon Stanley's ability to gain for Leopold trading rights with the local tribal chiefs stirred the interest of other European monarchs. The French dispatched Pierre de Brazza to the same area and established in 1881 a French base on the Congo River at what would become Brazzaville. That same year they also expanded their French reach in the north of Africa from Algeria eastward to Tunisia and in 1884 to the west of Africa in the region of today's Guinea.

The Berlin Conference of 1884-1885. When Germany began to show interest in the scramble for African territory, Bismarck invited fellow Europeans to hold another conference in Berlin to decide how to apportion spheres of European influence across the African continent.

	Representatives from America and nearly all of Europe gathered in Berlin in late 1884 to sit down with the sketchy map of Africa ... and decide on basic rules (including the requirement of "effective occupation") guiding the carving up of Africa into colonial domains. Leopold subsequently had his holdings in the Congo region (what would eventually become the Congo Free State) confirmed by fellow European monarchs. The Portuguese, the Dutch Boers and the British had their previous positions in southern Africa also confirmed. And Britain's position in Egypt, including assigned dominance in the Sudan and the upland sources of the Nile (but also reaching across Uganda and Kenya to the Indian Ocean) was also confirmed by the other Europeans. The rest of sub-Saharan Africa, east and west, was then divided among the English, French (the French getting most of Saharan West Africa), Germans, Spanish and Italians. Only Liberia (an American creation earlier in the century ... as a home for American slaves repatriated to Africa), the Sultanate of Morocco, and the Christian Kingdom of Ethiopia were left unassigned.

The imperial fallout

Now a race of sorts was on. Nationalist spirits were pumped up by a rivalry that was supposed to be orderly, following certain diplomatic rules, and involving literally the entire world as an object of European domination (the Americans also wanting into the game). Navies were critical to the ability to put a national player in position to follow imperial designs, and a naval race of sorts began to unfold among the Europeans ... much to the distress of Britain which felt its dominant position on the high seas threatened by all this buildup ... especially by the German buildup once Wilhelm II took over from Bismarck in 1890.

Alliances were beginning to be formed among the competitors, in the hope that these would advance the political leverage of the national contenders. In 1879 Bismarck signed a pledge with Austria-Hungary that promised German aid if Russia were to attack Austria (and vice-versa). The agreement was also that if Germany or Austria were to be attacked by some other European power, the partner in this alliance would at least remain neutral (the unspoken understanding being: "in case of an attack by France"). Bismarck knew how badly the French wanted the lost provinces of Alsace and Lorraine back ... and expected trouble from the French on that account. In 1882 the German-Austrian alliance was expanded to include Italy ... mostly to bring Italy into an alliance aimed at France (Italy purposely excluded Britain as a potential adversary).   This would be the beginning of an alliance system that would push the European powers dangerously close to a war that could ... and would ... quickly get out of hand. But for the moment, no one saw the dangers ... yet.

✳ ✳ ✳

THE MAJOR WESTERN POWERS AT THE TURN OF THE CENTURY

The United Kingdom (Great Britain)

The close of the Victorian Age. Under Victoria, Great Britain had thrived as something of a no-nonsense society, because the inspirer of the Victorian age was herself something of that kind of woman: sober, stiff, and always proper. Under Victoria, Britain had chosen to "go it alone," standing off from continental affairs while the nation focused on its particular world of heavy industry, commerce and finance ... in which it was the world's unchallenged master. But towards the end of Victoria's long reign other countries were quickly moving in a similar direction ... and seemed content to do so as if they were in purposeful competition with Britain. Diplomatically, Britain was finding itself isolated from its European partners.

Domestically, Britain was finding it increasingly difficult to maintain its position of economic dominance in the world. At mid-century, Britain (in part also because of the Irish Question) had been so confident of its economic position that it ended the Corn Laws that had protected British agriculture from foreign competition ... the only country to make such a move into "free trade." At that time, Britain was essentially self-sustaining in food production. But as the decades passed, Britain found itself less and less able to feed its population. Cheaper grain and meat products had flooded the British food market ... bankrupting many British farmers, who were forced to move to the rapidly expanding industrial cities in order to find work ... driving down workers' wages there in the process. Unemployment was increasing across the country ... and by the end of the century the nation's economy was suffering great strain.

At that point America had greatly overtaken Britain as an industrial nation ... and Germany was moving rapidly in a similar direction. Even France, though far behind Britain in total industrial output, was showing a strong rate of industrial growth.

Edward VII (1901-1910). When Edward took the throne upon his mother's death, he was already 60 years old. He had busied himself while waiting for the throne in a rather wild life ... wild that is in Victorian terms. Actually he had traveled much and thus knew far more about the world and its varied ways than did the average British politician. He also had a much warmer personality than his mother ... and soon found that he was able to cultivate considerable affection for himself and his rule that was largely lacking during the latter part of the Victorian age. The British came quickly to be fond of their king. But so did the French and other Europeans. Consequently, he ended the splendid isolation of Victorian Britain and engaged his nation more directly in the doings of the rest of European society, culturally as well as politically. Soon close (and ultimately strategic) relations developed with France and Russia. Only in his dealings with his German nephew Wilhelm did Edward find the going a bit rough.

George V and liberal reform in Britain. Edward's son George took the throne at age 45 when his father died in 1910. He was a bit of a reversion back to Victorian sobriety. Nonetheless he was dutiful in his royal office ... and supportive of the cabinet ministers that now effectively ran the nation.

Britain had been on a strong democratization campaign led by the Liberal Party, which dominated the House of Commons. In the first ten years of the twentieth century (but especially after the 1906 elections) the Liberals pushed through a number of bills designed to improve the conditions of the British working class, both workers and families: a legal minimum wage, accident insurance, injury compensation, old age pensions, workplace hours and conditions, slum clearance and housing renewal, public education, etc.

Ironically, much as in Germany and France, the harder the Liberals worked to improve life for the workers, the more the socialist leaders of the British working class seemed to draw political support that enabled them to increase the numbers of the members of the Labour Party sitting in the

House of Commons. For instance in the general elections of 1906, the Liberals won 366 seats and the Conservatives (still referred to as Tories) were reduced in number to 157 seats. But the new Labour Party was able to take 51 seats.

But at the time the real challenge to the Liberals was considered to be the strong Conservative Party loyalties of Britain's upper house, the House of Lords. Passage of the Liberal reform bills had been bitterly fought by the Lords ... and won by the Liberals over this Tory opposition only through much struggle. From the Liberal point of view, the House of Lords needed deep reforming ... especially the power of the Lords to veto or mutilate legislation passed in the House of Commons.

Finally in 1911 ... after the threat to the House of Lords was issued that if they continued their obstructionism the Liberals would simply direct the King to create a large number of new Lords to ensure passage of their bills ... the Lords backed down and accepted a new law restricting greatly their ability to block the work of the House of Commons: failure of the Lords to pass Commons' financial bills would automatically make them law after one month; they could slow up but not stop Commons' other legislation. In short governmental power was now given over fully to the people and their representatives in the House of Commons.

The French Third Republic at the turn of the century

The glory of Paris. Without question, Paris during this period was by far the most glamorous, most sophisticated, most artistic city ... not only in Europe but also the world. The city attracted writers, artists, musicians from all over Europe. Of a huge impact on the world of art were such French artists as Manet, Monet, Renoir, Degas, Pissarro, Morisot, Seurat, Cézanne, Gaugin, Toulouse-Lautrec, etc. And artists of other countries flocked to France to be part of the dynamic, Van Gogh (Dutch), Cassatt (American) etc. Paris's shops sold the finest clothing, perfumes, jewelry and other refinements, and its restaurants offered world-famous foods and wines – as did other towns in France.

But therein lay a major economic problem for France. At a time when the industrial age was turning countries such as England, Germany, and the United States into superpowers ... France was still producing only small-scale – often only hand-crafted – refinements. They were of a superior quality to be sure. But the days of mass production were overtaking such economic traditions ... and France would find itself left behind in the rapid growth of the economies of its fast-rising competitors. The Franco-Prussian war had demonstrated this clearly. Yet France was not in the mood to make such an economic shift. It was proud of its cultural achievements.

But these achievements would not be enough to protect France in the days ahead.

The Boulanger Affair (1888-1889). A number of major crises would hit the new republic during those times. The French were very angry over the loss of the eastern provinces of Alsace and Lorraine to the Germans. Eventually these sentiments seemed to draw forward a charismatic French general Boulanger, in whom many French placed their hope for something of a military revival, Napoleon-style ... even a political coup d'état or takeover of the government in order to get things rolling.

But charismatic did not mean courageous ... and when it became apparent that he was being pushed up against a strong set of resistant leaders, Boulanger lost his nerve and fled to Belgium (where he committed suicide).

The Dreyfus Affair (1894-1906). Among the many other issues which stirred troubles within the political circles of France, the biggest and most persistent was the case of the Jewish French military officer Alfred Dreyfus, accused of handing over to the Germans secret documents concerning France's military defense position. The evidence was sketchy and clearly biased by a mood of anti-Semitism.   But Captain Dreyfus nobly held his composure during the humiliating trial and sentencing, never wavering from his claim of innocence.

When he was sent off to solitary confinement in the French penal colony of Devil's Island (French Guiana, South America) the affair plunged France into a deep dispute, republicans generally in strong support of Dreyfus and the monarchists in opposition. Republican charges of anti-Semitism ... and monarchist (and Catholic) charges of Jewish money involvement ... were flung back and forth. Rumors (later proved to be true) began to appear that the military knew that someone else was guilty, but was unwilling to reopen the case. At this point the famous French author Zola wrote a strong defense of Dreyfus ... earning Zola a sentence of a year in jail (which he avoided with his escape to England!). Indeed at this point everyone was talking about the case. Soon French governments were rising and falling over the issue.

In 1899 Dreyfus was brought back to France, tried and again found guilty ... but then given a full pardon ... though not a reversal of the "guilty" verdict ... which ultimately satisfied none of the "Dreyfusards" (numerous authors, journalists and politicians of the "Left"). Finally in 1906, after much further digging into the evidence, he was found to be innocent of all charges and reinstated with the rank of major and awarded membership in the Legion of Honour. Thus it was that France was able to put behind it an affair that had torn at the heart of French politics for over a full decade.

But the Dreyfus Affair had achieved one distinct outcome: French monarchism, coupled with an intensely reactionary Catholic-French nationalism, was greatly reduced in stature and influence ... and French republicanism, with socialist and internationalist instincts, was in the same measure greatly strengthened. This controversy thus launched the career of the Socialist leader Jean Jaurès and led to the creation of the large French Socialist Party and the huge French trade union (the SFIO).

It also inspired the Austrian journalist Theodor Herzl, who had been present at Dreyfus' sentencing in 1895, to move from his advocacy of Jewish assimilation into Gentile society ... to the advocacy of the creation of a Jewish homeland in the biblical territory of Israel, where Jews could gather in order to get away from the strong anti-Semitism that seemed to threaten Jews constantly wherever they found themselves. Thus out of the Dreyfus Affair Zionism was born.

The (Second) German Empire or Reich

The German Empire that Bismarck had assembled under the Prussian monarchy contained 27 distinct political units: four kingdoms, twelve duchies, seven principalities, three cities, and the imperial territory of Alsace-Lorraine. At the heart of the Reich stood Prussia, the largest of the kingdoms in extent and population. The King of Prussia was thus also the Emperor who symbolized the union. But in addition to the imperial head, holding the whole thing together were the legislative institutions of the Reichstag (its representatives voted on by all adult German males) and the Bundesrat (with representatives sent by the 27 states) ... and a supreme court, the Reichsgericht. Eventually both a criminal law and a civil law code would be put into effect on a uniform basis throughout Germany.

Of course also holding it together was the pride of the German people who, having suffered for centuries the indignities of being considered something of a political and cultural backwater, sensed keenly the rapid rise of their new nation as a great European power. For that they had Bismarck to thank.

The *Kulturkampf* – struggle between Church and secular State. But not all went smoothly at first for Bismarck or the German people with respect to their new domestic politics. The Roman Church had been humiliated in the loss of its lands to the new Italian state ... and sought to recover some of its stature with the new declaration (1870) of the infallibility of the pope. The Church proclaimed that in all matters of faith and morals the pope's pronouncements were totally infallible ... thus not subject to change or even question within the church. Not all German Catholics were happy about this new dogma and their very "un-Catholic" protests were heard in Rome. In response, the pope demanded that the Prussian government remove these individuals from all positions of authority in schools and universities, and even in the German churches. This was something that Bismarck was not about to do, seeing in it the revival of the old investiture controversy. He informed Rome that the German emperor had no intentions whatsoever to ever again "go to Canossa"* physically or spiritually. A church-state battle of sorts was now on in Germany.

But there were numerous German Catholics willing to join with the pope and Vatican in their support of the views of the Catholic Church. In the Reichstag a large group of such Catholic representatives formed themselves into the Center Party (very conservative, but seated at the center of the array of representatives in the Reichstag). Their support of Rome Bismarck interpreted as a challenge to the German nation itself. He thus led the German parliament to pass a number of laws putting various restrictions on religious education, on the selection and functioning of the clergy, and on marriages (requiring a civil ceremony). The net result for Bismarck was not what he was hoping for ... because in the next elections the Center Party increased its seating in the Reichstag significantly. Bismarck, being ever the intuitive politician, recognized his loss in this matter and began to back down on the various restrictions ... and the Kulturkampf gradually died away.

Ritschl takes German theology further down the Liberal path. At around the same time, another German Protestant (Lutheran) theologian, Albrecht Ritschl, took Christian Liberalism further down its new path in stressing that Christianity's value was found actually rather rationally in its moral-ethical impact, and not on its unbending devotion to the "facts" of Scripture. Like Schleiermacher earlier in that century, Ritschl asserted that much of Scripture was simply the revelation of faith, not fact.

And like Schleiermacher, Ritschl saw faith as highly socially and culturally shaped, stressing the importance of collective faith. Thus the "truth" of faith is found simply in its serviceability to the Christian community.

He was quite direct in his opposition to the traditional adherents of *sola scriptura* ("by Scripture alone"), who saw Scripture as truthful in the same way that modern science approached the idea of "truth." Thus Ritschl hit hard when he claimed that the Gospel of Luke was simply derived from the discredited Gospel of Marcion, employing

---

*In reference to the event of 1077 when Holy Roman Emperor Henry IV went barefoot in the snow to Canossa Castle to ask forgiveness of the Roman Pope Gregory VII ... for Henry's earlier political challenge to the papacy.

the methodology of the rising field of text criticism: inspecting the material-cultural roots of the actual language found in Scripture.

Beyond that, Ritschl remained something of an agnostic, claiming to have no strong knowledge as to the truth of such things as the Eternity of Jesus as Christ's Son, or the validity of the Trinity of God the Father, Jesus the Son, and the Holy Spirit as three representations of the universal God. Likewise, he was dismissive of the idea of Jesus's birth to the virgin Mary. But to Ritschl, these were not the key issues of Christianity anyway. Faith inspired by the example of Jesus, not unverifiable historical fact, was key to Christian "truth."

Ritschl would have a tremendous impact not only on German Protestant theology, but also on Protestantism elsewhere, especially in heavily Protestant America – shaking that Protestantism to the core.

Bismarck and the Social Democrats (Marxists). Germany's move into the industrial age was phenomenal. In short order during the last quarter of the 1800s, Germany moved from being a mostly agricultural society to being the largest industrial society on the European continent. Industrial towns exploded with growth and activity ... changing the demographic character of German society just as quickly. And with that rapid change went all sorts of issues, economic, social and political. One of these was the rapid growth of Socialist political parties representing the interests of the fast-growing industrial working class. From such groupings would eventually emerge the rapidly growing (quite Marxist) Social Democratic Party.

Bismarck decided to meet the Socialist challenge by clamping down on their party's ability to meet and organize ... at the same time trying to steal their thunder by sponsoring a number of state programs similar to those advocated by the working class parties: workers' compensation for sickness and injury on the job, insurance for surviving relatives of a worker killed on the job, and old age pension. Bismarck blended funding from the state, from the industrial companies, and from the workers themselves to finance these programs.

But whereas Bismarck's own social programs were well received by the workers, they did little to undercut the popularity of the Social Democrats. Just as with his struggle with the Catholics, Bismarck, realizing that his strategy had gained him little, backed away from his program ... at least with respect to the clamping down on the politics of the workers' organizations. But when this easing up on the oppression yielded no positive results, he then reversed course a second time and came back hard on those organizations. This would ultimately become part of what would create a political distancing between him and the young German emperor Wilhelm II.

Bismarck and Wilhelm II. In 1888 a 29-year-old Wilhelm took command of Prussia and the German Reich when his grandfather died ... and then his father also died only three months later. Wilhelm was physically very energetic and had a very quick mind. Unfortunately, this would prove to be a major disability because Wilhelm trusted himself to be quicker than others in understanding a situation ... and thus did not tend to check things out deeply before acting.

Bismarck, who was long used to Wilhelm I allowing him to govern Germany, found himself up against the young emperor, who intended to rule Germany directly. Wilhelm did not want the strong-willed Bismarck to get in his way. They disagreed sharply over how to handle the Socialists (Wilhelm at first wanting to take a much softer approach to them) and whether the cabinet ministers were to report directly to Bismarck or to Wilhelm. Bismarck used to get his way with the old emperor by threatening to resign, backing down the emperor every time. But this tactic backfired on Bismarck when such an event in 1890 ended up with Wilhelm accepting his resignation! The Bismarck era in Germany thus came to an abrupt end. A new one under Wilhelm II was about to unfold.

Wilhelm and the shift in German foreign policy. On two other accounts Bismarck and Wilhelm II had disagreed sharply. Wilhelm was very interested in getting Germany involved in the game of European imperialism. Bismarck had thought such imperialism to be unnecessary and needlessly very expensive ... costing Germany vastly more than it yielded in benefits (Bismarck proved ultimately to be absolutely correct on this point). Of course to play the overseas game, a player needed a top-rate navy ... another matter for which Bismarck could see no particular benefits, especially given the cost involved. Wilhelm had disagreed vehemently ... and with Bismarck gone he proceeded to create a German navy that was second in size only to the British navy.

As for the British, their navy was considered vital to their nation's survival. They could see no similar need for such a huge German navy and became ever more suspicious of Wilhelm's goals.

Wilhelm also took the attitude that the German military needed to be strengthened even more than it had been under Bismarck ... claiming that this was the only way to guarantee Germany would never be attacked. Bismarck had been careful about how he sized German power, aware that too much buildup would merely lead other European nations to do the same ... leading to the greater possibility of an unplanned diplomatic catastrophe. Bismarck relied more on diplomatic skill than brute power. For Wilhelm, however, things were exactly reversed: Wilhelm was uninterested in diplomacy and keen on a buildup and demonstration of brute German power.

Here too, Bismarck would soon prove to have been the wiser in the design and use of German power. France immediately sensed a major threat coming again from Germany ... and began to react accordingly.

The Austro-Hungarian monarchy

Franz Joseph I (reigned 1848-1916) and the Austro-Hungarian Union. A young Franz Joseph inherited a very troubled Habsburg empire when his uncle Ferdinand abdicated as a result of the nationalist uprisings which swept Europe in 1848. Franz Joseph was expected to hold together a vast multinational empire on the basis of his personal strengths alone. However, political and economic institutions which would have provided him some degree of unifying support were largely lacking. At his accession to the Habsburg throne, he reigned over a multitude of very different societies, German, Hungarian, Czech, Moravian, Croatian and Italian in ethnic character. In an era of a rising nationalist spirit inflaming all European ethnic groups, such a multi-ethnic empire would find it extremely difficult to maintain the semblance of social order. Franz Joseph had a huge challenge ahead of him.

In 1867 the decision was made to combine into one the two main thrones of Franz Joseph: the Austrian empire and the Hungarian kingdom. Thus Austria-Hungary was born with a single head of state ... yet with two separate parliaments (in Vienna and Budapest) and two separate ministerial councils or cabinets. The two parts of this new kingdom were bound somewhat more closely economically with a customs union and a common currency.

Ethnic problems still remained despite this new union recognizing the separate national identities of the Austrians (German-speaking) and Hungarians. The Italian part of the problem had already been solved simply by the loss of Austria's lands in Italy in Austria's war with Sardinia-Piedmont and France (1859) and then Prussia and its new ally Italy (1866). But the question of the Slavic minorities (Polish, Czech, Croatian and other) remained unanswered by the new union. Slavic nationalism ... actively promoted in the Balkan region by Austria-Hungary's principle Slavic neighbor to the East, Russia ... would remain a major problem for the dual monarchy.

Franz Joseph sincerely attempted to meet the aspirations of the various national groupings making up his multi-national empire. But he found himself constantly challenged by the jealousies among the national groups themselves. His efforts to help one group would bring greater anger from other groups because of his "favoritism" than it ever brought gratitude from the national groups he was trying, one by one, to help. Though he personally was loved dearly by his people, his efforts to solve their political problems proved to be impossible.

Eventually this very matter would become the cause of the outbreak in 1914 of a war (World War One) that would destroy Austria-Hungary ... and much of the rest of Europe as well.

Italy

Italy was finding that as difficult as it had been to create Italy, it was proving to be even harder to create Italians. Most Italians saw themselves as Venetians, Genoese, Florentines, Sienese, Romans, Neapolitans, Sicilians, etc. well before they recognized themselves as Italians. These local identities had been at the heart of their economic competitions and wars for countless generations ... and it was very hard for them to rise above those local loyalties to take on the primary identity as Italian.

Also, Italy was a very Catholic country ... and the hatred of the Church for the constitutional monarchy that had taken away the Church's vast landholdings made it difficult for the devout Catholic Italians to love their new government. The new Italian state was constantly denounced from the local pulpits ... and particularly by Pope Pius IX (Pope:1846-1878) who hated what had been done to the Church and who considered himself a "prisoner of the Vatican."

Part of the Italian identity problem also was that those who had supported the Risorgimento had been mostly a relatively small group of urban upper-class intellectuals ... and not really the vast peasant population who simply watched the unfolding of events and the creation of Italy from the sidelines. Most Italians had not invested much personally in the creation of the new Italian state.

Also, now that the young political idealists had achieved the dream of a united Italy wrested from the hands of surrounding powers, they had no similar national challenges still facing them, ones that could continue to draw them together in a spirit of ongoing national unity. The Risorgimento had achieved its goals ... and there was no similar burning sense of what was supposed to happen next.

Poverty. Italy was a poor country. Industry was still in its infant stages and agriculture was the economic mainstay of the country ... though even here productivity was very low (a high mountain range running north and south through the middle of the country did not help matters). Much of the population lived near the starvation level and disease was rampant.

Nonetheless even in the face of these problems, the rate of population growth was extremely high ... pinching Italy even more. As a result, sadly one of Italy's major "exports" was its population, which went abroad in the hopes of finding a better life elsewhere. Expatriates did indeed help finance life in Italy, sending money back home to their families. Many would also return to retire in their homeland where their savings would carry them further in life.

Illiteracy. Literacy was very low, especially in the south where even as late as 1870 only about one tenth of the population could read and write. Even in the somewhat more prosperous north hardly half of the population could read and write at that time. But efforts to improve Italian education in the early years of the twentieth century would begin to have an impact on this problem... though even as late as 1914 over a third of the population was still illiterate.

Political corruption. Italian politicians tended to look only to their own political careers ... not being vitally interested in issues larger than their own personal success. Political parties were numerous and actually only small groupings centered around key individuals, the groupings held together by the favors these individuals drew from their political office and were able to pass on to their personal following. This in turn produced terrible political instability as governments in Rome rose and fell simply on the basis of personal politics.

Taxes were very heavy on the tightly-stretched Italian population ... and governments were not inclined to keep expenses in line with Italy's actual ability to afford the projects produced by the government. Thus for many Italians, the new Italian state seemed to be no less an oppressor than had been the earlier governments, whether local or foreign. In the south of Italy, people continued to look to the local Mafia organization to supervise local life rather than to the distant Italian government in Rome.

Real growth. And yet ... Italy did begin to register real growth as the 1800s closed out and the twentieth century opened up. Coming from so far behind economically it was of course easy to register high rates of growth ... but in fact Italy was definitely moving ahead in terms of industrial production (despite Italy's own lack of coal and iron deposits), railroad mileage, new port facilities, drainage of swampland and improvement of agricultural yield.

The monarchy. Victor Emmanuel II, who had led the Risorgimento to its victory, died in 1878 ... not long into the life of the new state. His place was taken by his son Umberto I, who reigned over Italy until his death in 1900 when he was killed by an anarchist's bullet (he had escaped two previous assassination attempts). His 22-year reign however had been much less illustrious than that of his father. Umberto was a very passive king who preferred to let the politicians do the heavy lifting while he mostly watched from the sidelines. Sadly he did little to pull Italy together as it slid into a political lethargy that threatened even more the thin unity holding the country together.

His place was taken by his son Victor Emmanuel III (reigned 1900-1946). Despite the high hopes the country had that this energetic young prince would be able to pull Italy back together, the passing of time proved that he really did not have the strength to discipline the chaos of the various party bosses ... including his prime minister Giovanni Giolitti, who was in and out of office five times in the period 1892-1921, and who also followed the political trend of using his office simply for his own personal political good.

Italy and the papacy. In the same year that Victor Emmanuel died, so did Pope Pius IX ... whose place was then taken by the nobly-born Giaocchino Pecci as Pope Leo XIII (pope 1878-1903). The new pope's political domain was now reduced to simply encouraging certain types of humanitarian social action around the still very broad Catholic realm.

Theologically, Leo followed the basic directions of his predecessor, Pius IX – in fact nearly all Catholic (and Orthodox) predecessors reaching back to the time of Constantine – in stressing the importance of personal devotion to the Virgin Mary. As "Mediatrix," she had the power to intercede for the faithful in their look to heaven for its blessings. In this regard, he stressed the importance (by way of eleven encyclicals he issued!) of the Rosary ... a prayer employing rosary beads to help keep correct count of the ten elements of the prayer ... or ten "Hail Marys." In short, the Catholic Church's Virgin Mary – not the new secular government in Rome, or in any other political center in the Western world – was where the faithful were to look for social justice, for personal and family blessings ... and ultimately for personal salvation.

This was the Catholic response to a new, highly Secular world unfolding across the "Christian West." It would need that spiritual support in the days that loomed ahead.

Italian imperialism. One of the keys to successful nationalism seemed at the time to be the securing of an overseas empire. Thus Italian nationalists put in place an imperial strategy ... but found the pickings overseas for Italian colonial territory to be quite slim. Most of the prime territory in Asia and Africa had already been grabbed. This left only the sandy wastes of North Africa and the horn of East Africa available for seizure. The Italians were most desirous of Tunisia, just opposite the Italian island of Sicily. But to the immense distress of Italy, the French grabbed that territory in 1881 ... which, by way of bitter reaction, drove Italy in 1882 to join with Germany and Austria-Hungary in forming the Triple Alliance.

This would mark the beginning of diplomatic troubles that would not only divide Europe into two contending camps ... but would ultimately lead Europe into the "Great War" (World War One).

Things at this point did not get much better for Italy in the imperial realm. An attempt to seize the Christian kingdom of Abyssinia (Ethiopia) resulted only in the humiliating defeat of Italian troops in 1896 by local Ethiopian troops, ending that venture (for a while anyway). Italy then (1912) moved its focus to the North African desert lands of Tripolitania and Cyrenaica (to the South of Italy, just across the Mediterranean) ... bombing Bedouin troops from their new airplanes (the Italians proved to be much better at aerial combat) ... and occupying the few towns located there. They would then unite and assign to this new piece of imperial territory the ancient Roman name "Libya."

Spain

In many ways Spain was the mirror of Italy ... complete with the same problems of a weakly developed industrial infrastructure, vast poverty and illiteracy, and a less than illustrious national leadership.

Carlists versus Liberals. A major complicating factor in the life of Spain was not however – as was the case in Italy – a feeble sense of national identity. A strong sense of Spanish national honor had been securely established centuries earlier. But in 1833 a problem would develop that would divide that national sense of identity into two warring camps ... a division that would tear at Spanish society for the next century and a half ... and bloody the nation more than once ... though particularly in the 1930s during the time of the murderous Spanish civil war.

The problem began simply over a dispute within the ruling Bourbon royal family when a dying Ferdinand VII found himself with no direct heir ... despite three previous marriages. But as he lay dying his fourth wife was pregnant ... and he made the national assembly or Cortes promise to designate the unborn heir, whether male or female (the latter a questionable principle under Salian law), as the new reigning monarch. His younger brother Don Carlos, however, put forward his own claim to the throne. And when a baby girl, Isabella, was born, a dynastic fight erupted. Supporting Isabella II and her regent mother were the Cortes (national parliament), much of the army, and most of the Spanish middle class. Supporting Don Carlos (and thus the "Carlists") were the Catholic Church and the landed nobility. A very nasty 7-year civil war followed, which divided bitterly the nation into very conservative (Carlist) and militantly Liberal camps.

Ultimately the Liberals won out politically. But the war left the country divided culturally as the ultra-Catholic Carlists would henceforth set their hearts on a highly romanticized dream of reviving the glories of a feudal Catholic Spain that existed three centuries earlier ... whereas the Liberals would be as intensely dedicated to moving Spain away from its deep conservatism and into the realm of modern industrial progressivism sweeping the cultures of northern Europe. This division ultimately would cripple Spain as a functioning society across many Spanish generations ... even up into the 1970s.

As it turned out, Isabella grew up to become a scandalous pursuer of sexual affairs and a ruler who seemed unable or unwilling to bring under control Spain's rampant political corruption (similar to the way Italy was given over to boss-controlled politics) ... until in 1868 a major Spanish uprising finally drove her into exile. Then despite the drafting of a new liberal constitution, political confusion followed when the search for someone to accept the Spanish throne yielded only many refusals. Finally Amadeo, younger brother of Victor Emmanuel of Italy, accepted ... but then abandoned the throne two years later, unhappy with his chilly reception by the Spanish. Then a republic was attempted ... which also was abandoned after two years. By this time (1874) Alfonso, son of Isabella, was of age and took the throne (Alfonso XII). Things then settled down as Alfonso came under a rather liberal constitution bringing Spain in line with the constitutional monarchies prevalent in the rest of Europe. Still, the problem of political bosses and the deep bitterness between the Liberals and the Carlists continued to plague Spanish politics.

Then only 28 at the time, Alfonso died in 1885, leaving behind a pregnant wife, Maria Christina, who would act as Spanish regent until the son born to her (Alfonso XIII) reached his majority (1902).

A post-imperial Spain. It was during this regency period that Spain lost the last of her major overseas colonies (Cuba, Puerto Rico and the Philippines) in a three-month war with America (1898) that the Spanish really did not support with any enthusiasm. Indeed, many of the Spanish were glad to be rid of the expensive burden of the colonies ... for they had not brought Spain anything but an ever-larger debt. The hope was even that with the colonies gone, the Spanish economy could finally begin to take off.

In fact, the coming of Alfonso XIII to the throne in 1902 marked the beginning of a gradual improvement in the Spanish economy. To be sure the movement was slow ... but perceptible. Yet Spain remained one of the poorest countries in Europe ... and a country so conflicted internally (Liberals versus Carlists) that it was unable to involve itself diplomatically or militarily in the tensions growing among the other major European powers. It was just as well. By staying outside of the conflict that was destined to become the Great War (World War One) Spain did itself a great favor.

Romanov Russia

Alexander III (1881-1894). With the assassination of Tsar Alexander II in 1881, the new Tsar Alexander III would bring Russia into a period of reaction (Alexander III was completely opposed to the Liberal reforms of his father Alexander II) ... something on the order of Nicholas I. Nicholas's almost forgotten doctrine of "autocracy, orthodoxy, and nationality" would be revived by Alexander III ... perhaps even more rigorously. To the new Alexander, anyone who did not honor the absolute power of the Tsar and was not Russian Orthodox in religion and Russian in language and culture was suspect in the tsar's eyes. He despised the internationalist mindset of the Russian Liberals, and did what he could to crush the spirit of Russian Liberalism.

His dedication to the cultivation of the Russian nationalist spirit was fierce. For an empire built on many different nationalities and ethnic groups, this would be a hard thing indeed. The Finns and Poles, for instance, who had earlier been promised co-equal status within the empire, would see their cultural-political rights removed one by one. Yet these very actions by Alexander would serve to increase the cultural sensitivities of the subject nations, not bring them to the point of assimilation into the larger Russian culture.

Jewish persecution. The worst-case scenario was that of the Jews in Russia ... where more than half of the world's Jews lived by the late 1800s. Jews had been brought under Russian dominion during the reign of Catherine the Great, with the second and third (1793-1795) partitions of Poland, where in Eastern Poland (at this point now absorbed into Russia as its Western region) there were numerous German-speaking Jewish settlements. Catherine then set out the boundaries of a "Pale of Settlement" to which Jews were restricted. Under Nicholas I, the restrictions against Jews serving in the military were finally lifted – and indeed Jews were required to perform military service under Nicholas's 1827 conscription law. Gradually Russian Jews began to adopt Russian ways – and under Alexander II were even freed up (along with the ending of serfdom in 1861) to the extent that many began to enter the ranks of the Russian upper middle class of merchants and intellectuals.

When then the reactionary Alexander III became tsar in 1881, the situation facing the Jews became harsh. Jews were falsely blamed for Alexander II's death ... and a mass of anti-Jewish "pogroms" (the random beatings of Jews and the plundering and burning of their homes) broke out across the south of Russia ... continuing until 1884, when the Russian "Christians" were finally satisfied as a new round of anti-Jewish laws went into effect. Jews were forced to abandon their farms and move into towns and cities ... then expelled from even some of these such as Kyiv in 1886 and Moscow in 1891. In 1887 highly restrictive quotas were placed on Jewish entrance into secondary and higher educational institutions and into a number of professions, particularly the legal profession. In 1892 restrictions were added, prohibiting the Jews from voting or holding elective office. Then a new wave of pogroms hit the Jewish community in the period 1903-1906. Thousands were killed or gravely wounded in the ordeal.

Meanwhile Jews were emigrating from Russia in mass numbers ... most of them to America, and some to other parts of Europe. But some also began to migrate (1882 and after) to the region of Palestine within the Ottoman Empire ... as part of the new "Zionist" movement.

Problems on the peasant farms. But the situation for the Russian peasants was not all that wonderful either. They were easily disillusioned when the formal end of serfdom did not bring about the gains they were expecting. In some cases the new freedom brought on economic hardships they were not accustomed to. Payments for the land, land scarcity and the small size of the farmers' plots of land, poor agricultural practices, and periods of bad weather made success in their new "business" of farming at times almost impossible. Thus peasant rebellions were constant and numerous in the latter part of the 1800s.

Nicholas II (1894-1917). When Nicholas came to the throne after his father's sudden death, there was hope that he would return Russia to the path of liberalization started by his grandfather Alexander II. That hope would soon fade away. Although Nicholas was not the suspicious reactionary that his father was, he had the very strong conviction that he was placed on the throne to serve God by preserving the old Russian order ... against the modernizing tendencies of the Liberals. Worse, he was easily manipulated by stronger personalities around him ... especially by his wife who possessed even stronger, virtually mystical, convictions that they were placed on the throne to carry out the will of God ... not the will of man.

Rapid social change. Meanwhile Liberalism was spreading within a growing population of educated Russians ... desiring Russia to be recast as a constitutional democracy on the model of Great Britain. Behind this growth was the slow emergence of the industrial revolution in Russia ... and the new wealth it was creating among the small upper middle class of "capitalists." But this group by comparison to the rest of Europe would remain tiny – and relatively politically incoherent (organizing themselves into a large number of small competing political parties). They also would never gain the economic leverage that this class had in the rest of Europe because most of the investment and industrial development came not out of their finances but rather from foreign investors – and the Romanov state – which together owned most of the newly accumulating industrial wealth of Russia.

This same industrial revolution was also producing another new and rising social class in Russia: the industrial worker. By the turn of the century this rapidly growing segment of Russian society was developing a very aggressive social and political agenda ... in great part because of that very fact that the companies they worked for seemed remote and insensitive to their needs, being foreign and state owned. Consequently, a quasi-Marxist ideology despising both capitalism and its supposed tool, the state, developed within the working class ... and among the intellectuals. This was particularly the case for the Social Democrats – (or "Communists") who felt called on to give voice to that working class.

The Ottoman Turk "Sick Man of Europe"

But if the Tsar was having a hard time hanging onto the lead in Russia, the Ottoman Sultan was having an even harder time maintaining his authority within the fast decaying Ottoman Empire. It seemed at times that the only thing holding the Empire together was the fear by France and Britain (especially Britain) that should the Ottoman Empire collapse, their major interests in the Eastern Mediterranean would be threatened deeply. Thus it was that they had intervened in the Crimean War between Turkey and Russia on Turkey's side ... not so much out of an interest in a Turkish victory as instead a fear of a Russian victory and the position that would give Russia in the Eastern Mediterranean.

Thus holding the decaying Ottoman Empire together was the fact that the European powers feared that carving up the empire (as they had done to Poland) would merely benefit their fellow European competitors more than themselves. Similarly, ethnic jealousies within the empire kept Turkish political reformers from acting in unison to revitalize their empire.

Strong leadership by the sultans would have helped greatly. But such leadership was sadly lacking. At a time (the 1400s and 1500s) when there was no moral argument being issued by political philosophers against the principle of rule by emperors, and when at the same time the Ottoman Empire was blessed by emperors or sultans of great ability, the Ottoman Empire was not only a stable political unit ... it was one of Europe's great powers. But by the end of the 1800s those days were over ... on both counts. Not only was rule by imperial figures under attack philosophically, the Ottoman Empire had developed in ways guaranteed to bring forward a whole series of sultans not really up to the demands of their office.

Corruption and decline. Moral rot had set in at numerous levels of the empire. A major problem was the Imperial Harem, made up of hundreds of wives, concubines, eunuchs and children belonging to the sultan. Presiding over all of it was the sultan's mother, the Valide Sultan, the second most powerful person in the empire. With all these possible inheritors of the sultan's throne, it was inevitable that the Harem would become a center of dangerous intrigue ... involving even the sultans themselves who moved from the palace to the harem supposedly to govern their empire. Little by little however the sultans found themselves spending more time managing the harem than they did managing their decaying empire.

The crushing weight of foreign debt. Another failing of the Ottoman sultanate ... not untypical of many governments unwilling to live within their own means ... was the massive debt that was run up by the sultan in his effort to live up to the high material standards he thought sovereign lords should be able to enjoy. Part of the independence he accorded Egypt in its political operations was in exchange for the tax revenues that Egypt promised to send to the sultan. As the Egyptian khedive was a major stockholder in the new Suez Canal Company, those revenues were expected to be substantial. Thus on the basis of those expected revenues, the sultan was able to engage massive loans to support his rule ... not aware of the huge dangers he was courting in doing so.

When the costs in building the canal proved to greatly exceed the revenue it subsequently received from those using the canal and the khedive was forced in 1875 to sell his shares (primarily to the British), that key source of revenue flow to the sultan ended abruptly. In turn the sultan was forced to default on his loans to the European banks, provoking the Great Eastern Crisis (1875-1878) ... in which the sultan himself was forced to commit "suicide" by some of his pashas (1876).

Finally in 1881 an international debt collection agency was set up by the European powers to collect the payments owed by the Ottoman Empire to its European creditors. But not only did this agency collect on debts, it also played a key role in finding financing for ongoing industrial and railroad projects for Turkey. While this served greatly to help modernize Turkey, it also compromised deeply the empire's political independence. But being the "Sick Man of Europe," the empire seemed to have no way to avoid this development.

The Young Ottomans. In the mid-1860s a group of Turkish intellectuals formed a secret society, the Young Ottomans, whose focus was on modernizing the political structure of the empire. They hoped not only to bring the empire up to the constitutional standards of the constitutional monarchies of Western Europe ... but also to create a broad Ottoman "nationalism" that would develop a sense of Ottoman pride, a super-nationalism designed to bridge the ethnic differences dividing the various national groupings within the empire. In 1876 they seemed to have made great progress toward that goal when the new Sultan Abdül Hamid II (reigned 1876-1909) did indeed extend to the empire a constitution designed to make the Ottoman government conform more closely to the West European version. But only two years later the sultan reversed himself completely in the face of a growing conflict with his new parliament and he simply suspended the new constitution and returned the empire under his rule as absolute monarch. At this point the animosities separating the various ethnic groups making up the empire simply magnified.

America

The Industrial Revolution. Across the Atlantic, America was very busy developing along economic lines very similar to Europe's. As already noted, America, in fact, was way ahead of Europe in this game of industrial development. But unlike Europe, this development had virtually nothing to do with governmental policy. It was all done under the control of very wealthy "private" entrepreneurs ... who felt themselves to be in no need whatsoever of government assistance in the development of their particular business interests. Personally-cultivated capitalism worked just fine for them.

But for the industrial workers, driven from the American farms by overpopulation and drawn from those escaping the "Old World" of Europe in the hope of finding in America a better opportunity for their own development, things were proving to be quite hard. A labor movement of sorts had developed in the 1880s ... but had not done well, and simply died.

Industrial greed benefits an ever-smaller percentage of American society. Tragically, the spread in the level of wealth between the great capitalists (the Vanderbilts, Andrew Carnegie, J.P. Morgan, the Rockefellers, etc.) and the industrial working-class families became outrageously high for a supposedly "democratic" America. Basically, the top one percent of the population earned fifty percent of the nation's wealth. The bottom half or lower fifty percent of the population together earned or possessed about one percent of the nation's wealth. This was morally unacceptable in a society posing itself as the model of "democracy."

Finally, the danger this posed to the "American way" was answered by the very ambitious and very active President Teddy Roosevelt (1901-1909), who undertook to push anti-trust legislation forward ... and aim it at a number of American industrial monopolies. And his replacement in the presidential office, Howard Taft (1909-1913), would push antitrust actions to an even greater extent.

Capitalism in America was a wonderful system. But it would have to function under various rules or restrictions designed to not let the pure greed of a few individuals or organizations take over the American economy.

So absorbed was America in its own fabulous industrial development that it treated international matters, especially the urge to imperialism, only as a rather secondary matter. However, developments in Hawaii, rebellion in China, revolt in Cuba, and dwindling Spanish power in the Philippines did stir enough interest in American political circles to get America involved ... though its involvement seemed rather minor in comparison to the actions abroad by the British and the French ... and the efforts of Germany to put itself in the same league with the British and the French.

Thus despite its massive industrial capacity, America was thought of by its fellow Westerners as being a national power of only a secondary order. There was, in fact, little interest in drawing America into the imperial game as a valuable ally. So ... the imperialist game seemed to move forward without great American involvement in the matter. But that would soon change.

America's own intellectual-spiritual challenges at the turn of the century. With the distancing in time from the Civil War, once again America fell back into a world of humanistic rationalism, pretty much along the same lines as what was developing in Europe. Again, the Christian faith in America found itself deeply challenged by this intellectual-spiritual shift.

America "Liberalism" was growing rapidly in the world of academics, government, and even religion. And it took on qualities not all that different from the political idealism of Karl Marx. Liberals, such as the prolific writer and lecturer John Dewey, blamed flaws in the social structure, not flaws in the human heart, as the cause of the social problems still facing the country. According to Dewey, if you reform the social structure then the problems will go away. True, some "education" of the masses will have to take place in order to release them from the grip of antiquated thinking.

Like Lenin, Dewey believed that this was the special responsibility of those already enlightened to society's truths. But (also like Lenin) he believed that this would be merely a temporary stage in social-cultural development that a society would have to go through, before the masses were ready to take on freely a fully enlightened world. Thus American Liberalism came to be understood as a program of deep social reform – reform led (just temporarily, of course) by the more enlightened of society.

On the governmental side of this same Liberalism was the Supreme Court Justice Oliver Wendel Holmes, who took a very "progressivist" view of the American Constitution, understanding that it needed to be constantly adjusted to fit the changing context of society's ever-changing dynamics. In short, the Constitution needed to be understood to be whatever the currently serving justices saw the need for it to be ... sort of a "Legal Realism" being their guide. Thus the real Constitution was not to be found in an ancient document, but in the hearts and minds of very wise Supreme Court justices!

Thus to a rising group of American Liberals, "democracy" was to be a social program "coming from above," not from the desires and actions of the unreformed masses.

This same kind of "Enlightened Realism" also found its way into the Christian world of America, not surprisingly among some of its leading voices of the day. Reason seemed once again to dictate the need to do some updating of the faith, getting it away from the ancient myths found in Scripture – in order to help the faith deal with the issues more at hand at the time. Thus Biblical "text-criticism" became the fashion in seminaries training a rising generation of pastors to be more "realistic" in their approach to Scripture, and thus their Christian walk (and preaching).

This was hardly a new development, something that had already shaken the Christian West back in the late 1600s and early 1700s. And of course it demonstrated amply the horrors of such "enlightenment" in the French Revolution, dedicated to exactly that same post-Christian enlightenment – which unsurprisingly the Enlightened Ones ended up slaughtering each other because they could not agree on the directions such enlightenment was supposed to take them.

But American Christianity had thankfully not really gone down that road very far, and subsequently – the mid-1700s to the mid-1800s – had been able to return to its more traditional understanding of life and its dynamics, in order to put America back on track as being a "Covenant Nation" ... and take on successfully the nation's accompanying challenges.

But here at the end of the 1800s, a fully settled America found itself once again back in the mood to repeat the ways of the earlier "Age of Enlightenment." The milder form this would take would be found in the development of the "Social Gospel" – an effort of Congregationalist pastor Washington Gladden, the Baptist pastor and seminary professor, Walter Rauschenbusch and the economist Richard Ely to find some kind of "middle ground" between Christian traditionalism and modern Secular science. They skirted theological controversy by simply emphasizing that Christianity was about social service, to the poor and hurting. Of course there was nothing particularly Christian about this, in the sense that any person of humane sentiments (Confucianist, Buddhist, Hindu, Muslim) would find themselves agreeing that this was a very important way to go at life. But ultimately it had nothing to do with Christ's eternal salvation. Indeed, the Social Gospel treated such a traditional concern as very problematic.

Then there was what appeared to most of the faithful as a very strong attack on Scripture as the foundation of all key Truths in life. The huge and very traditionalist Presbyterian denomination found itself deeply troubled by the "text-criticism" offered by Union Theological Seminary's professor Charles Briggs, who was perceived as treating Scripture as folklore rather than absolute truth. Briggs pointed out that Moses did not write the books attributed to him, but instead those writings were most likely put together many centuries after him – by drawing from four different traditions. And he also stated that the second half of the Book of Isaiah most likely had been put together after Isaiah's death by his disciples.

At a time when truth was coming to have a strongly material basis in the thinking of most Westerners, such attacks on the material or "factual" foundations of scripture appeared to most Christian Americans as being absolutely heretical. Thus the denomination in 1893 voted to excommunicate Briggs, and attempted to remove him from Union Seminary. Union Seminary, however, chose instead to remove itself from the Presbyterian denomination. And Briggs continued his studies and teaching there.

On the other hand, the very popular circuit preacher/evangelist Dwight L. Moody was able to take the rising social doctrines of Progressivism and combine them with the idea of cleaning up America's sins in anticipation of Christ's second coming, all without involving any commentary on the burning theological disputes of the day. This made a lot of sense to independent-minded "Middle Americans" who simply wanted to find in their Christian faith the guidance they needed personally to get through the changing times of the late 1800s, and prepare for the eternal life to come. Thus thousands came out to hear Moody's preaching.

Also, there was a most unusual (unusual in terms of more traditional Christianity) pentecostal or charismatic "awakening" which broke out with the Azusa Street Pentecostal revival in Los Angeles in 1906. And this in turn birthed the charismatic Assemblies of God denomination, which would grow – and is still growing to amazing size – not only in America but also internationally. Thus it was still understood by many Americans that its nation still had God's work to pursue

But most tragically, few of the Secular "Enlightened Ones" on the other side of the spiritual fence at this point had any sense of the collapse of all reasonable social order awaiting them only a few years into the future (the coming "Great War" of 1914-1918). They too were positive that they were moving into an "End Times," although not one delivered by God, but instead one delivered by the Human Reason by which they intended to guide the rest of society. But sadly, this march forward of history would hit the country tragically when the Liberally enlightened American President Woodrow Wilson would take America into the ghastly European War in 1917, to make the world "safe for democracy."

So it was that democracy ("democracy" as conceived by political experts) rather than God's covenantal program would come to take over as America's main program. The results would be very bloody, and ultimately very pointless.

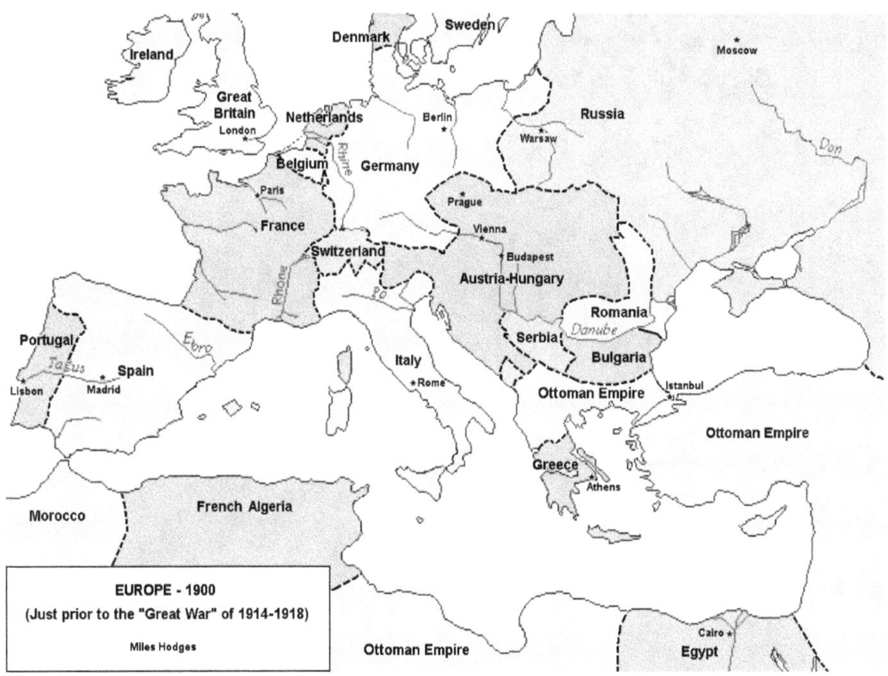

The Gilded Calm Before the Storm

So ... at the turn into the twentieth century most of Western society seemed to be clearly at the top of its game. Many already called this the "Gilded Age" ... where everything seemed to be gold-lined. True, the world was still engaged in rapid social change, and perfection had not yet been fully achieved. But all this change seemed to be in a direction entirely positive in character ... and seemed to promise that utopia was at hand. The common people were enjoying unprecedented new powers as designers of their own destiny. Even kings and emperors seemed to have been brought under the power of the people.

Wealth was clearly expanding, though reaching the lower classes only with difficulty. But even in this matter, just as the middle class had recently secured vital political and economic rights wrested from the old feudal order, socialist reformers were certain (Marx had clearly demonstrated to them how this all was an inevitable historical development) that soon the working classes would be wrestling those same political and economic rights from the middle class industrialists (or "capitalists"). Such utopian progress was certain ... and just around the corner.

But storm clouds were gathering that would change this game plan dramatically ... in a way few observers anticipated in those first years of the twentieth century. Europe was about to go through such a nightmare of events that even in finally getting through it all, Europe would never be the same.

The Gilded Age was about to come to a dramatic close.

CHAPTER THIRTEEN

THE "GREAT WAR" (WORLD WAR ONE)

* * *

THE PATH TO WORLD WAR

By the opening days of the twentieth century the Europeans and Americans had clearly put the political-cultural stamp of the Christian West on most of the rest of the world. This would mark the peak of Western glory. It would also mark the beginning of its political-cultural decline, at least with respect to Europe's part in the Western political-cultural dynamic.

Ironically, it was the very sense of Western "progressivism" that would be its undoing. The rising theory of the "sovereignty of the people" – as opposed to the sovereignty of their traditional lords (kings and emperors) – sounded so noble, so progressive. But it contained a set of social dynamics that no one seemed able either to understand or manage when set loose. Thus the first half of the twentieth century would be marked by not only levels of violence not seen in centuries, it would also bring the decline in global influence of those very groups who thought themselves, as Westerners, to be the teachers of "good citizenship" and "proper civilization" to the rest of the world ... "White Man's Burden" as Rudyard Kipling termed it in a poem of his (1899) directed to a rising America.

In the earlier days of the recognized importance of kings and emperors as the glue bonding numerous societies into a single whole – presumedly offering stability and peace for the common people in the process – kingdoms and empires made a great deal of political sense. They could unite the most varied of people, even ones who otherwise would be at each other's throats because of more local hatreds possessing deep historical roots. Thus just as the Austro-Hungarian Empire held together Germans, Hungarians, Poles, Bohemians (Czechs), Moravians, Ruthenians, etc. with Lutheran, Calvinist, Catholic, Orthodox religious self-identities as well, the Ottoman Empire united Turks, Arabs, Greeks, Armenians, Bulgarians, etc., also of a wide religious variety as Sunni, Shi'ite, Druze and Alawi Muslims and Catholic, Orthodox and Coptic Christians.

The problems of tribal "group-think" or "nationalism." Now with the arrival of the "Age of Nationalism," each of these smaller ethnic/religious sub-groups was expected to define, defend and promote its own "national" identity ... a task muddied greatly by the fact that there were no clear geographic borders separating these sub-groups into distinct national packages. While there were certainly points of concentration on the map for one or another of these sub-groups, they found themselves scattered amidst other sub-groups as you moved outward from these central points. Just trying to draw national boundaries among these subgroups was guaranteed to pit one group violently against another (or even several others!)

Furthermore, a kind of nationalist "Romanticism" had turned the very idea of the nation itself into a highly revered, even worshiped, object of social affection ("group think") ... something not really allowable during the previous centuries of dynastic rule in the West. But with the rise of the political urges of the masses – birthed by Napoleon and his "nationalist" armies in the early 1800s – dynastic governments now found themselves on a steady political retreat in Europe. The dynasties that continued in place no longer represented merely their own family interests ... but were there to cultivate this larger group-think, to bring the people they presided over to ever-grander political purpose. But these dynasties – untrained in the ways of popular democracy – possessed very little understanding, and in some cases no understanding at all, of the forces they were unleashing in their efforts to govern their increasingly nationalistic societies. Thus it was that the forces of nationalism constituted a powder keg waiting to explode.

Tragically the utopian idealists and nationalist dreamers were completely self-blinded on this subject (as they still are today). The theory of "the self-determination of peoples everywhere" sounded so noble ... especially to intellectuals far removed from the practical difficulties found in the realm of political actuality.

The basic requirements of social success. Self-government of a people is a great idea ... provided that the people themselves have a well-practiced habit of moral self-discipline, a habit built on the foundations of a well-supported system of laws and social boundaries ... ones that have proven themselves through the test of time. Trendy, and thus untested, political ideas and ideals must always be viewed with much caution.

The people must also possess a spirit of social compromise based on the understanding that they must first look to the larger challenges facing them collectively as a people ... rather than get caught up with more immediate local matters, ones that so much more easily draw their attention and arouse their emotions.

And political wisdom demands that this sense of collective challenge must not just stop at the national border ... but extend to other people groups, other societies, other tribes and nations besides their own. Working with others not only amplifies the social power available to a people to work with, it also tends to broaden a people's sense of political self-interest to a much higher realm – the lofty but complex realm of international politics.

The massive tragedy that was about to hit Europe – and bring its days as the world's power center into rapid decline – happened because this same wisdom, this vital realism, was lacking in Europe's various nations ... and especially in their leadership.

Indeed, excellent leadership is critical to a society trying to live to higher social standards. But finding such leadership is always a serious challenge facing any society.

To be a great leader, a person must possess not only a great intellect but also *a deep wisdom* ... a wisdom achieved through excellent early education, through the careful attention paid to earlier generations of a life of proven success, and then through considerable personal experience in seeing all those learned lessons of life put to the test.

But also to be a great leader, a person must possess *a high degree of personal ambition*, one able to keep a person going in the not-uncommon face of grand disappointments – even failures – in the early effort to find success ... and then in success, the ability not to give in to a reactive opposition that success naturally provokes in the hearts of other equally-ambitious competitors.

Thus importantly, it requires both wisdom and ambition to produce a great leader. But on the one hand, there are always wise ones in society who (maybe most wisely itself!) choose not to get involved in the rough-and-tumble game of politics. And on the other hand, there are always the very ambitious – but not so wise – ones ... ones who are so caught up in their own personal success that they possess none of the greater wisdom that society will need in facing its challenges. Tragically it is exactly this latter group that can actually bring a society to defeat, even to collapse.

So ... coming up with a great leader is not a matter easily secured for a society.

The challenges facing Western society at this point.   As it enters the twentieth century, the Western world will find itself facing exactly this very challenge. Indeed, lacking tested leadership in the newly rising world of "democracy," the move to self-government will become a formula for a savage breakdown in the European social order – in which thousands, hundreds of thousands, even millions of ordinary people will get sacrificed to the gods of rising nationalism.

But it was not just dreamy "Progressivists" who were guilty of shaping this terrible social disaster. It was also kings and emperors themselves who did not understand what was going on right under their noses, and so managed to do the worst of things at the worst of moments, activity well designed to make a complicated situation virtually unmanageable, and ultimately catastrophic.

Some leaders seemed particularly expert in this regard. Chief among them was Nicholas II of Russia (r. 1894-1917), who had virtually no understanding of the mentality of the Russian peasants he was reigning over.

There was also Franz Joseph, the Austro-Hungarian emperor, who though a man of some intelligence, was nonetheless in over his head leading an empire made up of a multitude of contending national groups, groups that had few political interests in common. And sadly, Franz Joseph's Austria-Hungary was not content in possessing this unmanageable bag of contending nationalities. Austria-Hungary seemed determined to acquire even additional national groups, such as the Serbs, just to the south of the Austrian-Hungarian border. Serbs, of course, had other thoughts on this matter, especially the hyper-nationalists among them.

In fact it would be this very problem brewing between the Austrians and the Serbs that would finally set off the fires of war, which once ignited, seemingly could not be put out. And so a pointless bloodletting ensued, dragging itself out for four whole years.

Finally America brought new blood into the exhausted mix, breaking the deadlock and tipping the balance of power in favor of one side over the other, bringing the war finally to an equally pointless end.

Tragically the war would cripple the participants so badly that Europe, even in the period of post-war "peace," would be unable to reclaim its former position of world influence. The decline of Europe thus got itself underway.

Tsar Nicholas II's Russia

The Russo-Japanese War (1904-1905). In its push to acquire additional territory, Russia had been reaching eastward across Asia and had arrived at the Pacific Ocean by the mid-1600s. Over the next two centuries migrating into Siberia were Russian fur traders, Cossacks, exiled criminals and farmers escaping serfdom and looking for inexpensive land. Resistance of the previous inhabitants, small nomadic communities mostly, was problematic but not unsurmountable. So was the resistance this Russian expansion drew from the Chinese emperor (who at the time was hard pressed by the Taiping Rebellion and the Opium War with Britain) resulting in the 1860 Treaty of Aigun, which favored Russian claims in Manchuria.

But the biggest difficulty facing Russia would come from the Japanese, who also had imperial interests in the same area. Under the direction of the Japanese emperor, Japan had been both industrializing and militarizing, using the very latest technology (acquired mostly from Bismarck's Germany) in the process. Their achievements were stupendous, very unexpected of a people who were not "White." The Europeans would be startled by the readiness of the Japanese to join them in putting down the Chinese Boxer Rebellion, the Japanese showing themselves to be as capable as any of the European powers in their own imperial behavior.

Since the Vladivostok port on the Pacific was usable only during the summer, the Russians had contracted with the Chinese the use of a port (Port Arthur) further to the south in the Liaodong Province. This brought them up against the Japanese who were interested in the same region. The Japanese proposed an agreement in which Russia would recognize Japanese control of Korea in return for Japan recognizing Russian dominance in Manchuria. But discussions went nowhere (meanwhile the Russians were building up their forces in the region).

Finally, in May of 1904 the Japanese conducted a surprise attack on – and a blockade of – the Russian position at Port Arthur, and also moved troops into Korea, taking that land for their own Japanese empire. Bombardment of the Russians at Port Arthur continued through the rest of the year, the Russians unable to break the siege. Then much to the surprise of everyone (including the Russians) at the beginning of January 1905, the Russian commander at Port Arthur simply surrendered to the Japanese. Then in February both sides (a total of 500,000 men) met at Mukden, and after three weeks of fighting the Russians abandoned their position there. Finally, the Russian Baltic Fleet arrived in the area and at the straits of Tsushima (the narrows between Korea and Japan) the two navies confronted each other in late May, again with disastrous results for the exhausted Russian navy. The Russians were now ready to quit.

American President Teddy Roosevelt hosted a peace conference in Portsmouth, New Hampshire (September 1905), in which the Russians got off with only the loss of their positions at Port Arthur and on the southern half of the Sakhalin Island. But the Russian humiliation cut deep nonetheless.

The Russian Revolution of 1905. The timing of the conflict with the Japanese could not have come at a worse time. Social agitation back in Russia had been building since even before the war over the sense of gross mistreatment of the Russian industrial worker by the new industrial lords. At the same time these new industrial owners had been agitating for Liberal constitutional reforms. Thus labor unions had been organizing as fast as liberal revolutionary societies, both groups pressing for a serious overhaul of the Russian social and political system.

The Tsar however seemed unable to gauge the seriousness of this agitation, presuming that simple police action would suffice to keep such radical tendencies in check. When in early 1905 a peaceful demonstration led by a Russian priest and involving about 50,000 men and women in St. Petersburg was met by the Tsar's soldiers, who killed hundreds and wounded over a thousand demonstrators (Bloody Sunday), Russia exploded. Russia seemed to be spinning out of control.

Workers' councils (soviets) appeared everywhere and Liberals grew louder in their demand for reform. In October (after the humiliating Portsmouth Treaty was signed with the Japanese) a general strike was held across the country, virtually shutting down the entire Russian economy. The army had to be called out and was put to work crushing brutally the protest movement. The Tsar ultimately responded (the October Manifesto) by promising a number of civil rights reforms, and by offering a new Constitution and creating a Duma (legislature), so eagerly sought by the Liberal reformers. For the time being things settled down.

But pro-labor agitators (this included Lenin, who returned from Geneva for the occasion) saw this backing down of the Tsar as a great opportunity to push for Socialist reforms, and scheduled a massive revolt for early December. But despite the huge turnout of workers and their soviet leaders to build street barricades in protest against the government, they were met by soldiers who blasted the positions of the protestors. Ultimately the workers' uprising failed, and the organizers decided to call off the protest. But feelings still ran deep.

In 1906 the First Duma met in St. Petersburg, but found the Tsar highly reactive to pleas for deeper reform. To protect the almost sacred legacy of "autocracy," he instead reduced the few rights of the Duma even further, and then simply dismissed the body. The next year (1907) the Duma again met, proving to be even more hostile to the Tsar. It too was soon dissolved. But before a Third Duma could meet, the Tsar reshaped it so that it represented only the more conservative members of the upper middle class.

Serious reform would have to wait. As for the Tsar's promised civil rights reforms, those simply got dropped. Police repression continued as it had before.

The Rasputin scandal. Clearly, the imperial family was losing touch with reality. Tragedy stalked the halls of the Tsar's Winter Palace. Adding to the tragedy was the scandal created by the presence of the mysterious Russian holy-man Grigori Efimovich Rasputin, who in 1907 had worked his way into the imperial household on the claim that he had mystical powers to heal the young prince Alexei, who suffered from the incurable illness of hemophilia (no ability to stop bleeding when injured). Soon Rasputin became a regular celebrity within the imperial circle, complements of the Tsarina, who was completely convinced of his divine powers. Being a very hard-headed woman, she would also hear of none of the rising complaints about how Rasputin's frequent presence in the imperial court was causing highly damaging rumors to spread wildly among the Russian people.

Little by little opposition to him began to brew within the imperial court. Yet as time went on, Rasputin – with the support of the Tsarina Alexandra – seemed to grow in influence in the matters of state, especially with the departure in August of 1915 of the Tsar for the front during the "Great War" (World War One, which had been underway since August of 1914).

Resentment among the men of the imperial court grew so great that finally in January of 1916, a small group of them plotted his murder, which proved not to be as easy as they had hoped (or so the legend goes). But indeed, finally he was gone. But by this time the Great War was giving Russia even bigger issues than Rasputin.

Ottoman Turkey

The Young Turks. With the power of the Turkish sultanate fading away, the Young Ottomans formed and reformed their secret political organizations, adding medical students and military officers to their rolls. They eventually created a political union, the Committee of Union and Progress (CUP) which in 1902 and 1907 held its first and second congresses (in France).

Then in 1908 the military wing, beginning to be termed the "Young Turks" – under the leadership of "the three pashas" (Talaat Pasha, Enver Pasha, and Djemal Pasha) – marched on the capital at Constantinople (Istanbul) and forced the sultan to restore the Constitution of 1876. While he agreed, he seemed to be encouraging reactionary elements in the military, who in 1909 attempted a counter-revolution against the Young Turks. The effort failed, and Abdül Hamid was forced to abdicate and go into exile. His brother, Mehmed V, was installed as sultan in his place. But Mehmed had no real power of his own. At this point the Young Turks were the actual governors of the decaying Ottoman Empire.

The Balkan Wars as prelude to the coming "Great War"

Romania. In close cooperation with the Greeks, the Wallachians had also risen up in revolt against the Turks in 1821, demanding a number of political reforms, though expressing continuing loyalty to the Sultan. Here too infighting among the Wallachians made it relatively easy for the Ottomans to restore Turkish order. Another attempt occurred in 1848, along with the general Liberal upheavals that shook Europe that year. This united the province of Moldavia with Wallachia to form the idea of a united "Romania." But the effort came to nothing, until after the Crimean War, when in 1859 electors from both provinces voted for a single leader, Alexander John Cuza, as Romanian prince (within the Ottoman Empire). In 1866, because of his social reforms disliked by the Romanian wealthy, he was forced out ... and replaced by prince Carol I of Romania (of the Prussian house of Hohenzollern).

The Russo-Turkish War of 1877-1878. In 1875 peasants in Herzegovina (just to the west of Serbia) rose up in revolt against the heavy Turkish taxes, and the revolt soon spread around the Balkans. The Turks reacted violently, their slaughter being especially heavy among the Bulgarians living just north of the Constantinople region. This not only shocked the Europeans, it drew the Russians into the melee as a champion of the persecuted Bulgarians. Russian intervention no doubt was also motivated not only by the desire to recover territories on the Black Sea lost during the Crimean War, it was also inspired by the eternal Russian dream of securing a foothold on the shores of the Eastern Mediterranean.

The Turks were soundly defeated. As a result, in the Treaty of San Stefano (1878), the Turks lost sovereignty over considerable sections of Balkan territory. Not only was Turkey forced to acknowledge the full independence of Romania, but also Serbia and Montenegro.

Bulgaria. To the Russian mind, even more important was the fact that the Slavic principality of Bulgaria (under the Bulgarian prince Ferdinand I) also was founded as a result, stretching across the southern reaches of the Balkan Peninsula just above Greece. But the British and the Austro-Hungarians were afraid of such an extensive client state of Russia and forced the replacement of the San Stefano treaty with the Treaty of Berlin, which recognized only a smaller Bulgarian Principality. This was designed to prevent the creation of a strong Slavic state in the Balkans, presumably playing to the interests of Russia, which the other European states wanted to avoid at all costs. The Bulgarians living in Macedonia were thus left out of the new Bulgarian state, a matter that would soon become the cause of serious strife among the emerging Balkan nations.

At the same time the British were accorded the right to occupy the strategic island of Cyprus (protecting the sea route passing nearby on its way to the Suez Canal in Egypt) and Austria-Hungary was given the right to "administer" the Ottoman territories of Bosnia and Herzegovina.

In theory Bulgaria was still under Ottoman authority, but it acted rather like an independent nation. Finally in 1908 Bulgaria declared its independence as the Kingdom of Bulgaria with Ferdinand now designated as Bulgarian Tsar.

The Balkan Wars of 1912 and 1913. There were two conflicts that broke out in the Balkans, the first (1912) between Turkey and a coalition of newly independent Balkan states (the Balkan League of Bulgaria, Greece, Montenegro and Serbia), the second (1913) a war within the community of Balkan states, pitting Greece and Serbia against Bulgaria in a dispute about the dividing of Macedonia as a result of the first war. Bulgaria was unhappy about the way Greece and Serbia took the largest portions of Macedonia, and decided to invade the area to incorporate Macedonia into Bulgaria. Seeing Bulgaria thus distracted, Romania – which had stayed out of the first war – decided to launch its own offensive against Bulgaria. And Turkey struck back at Bulgaria as well. The end result was the dividing up of Macedonia between Serbia and Greece, and the loss of Bulgarian territory to the Greeks, the Turks and the Romanians.

The major European powers had decided to stay out of the first war, fearing that their intervention would only complicate further a diplomatic standoff that was building among the larger powers themselves. In the second war, the major powers got indirectly involved, though not necessarily out of a desire to do so. The net result of this second war was the delivery of a huge blow to Russia, because of the Russian support of Serbia – which in turn had driven its former Bulgarian "protectorate" into the waiting hands of the Germans. This war also further deepened the divide between Serbia and its neighbor to the north, Austria-Hungary, which – with Germany – saw Serbia as a new Russian dependency and a possible ally in Russia's quest for a forward position in the Balkans.

Tensions were building fast. It would take only a small spark to set off a huge military conflagration. That spark was about to occur.

Growing tensions among the major European powers

The age of imperialism had conveniently served to direct rising national ambitions infecting the European continent away from Europe itself. But with the near completion of the global land grab by the end of the 1800s, it was perhaps inevitable that these European ambitions would turn to a question closer to home: the breakup of the Ottoman Empire and the territories it would free up for the taking. This matter was too close to home to keep it rather abstract in principle. With this contest right in its backyard, the danger of this turning into a brawl within Europe itself was great. It would require great diplomatic skill to prevent this contest from getting out of hand. But sadly, such skill was largely missing among those who led these European major powers.

The growing system of opposing alliances. The nationalist passions were heating up. The French had been unrelentingly bitter about their loss to Germany of Alsace and Lorraine in the 1870 Franco-Prussian War. To the French it was a matter of huge principle to get these lands back. Sensing the danger, in 1872 Bismarck promoted the creation of the *Dreikaiserbund* (Alliance of Three Emperors) made up of Germany, Russia and Austria as a counter to French ambitions. But when Russia and Austria-Hungary found themselves in opposition over the breakup of the Ottoman Empire, Bismarck decided to drop Russia and stay with his fellow German Austria. Thus in 1879 he formed the Dual Alliance between Germany and Austria-Hungary, and in 1882 he extended this alliance to include Italy, giving the alliance now the designation as the Triple Alliance. Italy was not a particularly enthusiastic partner. But necessity (Italy was fuming over the French seizure of Tunisia) seemed to dictate the relationship.

In the meantime, relations between France and Russia were warming up, mostly out of concern over the buildup of German military power and the growth of Austria-Hungary's interests in the Balkans. By the 1890s this French-Russian relationship had turned itself into a basic understanding or *entente*, including the plans for military cooperation. Basically, the entente was an agreement that if either France or Russia were attacked by a member of the Triple Alliance, the other would come to the aid of its partner.

At first the British found themselves caught in the middle of this growing split. Britain approached the alliance matter cautiously. But concern by both Britain and Japan over Russian involvement in Asia brought Britain to sign an alliance with Japan in 1902. Then as Wilhelm grew bolder in his development of the German navy, British nerves began to fray, and the British decided to enter into an anti-German entente with their long-time former opponent, the French, resulting in the Entente Cordiale of 1904. Finally, with Russia's defeat in the Russo-Japanese War, the British concern for Russian activities in Asia dwindled to the point that Britain was willing to enter yet another entente, this time with Russia. Thus in 1907 the Triple Entente of Britain, France and Russia entered into effect. Three years later the Japanese and Russians came to an agreement, and Japan thus decided to ally with the Triple Entente.

The First Moroccan crisis (1905-1906). Rising tensions among the European players of the nationalist game nearly turned to blows exchanged between Germany on the one hand and France and Spain (backed by Britain) on the other over the status of still-independent Morocco. Actually,

Morocco's independence came in the form of "protection" offered by France and Spain to Morocco in 1905 ... done without any "consultation" with Germany ... ignoring an earlier 1881 agreement which had included Germany as one of the guarantors of the Moroccan status quo. Wilhelm was not only insulted that Germany had been left out of the new arrangement ... but was seeing all this as simply another effort of France and its ally Britain to keep Germany from its natural "place in the sun." Thus in 1905, Wilhelm personally sailed to Morocco to offer the Moroccan sultan the same "protection."

A huge diplomatic crisis thus resulted. To avoid a mounting confrontation, it was finally decided to bring the matter early the next year (1906) to an international conference held at Algeciras in Spain (attended also by the U.S. President Teddy Roosevelt). The conference confirmed the sovereignty of Morocco, but in fact allowed for both Spain and France (not Germany) to serve as the protectors of that sovereignty. Germany was still excluded from a role there.

Bosnia-Herzegovina (1908). As tensions built in the Mediterranean, without any warning things exploded over on the other side of Europe ... when in 1908 Austria-Hungary simply announced the annexation of the former Turkish territory of Bosnia-Herzegovina. But land-locked Serbia had also been contemplating the same action ... in order to extend its own borders all the way to the Adriatic Sea (part of the Mediterranean Sea). Serbia was furious.

But this land grab also widened the divide between Austria and Russia (the latter being a strong supporter of Serbia), caused some consternation with Austria's ally Germany (which had not been consulted prior to the event), and forced France and Britain (both neither in a position to help Serbia nor willing yet to help Russia) to stand off, very unhappy over the event. And as for Turkey, it was rather content to receive monetary compensation from Austria for its loss of these two distant provinces.

The Second Moroccan Crisis (1911). Morocco was not doing well under French and Spanish protection. The sultan's finances were in crisis mode and unrest among the Moroccans was building. When rebellion broke out in Fez against the Sultan in April of 1911, the French moved troops to Morocco to "protect its citizens in Morocco" and to support the Sultan. This upset Wilhelm greatly, who saw this as simply a ploy for the French to add Morocco to their North African empire. Wilhelm countered the French move by sending the German gunboat *Panther* to Morocco "to protect German citizens."

This in turn angered deeply the French and Spanish, and also the

British who were lining up more closely with France (the *Entente Cordiale*). Consequently, France (with British backing) refused to be intimidated. Ultimately, Wilhelm once again had to back down.

Part of the dynamic in this incident was that Germany had been challenging British supremacy with its own rapid development of a German navy, increasing British nervousness about Wilhelm's intentions. Britain, being an island, was always very sensitive about international naval matters.

On the other hand, Wilhelm, in being forced to back down from his ambitions in the Mediterranean, chose to see this episode as simply more German "encirclement", and began looking to expand Germany's own diplomatic alignments to counter the close relationship of Britain, France and Spain.

Thus it was that things were pushing quickly toward the horrible events of 1914. Nationalists of all the major European countries seemed to want a street fight of some kind to finally settle the matter of Europe's power alignment. But what they failed to realize was that such a fight was not destined to be merely an afternoon sporting event. The powers seemed so evenly balanced at this point that once underway such a conflict would simply stalemate itself into a long, unrelenting bloodletting – the kind that could result only in a huge loss of political strength by all parties, the kind that would in the end (should there ever be an end) resolve nothing. But passions at this point had greatly overridden cool logic.

A war now seemed inevitable.

✳ ✳ ✳

THE "GREAT WAR" (WORLD WAR ONE) 1914-1918

The assassination of the Austrian Archduke Franz Ferdinand (June 28, 1914). The absorption of Bosnia-Herzegovina by Austria was by no means a finished matter. Serbia was in no mood to accept this development and Austria knew it had work to do to complete the absorption of these Balkan provinces. When in June it was announced that the Austrian Archduke Franz Ferdinand (acting on behalf of his 84-year-old uncle, the emperor Franz Joseph) would be visiting Sarajevo, the capital of Bosnia, a radical group of Serbian nationalists (including even members of the Serbian government) planned his assassination. They wished to disrupt Austria's plan to create a new Triple-Monarchy (Austria, Hungary and now also a Slavonic state) under the Austrian emperor's authority. Austria's plan would have ended the Serbian dream of an independent Greater Serbia (reaching down to the Adriatic Sea). Somehow Austria needed to be stopped.

But the plot nearly failed, but only nearly, for by accident one of the plotters (who was actually on his way away from the proposed action) was able to shoot the Archduke and his wife as they passed by him ... after having taking an "alternate" route – ironically out of the fear of just such an act. But the assassin was quickly caught ... and identified as a Serbian nationalist.

Austria's declaration of war on Serbia. At this point Austria wanted to destroy Serbia, but needed German backing. Wilhelm was reluctant to get involved in such a tangle but also knew that German support was vital in keeping the Austrian-Hungarian empire from falling apart. He had to support Austria. Aware of this backing, the Austrian cabinet placed extremely heavy demands on Serbia to allow Austria to take over the search in Serbia for the Serbian criminals (presuming a Serbian refusal, and thus in effect precipitating the war sought by Austria).

The Serbian government itself had authorized no such act ... and tried to meet the terms of an outraged Austria. Thus most of Austria's demands were agreed on by the Serbian government. But Austria insisted that not most – but all – of the demands be met by Serbia. When Serbia stalled, Austria decided that it had the justification it needed ... and on July 28 declared war on Serbia.

Austria supposed that this would remain a quick, local war, as most of the wars in the Balkans had been. But Austria foolishly had failed to take note of the fact that things were very different in the European diplomatic world at this point.

Russia joins in. It was now Russia's turn to decide what to do. Russia was not only the protector of Serbia, it saw in this outbreak of war the opportunity to take advantage of the crisis to seize Constantinople and complete its dream of its own port with direct access to the Mediterranean. But Russia was not really prepared for a major war, and Tsar Nicholas was well aware of this fact. Yet he could not hold back his own ministers who wanted war nonetheless. They demanded a general mobilization. Nicholas knew well that this would constitute a declaration of war, and by the terms of the Dual Alliance would automatically bring Germany into the war as well. But he finally gave in to his ministers and on July 29 the Russian cabinet called for mobilization. A few hours later he received a conciliatory letter from his German cousin Wilhelm. But it was too late to call off the mobilization. Russia was at war.

Germany joins in. Germany reacted immediately to the news of the Russian mobilization with a demand that the Russians immediately back down, and declared war (August 1) on Russia when Russia failed to do so.

Germany then sent a letter to France demanding to know whether or not France was intending to stay out of the conflict, received an ambiguous reply, and thus declared war on France (August 3).

Italy initially chooses to stay out of the conflict. Most wisely, Italy declined to honor its treaty with Germany and Austria-Hungary ... because it had agreed to act in accordance with the treaty only when it was a matter of national defense – not offense, as clearly was the case for Austria (and Germany also for that matter). Italy thus stayed neutral ... at least for a while.

Turkey joins the German-Austrian side. Turkey, meanwhile, having no formal commitments to either side, was at first unsure of where it stood in this new crisis. It looked to Britain as a friend (Britain had earlier defended Turkey against Russian expansion) ... but with Russia now a British ally, this confused matters a bit. Also, the Young Turks were very impressed with German military technology and general order, although Germany's alliance with Turkey's problematic neighbor Austria complicated matters here as well. But finally, Turkey chose to enter the war on the side of Germany ... although it had little to offer its new allies by way of military support – at least not at first.

The papacy stays neutral ... and humanitarian. Giacomo Chiesa had just been voted pope as Benedict XV in 1914 – in the very days that the war first broke out. He immediately declared the Catholic Church to be neutral in this nationalist contest. Indeed, pope Benedict tried on two occasions (1916 and 1917) to formally mediate the conflict ... but was rejected by both sides of the contest. Nationalist fervor hugely outranked the religious – even Catholic – loyalties of fired-up Europeans ... at least those of the political leadership of the nations involved.

Meanwhile, Benedict undertook to offer humanitarian aid to both soldiers (captured and/or wounded) and hungry civilians.

August 1914 – The "Great War" takes shape

The battle along the "Western Front." Germany supposedly was well-prepared for just such a conflict. According to a military plan (the Schlieffen Plan) drawn up years earlier in the expectation that war would eventually occur again between Germany and France over the provinces of Alsace and Lorraine, the Germans had designed plans to send German troops hurriedly through Belgium in order to grab Paris (located in the north of France, not far from the Belgian border) before the French had a chance to mobilize their war machine. This was basically what had happened in Prussia's war with France back in 1870. And Wilhelm knew that with Paris under German control, France would be unable to offer any resistance.

Wilhelm also knew of course that sending his troops through Belgium would be in total violation of that country's neutrality (Belgium had been purposely established as a buffer zone amidst Germany, France, the Netherlands and Britain). Violating Belgian neutrality would automatically mean war with Britain. But Wilhelm expected the German grab of Paris to happen so quickly that the war would be over before the British could get mobilized.

But what Wilhelm had not counted on was the stiff resistance offered by the Belgians ... and the rapidity of the French response to a call to arms in defense of France's borders (with France now also allowed by terms of the Belgian treaty to place its defenses further to the north, even in Belgium, against the German invaders). Thus the Schlieffen Plan failed to function as anticipated.

The German effort soon slowed down ... despite the horrible treatment the Germans gave the Belgians for their resistance, both military and civilians – immediately earning the Germans the term "Huns" because of their horrifying brutality.

And indeed the British were also quick to act ... sending part of their army, the British Expeditionary Force (BEF), to France and Western Belgium to help slow down the German momentum.

And indeed, by the end of August, the German invasion of northern France had come to a full halt – across a long line of action reaching from the Rhine River in the East to portions of western Belgium in the West ... and just north of the Paris suburbs. Paris was thus saved.

And there, along that long battle line, the action would bog down completely. In fact, over the next years this battle line would hardly budge one way or the other ... no matter how many men (millions were) sent to try to break through this highly defended line of deep trenches, barbed wire, machine guns, cannons, poisonous gas ... and multitudes of soldiers.

The Eastern Front. On the other hand, the long battle line reaching in the East from the Baltic Sea in the North to the Balkan Peninsula in the South, was much less a permanent matter, moving back and forth as pressure was applied here and there: Germans against Russians in the North, Austrians against Russians in the center of the line, and Austrians against Serbs in the South. Although Russia had a much larger army than the Germans and Austrians, and although Germany was deeply committed to action on the Western Front in France and Belgium, the Russians did very poorly in their contest with the Germans. At one point early in the conflict (at Tannenberg at the end of August) a Russian advance turned into a Russian defeat when a huge Russian army was skillfully surrounded and forced to surrender to its German opponents.

Russia still had more men to bring into the war. But this initial defeat would be merely the beginning of many troubles the Russians would experience in continuing a war they now had no idea of how to pull out of without a huge loss of national pride.

In the central part of the line of engagement, the Russians were facing an Austrian army of equally inferior quality, in great part because of its multinational character. Here the war bogged down along a line that reached from the Carpathian Mountains in the south to Silesia in the north, and efforts of both sides to move the line proved to be dismal failures.

In the South, the Serbs were able at first to hold back the Austrians. But the Serbs were vastly outnumbered by the Austrians in numbers of troops and weapons ... and bit by bit Serbia was forced into a step by step retreat in the Balkans.

1915/1916

The slaughter continues. As Christmas 1914 came and went, so with it went the idea that the war would be "over by Christmas." Along the entire Western Front soldiers had dug deep trenches and awaited orders to move up out of their trenches to face barbed wire, machine guns, and shell holes (with dead and decaying bodies in them) in order to advance on an enemy well entrenched in an opposing line of trenches. When nothing of strategic value was achieved in this butchery, troops still alive were called back, sent to a line of trenches in the rear in order to recover ... until called once again to the forward line of trenches ... where they sat in anticipation of poisonous gas coming their way or enemy canon shells to explode in their midst – while they awaited their next call to attack the enemy across "no-man's land."

It was the Germans that got the brilliant idea of bombarding the enemy with poisonous gas, with the hope of clearing the enemy trenches before their assaults. But while this proved deadly it did not prove as effective as they had hoped in clearing the enemy lines, and soon the British and French were attempting the same tactic, also now employing gas masks to protect themselves in the process.

Between the gas attacks and the constant barrage by enemy artillery, life on the front was a person's worst nightmare, one that refused to go away. There was no escaping the slaughter. The casualty lists soon numbered in the millions on both sides.

So life went on for millions of young Europeans (and colonials from around the world as well), day after day, week after week, month after month, and now year after year. Survival was not really expected.

Yet, more countries join in. It seems strange that with the horrifying experience of the Great War (as it was coming to be called) by this point a year old, any other countries would want to get involved. But political folly is not unknown in high political places.

For Bulgaria there was in fact a good reason for joining the war: to get back the lands that it had lost to Serbia and Greece in the Balkan wars. In this they largely succeeded, until the war turned against their German allies in 1918.

Italy, however, was another story. Italians were deeply divided about the war. In one of the many secret treaties being issued during the war, the British and French in April of 1915 promised the Italian government lands taken from Austria along the upper Adriatic Sea coast and along the southern slopes of the Alps, plus the possibility of picking up colonial territory from the Germans in Africa. And although many Italians were adamantly opposed to getting involved in the war for any reason, pro-war enthusiasts, led especially by the fiery Gabriele D'Annunzio, finally got most of Italy worked up for war. Finally in May, Italy declared war, coming in on the side of the British and French against Italy's former allies Germany and Austria. Not all Italians would be happy about this.

Italy was really not prepared mentally or physically for such a war. As it turned out, the Italians were unable to dislodge the Austrians from the mountainous Italian province of Trentino, despite repeated efforts. Finally they would find themselves in a humiliating retreat in the face of an advancing Austrian army in late 1917 after the fall of the Italian forward position at Caporetto.

Romania also decided to enter the war (August 1916) after promises for territorial compensation were made to it similar to those made to Italy. When in September Romania invaded Hungarian Transylvania to collect on those promises, they were only briefly successful in holding that territory, before they were thrown back by a joint attack of Austria and Bulgaria. Before the year was out Romania had to yield not only its capital city Bucharest but most of its land to the invading Bulgarian and Austro-Hungarian forces. Romania was effectively knocked out of the war.

But still ... promises are promises. And at war's end Romania was ranked among the "victors" and awarded the Hungarian lands originally promised to them by the British and French.

Gallipoli. Because of the murderous stalemate facing the British in their war against the Germans, the head of the British navy, Winston Churchill, came up with a plan to strengthen Russia's fighting capacity on the Eastern Front (helping to relieve German pressure on the Western Front) by opening up a direct line of supply to Russia from the Mediterranean through the Dardanelles. That would of course require taking out Turkey. But Churchill was convinced that with a surprise attack launched directly at Constantinople (March 1915), the Turks would be neutralized and the way then cleared for this supply line to be opened up. But the key to the strategy was speed. And things just did not go Churchill's way from the very start.

The Turks had mined the waters and these needed to be cleared before the small fleet of British and French ships could head on to Constantinople. The Turkish shoreline forts were quickly reduced, but clearing the mines proved to be more time consuming than anticipated. As days passed, British and French ships were sunk. The Turks seemed able to maintain a steady attack on the invading fleet, though it also seemed that the Turks might be running out of ammunition. However the word was out that German relief ships were heading toward the battle, and the local commanders convinced British headquarters that with bad weather and huge naval losses, the effort had failed and the fleet needed to pull back.

The plan now shifted to the idea of landing shore parties to march overland toward Constantinople, destroying Turkish positions as they went, and allowing the fleet to try again to open the Dardanelles to allied shipping. The new plan included bringing Australian and New Zealand soldiers up from the British command in Egypt to join the attack. Days went by as the commanders worked out the details of the plan, not realizing that the Turks – who were *not* the weak-willed Ottomans as the British and French had supposed – were also readying themselves to resist exactly the plan they by now had guessed that the British and French were working on. When finally at the end of April everything seemed ready, the Allied troops went ashore, only to discover that the Turks, under the command of Mustafa Kemal (the "hero of Gallipoli" and future Turkish leader), were well entrenched in the heights above the beaches and – armed with massive firepower – were eagerly awaiting them.

The Allies thus found themselves largely stranded along the Gallipoli shores, unable to make any serious progress against the Turks. More troops were brought in, on both sides. Gradually the Gallipoli Front was taking on the character of the Western front as both sides dug in deeply, neither side able to advance against the other, yet neither side willing to give up their positions either.

Now the Gallipoli campaign would drag on and on. With Bulgaria's entry into the war on Germany's side (September), supplies could now be brought directly from Germany to Turkey, ending all possibilities of the British simply wearing down the Turks to the point of surrender. When winter then came on (soldiers were dying in great numbers from disease and exposure) the decision was finally made to abandon the effort. In December the Allies pulled their troops out of Gallipoli, leaving behind only a memory that would never be forgotten by the parties involved, on both sides of the engagement.

Serbia is crushed. In the fall of 1915 Austria-Hungary and its allies Germany and Bulgaria joined forces to hit the Serbians hard. The Serbians were forced to retreat, leaving their capital Belgrade in enemy hands, even falling back into the Albanian mountains, and finally being chased down even there. Remnants of the Serbian army were finally, with British and French help, able to escape to Greece. In all, the Serbs lost over a million men (more than a quarter of its population and over half of its male population).

The Battles of Verdun and the Somme (1916). In the late winter (February) of 1916 the Germans opened up a massive offensive against the French line at the fortress city of Verdun. The Germans literally reduced to rubble the complex fortifications of Verdun, hoping to annihilate completely the French troops gathered there. It was expected that this would open such a huge hole in the French line that the French would be thrown in disarray and the Germans could then move on the French capital and end the war. Massive amounts of German power would be thrown into this operation.

But the Germans had not counted on the stiff resistance the French offered even amidst the rubble, and the French line held as more French divisions were brought into position by the determined French General Pétain.   By July the Germans were forced to back off on the effort ... because it had become very clear that the Germans were gaining nothing from the effort except a massive loss of men and war materials.

Anyway, by this time the scene of the greatest action had moved north along the battle line to the Somme River valley ... where the British had undertaken a massive countermove against the Germans – something on the scale of the German Verdun effort. Try and try again (just like Verdun) through August, September and October, even as the effort became heavier with time, nothing was achieved in the process. Finally, the November rains (and fields of knee-deep mud) brought the effort to a halt. And here too, the only result of the British Somme River offensive was the loss of massive numbers of men and supplies ... on both sides.

But something of note was introduced in the effort: the British tank. This automotive tank was brought into action in order to finally be able to cross barbed wire, face machine guns, and even overcome trench defenses ... except that the British military had not yet figured out the necessity of advancing foot-soldiers in accompaniment with the tanks. Thus the tank at first proved to be more a novelty than a breakthrough in military technology. But they would soon develop that technology (certainly by the spring and summer of 1918) ... at that point making the war in the West much more mobile.

The 1916 Brusilov Offensive in the East. The year 1915 did not go well for Russia. The Germans pushed the Russians out of Warsaw as well as the Polish lands further to the east.

But the Russians planned to open up an offensive in June of 1916 (the Brusilov Offensive) against the Austrians – involving a massive number of Russian soldiers and war materials – in the hopes not only of relieving the German-Austrian pressure on the vital wheat-producing economy of the Russian Ukraine region but also of retaking some of the lost Polish territory. And in part it was undertaken to relieve the pressure on the French at Verdun. And this was prompted by the belief that the Austrian-Hungarian war machine could yet be broken.

But whereas General Brusilov's Offensive ultimately (by September) did break much of Austria's power (forcing Austria to have to rely increasingly on German assistance in its sector) it also exhausted the Russian army so deeply that the Russians found themselves unable to mount much of an effort against their enemies after this point. And this, in turn, would lead to deep political troubles at home for Russia.

The Russian "February Revolution" - 1917

Although Russia's army greatly outnumbered its enemies, it lacked the supplies necessary to make it an effective fighting force. Weapons and ammunition were always in short supply, demoralizing the Russian soldier who was expected to fight on empty-handed. Russian civilians were well aware of these problems and were quick to blame the Tsar and his government for these scandalous shortcomings.

Very unwisely, in September of 1915, the Tsar decided that he personally must lead the military from the front and left the governing of Russia to his wife. And the Tsarina in turn left matters to Rasputin, who made and unmade governments with his own personal appointments, further scandalizing the Russians in their dwindling respect for their imperial government.

By the beginning of 1917, wartime shortages had hit the civilian population as cruelly as it had the military. Food in the cities was very difficult to obtain, and grumbling turned into a full-scale protest in March by Petrograd* workers, joined by masses of women. The protest built force over the next days, and soldiers sent to restore order began to join the protesters (reminiscent of the startup of the French Revolution!). At this point the Russian imperial social-political order simply began to break down.

The Russian legislature (the Duma) tried to bring order to the chaos by setting up a Provisional Government, on the same day that a Soviet (Council) of Workers was established in Petrograd.

The Tsar abdicates. Word then reached the Tsar at the front that even his own bodyguard had joined the revolt, and under advisement of his generals, Nicholas simply abdicated his throne (March 15). He had not been enjoying any of his governmental responsibilities for a long time ... and he was quite content to leave these agonizing matters for others to deal with.

At first Prince Lvov took command of the new Provisional Government ... who immediately undertook a number of social reforms that he hoped would cool down Russian tempers. These reforms included the calling of a national election, with the goal of a new Duma undertaking the task of composing a new Russian Constitution. So it gave the appearance at this point that Russia was no longer an autocracy, but was finally in the process of joining the ranks of the world's "democracies."

America joins the war (April 1917)

The British blockade of Germany. In violation of all traditional international law, Britain had taken up the strategy of blockading the shipment to Germany not only of any war materials from its previous suppliers (including importantly the United States), but out of sheer desperation in the March of 1915 announced that it was blockading the shipment of all overseas goods, even foodstuffs, to Germany. As Germany was highly dependent on imports of all varieties, the British intended to force Germany into submission by simply cutting off the foreign lifeline on which it depended.

America as a neutral nation protested vehemently. But Britain would not back down.

The German U-boat. The German navy was no match for the British navy and there was little likelihood that Germany would be able to break the

---

*Russia's imperial city had been changed in name from St. Petersburg to Petrograd because, under the rising nationalist impulse at the beginning of the war, "Petrograd" sounded so much more "Russian" than "St. Petersburg." Then with the coming to power of the Communists (and Lenin's subsequent death), the city would be renamed as "Leningrad." Finally it would have its original name, "St. Petersburg," restored with the fall of the Communist system at the beginning of the 1990s.

blockade, except through the development of their new sea weapon, the *Unterseeboot* (submarine) or U-boat. When in the early years of the war the U-boat took out a number of British cruisers, the Germans rushed to develop this new weapon. Just as the British announced a naval blockade on all commodities going to Germany, Germany announced that any ships entering British or Irish waters would be considered hostile and subject to sinking.

American "neutrality." Now caught in the middle of this was "neutral" America, with considerable interest in sea trade. What to do?

Despite America's own English ethnicity, America was actually a multi-ethnic society with multitudes of Irish and German Americans, who had reasons of their own for wanting to support Germany rather than England. Thus the best policy for America was to stay out of the war. But that would not be easy.

The sinking of the *Lusitania*. America (and much of the world) then found cause to rise in anger against Germany when in May of 1915 a German U-boat sank the passenger liner *Lusitania*, drowning nearly 1200 civilians … including over a hundred Americans – among them some of America's most prominent citizens. But the Germans had their own protests to issue in the matter … having warned beforehand that just as Britain had put in place a naval blockade against goods destined for Germany, so Germany was doing the same … using its U-boat to enforce its countering blockade. But somehow American opinions did not see these as equal matters … even when it was revealed that the *Lusitania* was carrying to Britain a massive amount of contraband war goods in its hold.

Noting the American reaction, and not wishing to turn America into a wartime enemy, Germany promised to end its blockade. Britain however did not end its blockade. So America's one-sided "neutrality" continued as before.

"He keeps us out of war." American President Wilson tried hard to maintain American neutrality not only abroad but also at home where opinions continued to be sharply divided. British propaganda about the bloody German Huns and their violation of helpless Belgium seemed to reach more ears than the German effort to counter this image with pro-German propaganda. Little by little American opinion was turning ever more hostile towards Germany (though hardly pro-English at the same time, for British violation of American rights as a neutral also angered Americans deeply). But Wilson still wanted to keep America from getting involved. Thus as late as November 1916 Wilson presented himself for reelection to the White

House on the basis of having successfully kept America out of the war. But things were about to change.

The resumption of the U-boat attacks. The British blockade of Germany was slowly driving Germany to starvation. The situation was so bad that the Germans now subsisted mostly on potatoes and turnips, except that in the summer of 1916 the potato crop failed. Thus the Germans were forced to go through a "turnip winter", made worse by the fact that the Germans also had no fuel to heat their homes. The blockade had to be broken or Germany would be broken. Thus in January of 1917 the Germans announced the resumption of U-boat attacks on the high seas.

America was furious. So was Wilson. In early February he went before Congress to announce the end of diplomatic relations with Germany, and stated that if things worsened, he would return to Congress to consider the next step (meaning war). Soon after that, Americans received news of a secret message intercepted by the British (who were careful to make sure it fell into American hands) in which Germany was proposing an absurd alliance with Mexico, with the promise that, at the end of the war, Mexico would be awarded the states of Texas, New Mexico and Arizona. Not surprisingly, Mexico was not interested in the proposal. However, Americans were now up in arms, demanding war against Germany (though not necessarily against Austria-Hungary and Turkey).

"To make the world safe for Democracy." Finally, with the change of government in Russia from autocracy to (supposedly) democracy in March, Wilson could turn American involvement into not just a desire for revenge for German U-boat attacks and national insults, but even something he personally loved greatly: a grand moral crusade to advance "democratic" progressivism. With Russian autocracy having been overthrown, Great Britain, France and now also Russia, together constituted a "democratic" front ... opposed to the remaining "autocracies" of Germany, Austria-Hungary and Turkey. If Americans were to now join forces with the "democracies," the war would be indeed a battle "to make the world safe for democracy."

"The war to end all wars." Furthermore, Wilson's (and other Idealists') understanding at that time was that with all the world coming to full democracy, the petty greed of autocrats (which was supposedly the cause of all wars) would end. Thus victory in this war would end up making it "the war to end all wars."

Thus on April 2nd, Wilson stood before Congress to ask for a declaration of war, which Congress four days later was more than glad to offer him.

Pure folly. In his speech before Congress, Wilson explained "democratic" matters this way:

> *Does not every American feel that assurance has been added to our hope for the future peace of the world by the wonderful and heartening things that have been happening within the last few weeks in Russia? Russia was known by those who knew it best to have been always in fact democratic at heart, in all the vital habits of her thought, in all the intimate relationships of her people that spoke their natural instinct, their habitual attitude towards life. The autocracy that crowned the summit of her political structure, long as it had stood and terrible as was the reality of its power, was not in fact Russian in origin, character, or purpose; and now it has been shaken off and the great, generous Russian people have been added in all their naive majesty and might to the forces that are fighting for freedom in the world, for justice, and for peace. Here is a fit partner for a league of honour.*

Here he was offering the usual Humanist creed ... that all people by their very instincts are democratic at heart. All they need is to be given the opportunity to put those democratic instincts into play in a newly "freed" social environment. Like the political Idealists of the French Revolution, Wilson had no idea whatsoever what would actually happen to a society if the power structure it had long lived under were to go away, were to collapse, were to be overthrown by "revolutionaries.

But oh how noble would be the American cause ... when it joined the mindless slaughter in the bloodied fields of Northern France. As Wilson put matters:

> *There are, it may be, many months of fiery trial and sacrifice ahead of us. It is a fearful thing to lead this great peaceful people into war, into the most terrible and disastrous of all wars, civilization itself seeming to be in the balance. But the right is more precious than peace, and we shall fight for the things which we have always carried nearest our hearts – for democracy, for the right of those who submit to authority to have a voice in their own governments, for the rights and liberties of small nations, for a universal dominion of right by such a concert of free peoples as shall bring peace and safety to all nations and make the world itself at last free. To such a task we can dedicate our lives and our fortunes, everything that we are and everything that we have, with the pride of those who know that the day has come when*

> *America is privileged to spend her blood and her might for the principles that gave her birth and happiness and the peace which she has treasured. God helping her, she can do no other.*

America's new "democratic" mission to the world. From this point forward, Americans would now see themselves as grand "missionaries" to the world. But it would be a mission not to spread the Christianity that had formed the country's very strong moral foundations on which American self-government had long been based ... but instead a mission to spread the doctrine of "democracy" – whatever that meant. And tragically, whatever "democracy" meant was not well understood by Americans. But a full understanding did not seem necessary ... because the word "democracy" itself had such a beautiful ring to it – so that it was easily seen as the noblest of all political-social-cultural causes, one worthy of even self-sacrifice in order to advance its place in the world. And tragically, there would be plenty of just such self-sacrifice that was going to take place for America's young Idealists in uniform seeking to support this noble cause.

Americans no longer understood why the country's Founding or Constitutional Fathers set up a "republic" directed by strong Constitutional Law ... and not a "democracy" run according to the inclinations of the people – one easily manipulated by the self-interests of ambitious individuals. The Fathers of the 1787 American Constitution were well aware of how democracy worked for the ancient "fathers of democracy": the Greeks. And they certainly were not surprised when, just as their new Constitutional Republic was coming into effect (1789), the "enlightened" French leaders overthrew their French monarchy in order to produce a new democratic Republic of their own in France – but instead produced only a bloody mess ... one that required the Napoleonic dictatorship to get France back in order.

Americans were failing to understand what Aristotle had come to understand after looking at the political dynamics of his own Greek days (the 300s BC) – and what the American Constitutional Fathers had also come to understand through their careful study of Aristotle and ancient Greek and Roman history – namely, that democracy (or any other social order) can be found to be "good" only when it is built on strong moral foundations. And moral foundations do not come just by decree, or by imposing it on others ... or by winning some kind war against "undemocratic" enemies (whatever that too actually means). Except in the case of a tyrant imposing a new moral order by brute force – and holding it in place by being able to strike fear in the hearts of those who would dare go up against this dictator's new social order – this is not going to happen overnight. It takes time, usually generations, for strong and deep moral foundations to develop for a society. And as the French Revolution made very clear, toppling one social order, no matter how inept or cruel it might be, does not automatically birth a new, more humane, social order. Chaos is the guaranteed result.

Thus Wilson taking America to war to bring down European "autocracies" was not going to lead automatically to democracy, or even peace ... and certainly not to "the war to end all wars."

Actually, both "autocratic" Germany and Austria-Hungary had parliaments, ones which did not differ greatly from the way the British parliament functioned. The Germans in fact had some of Europe's most progressive social programs in place ... at a time when Britain's own treatment of its industrial workers was still quite problematic. And Russia after the fall of the Tsar was hardly now a "democracy" – and in fact was headed towards a chaotic and highly murderous civil war, one which would kill more Russians than had the European war the Russians had just dropped out of. And even more tragically, this new Russian political dynamic would soon lead Russia not to democracy, but to one of the worst dictatorships in European history.

But Wilson saw exactly what he wanted to see in all of this. Unsurprisingly, and quite tragically, all of his beautiful Idealism would soon backfire on him.

America was now at war. But it had only a tiny army, fully involved at the moment along the American border with Mexico, trying to keep the chaos of a Mexican political revolution from spilling over into America. Despite the Declaration of War, it would be many months before America would be ready to enter full force into the European war as a British, French and Russian ally. At best, that could only be sometime in early 1918.

Russia's "October" Revolution – 1917

What the Russian intellectuals of the Provisional Government failed to understand was that the Russian people were not demanding democracy (whatever that might have even meant to them). They simply wanted out of this needless war. The decision of the Provisional Government to pursue the war in furtherance of the cause of democracy quickly put the new government in the estimation of the average Russian in the same category as the old Tsarist government. Failure of the Provisional Government to understand this basic fact would prove to be its undoing.

The initial reaction of the Russian people at the news of the downfall of the Tsarist government had been one of a heady euphoria. They supposed themselves now to be free from all the social suffering they had experienced under the old order, especially with the arrival of the war. Peasants simply assumed themselves now to be the owners of their own lands and refused payments to the landed nobility; industrial workers demanded control of their factories; and soldiers began to desert their posts to go home to their farms in order to take charge of their own new destinies. Truly Russia was in a state of major social revolution.

Thus the hope of the Provisional Government in May of 1917 in placing Alexander Kerensky at its head was that Kerensky's closer identity with the Russian revolutionaries (he was a member of the Social Revolutionary Party and vice-president of the Petrograd Soviet) might swing them finally in support of the Provisional Government's democratic revolution. But Kerensky was up against another group of revolutionaries even more formidable than his Social Revolutionaries: the Marxist Communists (or Bolsheviks) led by Vladimir Lenin and his close associate Leon Trotsky (who at the time was away in New York), two men who had long been underground or abroad planning for just such a revolutionary event.

Russian Bolsheviks were returning to Russia in mass numbers, now that the Provisional Government had liberalized its laws. But the Germans wanted to make sure that this influx included the most important Bolshevik of all, Lenin, and brought him secretly by train from Switzerland to Finland just across from Petrograd. The German goal was obvious, as Lenin had made very clear that his political objective was the building of a new Soviet society, not the continuance of an unnecessary war. The Germans knew quite well that any Russian pullback from the war would free up the vast number of German soldiers needed on the Western front. The Germans needed to conduct one last lunge at Paris to bring France to its knees before the American troops started to arrive in numbers in the coming spring (1918). They would need as many soldiers as they could possibly gather for this great offensive.

Once in Russia, Lenin began to make his move to take control of the Russian revolution. He promised the Russian people two things: land for the peasants and the coming home of the Russian soldiers. This was such a compelling program that the Provisional Government had no effective counter-offer for the people. Then Lenin and Trotsky began to organize the political support they would need to take control of Russia. Trotsky was able to gain complete control of the military committee of the powerful Petrograd Soviet before seizing power of all vital points in the nation's capital on the night of November 6-7 (October 24-25 on the Russian calendar). The members of the Provisional Government in the Winter Palace quietly surrendered the next day. Lenin's Bolsheviks were now in control of the Russian nerve center, and ready to spread their control over the rest of Russia.

1918: The war comes to an end

Russia drops out of the war. Lenin began almost immediately after taking control of the Russian capital to look for the best way out of the war with Germany. He sent Trotsky to negotiate with the Germans at Brest-Litovsk. In December both sides agreed to an armistice and an opening of peace negotiations. A war of nerves then ensued as the Germans demanded harsh terms from Russia in the form of territory to be given up and expensive reparations payments to be made to Germany. But the Germans were also in a hurry to get something agreed on. At one point negotiations broke down, and the Germans made ready to march towards Petrograd (the Russians at this point barely had an army to defend themselves by). Thus the Russians gave in first.

In early March the announcement was made to the world that a formal peace had been agreed on by the two parties. It would constitute a very huge loss for Russia. But it did give Lenin the peace he needed to pursue his revolution in Russia. And it gave the Germans the clearance they needed to vacate the Eastern Front and reposition their army in the West.

Wilson's Fourteen Points. Meanwhile, American President Wilson was working hard to make the American war effort a moral crusade rather than just a crude power play. The cynical nature of the war thus far had been amply revealed when the Bolsheviks published copies of the secret treaties that had been exchanged among the Allies, offering the bribes of land and payments in exchange for various forms of wartime support. Also, Lenin himself had, as an immediate follow-up to the Bolshevik seizing of control of Petrograd, delivered a speech promising Russian support for a new peace of equity and justice for the toiling classes of the world, one involving immediate peace without annexations (which he subsequently himself was unable to secure from the Germans). So pressure was mounting to get Wilson's own moral ideals in place as the higher light that would bring peace to the world.

On January 8, 1918 Wilson delivered a speech to Congress in which he clearly outlined similar but much more specific war goals of America in the form of Fourteen Points. He called for open rather than secret diplomacy, freedom of navigation and trade, reduction in armaments, the restoration of territories lost in the war by all parties, the restoration of Poland, and finally (Fourteenth Point) the creation of a general association of nations (the future League of Nations)

> *for the purpose of affording mutual guarantees of political independence and territorial integrity to great and small states alike.*

The speech had been prepared without any prior consultation with America's allies, who had, as part of their empires, numbers of great and small states (or provincial possessions). They clearly had no intentions whatsoever of setting these territories free as independent democracies, such as Wilson expected to happen as a result of America's involvement in this supposed moral battle for global democracy.

Nonetheless, despite Wilson's political presumptuousness, his declaration was well received by his allies. It helped give moral cover to what was otherwise a completely immoral war.

The German Spring Offensive of 1918 (Operation Michael). The Germans of course at that moment had other ideas than Wilson's. On March 21, the Germans began their assault on three points on the Western Front; at the Somme (March 21-April 5), the Lys (April 9-29) and the Aisne (May 27-June 4). However ... although these drove deep wedges into the Allied lines (especially at the Somme), they failed to break through French and British lines. By early June the Germans were exhausted.

America joins the counter offensive. The British and French merely assumed that the American one and a half million troops would be blended into their own ranks as reserves. But the American commander John Pershing insisted that Americans fight as an integral unit at various points along the front. Finally the allies relented and American troops took their positions along the line. The newly arrived troops were eager to go, and gave a fresh spirit to the allies as they pushed the Germans back at Belleau Wood at the center of the front (June-July), and at St. Mihiel (September), and at the Argonne Forest in the Verdun region (September-October).

The big push. Meanwhile the British, led into battle by their huge tanks, advanced strongly at the Somme (September), and the French, along lines just below the British, combined with the British to push the exhausted Germans back to the point that by the beginning of November the Germans were nearly out of France and much of Western Belgium. The German lines were collapsing rapidly.

ARMISTICE – NOVEMBER 11, 1918

Now Wilson's Fourteen Points looked very attractive to the Germans. They were running out of military supplies and food (the urban population back in Germany was struggling to survive near-famine conditions). Thus in early October Wilson received a message from Germany requesting an armistice and peace negotiations along the lines of Wilson's Fourteen Points. But Wilson was probing to see exactly on whose part the request was made: the German imperial government, or the German people.

Meanwhile U-boat attacks on American shipping continued, and Wilson hardened his terms for an armistice: he would deal only with a post-imperial government. Imperial Germany's hopes for an armistice were dashed. Meanwhile, protests began to rise from the German left calling for Wilhelm's abdication, and the creation of a German republic. Rebellion in the streets now spread rapidly and Bavaria became the first German state to proclaim itself a republic. Berlin then came under control by revolutionaries. It was time for Wilhelm to make his escape. But the military would not promise their protection. Finally on November 9th, Wilhelm was able to make his way into exile in the Netherlands.

Seeing the imminent collapse of Germany, Pershing wanted to push the war all the way into Germany to make it clear to the Germans that a new international status quo was now in force. But British commander Haig and French commanders Foche and Pétain felt that it was time to bring the war to an end, just where things presently stood.

Nonetheless on November 8th, the Allied commanders presented the German commanders in their discussions at Compiègne a number of very strong concessions imposed on Germany as terms required for a cease fire. The Germans were given until November 11th to respond. Finally in the early hours of the 11th, the Germans agreed to the terms, and a general armistice was announced to go into effect at 11:00 later that same morning. Tragically however the pointless shelling and slaughter continued right up to the very last minute of the war. But at 11:00 it was finally over.

CHAPTER FOURTEEN

ATTEMPTS AT RECOVERY (THE 1920s)

* * *

SHAPING THE POSTWAR PEACE

Four empires – Russian, German, Austrian and Turkish – had completely disappeared because of the four-year bloodletting. And what replaced them was hardly an immediate advance forward in peace and prosperity of the nations involved. Chaos, not peace and prosperity under new progressive governments, was what greeted the people with the loss of their former autocratic governments.

The Russian Civil War (1917-1922)

The worst case of post-war chaos was that of Russia, which fell into a four-year civil war that destroyed more Russian life than had the European war itself. Armies of Whites (a scattered coalition of supporters of Kerensky's Provisional Government, tsarists, Cossacks and an array of various conservative groups) and Reds (Lenin and Trotsky's Bolsheviks) ranged back and forth across Russia, pillaging, slaughtering, and burning farms and villages as they went, leaving behind pure desolation as they passed through to another battle with their enemies. Also involved were a number of foreign armies (British, American, Czech, Japanese) sent to Russia to support the Whites in the hope of keeping Russia in the war ... but who stayed on even after the war was over to continue that support.

Sadly, this participation of the foreign troops on the side of the Whites gave the war the appearance among Russians of the Bolsheviks fighting for the national rights of Russia against the efforts of Whites to put Russia under foreign rule. Adding to the confusion, a number of non-Russian national groups within the Russian Empire saws this as an opportunity to break free from Russian domination and establish national independence for themselves (opening up local political contests among themselves in the process). Thus the Russian Empire collapsed into a state of bloody chaos.

Lenin's move to secure his Soviet social order. In the meantime, Lenin set about immediately to put into force a social strategy he had worked out well beforehand. He decreed the transfer of the large landholdings (including lands belonging to the church) to the peasants who actually worked the farms ... not only winning the hearts of the peasants, but stirring fear in their hearts that if the Whites were to win the civil war the peasants would lose title to their lands. Lenin also moved quickly to put large industries under Bolshevik control, although workers' committees were set up to give the industrial workers a sense of ownership of the production of these industries ... again, to win the loyalties of the Russian working classes. Lenin also set up a bureaucracy of Bolshevik agents who were sent out in the country to monitor these changes. And finally, Trotsky was assigned the task of professionalizing the Bolshevik army (the Red Army), reshaping it quickly as an effective fighting force designed to protect the rights of the common people against the former ruling classes ... a task in which Trotsky succeeded brilliantly.

Lenin also moved quickly and ruthlessly to eliminate all members of the social classes (the nobility and the bourgeoisie or middle class that had not yet fled Russia) most likely to oppose his revolution. Even peasants considered to be suspicious of anti-revolutionary loyalties were executed or exiled to Siberia. All political parties other than the Bolsheviks were outlawed and the Russian press was brought into conformity with the Bolshevik revolution ... or shut down completely. The Cheka, Lenin's new secret police (modeled after the Tsarist secret police), was ordered to remove outspoken opponents of the new regime.[*] And on the night of July 16-17 (1918), the Tsar and his family, who had been arrested by the Bolsheviks and moved by their captors to the Russian interior, were ordered by the local Soviet to be executed ... because of concern that they might be rescued by an advancing White army.

The Orthodox Church and the Christian faith also became objects of Lenin's social revolution. The church had long been supporters of the Russian autocracy and thus according to Lenin's logic needed to be destroyed. But he was also opposed to the Christian faith itself, held dearly in the hearts of most Russians, for he feared that it harbored conservative attitudes that would stand in the way of the cultivation of a revolutionary conscience among the new class of proletarian comrades foundational to Lenin's rising social order.

----

[*]Since opponents of Lenin's regime were arrested secretly (usually in the middle of the night) no numbers were kept of the people "liquidated" (usually killed directly) by the Cheka. Estimates vary from 50 thousand to hundreds of thousands. So bad was its reputation that in 1921 its name was changed to the Government Political Office (GPU) ... as if a name change might improve the reputation of the Leninist regime.

Ultimately, little by little, Trotsky's Red Army was able to gain ground against the less well-organized White Armies. Kolchak's White army, at first successful in Siberia, was finally defeated by the Reds, as was a coalition of Whites in Ukraine (1919-1920). Remnants held out in the south until finally driven out of Crimea in late 1920. In October of 1922 the Reds were able to secure all of Siberia when the Japanese pulled out of the far eastern region and the last White army in Siberia at Vladivostok surrendered. From that point on only small scattered groups of Whites continued the struggle. Thus Lenin had finally secured his Soviet state.

But things were not going quite as well for Lenin as he had hoped for in those first years of the establishment of the Soviet state. The economic disruption of the civil war was immense. Industrial production dropped to one-fifth the level it had stood at in 1913 before the European war. Towns were deserted as workers fled to the countryside in the search for food. Even production on the farms was less than half what it had been before the war. There was no stable currency the farmers could count on or even manufactured goods they might want to buy, so most farmers reduced their food production to levels sufficient merely to feed their own families.

When the fighting finally slowed up and stopped (1922-1923), the war toll, the famine which hit the country (1920-1921), and the widespread malnourishment and disease that was rampant in the country ultimately claimed millions of lives (possibly as many as 10 million).

Lenin's New Economic Policy (NEP). By 1921 Lenin was ready to try another approach to industrial and agricultural production. He came up with a plan termed the New Economic Policy (NEP) which opened up the economy to the development of small private enterprises and private trading beyond the official state program. He put the ruble back into operation in order to facilitate that trade. He established a standard agricultural tax rather than the state requisitions of food products as payment to the state. He did maintain the state monopoly on the major industries however. Yet slowly the economy started signs of growth under the NEP, especially in the realm of agriculture where the revival was fairly quick. Even in the industrial sector, Russia was back up to 1913 production levels by 1927.

Lenin dies. However, Lenin would not live to see the fruit of his labors. His work took its toll on his health, which began to show signs of decline toward the end of 1921 ... and in May of 1922 he suffered a stroke which partially paralyzed him. He largely recovered ... though now he had to look to others to carry on much of the work. Then in early 1924 he died. Now would begin a struggle for power among the party elite that would have a highly determinative effect on the further development of the Russian Soviet Union.

The German Weimar Republic

The Germans themselves had not asked for a democracy or republican form of government. It had been pushed on to them as a pre-condition imposed by their enemies as the price required to secure the peace the Germans so eagerly sought. To be sure, there would be those (mostly intellectuals of the Socialist variety) who supported the idea of a German republic. But for most of the Germans this mattered little. Eventually (the early 1930s) the Republic would be considered even a bit treasonous because of its birth in what increasingly came to be understood as a wartime betrayal of Germany.

Actually, very little changed about German society because of this changeover to a republican government. Although the heads of the various states making up the German union were gone, their bureaucracies remained, conducting political business as usual in Germany.

The street violence that sent Wilhelm into exile continued to mount, giving opportunity (November 1918 to January 1919) to a group of leftist radicals (the Sparticists, led by Karl Liebknecht and Rosa Luxemburg) to attempt to spark a German revolution similar to Lenin's. But they ran into the stiff resistance of returning soldiers who formed themselves into anti-socialist units (the Freikorps or Free Corps) who went about gunning down radicals whenever they gathered. A similar attempt to establish a Soviet Republic in Bavaria (April-May 1919) was also taken out by the Freikorps. Thus the only events resembling something of a real revolution in Germany were quickly snuffed out.

Less radical Socialists quickly moved to fill the political void created by the departure of Wilhelm. A Provisional Government was quickly established and Friedrich Ebert, a Social Democrat, was made its head. Elections were soon held (January 1919), in which a number of parties (many makeovers of the parties of the days of Imperial Germany) took their seats in the Reichstag, although the Social Democrats were by far the largest. Ebert was elected as the republic's new President. Being concerned about how easily urban mobs (Paris, Petrograd and now Berlin) were able to dominate their nation's politics, he decided to move the task of writing a new constitution to the small town of Weimar.

The post-war treaties

Meanwhile Germany was waiting to see what were going to be the exact terms required of it in order to secure formally a new post-war peace. They were harsh.

Wilson's (and Americas') grand disappointment. Wilson had himself traveled to Paris to ensure personally that his promised Fourteen Points would be the terms by which the final peace settlement with Germany was shaped. Upon his arrival in Europe he was celebrated so wildly by the cheering crowds that he certainly expected to be supervising the treaty negotiations from a position of great strength. But his own idealism blinded him to the actual social dynamic taking place. The Europeans were cheering him because his American troops had seemingly tipped the balance of military power in Europe so as to finally give the Allies their long-sought victory. They saw in him their national victory ... not some abstract idea of a new world of international peace and understanding. Their sense of victory over a hated enemy was what excited them. Years of slaughter, of destruction of homes and villages, of wounded family and friends returning from the front, was what filled their minds.

The European leaders responsible for negotiating a peace with Germany understood what was expected of them. Their people wanted revenge ... not reconciliation and equity.

Sadly, Wilson at that point had nothing more to bring to the negotiating table. America had played its part ... and had departed, back to homes and towns unaffected by the war. America had not suffered as the Europeans had. It was thus easy for the Americans to be high-minded about a future peace. After all, that had been the motif of the American entry into the war from the beginning.

But that American high-mindedness was soon to turn to bitterness, not just by Wilson but by the American people who were shocked when they heard of the political deals being worked out among the British, French and Italians. Nothing had seemed to change in the behavior of the cynical Europeans. Americans had asked for nothing in its participation in the war except for the Europeans to join them in building a new and safer world. But the Old World seemed to have betrayed the Americans: glad to get American help but only to advance their own greedy national interests. Americans now grew bitter, ready to wash their hands of any further dealings with the cynical Old World.

Germany.   Indeed, the terms imposed on the Central Powers were harsh. In the Versailles Treaty, Germany was forced to acknowledge total responsibility in having started the war (remembering the Germans as bullying "Huns," Americans were as insistent as the Allies on this point). This then justified the subsequent punishment imposed on Germany (here the Americans differed): the loss of lands to the newly reconstituted state of Poland, of Alsace and Lorraine (plus for all practical purposes the coal rich Saar) to France, and small sections of Germany to Belgium (and in the future to Denmark). All the German colonies in Africa and Asia would be given over to one or another of the Allies (even the Japanese and Portuguese). The German army and navy were to be reduced in size to a point of uselessness. And massive reparations payments were to be made to the Allies for war damages inflicted by Germany (the precise amount to be determined by a special commission) ... and the heartland of German industry, the Rhineland, to be occupied for the next 15 years to ensure compliance with the reparations requirement.

In May of 1919 the German delegation received the terms prepared by the Allies, expecting to be part of a discussion of those terms ... and shocked when it was made clear that these were largely not negotiable. The German cabinet resigned rather than agree to these terms.

President Friedrich Ebert also wanted to resign but was persuaded not to do so because refusal to agree to these terms meant the resumption of the war. The French were ready at the border ... and the German army at this point was largely demobilized. The Germans were given until June 22nd to accept these terms, or the war would be resumed the next day. Thus very grudgingly did the Germans accept these terms on the 22nd, the Assembly voting 227 to 138 to accept.

Austria-Hungary.   As for Austria-Hungary, two separate treaties (Saint-Germain and Trianon) divided the empire into a number of independent states, including Austria and Hungary – which now existed as separate nations, each greatly reduced in size. Two new states were created from this dismemberment: "Czechoslovakia," combining Bohemia, Moravia and Slovakia and "Yugoslavia," combining Serbia with Slovenia, Croatia, Bosnia-Herzegovina, Montenegro and Macedonia.

Other provisions. Romania, as promised previously, was awarded the Hungarian lands of Transylvania.   And Italy was given land along the southern slope of the Alps and along the Adriatic Sea at Fiume – also as previously promised.

And Poland was brought back into being – having disappeared as a separate nation a century earlier (the late 1700s) – made up of lands taken from Germany, Austria-Hungary and Russia.

Bulgaria was also reshaped by the Treaty of Neuilly, with the new Yugoslavia receiving a section. But more importantly, Greece received a key portion of Bulgarian Thrace which had formerly given Bulgaria a position along the Aegean coast and thus also direct access to the Mediterranean. Consequently, Bulgaria had access only to the Black Sea and so now (like Russia) had to pass through Turkish waters to reach the Mediterranean and the high seas.

Although the Russians were not part of the post-war negotiations, the lands Russia had given up to Germany in its agreement ending its war with Germany came up for redistribution. Out of this land were carved the newly independent states of Finland, Estonia, Latvia, Lithuania ... and what would become the eastern portion of the newly recreated Poland.

In accordance with the Treaty of Sèvres, The Ottoman Empire was also dismembered, with the setting up of "independent" Arab kingdoms ... under French and British supervision (principally Iraq, Syria, Palestine, and Transjordan). And Greece was awarded huge sections of Western Asia Minor ... so that what was left for a Republic of Turkey was a greatly reduced territory comprising the interior Anatolian plateau of Asia Minor. But this treaty was never ratified by the Sultan, was rejected subsequently by the new Turkish Republic, and after a major Greek-Turkish war was finally redrawn as a less harsh 1923 Treaty of Lausanne.

Serious problems. Overall, the final treaties had left large groups of nationals in foreign territory, especially Germans, but also Bulgarians and Magyars (Hungarians). In rebirthing Poland (a result of France hoping to secure an ally to the east of Germany to help keep Germany in check), huge sections of German territory – the entire province of Posen and most of West Prussia, including the "Polish corridor" of the Danzig region, and of upper Silesia – were given over to Poland.

The vast majority of Germans would then flee Poland over the next years, straining even more the relations between the new German Republic and the new Republic of Poland. Austria was reduced to a third-rate power with the huge capital of Vienna, once the cultural and political center of a vast empire, now reduced to supervising a German-speaking hinterland only two times greater in population than the capital itself. Economically (and culturally) this was unsustainable.

Also a huge German-speaking population living in the Sudetenland had been incorporated into the new Slavic-speaking state of Czechoslovakia ... another sore point for the German world. Hungary too was badly sliced up in losing two-thirds of her land and population ... and like Austria, its capital Budapest greatly overshadowed the tiny country to which Hungary had been reduced. Also Bulgaria had not only lost its position on the Aegean it had lost 1.7 million Bulgarians to foreign rule. And Turkey would find itself in such a sour mood over the loss of its vast empire that it was a powder keg ready to explode ... which it did in 1922 – with devastating results for the Greeks who thought that victory in the Great War had set them up as the new major power in the Aegean.

All of this redrawing of Europe's political map meant one thing: in an age of nationalism these geographic revisions would serve to stir a bitter revanchist mood among those cut off from the nationalist heartland ... and an opportunity for demagogues to use such nationalist hurts to reopen wounds left behind by the Great War and its not-so-great peace treaties. Hitler in fact would depend on this revanchist spirit to get his political career up and running.

The League of Nations

Wilson was very unhappy at the way his "democratic" allies forced vengeful terms on the defeated "autocratic" powers. But he held on to one hope: that once nationalist passions settled down, cool-headed diplomats could use the new League of Nations to revisit these treaties foisted on the war-wearied Central Powers – and amend them in order to produce a more just outcome, one that would remove the temptation of the losers in this war to seek revenge in another war. In this he was also hoping that he had some kind of good news to return to the States with ... in order to justify the American sacrifices that had been made by his people.

But in fact he came home to an America so burned by the behavior at Versailles that it viewed with deep suspicion any kind of further American involvement in international affairs, much less European affairs ... especially when it looked as if Wilson's proposed League of Nations might possibly take away from Congress and the nation the sovereign right to decide for itself the nation's particular stand on matters of war and peace. Thus when the Versailles Treaty was put before the Senate for ratification, it was defeated by a vote of 55 to 39.[*] Further efforts to get it passed failed ... and eventually the matter was dropped. Thus not only did the U.S. not formally recognize peace between itself and Germany[†] ... it would not be joining Wilson's League of Nations (also part of the rejected Versailles treaty).

But forty-four nations did sign the League's Covenant in June of 1919 and then set up an international organization headquartered in Geneva, Switzerland. It included a League Assembly – where all the members had a voice. But it also included a League Council – where four "Permanent Members, Britain, France, Italy and Japan (America was originally expected to be its fifth Permanent Member) were joined by four (ultimately ten) other members rotated among the rest of the League membership ... this smaller body to take on the more sticky diplomatic matters as the "enforcers" of League policy. As matters brought to the Council for action were considered to be of a much more critical concern, decisions of the Council had to be fully unanimous ... except in cases where one of the members of the Council was involved. That nation was not entitled to vote on the matter.

─────────────────

[*]The vote fell eight short of the required two-thirds vote needed for the Senate's approval of any U.S. treaty.

[†]It would do so in a separate treaty with Germany in 1921.

Besides these representative bodies, there existed in Geneva a full-time staff or Permanent Secretariat to oversee the League's business on a daily basis.   These were bureaucracies authorized to act on a number of particular issues – such as health, education, labor, women's rights, the drug trade, slavery and other such social questions ... all very much in keeping with the rising spirit of Socialism in Europe (and Progressivism in America) in the early 1900s.

The League was also empowered to supervise a Permanent Court of International Justice (PCIJ) located in the Hague (the Netherlands) – a world court designed to try cases involving international law. Bringing cases before the PCIJ occurred frequently during the 1920s ... most concerning boundary questions raised by the treaties ending the Great War. But as matters became darker and more bitter in the 1930s, the PCIJ was involved less and less in the developing political dynamics.*

As long as these issues did not involve directly any of the major powers, they were settled more or less peacefully and equitably ... because it was in the interests of the major powers to see these issues resolved in this manner. But when the major powers were themselves involved, things did not work out so well ... often with one or another of the major powers resigning from the League in protest.†

Political reality vs. Humanist dreams

Thus the Wilsonian dream (and the dream of others like him) that a realm of reason could override narrower social interests proved to be exactly that: just a dream. Nationalist power considerations still prevailed in the international realm.

Two particular military crises that hit Europe immediately after the war give clear demonstration of this inconvenient reality.

The Polish-Soviet War. The fact that the newly constituted Poland was in part carved out of formerly Russian-held territory would push both Poland and Russia into conflict. Actually, the new Polish government under Józef Piłsudski took the initiative in 1919 in invading Lenin's Russia ... still caught up in its own civil war. Polish forces launched deep into Russia. But with

---

*The PCIJ was nonetheless highly respected and was one of the several League organizations that was carried over as part of the new United Nations when it was set up in 1945.

†A number of major powers party to disputes, in finding decisions going against their national interests, simply resigned: Japan (1933), Germany (1933), and Italy (1937). Soviet Russia was expelled by the League in 1939 when it refused to call off its invasion of Finland.

Lenin's Communists finally in full power in Russia, Lenin reversed the course of war, his Soviet troops throwing the Poles back all the way to their capital at Warsaw (July 1920).*

Although the Western powers seemed more sympathetic to Poland, they offered very little assistance in the midst of this crisis ... only a handful of military advisors (which included French officer Charles De Gaulle!).

But then the Soviets split over the larger strategy of the war ... and the Poles were able to use this confusion to their advantage ... with Polish General Władysław Sikorski, joined by Piłsudski, taking to the counteroffensive and pushing the Soviets back, deep into Russia.

However, the Russians were spared humiliation when the Polish troops now found themselves exhausted ... and Piłsudski's opponents at home forced him to agree to hand back territory to the Russians – leaving a million Poles within the Soviet Union to face subsequent persecution from the Bolshevik authorities. Likewise, Piłsudski's Ukrainian allies were also left in Bolshevik hands ... with sad results.

Nonetheless, in March of 1921 the Peace of Riga was signed between Poland and Russia, officially ending the war.

But very importantly for Europe as a whole, this Polish-Soviet Russian war served greatly to halt Lenin and Trotsky's plans to push their revolution westward into the heart of Europe. But it also supported Stalin in his dispute with his colleagues, in his effort to keep revolutionary matters focused solely on Russia itself.

But it also helped the newly established countries of central Europe secure their independence ... especially Lithuania which Lenin was planning to absorb – before Russia lost its war with Poland. And the war brought forward Piłsudski as Poland's national hero and once again future leader ... and also French military advisor Charles de Gaulle and Polish General Sikorski, both of whom would lead their national armies during World War Two.

The Greco-Turkish War (1919-1922). The Turks found themselves deeply divided politically when a group of Young Turks, under the leadership of the "hero of Galipoli," Mustafa Kemal (eventually given the title "Atatürk, "Father of the Turks") set up a government in Anatolia (central Turkey) at Ankara in mid-1919 – in opposition to the sultan's government in Istanbul (old Constantinople) ... the latter considered an embarrassment to Turkish pride in the way it gave in so easily to the Western powers at Paris.

Meanwhile next door, the Greeks were having their own post-war

---

*Very tragically, but quite characteristic of the times, the Poles at this point turned on the large Polish Jewish community – accusing it of being supportive of Russian Bolshevism!

problems. Originally they had entered the war on the side of the British on the basis of a British promise to extend Greek territory from its ancient position in coastal Asia Minor deeper to the East (pushing into Turkish Anatolia).* Originally, Greek King Constantine had opposed this offer, wanted to stay out of the war ... and thus strongman Eleftherios Venizelos had him deposed – and had his son Alexander take his place as a Venizelos puppet.

But the British had been promising others this and that ... including lands along Southern Asia Minor to the Italians ... as well as lands in Palestine – to the Arabs and to the European Jewish community at the same time (to secure various types of support during the war). With the end of the war, things in this region were very confusing.

Venizelos then simply decided to take matters into his own hands, sending 20,000 Greek troops in May of 1919 to push into the Anatolian interior ... where the exhausted and politically divided Turks were caught completely off guard.

Then things went badly for the Greeks ... when King Alexander died (bit by a monkey!), a national election was called, Venizelos lost the election, and Constantine was called back to power ... and mainland Greeks seemed at that point to have lost interest in the war with the Turks. At the same time, Atatürk dug his troops into a strong defensive position ... which not only stopped any further advance by the Greeks, but which led the Greeks to retreat. But once in that mode they could not find a position themselves to dig in and take a strong stand. The Turks continued to advance westward.

At this point Greek civilians in the west of Asia Minor began to panic. On came the Turks – even finally to the last Greek stronghold at Smyrna. There they crushed the last of the Greek resistance – and burned out the Greek and Armenian sections of this huge city. By mid-September (1922) the Greeks had lost everything.

The war was over – and a new treaty (Treaty of Lausanne) had to be drawn up between Turkey, Greece, Britain, France and Italy. It provided for the transfer of populations: 500 thousand Muslims to be relocated from Thrace to Asia Minor and over a million Greeks from Asia Minor to Thrace, Macedonia and Attica (Eastern Greece). Considering the scale of the ethnic cleansing that had occurred on both sides during this war (whole communities of Turks on the one hand and Greeks and Armenians on the other were completely obliterated) this transfer of populations, though cruel in execution, was preferable to remaining behind and being slaughtered in the heat of the intense Greek-Turkish hatred that now existed between these two peoples.

------

*Almost 20% of the population of Asia Minor/Anatolia was Greek Christian in language and religion at that time.

Atatürk then moves on to modernize Turkey. So completely taken was Turkey by Atatürk's success, that the Turks seemed most willing to follow whatever path he seemed to want to take the country down at this point. And for Atatürk, that meant modernization ... deep modernization.

There was no real opposition to his ending the Ottoman sultanate and replacing it with a new Turkish Republic (1922-1923), with himself as the Republic's new president (1923-1938), voted there through universal male adult suffrage ... adding women's suffrage to the dynamic in 1930.

He also understood that if Turkey were to be able to protect itself fully from Western intrusions, it was itself going to have to take on Western ways – economically and culturally as well as politically. That was not going to please Muslim traditionalists. But at this point they had nothing to offer in opposition to Atatürk's reforms.

Thus Atatürk redesigned the Turkish written language ... taking it from an Arabic alphabet to a Latin-based alphabet. He took on Western attire (the military had actually already done this) as a civilian political leader ... and extended this same updating in attire to women, no longer forced to wear Islamic attire. Education would now be conducted by public educators ... rather than by the traditional Muslim mullahs. And so it went with the "Kemalizing" of Turkey.

✳ ✳ ✳

THE EUROPEAN POWERS TRY TO REBUILD

The Great War had clearly left the European nations shaken socially and morally to the roots. Soldiers demobilized and returned to the farm and small towns that dotted Europe, disillusioned and bitter about the recent nightmare they had just been through, finding that the innocence of their former lives was not possible to recover. Too much social change had occurred in those four years. Farm and village life had become marginalized ... pushed to the side in its former dignity in favor of the fast-growing smoky industrial cities cranking out heavy materials used to manufacture a whole new range of goods enjoyed by a newly-rising middle class.

Many of those young men would turn to those very industrial cities to look for work, greeted mostly by meager employment possibilities and bitter about finding so little concern for their poor economic state after having given so much of themselves to national honor. Thus it was that many sensed that their homeland was on the edge of revolution ... especially by the endless ranks of industrial workers who were feeling exploited by the new fast-paced culture which, like the war, demanded so much from them and offered so little in return.

Middle class life, on the other hand, looked very glamorous. Yet there was something very reckless in the way the newly-rising middle class, especially its younger members, now wanted to have a go at life. Patriotism was dead ... associated with the excessive jingoism of the recent war which obsessed about the need for personal sacrifice and for serving the nation above all else. It was time now to look to personal goals and interests and forget about the needs of larger society. Shopping, partying, sports, and entertainment – and of course personal careers – filled their lives ... but most of it without any greater purpose than simply to place a thin layer of material happiness over deeper, haunting thoughts about what had just happened – and fears that it could happen again. After all, who saw it coming? What did it all mean? Did anyone understand how to keep such a grand accident from happening again?

Certainly Europe's politicians were well aware of this dynamic ... and the challenges it posed to their national governments. The people were very suspicious of the political professionals who had so recently led them into and through this nightmare. The people wanted peace, an unbreakable peace. And yet there was always the feeling that peace might at any time easily disintegrate again ... from a domestic crisis as likely as from a foreign crisis.

Europe's political leaders had their work cut out for them. Would they prove to be wise in the face of these challenges? What exactly would they do now? The people were waiting and watching closely.

Britain's recovery

In the first years after the war, Britain's economy did quite well – particularly as European countries on the continent had suffered considerable war damage ... and needed British products which Britain's untouched wartime factories were happy to produce.

But in fairly short order those continental countries had much of their productive capacity rebuilt ... except in the form of new factories with new machinery and new technology – which were thus much more productive that those of Britain's aging industrial system. Also Britain's huge coal mining industry – which was a major overseas income earner – now became hit deeply by the trend of other nations to move to oil and hydroelectric power to run their economies.

Thus a slow-up of British manufacture began to register itself ... at a time when Britain's import needs, especially of food, remained constant. Unemployment rates thus also began to climb perilously high ... and the British labor movement began to take on a much angrier tone as it searched for explanations and solutions concerning the growing unemployment problem.

In 1926 a General Strike was called by the British Trade Union Congress – shutting down the British economy and causing a fear of a Bolshevik-like workers' revolution. This merely stirred the British right-wing to an even greater interest in the doctrine of Fascism – threatening to radicalize British politics on both extremes of the political Right and the political Left.

Thus during this postwar period, the political spectrum in Britain changed deeply. In the 1922 elections, the wartime Liberal-Conservative coalition led since 1916 by the Liberal Party leader David Lloyd George went down to defeat … also largely ending the glory days of the Whigs or Liberal Party. Its place was first taken by a Conservative Party government led by Stanley Baldwin, which lasted only briefly – before having to form a coalition with the rising Labour Party led by Ramsay MacDonald. The Conservative Baldwin and the Labourite MacDonald were then to dominate British politics for the next fifteen years … years of extreme caution given the potential volatility of the political world both at home and abroad.

The Irish Question

A major problem troubling deeply the political waters of the British Empire was the Irish Question. The Irish saw themselves as long-suffering as a Catholic people at the hands of the Protestant British … and the British aristocrats who ruled Ireland in the most feudal way – treating the Irish as if they were simply a nation of peasants. The horrible Irish potato famine of the 1840s in which thousands of Irish died – without significant help from their British masters (not that there was really much that could have been done about the blight that attacked the potatoes that the Irish diet depended on so deeply).

During the Great War, Irish assistance was needed … and a promise that British Chancellor Gladstone had made back in 1885 promising Irish self-rule was brought back into play at the outbreak of the war. But the sacrifices required by the war itself only deepened the impatience of Irish militants.   Then in 1916 a small incident exploded into a major Irish uprising on Easter Day in the Irish capital, Dublin, leading rebels to declare the creation of an Irish Republic. However … a German promise of aid did not occur – and the Easter Rebellion was put down forcefully by British troops. But the Irish goal of independence was now fully set in the minds of a number of active Irish.

In Britain's national elections held at war's end in 1918, the Irish independence party, Sinn Féin – led by Arthur Griffith and American-born Éamon de Valera – won 73 of the 105 seats accorded to the Irish. But instead of taking their place in Parliament, Sinn Féin members founded in

Dublin a new Irish national assembly, the Dáil Éireann.

When British troops were sent to Dublin to shut down this new assembly, war was on – the Irish defended by the newly created Irish Republican Army (IRA), led by Michael Collins. Taking notes from the recent Boer War, the IRA now began to take guerrilla hits on British power wherever possible ... over the next months and then years.

In 1921 a highly divided and very tired Ireland signed a treaty with an equally tired Britain providing for the creation of an Irish Free State, largely independent and affiliated with the British crown on the same basis as the dominions of Canada, South Africa, Australia and New Zealand. But two problems remained. The six northern counties of the Ulster Province were largely Protestant in nature and chose to opt out of the new setup and remain British.

However, de Valera and the more radical elements of the IRA refused to accept Ireland as any part of the British domain, even as an independent dominion – and thus broke ranks with Ireland's new President Griffith and its head of the new Irish army, Collins. Thus Ireland fell into a state of civil war.

Although the majority of the Irish (and the Catholic Church) supported the treaty, the radical wing of the IRA did not – and assassinated Collins. Then even the radical wing of the IRA split into contending groups. Finally de Valera seemingly accepted the treaty-based Irish Free State by participating in the national elections of 1923. Thus things settled down a bit ... with the Irish Free State now joining the League of Nations as a new national member. But by 1926, de Valera was back pressing for a fully independent Irish Republic ... one including even the six heavily-Protestant Ulster counties. Thus Irish tensions lived on ... even well into the 1930s (and after).

France struggles to rebuild

The ravages of war in France. For the French, the "victory" in the recent war produced only a very empty feeling in the country. The northern part of France, where the war had raged for four horrible years, had been laid waste ... with hundreds of towns being simply piles of rubble. Deep trenches and unexploded ordnance covered the area, coal mines had been flooded, dynamited, filled with waste or even set ablaze, and steel mills and textile factories had been destroyed by the Germans. And of the nearly 8 million Frenchmen who had served in the French military, nearly 1.5 million of them had been killed or were missing and another 1.5 million of them seriously wounded. And overall, the French population during the war years dropped from 41.6 million to 38.6 million.

Unsurprisingly, France was in a very vengeful mood with respect to

Germany. The Germans were going to have to pay dearly for what they did to France. The fact that Germany itself was economically a disaster and thus unlikely to be able to meet that demand was to the French beside the point. They must pay.

The post-war splintering of French politics. Also, France was so shaken up by the war morally and intellectually that it was not sure what ideas or symbols to rebuild its post-war national honor around. The conservative political organization Action Française wanted the French Orléanist monarchy and Catholic Church restored to their former places of glory. On the other side of the political aisle (the "Left"), the large Socialist Party was split deeply over their Socialist goals – many of the Socialists inspired deeply by events in Lenin's Russia ... whereas others claimed that Lenin's party was not truly Marxist but merely opportunist. Finally in 1920, the majority of the Socialists decided to follow the Leninist model and reformed themselves as the French Communist Party.

Then there were the Radical-Socialists, in fact rather centrist (but tending to the Left) ... and the somewhat militarily oriented Croix-de-Feu, which was strongly conservative (monarchist and Catholic) but Bonapartist in sentiments and thus strongly opposed to Action Française.

Occupying something of the "center" of this widely-split political spectrum were the French Radicals (actually not very "radical" at all) – in coalition with other small centrist parties – and the more centrist remnants of the old French Socialist Party. These "centrists" actually supplied France with most of its prime ministers after the war (e.g. Raymond Poincaré, Édouard Herriot, and Édouard Daladier).

Rebuilding the French economy. Because of the huge expense of the war, the French government found itself deeply in debt. The hope was that German reparation payments might be a major solution to the problem. But those payments were never seriously forthcoming, not anywhere to the extent the French had hoped for anyway. The French franc fell perilously ... not to the extent of the German mark, but at least to the point that it was worth only a couple of cents (American) by 1926. Wartime leader Poincaré was brought out of retirement, put the government under tight financial discipline, and by early 1927 the French economy seemed to be stabilizing. Indeed the French economy began to pick up as business orders and tourism grew to prewar levels.

Then the Great Depression hit over the winter of 1929-1930. At first it looked as if France might escape its grip ... but by 1931 the French economy was slipping into the American-birthed Depression as well. The next few years would be extremely tough for France economically.

Weimar Germany struggles to get on its feet

Postwar chaos. The new Weimar government was having a very hard time finding loyalty from its German society. Conditions in Germany were horrible ... mass starvation even a threat – in great part because the British were maintaining a blockade against food imports to Germany until the Germans agreed to the terms of the peace treaty. In the meantime, it appeared to most Germans that the whole political setup, including the new Republic, was contrived to keep Germany humbled ... a stab in the back theory (the *Dolchstosslegende*). The final terms agreed on by the Weimar representatives at Paris only deepened the suspicions.

In those hard years after the war Germany struggled to avoid social collapse. The Left-wing socialist and communist paramilitary Red Guard and the Right-wing super-nationalist Freikorps battled with each other in the streets, catching innocent citizens in the brutal crossfire. General strikes were called by Leftist labor organizers ... and produced not better working conditions but instead merely crippled a German economy struggling to get back on its feet. Also, unsuccessful attempts were made by various political factions to take over one or another of the smaller states comprising the German union – further shaking the German social order.

Inflation and devaluation of the mark. On top of this was the horrifying drop in the value of the German national currency, when the new government began printing marks in huge numbers to meet the post-war industrialists' investment needs and workers' salary demands, and finally to meet reparations requirements imposed by the Versailles Treaty. At the beginning of 1922 the mark went from four to the dollar to 300 to the dollar by that June, then by the end of the year to 8,000 marks to the dollar. By the fall of the next year the mark was not even worth the cost of the paper it was printed on.

Then in the midst of this crisis, when the German government announced at the beginning of 1923 that it could no longer make reparation payments to the French, Belgians and others, both French and Belgian troops entered Germany's industrial region of the Ruhr to seize the industrial assets of Germany. This move in turn was met by general strikes of the German workers – which only drove the German economy further into the ground.

Ultimately at the end of 1923, the government took action by simply striking 12 zeros off the exchange rate of the mark (it was at that point 4 trillion marks to the dollar), bringing the value back to four marks to the dollar. This finally stopped the inflation. But in the process, multitudes of Germans lost their entire life savings.

Economic recovery ... but a widening social-moral divide. Eventually things settled down for Germany as the 1920s rolled along. Rural life in Germany recovered sufficiently so that it was finally able to take on its more traditional character. Urban life however looked in a different direction as life settled in. Urban Germany was excited about the new life-style offerings of post-war industry and commerce. New material goods such as cars, radios, home appliances – plus the exciting distractions of movies and cabarets – seemed to point to the opening up of a wonderful new world (which rural Germany did not fully understand or admire).

Traditional moral standards gave way as urban Germany experimented with new cultural ideas and behavior. Urban Germany was not prudish to begin with ... but its sexual freedoms – including rapidly spreading homosexuality – would become particularly bold and challenging to those holding traditional German understandings of how things were supposed to be. Indeed, traditional rural and small-town Germany found itself increasingly hostile to Germany's rising urban culture.

Later Hitler would play heavily on this moral divide, targeting particularly the rampant homosexuality that seemed to infect urban Germany (particularly Berlin), making himself even more popular with rural and small-town Germany in the process.

The "Jewish problem." Germans had already been highly suspicious of Jewish treachery … in that this had been part of their Protestant (Lutheran) outlook on Jews in general – plus the fact that a large number of Jews were part of the Socialist Party that had set up and now directed the largely unloved Weimar Republic. Also, the postwar migration into Germany of Jews from the East (principally escaping anti-Jewish persecution or pogroms in Russia and Poland) only heightened this attitude.

Jews had long suffered in Russia and Poland as a distinct religious minority, in that they were never allowed to secure stable property rights ... and thus were forced to invest their assets in things other than land: notably gold, jewelry and other mobile valuables. With the increase of the persecution of Jews during the heat of rising nationalism in Russia and Poland before and during the war, this mobility of Jewish wealth actually made it much easier for the Jews to make the decision to finally abandon their homes and head west. Urban Germany was a natural destination ... as most of them spoke Yiddish (actually Jüdisch) a German dialect, making assimilation into Germany a relatively easy move. On arriving in Germany, they were able to use their mobile assets to purchase German businesses that had fallen on hard times, deepening a bitterness among Germans who saw their neighbors lose their businesses to these Jewish intruders. It all seemed like further proof of a grand Jewish conspiracy to undermine Germany. Here too Hitler would play on these feelings to promote himself and his fiercely anti-Jewish Nazi program among bitter Germans.

Austria struggles to survive amidst the political ruins

Nationalism had been on the rise since the late 1800s. But the national fervor stirred by the war – plus Wilson's push for the rights of "national self-determination of people everywhere" at the peace talks in 1919 – brought to those peace talks national groups demanding national independence. Of course Britain's and France's multinational empires were untouchable. But this was not the case for the defeated powers Germany, Austria-Hungary and the Ottoman Empire.

Habsburg Austria-Hungary was therefore stripped down deeply ... with Hungary separated from the Habsburg union as a completely independent country. Czechoslovakia and Yugoslavia were created from some of the Habsburg lands. Thus when the carving up of the Habsburg empire was completed, there was very little left geographically of what was to carry on as "Austria." And what was left was heavily mountainous and devoid of much by way of natural assets. And her economy, once built around the empire's formerly huge internal trade zone, now found itself cut off from those same markets by tariff barriers erected by the newly independent nations once making up her empire. Economically, survival looked nearly impossible for the little rump state left over from the carve-up.

There was some thought of simply linking German-speaking Austria to the new German Weimar Republic ... but that idea was shot down by the Allies' fear of adding strength to a Germany which was supposed to be put under very tight oversight, to ensure that its "Hunnic instinct" would never rise again. Indeed, in the Versailles Treaty such union (*Anschluss*) of the two German states was strictly forbidden – except by express permission of the League of Nations ... which was very unlikely ever to occur.

Reparations had been imposed on the new Austrian Republic – similar to, though not of the same scale as those imposed on Germany – and, as with Germany, had invited an inflation that by 1922 had nearly bankrupted the new republic. The League agreed to suspend the reparations payments ... and the currency began to stabilize. The economy began then to pick up.

But politically Austria seemed unable to bridge an ideological gap that separated the Social Democrats from the Christian Socialists. The former were strongly supported by an urban-based industrial workers movement of the Marxist variety, whereas the latter represented the conservative interests of the Austrian countryside. The rivalry grew so bitter that Austria could never find a middle ground politically on which to move ahead.

The new Republic of Czechoslovakia

The newly created Czechoslovakia was a combination of Czech society in the West, Slovakian society in the East, Moravians in the middle, and other minorities here and there … including a huge number of Germans along the Czech borderlands north and west – the Sudetenland.

Though vastly Slavic in language, the country really had two distinct cultures: the Czech or Bohemian society in the West was very modern, highly industrialized and totally Westward-looking … and had been the industrial heartland of the former Habsburg Empire. Indeed, despite tariff barriers which abounded in the days after the war, the Czech industrialists were able to develop a large export business ... and the nation's currency became, alongside the Swiss franc, the most stable on the continent. On the other hand, the Slovakian society was rural and looked principally to the older Slavic world to the East.

Holding the country together were very capable leaders, Dr. Thomas Masaryk and Dr. Edvard Beneš, the former who would come to serve as the new Republic's first President (1918-1932) and the latter who would come to serve as the country's Foreign Minister (1918-1935) and then as its President (1935-1938), as its President-in-exile in London (1939-1945), and again as Czechoslovakia's President (1945-1948). Such leadership along with the country's highly developed industrial skills made for an outstanding postwar economic development in Czechoslovakia.

✳ ✳ ✳

THE BIRTH OF "POPULAR DICTATORSHIP"

Poland

We have already noted the war that broke out between Russia and the newly restored Poland. Finally, the Polish borders were recognized internationally by the Treaty of Riga (1921) ... along a line negotiated by British Foreign Secretary, Lord Curzon. Piłsudski and his military officers had hoped for better. But the political leaders of the Polish Republic were content – stirring feelings of hostility between the Polish military and the Polish civilian leaders.

Piłsudski takes control. The next five years was a time in which Poland attempted to discover what it truly meant to be a modern republic – and largely failed. The country was split politically into a number of contending power groups, and corruption within the ranks of the government was widespread. And the military was unwilling to submit itself to civilian authority. The blow finally came in 1926 when Piłsudski led a military coup overthrowing the civilian government – and Poland entered into a period of tight-fisted dictatorship under Piłsudski ... one that lasted until his death in 1935. Some degree of unity was forced on Poland, and it did undergo some economic growth – though not nearly at the rate that its population was growing. Also, it lived a very precarious existence squeezed between two naturally hostile powers, Germany and Russia. Non-aggression pacts were signed with both countries. But as events would soon prove, these pacts were meaningless.

Hungary

Kun takes control. When the newly instituted Hungarian Republic (carved out of the former Austro-Hungarian Empire) proved unable to protect itself from the seizing of Hungarian territory by its new neighbors Poland, Czechoslovakia, and Romania, the Communists took over the government. The Communist leader Béla Kun, a close friend of Lenin's, attempted to reorganize Hungary along Soviet lines ... but succeeded only in throwing the economy into massive inflation and disarray. He then in the summer of 1919 attempted to carry the Communist challenge into Romania ... but in realizing his motives, much of his army deserted – and the Romanians drove his weakened army into humiliating retreat. This soon undercut the last of his support in Budapest, and he and other Communist leaders were forced to flee Hungary.

Horthy takes control. This in turn inspired a campaign of violence (the "White Terror") against Communists ... but also against leftist Socialists and even Jews ... when Hungarian war hero Admiral Miklós Horthy was invited to take control of Hungary as "Regent." Horthy took the side of social-political conservatism and soon brought the country under his control, arresting massive numbers of Radicals and Liberals. He also undid most of the liberal reforms enacted during Kun's rule, including very importantly Kun's land reform, turning the land back over to the tiny but highly privileged class of landowners ... and as a result setting up a political controversy that would shake the country during the entire 1920s and 1930s. This in turn drove the Horthy regime deeper into dictatorship ... and a second ill-fated alliance with Germany.

Yugoslavia

Much like the other new states carved out of the divided up Austro-Hungarian Empire, Yugoslavia was itself actually a mix of a number of national subgroups, the most prominent being the dominant Serbs, but also the highly national self-aware Croatians and Slovenes ... plus the Montenegrins, Macedonians, Muslim Bosnians, Albanian Kosovars, Hungarians and others. On top of this, the country was divided into contending religious groups, 47% Eastern Orthodox, 39% Catholic and 11% Muslim.

Holding it all together was a constitutional monarchy, with the Serbian heir to the throne, Alexander, as king. The democratic aspect of the constitution was truly beyond the comprehension of the largely illiterate population and the national legislature in the capital Belgrade (also the Serbian capital) seemed to be responsive to no other interests than its own Serbian agenda. Finally in 1929, King Alexander simply suspended the constitution and attempted to enact social reforms on his own in the hopes of pulling his kingdom together ... then granting the country a new constitution in 1931 which changed very little about how the kingdom was actually governed.

Alexander's attempt to soften the cultural divisions actually seemed only to make them worse, driving the national groups into a stronger defensive posture as they sensed his effort to undercut their spirit of nationalism.

When Alexander was assassinated in 1934, his son Peter was too young to take the throne ... so a Regency under Alexander's cousin, Prince Paul, was established. Paul attempted to appease the minority nationalists by granting greater local autonomy ... especially to the most vocal of the national subgroups, the Croats. But this only irritated the Slovenes all the more when the same rights were not immediately extended to them. But then before that challenge could be addressed, World War Two intervened ... and the political agenda changed drastically.

Mussolini's Fascist Italy

Post-war frustration in Italy. Though on the "winning" side of the Great War, Italy was as convulsed after the war by the same political and social problems experienced by the "losers." Italy had joined the Entente of Britain and France in 1915 on the promise that Italy would receive a number of pieces of neighboring territories as part of an expanded Italy. But multiple promises were made by the British and French ... and when Yugoslavia, not Italy, received the Fiume province along the northern Adriatic Sea (near Venice) the Italians fumed. Especially angered was the Italian adventurer Gabriele d'Annunzio, who seized the territory and named himself its Duce (Italian: "Leader") and began promoting a philosophy of national unity through strength – a political idealism attempting to transcend the violent industrial-class politics which had set in heavily in Italy, much as in Russia and Germany. D'Annunzio was eventually deposed by the Italian military – but not before his philosophy had caught the attention of another aspiring Italian politician, Benito Mussolini.

Mussolini and the Fascist takeover of Italy (1922). Mussolini had started out as a Socialist propagandist (newspaper editor) – who turned against Socialism when it refused to support the Italian entry into the Great War. But he was just as opposed to the Liberalism spreading across postwar Europe with its spirit of democratic pacifism. He exalted strength – strength through conflict, strength through struggle – which would produce a warlike character among a people. This in turn would bring them to unity (fascism)* and greatness – greatness such as the ancient Romans had once exemplified. The key to this process was achieving an absolute unity of the people through unswerving loyalty to a great leader, a "Duce" such as Mussolini himself proposed to become. He promised Italians (prominently Italy's industrial leaders) to bring social unity to Italy through a policy of strict enforcement of that unity through the use of his street "toughs" (the "Blackshirts") who stood ready to strike total fear in the hearts of labor agitators and anarchists through whatever means were necessary to do so.

At first Mussolini headed up an actual parliamentary party, with 31 Fascist Party seats in the Italian Assembly. But from this position he began bullying the feeble Italian leadership – demanding full control of the government. Finally in September of 1922 some ten thousand Fascists descended on Rome demanding that control. But a supportive King Victor Emmanuel would not grant Prime Minister Facta the right to call out the army. As more Fascists gathered over the next couple of days, Facta resigned. The king now asked Mussolini to "save" the nation by becoming its new prime minister (and also the head of the home and foreign ministries).

From this point on, Mussolini saw to it that Fascist officials took over one then another political office … including most importantly the police and the military. All opposition was shut down – politicians, journalists, labor leaders, and the leaders of any organization not willing to fall in line in support of Mussolini and his Fascists. All of this was justified as not only the proper means to bring unity to a very divided Italy, but also a restored national strength … such as to bring the nation to prominence among the superpowers of the day.

Interestingly, Mussolini ended the long-standing church-state divorce

---

*From the Italian *fascio* or bundle … and also from the ancient Roman fasces or bundle of rods with an axe head lashed tightly together by leather thongs – which was carried into battle by a Roman commander.

between the Vatican and the Italian government when in 1929 both Mussolini and the Pope signed the Lateran Treaty. Mussolini actually came out in support of religious education, Catholic marriage, and the Church's property rights ... in exchange for the Church's support of Mussolini's government.

And thus it was that all Italians seemingly had come under the rule of the Fascist state, the only true protector of the Italian nation!

✻ ✻ ✻

THE STIRRING OF THE NON-WESTERN WORLD

India

India was more a subcontinent than a true nation. But its years of unity as the crown jewel of the British Empire had created something along those lines. Indians largely accepted their place in the imperial scheme of things as a people dependent on British political management ... even contributing 1.5 million troops loyal to the British cause during the recent war.

But the Japanese humiliation of the Russians in the Russo-Japanese War of 1904-1905 had done considerable damage to the idea that Europeans had, by their very nature, an equally natural place at the head of the various European empires found widely around the world. Then too, Wilson's grand crusade for "anti-imperial democracy" (aimed however only at America's enemy empires) certainly stirred the expectations at the postwar peace conferences for some kind of a move towards independence as a result of their contribution to the "democratic" cause of the Great War.

Among those hoping to see such a reward come to their own land was the Indian lawyer – and ultimately political guru – Mohandas Gandhi. He proved himself to be one of those 1920s charismatic leaders with a talent for mobilizing a spirit of intense nationalism among the common people ... though his methods were quite different than those of Mussolini, Horthy, or Piłsudski.

Born in India, Gandhi was sent off to London to study law ... and was eventually admitted to the prestigious bar of London's Inner Temple. But he then returned to India – where he ultimately found little success as a lawyer. He then moved his law practice to South Africa, where for the next 22 years he would represent members of the large Indian community living in the Natal Province.   Racial attitudes in South Africa stirred Gandhi's interest in fighting just those attitudes ... and there he first developed a political strategy of simple non-violent street protests in order to make his point. He also learned how to cultivate the British sense of shame when protests provoked police brutality. In short, he understood well how to employ the necessary tactics (*Satyagraha*) to succeed in his crusade.

During the Great War, in 1915, he gave up his practice in South Africa to return to India ... dressed not in a suit as a proper London-trained lawyer but in a towel-wrap typical of what Indians considered to be the proper attire of a Hindu holy man! For a while he continued to support the British effort in the war ... until a huge famine hit India, and the British did not respond with the support that Gandhi demanded of them. He countered British authority by then getting Indians to refuse to pay their taxes to the British government. He knew that without Indian support of the British government, British authority would not long hold in India. Such non-cooperation with the British authorities thus would become central to his campaign of Satyagraha. He went on to urge the Indians to refuse to buy British goods (for instance, to weave their own clothes, as he himself exemplified), to resign their positions in the British colonial administration, and to withdraw from British educational institutions in India.

In all this he was able (for a while anyway) to draw the huge Muslim portion of Indian society into his program ... exploiting the Muslim anger at the British for opposing Muslim Turkey and its sultan. Thus, being the only Indian truly able to reach across the Hindu-Muslim divide in India, he was given (1920) leadership of the newly rising Indian National Congress.

Yet Gandhi never could figure out how to control a protest movement that soon got caught up in militant and then violent action. The Indian National Congress was not a disciplining organization like Mussolini's Fascists or Hitler's Nazis ... and only the moral appeal of Gandhi personally gave whatever discipline his movement was able to enjoy. Consequently, despite his advocacy of nonviolence, Indian protests constantly turned violent. For instance, riots in Bombay in November of 1921 resulted in the death of 53 people and the wounding of hundreds of others. Finally, in 1922, as the violence spread, Gandhi was arrested and sentenced to six years in prison. Without their leader, the movement then settled down.

However, British efforts during the 1920s to recognize some degree of Indian self-rule was greeted typically by the Indian leadership as being too little, too late. Actually, seeing the British retreat merely encouraged the Indians to demand greater retreat. And when Gandhi was released from prison and retook the lead of the movement, he now demanded total independence (*Swaraj*) for India. He simply wanted the British to leave ("Quit India") and go back home to the British Isles.

In 1930 Gandhi started up again his protest campaign of civil disobedience – this time as a protest against the salt tax – by leading thousands of Indians on a long march to the sea to make their own salt. And once again the movement turned violent as crowds of Indians marched up against British troops trying to keep order. The violence was terrible (and well covered by the press) and over 60,000 Indians were arrested (though not Gandhi). Yet Gandhi's overall goal was achieved: the event shattered whatever loyalty was left for the British Empire in the hearts of multitudes of Indians.*

Chinese nationalism blossoms after the War

The Chinese meanwhile were trying to secure national independence from extensive Western intervention – but were themselves inspired in their efforts also not by one but by several conflicting programs of Chinese reform ... each built around several competing political leaders.

Clearly the Qing government was losing its grip over the country ... as the Chinese national spirit grew increasingly rebellious against this dynasty – which was Manchurian in origin, rather than of true Han Chinese descent. And its ineffectiveness in the face of the Western intervention only intensified this rebellious spirit ... for clearly to the Chinese, the weakness of the Qing made it clear that their dynasty had lost the all-important "mandate of Heaven." Thus rebellion broke out widely across China.

Yuan Shi-kai. The Chinese emperor then (1911) called on General Yuan Shi-kai to be his prime minister ... and crush the rebellion. Instead, Yuan sat down with some of the rebel leaders to work out the details for a Chinese Republic ... then getting the Qing emperor to abdicate, and finally making himself the president of this new republic (early 1912)! But Yuan was not happy with a huge victory in elections for the new National Assembly by the Chinese Nationalist Party – the Kuomintang or KMT. Its leader, Song Jiaoren, he had assassinated. Yuan then moved to bring the KMT under his personal control. Then as the Great War came to impact China, he tried to build the Chinese nationalist spirit around his personal rule ... in having his assembly designate him as the new Chinese emperor. But before he could actually have this move formalized in 1916, Yuan died of kidney failure. At this point chaos again spread across China.

Sun Yat-sen. But at this point a particularly active – and highly Westernized - medical doctor, Sun Yat-sen, returned from his exile in Japan to reorganize and take command of the scattered KMT. But he was facing numerous Chinese warlords – who saw the collapse of the Yuan government as also their great opportunity ... if not to rule all of China, at least portions of it. But bit by bit Dr. Sun was able to reorganize and rebuild the KMT ... so that by the early 1920s, he (with some help from some rebel leaders, some local

---

*American President Obama would later attest to the fact that Gandhi was a huge inspiration to his own campaign to equalize the races in America.

warlords, and from Lenin's Communist government) seemed to be able to secure more and more Chinese territory brought under KMT rule.

But by 1923 a dispute he was having with a supposed supporter among the warlords had reached crisis proportions. China found itself again in a state of civil war. But with the help of his Soviet advisors (who were as interested as the Chinese in ending all Western governmental involvement in Chinese affairs) – and in securing the much-needed assistance of the young but militarily very skillful General Chiang Kai-shek in organizing a more modern KMT military, led by young officers trained at the newly established Whampoa Military Academy – Sun seemed to be on the path to bringing China finally under KMT governance ... when in early 1925 he suddenly died (cancer).

Chiang Kai-shek. At first, a three-way struggle developed among KMT's potential leadership, with one assassinated, his assassin arrested, and the third, the Soviet-backed Communist Wang Jingwei, finally taking command of the KMT. Once in power, Wang then appointed fellow Communists to other key leadership posts.   At about the same time, false accusations concerning an event in southern China resulted in a call for Chiang's arrest (1926).

But rather than flee China (the expected recourse!), Chiang chose to take a stand and fight back against the KMT authorities coming after him. The results proved disastrous for the Communists – who, (including Wang) were arrested and imprisoned ... and the Soviet advisors (those who had not already fled) were expelled from the country. But oddly enough, the Soviet response was mixed ... with Soviet dictator Stalin still wanting to work with Chiang. Chiang then conquered China's warlords ... and brought nearly all of China under his own KMT authority by 1928.

But the problems with the Chinese Communists and the ambitious warlords would always have the potential of breaking forth at any moment.

The Pahlavi dynasty's modernization of Persia
... Persia eventually (1935) becoming "Iran"

Persia was also having troubles, stirred deeply by the Western political-cultural impact on the country. In the face of various challenges, the Qajar dynasty had proven itself unable to offer Persia serious leadership ... and the country thus found itself caught in a rising competition for power among unhappy groups of Persians.

Leading the conservatives was the Grand Ayatollah, who urged Persia to return to very strict traditional ways – certain that this was the only way that Allah would ever bring Persia out of its obvious mess and restore the

Persian empire to glory.

But the large reform or pro-modernization group found itself facing its own difficulties in that Western outsiders were not merely supporting Persia's modernization, they wanted full control of the process. For instance, during the Great War, both Russia and Britain controlled "neutral" Persia in order to move war materials and foodstuff between the two wartime allies. Also the British convinced the Qajar government to be content with receiving only 16% of the oil revenues coming from the British pumping of Persian oil. And so things went.

But with the success of the Soviets in Russia, Persian modernizers were eager to get the support of Lenin's Communists in the conduct of their own social revolution in Persia. Indeed, with Soviet help, Persian rebels were finally able to establish their own Republic in 1921, ending the reign of the Qajar shahs. But the challenge of bringing this disrupted political system back to order remained a huge problem.

Reza Shah Pahlavi (1925-1941). It would be the British, in a move to protect its extensive interests in Persia, that would make the move to bring forward the leader of a Persian Cossack Brigade, Reza Khan, to force the country back into some kind of order by 1923. So appreciative of his role in all this was the new Majlis (Parliament), that it asked him to assume the position as the country's Prime Minister. Then only two years later the Majlis changed its own constitution ... making itself a constitutional monarchy, with Reza Pahlavi called to be its new king or Shah.

With that, Persia found itself embarked on a new modernization program, very similar to the one going on next door in Turkey under Atatürk. Education was Westernized, clothing requirements (especially important for the women) were reshaped along Western lines, roads were built, industrial investment by new Persian banks expanded dramatically ... except in the oil industry, which remained still fully under British control. And with that he also changed the name of the country to "Iran" (Aryan) to indicate its distinct ethnic background. It was no longer an empire. It was now a "nation" ... under the rule, of course, of a new Pahlavi dynasty.

Naturally, all this change merely brought out the traditional clergy in anger. But – for the time being – there was little that the traditional clergy could do to oppose all this change. For the next 50 years these reforms would hold ... until events inside and outside of Iran would collapse that same Pahlavi dynasty – and deliver the nation into the hands of the ayatollahs and their militant Muslim supporters.

Japan begins its debate: pacifism or militarism?

Japan had chosen the side of England and France in the Great War – which involved in Asia simply the Japanese military seizing German colonial territories in the Far East (mostly islands in the Pacific). It had also joined its allies in their intervention in the Russian civil war (acting in the Russian Far East) – and was the last of the allies to leave Russia (1925), although Japan continued to occupy the Russian zone of Outer Manchuria and the whole of the island of Sakhalin (with its extensive oil resources) off the Russian Siberian coast.

From all outward appearances Japan was eager to present itself to the world as a modern constitutional democracy ... except that there were large elements of Japanese society – especially within the military – that resented deeply the intrusion of Western ways. This group looked back to the ancient days of Japanese honor – in particular to their ancient military ethic of *bushido* and their ancient religion of State Shinto involving total devotion to the Emperor. Like the Fascists and Nazis in Europe, these Japanese militarists had nothing but scorn for democracy and the rising trend of secular humanism with its dreams of global peace through human reason. They were particularly furious at the way their Japanese government gave in to the Western move to general disarmament ... agreeing to deep cuts in the Japanese army and navy.

✷ ✷ ✷

AMERICA TRIES TO RETURN TO "NORMALCY"

The postwar "Red Scare." As already noted, at war's end the Americans took on a very negative view concerning further international involvement. There was very little interest in getting involved with the new League of Nations ... and that organization's efforts to manage world peace. But serving to worsen this anti-foreign-involvement attitude were several incidents involving Italian anarchists (particularly immigrants influenced by the Italian anarchist Galleani) that set the country on edge. Attorney General Palmer even had his house blown up by an agitator ... determining him even more to break this "Red Scare." Thousands were arrested in the period November 1919 to February 1920. Then the case of a robbery and murder in a payroll heist in April of 1920 – leading to the arrest of two Italians with anarchist backgrounds, Nicola Sacco and Bartolomeo Vanzetti – would absorb the attention not only of all America but even much of the world. They were sentenced in the summer of 1921 but appeals dragged the case out until they were put to death six years later ... with the country much divided over the issue.

Depression in rural America. Adding to this negative attitude was a rising sense among "Middle-America" – that is, among traditional rural and small-town America – that America's own rising urban society was corrupt and even anti-American. Part of this was because of the huge number of immigrants moving to urban America and carving out strongly ethnic neighborhoods where English was seldom heard. For rural America, going to the city was like going to a foreign country. It was certainly not the America they knew.

Part of this sense of alienation from urban America was fueled by the growing economic disparity between city and country life in America. Farmers had prospered greatly during the war ... feeding much of Europe at a time when most of Europe's farmers were in uniform fighting the war. American agricultural business was so good that farmers took out loans and mortgages to buy more land and equipment. But after the war, as the European farmers returned to their fields, the demand for American farm products dropped away. Indeed, the oversupply of farm produce drove prices at times below even their production costs. On top of this, those loans and mortgages had to be paid off ... and the farmers had no money. Soon the lending banks found themselves in trouble as well. Bankruptcies among rural banks spread quickly around the country ... creating a rural depression that anticipated the 1930s industrial depression in America by ten years.   Thus in the 1920s, rural America already knew what a massive economic depression was all about.

The "Roaring Twenties"

Massive consumerism. By contrast, urban America seemed almost in a partying mood. America's industrial war machine was easily converted after the war to the production of a whole new line of consumer goods, which quickly flooded the market: automobiles, radios, washing machines, vacuum sweepers, stylish clothing, movies. For instance, by 1927, Ford had produced over 15 million of its Model-T Fords; by 1929 the A&P grocery stores numbered 15,000, Woolworth's 5 & 10 cent stores numbered nearly 2,000, and J.C. Penny department stores numbered almost 1,500; by 1930 13.8 million Americans owned radios.

New "freedoms." Also very visible about 1920s America (particularly urban America) was its strong emphasis that life was all about personal freedoms ... rather than heavy social responsibilities – ones such as the recent war had required of them. No ... there would now be no social rules that would prevent them from undertaking life entirely on their own – in whatever manner they chose to do so. Nationalism and patriotism were things to be avoided ... in order to secure the freest life possible. Yet (unsurprisingly), there was great conformity visible in their "free" hair styles, clothing styles, musical tastes, etc.

Corruption in the White House. Nonetheless the anti-social instincts also became quite visible during the brief presidency of Warren Harding (1921-1923), corruption in the Harding Administration (not so much in the person of Harding himself, however) seeming almost to be the word of the day ... though his presidency was cut short when he died of a heart attack on a visit across the country to try to put his administration in a better light.

His vice president Calvin Coolidge on becoming US. President did bring something akin to Puritanical dignity back to the high office ... though his was not exactly an activist presidency.

"The Lost Generation." But all this freedom and glitz and glitter did little to satisfy the burdened hearts of a number of members of America's artistic-intellectual community. Under the patronage of Gertrude Stein, a group she herself entitled "the Lost Generation" gathered in Paris, in the attempt to offer each other companionship and support (e.g., Hemingway, Fitzgerald, Dos Passos, Cummings, etc.). Others went down the dreamy path of Marxism ... with its anti-nationalism (Marx detested the way nationalism was dividing his working-class movement) ... which was an understandable instinct given the horrors of the nationalism-induced war the world had just gone through.

But disillusionment did not extend just to the newly rising nationalist spirit that had just infected the world. It also took on a struggling world of the Christian faith ... at a time that God seemed to be most distant.

Freud takes on the struggling world of Christendom. An individual that would have a tremendous impact on modern culture and how it understood human behavior – and life itself – was the Austrian psychiatrist, Sigmund Freud. He was a prolific writer ... whose ideas were widely accepted as "scientific truth" – although they were in fact only that ... just his ideas about things.

Freud went on the attack against Western "rationalism" ... the key understanding of human nature held by "enlightened" Westerners since even the 1600s. Freud instead posited the idea that we humans are actually driven not by reason but by deep forces within our "subconscious" realm ... forces that we are hardly aware of because they are buried so very deep in our being. Dreams however are actually these subconscious forces surfacing from that deeper realm ... and reveal the truer nature of our being. Thus in his "psychotherapy" with his patients, he would explore deeply their dream world.

Freud claimed that these deep forces originate with us in our earliest years as children ... as sexual thoughts – but ones that we are taught to repress as we become increasingly socialized during our childhood years. He claimed that boys have a natural sexual fixation with their moms (the "Oedipus complex") ... and girls with their fathers.

He also ventured into analysis of masculinity versus femininity ... tending to support the dominating role that men play in the social scheme of things ... something that later caused feminists to depart from his legacy because of this view of his.

In two respects Freud "spoke for his age." As already noted, sexual freedom was considered to be a basic right by the Jazz Age generation ... and Freud somehow justified it as a more natural, less Victorian or sexually repressed instinct ... that has every good reason to be simply released.

Secondly, he also had his own interesting views on religion, seeing Christianity derived from a more feminine instinct and Judaism (his own ethnic background) as derived from a more masculine instinct.

But in any case, Freud felt strongly that belief in a heavenly God – Jewish or Christian – was merely a form of escapism from hard reality ... into a prettier dream world. Such religion was simply delusional, a form of collective or social neurosis ... much like the nationalist spirit had been.

Thus it was that Freudian psychology spoke to the skeptical mindset that followed up the recent war. Hadn't each of the warring parties gone into battle, very certain that "Gott mit uns"/ "God with us"? So then, where indeed was God? He seemed to have been very silent during the horror of the war.

Thus the question was not something answered easily.   Perhaps Freud seemed to have it right. Perhaps the belief in God was simply a made-up belief that weak people dream up in order to comfort themselves in confronting a difficult world. Thus to a lot of people, Freud and his ideas made a lot of sense.

And thus also, fewer and fewer people headed to church on a Sunday to find themselves in God's company.

The 18th Amendment (1920). Watching all this was rural America – shocked at the number of speakeasies (illegal bars), operating in brazen defiance of the new 18th Amendment to the Constitution outlawing alcoholic beverages. Urban America interpreted the Amendment as a moral slap by rural and small-town Christian America against the libertarian behavior of an increasingly secular urban America ... and responded to the challenge with delight in seeing the law violated. Even the criminal underground generated by the law was regarded in urban America as almost heroic in its defiance of the law.

The Scopes "Monkey Trial" (1925).   An event occurred in Dayton, Tennessee, in 1925 – one that represented very accurately the social-moral division over this religious question digging deeply into American society ... and for that matter much of the rest of postwar Western society.

When the state legislature of Tennessee passed a law forbidding the teaching of the Darwinist view of the origin of life, a group of local town leaders decided to challenge the law ... as a way of bringing some needed attention to their town. They had no idea of just how much attention that would end up being. Immediately the very "Liberal" America Civil Liberties Union (ACLU) decided to take up the cause in defense of Darwinism,[*] by bringing in the famous New York criminal lawyer, Clarence Darrow, to argue their case. Brought in to represent the "Christian" or Biblical stand on the matter was the old national political figure, William Jennings Bryan. And the huge national press corps gathered to watch the proceedings ... for the case truly represented a very bitter battle going on in America between the older Christian worldview and the rising Secular-Humanist worldview.

Which side actually won the case was hard to say ... for the case itself decided very little legally.[†] Yet it did highlight the moral-spiritual crisis hitting Middle-America ... a traditionalist sector of American society attempting to not be swept aside by the rising Humanism worldview, the latter appealing to a much younger and increasingly urban sector of American society.

Participating in the world disarmament movement

Actually, the war had not made America truly isolationist ... but instead merely pacifist. Indeed, the general view of the times, both in America as well as Europe, was that the greatest danger to the peace that the world craved so deeply was to be found in the heavy militarization of the nations. "Take the weapons away and the nations will be forced to act peacefully with each other." This huge Humanist hope seemed very logical, especially when the nightmare of the Great War was still deep in people's thoughts. Thus America itself sponsored the Washington Conference (1921) outlawing the use of poisonous gas and setting limits on the number of naval vessels various nations were entitled to possess.

Although America did not participate in the Locarno Conference, it

---

[*]The trial gets its name from Darwinism's claim that man was not made complete in his present form at the dawn of history, but instead evolved slowly over the eons from some primal ape or "monkey."

[†]Sadly, five days after the close of the case, Bryan died in his sleep while on another speaking tour.

certainly supported the Locarno Agreement (1925), by which France, Britain, Germany, Italy and Belgium agreed that they would not resort to war in their relations with each other ... but would resolve their conflicts only by peaceful means.

Then in 1928 America entered into something similar to the Locarno Agreement when it signed the Kellogg-Briand Pact, in which American Secretary of State Frank Kellogg met with French Foreign Minister Aristide Briand and signed a pact agreeing to renounce war as a means of settling conflicts and to use peaceful means instead. Soon the Kellogg-Briand Pact was joined by 59 other nations (including Germany, Italy and Japan) – seemingly indicating that the world was finally coming to its senses. Never again would a war such as what the world had gone through ten years earlier ever have to happen again.

Yet all of this was simply humanistic illusion ... as events would soon prove. Serious conflicts of interest (such as contested boundaries and revanchist dreams of gathering nationals scattered in neighboring countries) were never really dealt with ... nor could they be by peaceful means in any case. Too much was at stake for nation-states not to attempt the use of physical force if push came to shove. And it soon did.

But in the meantime, those still shocked by the trauma of the Great War were happy to believe that they had solved rationally one of life's most critical problems ... forever.

THE EMERGING REALM OF QUANTUM MECHANICS

While the more popular world of science was confident that somehow it was increasingly able to bring life under human mastery, another – vastly more esoteric – realm of science was finding itself caught in a discussion, even a debate, about what exactly all of reality was built on. Interestingly, in the mid-1920s, the great German physicist Albert Einstein and his Danish physicist friend Niels Bohr found themselves in deep debate over the findings of the "quantum revolution" ... something that was actually forcing them to reconsider the most fundamental laws of physics ... the traditional laws of Newtonian physics that had lesser scientists certain that they not only understood but also could soon control the dynamics of the physical world.

Einstein and Bohr – but also others joining them in this debate, such as Werner Heisenberg, Erwin Schrödinger, and Max Born – found themselves much less certain about the predictability of the world of light, heat, mass, etc. ... because the very fundamental nature of the smallest element or quantum of life itself, an energy particle that moved at the speed of light –

which Einstein termed a "photon" – was hard to pin down.

But ... was it in fact a particle – or a wave of energy? And if a particle, where exactly was it, and where was it headed? Actually, Einstein and Schrödinger tended to the wave side of the debate ... although it was understood by most of this new group of scientists that it could be both!

Heisenberg demonstrated with his "uncertainty principle" that if you could locate its present position, you would be unable to identify its momentum – its speed or trajectory. Likewise, if you could get a sense of where it was headed and how fast it was moving, you could not simultaneously locate its present position. You could compute one or the other, position or momentum, but not both at the same time! It was thus a most "uncertain" matter!

Worse, the very act of the observer investigating the photon and its dynamics would itself impact those dynamics, prejudicing the outcome of the experiment (the "observer effect")!

Thus physics found itself working not with exact measurements, but only with probabilities of small variances in its calculations. True, those probabilistic variances were very, very tiny. But they were variances nonetheless!

Wow! There went the world of exact science out the window!

Of course, this was such an esoteric matter that it had almost no impact on the world of popular science at the time ... so certain was the world of popular science that it was on the edge of bringing life under full human mastery. There was no "probability" about that. That was a matter of absolute certainty!

But life was soon, once again, to undermine the cultural world of intellectual certainty.

CHAPTER FIFTEEN

DEPRESSION ... AND MORE DICTATORSHIP (THE 1930s)

✳ ✳ ✳

THE ONSET OF THE GREAT DEPRESSION IN AMERICA

The October 1929 stock market crash

During the 1920s, America was on a dizzying chase after wealth that seemed to be there simply for the snatching on the stock exchange of Wall Street. The price of industrial stocks climbed to fantastic heights as ordinary American citizens cashed in life savings to buy stocks and shares. They even borrowed heavily from commercial banks on the expectation of soon making a magnificent return on their investments.

The iron law of supply and demand. But America was not paying close attention to what was happening in the consumer world. By the end of the 1920s, the market for all these latest items was actually becoming "saturated" – as most of the potential consumers now had their car, their radio, their washing machine, etc. There would always be new faces entering the consumer market, but at nothing like the pace of the mid-1920s. Businesses now discovered that they were having a hard time finding new customers ... and lowered their prices so as to coax new buyers into the consumer market. But ultimately with lower demand they simply had to cut back on supply (production), which meant idling factories and letting workers go ... which in turn meant that, with less money, the workers would be taking themselves out of the consumer market ... dropping demand even further. And so the dizzying spin upward of industrial production of the early 1920s began to turn itself into a mournful spin downward of that same industrial production in the late 1920s.

Hoover's hesitancy

At this point, the economic depression rural and small-town America had been experiencing now began to extend itself to industrial urban America. By the beginning of the 1930s, America was finally entering the era known as the Great Depression.

Politically speaking, the fallout for this economic tragedy fell on the shoulders of Herbert Hoover, who had just taken office as U.S. president the year of the stock market crash. It was not his fault – though the nation looked to him for hope, for answers. But he was at a loss as to what to do ... refusing even to grant on an earlier basis the pension bonuses (promised to begin in 1941) to desperate veterans of the war – even at a reduced amount ... even when hundreds of desperate veterans camped out in Washington DC in the hopes of getting some kind of financial assistance. They were desperate.

But even when Hoover finally did attempt some kind of government programming to support a staggering economy ... his Democratic Party opponents in Congress – sensing Hoover's political vulnerability as the nation approached a new round of national elections – accused him loudly of practicing "Socialism."

Roosevelt's "New Deal"

Cashing in on the despair, the ever-smiling Democratic Party presidential candidate Franklin D. Roosevelt rode into the presidency promising a "New Deal" ... although the specifics of the matter were never very clear during the presidential campaign. In fact, they would soon reveal themselves to be even more "Socialist" than what the Democrats had so recently accused Hoover of attempting to put in place. In any case, a very discouraged American electorate turned out in huge numbers to support this most optimistic candidate – for there was little else at the time to be optimistic about.

The First 100 days. A vast number of Roosevelt's programs were easily put through a Democratic-Party-controlled Congress ... putting thousands of unemployed young men to work building national parks; Roosevelt and his "Brain Trust" of presidential advisors had dams and river plants built in order to generate both flood control and vast amounts of electrical energy for rural America; he put the American banking system under the protection of a Federal Deposit Insurance Corporation, the stock market under the regulation of a Securities Exchange Commission.

But that was just the beginning. He would in 1934 move on to create a home mortgage insurance commission (the Federal Housing

Administration); and in 1935 set up America's Social Security Trust Fund ... to prompt Americans to set aside part of their earnings in order to have a pension fund to draw from during the years of their retirement.

And then he went on to finance multitudes of various civil building projects, from swimming pools, to amphitheaters, to railroad improvements, to municipal parks, to municipal public office buildings, to roads, airports, etc., etc. ... to put unemployed Americans to work. And of course all this ran up the public debt to unprecedented heights.

Confrontation with the U.S. Supreme Court

The U.S. Supreme Court looked suspiciously at these projects, claiming that they had no constitutional warrant, and shot one down after another ... only to have Roosevelt come up with yet another program. Furious at this opposition, he threatened to simply reshape the membership of the Court ... shocking even members of his own party at this rather unconstitutional step. However, some changes in the makeup and viewpoint of the Court membership soon changed its position vis-a-vis his projects. Roosevelt, however, had lost a lot of political standing during his war with the Court ... a political war which did not go over too well with a lot of Americans.

A deep shift in the American sense of order

The Depression seemed to be a concrete support of the idea that the realm of social ideas and ideals that the country had been living under – virtually since its founding in the early 1600s – were "false gods" who clearly had failed. It was indeed time to go at life in very new, very "progressive" ways. Certainly that was the idea that justified Roosevelt's use of extensive federal powers to rebuild American society, almost from the ground up.

But the thinking did not just stop at political "progress" ... but under the guidance of self-appointed social prophets – with their grand social theories – the Depression promoted a deep spirit of progressivism in the realm of new social ideals ... and even in the realm of religion. For American intellectuals, this was exactly what they had spent years preparing for ... the opportunity to put their beautiful social ideals into action.

The *Humanist Manifesto* (1933). This intellectualist spirit of the times is best represented in the *Humanist Manifesto*, signed by 34 prominent individuals and published in America's mainstream media on May 1st, 1933. The signatories included some 9 professors of religion, theology, philosophy, etc. at Harvard, Chicago (3), Cornell, Michigan, Illinois, Pittsburgh, Smith, and Columbia (2 ... one of them being the very well-known John Dewey) –

plus 9 Unitarian pastors, plus 4 editors of prestigious journals, and a number of heads of various Liberal societies. In short, a group very representative of the highest realm of American social intellectualism.

Basically from the *Humanist Manifesto*'s point of view, capitalism had failed ... and so also had traditional Christianity. It was time for a deep revision in the social, moral and spiritual character of modern society.

Interestingly, the signers of the document start off by identifying themselves as "Religious humanists" ... believing that the universe was "self-existing and not created." It also affirms that "modern science makes unacceptable any supernatural or cosmic guarantees of human values." It also states that "there will be no uniquely religious emotions and attitudes of the kind hitherto associated with belief in the supernatural." And it affirms that "a socialized and cooperative economic order must be established to the end that the equitable distribution of means of life be possible." And so it concludes "So stand the theses of religious humanism."

This was not Middle America speaking. This was American Intellectualism speaking. And this amazing document made very clear the key features of Humanism ... and its ideals that serve as the underpinning worldview that has long directed "lofty" Intellectuals ... the same ideals that informed Rousseau, Jefferson, Marx, Wilson, and many others of this same intellectual nature.

The slide back into the Depression (the later 1930s). But this kind of Idealism would lose favor quickly (if it ever did have any favor at all with Middle America) ... because Idealist America found itself helpless in the face of hard reality.

First there was a huge and ongoing drought that descended in the mid-1930s upon a number of Midwestern states, from Texas in the south to North Dakota in the north. The topsoil was simply blown away by hot winds which turned the air into black clouds of choking dust. Farms were simply abandoned as destitute farmers headed west to California to look for work – any work. Most of them ended up living in migrant workers' camps under the worst conditions imaginable. People survived – but only by toughening up.

Then also by 1937-1938 America was running into new economic problems as government infrastructure projects came to completion and the need for new government work projects disappeared. America now had a largely complete network of national highways, dams at every likely spot where electricity could be generated, national parks for recreation in every likely location, etc. There was now little government work to be found ... and workers were sent home again.

And none of this seemed to activate America's "private sector" ... on which industrial America had previously built its national wealth. No new inventions, no new products, came on the shelves for eager consumers to purchase. Anyway, what money Americans did possess they refused to invest in the industrial world but instead simply put their earnings "under the mattress" ... where it would be safe from the unpredictable shocks of the world of financial investment.

Consequently, with little economic action beyond what the government was still trying to offer, the American economy slowly slid back down into its former stagnant level. The Great Depression was still on in America.

A shift in the presidential agenda

But by this point Roosevelt was turning his attention elsewhere ... to the international scene where Japanese behavior in China and the rise of Hitler in Europe were clearly alarming developments. Although America was in no mood to go sallying forth to try to save the world again (in fact the mood of America at this point was becoming increasingly "isolationist" in the face of these rising dangers abroad) Roosevelt himself kept close tabs on what was happening overseas. He had a sense that a largely unarmed America was soon going to find itself caught up in a mess for which it was totally unprepared. Thus it was that he personally followed these overseas doings very closely.

$$* \; * \; *$$

THE DEPRESSION'S IMPACT ON EUROPE

Britain

Britain would join the industrial world in the great catastrophe which fell upon the West at the beginning of the 1930s ... but would fare better than many of the other nations. At first the British financial and industrial sectors were hard hit by the panic of the capital markets ... and by the American decision to impose tariffs on non-American goods in the hope that this would protect struggling American goods against foreign products. But this merely produced the decision of other governments to do the same, drastically restricting global markets at a time when they needed to be more open than ever in order to invite production.

Britain responded by creating a protected trade region with its dominions overseas ... large enough to encourage the continuing movement of raw materials and finished products back and forth within the imperial zone. Thus Britain and the dominions fared better than much of the rest of the world ... though Britain still had to watch government expenditures (especially such items as military men and equipment in a time of "peace"). But British industry was also modernizing and developing new lines of efficiency that would help the British economy enormously.

France

At first it looked as if France might escape the impact of the Depression. But by 1931, the French economy was slipping as well. The coming years would be extremely tough for France economically.

By 1934 France was being shaken by political revolts ... especially after the revelation of the Stavinsky scandal in which a number of Leftist cabinet members were found to have been involved in the massive purchase of worthless bonds. This led to street riots which had to be dispersed by the force of arms ... resulting in the death of over 200 protesters and the wounding of over two thousand more.

This in turn divided France deeply politically, the Left accusing the Right of trying to take over France by Fascist means ... and the Right countering with accusations of similar Communist motivations on the part of the Left. Indeed, by 1935, the French Croix de Feu had developed from a postwar veterans' organization to a strongly Right-wing paramilitary organization of some 300,000 members, shaped along the lines of Mussolini's and Hitler's Fascist organizations. At the same time, the Communists, who had broken from the older French Socialist Party, seemed to be taking orders from Stalin. Consequently, the French political Middle found itself on shaky grounds.

The Popular Front. The French national elections of 1936 went strongly against the French Right ... resulting in a political coalition of Socialists, Radicals, and (thanks to Stalin's directives) a small number of Communists – under the premiership of the Socialist leader, Léon Blum.

This was an extremely difficult time for Blum to be given the responsibility of leading the nation. Employment levels in France were so low that only about a half of the French workers were employed full time. Unemployment payments by the government had again nearly completely drained the French treasury of its gold reserves. And workers' strikes were breaking out all over the country. Blum responded with legislation mandating the 40-hour work week, paid vacations, and collective bargaining ... which greatly settled the mood of the French industrial workers. Likewise for the French farmer, prices were set by the government so as to guarantee the price of the industry's all-important wheat crop. And a number of industries (such as the armaments industry) were nationalized ... or at least brought under strict government regulation.

Unfortunately for the French economy, these measures only ignited a huge French price inflation of all these regulated goods. Wheat prices were higher ... therefore so was the price of bread for the average Frenchman. Shortening the industrial work week forced industrialists to have to raise prices in order to draw any profit for their operations, which made French products less competitive on the open international market. Consequently, this French "New Deal" failed to solve the problem of widespread unemployment, industrial bankruptcy and the devaluation of the franc. Worse, it crippled the French armaments industry ... at a time that Germany was rapidly rearming under Hitler's direction.

French foreign policy did not fare much better during this time ... for the country was deeply split over the debate as to which of the rising powers to the East constituted the greater danger to France: Hitler's Fascist Germany or Stalin's Communist Russia. And crisis events of the day – most notably Mussolini's invasion of Ethiopia and the Spanish Civil War – only deepened the discord in France. Indeed, the failure of Blum to support the leftist Republicans in the Spanish Civil War caused the defection of the Communists and the collapse of the government in 1937. From that point on, leadership changed hands from Blum to the Radical Édouard Daladier ... as the French tried one political formula then another to bring the country back to unity. But that just was not destined to happen.

Austria

With the coming of the economic crisis of the early 1930s, a rising group of Austrian Fascists pressed for union (*Anschluss*) with Hitler's Nazi Germany ... with both the Christian Socialists and the Social Democrats fervently opposed. Christian Social leader Engelbert Dollfuss headed a coalition government in 1932 – but with such a slim majority that it made his position very shaky. Voting irregularities in the following year caused the coalition to collapse. But Dollfuss convinced the Austrian President, Miklas, to let him rule without parliament – as virtual dictator – pointing out the threat of a German Nazi takeover of Austria as the alternative (the Nazis were gaining popularity rapidly in Austria at this time).

However in 1934, Dollfuss was assassinated in an attempted German Nazi takeover of Austria, the "July Putsch." His assassins were arrested and the coup was thus thwarted.

Dr. Kurt von Schuschnigg then took over the office of Chancellor, and in 1935 was able to disband the Heimwehr, a paramilitary group similar to the Nazis, in an effort to get Austria settled down. But Schuschnigg was ultimately unable to hold back the rising Nazi spirit demanding the

Anschluss with Hitler's Germany. In short, Austria was facing a crisis it could not seem to overcome.

Czechoslovakia

As with the rest of Europe, the Depression hit Czechoslovakia hard. Fairly friendly relations that once united the cultural subgroups making up the Republic began to turn sour. The Slovaks and the Hungarians of the Ruthenian district in fact became increasingly bitter about the Czech domination within the Republic. And the Germans in the Sudetenland began to take a louder interest in an escape from Czech domination and an embrace of unity with Hitler's Germany. Hitler would eventually play this complaint to great personal and national advantage.

＊ ＊ ＊

STALIN'S SOVIET RUSSIA

Stalin's rise to power

During the Russian Revolution, Stalin had been assigned the less glorious task of overseeing personnel issues (selection and advancement of party members) by the Communist Party hierarchy. But Stalin had been using his position to place and promote individuals presumably loyal to himself personally – thereby building up a personal power base within the Party, a development to which the Bolshevik intellectuals directing the Party at its highest levels had not been paying much attention.

At Lenin's death in 1924 the party leaders expected Trotsky to take over Lenin's role. Lenin had even earlier given indication that he clearly favored Trotsky over Stalin (whom he did not trust). But Stalin had his own plans at this point.

A sick Trotsky's failure to appear at Lenin's funeral became the signal for Stalin to begin his campaign. First Stalin had the party remove Trotsky from his command of the Red Army (1925). Trotsky's complete fall after that happened quickly. Stalin intimidated his fellow Bolsheviks into agreeing to the need to focus on "revolution in one country" (Russia), to focus solely on the rapid industrialization of Russia, and to oust Trotsky – whose internationalism (focusing on the spread the revolution to the industrial societies to the West) threatened the security of the revolution in Russia. Thus in 1927 Trotsky and his supporters were forced from the party ... and in 1928 Trotsky was forced into exile. Stalin now held total control over the Community Party and the Soviet State.

Stalin's forced industrialization of Russia

Then with the introduction of his first Five Year Plan (1928-1932), Stalin took complete control of the wealth, the productivity, the very life of Russia – and completely reoriented its culture to his industrial agenda.   The plan was devoted entirely to the creation and management of the huge state-owned collective farms and the state-run heavy industries.   Missing was any focus on consumer goods for the people themselves.   Thus Russia's private industries and extensive farmlands were nationalized – put under the direction of Stalin's bureaucrats ... and anyone resisting this move was arrested and sent off to a Siberian work camp for his "anti-revolutionary" activity.

The results of the plan were mixed.   Iron and steel production was increased greatly ... and coal, oil and electrical production came close to meeting Stalin's goals.   But other areas, such as in textile manufacture, fell far short of his goals.   And agricultural production was a total disaster ... producing mass starvation in an economy once based largely on agriculture.

This was because the farmers naturally resisted having their lands turned over to and run as new "collectives" by Soviet authorities – for instance, farmers slaughtering their animals rather than turning them over to their new Soviet authorities.   But in any case, the Russian farmer now ranked simply as another common laborer in Stalin's "workers' paradise."

But it was no paradise ... with farming families unable even to feed their own families from the production required of them on their former lands.   Their production was now intended to feed the growing industrial work force ... not the farmers themselves.   Tragically, any family that did not look as if it was starving obviously was guilty of holding back part of its production to feed itself (the crime of "hoarding") ... and its members were arrested and sent off to one of Stalin's Siberian work camps ... where they died – on their way there or soon thereafter.

Thus possibly 12 million farmers and their families died from starvation or industrial slavery in the early 1930s ... in order to make way for the country's transition from traditional agriculture to modern industry.

The Soviet "grand illusion"

Stalin was careful to allow the larger world a picture only of "Communist" Russia's rapid industrial development ... a picture of steel plants, hydroelectric dams, urban housing, etc. going up in amazing speed and extent – in stark contrast to the idle economies of the "capitalist" West.   But Stalin's Communism had nothing to do with Marx's Communism, instead being simply a form of state capitalism.   Stalin's state now owned everything ...

and the workers themselves had no say in how their "worker's paradise" took shape – or the benefits they themselves would draw from the new system. This was political, economic and social dictatorship, pure and simple.

Sadly, many Western social philosophers were taken in by the picture that Stalin carefully presented ... and found themselves advocating eagerly for a similar policy of Communism – or at least its close cousin Socialism – to be instituted in their own countries. Many, of course, would one day come to regret deeply their having been so deceived ... for having identified themselves so closely with Communism in their writings and political activity.

But even more tragic, young Westerners – hearing from their intellectual mentors and teachers in America and in Europe of the glories of Stalin's Communism – traveled to Russia to see firsthand the Soviet wonder ... and stumbled upon what they were not supposed to see: the huge suffering that much of the country was experiencing in order to make Stalin's dream possible. Few of these idealists ever made it back alive to the West, but simply disappeared into Siberia in one or another of Stalin's gulags (concentration camps) where they died miserable deaths.

Stalin pushes ahead

In Stalin's second five-year plan (1933-1937) he at first made provision for the manufacture of some personal consumer items ... but soon backed away from this in watching Hitler's rise to power in Germany – and instead turned Soviet production more heavily in the direction of military goods. He did back off a bit on the agricultural world, allowing some private property (homes and animals) and also personal consumption or sale of any production exceeding the set quotas. This all succeeded in getting production by 1937 up to its best prewar levels. Furthermore, in the industrial sector most of the various producers were able to meet the expanded quotas. Stalin's Soviet Empire was indeed gearing up as a major industrial power.

The Third Five Year Plan (1938-1942) basically continued the Second ... except that a shift towards even more military production occurred as the situation in Hitler's Germany grew darker from the Russian perspective. Furthermore, much of the new industrial development was purposely placed to the east of the moderately protective Ural Mountains ... a wise choice given what would happen in the summer of 1941 (when Germany suddenly invaded Russia).

Stalin's purges (1936-1938)

Less wise was Stalin's decision in the second half of the 1930s to cleanse the party, the state, and the military of personnel that Stalin and his body of inspectors considered to be less than fully trustworthy. Stalin had originally been given the task of disciplining the lower ranks of the party ... and this had given him the opportunity to build up his own personal power base. Consequently, he would never forget the importance of maintaining tight discipline over his organization ... not merely for the strengthening of the party but for his own power purposes. Needless to say, when he found himself in charge of virtually everything that went on in Soviet Russia, this urge to discipline turned to a case of personal paranoia – in the extreme. Quickly eliminated (no questions asked) was anyone suspected of even the slightest disloyalty by Stalin and his personal police.

During the "Great Purge" (*Yezhovshchina* or "Period of Yezhov")* such elimination extended most importantly to the very highest circles of the party. Of the original members of the 1917 Politburo, only Stalin remained in power ... and of other members added to the Politburo since 1917 only two (Molotov and Kalinin) were still alive in 1938 ... the rest having been shot or otherwise eliminated (including former "heroes of the Revolution" such as Zinoviev, Kamenev, Bukharin and Marshal Tukhachevski).

This frightful behavior then led even local party officials to turn against each other ... in order to prove their loyalty to Stalin. Consequently, the Yezhovshchina extended deeply down the Communist Party ranks. But also eliminated were Orthodox clergy, intellectuals, and writers – even musicians and artists – by the thousands. Also, farmers of a too-independent nature (the Kulaks) were eliminated ... in the hundreds of thousands. But so were non-Russian minorities living in the Soviet Union: perhaps a quarter of a million of non-Russian minorities such as the Poles and the Crimean Tatars suffered a similar fate simply for the crime of being non-Russian.

These purges extended deeply into the Russian military as well – incredibly poor timing given the obvious danger Hitler's rise to the West posed for Russia. But Stalin could not contain his paranoia ... and had the vast majority of Russia's top generals, nearly all of the field commanders, admirals and division commanders – as well as the party's military commissars – removed from power (although a third of them, somehow survivors of the purges, would be allowed to return to command after Germany's attack on Russia in 1941).

It was very dangerous to be around Stalin ... even to be successful at what you did, as it would set off suspicions in the mind of Stalin that you might willingly or even inadvertently provide a rallying point for those who wanted to see Stalin gone.

At this point no one dared to even think to oppose Stalin, even on the

---

*Named after Nikolai Yezhov, who headed up Stalin's secret police or NKVD ... who ironically was himself eliminated by Stalin in the summer of 1938 – when Stalin was ready to bring the purges to an end.

smallest point or issue. This would of course be a danger for Russia ... in that it was too dangerous to bring to Stalin any thoughts, opinions or even news that he would be sure to dislike.

✳ ✳ ✳

HITLER'S GERMANY

One of the most notable of the attempted post-war coups occurred in Bavaria: the unsuccessful Munich Beer-Hall Putsch of November 1923. Bavaria was a German state caught in deep turmoil from the hyperinflation, with street protests gathering force, and plans of three local politicians, Kahr, Seisser and Lossow (the "triumvirate"), to seize power and establish a dictatorship. But Hitler was on the scene with his own similar plans – aided by the German wartime commander Erich Ludendorff (to add prestige to Hitler's bold plan) – to take over the Bavarian government and from there march against Berlin. With some 600 paramilitary under his command, Hitler surrounded a large meeting in the main Munich beer hall led by the three politicians. He hoped to convince the three to join him ... which reluctantly they did. The next morning Hitler marched 2,000 of his men on the Munich city hall ... and there shooting broke out – with four state police and sixteen Nazis killed in the exchange of fire. Hitler and many of his men were also wounded. Word spread quickly of Hitler's activities. Students protested the action, the Catholic Church sided with the Bavarian government, and the triumvirate began to lose its nerve. Now Hitler's move lost its momentum ... and Hitler was soon arrested and charged with high treason.

The trial which followed (February-April 1924) was covered widely by the nation's newspapers, elevating Hitler to the status of a political celebrity (placing him in the same company with Ludendorff who was also on trial with Hitler). As it turned out, the judge who heard and decided Hitler's case was sympathetic with the basic goals of the putsch, particularly as Hitler presented him a well laid out explanation of Hitler's desire to see Germany restored to greatness. Thus the judge went light in his sentencing of Hitler: five years of easy imprisonment (comfortable quarters and regular visitors daily) in Landsberg Prison.

Hitler took advantage of this time to sit down with his close associate Rudolf Hess to write out his memoirs, *Mein Kampf* (My Struggle), which clearly outlined his political thinking and political goals for Germany ... a major piece in Hitler's later rise to power. Then, only nine months into his imprisonment, Hitler was released from prison for good behavior! Hitler was something now of a changed man: no mere neighborhood rabble rouser, but an ambitious politician who understood clearly the path to power he must follow. He would use his ideas, rather than violent insurrection in the streets, to bring others alongside him in his quest to raise Germany once again to the greatness he dreamed of. He was confident that destiny (even God) was with him.

Hitler's rise to power

The Weimar Government had brought a degree of prosperity and some element of legitimacy to the democratic social order of the new Germany. But it could never remove the memory of its origins as a system basically imposed on Germany by its former enemies. Also, the horrible years (1922-1923) of the mark's inflation, which had ruined the life savings of millions of middle-class Germans, was an early legacy of the Weimar Republic which was difficult for those Germans to forgive and forget. The ambitious Hitler (like Mussolini) knew how to tap into this discontent ... and his book *Mein Kampf*, though a collection of rambling thoughts, laid out a program and promise of greatness awaiting the German *Volk* (people). The book soon became a best-seller in Germany ... and was a key source of income for Hitler and his growing Nazi Party.

Hitler was a colorful orator, even spell-binding in the hyper-emotionalism he seemed always to be able to rise to ... as if he were somehow divinely anointed or inspired. He spoke before public audiences often, loudly denouncing the multi-faceted conspiracy of: 1) the international clique of politicians and financiers (full of inferior Jews) whose goal as laid out in the infamous Versailles Treaty was to keep Germany in a servile condition; 2) the communists (also full of inferior Jews) who wanted to create an empire reaching from the Slavic East (also full of inferior Slavs) to all of Europe; and 3) various social sub-groups who wanted to mix racially with the pure-Aryan German (especially the inferior Jews). He cast democracy as a system, though existing widely in Europe, vastly inferior to the natural instincts of the superior German Volk. Democracy had been imposed on Germany by the Treaty of Versailles ... designed purely to allow inferior people to hinder the German rise to greatness. And he laid out clearly in *Mein Kampf* the strategy he had in mind for German success: to bring Germany under a great leader (*Führer*) who would direct Germany in its achievement of *Lebensraum* (living space) for an expanding German Volk, directed primarily toward the wheat and oil fields of the southwestern regions of the Soviet Empire. But France would have to be defeated first in order then to give Germany a free hand in seizing this Lebensraum. Sadly, few people of high political office paid much attention to, or took seriously, these grandiose dreams. But Hitler did. And so did his growing group of followers.

Taking a page from Mussolini and his quasi-military Blackshirt Fascists, Hitler's Nazis wore brown quasi-military uniforms, marched in formation at frequent rallies as a corps of Storm Troopers (*Sturmabteilung* or SA), with banners flying, marching music blaring, torches and searchlights lighting up the night sky if it were a nighttime rally. Dr. Joseph Goebbels was the master planner for such an event (his talents would have made him a very successful Hollywood producer if he had chosen to go a less offensive path in life!).

Then there was also the growing body of the SS (*Schutzstaffel* or Protection Units), a black uniformed elite corps whose sole purpose was to serve the cause not of Germany but of their Führer, Hitler. Hitler was planning to build the German nation around his own personal will ... as he saw things, give strength of purpose and solid unity to the German Volk as he and the nation became one.

At first there were sneering German critics who saw this all as dangerous nonsense. But when the Great Depression finally hit Germany at the beginning of the 1930s the critical tone began to change. For instance, in the 1928 national elections in Germany, Hitler's Nazi Party (National-Socialist German Workers' Party) received only 2.6% of the vote. But in elections two years later (September 1930) that figure was up to 18%, making the Nazi Party the second largest (among many parties) in the Reichstag.

But while the Nazis took the democratic path of standing for national elections, they were also busy in the streets terrorizing their political opponents ... notably members of the Communist Party of Germany (the KPD) with whom they had a particular grudge. Deaths occurred on both sides in these street battles and beerhall brawls. Jews were also favorite targets of the SA thugs. Laws were passed to outlaw many of the activities of these paramilitaries ... though they largely were ignored. It was beginning to look as if the Germans were headed toward all-out civil war.

In the presidential elections of 1932, in a run-off vote for the German Presidency, Hitler received 36.8% of the vote ... against German military hero Hindenburg's 53%. Hitler was gaining power. Likewise, the Nazi Party position in the Reichstag expanded to 230 seats. Hitler was asked by Germany's Catholic Center Party leader and newly appointed Chancellor Franz von Papen to participate with him in a coalition government as Vice Chancellor. But Hitler declined, assuming that in waiting, his party strength would only continue to grow ... so that he could then take the reins of government solely on his own terms.

But in the November elections of the same year – called because of the failure to find the formula for a stable government – his Nazis registered a decline in the vote (33%), losing 35 seats but remaining still the largest party in the Reichstag. On the Left, the Communists received 17% of the vote and the Social Democrats 20%. There was talk of the two parties of the Left trying to form a coalition government. But Stalin had given the order to the German Communists to avoid such a coalition.

Von Papen was at a loss as to what he could do to resolve the political impasse. He finally proposed to President Paul von Hindenburg the not very bright idea of asking Hitler to take the Chancellorship and he, Papen, would serve as Vice Chancellor ... though nearly all the other positions on the Cabinet would be held by members of his Catholic Center Party. He was certain that he could control Hitler. Thus Hitler became German Chancellor at the end of January 1933. That was a huge mistake ... though not Papen's only mistake. He allowed a Nazi to take the position of Minister of the Interior, the cabinet post that commanded the nation's police.

But the situation was still not stable ... and Hindenburg called for new elections for March. Hitler's Nazis campaigned on the basis of a supposed conspiracy of the Communists to take over Germany, which the Nazis claimed that they alone were prepared fully to ward off. Then conveniently a fire broke out in the Reichstag prior to the elections, a Dutch Communist was arrested, and Hitler proclaimed this event as the start of the expected Communist takeover. Hitler then gained from Hindenburg the emergency power to suspend all civil liberties ... and proceeded to arrest thousands of German Communists. With the Communists thus removed, the elections which followed allowed the Nazis and a small coalition partner (the Nationalists) to form a government based on their combined majority of 52% of the seats in the Reichstag. Then with the arrest or intimidation of a number of Social Democrat members of the Reichstag (and with even support from members of the Center Party) Hitler could now proceed to the passage of the Enabling Act (requiring a two-thirds vote) giving him the right to rule Germany by decree. On March 27, 1933, the Reichstag officially put Hitler in power as German dictator.

Hitler had both the Communist and Social Democrat Parties outlawed. But the Catholic Center Party and the Nationalist Party also agreed to disband ... and in July the Nazi Party was declared to be the only party allowed to operate in Germany.

When Hindenburg died the next year in August (1934) Hitler simply did away with the office of President ... and assumed for himself the title of Leader (Führer) of Germany.

Hitler's New Order (*Neuordnung*)

Although Hitler himself was a coarse man, or at least a leader of a very coarse group of Nazi German toughs, his policies seemed to have validated themselves in the way they got Germany back up and moving in strength as a society – something that many intellectuals in Europe and America felt was becoming increasingly beyond the reach of their own country. Hitler was very Darwinian in his understanding that nothing should stand in the way of the strong taking control of history – to promote the rising greatness of the *Übermenschen* (superior people) ... who according to Hitler were the Aryan Volk.

The increasingly shrill anti-Jewish ranting of Hitler disturbed many thoughtful intellectuals, though there was always an undercurrent of anti-Jewish sentiment that ran through even some of this group at this time. Thus many felt inclined to look the other way when it came to what Hitler was doing to the Jews in Germany during the 1930s: he had removed them from all positions of importance in German society and treated them – even the highly educated, even the highly decorated for their service to Germany in the Great War – as the vilest of Untermenschen (inferior people) unworthy of any sentimental concern on the part of a true Aryan German.

The military's take on Hitler. A key part of German society that was very ambivalent about Hitler's leadership of Germany was the regular army, the *Reichswehr*. The Reichswehr had always been something of a state within the state and had its own ideas about how the state-military relationship was to work. In general, it stood strongly with Hitler in his desire to continue to ramp up the remilitarization of Germany ... started secretly several years earlier by General Kurt von Schleicher. But the Reichswehr despised intensely the paramilitary SA corps and was deeply suspicious of the political authority assumed by Hitler's SS troops.

Sensing the deep dislike of the Reichwehr's professional officer corps, and under the threat of a possible call of Hindenburg for martial law to eliminate the 3 million strong SA, Hitler made the decision to resolve the standoff by having the majority of his SA leadership, including his close associate Ernest Röhm, eliminated. On the "Night of the Long Knives" (June 30, 1934) Hitler had his SS troops and the German state police (the Gestapo) arrest thousands of SA troops (as well as a number of Hitler's anti-Nazi opponents – including even briefly his Vice Chancellor Papen) ... and even murder a number of others (including General and former Chancellor Schleicher and his family and many of Papen's supporters). Röhm was arrested, but was murdered in his cell the next night.

Hitler announced to the German people that by his actions he had stayed an attempt by Röhm and Schleicher to overthrow their government – another bold Hitler lie that the German people found convenient to believe. But the Reichswehr was made happy – or at least happier – by this purge of the SA. But Hitler would face problems from the Reichswehr in the years ahead, as it appeared increasingly that he was heading Germany toward war.

Ultimately the German judiciary failed to bring to trial those responsible for the murders ... establishing the principle that Hitler and his government were above the law. It also made clear to German society that no one, no matter how highly placed in the German government or society, was immune from arrest or execution if Hitler deemed it necessary. Hitler and his SS/Gestapo arm could now move through society at will, performing whatever deeds the Nazi regime saw as necessary. All Germans were now completely at the mercy of the Führer.

German Christians respond.   Tragically, a large number of German Christians greeted Hitler's rise to power as something akin to divine deliverance, a "miracle of God."   In April of 1933 they held a national convention in Berlin, seeking to unite the numerous Protestant denominations into a single national church, complete with a single national bishop. Their hope was to generate a particularly German spirituality based on an Aryan version of Christianity. In June of that year Ludwig Müller, a strong Nazi, became the head of this new federation of "German Christians" ... and with the creation of a new constitution for this Protestant Reich Church, became the national bishop voted to that position by a German national synod. From this point on the program (the "Aryan Paragraph") was undertaken to eliminate from German ministry all "undesirables" having Jewish or Slavic backgrounds – in order to purify the Aryan character of German Christianity ... and to give full recognition that Hitler was lord over the German church. To secure his position in the Church, Hitler in July of 1933 called for new church elections ... to replace those elected in the *Landeskirche* or National Church only the previous November. The results were that the German Christians won the vital Prussian Synod seats, plus most of the other synod seats.

In response, the young Dietrich Bonhoeffer, widely recognized because of his anti-Nazi writings and speeches, was given the commission by the opposing members of the Landeskirche to draft a new confession (the Bethel Confession) ... which however got watered down greatly by fellow pastors. Bonhoeffer thus refused to sign his own work ... but did inspire others to try again.

Then when that November some 20,000 German Christians demanded the removal of the Old Testament from the Bible because of its Jewish origins, Martin Niemöller founded a pastors' league ... the beginning of an effort to organize an anti-Nazi opposition within the church.

The following May (1934), a group of predominantly German pastors – led by Karl Barth, Martin Niemöller, and Hans Asmussen – declared themselves at a meeting in Barmen (thus the *Barmen Declaration*): to be under the lordship of Jesus Christ and him alone; the Word of God was their only authoritative guide; and their Church was independent of and not subordinate to the State* ... thus giving birth to the *Bekennende Kirche* (Confessing Church).

This group would soon find itself in serious trouble with the Nazi authorities and many would eventually be either arrested (some 700 in 1935) or forced to flee Germany.

Sadly, the impact of their effort though very noble was rather slight. Of the 45 million Protestants in Germany at that time, only some 150,000 would come to actually constitute this Confessing Church – that is, only one half of one percent of the total number of German Protestants ... although about one fifth of the pastors supposedly identified themselves as part of the Confessing Church.

However, the Catholic Church – with its broader or international character and leadership in Rome, not Berlin – was less drawn into the Aryan appeal ... and traditionally was suspicious of Germany's majority Protestantism anyway. German Catholics had long identified politically with the Center Party, one of the main political parties that had originally stood in opposition to the Nazi Party.

However, Pope Pius XI did agree to a *Reichskonkordat* in 1933 with Hitler's Germany ... in the hopes of softening the persecution just underway against German Catholic clergy and Catholic politicians by the Nazis. But ultimately Hitler paid no attention to the terms of the agreement. Catholics, priests and parishioners, were arrested on wild charges ... solely to shut down all voices in Germany except Hitler's.

Finally, in 1937, Pius repudiated the Reichskonkordat, issuing a new encyclical, *Mit brennender Sorge* (*With Burning Anxiety*) condemning the political-ideological trends that had developed in Germany under the "mad prophet" (obviously referencing Hitler ... though neither he nor his Nazi party were specified in the encyclical) ... a document secretly distributed (300,000 copies in German) to be read from Germany's Catholic pulpits on Easter Sunday.[†] Hitler was furious ... and had his Gestapo seize all copies they could get their hands on ... and increased dramatically the oppression of the Catholic Church. Catholic schools were shut down. Catholic youth organizations were ended. But amazingly, Catholics seemed to stand with the pope in this matter ... at least for the present.

---

*In Germany, as in most of Europe, the Church had always been considered to be a key part of the governing system of the country ... even financed in its operations by state funding - in Germany, via the ancient Kirchensteuer or church tax.

†But pope Pius also quickly answered Hitler's accusations that the pope was pro-Communist ... in issuing another encyclical, *Divini Redemptoris*, specifically denouncing Communism as anti-religious, citing the persecution of the Church that accompanied the establishment of Communism in Russia.

✳ ✳ ✳

THE SPANISH CIVIL WAR (1936-1939)

Social stress in Spain. Spain had stayed out of the Great War ... and seemingly benefitted greatly economically as a result. Demand for Spanish industrial production, especially in armaments, stimulated greatly the growth of Spanish industry. However, most of the economic benefits went to a rising capitalist class and not the industrial workers ... and for that matter not the Spanish farmers either, whose almost medieval farming methods allowed them to produce no more than what could barely feed their families. And the Spanish worker was keenly aware of this problem of an unfair distribution of the nation's wealth. Consequently, rumors about how the Communists in Russia had overthrown a Russian economic system very similar to their own and were making great progress toward improving life in Russia (hardly true at all) were the kind of rumors perfectly designed to draw thousands of Spanish to the call of Communism.

Certainly it was apparent to all that the Spanish social and political system was in great need of reform. But reform was unlikely given that although Spain was on paper a constitutional monarchy – complete with a legislature (the Cortes) elected by universal male suffrage, a royal ministry responsible to the Cortes, and a supposedly independent judiciary – in actuality Spain was run by a system of local bosses (*caciques*) with ties all the way up to the capital Madrid. These caciques had little interest in reforming Spanish politics. Additionally, the rising nationalist spirit infecting Europe had touched deeply the Basques and Catalans, who did not consider themselves to be Spanish, thus tearing further at Spanish unity ... which because of the economic problems afflicting the country was disappearing rapidly. Spain seemed simply to be falling apart.

Rivera's coup d'état (1923). An event in Morocco triggered the political explosion which was waiting to occur. In 1921 a Spanish army of about 20 thousand troops was crushed by Riff tribesmen, a humiliation of Spanish military dignity so immense that a major inquiry was opened as to the causes of such a defeat. What was revealed was poor discipline and widespread corruption afflicting the Spanish army. But before a formal decision could be made on the matter, General Primo de Rivera carried off a coup d'état in September of 1923 and placed himself at the head of a military junta which now commanded all Spanish politics. He brought order back to Spain, rid the country of the worst of the caciques, and finally defeated the Riffs. He took up a role similar to Mussolini's ... though without all the boast and fanfare. He pushed for new industries, instituted a system of improved industrial worker-owner relations, and in general strengthened the Spanish economy.

But his firm hand on Spanish politics (which he at first promised was only temporary) drew increasing resentment as the years went by. Radical voices began to call not only for the dismissal of General Rivera but also for the end of the monarchy and the establishment of a Republic.

The creation of the Spanish Republic (1931). After seven years of Rivera's dictatorship, both Rivera and King Alfonso XIII were tired of the arrangement. In 1931 the Spanish people went to the polls to determine their political future. A majority of their votes went to the various Republican (anti-monarchist) parties.   The King accepted the verdict and chose to go into exile. A Republic was created, secular-socialist in character – and the new government under President Alcalá Zamora proceeded to take education away from the Church, dismiss or put under tight control various Catholic monastic orders (notably the Jesuits), and loosened up the laws of marriage and divorce. It also seized large estates and distributed them to landless agricultural workers ... though never as quickly as these workers expected, stirring the radicalism caused by expectations which rose faster than reality permitted. Reforms were met by strikes and riotous protests (led principally by a growing Communist segment of society) demanding greater action.

Naturally all these changes took place to the great displeasure of those of Spanish society who remained fervently monarchist and Catholic. The most radical of this group were the Falangists, headed by Jose Antonio Primo de Rivera, the son of the former dictator. Like the Fascists of Italy, the Falangists were a uniformed paramilitary organization, with a reputation as "toughs." Elections in late 1933 demonstrated the strength of this conservative sector of Spanish society when they won a large majority in the Cortes. On the basis of this electoral success a conservative government was formed with the goal of undoing the previous reforms ... only agitating the Communist-Socialist Left all the more.

Then in the elections of 1936 a reversal in the Left-Right balance of power brought in a "Popular Front" government made up of parties of the Left – including the Communists (who, under the direction of Stalin, were cooperating with the other leftist and centrist secular parties across Europe.) Immediately political conditions in Spain deteriorated – with on-going street battles running between the Falangists and the equally tough Republican police, the Asaltos. Terror and assassinations became increasingly the order of the day for Spanish politics.

The Spanish Civil War (1936-1939)

Franco intervenes (1936). When, in July of 1936, the Asaltos murdered a prominent Fascist politician, all hell broke loose. Soldiers in Morocco loyal to the monarchy, "Nationalists" as they called themselves, revolted against the Republican government in Madrid. This was the signal in Spain itself for the Catholic monarchists in the military to rise up in revolt against the Republican government – in accordance with a plan carefully worked out beforehand by a young general, Francisco Franco Bahamonde.

When Seville fell to the Nationalist troops, 200,000 workers (heavily Communist) were stirred to counter-action in Madrid by the passionate Dolores Irarruri ("la Pasionaria"). This was a call to arms of those loyal to the Leftist Republic.

Europe gets involved. Seeing a fellow Popular Front Government in Spain under threat by Rightist forces, Leon Blum's Leftist Popular Front government in France quickly sent 30 French planes and pilots to help the Republican government crush the rebels. But in turn, Franco called upon the Nazis of Germany and the Fascists of Italy to come to the aid of the Nationalists' cause.   By the end of July, German and Italian planes were arriving in Morocco to assist Franco in his revolt against the Republican government of Spain. Thus the Spanish civil war became from the very outset an international issue.

The Spanish Civil War became an international issue not just because foreign countries wanted to help out one side or the other in the struggle – but because the war in Spain gave a number of countries (Germany, Italy and Russia) the opportunity to develop and test larger political, military and diplomatic strategies of their own. The Spanish Civil War was becoming a dry run for a larger war which seemed to be once again headed Europe's way. Thus the Spanish suffered even greater anguish because of the military games played by these outside powers.

In November of 1936, Franco's Nationalists attempted to seize Madrid – but were held off by a Republican defense of the city at the Casa de Campo park and at the University. Then Franco attempted to cow the city into submission by bombing it (except the wealthy – and supposedly pro-Nationalist – parts of the city). But this only stiffened the resolve of the Republican forces to hold Madrid at all costs.

Battle of Guadalajara (March 1937). Mussolini's Italians and Franco's Nationalists combined forces to attack Madrid from Guadalajara. Vastly outnumbering the Republican forces, the Italians and Nationalists were at first successful in taking one small town after another. But bad weather – and the arrival of the International Brigade (with Russian volunteers involved) stiffened the Republican defense (though they were still outnumbered 2 to

1). The Republican air force was also operating from concrete runways – whereas their opponents were grounded with an airstrip of mud. Gradually the Republicans began to push the Italians and Nationalists into full retreat. The Italians lost some 6,000 men in the action – and Mussolini lost a huge amount of prestige, for he had personally organized the Italian effort in order to gain the prestige of what he originally thought was going to be a grand victory.

The bombing of Guernica (April 1937). The bombing of Guernica was an aerial attack by the German Luftwaffe squadron known as the Condor Legion against the Basque city of Guernica (Basque: Gernika). Guernica itself was of no particular strategic importance in the civil war itself, lying well outside the center of the struggle. But it did give the Germans and the Italians the opportunity to try out their new military weapons and assault techniques. Hundreds of civilians died in the bombardment ... much to the shock of the Europeans who still believed that wars should be fought only by armed troops. That view would now be greatly revised.

The battle of Teruel. The battle of Teruel was fought in and around the city of Teruel in December 1937-February 1938. It was one of the bloodiest actions of the war. The city changed hands several times, first falling to the Republicans and eventually being re-taken by the Nationalists. In the course of the fighting, Teruel was subjected to heavy artillery and aerial bombardment. The two sides suffered up to 100,000 casualties between them in the three-month battle.

Franco's victory (March 1939). Bit by bit the Nationalists began to gain ground against the Republicans. Catalonia was finally taken by Franco at the beginning of 1939 and Franco's forces then turned again to Madrid. But officers in the Republican army rose up in March against the Republican prime minister and created a junta to negotiate a peace with Franco. Communists now turned on their own Republican officers ... making it easier for Franco to move on Madrid, which was now in a state of political confusion. By the end of the month all of Spain was under Franco's absolutist control.

Countless thousands of Republicans were imprisoned, some 32 thousand executed, and half a million fled the country ... mostly to France where they were immediately put in internment camps (the shaky French Republic was in no condition to be able to absorb such a massive demographic invasion). There they were held even as World War Two broke out that fall ... and with France's surrender to Hitler in June of 1940 were turned over to the Germans, who carted them by the thousands off to the Mauthausen concentration camp ... where 5 thousand died.

CHAPTER SIXTEEN

WORLD WAR – ROUND TWO

✳ ✳ ✳

THE STEPS TOWARD ANOTHER WORLD WAR

Actually, the clouds of another terrible war had been gathering even before the Spanish civil war broke out. On a number of fronts, because of events developing there, it appeared increasingly that there was no way the West was going to be able to escape another horrifying conflict.

Mussolini and Ethiopia. All the way back in the mid-1930s, Mussolini found himself ruling over an Italian society growing critical of his overextended political regime. Given his strongman mindset, he concluded that a foreign war of conquest would provide the impetus to restore support for his government. And Ethiopia seemed just the place to wage such a war. Ethiopia had escaped the clutches of European imperialism – and its backwardness and lack of military preparedness made it an attractive target for Mussolini. Besides, he counted on the fact that France and Britain were more concerned about having Italy as an ally against a rising Hitlerian Germany and thus would be no problem if he simply made a grab at Ethiopia.

The Ethiopian Emperor Haile Selassie, seeing a huge buildup (some 300,000 troops assembling in neighboring Italian Somaliland) took his concerns to the League of Nations in mid-1935. But all he got was talk – and little else – in support of his darkening situation. Then that October, the Italians invaded Ethiopia.

In response, the League responded timidly. They could have ordered the Suez Canal closed, or placed strategic industrial goods (coal, steel and oil) on an embargo list. But Mussolini was right in his expectations of a weak diplomatic response. The Europeans did not want to alienate Mussolini – and the Americans did not want to lose any oil business (America was a major oil exporter at the time). And what minor items the League did place under embargo did little – except to rally a large number of Italians more closely behind the Duce Mussolini!

Also, an exposé revealing a secret agreement among British Foreign Secretary Samuel Hoare, French Foreign Minister Pierre Laval, and Mussolini – offering Italy most of Ethiopia – got leaked to the press ... embarrassing the British and French governments ... and giving the League the appearance of being fairly useless. Ultimately this was simply the signal for Mussolini to drop Italy's membership in the League.

Within seven months the Italians had worn the Ethiopians down. On May 5, 1936 the Italians entered the capital, Addis Ababa – and Italy declared itself victor.

Problems developing in India

The Muslim community in India had not joined Gandhi's salt march ... and in various parts of India Hindus attacked Muslims in anger. Gandhi had also made a move to bridge the caste system by eulogizing the Untouchables as Harijan (children of God) ... only to have the political leader of the Untouchable community B.R. Ambedkar accuse Gandhi of paternalism in making the Untouchables appear as children unable to care for themselves.

Then Gandhi resigned from the Indian National Congress, turning leadership over to Jawaharlal Nehru, who was more open to the admission of Indian intellectuals (including socialists and communists) into the party ranks.

Soon a clash arose with Subhas Bose, elected Congress's president in 1938, a strong militant who disagreed strongly with Gandhi's non-violent strategy. When Bose was reelected in 1939, many of Congress's leaders resigned in protest over his militancy ... this then causing Bose to resign. At this point Bose was becoming a strong supporter of Japanese and German fascism.

Growing war clouds in Asia

The Manchurian incident (1931). With the onset of the Depression and the obvious weakness of the Western democracies in dealing with the crisis, Japanese militarists grew bolder in their politics. They wanted action, they wanted honor, they wanted dominion. And they were going to go after it ... no matter what the policy was of the official government. In this they seemed to have the silent support of the Emperor. Thus without any warning, in 1931 they simply used an incident (probably set up by the Japanese themselves) along a rail line in Manchuria as an excuse to turn their role from their League-awarded "mandate" supervision over Manchuria – to full Japanese control ... in setting up a puppet state of Manchukuo. Thus China took its concern over this to the League – which favored China in the matter. But seeing nothing useful – nor in fear of any real consequences – Japan too simply dropped its membership in the League.

Cabinet government instability. On their own home front, the Japanese found politics becoming ever-bitter between the pro-Western group and the Japanese militarists. There was a rapid turnover of civilian leadership – including assassinations by the militarists. Then when young militarists involved in these plots got arrested, this brought the Japanese army into more complete control of the "civilian" governments that followed ... in order to "stabilize" matters.

China's Nationalist-Communist Civil War. And the fact that Chinese President Chiang was preoccupied with the Communists – and their effort to follow up Dr. Sun's government with their own form of workers' Socialism – made for a greatly weakened China. Finally (the beginning of the 1930s) Chiang was able to chase most of the Communists from the industrial cities of Eastern/Coastal China. But at this point, the young Mao Tse-tung (Zedong) stepped forward to take what was left of the Communist Party membership – plus a lot of peasant-farmers wanting to join him - and marched (his "Long March" of 1934-1935) the whole group off into the Chinese interior ... to begin the rebuilding of the Chinese Communist Party from a more protected position. Then too, Chiang's associates helped Mao immensely when they kidnapped Chiang – and would not release him until he agreed to stop chasing Communists and turn his attention to the growing Japanese threat to the north.

Japan invades China ... starting up World War II in Asia (1937). Using an incident at the Lugou Bridge separating China from Japan-held Manchuria, Japanese soldiers suddenly (July 1937) struck deep into China, beginning an 8-year war that would devastate both societies. The Japanese were ruthless, destroying everything (including bayonetting and beheading civilians along the way) their path as they made their way towards China's major commercial center, Shanghai. This city they also bombed and burned out ... as they then made their way towards Chiang's capital city, Nanjing. There they conducted the "Rape of Nanjing" – as many as 300,000 civilians being executed over a six-week period at the end of 1937.

Then they barely escaped a strong Chinese encirclement of their troops at Tai'erzhuang (March-April 1938) – forcing the Japanese to deny what had actually happened ... and causing a Japanese cabinet crisis. But it also inspired a new Chinese fighting spirit. Nonetheless, the Japanese were able to advance to Xuzhuo in May and then Wuhan in October. But then things stalled for the Japanese ... pretty much for the next seven years.

Russia and Japan become neutrals diplomatically. An attempt in May-August of 1939 of the Japanese to then attack Russia from Manchuria ... proved to be humiliating for the Japanese. Thus seeing no further gain to be made in that direction, the Japanese signed a neutrality pact with Russia in April of 1941. This would allow both countries to focus their attention on other mounting issues – Russia focusing on developments to the West and Japan to the South and East. Consequently, America and Europe's war with Japan (December 1941-September 1945) would be of no particular interest to Stalin ... until the very last days of that war.

Europe begins to realize that it has its own problems

France stumbles. Although most Europeans had made every effort to demilitarize after the Great War – hoping this would eliminate the temptation to ever go to war again – the French understood that Germany still remained as a huge threat ... especially since Germany's population (75 million) nearly doubled that of France's (41.4 million) – and the French birthrate was dropping rapidly. Thus to protect itself, France undertook the massive construction of the "Maginot Line" of very sophisticated defensive military installations along its eastern border with Germany.

At the same time, France depended very heavily on diplomatic support from a defense alliance with Belgium, Czechoslovakia, Romania and Yugoslavia ... a very weak grouping which served merely to strengthen Hitler's accusation of a conspiracy to surround and isolate Germany (which indeed it was designed to do). And France undertook to renew its former close relations with Russia – concluding commercial and defense treaties with Stalin.

But when Hitler moved in 1936 to seize the demilitarized Rhineland – under French supervision at the time – and France did nothing to block him, it became clear to all (Russia as well as Germany) that France really did not seem to have the will to resist Hitler. And instead, merely appealing to the League of Nations for help made it clear that France did not have the sovereign will to stand directly against German aggression.

Britain's "appeasement" of Hitler's Germany. Conservative Party leader Stanley Baldwin dominated English politics during much of the post-war period.* And understanding that the English were determined to never again go through a war such as they had just experienced, Baldwin took the

---

*Baldwin was Prime Minister 1924-1929. Then in 1931 he joined a cabinet coalition led by Labor leader Ramsay MacDonald ... tending even then to dominate British politics. Finally in 1935, Baldwin took over from the largely senile MacDonald – until his own retirement in 1937.

political position of "peace at any cost." Thus even as Germany was rapidly rebuilding its military (in total violation of the Versailles Treaty) Baldwin cut back deeply England's military spending and strength.

He and Winston Churchill were constantly at odds in Parliament (though both members of the Conservative Party) over this issue of England's pacifism in the face of German remilitarization. Baldwin viewed Churchill as a war-monger who wanted to drag England into an arms race and thus another war with Germany. Churchill viewed Baldwin as one who invited German military adventurism by the obvious lack of English resolve to stop Hitler before he became so strong that there would be no way to block his military ambitions. But nothing moved Baldwin from his anti-war position.

In 1937 Baldwin stepped down and Neville Chamberlain took his place. Now however, whereas Baldwin had been a pacifist, Chamberlain was actually rather pro-German – as had long been much of the royal family. Chamberlain viewed Communism as a greater threat to Europe than Fascism – and actually hoped that a strong working relationship with Hitler would serve everyone well in preventing the spread of Stalin's Communist realm. Churchill, who had previously taken a strong stand against Stalin's Communism, infuriated Chamberlain by now making it loud and clear that Hitler was by far the greater danger to the West. Thus Churchill remained sidelined politically by a resentful Chamberlain.

Hitler expands the Nazi Reich

The *Anschluss* with Austria (March 1938). Hitler had been laying the groundwork for a highly desired Germanic union (the *Anschluss*: closing or connection) with his native Austria ... a move expressly forbidden by the Versailles Treaty. He forced the Austrian Chancellor Kurt von Schuschnigg to take on pro-Nazi Arthur Seyss-Inquart as Austria's Minister of the Interior (state police) ... and release all Nazis previously arrested for their illegal activities. In response to this, neither the League nor Chamberlain did anything – leading British Foreign Minister Anthony Eden to resign.

Then when Schuschnigg decided to put the matter of an Anschluss with Germany in the hands of the Austrians themselves and hold a referendum on the matter, Hitler knew it was time to move ... two days prior to the elections forcing Schuschnigg to have Seyss-Inquart replace him in power – and then have Seyss-Inquart invite German troops into Austria "to restore order" (they were actually already into Austria when the order was given!). Austria was now an integral part of the German Reich.

Hitler then had that postponed referendum held ... which produced a most amazing 99.7% approval rating of the Anschluss by the Austrian voters.

The Munich Agreement (September 1938).   The new country of Czechoslovakia had a huge German population inhabiting its mountainous Sudetenland bordering Germany and Poland. It was here in the Sudetenland that the Czechs had constructed massive defense installations ... the Czechs fearing both their German and Polish neighbors. With Hitler now complaining loudly about how the Sudetenland Germans were being cruelly mistreated by the Czechs (a complete lie), Chamberlain was concerned that Hitler was simply creating the pretext for a takeover of the region. In that he was quite correct.

So he flew to Munich to attend a meeting of numerous heads of state – without any Czech representation however – to try to work out a "peaceful" settlement to the growing Czech "crisis." And there, most amazingly, Chamberlain signed an agreement letting Hitler take over the Sudetenland under Hitler's promise that this was all that he wanted of Czechoslovakia ... and under Chamberlain's promise that he would lean on the Czech president Beneš to peacefully deliver the Sudetenland to Germany.

On Chamberlain's return to London, he was wildly celebrated for having "saved" the world from war ... or as he put it, having secured "peace in our time." The Norwegian Nobel Committee was even so swept up in this strange mood that Chamberlain was then nominated to be the coming recipient of the Nobel Peace Prize.

The sad irony in all of this was that by agreeing to Hitler's demands for the German absorption into Hitler's Reich of the Czech Sudetenland, Chamberlain inadvertently undermined a plan for a coup against Hitler by a number of German generals who were positive that Hitler was going to lead Germany into a suicidal war. Tragically, the cost-free granting to Germany of Sudetenland by Chamberlain made Hitler all the more a hero to the average German. Had the generals moved as planned against Hitler at this point in his apparent "success" it would have made their actions appear totally treasonous in the eyes of the German nation. So their plot was put aside.

Thus Chamberlain foolishly not only undercut what would have probably been a stiff and embarrassing Czech resistance to Hitler's ambitions (the Czechs were ready to resist Hitler with some forty well-armed divisions – which Chamberlain forced the Czech to promise not to use – so as to avoid "war") but he also undercut what would have been an heroic move by true German patriots to remove this madman from power. How ironic Chamberlain's desire for peace – peace at all costs – would end up having just the opposite effect on Europe ... ironic, but unfortunately all too common a development in human history.

***Kristallnacht* (the night of broken glass).**   On November 7, 1938,

Herschel Grynszpan, a young Polish Jew in Paris, shot and killed the German 3rd secretary in the embassy there, providing the Nazi government the excuse to retaliate 2 days later against Jews everywhere in a night of well-organized Nazi terror known as *Kristallnacht* - for all the glass windows of Jewish stores destroyed. Synagogues were systematically burned, 7,500 shops were wrecked, perhaps as many as a hundred Jews were killed, thirty thousand were arrested and headed off to imprisonment in such places as the Buchenwald and Sachsenhausen concentration camps. On top of this, fines totaling a billion marks were levied on the Jews ... as if the Jews themselves had been responsible for all the damage. To add to the cruelty, all the insurance money paid to the Jews for the damage of Kristallnacht (five million marks) was confiscated by the government. Hitler's Germany was definitely taking the shape he had long dreamed it should be.

March 1939 – Hitler grabs all of the Czech lands. Hitler had no intention of honoring the Munich Agreement – and using the Slovakian desire for political independence from their Czech partners as his excuse, Hitler moved German (plus some Hungarian and Polish troops) into Czechoslovakia ... and placed the country under his authority as a German "protectorate."

Chamberlain then responded "boldly" by promising Poland (the most obvious next recipient of a German expansion) that the Poles would receive full aid from Britain if Hitler were to try to make a move on their country. Considering the fact that Britain would have no way of moving troops or even supplies past Germany to reach Poland, Chamberlain's promise not only was another empty one that he was prone to issue ... it came across to many simply as that of a very weak leader trying to present himself as a political strongman.

The Molotov-Ribbentrop Pact – August 23, 1939. Meanwhile, in April Churchill had come out in support of securing a strong working relationship with Russia – something that Soviet Foreign Minister Maxim Litvinov had also been trying to secure. But Chamberlain would have none of this, and did what he could to head off the idea.

In Russia, Stalin was trying to come up with his own solution to the growing German problem to the West ... and in early May dismissed Litvinov (after 9 years of service) to bring on Vyacheslav Molotov – who was a strong advocate of working out some kind of a deal with Hitler. Finally in August, Stalin was ready to undertake just such a deal ... and in Moscow signed an agreement drawn up between Molotov and German Foreign Minister Joachim von Ribbentrop – an agreement announced to the world as a "non-aggression pact."

But what the world did not know was that as part of this pact Hitler and Stalin had secretly agreed on respective spheres of German and Russian control in Eastern Europe, and in particular had agreed to divide up a conquered Poland between them, Germany taking the western half of the country and Russia taking the eastern half.

Stalin had entered this agreement with the understanding that a divided Poland would create a huge land buffer protecting Russia from further German expansion ... plus expecting (correctly) that, with German aggressions to the East well satisfied in the confiscation of much of Poland, Hitler would now take his aggressive instincts westward against France and Britain – to settle old scores with these former enemies. Stalin presumed (incorrectly) that some kind of stalemate would again develop on the Western front – one that would keep Hitler very busy for a very long time. But Stalin was yet to learn of German *Blitzkrieg* (Lightning War).

✳ ✳ ✳

BLITZKRIEG (1939-1940)

The War in Poland

The Germans invade Poland.   A week later, on September 1st, Hitler's troops invaded Poland without any formal warning - and began to blast Poland into bloody submission. England and France declared war against Germany on September 3rd for this action against Poland. But within two weeks Polish resistance to the German invaders was limited to several small pockets.

The Russians make their moves. There was a little over a two-week delay (until September 17) in the movement of the Soviet Red Army into Poland. The Poles did not know about the secret provisions of the Molotov-Ribbentrop Treaty by which Hitler and Stalin had decided to divide up Poland between them. When the Russians did finally cross into Poland, the Poles thought the Russians were coming to aid them against the Germans. Too late the Poles realized that the Russians were invaders as well.

The Germans and Russians finally closed forces against the Poles at Brest-Litovsk. By the 28th of September, the last Polish pocket of resistance was crushed. On the 29th Poland was formally partitioned between Germany and Russia.

Soviet Russia was just as guilty for its part in starting the war. And its treatment of the Poles would be no less cruel.* But the English and French

---

*Indeed, the Soviet Red Army massacred some 22,000 Polish officers, civil officials, intellectuals, etc. in taking over eastern Poland ... an act that the

would not declare war on Russia as they had on Germany for this invasion of Poland.

But Stalin was not finished. The following month (October), he pressed his neighbors, Estonia, Latvia, and Lithuania to sign three "Mutual Assistance Pacts" - which then legitimized the Russian Red Army's entry into those countries and their absorption into the Soviet Empire. He then turned on the Finns, demanding grants of land along the Soviet-Finnish border. When they refused, he attacked Finland, bombing Helsinki and sending troops into Finland. But winter, plus stiff Finnish resistance, proved ruinous to the Russians (losing a quarter of a million troops to Finland's loss of 25,000). But the next spring Stalin resumed the attacks … and this time the losses were heavier on the Finnish side. The Finns thus surrendered large strips of land to the Russians – and fell under Soviet domination. Then when the League tried to come to the aid of the Finns, Stalin simply pulled Russia out of the organization.

The "Sitzkrieg" or "Phony War" in the European West

Meanwhile, the powers of Western Europe, though at "war" technically did nothing at the time – missing an opportunity to hit Hitler hard from behind while he was occupied in the East. But in part that was because Hitler's victory in Poland was so swift that there really was not time to take action. And with Germany sitting so victorious at this point, there was little appetite for military action in the West – except in the case of Churchill, appointed First Lord of the Admiralty and thus in charge of the British navy. When a German U-boat was able to sink a battleship at the naval harbor of Scapa Flow, Churchill retaliated by having his navy take the offensive, trapping a German battleship off the coast of Uruguay (causing it to scuttle itself rather than be captured).

Otherwise the action was so minimal that the Germans mockingly called this war a Sitzkrieg ("Sitting War" – playing on the wording of Blitzkrieg!). The British termed it simply the "Phony War" … though they were beginning to realize that there was nothing phony about Churchill!

The End of the Sitzkrieg / Phony War

The Battle of Denmark and Norway (April 1940). Finally, Hitler made his move on the West … on April 9th, overrunning an unprepared Denmark in only two hours of action … on his way to Norway where plans were to grab

---

Russians tried to pin on the Germans when mass graves were discovered in 1943 in the Katyn Forest. It would not be in fact until 1990 that the Russians finally confessed that the massacre in the Katyn Forest (and other similar sites) had been specifically ordered by Stalin and Molotov.

that country as well – in order to reach via the ice-free port of Narvik the rich iron ore fields of "neutral" Sweden (the Baltic Sea separating Germany and Sweden was not ice free year round). But much to Hitler's surprise, the Norwegians put up a very stiff resistance. Ultimately, however, the Germans were able to drive many of the Norwegians into the mountainous interior … while others were able to escape to Britain (as did the royal family). Then Hitler turned a nominal Norwegian government over to the pro-Nazi Vidkun Quisling. Nonetheless, though Norway was now theoretically part of the Nazi Empire, the Norwegian resistance never let up for the duration of the war.

The Battle of the Netherlands and Belgium (May). Then a month later (May 9th), German troops invaded Belgium, the Netherlands, and Luxembourg, sweeping westward well to the north of the well-entrenched French Maginot Line. German parachute troops were dropped ahead of motorized German infantry, seizing airfields, strategic crossroads and bridges … as the Dutch countered by flooding their fields and trying to blow up bridges. But the Germans moved so quickly that mostly such efforts by the Dutch of self-defense availed little. Three days later, the Dutch Queen and cabinet ministers escaped to England and the next day Rotterdam was completely laid waste by the Germans as a demonstration to the Dutch of what resistance to the German occupiers would gain them. Thus the Dutch surrendered.

The Belgians experienced the same Blitzkrieg strategy of the Germans … though they held out for over two weeks against the Germans. Then on May 28th, Belgian King Leopold III surrendered himself to the Germans … and the Belgian resistance collapsed.

Churchill takes command in Britain (May). The British were stunned by these huge German successes. In England Chamberlain sensed growing opposition to his leadership and was rejected by Parliament in his effort to create a broad national-front cabinet. At this point Parliament wanted Churchill to lead the nation … and the King did indeed ask him to take over on the 10th of May. Three days later, in a speech before Parliament, the new Prime Minister told the country that he could offer no quick road to victory but only "blood, toil, tears and sweat." But his aim was complete victory … "for without victory there is no survival." The British were ready to stand strong with Churchill now leading them.

The Fall of France (June 1940)

Tragically, the French supposed that the Germans would repeat the invasion pattern of World War One and head across central Belgium in order to invade northern France. They moved troops up into the Netherlands (joined there by British troops), presuming to use those troops to swing behind the Germans as they made their way across Belgium. But Hitler had anticipated this move – and instead sent his motorized forces through the thick Ardennes Forest … undefended because it was believed that no troops could seriously make their way through such dense and rocky forest. Yet the Germans were able to move tanks and trucks very quickly through the Ardennes … and in two days (May 10th to the 12th) reached the Meuse River just outside of a largely defenseless Paris. In doing so, they bypassed the Maginot Line, – in fact came in behind it so as to cut it off from the rest of the French forces.

Dunkirk. And then – instead of completing his assault on Paris – Hitler headed his troops West towards the English Channel … in an attempt to destroy a combined British and French army trapped there. Oddly enough, Hitler then stopped his troops in their advance on this British-French force (was he hoping simply to get both parties, seeing the hopelessness of their positions, to capitulate?) … giving Churchill the opportunity at the port of Dunkirk to rally every possible ship, boat, or any floating device, to get his and France's trapped army (some half-million troops) to safety in Britain.

Vichy France. Then when the Germans finally turned towards a defenseless Paris (mid-June), the French troops posted there pulled out of Paris, not wanting to see it destroyed in a pointless battle. The French continued to fight on in the East behind the Maginot Line, but one by one French army units were forced to surrender, most of them by June 25th. For France, the war was over.

With the French cabinet now in flight south, Prime Minister Paul Reynaud resigned … allowing World War One hero Marshal Philippe Pétain to take over. Hitler then agreed to accept surrender terms from Pétain, signed at the very same railroad car where the Germans had signed the Armistice forced on them back in 1918. For Hitler this was major payback. For the French, a major humiliation.

France was then divided into two zones, the northern zone (where Paris and most of France's industry was located) under direct German occupation and administration, and the southern zone under a new French government based at the town of Vichy – and headed by Pétain. Additionally, some two million French soldiers were – as hostages – turned into forced labor prisoners in German occupied Europe … and France was required to send gold, food, and military supplies to Germany on a regular basis.

Although the Germany-Vichy France relationship was built solely on the basis of an armistice (thus theoretically still at war!), gradually and most tragically, Pétain's Vichy government came to align itself more closely with Hitler's regime, taking on a stronger fascist tone ... even becoming virulently anti-Jewish.

The French *Résistance*.   But numbers of French were most unwilling to bow to German dominance, and attempted to do what they could to undermine the German occupation. At first there was no real organization of the effort, inspiring Churchill to set up a section of British intelligence to help coordinate these groups. Then General De Gaulle, who had refused to recognize any form of French surrender and was now operating from London, was given the task of speaking to the French via the BBC's Radio Londres – giving some degree of direction to the résistance ... and in essence becoming something of its leader ... even the very symbol of a "Free France."   De Gaulle then began to organize a Free French Army and a French government-in-exile in London (Reynaud had been arrested by the Germans and was not a participant in the London government).

The "Battle of Britain" begins

Only the offshore island of Great Britain remained unconquered in the West. At first Hitler had expected a British request for an armistice ... and planned to be "generous" in the negotiations. But when, in his famous "finest hour" speech before Parliament on June 18th, Churchill made it again clear that – even with the fall of France – he refused to consider any notion except total victory in this war ... Hitler became determined to bring Britain as well to humiliating defeat. Operation Sea Lion was thus birthed in Hitler's mind.

Not understanding how very difficult a Channel crossing might be ... Hitler presumed to prepare the way for such a move by aerial bombardment of British airfields, docks, ships and industries. But the British RAF (Royal Air Force) fought back skillfully, as did the anti-aircraft gunners defending Britain from the ground. Consequently, the Luftwaffe's losses were huge. Furthermore, downed German pilots became prisoners in Britain ... but British pilots could parachute out of a downed plane and return to action with a new plane. In any case, the British showed no signs of yielding ... not even when on August 15th, Hitler sent a force of a thousand planes to attack Britain, losing 180 planes in the process. Indeed, in a week's time, the Germans lost 492 planes to the RAF's loss of 115 planes. Things clearly were not working out well for Hitler and his Operation Sea Lion.

Then the British retaliated by sending bombers to Berlin on August 25th ... materially not a matter of great significance, but spiritually a devastating blow to Hitler's Germany. This was the first time that the

Germans had felt the effects of war on their own ground since the days of Napoleon. Hitler was furious. On September 7th, Hitler shifted his attack from English airfields to London itself – more horrible in destruction – but a strategic distraction ... foolishly sparing British Fighter Command at a time that the British were actually having difficulty replacing lost fighter planes.

The Tripartite or "Axis" Pact - September 27, 1940

When on September 27, 1940, Germany, Italy and Japan signed a new "Tripartite Pact" ... the military alliance forming an "Axis" between Berlin and Rome now expanded to include Tokyo. While it was designed to support Japan's grab of the imperial holdings of the Western powers in Asia, it also served Hitler to weaken even further the Western powers he was holding under his grip. But it also meant that any war that Japan ultimately got involved in would bring the "Axis Powers" Germany and Italy into that same war as a Japanese ally.

American "neutrality"

American neutrality was a bit of a fiction – maintained by both sides of the European contest. Sensing the growing danger of war, America increased its defense budget from $2 billion to $10 billion in 1940 and established its first peacetime military draft. Likewise its economy was highly dependent on industrial sales abroad ... most of that destined to Britain – France now knocked out economically and Germany being as industrially self-reliant as possible. Hitler responded by pushing his U-boats to cut off the shipping going on between America and Britain – at least that portion conducted by British carriers – whose boats the Germans were sinking faster than the British could replace them.

Yet using its own carriers, America was able to increase its trade with Britain enormously – such as the millions of rounds of "surplus" ammunition it sent to Britain. Then there was the matter that same September of America turning over to the British some 50 of its "mothballed" navy destroyers ... in exchange for land rights offered by the British, ones allowing America to build numerous airbases within Britain's Empire.

Then also, Roosevelt announced in December that America was to be the "Arsenal for Democracy" and would thus be selling war materiel quite openly (to Britain obviously) in protection of the world's democracies against the recent rise in authoritarianism globally. This was hardly the policy of a "neutral" nation.

But Roosevelt had to proceed very cautiously, for there were numerous citizens (and congressmen) very isolationist in attitude ... committed fully to keeping America out of another European war ... no matter who the victor might be. But this group was losing out to a growing attitude within America that Western civilization itself was in great danger of being destroyed by Europe's (and Asia's) rising Fascism ... and that it was America's responsibility to see that this should never happen.

"Lend-Lease." The next year, 1941, Roosevelt was even able to get Congress (the majority Democrats at least, for most Republicans remained quite isolationist) to pass his "Lend-Lease" legislation. This authorized the president to sell, transfer title, exchange, lend, or lease to any government anything that he deemed strategically necessary to the defense of America. This therefore put America in full partnership with Britain. But it would soon also include China and Russia as well.

Finally, America went all out in repealing in October the last of the Neutrality Acts, ones that had been passed every year since the mid-1930s. And American merchant ships were now authorized to be fully armed ... and also to actually transport the war materials that had been going to Britain formerly only by British ships. Clearly, America's "neutrality" was pure fiction. But Hitler, a very busy man at the time (deeply caught up in his new war with Russia) chose still to ignore this American change in status.

The Atlantic Charter - August 1941. Another piece in the American move away from neutrality to active participation in the huge conflict going on in Europe and elsewhere was an agreement (soon termed the "Atlantic Charter") negotiated by Churchill and Roosevelt at a secret meeting in mid-August aboard a British warship anchored offshore from Newfoundland.*

This agreement outlined a vision for a post-World-War-II world, despite the fact that America had not yet entered the war.

In brief, the eight points of the agreement or declaration were:

1. no territorial gains sought by the United States or the United
      Kingdom;
2. territorial adjustments must be in accord with wishes of the people;
3. the right to self-determination of peoples;
4. trade barriers lowered;
5. global economic cooperation and advancement of social welfare;
6. freedom from want and fear;

---

*Official statements and government documents imply that Churchill and FDR signed the Atlantic Charter. Actually, no signed copies are known to exist. A British writer, H V Morton, who traveled with Churchill's party on the *Prince of Wales*, states that no signed version ever existed. The document was thrashed out through several drafts, says Morton, and the agreed text was telegraphed to London and Washington. The British War Cabinet replied with its approval and a similar acceptance was telegraphed from Washington.

7. freedom of the seas;

8. disarmament of aggressor nations, postwar common disarmament.

At a subsequent Inter-Allied Meeting in London on September 24, 1941, the governments of Belgium, Czechoslovakia, Greece, Luxembourg, the Netherlands, Norway, Poland, Soviet Union, and Yugoslavia, and representatives of General Charles de Gaulle, leader of the Free French, unanimously adopted the Charter. This agreement proved to be one of the first steps towards the formation of the United Nations ... including the use of the "United Nations" as the name of the grand alliance of those countries which joined together to fight the Axis Powers.

✳ ✳ ✳

1941: RUSSIA AND AMERICA ARE BROUGHT INTO THE WAR

Hitler attacks Russia (Operation Barbarossa)

Hitler's decision to head East. By September of 1940, with the British Royal Air Force still in the air and able to fight off German air cover needed for any invading ground forces, Hitler came to the conclusion that he would have to "postpone" the planned invasion of England. With this humiliation of not being able to deliver on a promised conquest of England, Hitler felt the pressure to strike elsewhere in testimony of Aryan greatness. By December of 1940 he was making plans (Operation Barbarossa) to make good on a long-standing promise to convert the Slavic lands to the East (principally Ukraine) into a "breadbasket" for Germany – and *Lebensraum* ("room for living") for an expanding Aryan German society and culture. Germans could also use the inferior people (*Untermenschen*) of the Slavic lands as a source of slave labor to strengthen Germany's industrial capabilities. And seized oil fields of Azerbaijan would also aid in this strengthening of Germany. Also, Hitler was certain that in seeing Russia defeated, England would finally lose heart and accept any kind of peace deal with Germany it could get.

Some of Hitler's generals prepared a study that demonstrated that the venture would cost more than it would gain. But Hitler, by this time positive that he had special (almost mystical) skills to see possibilities where other mortals – including importantly his generals – were blind, ignored their arguments. Plans were set for invasion of the East in mid-May of the next year (1941). Through the winter of 1940-1941 the Germans began amassing huge amounts of troops along the German-Russian occupation line in Poland.

The Yugoslav diversion. But Hitler did not get the operation underway as quickly as planned, because the movement of his troops on their way East was postponed when a Yugoslav political coup overthrew the Yugoslav King, who had been cooperating with Hitler. Consequently, Hitler in April turned his troops South toward the heartland of Yugoslavia in order to bring Yugoslavia back under "cooperation" with him and his operation.

But the delay would prove costly, because it would begin his operation much later into the season. It thus also pushed operations, in what he was expecting to be a quick victory over Stalin's Soviet army, into a deadly winter ... in fact, one that would cripple the momentum of the operation. Ultimately this delay proved to be disastrous for Hitler.

Stalin's response. But Stalin also seemed slow to respond. Actually, he had vastly more tanks and planes at hand than did the Germans, although because of his purges of the Red Army in 1937-1939, his officers were young and inexperienced. But still, Stalin was not really ready to face the possibility that war with Germany was at hand. Churchill warned Stalin that through his military intelligence he had every reason to believe that Hitler was indeed about to attack Russia. Stalin would not hear of it, claiming that Churchill was simply trying to start something between the Russians and Germans just to get the Germans off the English backs.

But indeed, on June 22nd, 1941 Hitler sent his troops rolling into Russian-controlled Poland. Their momentum soon had the Germans on Soviet soil itself. Part of Hitler's army raced toward the northeast, trying to seize Leningrad (St. Petersburg).

Hitler's arrogant stupidity in Ukraine.   Another section of his army made a lunge toward the southeast, through Ukraine. Amazingly, the Ukrainians came out to greet their "liberators" with flowers and cheers (the Ukrainians hated Stalin and his Russian Communists); equally amazing (not really!) Hitler was furious when he heard that his soldiers were fraternizing with the Ukrainians, and ordered them instead to start rounding up the Untermenschen for slave labor service. This bit of arrogance was a key factor in crippling Hitler's plan to overrun the Soviet Union – at least in the south.

Russian defenses. Rather than surrender, the Russians employed the same strategy that had worked so successfully when Napoleon and his French army invaded Russia back in 1812. The Russians fell back, burning their own lands to keep crops and herds from being of use to the invaders. Back they went, and then further back. German supply lines became overstretched – and lacking. Russian partisan groups began hit-and-run sniping and skirmishing with Germans patrols. Even the Ukrainians began to join the Partisans attacking vulnerable positions in the German lines. The Germans retaliated with incredible acts of cruel revenge enacted on the conquered civilians. The hatred between the two sides became intense.

Then the cold weather of Russia began to set in. Blitzkrieg soon lost its momentum. Hitler's troops were now entangled in a draining war in the East. With ammunition, fuel, food and warm clothing in very short supply, and the diesel engines in Hitler's tanks and trucks frozen up, the Germans found themselves unable to continue their advance. The offensive would have to wait until the spring thaw of 1942 before it could be resumed. But by that time Blitzkrieg would have lost its momentum and the Russians would be preparing a strong counter-offensive against the German invaders.

America enters the war

Growing tensions with Japan. Americans watched in horror as the Japanese took advantage of the new French Vichy government by requiring the French to give Japanese troops access to their colonial holdings in Southeast Asia (Vietnam, Cambodia and Laos) ... so that the Japanese could build military bases there from which they could then conduct attacks of China from the South. The Americans were very sympathetic to the Chinese ... and reacted by imposing an embargo on the sale to Japan of strategic goods: oil, scrap iron, minerals as well as military products such as aircraft parts – all vital to a resource-poor Japan. Now Japan had an "American problem" to deal with.

The Japanese could not at first come up with a counter move against this embargo that their military leadership could agree on. But there ultimately seemed to be no alternative but to hit America with such a military blow that it would force America to sue for peace ... and return things to where they were previously. They would also move on the Dutch possessions in Indonesia, where strategic oil was in abundance. But they would have to take out British holdings lying on the path to Indonesia ... plus the American position in the Philippines. This in turn would require them to take out the American naval fleet anchored in Hawaii ... leaving the Americans completely unable to respond to this bold Japanese move.

Not everyone was certain that this would work, notably the commanding Admiral Isoroku Yamamoto – who, having studied for two years at Harvard, felt he knew the Americans fairly well and had the fear that if this action failed to bring down American power it would instead merely awaken a sleeping lion. But ultimately he went along with the idea ... especially as it had the emperor Hirohito's full support.

"A date which will live in infamy." Thus it was that without any warning of a coming act of war (considered the "civilized" thing to do)* Japanese aircraft – in the early hours of Sunday, December 7th, 1941 – attacked the American naval-air station at Hawaii, sinking all of the battleships and destroying all the military aircraft based there.

But instead of bringing America to its knees in surrender it indeed awakened a great sleeping lion. On the following day, President Roosevelt went before Congress to request a declaration of war against the Japanese with the opening statement:

> *Yesterday, December 7, 1941 – a date which will live in infamy – the United States was suddenly and deliberately attacked by naval and air forces of the Empire of Japan.*

He made the American position and his own intentions quite clear:

> *I believe that I interpret the will of the Congress and of the people when I assert that we will not only defend ourselves to the uttermost but will make it very certain that this form of treachery shall never again endanger us.*
>
> *Hostilities exist. There is no blinking at the fact that our people, our territory and our interests are in grave danger.*
>
> *With confidence in our armed forces, with the unbounded determination of our people, we will gain the inevitable triumph so help us God.*

The Senate's vote on the matter was unanimous ... though the House of Representatives had one dissenting vote – the ever-pacifist/feminist Jeanette Rankin! As for the country itself, the rush of young men to sign up for the military gave clear indication that the American lion was fully awake.

Hitler declares war on America. In part due to the terms of the Axis's Tripartite Pact and in part due to Hitler's puffed up sense of personal military genius, three days later Hitler stood before the German Reichstag to call for war against America. Thus by Hitler's rather than America's choice in the matter, the war between America and Japan now extended also to Germany (and also Mussolini's Italy).

✳ ✳ ✳

THE WAR IN ASIA AND THE PACIFIC

---

*Actually, Japanese envoys were in Washington DC preparing a statement declaring war between the two countries ... though they had not finished their work until well after the attacks were completed.

The European and American retreat in Asia

Actually, the attack on Pearl Harbor took place at exactly the same time that the Japanese were making their moves in East Asia. Thus on that same day, the Japanese struck Thailand, Malaya, Singapore and Hong Kong. The greatly outnumbered British troops defending Hong Kong were brought to defeat by Christmas Day ... with many of the surrendering troops being massacred on the spot and others (eleven thousand) placed in prison camps ... where many would die of Japanese abuse. This then became the typical pattern as the Japanese advanced against the greatly defenseless Europeans.

The Japanese then made their way south through French Indo-China (permitted to do so by the Vichy French government) and took on a defenseless Singapore – its defenses being aimed at the sea and at not the land behind the Singapore citadel. By mid-February (1942) Singapore fell to the Japanese – with the same horrible consequences for the defeated British and Indian troops (some 130,000 of them).*

Next on the Japanese list were the islands of the Dutch East Indies (today's Indonesia) ... where the Japanese conducted multiple landings of small parties, making it impossible for the Dutch to organize an effective defense against the Japanese. Finally on the 1st of March, the Dutch surrendered.

The colony would remain in Japanese hands for the duration of the war as the action undertaken by the Allies to defeat Japan largely bypassed the region. For the Dutch, to whom the islands of Java and Sumatra had been for 300 years a vital part of their national economy (and even partly their culture), this would present major problems after the war because the Japanese, towards the end of the war when Japan was clearly in trouble, strongly encouraged anti-Dutch nationalism among the local non-Dutch population.

Meanwhile, the American "protectorate" of the Philippines came under the same Japanese assault ... though it would take considerably more time and effort to secure the Philippines for the Japanese Empire. The Filipinos were militarily capable (having given America considerable resistance only some two decades earlier) and fought with all their might against the Japanese war machine.

But the Japanese were persistent in their effort, and eventually the Filipinos and the 12,000 American troops stationed there found food and

---

*However, many (about 30,000) of the imprisoned Indian troops would come under the influence of Indian nationalist Subhas Bose and be released to join the Indian National Army ... and about 7,000 of those would actually join the Japanese in fighting against the British in the Burma Campaign and in northern India.

weapons resupply impossible because of the Japanese control of the Pacific at that point. Thus in early May the last holdout at the Corregidor fortress of both the Filipinos and Americans was forced to surrender.

What would follow was characteristic of the Japanese, who held in full contempt anyone who would not fight until death ... for in Japanese thinking, this was the only exit from a bad situation. Thus American and Filipino prisoners were force-marched 60 miles in heat without food or water to their prison in Bataan, with thousands dying along the way.[*]

But again, instead of breaking the will of the Americans, folks back home, when they heard of the Japanese atrocities, deepened their rage against the Japanese ... though at the moment there was little they could do.[†]

The Americans take to the counteroffensive

The Doolittle Raid (April 1942). Meanwhile, the Americans conducted an air raid on Japan (Tokyo and five other Japanese cities) by 16 B-25 bombers ... more a symbolic hit than a serious military strike. Their bombing was not terribly devastating – but achieved its psychological objective.

Because they had been forced to take off from the aircraft carrier *Hornet* well before their scheduled departure (fearing a Japanese fishing boat they encountered might warn Japan of the pending threat), these bombers ran out of fuel ... and crash-landed well before their planned landing sites. Finding themselves now in Japanese-controlled parts of China, local Chinese were quick to help the Americans get to safe territory ... but paid a huge price for this assistance – when the Japanese took revenge on the Chinese villagers who helped the Americans. As many as 250,000 Chinese paid with their lives for that assistance. All airfields in the region were also destroyed in order to prevent another such raid on Japan (none was planned ... as the raid was subsequently considered almost suicidal).

Doolittle initially thought that his raid was a total failure and expected to be court-martialed and stripped of command. But the raid was such a

---

[*]Figures vary widely, from 2,500 to 10,000, because many of the Filipinos were able to escape along the way, affecting the count. Also, the original number of prisoners is not known with any precision, varying from 60,000 to 80,000 in the best estimates.

[†]Tragically, some of that anti-Japanese wrath got directed toward the large number of Japanese-Americans living in America ... most of whom were loyal American citizens. But they would be taken from their homes and shops nonetheless and placed in internment camps during the course of the war. However, some young Japanese-Americans would still serve most honorably in the American military. But overall, this horrible treatment of its own Japanese citizens would be a most dark mark on America's moral profile ... not one easily wiped away even with time.

boost to American morale that instead, he received the Medal of Honor, a larger air command … and lasting fame!

Though Japan suffered relatively little material damage from the bombing, the humiliation was so great (how could the Japanese defense force have let this happen?) that it pushed the Japanese military to make the decision to perform a counter-strike against the Americans at Midway Island in June … which turned out to be an even bigger disaster for the Japanese military!

The Battle of the Coral Sea (May 4-8, 1942). Meanwhile, the Japanese were surprised to find four American aircraft carriers and other battleships awaiting them at their intended target of Port Moresby … not realizing that the Americans had cracked their military code and were aware of the general nature of this plan. Consequently in the ensuing battle, the Japanese lost one of their aircraft carriers … although the Americans had two of their own aircraft carriers badly damaged and would have to drop out of the action. But the Japanese had run low on planes and thus decided to break off the fight.

Actually, the Japanese came away from this action believing that it had scored a huge victory, losing only one carrier – whereas the Americans lost or had disabled two of their four carriers. This led them to thinking that another such engagement would finish off the American navy.

The Battle of Midway (June 4-7, 1942).   Again, not realizing that the Americans had intercepted messages sent to the Japanese fleet, the Japanese were stunned to find Americans waiting for them as they advanced on the very strategic island of Midway … hoping to use that island's airfield as a Japanese base to continue their attacks on the American presence in the Pacific. Over the next few days American pilots shot down over 300 Japanese airplanes and sank a Japanese battleship and three of Japan's five aircraft carriers.

True, America had lost the *Yorktown*, which sank from its damage on its return to base in Hawaii. But America was on its way to such levels of production that it would be able not only to replace but to increase vastly the number of battleships and carriers (and planes) that it would bring to action in this war. On the other hand, as for the Japanese, this was a huge loss. They would never again be able to assemble such a naval fleet in order to expand, much less be able to defend, their empire.

But the Japanese instead announced to their own unknowing citizenry that a great victory had been achieved over the Americans at Midway. But making such a lie believable would become increasingly difficult as the war dragged on in the Pacific.

Guadalcanal (up from the South). Although Midway had been a huge event in stopping Japan's expansion, the actual turning point in the war in the Pacific would not occur until the Allies' success in the battle of Guadalcanal (August 1942 to February 1943). Guadalcanal was a huge island located among the Solomon Islands to the north of the Coral Sea and East of New Guinea. This long-running battle finally resulted in an Allied victory which was very costly to the Japanese – and which indeed was the turning point in the war against Japan.

And although the Japanese were clearly in retreat after Guadalcanal, they fought fiercely for every inch of ground they gave up. The Japanese soldiers clearly demonstrated at Guadalcanal that whenever they would find themselves facing the likelihood of defeat, they would conduct a suicidal *banzai* charge against American machine guns rather than submit to the grand humiliation of surrender. Their military code of *bushido* demanded nothing less.

Tragically, not only did the loss of their fellow soldiers in this horrible war hit the Allied troops hard emotionally ... seeing the Japanese willing to be butchered by Allied hands, rather than surrender to those same hands, unnerved the Allied soldiers greatly. It all seemed so pointless, so evil.

Burma and India

At the very beginning of its offensive in December of 1941, Japan and its ally Thailand had attacked British Burma (today's Myanmar) and by April of 1942 had forced the British out of its colony there. The Chinese meanwhile were largely holding the line in the South against Japanese expansion in China.

Then from their position in Burma, in March of 1944 the Japanese attempted a new offensive against the Allies by attacking the British position in Assam (northeast India) which the Allies had been using as a base to fly supplies across the mountainous "hump" into China. To counter the Japanese, India itself provided over three million troops to the Allied cause, some of the most dedicated soldiers in the Allied cause.

Gandhi. Most amazing was the behavior of Mohandas Gandhi who, in 1942 – when the British were barely surviving in England under German bombardment and when the Japanese had the British on the run in Asia – decided that it was a perfect time to once again press for an end to British governance in India. In August of 1942, he announced the start of a "Quit India Movement" designed to drive the hard-pressed British from India through a campaign of civil disobedience, something that would make India ungovernable for the British ... and another easy Asian target for the

Japanese.

Sadly, Gandhi seemed to have no interest in looking at how the Japanese actually treated the Chinese – or any other non-Japanese people they had overrun. It was important to Gandhi only to get Britain to "Quit India" … no matter what the social costs. Tragically, a politically blinded Gandhi had no ability – or desire – to carefully study exactly the costs versus the benefits of his campaign (typical of all Idealists).

The campaign, however, proved to be a huge failure when the Indians themselves showed little interest in crippling British authority in the midst of the war, a war in which many Indians themselves were serving in the British Imperial army.

Ultimately, the British arrested and imprisoned Gandhi – which did inspire an Indian reaction finally – keeping him locked up until he was released for health reasons in 1944.

Bose's Indian National Army (INA) supports the Japanese. While all of this was developing, an Indian National Army (INA) was assembled under the leadership of pro-Fascist Subhas Chandra Bose, who (like Gandhi) had dedicated himself to getting the British out of India. The INA even went so far as to ally itself with the Japanese in fighting the British (and even fellow Indian troops) in neighboring Burma, even planning to cooperate with the Japanese in invading India itself! Given the Japanese treatment of non-Japanese, this was truly a highly risky – actually highly foolish – program of the Indian Nationalists.

Nonetheless by June of 1944, the offensive proved to be a colossal failure for the Japanese … and the INA. This effectively ended the Japanese ambitions in the region – and killed the momentum of the INA.

India divides. But by this time India was beginning to divide into a number of conflicting political, regional and religious parties: pro-British princely states with many Indian officers in the Imperial Army, pro-Soviet Communists, and millions of Muslims wanting to break from Gandhi's Hindu India … and Punjabi Sikhs – not sure of what would happen to them with Indian independence.

Obviously, Gandhi had given no thought as to the obvious social conflict that would descend on India with the British departure. But he would soon have the opportunity to witness the mass bloodshed that accompanied his political success … and ultimately experience his own political reward (assassination).

✳ ✳ ✳

THE WAR IN NORTH AFRICA AND ITALY

Both Roosevelt and Churchill agreed that though their countries had a vital interest in defeating the Japanese in Asia, their priority would be to concentrate on defeating Hitler in Europe. With Germans at the gates of Moscow and Leningrad (St. Petersburg) during the winter of 1941-1942, the Russian situation looked desperate. Stalin immediately began pushing the Americans and British to open up a front in the West so as to take some of the German pressure off the Russians. He was also growing suspicious that his new Western Allies were holding off confronting Hitler directly in the hope that while they dallied, both Germany and Russia would exhaust themselves in mutual conflict – a suspicion Stalin held deeply because it was exactly the strategy he had employed (in reverse) with the Molotov-Ribbentrop treaty!

The catastrophic Dieppe Raid (August 19, 1942). A move was thus made to send 6,000 Allied troops (mostly Canadian) across the Channel from England to the shores of France at Dieppe ... a move that turned into a disaster. It lacked the vital element of surprise, the German Luftwaffe was able to attack the landing party rather more easily than the British RAF could defends those same troops ... and thus the raid was called off the same morning it was launched. Tragically, 3,623 of the troops that got ashore were either killed, wounded or captured. Another 1000 didn't even get ashore but were still waiting in the landing craft when the Allies pulled back from Dieppe.

The failure of the Dieppe Raid would henceforth make the Allies very much more cautious about any such future venture, one which, to the great distress of Stalin, would have to wait another two years before it would be attempted again.

The North African Campaign (1942-1943). Attention was instead turned to the matter of Germany and its ally Italy's effort to move on Egypt – to cut off Britain's vital support coming from India, Australia, and New Zealand through the Suez Canal. Heading up the Axis effort was the German "Desert Fox" Erwin Rommel ... opposed by the equally determined British General Bernard Montgomery. A huge battle resulted (October 23, 1942) at Alamein ... in which the British broke through the Axis center. And by November 4th they had encircled huge numbers of German and Italian troops – and had others falling back rapidly across northern Libya to avoid total annihilation. At the Libyan port of Tobruk alone, nineteen thousand Italians and six thousand German troops were taken prisoner.

Meanwhile at that same time (November 8th), British and American troops landed in French North Africa , hoping to find the French accommodating to this Allied intrusion. The French Vichy government, under the thumb of Hitler, however turned out to be not at all accommodating – and "Operation Torch" met with serious Vichy French resistance in French Morocco and French Algeria.

An Allied effort to bring on French support through the takeover of the French navy by a more willing Admiral François Darlan, brought on such German fury that the Germans seized control of Vichy France. This in turn led another French Admiral to order the French fleet to be scuttled (77 ships sunk) in order to keep them out of German hands.

The Allies thus crossed Algeria and pushed on to Tunisia … where Rommel's forces joined other Germans trying to block the Allied advance. The Germans and Italians knew that they had to take a strong stand here – or lose their position along the entire southern Mediterranean. At first the Allies were forced back in the West (the still largely inexperienced Americans took a heavy beating at the Kasserine Pass) – but then on May 6th the Americans and British regrouped at Bizerte and Tunis and, having already cut off the German and Italian escape route by sea, soon had them completely surrounded. On the 13th, the Germans and Italians surrendered … and as a result the Allies found themselves in possession of a quarter of a million German and Italian prisoners.

The Allied advance in Italy.   Then the British and American troops pursued the retreating Germans and Italians across to the Island of Sicily … and within two weeks had taken control of the island (mid-August) … with Montgomery and American General George Patton seeming to be more interested in beating each other to the glory of victory than in merely defeating the enemy! In any case, the Germans were able to get most of their troops out of Sicily and over to Italy … though the Italians had most of their troops captured before completing what they could of the evacuation.

Mussolini overthrown. The Fascist Grand Council in Rome had seen the writing on the wall with the beginning of the Allied assault on Sicily and on July 24th (1943) voted Mussolini out of power. He was arrested the next day and then moved around as a prisoner from place to place to avoid being set free by either the Germans or pro-Mussolini Italians.

Then on September 3rd, just as the first of the British troops were landing in Southern Italy, the Italians indicated that they desired an armistice with the Allies. This created massive confusion among the Axis powers, forcing German troops to have to focus on disarming their former Italian allies at the same time the Americans and British were preparing their Italian campaign. Then on September 8th a full Italian armistice was announced ... taking the Italians out of the contest.

But the Germans learned of Mussolini's location (a ski resort high in the northern Apennine Mountains). They sent special-forces (mid-September) to the site and were able to retrieve him and bring him back to his friend Hitler – who himself was suffering from another assassination attempt that had nearly succeeded. Mussolini was then declared by the Germans to be the head of the Italian Social Republic ... a puppet state comprising the northern part of Italy still in German hands.

But in actuality, the Germans were now forced to fight in Italy on their own against the advancing Allied armies.

Very slow going. Meanwhile, Americans landed their troops on the Western coast of southern Italy ... just as the British began to move their troops up Italy's Eastern coast. But Italy was very mountainous and therefore much easier for the Germans to defend against the advancing Allies. Indeed, German General Albert Kesselring established not one line of defense across the peninsula but several, one behind the other. Consequently, progress for the Allies against the Germans in Italy over the next year and a half turned out to be slow, painfully slow.

In fact, the Allied advance was so slow that by the beginning of 1944, they had reached only as far north as the area where the ancient abbey of Monte Cassino was located, perched atop another of Italy's mountains. Tragically, they reduced this beautiful site to ashes, presuming Germans to be well situated there – although actually the Germans decided to take advantage of this precious position only after the Allies had destroyed the abbey. And in the end, all this did little to move the battle line further north.

Anzio. Thus it was that the Americans decided to do a coastal swing behind the German defenses by sending troops ashore further north at Anzio in mid-January of 1944. But once ashore, they foolishly delayed the push deeper into the surrounding countryside because the American commander insisted on securing more troops and supplies before pushing inland. This gave the Germans ample time to move troops into a strong defensive position around the Allied coastal position at Anzio ... thus creating another Gallipoli-like scenario. Tragically for the Allies, it would not be until four months later (May) – and a huge number of dead and wounded – that the Allied forces would be able to break out of their position at Anzio.

Rome. Then, rather than heading east across the Italian peninsula – to position themselves behind the Germans ... thereby encircling and capturing a huge German army, the decision was made to head the American troops north towards Rome instead. The capital was captured fairly easily (just two days before the massive landing of Allied troops on the Normandy beaches of France). This "liberation of Rome" was a great emotional success, but another military blunder … because it allowed the Germans to slip north out of the potential trap and reposition themselves in another well dug-in line north of Rome.

Indeed, the Germans were able to defend northern Italy unrelentingly until the war was finally ended with the German surrender to the Allies the following year (May 1945).

✳ ✳ ✳

THE WAR ON THE EASTERN FRONT

Stalingrad

In June of 1942, Hitler was ready to resume his offensive in Russia. But rather than making a final (and relatively short push) into either Moscow or Leningrad in the center and north, he focused his efforts on expanding the German position in the south. He wanted to reach the grain fields of the Kuban along the eastern coast of the Black Sea and the oil fields of the Caucasus further east along the Caspian Sea coast.

At first his armies (which included also huge numbers of Romanians as well as Italians and Hungarians) were very successful in overwhelming everything the Russians could throw against them … including utterly destroying the city of Sevastopol. Then at the end of July the Germans divided their army, Group A continuing south under General Kleist toward the old fields of Baku and Army Group B under General Friedrich Paulus heading east toward the city of Stalingrad (today's Volgograd) located strategically on the Volga River.

The latter, Stalingrad, was extremely strategic … to Stalin (besides the fact that it bore his name and thus reputation!) – because the Volga River offered Russia its last strong position of defense against an aggressive German army. And Hitler needed to cross that river in order to reach the oil fields and grain fields of southern Russia to supply his Reich in energy and food. Thus each side poured hundreds of thousands of men into the battle against the other. At first it looked as if things would soon favor the Germans ... who in October pushed the fighting even into the city of Stalingrad itself.

But winter set in with full force leaving unprepared Germans freezing … and reinforced only by a greatly exposed and poorly defended line of supply behind them. And they were exhausted. Indeed, at this point, Russian troops saw their advantage, and moved quickly to cut off that line of supply ... and leave the German troops at Stalingrad surrounded.

Worse ... Hitler, blinded with pride, refused to allow his army to retreat from Stalingrad but ordered them instead to wait for reinforcements – which never came because the Russians were able to hold them off. By February (1943) Paulus's army was hungry, sick and dying – bringing Paulus (to the fury of Hitler) to surrender to the Russians what was left of his army.

Stalingrad had been a monstrous event. Of the original nearly one million German, Romanian, Italian and Hungarians soldiers, only about 90,000 were still alive to be able to surrender (only about 5,000 of those would ever make it back to Germany ten years later, the vast majority dying within a few months of their capture). But the Russians had also lost big, with nearly a half a million soldiers killed and 650,000 wounded or sick – and countless numbers of Russian civilians also killed. But the Russians could absorb those losses. Germany could not.

The Soviet counter-offensive gets underway

Kursk. By the summer of 1943 the Germans were ready to try again – this time at the center of the Russian lines, aimed at Moscow. But the Russians did not give way and the Germans succeeded only in exhausting themselves. Now it was the turn of the Russians to go on the offensive. At Kursk the largest tank battle of record occurred: with each side deploying 3,000 tanks each! Though the loss of tanks by both sides was huge, the Russians held their position. And then Hitler strangely called off further action ... switching his focus to the Allied assault on the Island of Sicily.

The Dnieper River. But this pullback at Kursk was viewed by the Russians as a great victory and by the Germans as a strange loss, thus having a strong moralizing/demoralizing effect on both armies. The Germans then retreated to the long Dnieper River in September to try to achieve there what the Russians had achieved at Stalingrad. And for the next four months some nearly four million troops on both sides went at each other ... half that number on both sides ending up as casualties. But the Germans at this point were less able than the Russians to absorb such losses. However at this point, another Russian winter set in ... and the line held.

Into Poland

But with the coming of the next summer (1944), the high-spirited Russians were again ready to take to the offensive ... and a greatly dis-spirited German army quickly found itself in retreat. Indeed, by the end of August – when the Russians had rolled all the way up to the Vistula River in central

Poland – the Germans had lost approximately everything they had gained since June of 1941 when they had undertaken the invasion of Soviet-held territory in Poland and ultimately the Soviet Union itself. The Germans were in retreat everywhere in the East.

The destruction of Warsaw. Seeing the Russians approaching their capital, the Poles rose up in rebellion against their German occupiers (August 1944) … hoping to have put in place a Polish authority prior to the arrival of the Russians. But Stalin had other plans for Poland. He had his own obedient Polish government ready to put in place … and therefore cleverly halted the Russian progress against the Germans in order to give the brutal Germans ample time to put down the Polish uprising.

And it worked. The Germans killed some 150,000 to 200,000 Poles, sent off some 100,000 to labor camps, and some 60,000 sent to death camps. And Warsaw itself was nearly completely destroyed … by careful design of the Germans themselves – who torched the buildings that bombs had not destroyed. Then, in September, when the Germans had achieved Stalin's goals (destroying any ability of the Poles to resist his authoritarian grip over their county), he ordered his army to resume their advance.

Into the Balkans

Romania. At the same time (August 1944) Stalin headed some of his troops South against the German ally Romania … aided by a Romanian uprising against the pro-Nazi government – but in support of a return of the Romanian king. But the real victors were the Romanian Communists who, under Stalin and the Red Army's sponsorship, took charge of Romania step by step (the king was forced to abdicate three years later).

Bulgaria. A similar move in Bulgaria occurred in September when an uprising there was quickly brought under the control of a pro-Soviet administration backed up by Stalin's Red Army. The Bulgarian Army then even joined the Russians in their next move … against Yugoslavia.

Yugoslavia. Multi-ethnic Yugoslavia was a special case politically … having initially resisted fiercely their Italian, German, Hungarian and Bulgarian invaders. But over time, the Serbian Chetniks began to work with the Italian Fascists … and then with Germany after Italy's retreat from the war. This then brought other Yugoslavians to swing their support behind Jozip Broz Tito and his Communist Partisans. When in the summer of 1944 the Germans found themselves in retreat, Tito's Partisans were quick to take control of the southern part of their country while the Soviets and their new allies the Bulgarians took control in the north. Then the two groups came together in October when all German power in the country collapsed. Then, leaving Tito in charge of matters, Stalin's army turned its focus northward, toward Budapest in Hungary.

Hungary. Soon after this, the Red Army moved on toward Hungary … where the Hungarians and their German allies proved much more resistant to the Russian offensive. It was not until February of the following year (1945) that the Hungarian capital Budapest was taken by the Red Army and their new allies, the Romanians.

✳ ✳ ✳

THE WAR ON THE WESTERN FRONT

The Battle of France

Normandy. Stalin had long been pressing for the Allies to open a front in the West in France, to relieve the pressure on the Russians fighting the Germans in Eastern Europe. The Western Allies' focus on Italy seemed to Stalin to be simply a waste of assets designed solely to serve the commercial (and military) interests of Britain … or worse, to position the Allies so as to be able to head off a Russian movement into southeastern Europe (where Stalin was hoping to establish a foothold that would allow Russia finally to fulfill its long-held dream of direct access to the Mediterranean).

But the mishap at Dieppe had put serious caution in the plans of the British and American allies. Likewise, after Dieppe the Germans had seen to the emplacement of concrete bunkers housing artillery and machine guns all along the German's Atlantic Wall. Going ashore against the German defenses would be murderous for the Allies.

The Allies hoped to weaken the German line of defense along the Atlantic Wall by convincing the Germans that the crossing would occur way to the North of the area actually selected for the landing. They thus created a phony army of dummy tanks and trucks and false radio communications that they were hoping German intelligence was analyzing. The fact that Patton was appointed head of this phony army was thought (correctly) to be the most convincing part of the ploy. And indeed, Hitler was certain that the channel crossing of the Allies would be happening under Patton at Calais, the closest point in France opposite England.

Training for the channel crossing took place over many months. But as the summer of 1944 approached, Eisenhower, heading up the Allied action in Europe, knew it was time to move if they were to cross France and reach Germany before winter set in. But bad weather delayed the first date chosen for the crossing. Then a slight break in very bad weather finally gave Eisenhower the conditions he needed before the tides began to change and the crossing would have to be delayed by weeks. Because of that bad weather however the Germans were not expecting any action from the Allies. In fact Rommel took those days off to head back to Germany for a visit to his wife.

Thus in the early hours of June the 6th, 160,000 American, British, Canadian and French troops went ashore along a 50-mile strip of the coast of southern Normandy. The Normandy landing area was divided into five sectors: Utah (American), Omaha (American), Gold (British), Juno (Canadian) and Sword (British and some French). Omaha Beach and the Pointe du Hoc landing of Rangers (next to Omaha Beach) were the sectors with the highest Allied casualties because this area was defended by strong German emplacements atop very tall cliffs. Juno was almost as bad - due to the German network of bunkers along the seawall. Utah Beach produced the lightest Allied casualties. The Airborne divisions dropped behind German lines also suffered very high casualty rates.

But the landing succeeded. Hitler refused to reposition the troops gathered further north at Calais, considering the Allied landing to be merely a feint designed to draw troops away from Calais so as to make Patton's invasion easier (there was, of course, no such Patton invasion). For days Hitler hesitated before he finally came to the realization that this was the massive assault that the Germans had long been expecting. But by that time the Allies were well planted in Normandy and moving inland fairly quickly.

Several problems however complicated the Allied advance. The British were expected to liberate the city of Caen almost immediately. Their landing had been largely unopposed ... but in reaching the outskirts of Caen the Germans showed themselves prepared to put up a major fight. Consequently, this key hinge point took two months to bring under Allied control. Also, the farms of Normandy were outlined not by fences but by huge, thick centuries-old hedges that gave the Germans great defensive opportunities and made progress of the Allied tanks and infantry almost impossible ... until an immense steel fork was created to be placed on the front of the tanks, allowing them simply to plow through the hedges. With that innovation the advance against the Germans proceeded much more quickly.

At one point a huge German army was nearly surrounded by the advancing Allies. But failure to close quickly a gap in the circle allowed most of the Germans to escape and reorganize further east against the Allied advance. Nonetheless, the Germans were tiring and running out of men and supplies. At this point (August) the Allied move across France towards Germany was advancing quickly.

The decision to liberate Paris rather than head directly to a Rhine crossing. Eisenhower's original plan was to head Allied troops across central France in an effort to reach the Rhine River, certainly before the autumn season ended (and bad weather would bog down the Allied offensive) and then head quickly on to Berlin. But the French Resistance was pleading for help ... to rescue Paris before the Germans could destroy it – as they had done to other cities. But the French also needed help in resolving the growing division between the original members of the Resistance (just French patriots) led by De Gaulle ... and the Communist members of the Resistance led by Henri Tanguy (who joined the Resistance only after Germany attacked Russia in mid-1941) – who appeared to be motivated simply by the desire to bring France under Communist control ... which was something that neither the Americans nor the British wanted to see happen. Thus the decision was made to head their troops to Paris instead.

Speed, surprise, and caution in handling the situation were all called for. But de Gaulle and his Free French were already rapidly on the move toward Paris before Eisenhower finally came to the decision to divert the offensive away from the Rhine and toward Paris. De Gaulle had to get his troops into Paris before Tanguy's Communist Partisans could get themselves in position to take the city.

But things moved quickly ... especially as the Germans posted there were not themselves battle-hardened soldiers, having lived the good life as Paris occupiers for four years. And the Free French were so charged up with the thought of taking Paris from the Germans that their tanks kept pressing forward against the withering fire of the German artillery, simply overrunning the German guns in the process. And on to Paris center (August 25, 1944) they headed, catching the thinly spread Germans unready to offer serious resistance. Pockets of entrenched Germans (and snipers) put up a valiant last-ditch effort to hold the city, though there was little hope for their success - as the Parisians took to the streets and the Communist and Free French Resistance rose up and took the Paris districts by force. The Germans were brought quickly to surrender.

De Gaulle was quick to lead the victory march of his troops down the broad main street of Paris, the Champs-Elysées, putting himself out front prominently as the "Liberator" of Paris. The Communists were forced to settle for second place (a major political setback for them). And then when a few days later a long line of American tanks and troops also came down the Champs Elysées, there was no longer any possibility that the city would go Communist, but instead would go center-right in political orientation.

The cost of the decision to delay the Rhine crossing in order to liberate Paris was very, very high. This gave Hitler time to reorganize his troops in the West, snuff out British General Montgomery's hope to quickly cross the Rhine in the North in Holland before the Germans could react (and thus open a very direct and lightly defended path to Berlin), even give the Germans the time to organize enough for one last push to throw the Allied effort back to the Atlantic (a combination of V-2 bombs and the German winter offensive known in the West as the "Battle of the Bulge") ... and worst of all, give him that much more time to try to complete the eradication of the entire European Jewish community with his "Final Solution." Thus a lot of lives were lost elsewhere because of the decision to redirect the Allied war effort toward Paris.

In short, a precious, precious price was paid to spare a precious, precious Paris ... a hard but momentous decision.

The German V-1 and V-2 missiles

The Germans pushed hard for the development of long-range jet-propelled missiles, promised as "revenge" (*Vergeltung*) for the Allied bombing of German cities ... even though the work in developing such German missiles had begun well before the Allied bombings of Germany. Thus the *Vergeltungswaffe* was developed in two increasingly sophisticated forms: The Vergeltungswaffe 1 (V-1) and Vergeltungswaffe 2 (V-2).

The V-1 operation began after the Allied invasion of Normandy, the missiles launched from the French coast and aimed primarily at London. But the British developed anti-aircraft fire capable of bringing down many of nearly 10,000 V-1s headed their way (roughly three out of every four missiles were knocked out). Nonetheless, the 2,500 V-1s that did hit, terrorized the London population so profoundly that 1.5 million Londoners fled the city ... seeing their capital experiencing the horror of a "Second Blitz."

However, against the V-2, launched several months later from German sites in the Netherlands, the British had no defense. Flying three times the speed of sound, and dropping noiselessly from the heights, they did considerable damage not only to London, but also the port of Antwerp, their primary target (the Allied needed a large port to bring in supplies for their troops), Liege, and other European cities. But these missiles were expensive to build, used fully a third of Germany's fuel capacity, and ultimately were of no serious help strategically to a collapsing Germany.

But they did however, give the victors (American, British and Russian) a huge pool of German scientists to draw from in developing their own post-war missile systems ... weapons of mass destruction that became centerpieces (along with atomic explosives) in the Cold War that was soon to develop.

Troubles to the North

"Operation Market Garden" (September-November 1944). British General Montgomery, who commanded the northern flank of the Allied Army, was able to convince Allied Command that the best way to get across Germany's Rhine defenses was to cross that river in the lightly-defended Netherlands ... by dropping paratroopers to seize the bridges – at the same time moving troops north quickly to cross those bridges. Thus (with him in command of the operation)* they would be able to swing around Germany's lighter defenses in the North, encircle the heart of industrial Germany, and gain quick access to Berlin ... possibly bringing the war to an end before Christmas.

But it was a plan fated to fail. The Germans quickly caught on when Allied troops began their march north, with the Allied troops slowed greatly by having to move tanks and trucks along narrow roads elevated above surrounding fields ... and the fact that the Dutch poured out into the streets to celebrate their "liberation" by the Allied troops ... making troop movement almost impossible. Thus the whole strategy of catching the Germans by surprise failed.

The Germans blew up bridges and captured paratroopers waiting for reinforcements, ones that failed to appear. An effort now had to be made to rescue those paratroopers trapped behind German lines. Of the 10,000 troops that had been dropped at Arnhem, only a fifth of that number were rescued, the rest either killed or captured by the Germans.

The "Battle of the Bulge" (December 1944). The Germans proved themselves to be better at the game of surprise, when suddenly a massive number of German troops hit the very lightly defended Allied lines in the middle of the Ardennes Forest ... a place that worn-out Allied troops had been sent to rest and recover. The surprise was so complete that in a matter of a few days German tanks, trucks and infantry were able to push deep into the Forest. Hitler's goal was to reach the key port of Antwerp, shut down the Allies' vital operations there, and seize Allied supply bases (supplies greatly needed by an impoverished German army).

Hitler's generals tried to reason with Hitler concerning all of the

------

*This would infuriate American general Patton, whose tank corps was making good headway against the Germans as it advanced toward Germany itself ... for this meant not only diverting important supplies (especially fuel for his tanks) to his nemesis Montgomery but also the loss to Patton of the glory that both men sought on the battlefield!

dangers involved in such a move. But Hitler's mental state at this point was such that he again (like Operation Barbarossa) thought himself to be totally brilliant as a military strategist and ignored their warnings. In the end, his advisors proved right. It turned out to be a grand disaster for the Germans.

Protected by heavy cloud cover, which prevented Allied airpower from joining the fight, the Germans were able quickly to push westward. But the town of Bastogne, reinforced quickly by Allied paratroopers, was able to hold out. Bastogne being at the very center of the German expansion, this weakened the German offensive greatly. Then also the Germans tanks and trucks began to run out of fuel. And then the clouds lifted, allowing Allied planes to attack the stalled German line. The Germans were thus forced to retreat back into Germany … now as crippled in the West as they were in the East.

This would be the last grand attempt of the Germans to hold off the advance of the Western Allies into Germany. Nonetheless the Germans would continue to fight fiercely for every piece of ground now that the Allies were entering Germany.

✳ ✳ ✳

THE FULL ASSAULT ON JAPAN

Island hopping (in from the East). The general strategy of the Allies (largely American in this particular theater) against the Japanese in occupation of the numerous Pacific islands was not to take each island held by the Japanese one by one, but simply select a few islands that were strategically located in the group, and which offered excellent staging ground (by sea and by air) for their advance deeper into Japanese territory. As the Allies largely held control of the sea and air, Rabaul and the Pacific islands the Allies by-passed would find themselves cut off from Japanese resupply … and thus could be brought under full Allied control at a later date.

But the islands they did pick to undertake landings were always the scenes of considerable Japanese resistance, especially as the Japanese tended to dig in deeply … hoping to create impenetrable lines of defense against the advancing Allies. But the Allies bombed and torched (napalm) these defenses as they went. The death toll was tremendously high, especially on the Japanese side. But Allied losses were also very high.

With American Admiral Chester W. Nimitz in command, the objective was to secure islands close enough to Japan that the mainland, especially the industrial cities of coastal Japan (including the capital Tokyo), could be hit by long range American bombers.

Thus it was that Tarawa (November 1943), in the Gilbert Islands well south of this line of advance,* was the first target of this effort. This was followed up by the taking of the islands of Kwajalein and Eniwetok (February 1944). From there the Americans took the islands of Saipan (June-July), Tinian (July) and – most importantly – Guam (July-August). From this point on, the Japanese civilians found themselves as familiar as the Germans as to what it felt like to have the horrors of war inflicted on them and their homes and cities ... rather than just on their enemies. The Allied bombing of Japan would now be relentless.

Meanwhile, the Allied advance up from the South. A second command, coming up from just offshore from Dutch New Guinea , had as its object the retaking of the Philippines from the Japanese. For its commanding General Douglas MacArthur, the Philippines constituted something he held as a personal objective, for in leaving the Philippines in 1942, he had guaranteed the Filipinos: "I shall return."

The startup – from the huge island of Dutch New Guinea (just north of Australia) and to the east from the Solomon Islands (north of Guadalcanal) – was slow and also very bloody ... Bougainville being chief among these islands and taking from November 1943 to February of 1944 to secure.

In October of 1944, the Allies reached the Philippine island of Leyte ... but found the Japanese navy waiting for them. A huge sea battle resulted ... which the Japanese lost decisively.   But even then, it would not be until December that Leyte was fully in Allied hands. With much fanfare General MacArthur came ashore at Leyte Island, cameras recording the event with a properly dramatic effect. He had finally fulfilled his promise.

But the full liberation of the Philippines was yet ahead. From Leyte the Americans swung around the Philippines' main island of Luzon to land on its northern shore (January 1945) ... and then to advance south across the island toward the Philippine capital of Manila. In Manila itself, fierce house to house fighting followed until finally in late February the capital was cleared of the last of the Japanese troops ... with much horrifying destruction brought to the city and its people. And once again, the Japanese casualties were also enormously high, the Japanese resolved to fight to the last man standing rather than to surrender.

Closing in on Japan

Iwo Jima (February 1945). In mid-February, American Marines went ashore on the Island of Iwo Jima, the first truly Japanese island comprising the Japanese island group. Here Americans would discover what they

---

*Debate would be ongoing even till today as to whether or not it was absolutely necessary to spill American blood to seize this off-path objective.

could expect by way of Japanese resistance now that they were actually on Japanese soil. It would take almost six weeks to break the last of the Japanese resistance on the island. Approximately 90 per cent of the Japanese force of 20,000 was killed (or committed suicide) in the action.

Okinawa (April 1945). At the beginning of April, a huge armada of 1400 American ships sent troops ashore on the Japanese island of Okinawa. This large island was so strongly defended in the south that it took three months of battle to finally bring it under Allied control (the Japanese killed in action numbered fourteen times the Allies killed, a clear indicator of the Japanese resolve to fight).

Air and sea attacks on Japanese territory itself. By this point, the Americans were finding themselves closer to the Japanese heartland – and the Japanese air force offering little defense against the bombing runs of the Americans on their cities. Tokyo was being hit by intense fire-bombing which was turning the Japanese capital into a fiery inferno. Yet the Japanese showed no sign of weakening in their resistance to the advancing Americans.

Kamikaze. What air action that the Japanese did offer (at Okinawa) was suicidal ... a desperate effort of 4,000 young (and inexperienced) Japanese kamikaze ("divine wind") pilots to hurl themselves and their explosives laden planes at the American ships advancing on their islands. Only a small percentage were able to hit a ship. Nonetheless, the effort certainly unnerved the American sailors – with 30 ships sunk and over 300 others badly damaged by the fanatical kamikaze pilots.

Nonetheless, the Japanese naval attack on the American fleet failed to stop the American advance. By now it was clear that the Americans were unstoppable. But it was also clear that the Japanese did not seem willing to give up the fight as long as there were any Japanese still alive to fight. Even the women and youth were being trained in defense tactics. It looked as if the Allies were going to have to go village to village across the entirety of Japan to finally bring the war with Japan to an end. This might take years and millions of casualties to complete.

✳ ✳ ✳

PREPARING FOR A POST-WAR WORLD

Rooseveltian Idealism. Political necessity had quite naturally formed the tight alliance that existed among the Allied leaders Roosevelt, Stalin and Churchill. But Roosevelt's deep idealism was another important factor in the dynamic.   Roosevelt, like all well-educated (Groton Prep School and Harvard College) and socially quite comfortable (part of the Rooseveltian aristocracy of New York) Humanists, saw life as directed by basic rules of civilization that all good people follow by simple instinct. This sense of inevitable order was what, in fact, lay beneath the New Deal program that Roosevelt was certain would bring America out of the Great Depression (in fact it did not. It took putting the World War Two American war industry on its feet that did the trick).

The publicly very polite Stalin, indeed, played quite beautifully into this idealized picture held by Roosevelt ... who thought that he had charmed Stalin into a very close personal relationship. In fact, the cynicism that Churchill chose not to hide (it was clear that Churchill did not trust Stalin) annoyed Roosevelt greatly.

Indeed, Churchill's constant reference to the British "Empire" also annoyed Roosevelt greatly. Americans, including their President, were by their own political perspective supposed to be highly opposed to the idea of "empire."

Thus it was that Roosevelt believed that he shared a certain natural understanding with Stalin as to how a post-war world should come into being. Indeed, he often met privately with only Stalin to talk about the more serious issues facing the American and Soviet superpowers ... Britain – like France – now being viewed as secondary-level powers.

The United Nations Organization. Another piece arising out of Roosevelt's world of Idealism was the new United Nations Organization that Roosevelt had planned as key to the building of a post-war world.* In most ways his proposed organization resembled the now-defunct League of Nations ... with a General Assembly offered as a political forum for all of the organization's member countries – and a special Security Council to take on the trickier political issues facing the world. And the latter component, like the League Council, would be led by a small group of key powers, "Permanent Members" who would always have a seat on the Security Council (but joined on the Council by ten rotating members). And by Roosevelt's own design, those Permanent Members would be America and Soviet Russia ... but also Great Britain, France and China.

These "Big Five" in fact would hold supremely important veto powers over proposed Security Council actions. This veto power was awarded to

----

*Actually Roosevelt had come up with a draft proposal for just such an organization only a few weeks after America's entry into World War Two in early December of 1941, and on New Year's Day 1942 his proposed organization was formalized as the "United Nations" when America, Great Britain, Soviet Russia and China signed a document soon to be known as the United Nations Declaration – which then representatives of twenty-one other nations also signed the very next day.

them to make sure that a rising political issue would not break the relationship between these key powers and the new United Nations Organization ... the way such matters had led to the resignation of the great powers from the League in the 1930s.

But Roosevelt personally believed that, in any case, it would be the natural diplomatic alliance between America and Soviet Russia that would actually direct the post-war world. In this he would prove correct ... in that it would be America and Soviet Russia that would direct that world – but not as the allies he thought they would be.

Bretton Woods (July 1944). In July of 1944, delegates from the 44 "United Nations" Allies gathered at Bretton Woods, New Hampshire, for a three-week conference to put together plans to rebuild a war-torn world. The focus was economics, especially ways of freeing international trade and the exchange of currencies. And thus the International Monetary Fund (IMF) and the International Bank for Reconstruction and Development (IBRD) were born. And the foundation of this international world would be the American dollar. All exchange rates would be set in relation to the dollar ... rates that could not be changed except by agreement with the IMF.

And that would be a big problem for Stalin ... who stepped back from this development because he saw how this played into the hands of American capitalism. Stalin would have none of that. Thus the first glitch in Roosevelt's Soviet-American post-war dream world took place. There would soon be more such glitches ... many more.

Yalta (February 1945). By the beginning of 1945 it was quite clear that the Nazi Reich was not going to last much longer. With the collapse of the Reich, much of Europe would find itself without government. Considering the great extent of the destruction of Europe caused by the war it was expected that immense social and political dislocation would result, threatening the peace that the Allies were striving for. Roosevelt, Stalin and Churchill understood that an administrative plan of sorts would have to be laid out to provide some kind of transition to a stable post-war Europe.

But while it looked like the war in Europe was about to come to an end, this was hardly the case in Asia. The way the Japanese were fighting to the last man (and often women) it appeared that the war in Asia might drag on for many more months, even years. Thus it was hoped by Roosevelt that Stalin might bring Russia into the Asian war (up to that point Russia had not been at war with Japan). But as Stalin saw no particular advantage for Russia in joining in, both Roosevelt and Stalin knew that they would have to offer Russia some incentives for doing so.

In February of 1945, Roosevelt, Stalin and Churchill met at the Black

Sea resort of Yalta to go over the problems of how to oversee the rebuilding of a post-war Europe. But also on the agenda was this matter of the war in Asia.

With respect to Europe, they basically agreed that areas under the control of one or other of their armies (primarily American, British and Soviet) would remain under that control or governance during a time of "temporary" occupation. Thus most of Eastern Europe would come under Soviet governance. Italy would come under American governance. And Germany would be divided among Russia, America and Britain (with France soon added by giving it portions of the British and American zones) on the basis of their actual military occupation at war's end. As for the most strategic part of Germany, its capital city of Berlin, although the city fell entirely within the Russian zone of occupation, they agreed to divide the city itself into three (then four) zones of occupation. All of this however was supposed to be of a temporary nature ... that is, until Europe's societies could get themselves up and running again.

As for the matter of enticing Stalin to bring Russia into the war against Japan, an agreement was struck that as a result of Russian involvement in the Asian war, Russia would be given post-war administrative rights in the northern half of Japanese-occupied Korea (America administering the southern half) ... and also in the entire region of Manchuria. Indeed, Stalin promised that within two or three months of Germany's defeat, Russia would come into the anti-Japanese action in Asia. The hope now was that the war there would be over much sooner than the brutal two-year period (or more) that they were fearing it would take to bring Japan to full defeat.

✳ ✳ ✳

WORLD WAR TWO FINALLY COMES TO AN END

Truman takes over from Roosevelt

Roosevelt's Death (April 1945). Roosevelt's greyness at the Yalta Conference certainly indicated that something was wrong with his health ... although America tended to take no notice of this – caught up in the glories of a war in Europe clearly about to come to an end. Then without warning, while on a trip to his Warm Springs spa in Georgia, Roosevelt suddenly died (April 12, 1945). Americans were deeply shocked.

President Truman. In accordance with the American Constitution, his recently-installed Vice President, Harry Truman, now became American President. But who exactly was Harry Truman?

Americans could not believe that not only had they lost their beloved commander-in-chief while the war was still underway, but that they were now being led by a politician largely unknown to most Americans, a man who in fact, just to look at him, seemed to be a most unexceptional individual. In this estimation the Americans were quite wrong.

Truman was himself shocked that such a heavy post-Rooseveltian legacy fell on his shoulders. He was fully aware of the heavy responsibilities falling on the presidential office ... and was unsure of the level of support he would receive in having to fulfill those responsibilities. But he was one who had learned to accomplish much ... especially when so little was expected of him. He had been a decorated officer in the Great War, had gone home to Missouri after the war to study and practice law ... and had been given special career support in politics by corrupt Kansas City boss Tom Pendergast, who admired Truman – for Truman's personal integrity! Being a Pendergast protégé, Truman had to prove himself to his fellow U.S. senators when he arrived in Washington as a freshman senator from Missouri. But little by little he earned the admiration of his fellow senators with his hard work ... and his integrity.

Truman's Hard-Nosed Realism. In the U.S. Senate, Truman served during the war as head of a committee investigating war-time graft and corruption in the business of supplying the U.S. government with war goods. He was always very perceptive of subtle power plays going on behind the scenes. Having entered national politics as a close observer of the roughshod ways of Boss Pendergast's Kansas City machine politics, Truman understood the power game well ... actually much better than Roosevelt, who tended to see only the best in people – including Stalin. As events would prove, Truman would read the real Stalin much better than Roosevelt would have, had he lived to lead the country in the post-war era.

The collapse of the Nazi Empire. The war with Germany was largely over, with the Russian armies flooding across eastern Germany and with Russian-German street fighting already taking place in Berlin as Truman took office ... and with the Allied Armies now in occupation of the rest of the country to the west of the Russian line. Hitler was in hiding and no longer governing Germany's war effort (he committed suicide at the end of April).

The question was thus one not of defeating Germany (a foregone conclusion) but rather of how the Allies were to govern a devastated German society ... and the other societies that had been under Nazi domination for the previous five, six or seven years. The Allied armies had been assigned administrative duties in these various societies. But the militaries were designed to fight, not govern. Further, they were going to have to transfer most of these occupational troops to the Asian theater of war. What then would be left to govern a hungry, sick, and homeless world in Europe? All kinds of political mischief could be expected to arise under these kinds of conditions. The post-war 1920s had illustrated very clearly the dangers awaiting just such a post-war world ... except that this coming post-war world was vastly more devastated than Europe had been during the period after the Great War. The problems would thus likely turn out to be monumental in size.

And the on-going fight with Japan. Then there was this matter of the war with Japan that Truman was expected to deal with. Strategic bombing of Japan (thus the firestorm of Tokyo that left hundreds of thousands dead and a million or more homeless) by conventional bombing, no matter how intense, seemed unable to shake the will of Japan to resist down to the last man, woman and child. And lots of American lives would be lost in the process of breaking just such Japanese determination.

In the process of trying to digest the meaning of these huge challenges, he also got word that a group of scientists had been working secretly in the desert of New Mexico to develop a new nuclear device, one so horrible in firepower that it might finally bring the Japanese to surrender ... though at this point no one working on the project was entirely sure of whether this bomb would work or not. Also there was another concern accompanying this project, namely that this device was so powerful that it might set off an explosive chain reaction, one that might not be easily brought under control. Thus even if it could be developed in the very near future, should it be used or not? This was quite a decision facing the new president!

The Potsdam Conference (17 July - 2 August 1945)

As a follow-up to the Yalta Conference in February, Truman, Churchill and Stalin gathered in the Berlin suburb of Potsdam in mid-July to work out specific details concerning the governing of a post-war Europe ... and the conduct of the ongoing war with Japan. Truman was the new kid on the block, but took up an immediate liking of Churchill ... and then a deep distrust of Stalin – a virtual reversal of the position Roosevelt had moved to in the latter days of the war. Truman understood that with their common enemy Hitler gone, the dynamics holding the Soviet-American (and British) alliance together would dissolve over the question of post-war governance of Europe. Truman knew that either American troops would be shifted to the Pacific front ... or they would be coming home under pressure from the soldiers' families in America. And he knew that Stalin knew this as well

... and was counting on the American departure to leave Russia sitting in a dominant position not only in the East of Europe but possibly in all of Europe. Truman immediately saw the dangers of defeating Hitler's empire in Europe ... only to have it replaced by Stalin's empire.

Churchill out ... Attlee in. Churchill promised what he could of British support of the Western position in Europe. But the British were tired ... and, like the Americans, wanted simply to go home and forget about the whole nightmare. Consequently, parliamentary elections held in July in Britain, the first since before the war started (actually since 1935), went strongly against Churchill's Tory Conservatives ... and in favor of the Labour Party under Clement Attlee, who had promised the British people that, under the governance of him and his party, national efforts would be turned inward toward post-war social improvements in Britain and away from Britain's long involvement in international affairs led by such "imperialists" as Churchill. It was a sad repudiation of the man who had led Britain through the darkest days of the war. Nonetheless that was what the British voters wanted ... and thus Attlee replaced Churchill during the middle of the Potsdam Conference itself.

At this point Truman knew that America would be facing Russia alone: two huge superpowers attempting to define the post-war world according to their respective (and highly conflicting) goals for that world.

It was in the context of this growing tension that Truman casually mentioned to Stalin that the Americans had successfully tested an enormous bomb (news of a successful test of the bomb reached Truman during the Potsdam Conference itself) that would likely shift in America's distinct favor the whole balance of power relationship with Japan ... and by implication, with Europe as well. Stalin seemed to show no reaction to the news, either because of his steely disposition ... or because he already knew of it, thanks to pro-Soviet informers within the circle working on the American project.

The end of the war with Japan

The bomb. But this was a significant shift in power toward America, both in Japan and in Europe. Of course to be a true power factor, it would have to be more than just a possibility. It would have to be an actuality. And Stalin did not believe Americans strong enough in willpower to actually use such a device. Thus Stalin seemed unalarmed. There was little or no deterrent value in simply possessing a nuclear device ... if you had no plans to actually use it.

But indeed, Truman soon demonstrated that he did indeed intend such use.* After warnings about "utter destruction" sent by the Allies to the Japanese emperor were ignored, on August 6th an atomic bomb was dropped over Hiroshima, killing an estimated 100,000 to 150,000 Japanese (half that number on the first day, the rest through burns and radiation poisoning over the next weeks). Another warning was sent, this time directly by Truman to the Emperor. But it too was not answered. And thus on August 9th a second atomic bomb was dropped, this time over Nagasaki, killing an estimated 40,000 to 80,000 Japanese.

Stalin jumps in. With the bombing of Hiroshima, Stalin had an idea that the war would likely be over very soon. He thus declared war on Japan. He was not going to be left out in the sharing of the goodies grabbed from a defeated Japan.

Japan surrenders. Within a week after the Nagasaki bombing, the Japanese announced (August 15th) their unconditional surrender to the Allies. And on September 2nd, Japanese representatives came aboard the U.S. Battleship *Missouri* to sign the instrument of surrender.

Counting the costs

This was a hugely devastating war … not just in terms of soldiers lost in battle … but also in terms of civilians caught in the crossfire. It is estimated that somewhere between 70 to 85 million people died as a result of the war – troops lost in action, troops who died in captivity … and civilians caught in the bombings, and those who died as forced labor or as prisoners in concentration camps.

The best estimates are that the Soviets suffered almost 11 million military deaths – but over 12 million civilian deaths. China's loss was almost as big … nearly 4 million troops and approximately 8 million civilians killed in the fighting … plus another 10 million who died simply from the famine and disease unleashed by the war. Germany lost 5.5 million troops and approximately 2 million civilians for a total of almost 11% of its population. Poland lost approximately 5.6 million people – nearly all civilians … and the highest percentage rate of all participants, losing over 18% of its population – the majority being its Jewish population (approximately 3 million … or half of the Jews killed in the Holocaust). Japan lost approximately 2 million

---

*Actually, records later revealed that Truman, and the group of advisors around him, in no ways seemed to have been hesitant about putting the bomb to use to end the war in Japan. Only Eisenhower, at the time, seemed hesitant about using the bomb, although later as President in the 1950s, he himself would include the real possibility of nuclear war as part of his Cold War strategy.

troops – and another half-million civilians for just under 6% of its population. Italy lost 457 thousand, over 301 thousand of that being military.

French Indochina and the Dutch East Indies lost 1-1.5 million and 3-4 million respectively … nearly all civilians caught in the crossfire.

Although all countries experienced the tragedy of such loss, for the Allies America, Britain, and France the numbers were much smaller. America suffered just under 420 thousand deaths, nearly all military. Britain lost over 450 thousand people, 67 thousand of that being civilians killed in Germany's bombings. France lost nearly 568 thousand, over half of that being civilians caught in the crossfire (and those who died in work camps and death camps).

Eleven million of those deaths took place in Germany's concentration camps. Approximately 6 million of those were Jews. The other 5 million were mostly prisoners of war (also mostly Soviet) … but also the physically and mentally disabled, homosexuals, Romany (Gypsies), Jehovah's Witnesses, and other "undesirables" – as defined by the Nazi regime. German politicians falling out of favor (if not killed on the spot) also ended up in just such camps (thousands of camps across German-occupied Europe).

And that's just deaths. Harder to calculate are those who were wounded … oftentimes severely so. And what about the damage in homes, industries, farms, towns and cities? The size of that loss is actually incalculable.

But at least the worst seemed over. Hopefully now the world could move on into an era of much-needed peace.

CHAPTER SEVENTEEN

THE POSTWAR WORLD

* * *

BRINGING THE ALLIES' FORMER ENEMIES UNDER A NEW ORDER

The "Morgenthau Plan." As victory against Germany became evident, plans were assembled as to what to do with Germany after the war. In 1944 Treasury Secretary Henry Morgenthau came up with a plan to divide Germany into two separate states, to either internationalize or integrate other parts of Germany with neighboring countries and to de-industrialize Germany by turning it into an essentially agricultural country (or countries). Churchill amended the idea in several ways - though it is still remembered as the "Morgenthau Plan."

The Potsdam decision.   But in 1945, when the Allies gathered in Potsdam after Germany's defeat, the allies came up with a different plan for dividing Germany, though most of it merely into temporary occupational or "administrative" zones.

However, Germany was actually to lose a considerable amount of territory, particularly in the East where huge portions would be handed over to the newly revised Poland. Thus it was that the world got to see ancient German cities now renamed as Polish cities.

In part, this was all done in compensation for the fact that Poland itself would not recover the land it lost to Russia in Stalin and Hitler's earlier agreement to divide up and take control of the Eastern and Western halves of Poland. The half of Poland lost to the Russians in 1939 stayed permanently in the hands of Stalin's Russia and his occupational troops there. And no one was in a position to contest that hard reality. So Poland instead received huge sections of the German East.

Even the Russians got in on this deal directly, awarding themselves the northern half of the huge province of German East Prussia as now part of Russia, with the old East-Prussian capital city of Königsberg given the Russian name Kaliningrad!

And the French got back the lands of Alsace and Lorraine lying along the French-German border ... which had swung back and forth between the two peoples many times.

Mass migrations. These territorial assignments meant that there would be millions of Europeans that would find themselves now as "minorities" in newly reconstituted nations. Millions of Germans now found themselves at the mercy of the very people they had been so cruel and condescending to. But Poles would find the certification of Poland's East now as Soviet territory to be no less troubling.

Thus the roads of Eastern Europe were filled with refugees attempting to escape the requirements of the Potsdam peace. Estimates are that some 12-14 million people became just such migrants or "displaced persons" (DP's), Germans moving in from Germany's lost lands in the East (Poland, Czechoslovakia and Hungary). Most of those coming to the Soviet-occupied zone tried to keep moving – until they arrived in what they considered to be the more hospitable zones in the West, zones administered by the British, French and Americans. But that put an even greater burden on those same zones. In this move, some 2 million of them simply died of hunger, exhaustion, or disease.

Then there were also some 8 million DPs in the former German Reich who were non-German foreigners released from work and death camps ... confused about their future. And the death toll from this horrible situation – from hunger, exposure, disease, and just local mischief – was enormous ... though the statistics are merely guesswork, the lowest figures being somewhere around 5 to 6 hundred thousand ... the highest around 2 to 2.5 million. It was all very sad ... the results of a war that should never have happened in the first place.

The post-war German economy. Not helping the situation any was the Allies' authorization for Russia to rebuild its war-devastated industrial infrastructure – by receiving $300 million in reparation payments from Germany ... plus by stripping the portion of Germany it occupied of whatever industrial items it might find useful. This proceeded very rapidly – leaving Soviet-occupied Germany with little by which to put itself back together again – until the Soviets realized that they were creating a situation in East Germany that threatened to make their occupation (and desire to inspire Communism among German workers) totally unworkable. So they slowed things down a bit.

The Western sectors undertook pretty much the same program of stripping Germany of whatever industrial items it might find useful ... but also slowed up when they came to the same conclusion as the Soviets about this kind of policy. In fact, in the French sector, the French authorities actually encouraged the Germans to get back to the business of farming, coal mining and steel manufacture ... actually very beneficial to French industry and its own profitability. Things picked up quickly in this sector ... noted carefully by the occupational authorities – at least in the West.

Bringing the former Nazi leaders to justice. There still remained the matter of what to do about the worst of the Nazis. Hitler and his mistress Eva Braun and Hitler's propagandist, Joseph Goebbels (and family) had solved that portion of the problem with their suicides. But subsequently, 24 others were arrested, imprisoned, and then put on trial in November of 1945. Air Marshal Hermann Göring committed suicide during the trial and Labor leader Robert Ley had done so prior to the trial ... leaving twelve others ultimately to be hanged, seven given lengthy prison sentences (three for life) and three were ultimately acquitted. And with that, the matter of bringing Germany to justice for its behavior came to something of an end (there would be many local acts of "justice" of course that would take place). There were new challenges to be dealt with.

Securing "justice" with other Axis nations. Italy made the matter a lot easier with its own capture and execution of dictator Mussolini, his mistress Clara Petacci, and several other Fascist notables just prior to the end of the war. And Italy was outside the realm of actual Soviet military occupation ... simplifying matters greatly in getting Italy pieced back together again.

In any case, an all-important Allied meeting was held in Paris (July-October) to work out "justice" for the Axis nations Germany, Italy, Austria, Romania, Bulgaria, Hungary and Finland. This was when the $300 million German reparations payment was decided. Russia demanded a similar reparations payment of $300 million from Italy ... which was turned down by the Western allies. Russia also wanted the Italian colony of Libya – nicely located on the southern shores of the Mediterranean. But that too was an idea that got no support from the Western Allies.

Nonetheless, allies Yugoslavia, Czechoslovakia and Greece were recipients of reparations payments ... plus territorial exchanges taken from Italy and Austria. Thus in the end, even the Italians had to come up with reparations payments: $100 million to Soviet Russia, $105 million to Greece and $125 million to Yugoslavia.

And most cruelly, Finland, a country that had been invaded by its neighbor Russia during the opening days of the Stalin-Hitler alliance – a Soviet invasion condemned by the League of Nations – which led Finland subsequently to look to Hitler's German for protection ... was therefore forced to pay Russia $300 million in various reparation forms and surrender border territory to Russia for its "crimes."

Taking over the former Japanese Empire. The Russians had come into the war effort in China so late (entering only one week prior to its termination) that they would have little voice in how the post-war Japanese Empire was to be administered. They did get the promised territory in North Korea and Manchuria. But they had no real say in matters beyond that. The French and Dutch had been so badly weakened by the war that, although they certainly were looking forward to regaining their imperial territories in Southeast Asia, they would have a hard time realizing those particular goals. As for the British, having come under Clement Attlee's British Labour Party, they would instead take a rather anti-imperialist path ... having long believed (the Labour Party anyway) that Britain's economic activities in imperial India actually undercut employment back in Great Britain. Therefore, the best policy for Britain was to step back from its former imperial role. Ironically, they failed to realize that economic relations with India were vital to British industrialism – including very importantly jobs for British workers. But the Labour Party was ideologically blind to this fundamental economic reality.

Thus, basically the overall management of Japan's former empire would fall to America ... whether it wanted this post-war responsibility or not. Most Americans had little concern about the sad state of post-war Japanese society. They did feel however that Japan should be brought to justice ... in particular Emperor Hirohito, who directed the murderous Japanese military during the war.

But both President Truman, and General MacArthur (the latter in command of occupied Japan) knew that managing post-war Japan would be exhausting if they did not have local leadership assisting them in this endeavor. And getting help from the emperor himself would greatly facilitate the occupational effort. Thus talk of imprisoning and probably executing the emperor was blocked by both Truman and MacArthur. Indeed, MacArthur was sent off to Japan to see if he could bring the emperor into American plans.

There were conditions associated with the emperor's "forgiveness." He would have to give up the pretense of being some kind of "god" ... and become more "democratic" (as America understood the term) in his dealing with his people. And indeed, the emperor seemed most willing to make this switch in his role, even heading out to be among the people at various events – even just taking walks in the streets of Japan's local communities in order to meet his people.

Actually, the Japanese people themselves seemed to switch their feelings about the Americans from hatred to acceptance – and even a willingness to learn from those Americans who now stood over them. Also, MacArthur was himself quite familiar with Asian ways (his earlier career having given him much time spent there), and was well familiar with what Asians wanted in their leadership: an individual strong, noble and visibly concerned about the welfare of the people under him. Thus MacArthur, in taking up exactly that role, was able to bring himself comfortably alongside Hirohito ... in a way that made it appear that Japan had "two emperors." This worked very well for the Japanese.

Thus it was that administering post-war Japan turned out to be a very simple, straightforward task for the American occupation.

Bringing the former Japanese leadership to justice. Nonetheless there still remained the question as to what should be done with other portions of Japan's leadership, notably its military leadership ... which had been quickly rounded up in Japan in the days just after the war's end. Finally, MacArthur set up a military tribunal in Japan to hear the cases of some 28 individuals, testimonies running from May of 1946 to November of 1948. Ultimately, seven defendants (including Tojo) were sentenced to death by hanging, and 16 defendants were sentenced to life imprisonment. However, America's allies also held local trials here and there in Asia of mostly lower-ranking military officials ... resulting in over 5,000 convictions and nearly 1,000 executions.

✳ ✳ ✳

POSTWAR EFFORTS TO GET THINGS BACK TO NORMAL

Post-war America

Labor issues. The war had smoothed over former ideological antagonisms separating American capitalists and the American workers ... bringing Depression-scorned capitalism back into national favor ... but also labor union membership and labor wages growth also to new heights. And war-time patriotism had kept both groups working in harmony. But now with the war over, old attitudes began to resurface ... especially with the huge concern over the direction America's post-war economy might take. What now would happen when the postwar world no longer needed the goods produced by America's massive war industry? And what would the "boys coming home" from the war find by way of work? Would America sink back into the Great Depression?

Indeed, during the period 1945-1946, America was hit with a wave of labor union strikes, involving around five million workers – angry at the job reductions that accompanied the shutting down of America's industrial war machine. But a number of factors would quickly bring America out of this contentious mood ... well in advance of the developments found elsewhere in the postwar world. It was a similar labor turmoil abroad that America was witnessing that began to put questions in American minds ... as it became increasingly clear that this labor strife was not just about jobs – but about political takeovers ... notably by the Moscow-directed Communists, active everywhere. American labor definitely did not want to be identified with any of that ... especially when the Cold War began to crank up (1947 and after).

Republican Party gains. Actually, this played strongly into the hands of "Middle America" ... and also fed the huge Republican Party sweep of post-war elections across the country – and brought Congress under a strong Republican Party majority. And that in turn led to the passage in 1947 of the Taft-Hartley Act, overturning the pro-labor Wagner Act of 1935 and placing America's labor unions under a number of restrictions. Truman vetoed the bill ... but Congress's 2/3rds vote overrode his veto.[*]

The G.I. Bill. But a kinder approach to the unemployment problem had already been put in place with the passage of the Servicemen's Readjustment Act of 1944 – popularly known as the "G.I. Bill." The government offered veterans free education – either college or technical school – covering both tuition and expenses. This gave returning G.I.s ("Government Issue"!) a great alternative to unemployment ... actually building considerably America's skill-level nationally. It was a very wise government investment ... and a way for young Americans to achieve the American dream: to train for work that would bring them to full membership in Middle America.

The huge consumer market. Also, and most importantly, American industry was quick to turn to the mass production of low-cost consumer goods ... ones whose production had been abruptly halted with America's entry into the war in order to focus American industry on war production. For instance, virtually no American automobile production took place during the war years (building trucks and tanks instead of sedans!). Consequently, there was a huge buildup in the postwar demand for cars, refrigerators, washing machines, etc. This was especially the case for single-family homes ... which in the post-war period were constructed in the thousands, hundreds of thousands even! Low interest mortgages and personal loans (again, thanks to the G.I. Bill) made all this very accessible to young Americans.

This dynamic also reached deeply down into America's labor segment ... which also very quickly saw for itself the open path to Middle American membership ... softening considerably American labor-management

---

[*]But then Truman himself during the remainder of his presidency would use the Taft-Hartley Act twelve times in his own confrontation with American unions.

tensions. Thus Middle America, which now included most all Americans (except most tragically, American Blacks), found itself flying high.

Vets and Boomers. Something else that had been put aside during the war were marriages among young Americans. But with the return from the war of hundreds of thousands of veterans – or "Vets" as they can be properly termed as a generation-group – that shortfall was corrected immediately! And with that (beginning at least 9 months later!) there occurred a huge explosion in the number of births in America ... a literal "Baby Boom."

But this would produce a new generation of young Americans who would differ greatly – radically so – from their parents in how they understood and went at life. The parents of these "Baby Boomers" – the "Vets" – were a tough breed ... having their own growing-up years take place during the Great Depression. And then as young adults, they were called to intense patriotic duty in the war ... offering themselves, even the possibility of forfeiting their lives, in service to the nation's call. Indeed ... these Vets would come to be identified (and rightly so) as "the Greatest Generation" – providing the last huge step in bringing America itself to greatness.

But their Boomer children will come to know virtually nothing of such larger social service ... growing up materially in the very best of times, lacking nothing, even indulged greatly by their Vet parents – who remember their own shortages and suffering in their younger years ... and want none of that for their children. Thus the Boomers will grow up (entering adulthood in the mid-1960s) as a very "entitled" generation ... naturally assuming that life will always owe them the kind of security and material payoff they experienced growing up. Self-sacrificing for the greater good will not register with them. Their world will center on themselves, their personal rights, their personal freedoms. Society will just have to take care of itself. Better yet, the government can do that for them. To the Boomer, that becomes the very purpose of government: to continue to provide the care they experienced at home growing up. Somehow this is what life owed them.

On the other hand, having just gone through the most challenging of times, the Vets made no assumptions that they themselves were automatically entitled to life's blessings ... or that they personally held the solutions to life's challenges. The design of the war, the nation's economy, society itself, they understood as belonging in higher hands ... their officers, their president (and his men), even their corporate bosses and local officials. However, the Vets were most willing to "do their part" in supporting the effort of those above them to meet those challenges. Thus they were intensely loyal to and supremely supportive of those whom they were called to serve.

Typically (and quite unlike their Boomer offspring), they would also live in the same community, work the same job until retirement, and hold true to their spouses for a lifetime.

American Christianity. But ultimately, life itself was understood by the Vets as belonging to an even higher authority ... to a sovereign God. And just as they had put on a uniform to serve their country, they continued to offer loyal service to God through obedient service to Jesus Christ (and the Church) – in how they saw that they were expected to live out their lives. The Vets faithfully attended church on Sundays. Sunday was, after all, the Lord's Day ... and most everything else, except most notably the restaurants where they could take lunch after church, was thus closed on Sundays.

But the same held true at the higher levels of American society. American businessmen had taken up the practice of holding prayer breakfasts – all the way back in the troubled days of the Depression. Likewise, this same businessmen's prayer-breakfast phenomenon had continued during the war. And political leaders (including numerous U.S. Congressmen) either joined them or set up their own prayer breakfasts ... also understanding that the huge challenges they faced needed God to go ahead of them to open and shut the necessary doors that laid in their paths – paths that only God could see clearly. But their faith was such that they had full confidence that their trust in God would get them where they needed to get. Indeed, they truly lived the American motto "In God We Trust."[*]

Post-war Great Britain

Britain's post-war economy was a grand mess. German bombing had destroyed or deeply damaged Britain's inventory of homes, industrial and commercial buildings, airports, shipping ports, railroads, roads, bridges, etc. ... in short, the fundamental infrastructure on which modern life depends. And government funds available to rebuild that infrastructure were just not there ... especially after funding coming from America's Lend-Lease Program – funds or goods (over $30 billion) that had helped Britain conduct its war effort – was terminated in 1945.

And with the war over, there would be many young soldiers looking for civilian employment ... at a time when the British economy seemed deeply stalled. A high level of unemployment – and probably accompanying labor strife – was a great possibility facing postwar Britain.

---

[*]In fact, the Vet generation made "In God We Trust" the nation's official motto in 1957 ... although the phrase had been in active use since the mid-1800s – especially during the Civil War, when the North's *Battle Hymn of the Republic* was about God's truth and justice going on before them.

According to the economic theories put forward by the economist John Maynard Keynes – theories that Britain (and most of the West) had been following since the mid-1930s – this situation indicated that it was time for the government to step in and take over the task of rebuilding those infrastructure items ... not just public roads and buildings but even family housing. But where would the funds be coming from that would finance just such an effort? Raising taxes on an impoverished citizenry was definitely out of the question.

And even to the extent that the government could finance some rebuilding ... where were the basic materials going to come from? The industries that provided such basic materials were themselves in massive disrepair. Even food to feed the working population and their families was short ... strangely shorter than what it had been during the course of the war itself. Almost every food item was now in short supply ... and thus food rationing would have to be deepened further in meeting the most basic needs of the British citizenry.

Then there was the matter of Britain's commitments abroad ... naturally expected of what was supposed to be a "great power." The British government was responsible not only for the care of its own citizens, it was handed the responsibility of getting the British portion of occupied Germany up and running. And for Germany it was not a matter of little food available. It was a matter of no food available for the Germans under British jurisdiction. Indeed, British domestic rationing even of bread was necessary in order to feed a starving German society.

And of course there were the long-standing responsibilities of empire ... something that offered Britain great prestige – but seemingly little else at a time of enormous shortages. How could the expenses of managing a huge empire abroad be justified in the face of these shortages at home? This would be a very big point of political debate within the British Parliament.

Attlee's Socialist program. Although Attlee was a deeply committed Socialist at heart, as Vice Chancellor under Churchill, he had toned down much of Socialism's anti-capitalist rhetoric. Now as Chancellor, he focused on putting some basic social services in place, ones he had promised his supporters during the war. Actually in this matter, Churchill had been himself in general agreement. Thus one of the first things Attlee got up and running was the extension by way of the National Insurance Act (1946) of welfare support for the unemployed, for the sick or disabled, for retirees, and for family child support.

Then he undertook an even greater challenge in bringing the British health care industry under government management ... offering the British citizens free "cradle to grave" health care (dental and eye care not covered however). He was able to answer the strong opposition posed at first by the medical profession by offering doctors the right to continue to run private practices – while hospitals and major health centers came under full governmental management (its National Health Service) in 1948. And the pharmaceutical industry was brought under governmental regulation in terms of its pricing of drugs, etc. In this too he had the support not only of his Labour Party but also Churchill's Conservative Party.

But being a Socialist, it was inevitable that Attlee would also want to take on capitalism's world of industry and finance ... and "nationalize" it all. Actually, much of that industrial world was not doing well ... especially the coal industry which was at a point of bankruptcy when it was nationalized in 1946. And the all-important Bank of England was taken out of the hands of private investors and simply made into an entirely government-directed operation (also 1946). From that he moved on to bring Britain's international airlines under government management as the company, British European Airways (1946), similarly electrical and gas services under the British Electricity Authority and the Gas Council (1948), and railroads merged into a single government-run company, "British Railways" (1948). In general, these actions received widespread British support.

Where Attlee ran into trouble was his nationalizing of the British iron and steel industry in 1949 as the British Iron and Steel Corporation of Great Britain. This industry had been running on its own ... and quite profitably so! Not only industrial owners but also the Conservative Party opposed this move strongly ... although with Labour holding a strong majority in Parliament there really was very little that the opposition could do about this move.

The social-cultural picture. In many ways the social picture of Britain in the postwar years was not all that different from America's. Home, family, community, and social-religious behavior remained quite traditional and quite central in importance. And the rigorous requirements of getting through the recent war – and now the austerity of the postwar period – only strengthened those social instincts. Even the feminism of the day was mostly about helping women operate a stronger home. And the British considered themselves strongly Christian ... not only in social performance but also in personal faith.

But these same instincts will not be passed on to the next generation ... also much like the situation in America.

But for the time being, the British will find themselves preoccupied with the challenge of just getting things back to normal as quickly as possible.

France sets up its Fourth Republic

The Provisional Government of the Republic of France. With Paris just liberated and the Allied armies moving fairly quickly against the retreating Germans – and the flight (and capture) of French officials who had served in the Vichy Government – a new Provisional Government was set up in September of 1944 … formed basically from the French Committee of National Liberation headed by De Gaulle (in partnership with General Henri Giraud), the latter organization set up in London in June of 1943. It was well understood by all that De Gaulle would head up the new Provisional Government … assigned the task of getting France back to normal – and coming up with a new Constitution.

Bringing the Vichy French to justice. There would have to be the Vichy legacy to deal with … both the individuals who directed that government and the matter of the legal standing of the laws enacted under that regime. Even prior to the setup of the Provisional Government there had been thousands of acts of local "justice" … when possibly as many as 10,000 collaborators were killed – although the exact numbers are hard to come by. In any case, some 300,000 individuals were brought to formal trial in the next years, with over 6,000 individuals sentenced to death … although only 791 executions were ever actually carried out. Those executions included Pierre Laval, who served at various times as French prime minister during the 1930s … and who continued in that same capacity during the Vichy era. And the heroic-tragic individual Pétain would be sentenced to death – but have his sentence commuted by De Gaulle to life imprisonment.

The Provisional Government attempted to secure a line of legal legitimacy connected to France's Republican past (the former Third Republic) … but found passing that line through the Vichy era to be very tricky. It finally dismissed the whole matter by simply declaring all acts issued by the Vichy government to be illegitimate and thus null and void – despite the Vichy government having actually been authorized legally by a popular referendum in 1940. Was therefore France as a nation guilty or not for what had transpired during the Vichy years? The answer was to be "not guilty."

Constituting a new Fourth Republic. Elections were held in October of 1945 to either restore the old Third Republic – or form a new constituent assembly to design a new, Fourth Republic. The results were that 96% of the voters were in favor of forming a new constitution. In the same vote the French Communist Party, headed by Maurice Thorez, secured 26% of the vote and thus the same percentage of seats in a new constituent assembly. The Socialist SFIO (French Section of the Worker's International), headed by Guy Mollet, gained nearly 24% of the vote. And the Centrist/Catholic MRP (Popular Republican Movement), headed by Robert Schuman, gained nearly 25% of the vote. These three parties then decided simply to work together as a governing coalition. Now the country could get to the task of designing a new French Republic.

It became quickly apparent that the coalition partners wanted to see basically a continuation of the structure of the Third Republic ... run by a very "democratic" National Assembly, one that represented exactly the variation and spread of France's numerous political groupings.

This was exactly what De Gaulle did not want to see happen. He was hoping to see a government directed by a strong presidential figure (with guess who as that president!) ... not by an assembly made up of a confusing array of various parties, small groups constantly coalescing and then breaking up over every matter that the French government was assigned to deal with. French governments of the Third Republic seemed to last only months – not years - making for political instability and weakness. De Gaulle pointed out that this was the very same arrangement that had crippled the French Third Republic when faced with the growing dangers in the 1930s of both Stalin's Communism and Hitler's Fascism. But he got nowhere with those elected to decide this matter. To most of the French, democracy and parliamentary government were totally synonymous. Indeed, he was even accused of being a latter-day Bonapartist ... seeking like the former Napoleons to want to direct the nation personally. Being thus spurned, he withdrew from French leadership in January of 1946.

Then the first draft of a new constitution, put before the French voters in May, found itself actively opposed by the Gaullists – but also by the centrist MRP and by conservative voters – because it provided for only a single legislative body ... dismissing a Senate as a second and possibly counterbalancing parliamentary body. In any case, the voters turned down the new constitutional proposal.

Consequently, a second round of elections for another constituent assembly was held the next month. This election however strengthened the Catholic and centrist MRP somewhat, also (but only slightly) the Communists, but weakened the Socialist SFIO a bit.

And it restored the role of a second chamber or Senate in the new Republic. But it still made the President simply a symbolic figure – as he had been in France's Third Republic – with France's executive power held in the hands of a prime minister ... someone supported in power (usually briefly) by an ever-changing array of political coalitions. But this time, when the proposal was put before the French that October, it was approved - despite De Gaulle's active opposition. But it was approved only by 53% of the voters, with 31% actually failing to vote at all. Not a good start.

De Gaulle would go on to create his own political party, the Rally of the French People (RPF) in April of 1947 ... hoping yet to get some kind of revision of the constitution more in line with his own thinking. The RPF did fairly well, particularly in the local municipal elections. But it would never acquire the dominating vote needed by De Gaulle to do the constitutional work he was hoping to see. The MRP seemed unable to hang onto the centrist/conservative support that De Gaulle was hoping would swing behind his RPF.

Getting France back up and running again. Like Britain, France had been hit hard by the war ... especially as the battles raged across the land after the Normandy landing in June of 1944. Much of the country's infrastructure, factories and housing was laid waste.

Getting the French economy back in proper order was going to be very expensive ... at a time that France's wealth was deeply depleted. Its overall national income in 1945 was estimated to be only half of what it was in 1929 ... just prior to the beginning of the Great Depression.

America's Lend-Lease assistance ended in mid-1945 and a Republican-controlled Congress was not interested in sending more money abroad (at least at this point). That was a shock to the French economy. However, America did rather immediately extend to France some $2 billion in loans, which certainly helped.

The French government – like most of Europe's governments – tended to see an economic comeback in the government's *nationalization* of the country's various industries ... in order to put them under a larger developmental program and not just under individualistic entrepreneurial development, as America tended to go at things. We have seen how this was the case in Attlee's Britain ... although actually the French had started down this path even before the start of World War Two ... with the nationalizing in 1937 of France's unprofitable railroad industry. Elements of the armaments and aeronautics industries were also nationalized during that same period.

In any case, the need for planned redevelopment seemed so natural to the French that the program of nationalization put in place after the war by Jean Monnet, head of the French Planning Commission, met generally with French approval. Thus the gas and electricity sectors were nationalized in 1946 ... with the nationalizing of the country's coal and steel industries – as well as its banking and insurance industries – following soon thereafter. However other industries – car, oil, and pharmaceuticals, for instance – were judged to be able to restore themselves ... and thus were left out of the nationalization program.

But – as elsewhere in Europe – France was hit hard by a fall in its economy in 1947 ... a huge drought and consequently the worst harvest in 150 years – and massive inflation due to rapidly rising demand greatly exceeding available supply. Not surprisingly, France would be hit (much like the rest of Western Europe) by workers' discontent ... reaching riotous levels by late April of 1947.

This in turn potentially played well into Communist hands. But this quite visible possibility of Communism's expansion across Western Europe also stirred America to take a strong counteraction: the Marshall Plan (1948). Just under $3 billion was eventually extended by America to France as purely a gift – but accompanied by expectations of a carefully planned use of the gift ... not really a problem for the French, who were already heading down that path! This Marshall Plan aid helped France enormously to get its economy back up and running ... and defuse the worker unrest – the primary reason for the aid in the first place!

Italy rebuilds

A republic instead of a monarchy. Much like France having to deal with the legacy of the Vichy government, Italy had to deal with the legacy of its King Victor Emmanuel III having been a close ally of Mussolini since 1922 when the king asked Mussolini and his Fascists to take charge of Italy's government. That alliance, having continued during the early days of the war, only made the king an Italian traitor in the eyes of many Italians.

However, with the Allied invasion of Italy in 1943, the king forced Mussolini to step down from his position ... and then signed an armistice with the Allies. The Germans were not happy about this ... and struck back at the post-Mussolini Italian government, forcing the king and his government to have to flee south to Allied lines ... and allowing the Germans to set up a puppet state in German-held northern Italy under Mussolini – once they had rescued him from prison.

But the king found himself frequently in disagreement with the Allied commanders. Thus in June of 1944 he turned most of his activities over to his son Umberto. ... and distanced himself from all the political dynamics of the day.

The very depth of the wartime destruction of Italy however only heightened the bitterness of many Italians toward their government ... and the king, hoping to save the monarchy, formally abdicated his throne to Umberto (May 1946) ... at the same time promising to call for a national referendum on this matter of monarchy versus republic. But the referendum, held only a month later, went 54% in favor of a republic. Both he and his son then went into exile.

But it was a very close election, with some questions about the results ... and indicating a sharp division in Italy on the matter, the industrial North highly supportive of a republic and the rural South highly supportive of the monarchy. But the decision in favor of a republic would stand nonetheless.

What shaped up next followed lines very similar to France's ... representation to the Constituent Assembly being made up heavily of Communists (19%), Socialists (21%), Christian Democrats (37%) ... and an array of a number of smaller conservative parties.

The shape of the final constitution was also similar to France's: a bicameral legislature or Parliament of a Chamber of Deputies and a Senate, with the government actually in the hands of a prime minister and his ministerial council (or cabinet). The president (elected by the legislature) would hold mostly just ceremonial powers.

Cleansing Italy of the Fascist legacy. Needless to say there would be serious reprisals taken against those who had supported the Fascist regime. But this would be a very complicated matter because Fascist membership had been an absolute requirement of anyone wanting to hold a job in the major professions. And the Italian resistance had not been that fair in its handling of its opponents either. Many of them had to be arrested as well.

Nonetheless, some 15,000 individuals were purged, even killed ... and like the French, any woman having relations with a German during the war years (often necessary to secure food for a girl's family) was humiliated by having her hair shaved off and being displayed in the streets as a traitor-prostitute.

But the new regime, under Christian Democrat leader Alcide De Gasperi,* opposed this dynamic ... and the Communist minister of justice Palmiro Togliatti was given the lead in this matter. And things then settled down in Italy ... pleasing the occupying Allied authorities greatly.

Trying to get Italy back to normal. And like France, economic conditions in Italy were horrible because of all the fighting that took place on Italian soil. Then too there was some "punishment" delivered to Italy for its pro-Fascist role in the war ... Italy losing territory as payoff to its neighbors, particularly the Yugoslavs. The award of sections of northeast Italy to Yugoslavia produced the emigration of 200,000 to 300,000 Italians from the areas awarded to Yugoslavia ... worsening the economic picture for an Italy that was already having trouble feeding its population.   And it lost all of its colonial holdings.

And like France, Italy would go through intense labor strife in the May-June general strike of 1947. But then (beginning also in 1948) it would receive Marshall Plan aid totaling $1.2 billion ... helping Italy move into a period of phenomenal economic growth (beginning around 1950 and

---

*But unlike France, Italy would get the continuing service of its prime minister De Gasperi from 1945 all the way to 1953 ... stabilizing Italian politics greatly.

continuing another 20 years).

Some of the other countries in the new European "West"

The Netherlands. During the war, the Dutch had been as active as possible against the Japanese, at least in the early stages of the war. But they could neither replace their naval losses in battleships (although their submarines survived and continued to serve) nor resupply their troops in Indonesia ... and lost out to the Japanese, who overran their Indonesian Empire. The results of this would be horrible to the Dutch, both military and civilian, who were carried off to horrible work camps ... and to the local Javanese, who were forced in the millions to work under the most horrible conditions for the Japanese (many women forced into prostitution as well). Thus the high death rate in the Dutch East Indies.

As for the situation in Europe, the Dutch had been hoping for either large reparations payments or the acquisition of German territory – reaching possibly as far as Germany's industrial Rhineland – in compensation for the destruction of both human life and social infrastructure.*   But with American rejection of the plan, that idea was quickly dropped.

The Dutch, like the French, had large numbers of both collaborators and members of the underground resistance ... making it difficult at war's end to be sure of which role an individual might have actually played, because the resistance had to appear as collaborators in order to get vital information from – or even just survive – their German occupiers.

Thankfully the Dutch royal family and parliamentary government had chosen to escape to Great Britain in May of 1940 ... and serve the Allied effort from there for the duration of the war. After the war, the royal family returned to the Netherlands to resume their former roles and a ministry was formed from among the London Dutch ... making the postwar political situation in the Netherlands much less troubled than elsewhere.

But still, economic conditions in the country were terrible ... with little food available. The harsh winter of 1944-1945 ... and German reprisals against the Dutch helping the Allies liberating their land (food and supplies cut off in the lands still under German occupation) did not help matters any. And thus some 50,000 Dutch civilians died of starvation or cold and disease that winter.

Even with the end of the war, deep rationing was required ... and the Dutch were encouraged to emigrate – some half million going mostly to

---

*For instance, the Germans had literally leveled Rotterdam to the ground in their attack on the city in May of 1940 ... and had required some half million men to work as forced-labor in German factories. Also the Germans had wiped out whole villages in reprisal against actions undertaken by the Dutch Resistance.

Canada, Australia and New Zealand.

The Catholic People's Party directed the government (1946-1948) in coalition with the Socialist Labor Party ... undertaking the challenge of getting the Dutch economy back up and running – and the Dutch East Indies back under Dutch control* ... both of them almost impossible tasks.

Belgium. Belgium had laid across Germany's path in its effort to conquer France ... and Belgium had paid a huge price. Likewise, Belgium lay across the Allied path on its way to the conquest of Nazi Germany ... and again paid a huge price for that.

Belgium also suffered from the fact that many Belgians collaborated with their Nazi occupiers, whereas others were very active in Belgium's resistance movement. Tragically, this collaboration/resistance dualism tended somewhat (though not exactly) to follow Belgium's ethnic dualism – long-dividing the country along north (Dutch-speaking Flanders) and south (French-speaking Wallonia) lines.

But the Germans had been very oppressive to both groups ... taxing the Belgians for German war operations to a point that very little was left for Belgium's maintenance itself. Also some 375,000 Belgians worked in German factories ... half that number having signed up for such work and half being conscripted after the 1941 conscription order.

Of course Allied bombs made no distinction as to German workers and conscripted foreign workers ... and many Belgians died as a result. Also Allied bombing of strategic sites in Belgium created unintended civilian casualties (as it did also in France and the Netherlands).

Thus, coming out of the war, Belgium had some major issues to face. Not only did the country have to deal with the problems of hunger, homelessness and unemployment, it again had to deal with those cultural/ linguistic sensitivities dividing the north and south of Belgium ... made worse by the question as to what to do about Belgian King Leopold III.

Leopold had defied his government's demands to take his government to London, but instead remained in Belgium to continue to lead his military. Ultimately, there was no way he and his army could hold off the Germans and he and his army were forced to surrender. At that point his government fled to London ... and Leopold came under house arrest at his royal palace.

To many Belgians (and others, including Churchill), Leopold's behavior seemed to be a cowardly – as well as unconstitutional – act (defying the will of his government). This was especially so when compared to the

---

*With the surrender of the Japanese government in August of 1945, the Japanese military authorities in the Dutch East Indies helped to organize an anti-Dutch Javanese independence movement led by Sukarno ... as simply a piece of final reprisal against their European enemies.

continuing anti-German inspiration offered by the Dutch royal family from their position in London.

However, Leopold actually used whatever influence he still commanded to get Hitler to back off from his plans to deport a half-million women and children to work in German munitions factories. He also visited Hitler to plead for the freeing of Belgian prisoners of war.

After the war there was a huge dispute within Belgium as to whether or not to continue with Leopold as king. Leopold and his young family went into exile in Switzerland … while the debate over his rightful status continued. Clearly, the Flemings wanted him back, and the Walloons wanted him gone. Finally the matter was submitted to a national referendum in 1950, Leopold then narrowly being confirmed in his role by a 57% favorable vote. But that vote was divided, 70% of the Flemings in favor and only 42% of the Walloons willing to see him resume his royal role.

On returning to Belgium in July of 1950, he was met by a huge general strike, with three people killed and the country looking as if it were moving to some kind of civil war. Thus in August – to spare the country from further turmoil – Leopold announced his decision to step down and have his son Baudouin replace him the coming July (1951). Belgium could now move on to other matters.

Denmark. Denmark, recognizing its own vulnerability (no land barriers between itself and Germany) had agreed to Hitler's offer of a non-aggression pact in 1939 … and then tried to remain as neutral as possible when war finally broke out. Thus Danish resistance was slight when the Germans took possession of the country in order to open a German path to a resistant Norway.

At this point, the British – deeply concerned about the status of the North Atlantic – took control of the Danish colony of Iceland (1940) … ultimately sparking the decision of Iceland to declare its independence in 1944.

At first, Hitler allowed King Christian X and the Danish parliament (its Folketing) to continue in power … at least partially so – as the Danish Communist Party was expelled when Hitler opened his war with Russia in 1941. And the Danish police mostly remained a national force … although some 2,000 police who resisted Nazi oversight were sent off to concentration camps.

By 1943, the Danish government was tired of the game … and simply resigned, with the Germans then taking over the Danish government themselves.

At about this same time Denmark was able secretly to send most of its 7,800 Jews to safety in Sweden … where neutrality in the war was seriously upheld.

Ultimately, Denmark was spared the destruction that hit so much of Europe ... and found the postwar period to be more or less a continuation of things. But therefore Denmark appeared to be a hopeful place of refuge for thousands of German DPs who flooded Denmark at the war's end. But a huge death rate accompanied those who arrived very weak and sick – over 13,000 dying ... of whom more than a half were children under five.

Sweden. Sweden remained "neutral" during the war ... preserving that neutrality from Hitlerian ambitions by selling precious iron ore to German steel plants during the war. That was a matter of great importance to Germany.

Sweden did help save its image after the war by its help in receiving Jewish refugees from Denmark and Norway during the war ... although the numbers involved were relatively small in comparison to the larger count of European Jews finding themselves in deep danger.

Unfortunately also for its standing, officially it offered rather small support to its neighboring Finland (actually once a part of Sweden itself) in the Finns' attempt to ward off the attack by Soviet Russians in 1939. Sweden did send military supplies to the Finns ... and some 8,000 Swedes took it upon themselves to join the fight on the Finnish side. And then it did take in some 70,000 Finnish children attempting to escape Soviet control during the war years.

Towards the end of the war, its "neutrality" began to swing to the Allied side in the way it allowed Norwegians to receive military training in its country and how it allowed American planes to use Swedish air bases to attack German positions in Norway (early-1944 and after).

Norway. Norway was another matter ... because the Norwegians tried very, very hard to hold back the assaulting Germans. And even when the Germans were able to position themselves at strategic points in and around Norway, the Norwegians continued to conduct underground warfare against their occupiers. It was savage at times.

Worse, Norway was theoretically controlled by a collaborationist government, headed by Vidkun Quisling, a government that the Norwegians would come to hate deeply. Quisling and his "Quislings" (now a term of contempt for such traitors) cooperated actively with the Fascists ... including sending Norwegian Jews to German death camps.

There existed also a Norwegian government-in-exile (Socialist or Laborite), plus the royal family of King Haakon VII, all located in London. Thus those hostile to the Quisling regime had something to rally around.

At war's end Quisling and the "Quislings" would be tried and sentenced

... many to death (such as Quisling himself).

And the Socialist character of the returned government naturally inclined it towards a social program of government ownership of Norway's vast natural resources ... plus a commitment to cradle-to-grave governmental care ... making Norway a leader in this kind of social policy.

Spain. Spain stayed neutral during World War Two ... and Hitler was willing to keep things that way for the duration of the war – especially as Spanish dictator Francisco Franco diplomatically had strong pro-Hitler sentiments. The Nazis and Mussolini's Fascists had, after all, helped Franco's own rise to power.

But Franco was no fool, and made it clear that Spain would not allow any expansion of Hitler's Reich into Spanish territory. Franco also knew that any actual move in support of Germany would bring British reprisals ... especially coming from British-held Gibraltar – Gibraltar considered a matter of absolute necessity to the British Empire. Spain was just recovering from its violent civil war (1936-1939), and Franco knew that Spain was thus in no position to take on the British. Also, the threat of the withholding of American oil sales if Franco betrayed his "neutrality" was a sobering matter to Franco.

He did however help the Germans to the extent that he sent a full division of his troops to help Germany fight Soviet Russia when fighting broke out between those two powers in 1941. But he made it clear that they were to be used only to fight Communist Russia ... and nobody else.

But as the war advanced – particularly after the Germans and Italians were defeated in North Africa in mid-1942 – Franco began to shift his "neutrality" to the Allied side ... at least to the extent of ending further aid to Germany's cause.

But he ultimately paid a price for his "neutrality" ... at first not being allowed to join the pro-Allied United Nations. Indeed, Spain underwent diplomatic isolation ... at least until the mid-1950s, when the Cold War was running quite strongly and Franco's anti-Communism appeared more appealing to an anti-Communist West.

✳ ✳ ✳

STALIN TIGHTENS HIS GRIP ON A SOVIET-CONTROLLED EAST

Soviet Russia's quest for security. For Soviet Russia's Stalin, the matter of what was to happen after Germany was defeated was quite simple. The Soviet Red Army was in occupation of nearly all of Eastern Europe – offering him and his people a sense of security that they had never felt since Russia began opening up to Western culture in the 1500s. There was no way, despite the promises he made to hold free elections throughout Eastern Europe, that Stalin (who was massively paranoid anyway) was going to allow any but the most Moscow-dependent (even Stalin-dependent) regimes to be "elected" to high office in those countries that his Red Army now controlled. In one country after another, Stalinist "puppets" would appear at the head of each of the new governments of Eastern Europe.

Poland. World War Two changed Poland deeply. Prior to the war, Poland was a rather tolerant, multi-cultural society – with one third of its population being non-Polish minorities. But the war changed all that. The country lost the eastern half of its territory to the Soviet Union, never to recover that land ... ever. It also lost an enormous portion of its population during the war. Then after the war it was expanded ... but only westward into German lands – leaving the Germans to decide what they wanted to do now that they were living in "Poland." Nearly all fled. But this opened up property to Poles who wanted to leave the Russianized East ... which about 2 million did (millions more to do so in later years). And with the decision of the large Jewish population that survived the Holocaust to head off to Palestine, this left (Catholic) Poland now for the first time with a largely ethnically homogenous population.

With much of its active population and the country's physical infrastructure destroyed (including its beautiful architectural heritage: for instance, 80% of Warsaw was destroyed) – and with Soviet troops occupying the country – Poland found itself in deep trouble at war's end.

Actually, Stalin had to do some rebuilding of Poland himself ... because, in his extensive paranoia-inspired purges in 1938 of the Communist ranks under him, he nearly destroyed the Polish Communist Party – when 5,000 Polish Communists were brought to Russia and killed there. Thus in 1942 he supported the rebuilding of a new Polish Workers' Party, under the leadership of Władysław Gomułka (who survived Stalin's purges because he was in prison at the time) ... although Gomulka, understandably, was a bit wary of Stalin's hand in Polish affairs.

Another problem was that in the first days of post-war Poland, Stalin's Polish Communists had very little appeal within the larger population. But at the same time, the London Poles suffered from a bad image as politicians who had earlier "failed" their people ... although there was little they could have done against the Hitler-Stalin program.

In any case, the Polish Workers' Party was given key positions in the (appointed rather than elected) post-war Polish Provisional Government of National Unity ... which the party used to begin the buildup of the Communist position in Poland. Also, tens of thousands of the members of the Polish resistance were arrested and sent off to Soviet prisons by the occupying Soviet authorities ... for their "collaboration" with the Nazis ... the most flagrant of lies – but the excuse that was offered anyway in order to further undercut any serious opposition to the Communist political buildup in Poland. By 1946, all Polish conservative parties had been outlawed.

In 1947, Poland had its first election under its new constitution ... with an astounding victory of the Polish Workers' Party. According to Stalin, the Communists had won 80% of the vote. America, Britain and France protested these obviously inflated results (the actual count would never be known). But there was little they could do about matters. With that, Poland officially came under Communist (thus Stalinist) control.

Ultimately, a widely popular social program of family and worker support was put in place. But as for the people having any say in how Poland was to be governed ... in that they had no say. But that was hardly a new thing ... for actual democracy had very little to do with the way much of Europe had been governed, at least until very recently – and even then when it finally did come into "democracy," it did so only on a very limited basis. So Communist authoritarianism was simply business-as-usual in Poland.

Romania. When war broke out in 1939, the country – under King Carol II – declared its neutrality ... not realizing that the Hitler-Stalin treaty had already designated the area as belonging to the Soviet sphere of control. With France's fall, Romania no longer had a protector ... and its land was carved up – with half of the country going either to Hungary or the Soviet Union and a small portion to Bulgaria.

This in turn stirred the ultra-conservative Iron Guard to action ... resulting in a bloody civil war, plus huge attacks against Romania's Jewish population[*] ... and the forced abdication of King Carol (his son Michael replaced him) and his exile.

From this point on, Romania moved towards a strong pro-Axis position ... making it official in November (1940). And in 1941, the Romanians sent a large number of their own troops – ultimately 1.2 million troops – to join Hitler in his assault on the Soviet Union ... all the way to Stalingrad. At this point, Romania underwent intense Allied bombing – its vital oil fields at Ploiesti being a particular target.

Then when the Soviets swung through Romania in their counter-assault against Germany, King Michael forced Romania to switch sides and join the Allies (August 1944). But still, the Soviets would cart off some

---

[*]Estimates are that between 300,000 and 400,000 Romanian Jews were murdered or died under orders of the Romanian authorities in the course of the war.

130,000 Romanian soldiers to Russian prison camps. Few would survive.

After the war, Romania followed lines very similar to Poland's. An agreement to hold elections for a new Romanian government was supposedly confirmed at both Yalta and Potsdam in 1945. But with Soviet troops occupying Romania, the outcome of any election was a foregone conclusion.

At war's end, Romanians were highly supportive of the National Peasants Party; the Romanian Communists were merely a tiny group. The National Peasants wanted national elections as early as 1944. But Soviet administrators blocked that move, insisting instead on the inclusion of more Communists in the Romanian government. Then when King Michael scheduled national elections for February 1945, contending sides came out to contest each other in the streets of Bucharest, prompting the Soviets to move Russian tanks into the capital ... and insist that the king appoint Communist Petru Groza as prime minister and postpone elections. The king had no choice but to comply.

Meanwhile, from that point on and step by step, the country was brought under total Communist control. Finally, in November of 1946, Romania was "ready" to hold national elections ... which went unsurprisingly 90% in support of the Communists – the National Peasants gaining less than 7% of the seats.

Now securely in power, the Communists undertook land reform, expropriating huge amounts of farmland, then distributing this as small landholdings to some 800,000 peasants – in order to secure their support. Then in mid-1947, the Romanian Communists began their program of eliminating all opposition to their rule ... filling the prisons and work camps with such individuals. And King Michael was forced to abdicate that December. Romania was now a fully-Communist dictatorship.

Bulgaria. During the war, Bulgaria had followed a very cautious path – in part because while the government of Tsar Boris III was pro-German (allowing German troops to pass through Bulgaria to take on the Greeks ... for which Bulgaria received the highly coveted lands of Thrace along the Aegean Sea), while the general population tended to be pro-Russian ... at least once the war broke out between these two powers in 1941. But Boris's death in 1943 and the advance of Russia against Germany at that time threw confusion into the Bulgarian government and society. This was resolved the following year when the Fatherland Front (mostly Communist in membership) took control, ended the monarchy, executed thousands of political enemies ... and brought Bulgaria into alliance with the Allies. Consequently, other than once again losing the coastal lands of the Aegean Sea, Bulgaria suffered no other post-war loss.

The Bulgarians then moved to being a one-party (Communist) people's republic under Georgi Dimitrov (1946-1949) – which lined itself up closely with Stalin ... and took on a very oppressive political character.

Yugoslavia. At war's end, Tito's Partisans took control of all of Yugoslavia ... including the region of Trieste (land claimed by the Italians). But Stalin, not wanting to strain relations with his allies, forced him to give Trieste over to the Italians.   That November (1945), Yugoslav national elections were held, in which Tito's Communists were the only ones on the ballot ... which led inevitably to the end of the monarchy and the establishment of the Federal People's Republic of Yugoslavia (six separate republics) ... shaped and run along lines similar to Soviet Russia's.

Tito then turned his attention southward ... first towards Albania (simply forming a close alliance with fellow-Communist Albania) and then beginning an assault on royalist Greece ... with the intention at least of turning Greece into a fellow Communist society. But here Tito would run into serious opposition from Truman's America.

Greece. Hitler's troops had taken control of Greece in April of 1941 ... in part to give muscle to Mussolini's unsuccessful efforts undertaken since October of 1940 to bring Greece under his control. This in turn had sparked a huge Greek Resistance Movement – the EAM, which opposed fiercely the Greek puppet government set up by the Italians and Germans. But the huge Communist element in the EAM (the KKE) also refused to cooperate with King George II's government-in-exile based in Egypt. This in turn led to a deep division within the EAM ... which evolved into a Greek civil war among the Greeks themselves – especially after the retreat from Greece by the Germans in October 1944. Who would now control a postwar Greece: the Communists or the Royalists?

The British did what they could to support the Royalist government, a government recognized internationally after the 1946 elections – elections which the Communists (the KKE) had boycotted, thus resulting in a resounding Royalist victory. But this outcome the KKE refused to accept. Thus the Greek civil war continued ... with Yugoslavia's Tito supporting the KKE (Stalin actually not happy about Tito's involvement) – and Truman's America taking over from an exhausted Britain the support of the Royalist government in 1947.

Hungary. Hungary had been an Axis ally from the start of the war (even sending a half million Jews off to German concentration camps) ... until German losses in the war caused the Hungarian government secretly to try to switch sides. However, the Germans learned of this and took direct control over Horthy's government in March of 1944.

But the Russians hit Hungary hard in late 1944, with the capital Budapest surrendering to the Russians in February of 1945.

With the end of the war, and with the Soviet Red Army in full control of the country, huge transfers in population took place: 200,000 Hungarians coming from Czechoslovakia, 70,000 Slovakians in turn leaving Hungary, and over 200,000 Germans expelled from Hungary.

The monarchy was terminated (vacant anyway since 1918) and a Second Hungarian Republic instituted in its place ... dominated by the Independent Smallholders' Party – brought to power by a huge victory in the 1945 elections.   But Stalin insisted that the Communists be given key positions on the Cabinet ... including Mátyás Rákosi as vice-premier and László Rajk as minister of the interior (responsible for the nation's police). Thus step by step, political opponents were eliminated ... and then new elections held (1947) – with the Communists emerging officially as the largest Hungarian party.

Czechoslovakia. With Hitler's seizure of all of Czechoslovakia in March of 1939, the country became officially a "German protectorate." Naturally a resistance movement developed – carefully directed from London by the Czech president Edvard Beneš and Czech military officers. German reprisals were extremely harsh – against Jews of course, nearly all of whom were murdered – and then against the organized resistance movement (ÚVOD), particularly after the Nazi "protector" Reinhard Heydrich was assassinated in May of 1942. The German response was not only to completely level two Czech towns but to make a supreme effort to track down and destroy all members of ÚVOD ... which the Germans basically succeeded in doing.

But Partisan activity continued on an unorganized and local basis – Czechs attacking trains, tracks, bridges, etc., in order to disrupt German troop movements.

Then (May 5-8 1945), with the Russians moving in on their country, the Czechs conducted a massive and very bloody uprising, finally getting the Germans to agree to withdraw from Prague (actually, the Germans had just surrendered to the Allies in Berlin) ... leaving the city in Czech hands prior to the arrival of the Russians on the 9th.

Ultimately however, it would be the Russians who would be depicted (by the Czech Communists) as their country's true liberators. The Westerners would be depicted as indifferent to the welfare of the Czech nation.* This political imagery would play big in the country's political development over

---

*Churchill wanted American troops, already in Czechoslovakia, to be the ones to liberate Prague. But Stalin insisted that his troops should be the liberators. And Eisenhower, wanting to keep American losses to a minimum and not wanting to antagonize Stalin, agreed to hold up Patton's advance and let the Russians take the city ... a huge political mistake.

the coming years.

But more immediately, it would give the Communists (the KSČ, under the leadership of Klement Gottwald) 38% of the vote in the 1946 elections … making it the largest party in the country. Consequently, the KSČ was, for the time being, confident enough in its own position that it was willing to work cooperatively with other Czech political parties (just like the Communist Parties of France and Italy). But eventually (1948) the KSČ would make its move to bring the country under full Communist mastery.

Austria. Now part of Germany after Hitler's Anschluss, Austria behaved exactly the same way as Germany in its politics, Austrians contributing important personnel to the running of the Third Reich (including Hitler himself), producing vast amounts of the war material Germany needed to fight the war (Austria was a bit beyond the reach of many of the Allied bombers) … and destroying the world of the Austrian Jews every way possible (and providing an extremely high percentage of the guards at the Nazi concentration camps).

But that all changed with the advance of the Soviet Red Army (and Romanian Army) on Austria from the East (mid-March to mid-April 1945) and its capture of Vienna.

At the same time, former Austrian chancellor (1918-1920), Karl Renner, was instructed by Stalin to form a provisional government (there was no government-in-exile to deal with) … with a third of his cabinet being Communists – including, of course, the position of Minister of the Interior. Stalin's Western Allies, who had not been consulted on this matter, at first were unwilling to recognize Renner's government (he had, after all, worked with the Nazis during the war).

But eventually Austria, including its capital Vienna, was placed under a joint commission of US, British, French and Russian military authorities … and in October (1945) the Renner government was recognized by all parties. Renner would then govern as Austrian President until his death in 1950 ... and Austria would remain under joint Allied occupation until 1955. But this at least kept Austria from becoming a Soviet satellite state.

✳ ✳ ✳

**THE ASIAN EAST MOVES AWAY
FROM ITS DEPENDENCE ON THE WEST**

America's "anti-imperialism"

America could be irritating to its allies at times. Something of the old

Wilsonian Idealism lingered on in America when it came to the idea of "making the world safe for democracy." America had always been uneasy about its European allies' empires in Asia and Africa. Yet at the same time, America never admitted that it had a "sphere of influence" in Latin America (and elsewhere) that often did not operate much differently than did the European Afro-Asian empires!

The Philippines. The classic example of this is the Philippines … taken from Spain by the Americans in the Spanish-American War (1898) and then placed under American "protection" … to the astonishment and anger of the Filipinos who had believed that American involvement in that war was designed solely to bring about Philippine independence … not dependence. Thus a new and quite ugly war broke out, Filipinos now against their American "liberators."

This finally embarrassed America enough that it made some promises to bring the Philippines – in stages – to full independence.

The outbreak of World War Two interrupted the final move of America to bring the Philippines to full independence. But with the end of the war – and with great fanfare – the Americans finally took down the American flag in Manila (July 4, 1946) and raised in its place the Philippine national flag … formally ending the status of the Philippines as some kind of American dependency.

And the Americans were loud in announcing how this move to national independence (and supposedly thus – automatically – also to full "democracy") of the Philippines was to be a model to all … friend and former foe alike. A new era was upon the world. President Wilson's earlier "universal right of self-determination" was now the new norm that would prevail everywhere … as the sure and certain guarantee that this time around, a true and lasting (eternal even?) peace and brotherhood for all peoples of the world was about to finally take place. Thus the world needed to get on board with the American train heading to such global glory.

The political Idealism of the new American superpower. Most sadly, as a new global superpower that the Western world would look to for its protection from rising aggressions coming from the Stalinist East, the ability of Americans to disregard the hard political lessons of their nation's own rise to power was (and still is) truly alarming. Idealistic Americans conveniently forgot about their own spread across the North American continent – brutally driving Indians tribes from their lands in order to make room for incoming European settlers (also forgetting the brutality of the "gentle" Indians themselves in their own fight to hang onto those same lands). These Americans conveniently forgot the cost in human lives of the war in their own country over the matter of ending slavery in America once and for all. And somehow they once again believed that the recent horrific spilling of blood in Europe and Asia was some kind of final price to be paid – for a peace that would never again require such a cost to maintain.

At the same time, they chose to see themselves and their country in its rise to prominence simply as a result of the wonderful "democratic" character of the American people … a proper moral – and certainly political – example for the other peoples and nations of the world to follow.

In short, to the thinking of the Americans – with a whole new postwar world unfolding before them – the world had, once again, the opportunity (which it had squandered at the end of World War One) to set a course that would finally bring truly-lasting global peace.

But that would require their European friends, the British, French, Dutch, Portuguese, Belgians, etc., to close down their empires in order to give the remaining oppressed people of the world the right to come to their own self-determination (self-government) as independent – and thus naturally also a democratic and peace-loving – people. There was no other path to world peace.

Gandhi's India

Atlee as Gandhi's most important ally. Actually, Gandhi had an ally in the British government itself, one that took control in London in the days immediately after the Nazi political collapse in Europe … namely the new Labour government led by Clement Atlee. Atlee understood himself to be in power solely to represent the working classes of Great Britain … and little beyond that. He had no interest in supporting the larger world of the British Empire. In fact, as already noted, he held the firm belief that it was the Empire itself that had served to keep the British worker in poverty … as Indian labor could always be counted on as being much cheaper for capitalism to find its profits. Thus to Atlee's thinking, the best thing Britain could do was to send India on its way … as soon as possible. Thus Gandhi's "Quit India" program had an invaluable ally at the very heart of Britain itself.

Major difficulties with Gandhi's Indian nationalist dream. A major problem, as also already noted, existed in the fact that India was not actually a nation at all, but a European-sized subcontinent made up of hundreds of long-standing states, large and small, ones that Britain had managed to bring together as a single political unit. In eliminating that British-enforced unity, a huge problem of different languages, different religions, and long-standing local rivalries would be brought forward … violently.

Certainly Gandhi was aware of this potential for trouble ... horrible trouble. But, like all such political "saviors," he somehow believed that he had the charismatic power to keep his India unified and moving forward once the British were out of the picture.

In any case, the problems hit just as soon as there was some indication that the British were indeed going to Quit India. Most importantly, there were numerous Muslim communities located here and there around the Indian subcontinent ... Muslim communities that were concerned about what would happen to them in coming under the mastery of the very symbol of traditional Hinduism, Gandhi.

The British had been rather willing to let the various religious traditions of the Indians continue as before ... not something that the Muslims expected to continue once the British departed. Thus they immediately pressed the British for guarantees that they could go their own Muslim way with the British departure. In short, they wanted separate Muslim states (or state) of their own to be set up – quite apart from Gandhi's India.

But how that was to happen was not exactly clear. Not only were there distinct Muslim states located here and there in both the East and the West of India, but Hindus and Muslims were to be found in some kind of combination mostly across all of India. Thus to set up a separate Muslim State – which the Muslim were calling "Pakistan"* – was not going to be an easy matter ... especially with Gandhi deeply opposed to the idea.

And what about the large community of Sikhs ... found mostly in the also highly Muslim world of the Indian northwest ... Sikhs who once had a huge empire reaching across northern India and southern Afghanistan? Where did they belong in the midst of any Hindu-Muslim division of British India?

But the British were quickly losing interest in resolving these difficult questions ... being simply in a hurry to get out of the matter as soon as possible. Thus British Lord Mountbatten (a member of the British royal family and Viceroy of India) was given instructions by Atlee's government to prepare India for independence by at least 1948 ... but preferably sooner if possible. Thus in June of 1947, Mountbatten pushed representatives of the various Indian communities (Gandhi did not participate – being adamantly opposed to any division of his India) to agree to accept various state boundaries ... for the British would be soon departing (August 15 of that same year).

Seeing this division headed their way, very quickly India became the

---

*Part of the name came from *istan* meaning place or land; Pak has a dual source as both the Urdu word for pure (thus Land of the Pure) or simply the acronym for the northeast region of Punjab, Afghanistan and Kashmir ... or cleverly, both.

scene of millions* of Indians scurrying to relocate themselves to one or another community, according to their religious identities ... with the Sikhs having no place in particular designated for them. Tragically, hundreds of thousands[†] would die in the chaos that accompanied this mass movement.

Gandhi, not understanding the forces he had unleashed, tried to bring down the level of hatred involved in this new dynamic by going into another one of his fasts (merely five days, however) – which had been able previously to redirect British policies ... but which had absolutely no impact whatsoever on the present chaos.

Gandhi is assassinated. Then in early 1948, with popular passions still running hot, Gandhi himself was gunned down by a Hindu fanatic, Nathuram Godse, a Brahmin who was embittered by Gandhi's toleration of Muslims ... plus his own social slippage due to personal business failures and the general loss of Brahmin caste privilege under the impact of the modern world.

Actually, it was merciful that it was a Hindu who gunned Gandhi down, for had it been a Muslim, the violence would have been explosive in the extreme.

But actually Gandhi's removal from the scene did India something of a favor ... for not only did it sober up the extremists a bit, it brought Jawaharlal Nehru forward as India's new leader ... someone ultimately dedicated to the idea of moving India forward into the rising industrial age – and not forcing it back into Gandhi's highly romanticized agrarian past – an issue that would soon have divided India into two strongly opposing pro-Gandhi and pro-Nehru parties. And it certainly spared India from the economic catastrophe (mass starvation) that would have occurred if Gandhi had succeeded in moving India in his direction.

In any case, as it turned out, India would continue under the guidance of Nehru until his death in 1964 ... and then under members of his family after that date.

But as it also turned out, it would create a vicious rivalry between Hindu India and the two Muslim Pakistans (East and West) existing on both sides of India ... a rivalry that produced numerous wars – and the decision of both India and Pakistan to go nuclear in their military programming ... a program prompted by this same Indian-Pakistani rivalry.

The Dutch lose Indonesia

---

*The United Nations estimated that 14 million people were displaced during this migration.

[†]The exact death count is hard to calculate. The numbers vary from a low of 200,000 to a high of 2 million.

On the other hand, the Dutch were not as ready to give up their overseas holdings in Asia as had been the British. For the Dutch, their investment in their extensive holdings in Southeast Asia had been built up over a period of three centuries ... much longer than even the British involvement in India. And over that long period a very deep cultural, economic, and political link between the Netherlands and the Dutch East Indies had served both societies quite well ... because the Dutch had proven very effective in keeping a quite tight control over the entire region.

And the Dutch quite naturally felt that, with the war over, they would simply put that same relationship back in place.

Of course the three-and-a-half-year period of Japanese occupation of that same region had done much (quite purposely on the part of the Japanese) to undermine that linkage between the Netherlands and its Asian colony. And the Japanese, even in defeat, worked very hard in their last days of occupation of the region to leave behind as much of an anti-Western social legacy there as possible. Indeed, still in occupation of the region after the formal surrender of Japan to the Allies, the Japanese supported strongly the efforts of a local nationalist leader, Sukarno (active even before the start of the war in an anti-Dutch independence movement) and his close associate Mohammad Hatta, to establish an independent "Indonesia" ... Sukarno declaring himself president of the new republic and Hatta vice president. Furthermore, the weapons that the Japanese had to turn over to their victors went mostly to arm the Indonesian nationalists.

But the situation – for both Sukarno and the Dutch – was a very complicated matter ... because the region was hardly a unified social entity. Languages across the region varied, as did the religion ... though mostly it was Muslim in character. But many of the islands making up the region were Christian. And there was a huge Chinese sector of the population. And of course there were many European Dutch who had long made the area their home. Thus the region quickly became the scene of frequent ethnic massacres.[*]

And the Dutch, whose homeland had been demolished by the Germans, found themselves absorbed back in Europe with rebuilding their society. Indeed, since the war's end, the Dutch had been forced to rely on the rather limited support of British Indian and Commonwealth troops in their East Indies colony ... largely sent to the region just to oversee the Japanese surrender. And thus it was not until early 1946 that the Dutch were finally

---

[*]Tens of thousands were reported killed or missing in the first year after the war alone. Several thousand Europeans were known specifically to have been tortured and executed and as many as 20,000 of mixed European-Asian ancestry were killed or went missing (those missing probably suffering a similar fate, though most likely their bodies were thrown into the sea; some mass graves were later uncovered).

able to send their own troops to their colony in an effort to bring things back under full Dutch control.

Actually, by 1947, the Dutch seemed to be largely succeeding in their effort, having brought the major islands of Java and Sumatra back under Dutch control. But they found that local resistance was now being replaced by international resistance … in particular in the New United Nations, where Sukarno and his Republicans seemed to be finding a lot of support. Australia, newly independent India, the Soviet Union – and even America – were tending to side with Sukarno and the Republicans. Finally, the Dutch bent to U.N. efforts to secure a cease-fire between the two parties, put in place largely along the lines where one or the other party seemed to be in control.

But Sukarno, enjoying rather significant international support (and growing support at home), was not really interested in respecting the cease-fire … and continued to press forward his nationalist movement.

The Dutch, seeing themselves facing an increasingly desperate situation, thus decided in late 1948 to make a huge push to put themselves back in command – regaining much of the urban regions in the process, though finding themselves stalled in the countryside … and worse, coming under ever-stronger opposition in the UN. At this point, America not only cut off all Marshall Plan aid designated for the rebuilding of the Dutch colony, but threatened to do the same for the rebuilding of the Netherlands itself. Americans were highly incensed by the idea that probably half of the budget designated for the rebuilding of Indonesia was going to support Dutch military efforts in the region. That was imperialism … and there was no way that America would ever support such a program.

By the summer of 1949, the Dutch were ready to quit. They ultimately (November 1949) worked out an agreement recognizing an independent Indonesia, under the presidency of Sukarno … the man who would continue to rule the Republic of Indonesia as a dictator – all the way up until 1967, when he was forced out of power by another Indonesian strongman, Suharto – who would then rule Indonesia for the next thirty-one years.

So maybe European imperialism got put aside in Indonesia through this effort of America and others. But that move hardly led automatically to the replacement of imperialism with national democracy. But America largely ignored events in Indonesia in the days and years that followed … thus learning nothing from the experience. And the Netherlands – no longer a global power – had to decide how then to move into a deeply reshaped future.

Troubles in French Indo-China

Also naturally, the French had the full intention after the war, as had the Dutch, to return to their holdings in Southeast Asia ... to French Indo-China.* But there too the European colonials found independence movements well underway ... helped greatly by Japan's encouragement – but also by the weak hand there of the wartime French Vichy government ... which had simply let the Japanese take over their colony during the war.

But even before the end of the war, Roosevelt had made it quite clear to the French that America would oppose any effort of the French to retake their colony in Indochina. In addition to the fact that America was deeply opposed to such imperialism, the Roosevelt government had been working closely with the anti-Japanese resistance – the Viet Minh, made up of Vietnamese nationalists led by the Communist Hồ Chí Minh. This group was expecting international recognition of the region's independence from the French. And America was willing to accord them just such recognition.

Thus just as the Japanese issued their formal surrender (September 1945) – and also turning their weapons over to the Viet Minh – Ho declared the independence of a Vietnamese Republic. He quickly took control of the city of Hanoi in the North ... just as the French (also assisted by British colonial troops) arrived on the scene to receive the Japanese surrender

At first Hồ hoped that the mutual sufferings of the French and the Vietnamese would incline the French to be sympathetic toward his efforts on behalf of Vietnamese independence. He also placed high hopes in the French Communist Party and their electoral victory back in France as insurance against a resurgent French colonialist impulse.

But negotiations over the summer of 1946 began to reveal to him that the French had no intentions of granting the Vietnamese their independence.

Fighting thus broke out (mostly in Tonkin in the North) not only between the Viet Minh and the French but also between the Viet Minh and the supporters of the young Vietnamese Emperor Bảo Đại – a curious political figure who had served as a Japanese puppet during the war but who now found himself in alliance with the French after the war (willing to serve again as a puppet?).

The fighting was mostly sporadic ...except for the one incident in 1946 in which the French bombed the port city of Haiphong, killing 6,000 citizens and scattering the Viet Minh into the countryside ... making the ability of the French to run down their enemy even more complicated.

In 1949, the French attempted to counter Hồ's nationalist appeal by establishing the Republic of Vietnam – under the Emperor Bảo Đại – as an Associated State within the French Union. They also set up a Vietnamese National Army to support the new regime. Likewise, Laos and Cambodia

---

*Laos and Cambodia, plus the three Vietnamese coastal regions of Tonkin in the north, Annam in the center, and Cochinchina in the south.

were also set up separately as Associated States within the French Union.

But the victory in China of Mao's Communists that same year (1949) encouraged the Viet Minh enormously.   Meanwhile, Truman had been approached for support of the Vietnamese independence movement. But by the late 1940s the idea of supporting any independence movement that might benefit the Communists was now politically taboo in America. Indeed, by the early 1950s, America was now also supporting the other side – that of the French ... as clearly a "Cold War" had set in dividing the world into the "Free" and their opponents, the "Communists." Things now turned very messy in the region.

The Chinese Civil War (1946-1949)

At war's end in 1945, Chiang Kai-shek's government faced a serious problem: the loss of deep esteem in the eyes of the Chinese themselves. The failure of his Nationalist or Kuomintang army to stop the Japanese takeover of the highly urbanized coastal regions of China – and having to rely on foreigners (principally the Americans) and local warlords – were matters of deep shame in the Chinese political honor code. To most Chinese, such failure indicated Chiang's loss of the sacred *Tianming* (Mandate of Heaven), that is, the powers of Heaven that Chinese dynasties traditionally built their moral and thus political foundations on.

Meanwhile Mao and his Communist troops, who had retreated deep into the Chinese rural interior, had carefully avoided serious engagement with the Japanese, merely conducting local hit and run tactics ... thus not tarnishing their reputation. Of course that was of little help to Chiang in his struggles with the Japanese. But Mao knew exactly what he was doing. He had built up his political reputation considerably in the world of rural China ... at the same time that Chiang had lost that reputation in the world of urban China – formerly Chiang's power base.

Also, the huge inflation that hit China at the war's end destroyed the life savings of that same urban middle class ... making Chang's inability to bring it under control – as any political leader was expected to do – weaken even further his all-important urban support.

Then too, Mao promised his peasant followers that, once in power, he would confiscate the large holdings of the Chinese landowners, and distribute their lands to the peasants as their own personal property ... making Mao very popular among rural Chinese.

There were attempts at war's end to bring Mao and Chiang together in some kind of political settlement – especially by U.S. General George Marshall, sent to China for that express purpose. But Chiang hated Mao deeply. And Mao sensed that he had the political future on his side. And

Stalin, although he supposedly supported the Allied-recognized government of Chiang, did the same thing as the Japanese had done in Dutch Indonesia and French Indochina: see that surrendered Japanese weapons fell into the right hands. And for Stalin, that meant Mao ... not Chiang. And having been given occupational rights in the vital province of Manchuria, Stalin turned as much as he could of the area of Manchuria over to Mao.

Meanwhile, the Americans airlifted thousands of Chiang's Nationalist troops into eastern Manchuria to "balance" the picture. But beyond that, there was little that the Americans felt that they could do to improve the situation for Chiang. They were quite aware of how bad things were for Chiang. And choices would have to be made ... and the "Realist" Truman and his advisors* were keenly aware that American interests in European recovery were far greater than those they held for China.

Step by step, China found itself caught in a widening civil war ... with Chiang on the retreat widely across the countryside and Mao continuing to build the size of his army and its holdings of Chinese territory. Then by 1948, Mao was ready to take on urban China, one city after another falling to Mao's Communist troops. In the time period alone running from early December to late January, numerous cities fell to the Communists, including the key city of Beiping (Beijing). And by April, Mao's troops were able to capture the Republic's capital of Nanjing ... forcing Chiang and what was left of his army to retreat south all the way to Canton. From there (and other places) some two million Chinese were able to escape the Chinese mainland and make their way to the island of Taiwan.

On October 1st (1949), Mao announced the creation of the new People's Republic of China ... bringing China fully into a Russian-American Cold War that was well underway by that point. The Soviet Russians would give full support to Mao's China ... whereas America (and its allies) would continue to support Chiang as the only legitimate voice of China – even though his political base was now located at Taipei, the capital of Taiwan.

✳ ✳ ✳

THE ISRAELI-PALESTINIAN QUESTION

The region known variously as Palestine or Israel has long been sacred to three major religions ... religions seldom in agreement about matters – but

---

*Truman's small society of foreign policy advisors was outstanding: besides George Marshall, Dean Acheson, Robert Lovett and George Kennan, the list included Chip Bohlen, Averell Harriman, Paul Nitze, John McCloy and many other highly talented American statesmen. Most of these men served as advisors in some capacity from the Roosevelt Administration in the 1930s all the way to the Johnson Administration in the mid-1960s.

especially about the matter of which of those religions does this vital area belong to. To the Jews, this is their homeland, the place of birth of their very religion. To the Christians, this is where their Lord and Savior Jesus was born, raised, taught, died and was resurrected as the birthing of their Christian religion. And to the Muslims, Jerusalem is the third most holy city in all of Islam ... because (among other things) of the nighttime ride of their founding Prophet Muhammad in and around Jerusalem. And basically, it has been the Muslims (minus the brief period of the crusades) that have been the victors in this debate since the 600s.

But the Great War changed matters ... deeply. When the Ottoman Turks joined Germany in that war, they decided the fate of both Islam's political presiding Ottoman Sultan and its religiously presiding Ottoman Caliph. As losers in that war they lost to both a modern Britain abroad and a modernizing Turkish leader Atatürk at home ... leaving Islam headless – and the Holy Land of Palestine in British hands as its mandated "protector."

Actually (as already noted), problems had already begun to arise a bit earlier when persecuted Jews decided to leave Europe (late 1800s and early 1900s) and head to their holy homeland, "Zion." Thus the Zionist Movement was born.

The Palestinian issue was not, however, a religious matter ... but simply one of property rights ... at least not originally. Something resembling religious toleration had actually long existed in the land. The capital city, Jerusalem, was itself divided into religious quarters, one Jewish, one Muslim, one Christian, and one Armenian (but also Christian). And relations among those groups tended to be friendly ... if not a bit distant.

Most unsurprisingly, immigrants coming from Europe to Palestine found the region fully occupied. The only uninhabited areas where Zionists could possibly settle were basically desert.

True, Zionists did set up numerous small communities (Kibbutzim), sustained by channeling water from the Jordan River – which flowed right through the middle of that desert, from the heights of the mountains in the north to the Dead Sea in the south. But this method could support only small numbers of those trying to settle in Palestine ... and would also drain down the river deeply.

But the Zionists also knew that the peasants working the farmlands of Palestine did not generally own the land. Land-ownership belonged to wealthy families, living not locally – but off in one or another city. So the Zionists used funds to purchase that land from these absentee landlords ... and then remove the Palestinian peasants working the lands in order to make way for Jewish settlers. Needless to say, this stirred up considerable anger ... and the beginning of an ongoing war over the land (much like the one between the Indians and the European settlers in America).

Then during the Great War, the British took it upon themselves to take charge of the region, using that position to get various war support against the Turks ... in exchange, promising British support of the ambitions of one group and then another involved in the Palestinian question. To the Jews, they promised (the 1917 Balfour Declaration) to support the idea of a Jewish homeland somewhere in Palestine ... in exchange for much-needed financial support from the fabulously wealthy Jewish Rothschild banking family of Paris. But they made a similar offer to local Palestinians ... in exchange for their rising up against their former Ottoman Turkish rulers. And they made the same offer to themselves ... in their own desire to expand their British Empire into the coastlands of the Eastern Mediterranean – close to their Suez Canal and the Egyptian government they already had under British wings.

This triple promise only guaranteed that even greater political confusion would follow in the postwar years. The bitterness deepened in Palestine even further in the 1930s when the global Great Depression upset the economies of people everywhere. In 1936, the British had to put down a major Arab revolt against the incoming Jews, leading the Jews to form David Ben-Gurion's Jewish Agency, and the development of a skilled Jewish army, the Haganah ... set up supposedly to help the British put down the revolt. But the British then (1939) put in place a 15,000-person limit to Jewish immigration into British Palestine ... deeply upsetting the Jewish world which was suffering from the intense Nazi persecution of Jews in Europe. But even 15,000 new settlers coming into Palestine annually would mean a somewhat similar number of Palestinians displaced from their homes and lands.

Then World War Two hit ... and much of the movement was blocked by military developments.

But after the war, the situation would become explosive ... on a monumental basis. Opening the Nazi concentration camps put muscle behind the Zionist movement ... that plus the reluctance of others, even those who had themselves suffered under the Nazis, to receive the Jews back to their homes (Poland was highly problematic in this regard). Thus tens of thousands of Jews became determined to reach a place of greater security, a place they could truly call their Jewish homeland.

But the British were caught in the middle ... with not only their Arab friends furious that the British would allow this mass migration (the British were actually doing all they could to slow down the movement) ... and getting shot at now by their wartime allies, the Jewish Haganah – and the Jewish terrorist organizations, Irgun and the Stern Gang (or Lehi). And this came at a time when the British Prime Minister Atlee was doing everything he could to get Britain out of its international commitments ... so that it could focus on problems at home. Thus the decision was finally announced in London (February 1947) that Britain was turning the matter over to the new United Nations … and would be getting out of Palestine as soon as possible.

But the new U.N. found itself in no better of a place than the British in taking on this political challenge. Efforts were made to divide Palestine into distinct Arab and Jewish territories, the foundations for future states. But neither party was willing to give up its goal of holding the entire region … and thus the fighting merely worsened.

At this point Britain announced that it would be leaving the area as of May 14th 1948. This it did … and on that same day the Jews announced the establishment of the Jewish state of Israel. Both Soviet Russia and America were quick to recognize the new government.

But this did not mean the end of the fighting … for all of the Arabs, including those of the surrounding states, refused to recognize the State of Israel. And thus the fighting merely intensified. And it also meant the disregard by the Jews of even the borderlines set out by the U.N. in its proposal to divide Palestine into two states.

Meanwhile Palestinians fled the scenes of battle, especially after the rumor spread rapidly of the massacre of an entire Palestinian village (Deir Yassin) by Jewish terrorists. And the Mediterranean coastal city of Jaffa – supposedly designated by the U.N. plan to be included in the new Palestinian state – was terrorized by Irgun and Lehi* … and the city's Arab population of 70,000 was soon reduced to a mere 4,000. And across the countryside, some 700,000 Arabs that had fled their homes would find themselves blocked by Israeli authorities from returning to their homes – despite a U.N. resolution calling on Israel to allow them to return to their homes. Instead, the refugees would have to take "temporary" residence in UN-run refugee camps … camps which would in fact become permanent homes to a huge Palestinian society unable to take care of itself (these camps were mostly located on desert land).

No soil for farming, no jobs of any kind, no hope at all awaited these lost Palestinians. This was perfect material for a long and lasting Arab-Israeli conflict.

----

*It is interesting to note that the Irgun leader Menachem Begin, who ordered the destruction of the King David Hotel (and 91 lives, including even Jews as well as British and Arabs) would become Israeli Prime Minister in 1977... and ironically become winner of the Nobel Peace Prize in 1979. Also a former Lehi leader Yitzhak Shamir would follow Begin as Israeli Prime Minister in 1983, a man who ordered the assassination in 1944 of the British Minister for Middle East Affairs, Lord Moyne, and in 1948 the United Nations peace negotiator, Swedish Count Bernadotte.

CHAPTER EIGHTEEN

A COLD WAR DEVELOPS

* * *

AN EAST-WEST IDEOLOGICAL DIVIDE BECOMES A "COLD WAR"

Iran

Actually, a deep political-ideological division between Soviet Russia and America got going during the early years of World War Two. During the war, a path that led across Iran from the Persian Gulf to Soviet Azerbaijan allowed Great Britain and America to ship war material to Russia ... to help support the Soviets on the Eastern Front. But this angered deeply the Iranian Shah Pahlavi ... who was a strong supporter of Hitler. Ultimately the problem was solved simply and quickly by the removal from power of the Shah in August of 1941 by the Soviets (largely) and the British. The country was then partitioned between the Soviets and the British ... and the Crown Prince Mohammed Reza Pahlavi was placed on the throne – with the understanding that the Soviet and British occupation would be temporary and would terminate no more than six months after the end of the war. Full sovereignty would be returned to Iran at that point.

But Stalin saw the Soviet position in Iran as highly strategic, offering his country another exit from its locked-in position in northeastern Europe. However, rather than violating directly the terms of the agreement, with the war over and the time of occupation coming to an end, Stalin simply moved to set up a Communist-governed Azerbaijan People's Republic (November 1945) ... independent of Pahlavi Iran – and destined to be placed under Soviet "protection" for the time being ... much the way Arab states found themselves under French (Lebanon and Syria) and British (Iraq, Jordan, and basically Egypt) "protection."

Truman quickly understood how all this was a problem for the Western world ... for this would put the Persian Gulf – through which the vital oil flow coming out of this region that Western Europe depended on – under Soviet control. It would even give the Soviets the ability to move its dominating influence from the Persian Gulf to the Indian Ocean, the West's vital path to India, China and Southeast Asia (and the British dominions Australia and New Zealand).

Truman took the matter to the U.N. Security Council (January 1946) ... where he was hoping that the support of China, Great Britain, France, and other members of the Council would back the Soviets down from this move. Indeed, the Soviets did pull out their military support in March ... with the new Communist Republic ultimately losing to mounting Iranian power that December. Thus Iran regained its lost territory.

But it would be the last time that the Soviets would back down in the face of such a challenge. From that point on, the Soviets would become fabled for their use of the veto power to block further U.N. moves against Soviet interests. But this also meant that the U.N. would now prove useless in providing what formerly Roosevelt had hoped was the grand formula for world peace.

From this point forward, direct diplomacy – state-to-state rather than through the U.N. – would have to be the route for any efforts to resolve the world's conflicts ... which would grow in number and intensity as a "Cold War" deepened.

Churchill's "Iron Curtain" warning (March 1946)

An early warning about this growing East-West problem – and the accompanying danger to world peace – occurred in March of 1946. Churchill, then no longer in political office thanks to the British voters, came to America and then accompanied Truman to Westminster College in Truman's home state of Missouri. Churchill was due to receive an honorary degree from the college ... and deliver what would become one of the world's greatest speeches.

In his acceptance speech, he warned America of a growing danger coming from Stalin's ambitions ... an "Iron Curtain" that was descending on Europe – stretching across central Europe from the Baltic Sea in the North to the Adriatic Sea in the south ... separating democratic Western Europe from a heavily Soviet-controlled Eastern Europe.

In effect, he was appealing to America to take up Britain's old role of "balancer of power" on the European continent ... for a tired Britain was no longer up to the challenge. Americans needed to understand Stalin's broken promises about free elections in Europe as a gauntlet thrown down in challenge at the feet of his former allies. And Americans needed to know that only America was fully equipped to take on that Soviet challenge. America had the power, the kind of power that Stalin respected – the only thing, in fact, that he respected.

And if America did not quickly move to exercise that counter-balancing power, the West (including America) would soon enough find itself involved in yet a third – and far more vicious – world war. Britain would stand with America. But America would have to take the lead.

But a very Idealistic American press at that time responded quite negatively to this speech. They were shocked that Churchill would talk so openly in such a hostile manner about our Russian or Soviet Communist friends.   They still saw the post-war peace in the idealistic terms that Roosevelt himself had laid out for Americans to expect. The press even accused Churchill of "grandstanding" – using his Iron Curtain speech to promote himself so as to gain entrance back into the halls of British power ... exactly the same accusation leveled against Churchill in the 1930s when he was trying to warn Britain of the growing dangers posed by Hitler and his Nazis.

Truman, meanwhile, had to move very cautiously on the matter. He was in full agreement with Churchill in seeing the dangers Stalin's ambitions posed to the West. But he was still viewed as an "accidental president" ... with little regard or support for him coming from a nervous American citizenry. But Truman was not playing the political game of doing whatever was necessary to win greater popular support. As president of the United States, he had a job to do ... and intended to do his best as such.

Early steps in the "containment" of Communism

Truman himself had never any intention of starting up a shooting war with Russia. But soon after his arrival in office in 1945, he had made up his mind to block Stalin's plans to expand his influence much beyond a theoretical line drawn around the Soviet Russian position as it found itself at the war's end in mid-1945 – that is, a political line that Churchill would describe in detail in his Iron Curtain speech. In short, Truman was already planning to "contain" Soviet influence ... as he clearly demonstrated in his response to Stalin's Iranian involvement.

Actually the term for just this policy of "containment" came from a State Department official posted in Kiev, George F. Kennan. He answered a request by the U.S. Treasury Department to explain why the Soviets were unwilling to cooperate with the new World Bank (IBRD) and the International Monetary Fund (IMF). Kennan's response was quite bold ... given the State Department's presumption at that time that the dream of friendship with the Soviets would continue as it had during the war years.

In Kennan's *Long Telegram*, he discussed the Soviet's anti-capitalist mindset – reinforced by Russian nationalist instincts – as the basis of the problem. He also described the dangers facing America and Europe if these very expansive Soviet-Russian instincts were not somehow "contained."

This paper in turn inspired a larger Kennan study (September 1946) of Soviet goals and possible strategies. This was intended for the president's eyes only. But so clear in its analysis and strategic thinking – and useful as a tool to get this understanding out to the American public – that the decision was made to have it published anonymously. Thus – with its author identified only as "X" – it was presented to the larger American world in the prestigious journal, *Foreign Affairs* (July 1947).

So it was that America was step by step led to understand that, although World War Two was over, America could not just "go home" ... but needed to take the lead in helping Europe not fall under Stalin's tyrannical grip (much like what Hitler had just done to Europe and the world) ... and – by responding quickly to this rising challenge coming from the Soviet East – also help the world not fall into yet a Third World War.

Crisis in Greece and Turkey ... and the Truman Doctrine

This awakening was furthered greatly by developments taking place at the eastern end of the Mediterranean. Communists were attempting to take over Greece – which would clearly expand Stalin's Communist realm ... the supposition being that any advance of Communism was automatically an advance of Stalinism, a supposition that not only Americans but also Stalin himself held.

Also ... with Iran no longer a possibility for Russia to break out of its continental isolation, Turkey looked like a possibility for Stalin ... if Turkey would yield to Soviet pressure and surrender its sovereign rights over the Dardanelles passage from the Black Sea to the Aegean Sea and thus the very strategic Mediterranean Sea as well.

In both instances the situation was a bit trickier for Stalin ... for there were no Soviet troops in occupation of either country. He would have to rely on local Communist organizations to do the work for him.

Actually, in the case of Greece, he had the support of the Communist Yugoslav president Marshall Josip Broz Tito ... who was sending his men and finances into neighboring Greece to help the Greek Communists in their effort to overthrow the newly elected (1946) Greek government. There were Communists also in Turkey ... though their position there was weak.

Traditionally, it was Britain that was expected to monitor such developments in the Eastern Mediterranean ... as it had done in the mid-1800s in protecting the Turks from Russian expansion in the Crimean War. And the British were traditionally looked to for help in stabilizing Greek politics when it got unruly. But it was a different Britain now, with Atlee and his Labour Party having taken over the British government.

Truman, however, was quick to take up this Communist challenge directly. On March 12, 1947, he appeared before Congress to request $400 million in American military and economic assistance to combat the takeover of those two countries by agents of coercion. He explained his program as America's determination to see that free peoples everywhere remained free ... and that America would never allow any free country to fall under the power of totalitarian tyranny. "Communism" was not specifically mentioned as the problem – nor were the Soviets or Yugoslavs – though by this time most people clearly understood at whom or at what the program was aimed. Specifically, Truman announced that America would directly aid Greece in its putting down any insurrection aimed at overthrowing the legitimate government of that country ... and would support Turkey in maintaining its military strength - and thus its national sovereignty.

It took two months for the formerly isolationist Republican Party majority in Congress to agree to fund his financial assistance program to Greece and Turkey. But it held back the offer of direct military assistance to either country ... at least for a little while. But the Republican Party was quickly coming around to an internationalist position. And soon American troops were authorized ... as advisors (not warriors) to the Greeks. And the financial-material assistance to the Turkish military improved the Turkish position greatly ... shutting down Stalin's program of intimidation.

This move to take up the traditional role of Britain as balancer and stabilizer of power in the Mediterranean Truman had now made official American policy.   He had established a major post-war principle directing American diplomatic and military programming, a principle that the world came to term "the Truman Doctrine."

America now sees itself involved in a "Cold War."   By 1947, it was beginning slowly to dawn on an increasing number of Americans how right Churchill had been about this growing problem with Stalin's Russia. It was increasingly clear that "Stalinists" now ruled in most of the Eastern European countries behind the "Iron Curtain." The press now began to describe quite readily how these "Iron Curtain" countries had become in effect Soviet "satellite" countries, drawing their political direction entirely from Moscow.

**Serious economic problems – and labor strife -
in post-war Europe**

At first it looked as if the Western European countries coming out of the war would be able to rebuild fairly quickly. With much war damage to be repaired, there would be great need for full employment of the soldiers returning to civilian life. And financing this reconstruction were the war credits still enjoyed by the governments of these countries.

But by the winter of 1946-1947, most of this funding was drying up … with that funding ending up in American hands through the massive purchase of much-needed industrial items from the American factories still in full operation. A huge shortage of dollars needed to continue to purchase those infrastructure items had thus developed

Consequently, the economic rebound collapsed and employers had to reduce workers' wages … and even let go thousands of their workers. Trouble – big trouble – now developed.

In April of 1947 many of the 30,000 French workers at the nationalized Renault plant went on strike … in response to the reduction in the bread rationing decreed by the Paul Ramadier cabinet … and just in general because of the deep Communist involvement in the French workers' world – always ready to blame capitalism as the cause of worker misery. Reacting to the ideological component in this event, Ramadier dismissed the Communists from his cabinet (early May).

Then, although the government was quick to answer some of the workers' wage demands and bring the Renault strike to a close (mid-May), the idea of a general workers' strike itself spread widely across France. Again … the motif was both financial and ideological – with a formerly hesitant French Communist Party now fully behind these strikes … with Stalin also doing what he could to direct this dynamic.

Meanwhile in Italy, Italian premier Alcide De Gasperi, had visited America at the beginning of 1947 … to plead for gentler terms in the treaty formally ending the Allies' war with Italy – and to petition the Americans for serious financial assistance. The $150 million he was authorized increased immensely De Gasperi's standing before the Italian electorate. But it also clearly put him in America's growing anti-Communist camp … made even clearer when Truman responded to the spreading workers' strikes in Europe (and in Italy no less) in May by pressing De Gasperi to remove the Communists from his government … joining the Vatican – which was demanding the same move against the Communists.

The creation of the Marshall Plan

At this point, Europe's central banks had financed all that they could in the effort to rebuild their war-torn economies. In fact many of them stood at the threshold of bankruptcy. Truman, sensing the danger that this posed to what was increasingly coming to be termed "The Free World," knew that it was time to swing substantial American financial support (the American economy in fact was booming at the time) behind these staggering Western governments. Indeed, the European worker's strikes which broke out in May of 1947 – and their obvious Communist (and Stalinist) support and direction behind them – made such countering American financial support an immediate necessity.

Marshall's Harvard speech. Thus in early June of 1947, U.S. Secretary of State George Marshall, at a commencement address at Harvard University, informed the nation (and the world) of the need for America to bring such support to war-torn Europe ... or disaster would result.

> *The truth of the matter is that Europe's requirements for the next three or four years of foreign food and other essential products – principally from America – are so much greater than her present ability to pay that she must have substantial additional help or face economic, social, and political deterioration of a very grave character.*

Marshall did not mention specifically the spread of Communism under these dire conditions ... but few people missed the underlying assumptions about just such a challenge to the Free World. Indeed, the "Marshall Plan" as it was soon entitled,* initially appeared to be no less open to the Soviet World than to the countries of Western Europe. And at first it appeared that countries of the Soviet bloc might be actually participating in the Marshall Plan.

Nonetheless, in July of that year, 16 Western European countries gathered in Paris to discuss the Plan ... and set up the means of international cooperation among their nations required under the Plan. Thus billions of U.S. dollars would be granted to Plan participants, not only to rebuild their respective nations but to provide the impetus for strong economic cooperation ... overseen by the new Organization of European Economic Co-Operation (OEEC). Thus it was that a new European unity movement was birthed.

The Soviets answer with the Cominform and the Molotov Plan. Stalin was quick to respond to this American challenge by setting up his own organization, the Communist Information Bureau or "Cominform," established at a meeting he held in September of 1947 in Poland with leaders of the Communist Parties of both the Soviet "Bloc" (Poland, Hungary, Romania, Bulgaria, Czechoslovakia, and Yugoslavia) and the Western

---

*Truman himself called for the Plan to go under Marshall's name, knowing that Marshall had a much better standing than he did with the frugal Republicans of Congress, who would have to approve the huge spending that the Plan called for.

countries, France and Italy.* Although the purpose of the Cominform was ostensibly only ideological – to help coordinate Communist doctrine and programming across the Communist world – it also had to be economic, to the extent of offering some response to the Marshall Plan ... which was why the meeting was held in the first place.

What specifically evolved along these lines was what would come to be termed the "Molotov Plan." Basically it was a system of trade agreements between Soviet Russia and the Soviet satellite states ... designed to direct economic development in a way that strengthened the ties of the Eastern Bloc nations to the Soviet Union. As far as actually achieving strong economic development (which certainly the Marshall Plan did) the problem remained that economic assistance was easily offset by reparations payments those same nations were required to make to Soviet Russia ... because a number of them had been former allies (willing or not) of Hitler.

America reorganizes its foreign policy instruments with its National Security Act (1947). Recognizing America's heightened responsibilities in global affairs, Truman put together (1946) and Congress approved (July 1947) a proposal to unite the various military branches (army, navy, and army air force) into a single National Military Establishment,[†] headed by a new Secretary of Defense (James Forrestal, 1947-1949). The Act also established a Central Intelligence Agency (CIA), upgrading the Central Intelligence Group set up the previous year ... the new CIA under a Director of Central Intelligence (Roscoe Hillenkoetter, 1947-1950). It also established a National Security Council (NSC), uniting the heads of the various foreign policy agencies (State, CIA, Defense, etc.) in mutual service as foreign policy advisors to the president.

The Communist coup in Czechoslovakia

Czechoslovakia was a Slavic society with industrial ties to the West and ethnic ties to the East. Its economy was a mixture of capitalism and socialism and it possessed a Western-style parliamentary democracy and a solid tradition of popular democracy. At war's end in 1945, not only the Americans but also even the Soviets withdrew their troops from Czechoslovakia. In 1946's national elections, long-time leader Edvard Beneš was elected President.

---

*The Cominform was actually replacing the older Soviet-run Communist International (Comintern) that had been disbanded during the war in 1943 ... in order to improve Soviet relations with its wartime allies in the West.

†Supposedly, the National Military Establishment (NME) was renamed in 1949 as the Department of Defense (DOD) ... because the initials NME sounded like the word "enemy"!

Communist leader Klement Gottwald (whose Communists had won 38 percent of the vote) was asked to form a coalition cabinet (principally with the Social Democrats, who had won an additional 12.8 percent of the vote).

For a while it appeared that Czechoslovakia would be able to enjoy good relations with both the Soviet and the Western world. But in 1947, with America's invitation to all of Europe to receive Marshall Plan aid, troubles began. The Czechoslovak cabinet voted unanimously to meet in Paris to discuss the offer – without first having consulted with Moscow about what their response to the offer should be. This angered Stalin enormously. Receiving the full fury of Stalin's anger, Gottwald backed away from the Marshall Plan. But Stalin's paranoid distrust had now been triggered by this episode. His "tolerant" attitude about an independent (though Communist-led) Czechoslovakia abruptly ended.

To make matters worse, a poll taken of Czech public opinion indicated a drop in Communist popularity due to the economic troubles facing the country. With national elections coming up in May of 1948, Stalin began to fear that Czech politics might move in the direction of a closer relationship with the West - in particular through involvement in the Marshall Plan.

The Communists began to tighten their grip on the country in early 1948 when the Communist Minister of the Interior replaced non-Communist police chiefs with Communists. In turn the non-Communists on the national Cabinet resigned in protest, hoping to force the creation of a new Cabinet. This merely turned up the Communist heat on Czechoslovakia. Armed Communist "Peoples' Militias" staged demonstrations and riots around the country, threatening a violent takeover of the government (an event with which all of Europe was well familiar). It also produced a visit from Soviet emissary Valerian Zorin. Zorin threatened Czech President Beneš with warnings of Soviet military intervention to protect Czech "independence" if the country found itself being drawn to the West. Beneš yielded to the pressure and reformed the nation's Cabinet – with an even stronger Communist makeup.

Thus a Communist "coup" took place in Czechoslovakia, delivering the country over to Stalin's control. The Czechs were now trapped in the Soviet "orbit" of dependent or "satellite" states. Americans were horrified.

The only notable non-Communist still included on the cabinet at this point was the highly respected Foreign Minister Jan Masaryk, son of the country's first President and a beloved patriot by his own right. But two weeks after this shift toward Moscow, Masaryk was found dead in the courtyard of his official residence. It was announced that he had committed suicide by jumping from the window of his apartment several stories up. As "defenestration" (throwing someone out a high window) had a long history among the Czechs, the story was greeted with great skepticism.

The assumption in America and West Europe was that more probably he was murdered ... as a signal to others who might have had any thoughts about crossing Stalin (after the fall of the Soviet empire in 1991, proof was brought forward that indeed Masaryk had been murdered).

With Masaryk's death there were no further obstacles to a complete Communist takeover of all organs of government in Czechoslovakia.

The West was shocked at this development – more so than the disappearance of any other country behind the Iron Curtain, because Czechoslovakia had been so closely connected to Western European events – reaching back all the way to the Protestant Reformation in the 1500s and even the Holy Roman Empire before that. Now Czechoslovakia had disappeared into the Stalinist *gulag*. It would not re-emerge as a fully independent society until the collapse of the Soviet system forty years later.

However ... Tito's Communist Yugoslavia goes its own way

Although Tito was a fellow Communist, the ideology that he supposedly shared with Stalin did not mean that they shared the same political interests. Actually the opposite was quite the case ... although for the longest time they characterized publicly their disagreements as being simply minor ideological disagreements.

The problem arose at the end of the war over Tito's ambitions in the Trieste borderlands along the northern Adriatic coast. Both Italy and Yugoslavia wanted the area. Stalin, fearing a needless confrontation with the West and the possibility of this undercutting the Communist position in Italy, pressured Tito to give up the contest for the area with Italy. Tito was not happy, but complied.

Then there was the matter of the Southern Balkans ... and Stalin's concerns that Tito's ambitions there at the same time would result in a Western (at first British but then American) intervention in the region. Thus Tito's attempts to put Greece under a Communist regime was actively (but secretly) opposed by Stalin. And Indeed, with American involvement in Greece under the Truman Doctrine in 1947, Stalin proved correct in his expectations as to how things would ultimately develop. The Greek Communists were humiliated.

Problems also arose over Tito's plan to incorporate Albania into his multinational Yugoslavia ... in countering the idea of incorporating the southern Albanian-speaking Yugoslavian region of Kosovo into Albania. Actually, the Albanian Communist dictator Enver Hoxha (HO-djah) agreed to work closely with Yugoslavia under Tito's plan ... without first consulting Stalin in the matter. Then when Tito and Communist Bulgaria also agreed in 1947 to work together in a number of areas, this was done also without

Stalin first being consulted ... leading Soviet foreign minister Molotov to denounce the agreement.

When Hoxha however began to have problems within his own party, Stalin sent Soviet agents to Albania (mid-1947) in support of someone working secretly to overthrow Hoxha ... someone who suddenly died most mysteriously. Ultimately things quieted down when Stalin and a Yugoslavian envoy, Milovan Ðilas (or Djilas),* agreed to continue supporting Hoxha.

But from Stalin's point of view, things were getting horribly out of hand in the Balkans ... when Bulgarian leader Georgi Dimitrov spoke publicly about the formation of a federally organized state across the Balkans. But Dimitrov and Tito could not agree on the status of Macedonia ... and of Bulgaria itself, Dimitrov seeking Bulgaria to be a coequal with Yugoslavia in the deal. But Tito viewed all this as simply an extended Yugoslavian ("South Slavian") federation ... including in it sections of Greek Macedonia.

Stalin was alarmed ... and demanded that Tito and Dimitrov meet with him in Moscow (February 1948). To this meeting, however, Tito sent only a representative. The meeting was rough, Stalin making numerous demands ... which subsequently failed to be met – at least to Stalin's satisfaction.

Now Stalin began to oppose Tito openly ... finally making the decision to bring his dispute with Tito forward at the next meeting (June 1948) of the Cominform. Tito refused to attend ... and the Tito-Stalinist split was now complete ... never to be reconciled.

At this point there was an attempt to overthrow Tito by pro-Soviet Communists in 1948. But it failed ... moving Tito to begin the purge of suspected pro-Soviet Communists in his organization ... with as many as 50,000 Yugoslav Communists either killed, imprisoned or sentenced to force labor in the process. But Tito was now securely in command in Yugoslavia.

Then he turned to America for help ... its Marshall Plan in fact. The Communist split had created huge setbacks for Yugoslavia economically ... and Tito needed all the help he could get. And America agreed in 1949 to support Tito in his new 5-year plan and in Tito's successful bid for a seat on the U.N. Security Council – which Stalin opposed. That same year Tito ended his support of the Greek Communists ... collapsing their efforts to bring their country under Communism.

THE COLD WAR INTENSIFIES

---

*Ðilas would go on to become famous in the West for the way he came up so strongly against his own Communist formation ... writing extensively on the way Communism had very adversely affected Western Civilization.

The Berlin Blockade (1948-1949)

It was gradually coming to Stalin the idea that his wartime Allies Britain, France and America were not viewing their presence in Germany, and especially in Berlin, as temporary ... but were planning to stay there until all of Germany could be reunited and then – and only then – the occupying powers would depart. And the situation was worsened in the eyes of Stalin when pressures he put on the West's occupation of Berlin (in his sector after all!) by stopping the deliverance of food items to Berlin were countered by the stopping of the surrender of German machinery from the Western zones of Germany to the Russians. Worse, all indications were that the Berlin municipal elections coming up would not be beneficial to the Communists, who were rapidly losing support among the Berliners.

Then in early 1948, the three Western powers were clearly making plans to unite their zones into a single German political unit, with its own German currency ... in preparation to bringing it into the Marshall Plan. Stalin reacted (April 1948) by shutting down the West's access by way of rail, highway and canal from what was beginning to be termed "West Germany" to the Western-held zones of Berlin.

He had, however, no way of stopping flights into Germany without crossing a very dangerous political line ... and thus the Western powers began to fly needed food and material into Berlin. Thus – for a while – the Soviets backed down somewhat on the effort to blockade Berlin. But with the introduction of the new German Mark – in Berlin as well as in the West – Stalin was so angered that he once again (June) shut down all access – except, again, by air – into West Berlin.

He could not stop the flights. But the operation was very expensive and could not possibly last long – or so Stalin believed. But he miscalculated greatly Truman's resolve to defend West Berlin as a symbol of the West's strong determination not to be beaten into submission by an aggressive Stalin.

Indeed, Stalin had given the West a grand opportunity to demonstrate its enormous muscle ... even bringing into Berlin by way of non-stop flights the coal needed to get Berlin through one of its hard winters. Indeed, so thrilled by this display of Western resolve were the Berliners that the December 1948 West Berlin elections led to a complete victory of the pro-Western candidates.[*]

---

[*]The Social Democratic Party (Socialists) - 64.5%; The Christian Democratic Union (Conservatives) - 19.4%; the Free Democratic Party (Liberals) - 16.1%. The Communists, who called themselves the Socialist Unity Party, boycotted the elections.

Of course the Communists responded by setting up their own Berlin municipal government in the Soviet Eastern sector of the city. Berlin would therefore be a deeply divided city for the next 40 years (although movement between the two sectors would continue – until the building of the Berlin Wall in 1961).

But it was a huge loss politically for Stalin. It closed tightly the ranks of the Americans, British and French as Cold War allies. And it helped the Germans to see these three powers not as their occupiers but as their liberators. And it pushed ahead the creation of a very pro-Western German Federal Republic ("West Germany") in May of the next year (1949).

This in turn signaled the willingness of the Soviets to end the blockade ... deeply aware that politically their blockade had cost them badly. So the blockade came to an end. But just in case, the Allies continued to fly more supplies into West Berlin ... a 3-month reserve just to make the status of West Berlin very clear to the Soviets.

The Creation of NATO (1949)

At this point the division of the world into two political sectors, "East" and "West," made it clear that no amount of diplomacy was going to resolve this rising Cold War. The United Nations itself was divided accordingly ... and thus of no use in promoting the dream of world peace that Roosevelt had felt would come into being with this institution finding itself in place at the heart of the world's doings. The divisive ideology – backed up with massive military muscle (including atomic weapons ... which the Soviets themselves finally attained in August of 1949) – put this rivalry beyond the realm of reasoned diplomacy ... much like the two world wars earlier that century.

Since military muscle rather than persuasive diplomacy reigned at the heart of the Cold War, it was rather inevitable that the Western powers, mostly demilitarized since the end of World War Two because of a general animosity toward more military infighting, saw the need to do something about the fact that a huge military establishment faced them – and their rights as free people – in the hostile form of the huge Soviet military buildup in the East. They would need something big to counter this Soviet challenge facing them (Czechoslovakia and Berlin had greatly awakened them to this danger). Their own national armies were hardly up to the task.

Thus on April 4th, 1949, diplomats of twelve "Western" nations* met in Washington to sign the North Atlantic Treaty ... uniting them in such a way that an attack on any one of them was an attack on them all. And because

---

*America, Canada, Iceland, Great Britain, Norway, Denmark, Portugal, Italy, France, Belgium, the Netherlands, and Luxembourg.

America was part (actually the key part) of this arrangement, these nations felt that they had provided themselves a quite sufficient response to the Soviet challenge.

Actually, the British, French, Dutch, Belgians and Luxembourgers had already put together a military pact (The Treaty of Brussels) in March of 1948 ... although it was motived by a fear of a revived Germany as much as it was of the Soviet threat further East. They even went so far as to set up a joint military command structure, the Western Union Defense Organization.

The new North Atlantic Treaty was an amazing "peacetime" step for Americans out of their former isolationism. But a combination of the Czech Communist coup, the Berlin Blockade, and the distinct change in early 1948 of the Republican Chairman of the Senate Foreign Relations Committee, Arthur Vandenburg, from isolationist to internationalist, all served to push that American transition ahead. Indeed, it was the Vandenberg Resolution of June 1948, approved in the Senate 82-13, that opened the way for just that American resolve to see to the defense of a "Free West."

Then when in 1950 the Korean War broke out, the new Alliance saw the need to push ahead (like the Western Union Defense Organization) and form a joint military command structure – now termed the North Atlantic Treaty Organization (NATO) ... bringing together 35 military divisions under the new NATO Supreme Commander, Gen. Eisenhower – working out of the France-based Supreme Headquarters of the Allied Powers of Europe (SHAPE) ... itself headed up by Churchill's primary wartime military assistant, Lord Hastings Ismay, who would serve as NATO's Secretary General (1952-1957).

Nuclear deterrence

Backing up the threat of American retaliation – something that undercut deeply Stalin's ability simply to use his huge military shadow thrown over Eastern Europe to intimidate Western Europe – was always the implicit threat of the use of nuclear weapons such as America used against Japan in 1945. The possession of these awesome weapons – and the willingness of American President Truman to actually use them, as he clearly demonstrated in the conflict with the Japanese – gave America and its Western allies a strong sense of security when contemplating trouble with any new rising power wanting to take over the world.

But when in 1949 the Soviets exploded their own atomic bomb, the nuclear threat now worked both against as well as for American power. American attitudes about the bomb went directly from happy confidence to terrible fear as Americans realized that atomic weapons could now be used on them.

The Korean War (1950-1953)

The post-war North-South division.   Initially, as the Cold War first developed, Korea was not a country that factored greatly in American strategic thinking. In fact, a speech by American Secretary of State Dean Acheson (January 1950), in detailing America's zone of interest in Asia, did not even mention Korea. But that was about to change.

At the end of World War Two, Japanese-occupied Korea (annexed to the Empire of Japan in 1910) was demilitarized under the supervision of both America and Russia ... Stalin getting jurisdiction in the northern half of the country (part of the sweetener offered Stalin by Roosevelt at Yalta to get Russia to join America in its war against Japan), with America seeing to the demilitarization of the southern half ... Korea thus "temporarily" divided equally North and South at the 38th parallel.

But the Koreans themselves were very divided on this matter of this Soviet-American arrangement and in 1946 took to the streets in protest ... some supportive, some opposed (yes, there were pro-Communists in the South as well as many pro-democracy Koreans in the North). Thus America, distracted by events developing in Europe, simply decided in 1947 to turn the matter over to the U.N. ... and call for elections to unite the country the following year. But when election time came, the Soviets claimed that the northern half of the country was not ready for elections ... and thus the 1948 elections were held only in the South.   There the conservative politician Syngman Rhee was the winner – someone that the Americans were not wild about – but willing to offer support to nonetheless.

But surprisingly, the Korean north found itself "now ready" for such an election ... only months after blocking the U.N. elections in the North! And there the Communists were majorly victorious. The Communist politician Kim Il-sung won handily, on the promise that he would confiscate all the lands owned by Korea's small aristocracy ... and turn them over to the peasants as their own property.[*]

In short, Korea was now divided into two distinct societies, with very different governments ruling in the North and in the South.

America protested. But there was little it could do. The leverage that America once held in its nuclear monopoly was now gone due to the Soviets being able to match that achievement themselves now.

Worse, and quite unknown to the Americans, the Soviets had been training a very well-equipped and quite massive North Korean Army in

---

[*]Of course, once securely in power, Kim would follow the Soviet model and "collective" all that property ... turning ownership over to his Socialist state and transforming Korean peasants into true Communist "laborers." This of course was also the course that Mao took in China.

preparation for a move to "unify" all of Korea under Kim Il-sung. And rightly so, Kim expected the task to be accomplished fairly easily ... for the South Korean Army was poorly trained and even more poorly equipped. And Kim planned the move to be a total surprise ... probably allowing his troops to complete the task in a matter of only a few weeks, perhaps even days.

The war breaks out (1950). He almost achieved his goal, when on June 25, 1950 – without any warning - a huge number of North Korean troops invaded the South ... quickly capturing the capital city of Seoul (just immediately below the North-South border) and then flooding South. They equally quickly scattered the ill-prepared South Korean forces – reducing their numbers from 95,000 down to about 22,000 (most simply fled ... or even joined the North Korean forces).

But, seeing the danger that a Communist victory in Korea would pose to the region around the North China Sea, Truman was just as quick to respond. He immediately took the matter to the U.N. Security Council ... which the Russians had been boycotting, since the West had blocked the effort to turn the vital China seat on the Security Council over to Mao's government. Thus the Russians were not there to issue yet another veto against U.N. action. Quickly the Security Council moved to bring military support to the UN-sponsored South Korean government ... and Truman was already answering that authorization with the rapid movement of troops from neighboring Japan to South Korea.

But it took some effort of those American troops, joined by a small number of British and other troops, to slow up and then stop the North Korean momentum. But finally, in early August, they brought the invasion to a halt ... with only the region around the port city of Busan still in what was now termed "U.N." military hands.

The situation at this point was tricky for everyone. Since it was not just America defending the South but the U.N. itself, Stalin found himself unwilling to authorize direct Soviet Russian action against those U.N. forces. For Mao's China and Kim's North Korea this posed something of the same diplomatic problem ... which China resolved by also staying out of the matter (for the time being). But North Korea was caught in a bind ... not able or willing to retreat, because to do so would count as a huge political shaming of Kim's regime. So, the North Koreans fought on.

The landing at Inchon and the North Korean retreat. But the situation was just as tricky for the U.N. troops ... which were finding that coming up against a North Korean enemy well entrenched in the mountains of the Korean interior posed the same serious problem that the advance against Nazi troops in mountainous Italy had recently posed. Thus once again it was decided to launch a sea landing of U.N. troops on the Korean shores well to the North of the present line of battle (September 15) ... and then swing them behind the North Korean troops. But this time, unlike the stupid delay that took place at the Italian beach at Anzio, American Gen. MacArthur moved his 75,000 American troops immediately off the beaches they had secured and had them quickly headed to the lightly defended interior well above the North Korean Army ... which at this point, fearing entrapment, panicked and fell into rapid retreat.

Seoul was soon liberated after a vicious battle ... and then the U.N. and South Korean (ROK or Republic of Korea) troops crossed the 38th parallel and headed into North Korea ... despite a Chinese warning not to do so. Two weeks later the North Korean capital at Pyongyang was taken ... along with 135,000 North Korean troops.

Problems with the Chinese ... and with MacArthur. Now the hero MacArthur spoke to an adoring press about the need to move even across the North Korean border into China ... in order to capture the bases in China that had been supporting the North Korean effort. Truman was upset because, in the larger context of the Cold War which was going on back in Europe, he did not want to invite a military conflict with the Chinese. But MacArthur answered back that he was certain that, lacking proper air cover, the Chinese would never dare to take on the U.N. forces. In this MacArthur proved to be totally blind and dead wrong.

As the U.N. forces headed north towards the North Korean border with China, Chinese "volunteer" troops began to be encountered ... at first in small numbers and then further north in larger numbers until finally at the frozen Chosin Reservoir 30,000 American troops encountered some 120,000 Chinese troops – and a deadly winter – that stopped the American advance ... in fact forced it into retreat – with half of those American troops being killed or wounded in the process. By mid-December the American forces had fallen all the way back to the 38th parallel ... and China had set Kim aside in order to take command of the Communist forces in the North.

Then as the battle swung back and forth along the 38th parallel (Seoul taken and retaken by both sides) MacArthur ignored Truman by seemingly taking command of the entire military operation ... talking openly to the press about taking the war to China itself ... even using atomic weapons if necessary. Tragically MacArthur was again blinded by the fact that Asia – not Europe – was the only world that he really knew ... and that brought his full devotion.

But Truman was U.S. President – not MacArthur. And with MacArthur ignoring Truman's efforts to get him to back down (it was even Truman who had to fly to meet MacArthur rather than MacArthur coming to Truman to confer over this matter) finally Truman simply relieved MacArthur from command ... knowing what this would do to himself politically in firing the new American military hero MacArthur.* But it had to be done. America could not afford to divide its forces in conducting its side of the Cold War. And defending Europe – not starting a war with China – was what America needed to stay focused on.

Armistice.   Thankfully, the effort of some 700,000 Chinese troops to take on the U.N. forces at the 38th parallel the next April (1951) moved very little of the line of battle separating the two halves of the country. Huge numbers of Chinese troops were lost (death in battle, disease and desertion). Thus a stalemate set in ... one not likely to be moved by further military action – action by either side. Consequently in July of 1951, U.N. representatives met with Chinese and North Korean representatives at the city of Panmunjom located near the line of battle ... to begin discussions about a possible armistice.

But the discussions dragged on for two more years ... as each side could not completely give up the idea of gaining some advantage with a bit more fighting along the battle front. But again, as clearly nothing much was developing, finally in July of 1953 both parties came to an armistice agreement establishing a demilitarized zone (DMZ) along roughly the same 38th parallel ... a DMZ still separating the two Koreas to this very day.

* * *

MEANWHILE ... SHIFTING SOCIAL IDENTITIES

What was happening in the European world in the latter part of the 1940s was that the military reality of a Europe divided into sectors of military occupation and control was slowly turning itself into a political reality of two distinct ideas of how a post-war world should eventually take shape. And this in turn was becoming increasingly frustrating for all parties involved ... even bitter for those having the chief responsibilities for directing the development of this postwar world – Soviet Russia in the East and America in the West.

This East-West division was not primarily military in nature the way things had developed in the buildup to World War Two ... although there were strong military components to this developing East-West rivalry. It

---

*Because of this action, many Americans came to view Truman as a coward, if not almost a traitor. But a Congressional investigation ultimately concluded that Truman had indeed acted constitutionally, and correctly, and that MacArthur (who actually spent all his time in Tokyo) was out of touch with the military realities in Korea, as well as the critical challenges facing America in the rest of the world.

was a division that was most importantly political, economic, social and especially ideological. But it was warlike in the attitudes by which the major players in this East-West game began to see and respond to each other. Thus it was indeed a "Cold War."

"Democracy" the central issue

Interestingly, both sides in this contest saw themselves as defending some version of "democracy." But the problem was that one side (America and its Western Allies) saw democracy as government *by* the people. The other side (Soviet Russia and its People's Republics) saw democracy as government *for* the people.

Communism's "government *for* the people." As hard as it is to believe that the paranoid and murderous Stalin was in any way interested in democracy, he truly thought that he somehow was carrying on Lenin's Communist legacy. Lenin of course, back in the beginning of the 1920s – just after having fought a bitter battle with forces representing an ancient Czarist political universe and a small but rising middle class – knew that in attempting to construct a workers' democracy he was up against a Russia that had virtually no real experience in self-government. Russia was going to need some guidance from socially and historically enlightened leadership before the Russian people would be able to take on the incredibly difficult challenge of self-government. Russia needed to experience deep change … to move in a new direction, a direction that supposedly only a handful of Marxist-trained leaders had the background and perspective to understand. Thus Russia would have to be in their hands … until such time that the State could finally wither away and leave a classless society to govern itself. But that was going to take some real doing … something that was also going to take some time … lots of time.*

Stalinist "democracy." Then Lenin's early death in 1924 threw newly established Soviet Russia into a dispute as to the direction their Communist – or at least Socialist – Revolution should then take them. Trotsky wanted

---

*Clearly Lenin did not hold the utopian or "Humanist" view of Communism's founder Karl Marx that democracy was instinctive to all people – and that the only barrier to such democracy was the authoritarian rule of a self-interested governing class … and that once that class was removed from power, the natural human instinct for democracy would automatically come into play. Obviously, Marx ignored the strongly contradicting example of the French Revolution, a tragic event that had occurred only a mere a half-century earlier than his famous *Communist Manifesto*. Lenin was not so easily blinded by such Humanism … which was rampant among intellectuals of those days (and in many cases since then).

to use Russian developments only as a springboard to greater revolution undertaken in the rest of Europe lying to the west. Stalin opposed him and his supporters ... because Stalin was personally a strong Russian nationalist – interested really only in protecting the political achievements recently secured in Russia. He wanted to build up Russian Socialism ... not spend valuable Soviet Russian assets outside the country. As we have already seen, this debate grew brutal.

After the Second World War, with Stalin and his army in command of huge sections of Europe, his understanding of democracy was deeply immersed in that same spirit of Russian nationalism – protecting and directing social "revolution" from the Kremlin headquarters in Moscow. Stalin was willing to support "proletarian democracy" in other countries ... but only to the extent that it deepened that sense of Soviet Russian protection and control.

Was there anything unusual about those instincts? Not really. Politicians played that same game everywhere ... at least to the extent that their actual power base allowed them to do so.

American "democracy" becomes its own form of nationalism. America was an English-speaking nation ... though in general it was not pushy about extending the English-speaking world. At home, immigrants coming to America took up the English language ... though simply because it made life in America easier to work with. There was no absolute insistence on the matter from America itself.

Certainly being "White" mattered ... at least to the multitudes of descendants of the Africans brought earlier to America as slaves. But beyond that, immigrants to America quickly found their way to their own White world.

For a very long time Americans were deeply involved in spreading their unique society across the North American continent ... utilizing the same nationalist energies stirring across the world among the world's commoner classes. Indians and Mexicans felt the enormous pressure of just such an American nationalist urge. So that's how America did the nationalist "thing" pretty much up until the 20th century.

It was Wilson who then made "democracy" – such as Americans understood the term – as the Absolute on which he intended to build a rising American national spirit ... as America entered the larger world stage. Although such nationalism was built on no restrictive linguistic or religious foundations, it certainly laid down a strong social spirit on "Democratic" political-ideological lines ... similar to the way the Soviets did so along "Communist" political-ideological lines. Expanding globally American-style constitutional democracy would be the very ideal that would underpin the

American urge to international involvement.

America's Anti-Authoritarian Democracy. Actually, with the end of the Great War in 1918, America became quite isolationist ... except in instances of upper-level diplomatic efforts to reduce the ability of nations to go to war.

But with the attack of Japan on Pearl Harbor in 1941 – and Hitler's declaration of war against America three days later – all that changed ... deeply. Authoritarian Nazism or Fascism was now easily defined as the great evil that America must help the other "democratic" nations fight against. Such symbols of evil gave great moral clarity to the effort patriotic Americans were willing to bring to the war.

But that "democratic" alliance included Stalin. Thus, with the help of Roosevelt, the authoritarian character of Stalin's rule was quietly overlooked in the thinking of Americans. Stalin was simply the leader of one of our key allies, the Russians, in this war against authoritarian Germany.

But that thinking would run into deep trouble after the war ... not immediately, but step by step. Confusion thus accompanied this shift. Clearly now, Stalin was simply just another authoritarian dictator ... of the same order of Hitler and Mussolini. How had they not seen this before?

Political ideology becomes the new game. Thus it was that with the development of the Cold War, the world was actually dealing with a new version of the social spirit ... built on ideological rather than linguistic or religious foundations, ideologies sponsored by one or the other of the world's two new superpowers, America and Soviet Russia.

How dangerous this actually was for the world was never fully appreciated by the new superpowers themselves. Ideology knows no geographic bounds. Thus the game could in fact find itself played out not just in this area or that ... but across the entire globe.

Indeed, as the Cold War developed, it seemed that there was no event, large or small, that did not invite the superpowers to calculate for themselves the degree of win or loss such events meant for each of them.

And the words "Communism," (and for the Americans, also "Socialism"), "Capitalism," "Democracy," "Iron Curtain," "Free-World," etc. took on highly emotional content ... so much so that just as nations fought each other in World War One just because their enemies spoke a different language, so in the Cold War they fought each other because either "Communism" or "Free World Democracy" was to gain or lose position with every rising development.

Thus whether Vietnamese independence from France should be supported or opposed by America, ultimately depended on which of the ideologies it would choose to identify itself by. Never mind that the

Communist Vietnamese were not close associates with the Communist Chinese. In fact the Vietnamese disliked rather deeply their Communist neighbors to the North.

And the fact that Communist China was not taking orders from Communist Russia never factored into the American thinking or understanding of Chinese developments. To Americans, all Communists are evil ... and thus must be opposed by the Democratic Free World. On the other hand, according to Soviet thinking ... all Capitalists are evil ... and must be opposed by the oppressed working classes (the Socialist-Communists) of the world. Thus the only thing that mattered to the superpowers was which label would this or that government take on for itself ... or which side in this great ideological battle was to benefit from this or that development. Everything depended on that single factor.

Ideological paranoia at home. Making the situation even more difficult to deal with, there were a number of Americans who had gone deeply into some kind of working relationship with the ally Stalin during the war. That now as the Cold War developed raised questions as to where they presently stood in this matter of finding the American nation in deep opposition to everything that Stalin represented. Could these individuals be trusted ... intellectuals mostly, found in both government service and the cultural services (the world of literature and the movie industry principally)?

Thus it was that Congress's House Un-American Activities Committee (HUAC ... actually founded just before the war) was called on by 1947 to begin looking into the matter – cheering Middle Americans ... but alarming much of the world of intellectualism. Brought under critical inspection was the Hollywood filming industry ... where writers were known to have strong Leftist sympathies. Then the following year (1948), as the Cold War intensified, HUAC brought charges of Communist sympathies (even spying for Stalin) against a number of Roosevelt's wartime advisors (the "Ware Group"), ultimately including Alger Hiss ... accused by Time magazine writer-editor Whittaker Chambers, who admitted that he himself had once been a Communist and a Soviet spy. He offered personal proof of Hiss's similar allegiance. However ... the American intellectual community strongly defended Hiss as being falsely accused by lowbrow "anti-Communist" rabble rousers – and in particular by Congressman Richard Nixon, who was leading the Hiss investigation.[*]

Thus America was dividing socially. And it would only get worse in the years ahead.

------

[*]The rising American intellectualist Left would never forgive Nixon ... and do everything possible to bring him down when he actually became U.S. President.

West Europe's position

Although most of West Europe would place its strategic military defenses in the hands of NATO, it would never become quite as "anti-Communist" as America. Suspicious of Stalin, yes. But fervently anti-Communist, no ... something that Americans would always have a hard time understanding.

Indeed, in both France and Italy, Communist Parties operated freely ... and widely, being the largest and best organized of those country's parliamentary parties – even occupying typically a third of the seats of their multi-party parliaments. And first-cousin Socialist parties (typically "Social Democrats" ... but in Britain the "Labor Party") operated widely across West Europe ... not infrequently the actual parties in power there. And that idea would not change substantially over the years.

Nonetheless, in the matter of nation defense, American-supported (and led) NATO was a very useful institution for West Europeans. Simply, it allowed European members to focus postwar development on rebuilding their destroyed economic and social infrastructure rather than spending huge amounts of money on national defense ... which at this point they felt that there was no way they could succeed anyway in going it alone on their own national basis against the Stalinist power buildup in the East. Their national defense was now an international matter (thus NATO) ... no longer just a national matter.

Indeed, in West Europe, nationalist impulses were quieted down deeply ... partly out of exhaustion and partly out of the understanding at this point that their European world worked best when they all cooperated, rather than opposed each other. And the Germans were more than just supportive of the idea ... because they had a huge national guilt to get past – and a fear of what would happen if they got caught up in some kind of German "thing" again.

West European internationalism: The ECSC. Thus it was that in 1950, French Foreign Minister Robert Schuman put forward the idea (the Schuman Plan) of uniting the strategic national industries of coal and steel production (absolutely vital for military purposes) ... by removing all trade restrictions – and even placing such operations under some kind of international authority. Thus it was that the following year (1951), Belgium, France, Italy, Luxembourg, the Netherlands and West Germany signed the Treaty of Paris, setting up the European Coal and Steel Community (ECSC), these vital industries now operating under the command of a High Authority, directed by both a Common Assembly and Special Council of member nations, and monitored by a Court of Justice.

A very strong European unity movement was now up and running ...

and would merely expand over the years ahead.

✳ ✳ ✳

THE WEST'S "CHRISTIAN" IDENTITY

Christianity's decline in Europe

Where did all of this leave the deeper Christian identity that – for centuries – had been so crucial to the idea of Western society? Nationalism certainly had succeeded in becoming itself something of a religion ... that masses of people were willing to live and die for. Where did such nationalism leave a Westerner's Christian identity ... and all the moral-spiritual aspects that went with it? Or ... then if nationalism was being replaced by a quite pragmatic sense of multi-nationalism, the same question still remains. What was it exactly that Westerners were to understand as their ultimate call in life? What was it that now constituted their foundational cosmology (view or understanding of all of life)?

Not surprisingly, the vast majority of Westerners still identified themselves as "Christian." But what that actually meant in their daily lives varied widely across the Christian world.

For the Germans, who had linked their Christian identities with Hitler's program ... the post-war period was one of deep shame. But conservative Catholics in Italy also had little to be proud of.

Indeed it was very hard for all Europeans – Christians as well as Jews – to link the idea of the full sovereignty of God with the horrors of the Holocaust and the widespread destruction that took place across Europe. Why hadn't God intervened? Why did he allow this to happen? Was, in fact, God really that crucial to the way things went here on earth?

Likewise, the gradual, then increasingly rapid, economic climb of Western Europe back to some kind of prosperity seemed to be more a matter of human planning than anything God was involved with.

True, self-identified Christian Democrats (or some version of such a political party) were deeply involved widely across Europe in these new political dynamics – alongside the agnostic or atheistic Social Democrats. But their leadership did not seem to serve to bring the common people back to some kind of strongly Christian personal and social life. Even Easter and Christmas celebrations seemed to be a declining matter of interest to an increasing number of Europeans. Clearly, by the 1950s, Christianity appeared to be on a serious decline ... in both Catholic and Protestant Europe – but especially in the latter.

Of course in Eastern Europe ... this was not even a factor ... where the Communist Party had put itself in the role as some kind of political priesthood serving Marx's religious Secularism. True, underneath it all were many dedicated Christians ... waiting for an opportunity to get things back to their pre-Soviet days. And in time they would have just that opportunity. But now was not the time.

Christianity running strong in America

However in America, the "Christian" situation there seemed to be going in a direction opposite the one going on in Europe. Christianity seemed to be ever stronger than it was during the pre-war period.

Perhaps this was because the war's impact on American society was very different than the impact it had on European society. No towns or cities were bombed. No huge elements of the population were carted off to slave camps. Indeed, the war itself had prospered America greatly, putting industrial America not only back on its feet ... but way ahead of the rest of the world in its magnificence. Indeed, by 1950, America alone seemed to be producing around 50% of the world's industrial capacity.

Certainly human hands had built up this grand industrial society. Yes, capitalists and government officials had played important roles in all this development.

But in the American heart, it was easy to see God's favor in all of this. In putting on those uniforms and – at great personal risk – taking on those fascist powers Japan, Germany, and Italy, they had trusted God greatly to protect them ... or at least guide them in this dangerous enterprise. And it was easy to see in the victory that came to them in this war the very hand of God as provider and protector.

Thus indeed, "Middle Americans" were outstandingly loyal in their Christian devotion – tending to be very regular Sunday Church goers ... and quite observant of what were understood as Christian social rules and responsibilities.

Truman. The fact that American leadership was strongly Christian – in quite different ways – was of major importance in this Christian character of Middle America. President Truman on several occasions called for a National Day of Prayer ... asking the nation to call on God to help the nation know what to do in the face of the many challenges confronting it. True, he was not a very active church-going Baptist while in the White House ... but explained this as simply having no time to get away from the job (he was indeed truly a workaholic!). But his faith was sincere and not just public performance ... for like Lincoln, Washington and others before him, he understood the importance of looking to God for his lead in matters.

He truly believed that if the world would simply live by Jesus's Sermon on the Mount (Matthew chapters 7, 8 and 9) peace would prevail across the world. But this only brought on public contempt of more sophisticated souls who saw in his Biblical comments only foolish ignorance … especially in his hope that living according to Biblical principles would bring the world a better peace.

But American Christianity itself was not a single phenomenon. Most sadly, a terrible split would occur between Truman and his long-time Baptist pastor Edward Pruden … when Truman appointed General Mark Clark as his personal representative to the Vatican. While this pleased America's twenty-five million Catholics immensely, it upset greatly many Protestant conservatives who were deeply suspicious of any Catholic pro-Vatican "popery."

The Graham crusades. Helping keep the Christian spirit alive in Middle America was the very young traveling evangelist Billy Graham. He had started out with an amazing revival – or crusade as he called it – in 1949 in Los Angeles which over an eight-week period had drawn over 350 thousand people. The next year he covered the country with his crusades, from Boston, to Columbia (South Carolina), to Portland, to Atlanta, to other points in between. By the next year, the Graham name was well-known across the country, and his crusades were so fully attended that often masses of people had to be turned away when the stadiums had become completely filled.

Vereide's prayer breakfast movement. Another person to have a huge impact in developing the Christian character of America … especially among its corporate and political leaders was the Norwegian-born Methodist minister Abraham Vereide. Actually he got his start during a visit to San Francisco – caught up in a very violent longshoremen's strike in 1934. There he found himself leading dispirited businessmen together (capitalists were in great political-social disfavor at the time!) in extensive prayer – for the local community, the nation and the world. Upon his return to Seattle he decided to turn such an event into a regular occurrence, "prayer breakfasts" … designed to keep up the spirits of wearied business executives. These proved to be so successful that soon local politicians found themselves joining these breakfasts.

Then the war itself served to greatly increase the sense of need of these kinds of prayer movements, and Vereide's prayer breakfasts spread widely across America, from city to city … eventually becoming a regular part of the nation's religious and political scene.

Graham and Vereide working together. In early 1952 Graham found himself in Washington, conducting another one of his crusades ... in which about a third of the senators and a good number of congressmen – and another half-million people were in attendance (along with millions more listening on the radio). While there, he found himself also working closely with Vereide in helping various political leaders focus on key issues needing a strong Christian touch.

This then inspired Congress to come up with the idea of a National Day of Prayer as an official act ... to which Truman – who generally did not like public displays of religiosity – ultimately gave his approval. And thus began the annual National Day of Prayer – eventually scheduled for the first Thursday in May.

And that same year Vereide was able to get Congress to support the idea of a National Prayer Breakfast, to be held the following February (1953) in the nation's capital. And so successful was that event that it has been held annually ever since.

Eisenhower. At this point (the beginning of 1953) Eisenhower was on the scene as the American president. And he was very supportive of these Christian-based events and the key role that they were designed to play in the shaping of the American nation. Indeed, it would be during his presidency that the words "under God" would be added to the Pledge of Allegiance in 1954, and "In God We Trust" would be confirmed as the nation's motto in 1956.

The tragic split between Middle America and Intellectualist America

1984. Meanwhile the Cold War paranoia was merely building in America during this time. Not helping matters much was the popularity of a book, entitled simply *1984*, written by British author George Orwell. The book portrayed a coming world (the year 1984 ... some mere 35 years in the future) in which the move towards increasing authoritarianism would ultimately produce full totalitarianism under "Big Brother." This was a monstrous individual who had at that point completely taken over the thoughts and actions of what was now basically a global slave society, one caught in perpetual war with itself.

Certainly there were already plenty of examples of how that worked. But to think that this was an inevitable development for everyone frightened enormously the readers (heavily American).

McCarthyism. In fact, that same fear was doing some of the work in driving forward in that very direction even America itself. Cashing in on this fear was a U.S. Senator from Wisconsin, Joseph McCarthy, who was looking to increase his importance ... when in 1950 he took up the cause of uncovering a supposedly wide realm of pro-Communist Americans plotting to overturn their own nation.

Quickly his behavior drew forward great public interest ... which he played to the fullest. He claimed to have a huge list of such traitors ... though the names were never actually revealed – except that he destroyed the political career of at least one fellow senator with very false accusations. He would even go forward to make the bold claim that the U.S. military command structure itself was filled with individuals "soft on Communism." Tragically, so fearful of this man and his threats was American officialdom, that little was done to stop him ... not for several years anyway.

More spying in high places. Not helping the situation any was the discovery of what would come eventually to be termed the "Cambridge Five" ... the discovery that a number of British Cambridge University students had sold their souls to Communism in the 1930s ... and had been recruited by Soviet agents to spy on their own government in which they served as intelligence agents. The uncovering of this plot began in 1951 when Donald Maclean and Guy Burgess were discovered sending intelligence information to the Soviets (there would be others, such as Kim Philby, Anthony Blunt and then John Cairncross discovered in future years).

Around the same time (1950-1951) – compliments of the Venona Project which had cracked the Soviet code and thus was able to expose spying going on in the West – a German working in the American nuclear program, Klaus Fuchs, was caught ... and then confessed. But in doing so, he also implicated Harry Gold – which then led to the discovery of the role of David Greenglass in the spying ... and then ultimately Greenglass's sister Ethel Rosenberg and her husband Julius. These, and then others as well, were found to have been passing on to the Soviets all sorts of nuclear secrets ... although only Julius and Ethel Rosenberg – despite their claims of being innocent[*] – were executed for their crimes – despite a huge international cry for clemency.

Ultimately, all of this merely confirmed the suspicions of Middle American Vets about how easily intellectuals were seduced and brought into service by Communism's supposed high Idealism. This then deepened even further a social-cultural divide between those two key American groups ... the Middle-American Vets and much of America's intellectual community.

---

[*]With the fall of the Soviet Union in the early 1990s, it was finally revealed that the Rosenbergs (or at least Julius Rosenberg) had indeed been Soviet spies.

The Intellectualist counterstroke: *The Crucible*. The intellectuals, of course, fought back – but very carefully, for they were still in a minority position politically as well as socially.

A major intellectualist counterstroke was issued by the playwright Arthur Miller, extremely upset that a close friend of his, Elia Kazan, had given HUAC the names of eight members of his Theater Group who were fellow Communists. To Miller, this all smacked of a witch hunt ... and wrote about just such a horrible event that had taken place in Puritan America 2½ centuries earlier (the late 1600s) in Salem, Massachusetts ... bringing this long-forgotten event back into remembrance with his 1953 play, *The Crucible*.

Interestingly, the play did not do particularly well in the 1950s. But it would be brought back into action in the 1960s ... and become a major weapon of Liberal America against a still very traditionalist Middle America – ultimately passed on as required reading to rising American generations (the Boomers, Gen-Xers, Millennials, and now the Gen-Z) in order to reshape their perception (very negatively) of "Puritanical" Middle America itself. Thus ultimately, intellectualist America would win big in its battle with Middle America.

McCarthy finally brought down. Tragically, it would take until mid-1954 that the assault on Intellectualist America by McCarthy could be brought to a halt. By that time, McCarthy was losing face, when CBS news host Edward R. Murrow concluded a series of his, *See It Now*, with a warning to America of the dangers to American freedom posed by the type of behavior that McCarthy exemplified. Then in June, during the well-televised Army-McCarthy hearings, army lawyer Joseph Welch actually went on the counter-attack, accusing a stunned McCarthy of doctoring his evidence and just in general acting the part of a charlatan. This then emboldened fellow senators to make their move, conducting a hearing that summer concerning McCarthy's senatorial behavior ... and voting a rare act of censure that December.   McCarthy would nonetheless continue to serve – in political isolation – then die an alcoholic's death in 1957.

The bringing down of McCarthy would ease greatly the Red Scare inflicting America ... at least that part concerning Communism in America itself. But it would nonetheless still leave a bitterness between the frightened Middle Americans that had been supportive of McCarthy's Red Scare ... and the angry intellectuals who had been the target of that most unfortunate political period. This would be a bitterness that would not really disappear.

*** * ***

NEW DYNAMICS IN THE INTERNATIONAL REALM

Stalin dies

In early March of 1953 Stalin experienced a stroke … and died five days later … with much mystery surrounding the unexpected development. Apparently, he was considering another round of extensive purges within the upper circles of Communist leadership to further fortify his position and it was thus rumored that he had been poisoned … a rumor easy to believe given the way political fortunes in those days rose and fell in the most deadly of ways.

In any case it raised the question: who was now in charge of the Soviet Empire? It was immediately announced that Georgy Malenkov was the new Chairman of the Council of Ministers (something like a Prime Minister) … with Lavrentiy Beria continuing in his position both as Deputy Chairman of the Council of Ministers … and as head of Internal Affairs (operating the NKVD or secret police). The Foreign Ministry would continue to be directed by Molotov.

Nikita Khrushchev (Soviet leader 1953-1964)

Yet while Soviet public office was important, Communist Party leadership was vastly more important. And here, Nikita Khrushchev was quick to take the position of leader of the party Presidium … that September (1953) taking the position as the party's First Secretary (Stalin's former position).

But Beria as head of the NKVD was a dangerous contender for power … and Khrushchev and Malenkov – fearing that Beria was actually planning a full takeover (and their deaths) – worked together in having Beria arrested (late June), tried, and then shot (that December).

But this now put Khrushchev and Malenkov in political competition … as Malenkov attempted to have the State take the lead in a post-Stalinist Soviet Empire … offering a program of social reforms. But Khrushchev countered by offering his own "reform" program … at the same time securing his position among the lower ranks of the party (following Stalin's example). Bit by bit, Malenkov lost status in the political dynamic … until in January of 1955, Khrushchev was able to get the Supreme Soviet to replace Malenkov with a Khrushchev loyalist, Nikolai Bulganin … offering Malenkov only a less important position in the state presidium (cabinet). Clearly now Khrushchev had full control of the Soviet regime, both party and state.

A workers' uprising in East Germany (June 1953)

Meanwhile, having heard talk of a possible loosening of Moscow's political hand since Stalin's death, East German workers – ultimately nearly a million of them – took to the streets, demanding that the Communist dictator commanding their country, Walter Ulbricht, also loosen up on his oppression.

Actually, the event had been building to the point of such explosion since the previous year.

There had been much talk of rearming West Germany ... possibly as part of a new (West) European Defense Community. But the fear of a rearmed West Germany was what brought dictator Ulbricht to tighten his grip on East Germany, taking greater control over his country's industries – and even undertaking the collectivization of East Germany's farmlands. But the latter move sparked farmer resistance by their cutting back on food production, which in turn led to deep hunger in urban East Germany. East Germany was thus very restless as it entered 1953.

When a massive revolt finally broke out across East Germany on the 16th of June, the Soviet collective leadership was quick to respond by sending on the following day 20,000 Russian troops to join some 8,000 East German police ... and quickly and ruthlessly suppressing the rebellion. In the process, the arrest, imprisonment, and even execution of East German participants was extensive.

Ulbricht was quick to blame the West for inciting the rioting with its propaganda campaign conducted by Western literature distribution and radio programs directed at Eastern Europe ... and did what he could to block such Western efforts.

But for the new American President Eisenhower, the game was not over. In July he announced the offering of food supplies to any East Germans able to get to American distribution centers in West Germany. Of course Ulbricht did what he could to stop this maneuver. But it even made Eisenhower's European allies concerned that this move merely increased East-West tensions, rather than relaxing them the way they were hoping a change in Soviet leadership might produce. Thus Eisenhower terminated the food program that October.

All in all, nothing much seemed to have resulted from all of this ... and things quickly settled back to more normal patterns in Europe.

The 1953 Iranian coup d'état

But that was also because Cold War tensions were rising elsewhere at that point: the Shah's Iran. Iran found itself in a very tricky position. The Soviets had demonstrated their strong interests in the country – neighboring Iran sitting atop huge oil reserves, plus commanding a strategic position overlooking the flow of much of the rest of Europe's oil resources out of the Persian Gulf. At the same time, the British actually controlled Iran's oil production ... vital to British industrial capacity – but also a major sore point for the Iranians themselves. And Truman's America was rather unsupportive of such European imperialism ... although Truman was growing increasingly concerned that every step-back of its European allies from their imperial positions abroad usually resulted not in constitutional democracy coming into being but instead a nationalist dictatorship taking over the "liberated" country ... a dictatorship strongly supported by the Kremlin. And now as Iran entered the 1950s, it looked as if that same challenge was about to hit that country.

Iranian politics themselves were indeed quite tricky. There were several political interests lining themselves up against each other in a bid to take over the country. The young Shah himself actually played a rather restrained part in Iranian politics ... allowing the Majlis (parliament) and the prime minister to take the lead in shaping Iranian politics.

But Iran's Prime Minister, Mohammad Mosaddegh, (as of 1951) was intent on building up his own power position even more by playing up Iranian nationalist sentiments massively through an effort to have Britain's oil industry in Iran nationalized. The previous prime minister, who had opposed such nationalization, was assassinated by a militant Shi'ite group headed up by the Ayatollah (Iran's religious leader) Abol-Ghasem Kashani,[*] who was working hard to bring his Shi'ites to power as Iran's governing group. And then there was the Iranian Communist Tudeh Party, also pursuing the same goal ... although politically they were a relatively small group.

When in late 1951 Mossadegh's National Front finally nationalized Iran's oil industry, all this tension exploded. The British did all they could to stop the move – pulling out their technicians and imposing an embargo on Iranian oil in the hope of forcing Mossadegh to return things to British control. Then they found themselves deeply disappointed when Truman was unwilling to support them in this effort ... despite the fact that they were supporting American troops in Korea. But Truman was more focused on Korea than Iran at the time. And besides, all this helped to promote the American oil industry greatly!

As for Iran itself, the embargo brought deep financial trouble to the country ... as well as much political turmoil – as the various groups accused each other for the mess that was clearly developing. And both Kashani's Shi'ite Party and the Tudeh Party were gaining strength in the process. Consequently, Mossadegh countered by hardening his grip on Iran, in mid-1953 closing down the Majlis and arresting political opponents ... merely deepening the anger tearing the country apart.

------

[*]Kashani was the mentor of the Ayatollah Ruhollah Khomeini, who would take control of the country after the Shah was overthrown in 1979.

At this point, the American CIA, under orders of America's new President Eisenhower – with cooperation from Churchill, who had returned to power as British prime minister in 1951 – pressured the Shah to dismiss Mosaddegh (which the Shah had every right to do) and appoint in his place Faziollah Zahedi (mid-August 1953). But Mosaddegh refused to leave office, arrested a number of political figures, forced Zahedi into hiding ... and encouraged his supporters to take to the streets in loud protest over the "attempted coup."

At this point, the Shah decided to head off to Italy to wait out the crisis! And then things quieted down with Mosaddegh securely in power.

But here too, the game was not over. The CIA used its funds to encourage an unsuspecting Tudeh Party to take to the streets to demonstrate clearly their own support of Mosaddegh ... which the CIA then used most cleverly by portraying Iran as facing a possible Mosaddegh-supported Communist coup ... something the CIA knew would enrage the vast majority of Iranians! Of course Mosaddegh had no such interest in a Tudeh Party coup. But the ruse worked. In reaction to this supposed Mosaddegh-Tudeh plot, huge numbers of pro-Shah protesters (joined by Muslim protesters) took to the streets, at the same time allowing Iranian military officers to have Mosaddegh arrested and imprisoned (August 19) ... and replaced by Zahedi as Iranian prime minister. So ... the crisis was over.

The Shah then returned to Iran – accompanied by the American Secretary of State John Foster Dulles. America now had a very strong ally in the form of the young Shah of Iran!

The French abandon Indochina (1954)

Neither the French nor the Vietnamese had given up in their fight for control of Indochina ... with battles raging back and forth between the two parties. But from the Vietnamese point of view, they had nothing to lose by continuing the battle ... whereas the French were finding the effort very expensive, with no real rewards for the effort ... and consequently were growing tired of the enterprise. The French were good at running down and defeating small groups of the Viet Minh ... but more would continue to pop up. At one point Vietnamese General Võ Nguyên Giáp even extended the battle into Laos, just to wear down further the French resolve to hold its position in Indochina. Then when fairly successful French General Jean De Lattre grew ill and died, the French resolve declined further.

Dien Bien Phu (1954). At this point (November 1953) the French attempted one major assault into Vietnamese territory, dropping 1800 paratroops into the huge and strategically placed Dien Bien Phu valley ...

from which they could send out patrols to hunt down Viet Minh units. But Giáp realized immediately that the French had put themselves in a very vulnerable position, with the valley surrounded by high hills from which Vietnamese artillery could bombard the French stations ... as well as destroy the airstrip by which the French received ongoing supplies – food as well as war materiel. And finally well positioned to undertake such an attack on the French, in March of 1954 Giáp began his attack on the well-surrounded French forces. With the monsoon season also beginning at this point, there was no way that French supplies could even be dropped successfully into the valley.

The 1954 Geneva Accords. It took only two months for the French to realize that they had been defeated in a most humiliating way ... at a time in which discussions were already underway in Geneva concerning the future of Indochina. The French were finally ready to admit defeat.

In the 1954 Geneva Accords, Vietnam was divided North and South temporarily ... "North Vietnam" designated as the Democratic Republic of Vietnam, under the presidency of Hồ Chí Minh, and "South Vietnam" designated as the State of Vietnam, under the Emperor Bảo Đại. But elections were to be held throughout Vietnam no later than July of 1956 to unite the two halves of the country.

Failed national elections. But in October of 1955, Bảo Đại's prime minister Ngô Đình Diệm deposed the emperor, proclaiming the Republic of Vietnam with himself as president.

Then as it came time to hold the 1956 elections, it was very clear that the elections would go strongly in favor of Hồ Chí Minh as the president of a united Vietnam. Thus Diệm refused to hold elections in the south, claiming that his part of the country was "not ready" for such elections. His people needed a bit more time in order to understand fully the dangers involved in a vote destined to bring on a Communist victory.

Does this sound familiar? This was the same excuse the Communists used earlier in blocking such elections in Korea. Anyway, now it was Diệm's turn to put forward this lame excuse ... because he had the full backing of Eisenhower's America in taking this position.

The "Third World" forms at Bandung – April 1955

With the former imperial nations of West Europe on clear retreat internationally and with America and Russia caught up in a Cold War of their own, it was decided by Indonesian president Sukarno, in getting mutual support from India's prime minister Nehru, to call a conference at Bandung in Indonesia ... inviting African and Asian leaders to come and discuss the possibilities of working together both economically and diplomatically as the rising new world. They were proposing the creation of an international alliance of nations "non-aligned" in the larger Cold War ... an alliance that would constitute what would come to be termed a "Third World."

Ultimately attending this week-long conference were leaders of 29 Asian and African nations.

This included China ... which did not want to be left out of this opportunity to register its importance internationally, seeing itself as the potential leader of what constituted basically an anti-European (both anti-East and West) independence movement.   Thus, besides helping organize this event, Mao sent his foreign secretary Zhou Enlai to the conference to align more nations in support of Mao's efforts to counter Eisenhower's strong support of Taipei rather than Beijing as the voice of China.   And indeed, in this matter Zhou succeeded grandly.

But other issues rallying the group were: the efforts of France to hold onto its North African territory (mostly importantly Algeria); the Dutch about to offer independence to its West New Guinea colony (which Sukarno wanted to be included as part of Indonesia); and even the Soviet Union's treatment of Muslim societies ... the latter however the conference ultimately failing to touch on – instead simply taking the position that it was opposed to colonialism of any kind, Eastern or Western.

The conference actually achieved a diplomatic breakthrough on a very touchy issue ... in getting Sukarno and Zhou to agree to require the huge Chinese portion of the Indonesian population to end their dual citizenship status and decide whether they would continue as Chinese or Indonesian citizens.   That would help solve a huge matter of tension between these two countries (for a while at least).

But otherwise, the conference produced simply a broad agreement among these countries to work together on this matter of anti-colonialism. They would stand united as members of the "Third World."*

The rearming of Germany ...
and the creation of the Warsaw Pact (1955)

Most interestingly, the creation of NATO in 1949 did not seem to require a Soviet response.   However, the move in 1955 to bring a fully rearmed West Germany into NATO did in fact inspire a very strong response ... from neighboring Czechoslovakia, East Germany, and Poland – still recoiling from

---

*Over time, various issues weakened the unity of this Third World front ... the term "Third World" ultimately coming to be merely a term referring to the poverty and violence that afflicted so many of the Third World nations.

the horror of the Nazi era – who wanted some kind of security pact designed to counter possible West German expansion.

This all started back in May of 1952, when Truman – drawing on an earlier plan (1950) of French prime minister René Pleven – pushed hard to get his European allies to bring West German military potential to play in the Cold War ... by getting them to create their own European Defense Community (EDC) – with West Germany as one of its members. But this military union would come fully under the control of an international authority ... just like its strategic coal and steel industries had been restored – and unified – under the Schuman Plan's ECSC. However, even for the French, the "Pleven Plan" was a bit too frightening. Thus in August of 1954 the French National Assembly voted "no" in the attempt to ratify the EDC treaty. Italy then simply refused to put the matter to a vote. The EDC was dead.

Then in 1954, Soviet foreign minister Molotov had proposed the idea of ending all military alliances of Europeans aimed at other Europeans, and instead having the Europeans join some kind of larger collective – but non-military – security organization ... one which would include a reunited (but disarmed) "neutral" Germany, East and West. This would take place with the withdrawal from Germany of all four occupying powers and the holding of national elections across Germany.

But in "demilitarizing" Europe (all except the Soviet Union of course) it was clearly designed to undercut the reason for the existence of NATO. There was no way that West Europe was willing however to leave itself without any means of military self-defense. No ... NATO was not going to go away. In fact, with the failure of the Pleven Plan, it would have to be NATO, not the EDC, which would have to serve as the means of bringing West Germany forward as a Western military ally. And thus it was that in May of 1955, West Germany was brought into NATO as a fully armed military member.

In response to this development, at the very same time (also May of 1955), Soviet Russia and seven other countries of the Eastern Bloc (Communist Yugoslavia, of course, would not participate) came together in Warsaw to sign a treaty setting up the Warsaw Treaty Organization (WTO) ... or just simply "the Warsaw Pact."

This now made the military union of the Soviets and their satellite nations official. And it gave the world a new name for those satellite nations. They were now the Warsaw Pact nations.

The Suez Crisis ... and the Hungarian Uprising
(October-November 1956)

Khrushchev's "New Look" ... and a supposed "thaw" in the Cold War.
At the 20th Party Congress in late February of 1956, Khrushchev stunned
everyone by strongly denouncing Stalinism in the harshest of terms. As
he saw things, it was time for the Soviets to recognize that the challenges
they faced were ideological, not military or police matters. There were
societies out there watching and deciding whether they wanted to go the
Communist rather than Capitalist route. Thus it was imperative for Soviet
Russia to show that world the great benefits – not the horrors – of taking
the Communist route. There was a battle going on out there for the minds
of men and women everywhere. In short, it was time for a post-Stalinist
"new look."

Although this address was supposedly delivered to a closed gathering,
in fact it easily found its way to the outside world (as Khrushchev actually
intended) ... causing quite a stir within the ranks of the Party, both in Russia
and in the Eastern Bloc. But it also stirred the larger world – which was
trying to interpret what this all meant with respect to the Cold War that had
long been raging.   Was this some kind of "thaw" in that icy Cold War?

The British ... and Nasser's Egypt. An area of particular interest to
Khrushchev – and equally to the West – was the Middle East. There, Arab
nationalism was stirring strongly ... offering the Soviets a grand opportunity
to put themselves in the middle of political and economic developments
which potentially had a distinctly anti-imperialist (meaning anti-Western)
character to them.

The British had long held a very strong interest in that part of the
world ... as it lay directly across the British path to its grand empire in India.
Although the British had not built the vital Suez Canal which strategically
linked India with Europe – in fact it was French engineers who designed and
supervised its construction in the 1860s – the British were able to buy out
the half-ownership of the Canal owned by the Egyptian king in 1875 – when
he fell into huge economic difficulties. Thus it had been under joint French-
British control since that time. In fact it was this interest in this strategic
position that determined Britain to put itself in the position of "protector" of
the Egyptian government – and the region around it – since then.

Of course under Atlee's Labour Government, that role had declined
greatly – in line with Britain's departure from Palestine in 1947.

But the British – once again (since 1951) under Churchill and his
Conservative Party – were doing what they could to get themselves back
into a pivotal position in the Middle East. Indeed, Churchill had succeeded
in February of 1955 in putting together a Middle East Treaty Organization
(METO) – better known as the Baghdad Pact – a military alliance of Britain,
Iran, Iraq, Pakistan, and Turkey. America had supported the venture but

had not joined, due to what Secretary of State Dulles termed the pro-Israel lobby in Congress. Egypt's president Gamal Abdel Nasser had been asked to join … but he refused to be closely aligned with Iraq's president Nuri al-Said – with whom he saw himself in competition for the leadership of the broader Arab world.

Nassar's refusal to join the Baghdad Pact would draw Egypt away from its former close relations with Britain. And it would certainly also undercut the importance of METO – which never really developed as a key player in the international game. But it also inspired Nasser to begin to portray Egypt's former ally Britain as the Arab world's biggest problem in its quest to unite the numerous Arab "nations" that the imperialist British (but joined by the French) had set up after World War One in order to give themselves the role of "protector" … when in fact there was only one true Arab "nation" – namely all of the Arab-speaking world. Nasser saw it as his job to unite that Arab nation into a single political entity. But this was what Britain's Iraqi friend al-Said was also trying to do. Consequently, relations between Egypt and Britain – the latter since mid-1955 now under Churchill's former deputy, Anthony Eden – grew hostile.

French problems in North Africa. But things in the Arab world were just as problematic for France … actually even more so. Algeria, which was located across the Mediterranean just opposite southern France, had since 1848 been considered an integral part of France (three of its *départements*) … and had been duly "Frenchified." In fact, neighboring Tunisia and parts of Morocco – and much of West Africa - also found themselves under strong French influence.

At this point, some one million ethnic Frenchmen (the *colons*) – approximately 10% of the Algerian population (but a much larger percentage of Algeria's urban population) – lived in Algeria as fairly successful farmers, shopkeepers, and civil servants. Additionally, some of the Arab population was well assimilated into French culture. On the other hand, some of it was truly still wed to ancient Muslim ways (especially the Bedouin tribesmen of the interior). But most of the Arab population simply served relatively silently within the larger, and still mostly alien French culture that dominated the land.

But by the mid-1950s, the situation in Algeria was becoming increasingly tense, with the colons and pro-French Arabs finding themselves targeted by Arab nationalists fighting for Algerian independence. The independence of Vietnam in 1954, had greatly inspired the Algerian nationalist groups. But the granting of independence to Morocco and Tunisia in 1956 had made the Algerian independence movement even stronger. In response, by this time, France had over 500,000 troops in Algeria trying to crush the rebellion.

But this merely made an ever-stronger case for Algerian independence in the thinking of the Algerian Arab population. And Nasser was playing up this Arab nationalist political potential in Algeria – to his own personal advantage, of course – as fully as possible.

Nasser and the Cold War. Meanwhile, Eisenhower and Dulles had become increasingly concerned about how the Cold War was reshaping itself into an East-West ideological contest for the loyalties of the rising nations of the Third World ... with the greatest potential for trouble in the rising Middle East. Originally America wanted to build an Arab military alliance with Nasser's Egypt as its key component ... but found that Nasser was interested in being seen as "unaligned."

However, Nassar's interest in building a high dam across the Nile River to provide the country with electricity did give Eisenhower and Nasser the possibility of working closely together. Thus America (joined by Britain) offered a loan of $270 million to Nasser to build that dam.

But Nasser was also interested in taking on military leadership in the Arab world ... and sought the weaponry designed to give him that role. Again he looked to America for that aid ... but found he did not like the conditions Americans demanded in the deal. They were to be used for defensive purposes only and granted only under American training and supervision. Nasser then turned to the Soviets ... and in September of 1955 was pleased to announce the completion of an arms deal with the Russians.

Running out of options, in December, America and Britain announced the pledge of $70 million towards the dam – in the hopes of luring Nasser Westward. But things did not improve. America was furious that Nasser extended recognition to Mao's government in China. And when, in June the following year (1956), the Soviets offered their own 2% loan worth $1.12 billion to build the dam ... in July, America backed out of its offer of support.

The beginning of the Suez Crisis (July 1956). This determined Nasser at the end of July to announce the takeover of the Suez Canal in order to complete the funding for the Aswan Dam project. He stated that the former owners (Britain and France) would be compensated for their loss over time. But Britain and France were not about to be bullied by the seizure ... and planned secretly – with Israel joining in the venture – to take back the canal and occupy the canal zone to protect their interests there.

Also motivating the event was that France was furious with Nasser for the encouragement he gave the Algerian insurrectionists and wanted him stopped. And Israel was also angry at the support Nasser gave the Palestinian fedayeen ... and for his blocking of their exit at the Straits of Tiran into the Red Sea

Sensing a growing international crisis, America tried to get Britain and France to ease up on any plans for what would constitute an act of war. Attempts were made to find an international compromise concerning the administration of the canal and the distribution of the canal's finances. But none of this proved able to shake British and French resolve to bring down Nasser.

Indeed, French premier Guy Mollet was deeply disappointed that his NATO partner America did not understand the importance to France of bringing Nasser down. After all, Mollet had turned down a Soviet offer to end their support of the Arab nationalists if they would drop out of NATO.

And thus their military plans continued to develop ... even while they went through the meaningless motions of sitting through diplomatic meetings. Also, Israel's planned military role in this whole affair was as yet unknown to any but the British and French.

Meanwhile – a student uprising in Hungary (October 1956). Totally unrelated to what was developing in the Middle East was what was developing elsewhere ... in Soviet-occupied East Europe. Since Khrushchev's "new look" speech, attitudes had been growing in East Europe that post-Stalinization also meant post-Sovietization. And thus on 23 October – at exactly the same time that the world was focused on the Suez crisis – 20,000 Hungarian students took to the streets to call for an end of the Soviet occupation of their country. By that evening about ten times that number had joined the protest.

This did not happen of course without some kind of buildup. And that buildup had actually been pushed by America itself ... through the broadcasts of its news network, Radio Free Europe (RFE). Dulles had issued promises through the RFE that America stood ready to help any people in overthrowing the Soviet tyranny that oppressed them so deeply. And the Hungarian students naturally thought that such help meant direct intervention in case the Soviets should attempt a counter-move.

Taken by surprise by this event, Khrushchev's response at first was quite timid, sending in some troops to try to put some sense in things there ... but not in such a way that it would give the appearance that Stalinism was still quite alive in Soviet Russia. But things merely worsened for Khrushchev day by day. The purging of pro-Soviet leaders was increasing and independent governing councils were rapidly being established in the country. The killing of pro-Soviet agents and the RFE broadcasts were also becoming very dramatic indicators of where things stood in Hungary ... and in the rest of East Europe. Something needed to be done. But what?

Simultaneous action at the Suez Canal and in Hungary. Meanwhile, with winter coming on and with increasing pressure in Parliament for the Eden government to do something about developments at the Suez Canal, clearly it was high time to make a move. Thus on 29 October the Israelis struck first, sweeping across the vast Sinai Desert and hitting an unprepared Egyptian army, forcing it back in fast retreat. Three days later (November 1st) the British struck the Egyptian army from the air, finishing off the Egyptian army ... and then several days later dropped British and French paratroopers near the canal in order to seize it. The action was an immediate and huge military success for the Israelis, British and French.

But politically and diplomatically, it would prove to be a huge disaster.

Meanwhile on the Hungarian front, Khrushchev remained hesitant about responding to the rapidly deteriorating situation in Hungary. Mao was even chiding Khrushchev for looking like such a weak leader. Then two events finally determined Khrushchev to make a very strong move on Hungary. One was Hungary's announcement that it would be leaving the Soviet bloc ... and planned to continue as a neutral nation in international affairs. That was totally inadmissible to Khrushchev. The other was the British, French and Israeli assault on Egypt – which not only had the world distracted but which he hoped would also make a Soviet move on Hungary appear to be no more imperialistic than the simultaneous British, French and Israeli move on Egypt.

Thus on November 4th, Khrushchev sent thousands of tanks and hundreds of thousands of Soviet troops into Hungary to crush the rebellion. It was a very bloody affair. Over 2,500 Hungarians were killed (but also 700 Soviet troops) and 20,000 Hungarians wounded (as well as 1,400 Soviet troops). Thousands (20,000 to 30,000?) were arrested, hundreds executed, and some 200,000 Hungarians fled the country, never to return.

And although this undercut deeply Khrushchev's "new look" ... it brought things quite quickly back into a proper Soviet order. Nonetheless, Khrushchev would continue to affirm that he still stood on the principle of his "new look" ... whatever that now meant – for clearly this had been an action of the Stalinist variety.

The "help" promised by America's RFE never materialized ... although the matter was taken to the U.N. – where of course a call for action was naturally vetoed by the Soviets. In short, the American superpower seemed not to be so super-powerful.

Worse, at the same time, America joined with Russia in bringing a resolution to the U.N. Security Council calling for a ceasefire and an immediate withdrawal of Britain, France and Israel from Egypt – with both resolutions vetoed by the British and French. But Eisenhower remained upset that the actions of the British and French allies had done far more damage in driving the Arab world into the arms of the Soviets than what regaining the canal ever offered the British and French. Furthermore, he was afraid that America's NATO commitments could have dragged them into a conflict in Egypt in which America had absolutely no interest whatsoever as a military action. Eisenhower even went so far as to threaten economic reprisals against Britain and France if they did not immediately withdraw from Egypt.

The political-diplomatic fallout from these events. Facing such pressure from America – and from the home-front where thousands of British had turned out to protest their government's action in Egypt – Eden's government had to acknowledge that Nasser's government was now the owner of the canal ... and that the British (and French) would withdraw. For Eden, and for the British in general, this was a humiliating defeat. Indeed, the event made it quite clear that the days of Britain as a great world power were over. It was now simply just another one of the many European nations – nothing more.

As for France, it too was stung deeply by America standing against it in the Suez Crisis. And that sting would come to be played for as much political gain as possible by De Gaulle when he soon returned to power (1958). He distinctly did not trust – or even much care for – America.

As for America, it lost considerable face by using none of its power to counter the Soviet crushing of the Hungarian uprising. Consequently, any hopes of the Eastern Europeans for American help in loosening the Soviet grip on their nations was now dead. At the same time America gained nothing from the Arab world (or the Third World in general ... as Eisenhower wished so much could have been the case) in its siding with the Soviets in coming up against its British and French allies (Israel was not yet considered any kind of American ally at the time).

Indeed, America's behavior raised all kinds of questions as to exactly where it stood on matters – and exactly how it could be counted on to support or oppose certain key diplomatic matters. Would America continue to respect the "all for one – one for all" notion that underpinned NATO? Or would America act only on the basis of its own national interest – and on that alone. Basically, all of America's NATO allies in giving over much of their military sovereignty to the American-directed military alliance had placed themselves under what they thought was, in compensation, the promise of American backing in the conduct of their own national diplomacy. But no such broader interest was shown by America to its British and French NATO allies in the Suez Crisis, when their traditional national interests were involved deeply and a military solution was the only serious option in the support of those interests. America actually opposed them.

Sadly, German Chancellor Konrad Adenauer thus grew uneasy about trusting America to come to Europe's aid (as required by NATO). Indeed, he became very bitter about America lining itself up with the Soviets in the Suez Crisis. All of this ultimately influenced deeply the German decision to draw closer to France in a special European relationship – one that would grow even deeper between Germany and France after De Gaulle took over in France.

At the same time, Soviet Russia played big to the Arab world its support of Nasser … making it appear that the Soviets were their best friends in their efforts to come out from under Western imperialism. And though actually the Soviets played the role of oppressor in the Hungarian matter, it made quite clear that nothing was seriously going to change in the Soviet mastery of East Europe. And if anything, it reconfirmed to a rather impressed world that indeed, under Khrushchev, the Soviets continued to be one of the world's great superpowers.

And of course now Nasser stood out in the Arab mind as the one person best able to bring about the Arab dream of an all-Arab republic. Indeed in 1958, Syria would join with Egypt in setting up just such a United Arab Republic under the presidency of Nasser.

American paternalism in the Western Hemisphere

Ever since America's issuing of the Monroe Doctrine in 1823, America had taken on a "protective" role with respect to its Latin-American neighbors to the south … a protection that differed hardly at all from what the Europeans saw as their role in Asia and Africa. But that protection had the qualities of looking out in particular for the economic interests driving those countries … economic interests frequently built on American investments in those lands – and the local officials willing to play the American game and protect those economic interests from local groups that wanted to seize those assets.

America talked a lot about its grand mission to spread democracy around the world. But with respect to the governments of these Latin-American neighbors, America tended to always look the other way because their associated officials were very dictatorial. In part this was because dictatorial government was part of their Hispanic political tradition. But it was also due to the fact that dictatorship was more or less required of these officials in order to guarantee the political and economic "stability" that those American investments required.

And when things did not always measure up to these American expectations – it was always easiest simply to send in U.S. Marines to straighten things out!

Castro's Cuban Revolution

But the situation could become embarrassingly corrupt … such as in the case of the Cuban government of Fulgencio Batista. Under his government not only extensive American interests in a vast number of industries were put under his protection, but so also was the Mafia in its business of prostitution, gambling and drugs. Thus Batista was a very corrupt, but very rich man. It had even come to a point that the American government itself was becoming quite embarrassed by his behavior.

Of course there was much local resistance against the Batista regime … and much sympathy in America toward those who wanted to get rid of Batista. But the Cold War was also raging at the time (the mid-1950s) and thus there was equal concern that efforts to dump Batista might once again profit only the eager Soviets. Caution was thus required.

One group attempting the overthrow of Batista was led by the young Socialist lawyer Fidel Castro. He and his brother Raul had attempted a coup in 1953, had failed and subsequently were imprisoned, then were released after two years. But once again (1956) they were trying to remove Batista – Castro now joined by the very colorful Argentinian doctor Ernesto Che Guevara.

Finally (1958), Eisenhower himself took action to bring Batista under control, placing an arms embargo on Cuba … and even encouraging the anti-Batista groups (even Castro's) to rise up against Batista's corrupt regime. At this point the crusading American press discovered the colorful Castro, and jumped into the matter, portraying Fidel Castro in very heroic terms.

Little by little the various groups advanced against a weakening Cuban army … with Castro's group receiving the greatest attention in the process. Finally on the first day of January 1959, Batista fled the country … and, to the roar of the crowds, Castro then entered the capital Havana as Cuba's new prime minister.

This was the beginning of the purging and even execution of former Batista officials (state and military). The casinos and hotels were also shut down … undercutting the Cuban economy greatly. But with Castro finally able to take full command of the government, in the typical Socialist manner, huge estates were redistributed as small plots to the small farmers. But so were even the small independent farms of Cuba's humbler classes. And although Castro claimed that he was no Communist, he certainly filled a number of positions on his cabinet with Communists.

Now opposition to these "reforms" began to grow … as Castro turned on not only members of the middle and lower-middle classes but also on other anti-Batista revolutionaries. As Castro's grip on Cuban society tightened, he forced hundreds, then thousands, to take to the hills … and even in vast numbers to nearby Florida.

Then when Eisenhower refused to lift the arms embargo he had earlier imposed on Cuba, Castro turned to the Soviets for military assistance. Needless to say, Khrushchev was more than happy to make Russia of great use to a nation just off the coast of America.

Eisenhower then struck back against Castro, cutting back America's purchase of sugar and the sale of American oil to Cuba ... in order to undercut Castro economically. But this merely opened another door of opportunity for the Russians – who were quick to purchase that sugar and sell Cuba oil from Russia's vast reserves. Then (August-October 1960) when American refineries refused to refine the Soviet oil, Castro simply nationalized these ... plus all other major American assets in his country (homes, banks, sugar and coffee plantations).

In turn, Eisenhower closed down all trade between America and Cuba (October 1960) ... and directed the Central Intelligence Agency (CIA) to gather and train (in Guatemala and Honduras) anti-Castro Cubans in order to overthrow this growing problem in Cuba. And he set plans to unleash this liberation force in early 1961 ... although he would be out of office by then.

CHAPTER NINETEEN

THE SETTLING IN
OF A BIPOLAR WORLD

* * *

EUROPEAN UNITY MOVES AHEAD

The Treaty of Rome founding the European "Common Market" (1957). On 25 March 1957, representatives of Belgium, France, Italy, Luxembourg, the Netherlands, and West Germany formally signed at Rome a new treaty, proposing to unite in numerous ways the economies of these six participating European nations. With the signing of this treaty, the European Economic Community (EEC) or "European Common Market" was scheduled to come into existence on 1 January 1958.

This was all part of the mood to create something of a United States of Europe, begun with the Schuman Plan which led to the creation of the ECSC in 1952, and the Pleven Plan, which attempted to unify the military of the same nations ... but which failed when the French National Assembly would not ratify the EDC treaty.

The latter failure however did not discourage those still seeking to unify a post-World-War-Two Europe. Under no circumstances was a politically vulnerable national spirit to be allowed to push the Europeans into another such war. Internationalism – not nationalism – was to be the new spirit directing European development.

As a result of a European conference at Messina in 1955, Belgian politician Paul-Henri Spaak was directed to come up with a plan at least to unify quite broadly the economies of West Europe into a Common Market. Spaak's Plan then led to a conference the following year ... in which some of the ECSC's institutions and that of the European Court of Justice would be used to form just such a Common Market ...although it was decided to keep the matter of vital atomic energy development separate from the rest of the economic realm. Thus two separate organizations, Euratom and the EEC were designed to move things forward.

Thus it was that at Rome in March of 1957, the Treaty bringing both organizations into being was signed ... and then submitted to the parliaments of the various participants for ratification. This time ratification was done quickly by all participants. Now the trade in European products could move without any tariff restrictions (eventually the move of labor across national borders would also take place as part of the deal).

Britain tries to go its own way. But Britain was not one of those EEC participants ... preferring to stay focused on its economic relations with its Commonwealth partners, to continue to give its farmers trade protection ... and a sentiment that Britain did best when working with America. And as an alternative to the EEC, Britain instead in 1959 helped put together its own European trade organization, the European Free Trade Area (EFTA), designed to promote trade among the members ... without having to impose a single or unified tariff such as was central to the EEC program. EFTA was thus designed to move forward in mutual economic support the European nations of Britain, Austria, Denmark, Norway, Portugal, Sweden and Switzerland (and eventually Finland). However, it soon proved that the amount of trade among those nations was not very substantial. Thus EFTA came to be a rather insignificant organization.

Finally, in 1961, seeing France and Germany develop economically vastly more rapidly than Britain, British Prime Minister Harold Macmillan made the decision to begin the process of gaining British entry into the EEC. But in 1963 a quite anti-Anglo-Saxon de Gaulle (who rather despised both Britain and America) vetoed the British application. And there was nothing further that could be done on the matter ... as long as de Gaulle remained France's leader.

$$* \; * \; *$$

THE CONGO CRISIS
(JUNE 1960 TO THE MID-1960s)

Intense personal political rivalry. Another major crisis to keep deeply the world's attention took place at about the same time in Sub-Saharan Africa ... when the Belgians finally gave over their Congo colony in June of 1960 to a hopeful coalition of local Congolese leaders, supposedly constituting the leadership team of a new Republic of the Congo. But with the departure of the Belgians, Congo society immediately broke down into a number of contending political groups ... principally between the new Congo President, Joseph Kasavubu, the new Prime Minister, Patrice Lumumba, and Moïse Tshombe, the leader of the secessionist Katanga Province. The

Katanga Province was where most of the vast mineral wealth of the Congo was located. And Tshombe's desire to have his Katanga go its own way as an independent country in Africa was seen as a clever way designed by the Belgians to continue to hold on to their key economic interests in their former colony. Also another smaller but also mineral-rich province, Kasai, was similarly attempting to set itself up as an independent state. And ultimately there was the staff of the new Congolese army, anxious to play a key role in the Congo's political development.   Things got very messy, very quickly.

The competition for power that developed among these leaders was of course personal, but also ideological, economic and ultimately (and most cruelly) tribal ... leading to an outbreak of ethnic cleansing undertaken by the Bakongo and the Baluba tribesmen (especially the Baluba of Kasai who were slaughtered by the thousands) ... and full revolt of sections of the new Congolese army.

Belgian Whites also found themselves caught in the middle of the strife ... with the Belgians themselves accused of playing the Congolese contentions to their own economic and political advantage.

The U.N. intervenes. In mid-July of 1960 the U.N. Security Council approved a U.N. peacekeeping force to place itself in the Congo to try to stabilize the quickly collapsing political situation there. Lumumba was hoping that these U.N. troops would help him put down the secessionist movements of the Kasai and Katanga provinces. But the U.N. Secretary-General Dag Hammarskjöld insisted that they had no authorization to serve in this capacity. So Lumumba turned to America for support ... but found Eisenhower reluctant to put America to such service, especially to a known "Socialist." Lumumba thus did the one thing designed to make America crazy: turn to the Soviets for assistance. Khrushchev was more than happy to help out, immediately sending some 1000 military "advisers" to the Congo to help Lumumba secure the unity of the Congo.

America now saw the Congo as going in the direction of Cuba: taking aid from the Soviets and thus joining the Soviet camp ... and in the eyes of America also becoming "Communist" in the process.

Mobutu takes action. Then in early September Colonel Mobutu Sese Seko seized control and had the feuding Kasavubu and Lumumba removed from office – and a new council put in their place to try to bring things back under control ... with Mobutu actually dominating things politically from behind the scenes. Now began the very unsteady process of trying to get the various leaders to work together – minus Lumumba, who was arrested (September). Lumumba then escaped to the Eastern Congo to set up his own government at Stanleyville. But he was captured in December by Mobutu's forces. Lumumba's fate now stirred considerable action in the U.N. ... and between America and the Soviets. Then in early 1961 Lumumba was sent to Katanga ... where he was immediately but quietly executed (January 1961) by Tshombe's troops. When news of Lumumba's execution finally emerged, the international outrage at this point was huge. It also inspired the rapid spread of the pro-Lumumba Simba Rebellion across the Eastern Congo.

The U.N. presses for a solution. Now Hammarskjöld attempted to undertake some personal diplomacy (mid-September 1961) to get the civil war to come to a halt ... but in flying to Africa, his plane crashed – with all aboard killed. Likewise, the attack on Irish U.N. troops (November 1960) and the killing of 13 Italian U.N. pilots a year later intensified the international call for someone or something to bring the crisis to a close.

More talks with Tshombe to bring his Katanga Province back into the Congo Republic went back and forth during the next year (1962) ... resulting in little real progress. Thus U.N. troops (20,000 at this point) became more aggressive in their move against Tshombe ... and in early 1963 Tshombe was forced to give up his independence movement.

Finally getting things settled down. A new constitution was drafted and approved the following year ... and Tshombe himself was called on to be the new Prime Minister! This in turn sparked new tribal and political factional rebellions ... and a new "People's Republic of the Congo" was declared by leftist rebels – quickly recognized and then supported by the Soviets, by Mao's Chinese Communists, and by Castro's Cubans.

At this point the Cold War was in full swing ... with America supporting the government of Tshombe and his military under Mobutu – also aided by Belgian troops and a large group of White mercenary troops.

Finally, in late 1964, a Simba rebellion in the Eastern Congo was finally broken by the Belgian troops – who were then accused of "neo-colonialism" by leftists everywhere. But it settled the crisis down considerably.

However, growing tensions between Kasavubu and Tshombe created such a political stalemate that once again Mobutu was moved to take control (November 1965) ... and over the next years bring all governmental powers into his own hands. He would continue to govern the Congo (the Congo undergoing a name change in 1971 as "Zaire") until his death in 1997!

✳ ✳ ✳

THE BIPOLAR WORLD IN TRANSITION

Eisenhower's last years in office

People to People (1956). Although a military man, Eisenhower – like most Americans (and others) at the time – understood the Cold War to be fought not on a military battlefield but instead a war fought in the minds of men and women in the realm of ideas ... ideas involving economic assistance programs, educational programs, media presentation (he was a huge supporter of Radio Free Europe) ... and ultimately simply the personal exchange of ideas by Americans with others of the world around him.

Thus it was that in 1955 Eisenhower organized a "People to People" conference to look at the idea of such personal exchange ... and the following year announced the actual establishment of a new government program of that same name operating under the United States Information Agency,[*] given the task of connecting ordinary American citizens with people overseas ... connecting them through sporting events, musical concerts, theatrical tours, "sister-cities" twinning ... and even just by way of individuals writing to each other as pen-pals. And after Eisenhower himself suffered a heart attack, he expanded it to include medical service abroad. Backing this program over the years were major American leaders in all forms of social activities (from the actor Bob Hope, to the Peanuts cartoonist Charles Schulz, to Walt Disney and many others)!

This was very indicative of the American mindset of the times ... shaped by America's original or founding Puritan (Protestant Christian) mindset, one that expected society to be built on the faithful service of its active citizens ... not on the commands coming from a ruling class or organization of some form or other. This traditional Christian mindset formed the foundations of the idea of "democracy" that America was so eager to bring to the world.

But as we have already noted, this American mindset was not something found commonly in the larger world. And there was nothing instinctive about such a mindset. Quite importantly, Eisenhower was correct in understanding that this would have to be taught to the larger world ... not brought to them by the force of arms. Unfortunately, this critically important understanding of the social dynamics of the larger world would be missing to most Americans, who – having never known any other world than their own – just supposed that the world "out there" was by all natural instincts ready to become like them ... only if freed from a tyrannical social order preventing them from developing along these "Christian" (at this point actually quite "Humanist") lines. Thus having a strong tendency to go down this Idealistic path, confusion and serious political-diplomatic

---

[*]But before leaving office in 1961 Eisenhower saw to it that the People-to-People Program was privatized as a non-profit organization, overseen by a Board of Directors located not in DC but in Missouri!

problems would soon result for the rising American power.

Sputnik. In October of 1957, Americans woke up to the shocking news that the Soviets had launched into orbit around the earth the world's first man-made satellite, the Sputnik. This was a double shock to Americans because it meant not only that the Soviets beat America in this critically important part of the race to show the world which society – Soviet or American – was more effective in advancing the realm of technology. It also meant that America no longer had protection from a nuclear attack – for certainly the rockets carrying Sputnik into orbit could also send nuclear bombs to America.

This was also a surprise because Soviet missile tests leading to this event had been conducted secretly (hiding the fact of the numerous catastrophes that had previously occurred) ... whereas American tests were conducted publicly – and cautiously for fear of just such a public disaster. And indeed there occurred just such a media-covered disaster that same December ... soon after the Soviets had launched yet another satellite in November with a dog aboard (which lived only a short time in space).

Americans were not sure whom to blame ... but certainly someone was responsible for this grand American failure. What Americans did not – or could not – understand was that such rocketry was a very complex matter in areas not quite so visible ... areas in which America was quite advanced in its technological development.

Nonetheless, Eisenhower, in mid-1958, gave the American public his answer in setting up the National Aeronautics and Space Administration (NASA) ... emphasizing the fact that NASA was to focus on science – not warfare – in its research. This helped some ... but still left Americans sensing their vulnerability to a Soviet nuclear attack.

"Peaceful coexistence." Nonetheless, there was good cause to hope that both Americans and the Soviets were going to be able to put the Cold War aside, at least the portion that had the two superpowers aiming at each other militarily. Seeing things now as a matter of competing ideas rather than guns, there was some hope that the two sides could find that the realm of ideas offered them the opportunity to work together in building the new world ... rather than standing in opposition to each other over every matter.

Thus it was that in July of 1959 Vice President Nixon traveled to Russia to support an American display of a typical American home at Moscow's National Exhibition ... and there also to conduct a friendly debate (the famous "Kitchen Debate") with Khrushchev about the differences in the lifestyle of the two countries. Then that same September, Khrushchev returned the favor by coming to America to see firsthand the "American Way" ... from corn farming to the Hollywood movie industry.

"Peaceful co-existence" seemed so completely the new international mood, that an international conference to be held in Paris the coming May (1960) was announced, one designed to bring Russia, America, Britain and France together to investigate ways to improve world peace.

The U-2 incident.   Then just two weeks before the scheduled Paris conference, the Russians announced that they had shot down a very high-flying American U-2 plane over Russian territory ... spying on Russia, to be sure. Thus the mood that was supposed to guide the upcoming conference was changed considerably.

But the situation only worsened when Eisenhower, believing that neither the plane nor its pilot could have survived the fall from such heights, claimed that this was not a spy plane but instead only a weather plane that had flown off course. But the pilot did survive – as well as critical sections of the plane – both of which confirmed that Russia had indeed brought down a spy plane.

At this point Khrushchev made as much as he could of the fact that he had caught Eisenhower issuing what the president knew quite clearly to be a lie. Thus Khrushchev announced that Russia would be withdrawing from the upcoming conference.

"Peaceful coexistence" thus took a huge hit ... as well as Eisenhower politically. Sadly, the "era of good feelings" that Eisenhower was hoping to leave behind as his presidential legacy was just not to be.

✳ ✳ ✳

DE GAULLE'S FRANCE

The worsening situation in Algeria.   By 1957, acts of terrorism were spreading not only through Algeria but even France itself as Arab nationalists – members of the FLN (*Front de libération nationale*) – and French die-hards – members of the OAS (*Organisation armée secrète*) – fought each other in the streets over the issue of Algerian independence.

Then when it looked as if the French government was interested in negotiating a settlement with the FLN, on 13 May 1958, angry Algerian French (soldiers and civilians) seized the government buildings in Algiers and formed a new governing committee, headed by General Jacques Massau – who the previous year had his paratroopers deliver a major blow to the FLN. Infuriated over the idea that France was going to abandon Algeria the way it did Vietnam, Massau now called on de Gaulle to come out of retirement to save France. The expectation was that de Gaulle would take the hard line against Arab nationalism that the political leaders of the French 4th Republic seemed unwilling or unable to assume.

In support of this move, French paratroopers took control in Corsica – and rumors began to spread that they were readying themselves to take control in Paris. A military coup in the heart of modern France ... how humiliating (and dangerous)! All eyes began to turn to de Gaulle. Only he seemed to have the power to avert a horrible national catastrophe. Thus it was that the French President René Coty called on de Gaulle to take over as the Fourth Republic's prime minister.

De Gaulle's Fifth Republic. De Gaulle was more than willing to answer the call to serve once again as France's "savior" ... but not unless he was granted six months of emergency powers and unless a new constitution was drafted and approved that would then give the French national executive the powers needed to lead France. France seemed to have no other choice but to grant de Gaulle his conditions. The French parliament voted its approval of these terms ... and thus at the beginning of June, de Gaulle took over the French political process.

A new constitution was quickly drafted under the guidance of de Gaulle's supporter Michel Debré, and in September (1958) was approved in a national referendum by 78% of the French vote. In December de Gaulle was elected President of the new French 5th Republic.

There were of course many issues confronting France at that time, and de Gaulle set out to meet these challenges one by one (economic recovery, relations with the Germans, with the Americans, with the British, with France's African colonies). But definitely the biggest challenge was Algeria ... and the general matter of African independence. Algeria was not considered a colony and thus handled differently than France's sub-Saharan African colonies ... which were immediately given the opportunity to go their way as newly independent nations ... although they would remain in a diplomatic union with France as part of the French Community.[*]

Algerian independence. Now France and the world waited to see how de Gaulle was going to tackle the thorny problem of Algeria.

It soon became apparent that de Gaulle was leaning in the direction of granting independence to Algeria. Consequently, the Algerian French and sections of the French military felt betrayed – and became bitter and rebellious ... to the point of attempting a major military coup against de

---

[*]Only the African colony of Guinée (Guinea) chose full independence at this point, coming under the authoritarian rule of Ahmed Sékou Touré from 1958 until his death in 1984 – a time period in which he allied closely with the Soviet Union ... although in his last years he increasingly looked to America and the West for economic assistance in the form of investments in his country.

Gaulle (April 1961). Numerous assassination attempts were also made on de Gaulle. But de Gaulle remained in tight control of the situation, crushing rebellions – even violently, such as the bloody suppression of an Algerian uprising in Paris in October of 1961 – of both Algerian nationalists on the one hand and the very unhappy French Algerians (*colons* – also known as the *pieds-noirs**) on the other.

Finally, in March of 1962, de Gaulle's decision in favor of Algerian independence was confirmed in the Evian Accords. In April, a national referendum was held throughout France - with nearly 18 million "yeses" to less than 3 million "nos." Then in July the Algerians voted on the Accords, with nearly six million "yeses" and less than 17 thousand "nos."

It was official. Algeria was independent. And France could move on. But so would a million pieds-noirs who abandoned their homes and businesses in Algeria and headed for France, to try to start up a new life there. And de Gaulle would have to face yet another (very serious) assassination attempt on 22 August 1962.

$$* \; * \; *$$

THE BRIEF KENNEDY ERA (1961-1963)

Kennedy's "New Frontier." The presidential election of 1960 pitted Vice President Nixon against Massachusetts Senator John (or "Jack") Kennedy. Certainly Kennedy's youthfulness and personal glamor (and that of his beautiful wife Jacqueline) made him a very attractive candidate. But he was a Roman Catholic – which made many Protestant Americans uneasy. However, Kennedy made it clear that his Catholicism would have nothing to do with the way he conducted his office.

Ultimately, America decided – in a very close vote that November – that Kennedy, not Nixon, would be the one to lead the country forward.

In taking office (January 1961), Kennedy also made it very clear that he would continue the idea of Americans themselves being the chief political tool he would use in promoting America abroad. He reaffirmed that the challenge America faced was the "New Frontier" ... calling on Americans to action abroad. And he issued his famous challenge: "Ask not what your country can do for you, but what you can do for your country."

And that challenge would take immediate form (March 1961) as Kennedy's Peace Corps program, going even further than Eisenhower's People to People program in the way his program was designed to send young Americans abroad – to show Third World villagers the "American

---

*"Black feet" ... a pejorative term long applied to the colons – the original source of the term still something of a mystery ... or at least under debate.

way" ... by coming to live and work among them for a couple of years. These Peace Corps volunteers would be taught the local language of a Third World country and then be sent there to undertake the task of teaching villagers economic and social skills that would help bring them successfully into the 20th century ... on the American side in the competition with the Soviets, of course. And indeed, tens of thousands of recent college graduates joined ... eager to be of just such American service abroad.

The in-between "Silent Generation." This age group of young Americans, termed the "Silents," were too young to have served in World War Two or even Korea, like the older Vets. But then the Silents too were older than – and quite different from – the younger "Boomer" age group coming up behind them ... Boomers who would begin to take their place as young adults only in the mid-1960s. In the early-1960s, the older Silents indeed went about the business of serving the nation and the larger world quietly but determinedly ... whereas the younger Boomers would soon distinguish themselves in the way they challenged quite loudly their own American nation and its "authoritarian" or "Fascist" social traditions ... in every way imaginable. And America would feel deeply the effect of this shocking generational development ... the first of many coming its way.

The Bay of Pigs Fiasco (April 1961). But also in his first days in office, Kennedy was to learn that a militia of 1,400 American-trained Cubans was scheduled quite soon to be unleashed on Castro's Cuba ... with full American support. Kennedy contemplated the idea of calling this off – realizing that this would put America in something of the same light as Russia with its invasion of Hungary in 1956. But something needed to be done about this society just opposite Florida – that was clearly moving itself into the Soviet Orbit. So he gave the go-ahead to the operation.

But try as he might, his effort to keep America's involvement appear to be minimal was not working. And thus with Castro's military able to stall the militia at the beaches, on the third day of the operation Kennedy called off the American air-cover and resupply of ammunition needed by the militia. The results militarily were disastrous for the militia ... who were easily defeated and then paraded as prisoners in front of the world press. And the results were just as disastrous diplomatically for America ... as the details of the operation from the beginning (American training of the militia in Honduras and Guatemala) to the end (the withdrawal of full American support) became well known to all. Furthermore, it all made the new young President Kennedy appear to be quite amateurish as a national leader.

A failed East-West summit in Vienna (June 1961). But Kennedy still pushed forward the idea of keeping the Cold War from building back up again ... especially with Khrushchev's announcement that he intended to close down the exit of East Berliners – and East Germans in general – into West Berlin (too much East German professional talent was escaping to the West through West Berlin). Thus Kennedy proposed a summit conference with Khrushchev to be held in Vienna in June ... which Khrushchev accepted. On Kennedy's way to Vienna, he and Jackie paid a "goodwill" visit to de Gaulle in Paris ... where de Gaulle warned Kennedy about Khrushchev's tough style.

And indeed, Kennedy came away from Vienna with no gains coming from Khrushchev. Worse, the meeting simply confirmed Khrushchev's opinion of Kennedy as a very weak leader. Thus the Berlin closing moved ahead as scheduled ... despite Kennedy's effort to show some degree of diplomatic muscle in announcing that America would be strengthening considerably its support of NATO in Germany.

The Berlin Wall goes up (August 1961). Following the announcement that indeed all exits into West Berlin would soon be closed, tens of thousands of East Europeans fled into West Berlin. But finally, on 13 August, East German police began to put up barbed wire across all the exits ... and then began building a huge wall encircling West Berlin, armed with watch towers and minefields as additional restraints. And indeed, that closed completely the last door of escape from the Soviet side of the Iron Curtain into the West.

The world watched closely to see how Kennedy would respond to this challenge. Would he have American bulldozers and tanks take down the wall? Ultimately the only thing Kennedy did was to march NATO troops to Berlin ... daring Khrushchev to try to block the West's military access into West Berlin. But otherwise he did nothing in particular about the wall itself.

The Cuban Missile Crisis (October 1962). Castro's Cuba remained a thorn in the American side, and despite the Bay of Pigs failure, Kennedy and the CIA remained intent on bringing Castro down. But this made it very easy for Khrushchev to convince Castro in the summer of 1962 to accept the Soviet plan to place strategic nuclear-tipped ICBMs (Inter-Continental Ballistic Missiles) in Cuba ... able to reach most of the U.S. That would not only protect Castro from a direct American military assault, it would neutralize the American ICBMs placed in Turkey aimed at the USSR ... and it would give Khrushchev additional political leverage in conducting his Cold War against America on all fronts.

Even then Khrushchev had to be very careful in undertaking this venture ... first having to convince his fellow party leaders that there was nothing to fear in this – given the weak character of Kennedy – and much to gain in the way this would bring America under the nuclear gun. Also it would involve the development of considerable infrastructure ... including the placing in Cuba of tactical missiles to protect the project in its developmental phase.

American U-2 spy planes detected the placement of these tactical rockets ... presuming them to be there to bring down more of their U-2 planes ... and backed off a bit in their overflights. Also a cloud cover moved in over Cuba ... blocking any ability to see what was going on below. In the meantime, a number of Soviet missiles were brought in to Cuba to the first 12 of 40 proposed launch sites.

Then on 14 October the cloud cover cleared over Cuba ... and America immediately knew what was underway there. But what then to do about the situation? Debate now got underway within the Kennedy cabinet about how this or that response would produce this or that result, politically as well as militarily. Meanwhile, rumors about the Cuban situation were already hitting the American press. Deep anxiety was building in America.

When Soviet Foreign minister Andrei Gromyko was confronted over the matter, he continued to offer the Soviet excuse that all of this was just tactical weaponry ... which of course he knew that the Americans already knew was not true. In short, the Soviets were not really ready to engage in any serious diplomatic discussion over the matter.

Finally, on the 21st, the decision was made to place a naval blockade around Cuba in order to block further shipment of missiles and material to Cuba from Russia. This actually constituted an act of war ... though the Kennedy team knew that it was not sufficiently provocative to initiate a nuclear war ... with America having some 15 times the number of Soviet nuclear warheads – and an already operational delivery base in Turkey.

The next day America's Latin American neighbors forming the Organization of American States (OAS) met ... and decided to give full support to Kennedy's "quarantine" isolating Cuba – a severe blow to Castro diplomatically. Then that evening, Kennedy went before the American people (and the world) to describe in detail the problem ... and the decided American response.

Things got very tense over the next days. The American naval blockade was put in place immediately ... and stopped some ships headed for Cuban ports – but let them pass when it was discovered that they were carrying no strategic materials. But Soviet ships carrying the ICBMs were still headed toward Cuba ... with the world watching nervously as they drew closer to Cuba. Meanwhile, construction at the launch sites continued.

Indeed, Castro became so convinced of a pending American military assault on Cuba that he called on Khrushchev to issue orders for a nuclear strike on America, even if conducted only by the smaller nuclear missiles presently in place, missiles which could probably reach no further than Miami. That was truly a strange request – for it would have meant a full nuclear attack in response, one that would have completely destroyed Cuba … and one starting an all-out nuclear war between Russia and America. There was no way that Khrushchev was willing to go down that road.

Finally, on the 27th, Khrushchev came out with a diplomatic counter-offer: he would remove his missile from Cuba if America did the same with its missiles in Turkey.

Castro was deeply angered that this offer had been made without prior consultation with him by Khrushchev … although there was little that Castro could do about the matter. But clearly, he was ready to see Cuba destroyed … if it meant that America – and much of the rest of the world – were also destroyed in the process.[*]

Now the back-and-forth got very serious when on that same day a U-2 plane was shot down over Cuba … Khrushchev being quick to claim that it had been a Cuban action, not a Soviet action (although only the Soviets had the power to conduct such a strike). A furious America then responded that if another plane were shot down, then the Americans would have to attack all the missile sites … killing numerous Soviet technicians as well as the missile infrastructure. At this point Khrushchev realized that he was not up against just some young, weak American president. This was serious business.

But at the same time, the American threat was counterbalanced by America's acceptance of Khrushchev's offer to remove the Soviet missiles. The Turkish removal was not mentioned specifically, but was implied as an exchange to be conducted "voluntarily." The next day (the 28th) Khrushchev announced his approval of the deal … including specifically the Turkey-missile removal in exchange.

But still, Soviet ships with ICBMs continued to head toward Cuba … and the American blockade also continued. Finally, as the Soviet ships approached the blockade, they were ordered to turn around. The Soviet-American agreement was indeed now effectively in place.

But what was not known to America was that smaller nuclear-armed rockets, not part of the accord, Castro wanted to have under his own command in case of the continuing possibility of an American assault on his

---

[*]What is especially terrifying about this experience is that it makes clear the fact that such socially suicidal instincts as Castro's are not unknown among self-important political leaders willing to bring down the rest of humanity rather than deal with the failure of their own leadership (Hitler being clearly a recent example, not to mention Castro). With nuclear weapons in the hands of such individuals, the world would find its very survival quite problematic. Hopefully the world will be able to keep nuclear weapons out of the hands of such individuals, although in the end only God can offer mankind such protection.

regime. This startled Khrushchev sufficiently to have even these removed on the 22nd!

Also what was not known in America was how close America and the world had come to a full nuclear engagement ... when an American ship dropped depth charges in Cuban waters – unknowingly nearly hitting a Soviet submarine located there. The submarine had orders to launch its nuclear-tipped missiles if it came under attack ... but an order that could be given only if all three commanding officers agreed to the attack. Two did. Thankfully, a third did not ... sparing the world a nuclear attack that would most likely have quickly spun itself into a global nuclear holocaust.

Anyway, with the Kennedy-Khrushchev agreement in place, now began the dismantling of the Soviet missile sites in Cuba and the 150 nuclear warheads based there. Even Soviet bombers based in Cuba were flown home. Thus by 20 November, Kennedy was able to announce to the world that the blockade was being lifted. And at this point then began the more complicated removal of the American missiles based in Turkey ... the project completed by the spring of the following year (1963). Thus the Cuban Missile Crisis and its diplomatic outfall was over.

Overall, the event played strongly in Kennedy's favor, strengthening his image as a very strong American president. And it would likewise undercut Khrushchev's standing at the Kremlin, indeed being one of the reasons his fellow party members cited in demanding Khrushchev's retirement in 1964.

Khrushchev would be the first, however, to be retired from Soviet power alive – being allowed to live out his life comfortably (but sadly) at home and at his dacha resort ... although politically and historically he would immediately become a "non-person" – carefully and fully forgotten by the society he once led.

The worsening situation in Indochina. The withdrawal of France in 1954 from its Indochinese colony under the terms of the Geneva Peace Accords did not, however, change the ambitions of the local Indochinese powers-that-be ... nor end the concerns of America that the area was about to come under Communist expansion ... in accordance with Eisenhower's term "the falling domino principle" that he used in April of 1954 in explaining the dangers of not acting immediately in the matter of Communist expansion in Indochina. Like a line of dominoes, if one falls, then so does the next one, and the one then next to that, etc. Thus was born the "domino theory" – something that would become so very important in American foreign policy thinking.

And indeed, going into the 1960s, Indochina was experiencing considerable political-military disruption at the time. For instance, there was no way that North Vietnam leader Hồ Chi Minh was going to give up on the idea of uniting both the northern and southern regions of Vietnam under his Communist rule. Meanwhile, in the Vietnamese South, rather dictatorial President Ngô Đình Diệm had undertaken land reform in order to make himself more popular (his Roman Catholicism did not go over well with the largely Buddhist population) ... limiting the size of the rice farms and allowing land to be purchased by the peasants. But slowly over time, the farmlands basically fell into the hands of a number of Diệm's largest supporters – deeply alienating the peasants.

Diệm's regime did however enjoy American support – even if lukewarm. Eisenhower and his Secretary of State Dulles were not pleased by Diệm's presidential performance ... but felt that they had no alternative candidate.

Meanwhile, in terms of the domino effect, the first domino that looked as if it might fall was the Kingdom of Laos, not Vietnam. There a civil war was building among the three sons of Laotian king Sisavang Vong: Prince Boun Oum was leading the rather pro-French conservatives; Prince Souvanna Phouma was prime minister and leader of what was considered the "neutrals"; and Prince Souphanouvong was leading the left-wing Lao Patriotic Front and its Pathet Lao troops – supported strongly by Hồ Chi Minh, Mao, and Khrushchev.

For a period of time, 1956-1959, something of a coalition government of the three groups was put in place. But tensions were building as the North Vietnamese were doing everything possible to strengthen the Communist position in Laos, even sending some 30,000 to 40,000 of their troops into Laos. The situation only worsened in 1960 when "neutrals" in the contest attempted a political coup ... but political confusion tended to move the outcome in favor of the Communist Pathet Lao.

A Communist outcome in Laos was very important to Hồ Chi Minh ... for the "Ho Chi Minh Trail" that ran north and south through eastern Laos enabled Ho to move his army and supplies from the north all the way to the southern region of Vietnam. In short, securing a friendly Laos was vital to Ho's effort to take over South Vietnam. But at the same time, America was doing what it could to support financially the Royal Lao Government, some of it directly, some of its through French advisors in Laos.

By 1961, Soviet-American involvement was running deep in Laos, the Soviets supplying the Pathet Lao with arms, Americans doing the same for the Laotian Royal Army ... plus for a growing Hmong* militia that had joined the action.

---

*A distinct ethnic group – made up of many competing clans – not part of the surrounding Laotian, Vietnamese, or Chinese peoples. America enlisted and trained many Hmong to fight the Pathet Lao – though many others of the Hmong decided to join the Pathet Lao.

But by 1962 the Royal Army, despite direct American military aid, was constantly failing in its encounters with the Pathet Lao ... and thus Kennedy pressured the Royalists and the Neutrals into a political coalition with the Pathet Lao ... under the International Agreement on the Neutrality of Laos (23 July 1962). According to the Agreement, all non-Laotian parties were to withdraw from Laos. Thus America took its men out of Laos ... but the North Vietnamese did not.

Next door in South Vietnam, not much had changed. Diệm was still in power ... and not doing well. Kennedy was not as focused on Vietnam as he was on Laos ... and in 1961 merely put forward a simple program in South Vietnam that hopefully would protect – actually isolate – the Vietnamese peasants from the Communist insurgents operating in the South, the Viet Cong ... by relocating the peasants to fortified villages. But by 1963 the program was clearly achieving little strategically.

The South Vietnamese army (the ARVN – Army of the Republic of Vietnam) was not doing well ... losing an important battle in January of 1963 to a much smaller group of Viet Cong. Morale in the ARVN was low. And tensions between the small but governing Catholic regime and the Buddhist populace was also rising ... with the ARVN under Diệm's brother (who was also serving as Vietnam's Archbishop) attacking Buddhist pagodas around the country. The situation was becoming so bad that a Buddhist monk even publicly torched himself in Saigon in June of 1963.

Thus it was beginning to look in the eyes of the Kennedy administration like it was time for a regime change!

Consequently, CIA instructions went out to some of ARVN's generals to remove both Diệm brothers from power ... which they did on 2 November 1963 – executing both brothers in the process. Kennedy was shocked by the killings, but rebounded in having his Ambassador Henry Cabot Lodge congratulate the coup leaders.

But leaderless, the situation in South Vietnam quickly grew chaotic. But what Kennedy was planning to do at this point will never be known.

Kennedy is assassinated. A mere three weeks after Diệm's murder, Kennedy would experience the same tragedy (November 22nd). On a visit to Dallas to repair political relations with the Texas Democrats, Kennedy was shot and killed riding in an open convertible through the streets lined with cheering crowds with his wife – and with Texas Governor John Connally (who was also wounded). The presumed assassin, who shot from the upper story of a building along the route, was Lee Harvey Oswald. He was tracked to a movie theater, was arrested ... and then two days later was assassinated by Jack Ruby as Oswald was being transferred at the Dallas police headquarters to the county sheriff.

The matter was not only shocking in the extreme, it all made little sense. Oswald was known to have Cuban political connections. Was this then a Communist plot? What about Jack Ruby ... known to have mob connections? Was Oswald's killing a move of the mob (or some other source) to silence Oswald before he could reveal what was actually behind the whole affair?

Ultimately an investigation into the matter directed by Supreme Court Chief Justice Earl Warren concluded ten months later that it all seemed to have been merely the personal acts of those two individuals. But the Warren Commission's report did not really answer a lot of conspiracy theories abounding everywhere. But there was nothing of substance that could be found to truly challenge the Commission's findings.

In any case, Kennedy's death meant that America was about to enter a whole new world politically under a new national leader – a new world that would change America deeply.

Deep social-spiritual change underway in America

The struggle to end racism. America understood itself not only as the supreme power called by God to protect Western civilization from the evil powers of authoritarianism (Communism specifically at that point) ... but also as having the responsibility of serving as a social model designed specifically to inspire and guide other societies in their quest for "democratic modernization."

In this modeling role, America knew itself to be far from perfect. Highly embarrassing was the place that American Blacks found in American society ... something that certainly darkened America's image in Africa (to the extent that Africans even cared about the matter). The horrible Civil War of 1861-1865 had ended the horror of slavery ... but had not changed substantially the miserable place Blacks occupied at the very bottom of the social status system of the American South. But racism ran almost as deep in the North, especially in the slums of Northern cities. Indeed, Blacks found themselves quite generally unwanted by the White world as friends or neighbors.

But key American leaders knew deeply that this all had to change ... and change deeply. And understanding the American political process as the heart of social reform, social reformers began to push forward the process of getting members of the Black community out to vote ... vote for a better world for themselves.

But even beyond the political process was the one of moral-spiritual change in the hearts of the American people themselves. And there to lead that campaign (when not also involved in voting rights actions) was the Baptist minister, the Rev. Dr. Martin Luther King, Jr. And truly powerful was his challenge to America, offered in August of 1963 before a massive gathering and a widely TV-viewing America from the steps of the Lincoln Memorial in DC ... to bring to reality his dream of an America where all its citizens, Blacks and Whites, lived and worked together as equals ... even as brothers and sisters. And why not. It all seemed not only so reasonable as a challenge, it seemed by most Americans to be a necessity.

The slow move from Christianity to Humanism as America's guiding religion or worldview. But there were also other changes underway at the time ... ones arising from America's now long-standing contest between Middle America's Christianity and Intellectual America's Humanism. And the Supreme Court was already in the process of becoming the most important scene of battle between the two parties ... with Congress itself trying (not very successfully) to keep up with the game.

And the reason for the Supreme Court taking the lead in the matter of social-cultural "progress" was because of the action of the leading legal instrument of Intellectual America, the American Civil Liberties Union (ACLU). As we have already noted, the ACLU was already long committed to removing Christianity as America's foundational worldview and culture ... and replacing that with Humanism. And since the late 1950s, the ACLU was finding willing support for its program among the body of justices making up the Earl Warren Court. In the case of *Engel v. Vitale* (1962), originated in the lower courts in 1959, and finally reaching the Warren Court in 1962, the ACLU got the Supreme Court to rule that public schools have no right to authorize a school prayer for the children to recite. Then the next year the Warren Court went further in two more cases in 1963, (one brought by the ACLU the other by the atheist Madalyn Murray O'Hair and her young son William[*]) reaffirming the rule of no school prayer, adding also that Bible reading is likewise forbidden.[†]

---

[*]A chilling irony in the story of the life of Madalyn Murray O'Hair and her children was that in 1995 she, and another of her sons Jon, and granddaughter Robin disappeared, and only six years later their bodies found buried – after having been executed by their murderers, one of them an officer in her American Atheists organization. Also ironic was that earlier (in 1980) her son William (Bill) became a Christian (Baptist), eventually becoming even an evangelist and Christian writer – and today chairman of the Washington-D.C.-based Religious Freedom Coalition, lobbying Congress for aid to Christians persecuted in Communist and Islamic countries!

[†]The First Amendment actually reads: "Congress shall make no law respecting an establishment of religion, or prohibiting the free exercise thereof; or abridging the freedom of speech, or of the press; or the right of the people peaceably to assemble, and to petition the Government for a redress of grievances."

Thus, according to the Supreme Court, Jefferson's proclaimed "wall of separation" (1802) between America's religions and America's federal government was designed not to protect religion from government action, but instead to protect government action (which, by the 1960s, was a process undergoing rapid expansion through the efforts of Intellectual America) from the realm of religion. That meant that Christianity should have no place in the public world of America. Thus effectively, the ACLU got the Supreme Court to reinterpret America's *religious protections* – clearly stated in the 1st Amendment of the American Constitution – to now read as *religious restrictions*! However ... the ACLU's Humanism was quite happy to take over Christianity's traditional role in American society ... because it was not "religion." It was Truth itself ... scientific truth!

Congress, supposedly America's only Federal body authorized by the Constitution to make or revise the law,* tried to take action to counter this move taken by the Supreme Court. Congressman Frank Becker in 1963 undertook the nearly impossible task of amending the Constitution in order to make the matter of religious freedom (allowing prayer and Bible-reading in the public schools) quite clear ... but had the chairman of the Senate Judiciary Committee hold up hearings on the matter for a year until all momentum was effectively lost. Then in 1966, Republican Senate Minority Leader Everett Dirksen took on the same challenge ... which was supported by nearly all Republicans and Southern Democrats – but opposed by the "Liberal" Democrats – thus failing to get the required 2/3rds vote necessary to move it along. No further efforts would be undertaken until the early 1980s when President Reagan would undertake – and fail at – a similar attempt.

✳ ✳ ✳

THE JOHNSON (LBJ) ERA (1963-1969)

Johnson – the Washington insider. With Vice President Lyndon B. Johnson (LBJ) now taking office as U.S. President, Kennedy's international sophistication will be replaced by Johnson's air of Texas "good-old-boy" plainness. But there was nothing plain about LBJ ... having been chosen as

---

*According to the Constitution, the President is authorized only to execute or apply the written law ... and the Judiciary (the Supreme Court and the Circuit and District Courts) is authorized only to judge cases of its violation or contested execution. Neither the President nor the Judiciary have Constitutional authorization to make or revise the law itself ... or read it in such a way that it creates new legal principles. In America's democracy, only the people's elected representatives to Congress have that right ... something which often goes unobserved by the Executive and Judicial branches of American government ... which have a tendency to want to do "democracy from above."

the Democratic Party's Senate Minority Leader in 1953 (at 44, the youngest ever to hold that powerful position) and then, with the Democratic Party election victory in 1954, the Senate Majority Leader – the most powerful man in the Senate ... holding that position all the way up to his installation as Kennedy's Vice President in early 1961. But as Vice President, he had played only a minimal political role (the Kennedys actually did not like him very much). But now, with Kennedy's death, he was U.S. President. And he was determined to show America what a Real President was capable of!

The "Great Society." What Johnson lacked in charisma he more than made up for in political skill – quite able to get the Democratic-Party majority in Congress to follow his lead ... the way Kennedy as President was never able to achieve. But he was not only powerful, he had a very strong caring heart for the poor (having been brought up in tough circumstances himself) ... and planned to use all the power he had in Washington to see "progressive" social programs put into action.

He had also been brought into the world of politics – and was shaped deeply by Roosevelt's New Deal. He understood extensive government management of American society as government's proper role ... although a very prosperous America of the 1960s was going through none of the social emergencies that supposedly had justified the New Deal's takeover of much of the country's social dynamics in the 1930s ... or the Federal government's commanding role during the years of World War Two. But from his point of view, there was still much work to be done to bring America to perfection as a social model to the larger world. Washington had a lot of work to do to get things to just such perfection.

And his wife "Lady Bird" was determined by her own Southern aristocratic instincts to turn the rather humble American capital city into something of a great metropolis, on the order of London, Paris, Rome, Vienna, etc. Under the Johnsons, DC was to become a culturally majestic as well as a politically powerful city ... more appropriate to its position as the leader of the Free World.

Thus it was that on 22 May 1964, addressing a University of Michigan graduating class, Johnson announced the basic design of what was to be his Great Society Program. The program was intended not only to end all poverty and racial injustice in America – but to improve America's educational and professional development; to protect its natural beauty from pollution, overcrowding and loss of fields and forests; and to shape America's rapidly developing urban life ... offering housing for all, improved urban infrastructure, and enhancement of a urban cultural growth – even the promotion of a spirit of urban community-mindedness.

And how was he going to do this? In the speech he claimed that he did not intend to make this a matter of federal government programming … but a social movement that would build itself on the support of cities and states all across the nation.

The only problem with this grand approach was that while Johnson commanded great power in DC, he had no such influence out in those very cities and states. Consequently, he had to have known at the time he made this promise that in fact it would be the DC government that would be given the responsibility to see his programs put into action. And this was going to require an enormous expansion of DC's bureaucratic infrastructure to make this happen.

And indeed, DC's population (especially in the realm of the legal profession) expanded enormously … and very quickly. Washington was taking command in America's development as a Great Society.

The Black-Power Movement. Another development that would shake America deeply was the growth of a very militant Black power "revolution of rising expectations" … in particular the more active of the movement that identified themselves as the "Black Panthers." Despite the quite visible progress in getting a much more affirmative pro-Black cultural shift underway, the progress was never fast enough for young Blacks for whom expectations for social equality were that it was to take place immediately … something that was guaranteed not to happen. In response, their anger against White society produced a rapidly rising incidence of urban violence … attacks on White (or Asian) businesses located in their neighborhoods, attacking, pillaging and burning them with great abandon – as if it constituted some right of theirs to enact such "justice" against White society. Thus to the tune of police and fire engine sirens rushing to burning inner-city Detroit or Newark or Watts could be heard the Black Panther refrain, "burn baby, burn"!

Of course this merely made the social conditions in such Black communities much worse … as gangs rose quickly to allow young Black males to get on the "right" side of such local dynamics. Consequently, the murder rate in Black urban America skyrocketed to new heights.

Tragically, the "White guilt" experienced by more "socially-enlightened" Whites led them to form an unusual political alliance with these young Black revolutionaries[*] – making it even harder to bring some kind of social order to the social disorder that descended on Black urban societies in the mid-1960s … not even when things got worse in these neighborhoods – much, much worse.

───────────────

[*]Malcolm-X, LeRoi Jones, H. Rap Brown, Ron Karenga, Bobby Seale, and Stokely Carmichael became prominent national figures as a result of the development of the Black Power Movement.

Vietnam. As far as foreign policy went for Johnson, the single, all-absorbing issue was the Vietnam mess he inherited when he became president. And his response to that challenge paralleled his approach to American politics at home: when you need to get something done, simply hit it hard. Thus to Johnson the issue was quite straightforward: increase the American military presence in South Vietnam to the level needed to simply defeat the Communist Viet Cong.

Somehow it never occurred to Johnson that the situation was in fact quite complex. And he was oblivious to the fact that no matter what America chose to do, it had better be focused on achieving one goal: getting the South Vietnamese population to support the American effort. Otherwise, no matter what America did, it would have no lasting quality ... unless America was planning to undertake full control of South Vietnamese society – like the European colonial powers before them had held their positions in Asia. In other words, this was not really about bringing democracy to a foreign land. It was about making sure that this foreign land never fell under the sway of Communism. Period.

But to get Congress on board in support of his intended response to the Vietnam situation, he was going to need something dramatic to happen to muster such Congressional support. That finally came when he was able to report two incidents occurring in early August 1964 when American destroyers were fired on by North Vietnamese at the Gulf of Tonkin. [Actually, only one of these reported incidents was partially true; the second never happened at all.] This demanded a full response. And Johnson got his needed Resolution from Congress to take whatever action was necessary to protect any of the countries of the region from Communist aggression.

A very serious mistake he then made was in selling his military response in Vietnam as simply a "police action" ... not full-out war – as what recently happened in Korea. But nonetheless, he would be sending American boys off to fight a war – without having the national consensus to make their sacrifices seem worthy of the cause.

Yet another mistake he (and his military advisors) made was nonetheless to go at this the way America had gone at the Korean challenge. It all seemed quite clear looking at a map of Vietnam that the object of the "police action" was to unload American troops at various points along the coast of South Vietnam's long but narrow profile – and then branch out from there until they had brought the entire country under American military command.

The only problem with this very conventional military approach was that the Viet Cong wore no military uniforms ... and thus were indistinguishable from the people American soldiers were trying to save from Communism. Thus, beginning in March of 1965, as they moved forward from their beachheads, supposedly securing village after village, American troops soon found themselves being shot at from behind … by what they previously had supposed were friendly Vietnamese. Gradually it dawned on the American troops that they in fact had secured nothing at all in this conventional military sweep.

In the end they simply set up military camps here and there in the land, ventured out from there upon occasions to shoot at supposed Communist guerrillas … then return to camp. And this would be the profile that would literally never change over the coming years of American involvement in Vietnam.

Faced with this disappointing result, Johnson simply upped the number of American boys drafted and sent to Vietnam to kill Communist guerrillas … until by early 1968 there were over a half-million American troops in Vietnam. But their action was combined with extensive aerial bombardment of suspected Communist sites (whole villages) … and also the spraying of Agent Orange to kill the forests that allowed the Viet Cong to hide in them – and the fields that fed them. All in all, it was a very nasty war.

Ultimately, the only "good news" that the American action was able to produce was that Americans were killing more Vietnamese enemies than the Vietnamese enemies were killing American troops. It was now just a numbers game … one clearly going nowhere.

Quite naturally, as the darkness of this effort became increasingly apparent, it brought not just severe criticism from a growing Congressional opposition to the war … but campus and street protests by young Americans (and their adult mentors) fervently opposed to the military draft that was sending those young men off to a war that was making no sense at all. "Hey, hey, LBJ … how many kids did you kill today" was the chant that echoed across the country – as well as by protesters gathered opposite the White House.

Then in October of 1967, thousands of American youth gathered at the Lincoln Memorial in DC and then, under "Yippie" leaders Abbie Hoffman, Jerry Rubin, Allen Ginsburg and others, marched across the Potomac River to the Pentagon military headquarters to protest the war. Thankfully, things remained peaceful … despite the huge number of young Americans (over 50,000?) and military police and U.S. marshals facing each other at the Pentagon.

Things at this point were not going well for Johnson.

MAO'S CHINA

The disastrous "Great Leap Forward." But the same could be said for China's dictator, Mao Tse-Tung (Zedong). Having secured Communist rule for China in 1949 by leading basically a huge peasant army to victory, it seemed by the mid-1950s to the more "conventional" Marxists of China that it was time now to turn the dynamic over to the industrial-urban (not rural peasant) world ... where Marxist history was supposed to unfold. Thus Mao found himself being put aside. He was still considered to be a heroic figure – but not someone destined to take the Chinese revolution forward along truly Marxist lines. Needless to say, this was not a political trend that Mao was going to let happen.

Somehow he was able to convince the Party leaders that he could push rapid Chinese industrialization ahead as effectively as he had won China for the Party with his peasant army. What he proposed to do as a new 5-year plan was to collectivize all the independent farms (even those recently turned over to his peasant followers) in order to make them part of the State's communal property ... and then conduct an industrial revolution there ... as well as in urban China. In fact with the huge rural workforce now employed as state laborers, the industrial revolution would move ahead even more quickly than if it were conducted solely as an urban operation.

And the test or measure of the ingenious character of this new plan was that China's iron production – which Mao convinced his colleagues that all industry was ultimately based on – could take place across the nation's vast number of rural villages. True, the furnaces would be small. But they would be so numeric that the total production would put China way ahead as a major industrial producer.

And so in 1958 his plan went into action as the "Great Leap Forward." But a leap forward it turned out not to be. First of all, the quality of the iron produced in these small rural furnaces was so inferior that it was totally useless for industrial purposes. But even worse, running those blast furnaces took a lot of peasant attention away from their fields ... reducing enormously China's food production to near starvation levels. Consequently, the whole venture turned itself into a national disaster. Starvation and just sheer exhaustion cut through the Chinese population ... killing millions of Chinese.[*]

Although the program was due to run until 1963, it was put aside in 1961 ... as was also Mao once again.

The equally disastrous "Cultural Revolution." But Mao was not one to be put aside. And watching how the Soviets removed Khrushchev from power in 1964, Mao knew that he had to make some kind of comeback ... or

---

[*]The estimated figures run from a low of 22 million to a higher figure of 42 million ... although the numbers were so large and the statistics so poor that the exact number of Chinese deaths would never be known.

he too might end up being "retired"

He skillfully played on the fears of the Party's leadership of there being a number of "anti-party" members among them … and they needed to be purged before they could bring the party to ruin … and the Great Chinese Revolution to an end. Indeed, with his actress wife, Jiang Qing, he took this latter matter – the danger to the Great Chinese Revolution caused by wrong-thinking individuals – to the Chinese people themselves … to enlist their support in his "cleansing" operation.

He even had a *Little Red Book* published that contained Confucius-like quotes from the Great Leader Mao himself, that the Chinese youth were supposed to learn and repeat in order to develop right-mindedness … especially necessary given the "capitalist" mindset that still lived on among many of China's older citizens. Indeed, these youth were ordered to form themselves into small companies of "Red Guards," designed to search out and bring to public shame individuals they discovered harboring such anti-revolutionary thought.

In short, Mao was conducting a huge "Cultural Revolution" in China … through the loyal service of fired-up Chinese youth.

Basically, Chinese society turned itself into an ongoing Revolutionary Festival, shutting down much of its industrial operation, local government, and formal schooling … in order to focus the nation's attention on street marches, bands playing, everyone singing, along streets lined with giant posters of the Great Leader himself.

Consequently, all the fun was causing the Chinese economy once again to go into deep retreat.

But the Cultural Revolution was also brutal in its treatment of suspected anti-revolutionary individuals … hundreds of thousands (maybe even a million) killed by self-appointed members of the Red Guard. But Party officials also underwent a process of Maoist purging … including the party's General Secretary Deng Xiaoping (1966) and the Chinese President Liu Shaoqi (1967).

In 1966 Mao appointed military commander Lin Biao to be next in command behind himself in the party hierarchy and First Vice President of the People's Republic of China. Mao's intention was that Lin would use his military resources to bring some degree of order back to a China that was spinning out of control. This Lin did. But becoming quite successful as a Chinese leader was a very dangerous achievement … as Lin was soon to find out.

However, in all of this, the Western World simply looked on these events in China as interesting … but otherwise of no great concern to the West itself. Developments in Vietnam were of far greater interest … especially for America.

$$* \quad * \quad *$$

DE GAULLE CHALLENGES AMERICAN LEADERSHIP IN EUROPE

Seeing Johnson's America so caught up in the Vietnam crisis, de Gaulle realized that he had a grand opportunity to pull Europe away from its dependence on America ... and instead bring his fellow European nations under French leadership – especially in the realm of military affairs.

In general, de Gaulle was not pleased with European integration and its attempt to move Europe beyond its national self-interest (the cause of two horrible world wars in the 20th century alone) by bringing Europe under some kind of bureaucratically united all-European government. Instead, he supported the idea simply of a well-administered diplomatic program uniting the various fully-sovereign European nations ... a program, however, that excluded the Anglo world of America and Britain that he despised so much.

He particularly resented the role that NATO played in Europe ... even despite the fact that NATO's operational headquarters were based in France. For de Gaulle, NATO involved way too much American intrusion into Europe's affairs. Thus soon after arriving in power, the following year (1959) he took France's Mediterranean naval fleet out of NATO command. At the same time, he also demanded that the Americans and British remove all of their nuclear weapons from France ... supposedly leaving only France's nuclear "Force de Frappe" to counterbalance the Soviet nuclear position in Europe.

De Gaulle also worked hard to bring German Chancellor Konrad Adenauer (German leader, 1949-1963) on board with his program of pushing America out of Europe. Certainly Adenauer and de Gaulle were friendly colleagues. But it soon became clear that Adenauer had no interest in exchanging American protection with French protection ... not if he hoped to keep a very aggressive Soviet Empire from attempting to extend its grip into West Germany. French power was not a serious alternative to American power.

And at the same time, de Gaulle used French authority to block in 1963 Britain's efforts finally to join the European Common Market ... vetoing Prime Minister's Macmillan's British application and leaving an embarrassed Britain out in the cold. He was finally getting his revenge for having been excluded from the Big Power triumvirate of Roosevelt, Stalin and Churchill during World War Two.

That same year he also made another move against NATO, withdrawing France's much more strategically important Atlantic fleet from NATO ... hoping that other NATO members would do the same. None did.

Also in grand defiance to America (now led by Johnson) in 1964 de Gaulle broke from the anti-Communist alliance supporting Taiwan's Nationalist Government and opposing Mao's regime ... instead, terminating French recognition of the Taiwan government and extending full diplomatic recognition to Mao's Chinese government in Beijing. He also made a trip to Moscow that same year ... reportedly restoring France's traditional and quite close relationship with Russia. He even posed France as neutral in the Cold War ... referring to the Soviet Union simply as "Russia," purposely ignoring the ideological differences separating Soviet Russia from Gaullist France. Then to add further insult to America, he traveled to Latin America ... to taunt America's southern neighbors for having allowed themselves to fall under American political and economic domination.

In February of 1965 he attacked even more directly Johnson's America by demanding the exchange of the dollar reserves held by France for America's gold reserves ... hoping that other nations would follow, thereby bringing down the international status of the dollar – and the American economy itself. No other nation followed his lead. Nonetheless it was a grand humiliation for America to have the French navy come to America to take away its share of America's gold reserves.

That same year he then pulled France out of SEATO (the Southeast Asia Treaty Organization) that had been formed in 1955 as an anti-Communist follow-up to the Korean War and the French withdrawal from Indochina. But again, none of the other members (Britain, Australia, New Zealand, the Philippines, Thailand, Pakistan ... and America of course) followed de Gaulle's lead.

Finally in 1966 de Gaulle made his biggest strike against the American-led West when he demanded that all NATO troops be removed from France.[*] His order did not include the NATO civilian staff located in France ... but they too sensed that humiliation would be soon coming their way – and simply moved their offices to Belgium, just south of Brussels ... where with the EEC's headquarters also located in Brussels, ended up making Brussels something of Europe's new administrative center!

De Gaulle meanwhile indicated that France would remain part of the North Atlantic Treaty ... but just not its organization NATO.

Certainly all this behavior turned many of the French into fervently anti-Anglo nationalists – as de Gaulle fully intended. But as he would soon find out, not every Frenchman was sold on de Gaulle's supposed importance to France ... and its new anti-Anglo identity.

____

[*]American Secretary of State Dean Rusk sarcastically asked de Gaulle: did this order to evacuate all U.S. troops from France include the 50,000 American war dead buried in French cemeteries?

THE ARAB-ISRAELI SIX-DAY (OR JUNE) WAR OF 1967

In general, Americans had been rather "neutral" in the matter of the dispute going on between the Arab Palestinians and the European Jews over the rights to the land of Palestine/Israel. Americans were very understanding of the plight that the Jews found themselves in ... especially with the shocking liberation of the German death camps. But the Palestinians were understood to have the same rights to govern their own lands as any other people in the world. Indeed, Palestine included a good number of Christians ... favorite tourist sites Bethlehem and Nazareth in fact being quite Christian Arab. And the capital Jerusalem had long been quite peacefully divided among Christians, Muslims, and Jews... each possessing their own "quarter" of the city (Christians actually possessing two of those quarters). So there was plenty of reasons for Americans to be as sympathetic to the Arab Palestinians as they were to the Jews flooding into Palestine.

Of course it was, and had been since the beginning of the 20th century, this "flood" of European Jews into the land that had shattered that communal peace. And the UN's 1947 proposed division of Palestine into two separate countries had not brought any peace to the land. The Arabs were furious that U.N. "outsiders" had once again dictated their own Arab destinies.

Then too, this Arab-Israeli dispute had served quite well the cause of Arab nationalism, giving the Arab world across the entire Middle East an issue to rally around ... and would-be Arab leaders a cause that they could use to promote their own political careers. And the master of that strategy was Nasser, President of his new United Arab Republic (the UAR of Egypt plus Syria).

Most loudly Nasser took the lead in building up the military capabilities of his UAR ... the presumption being that he was thinking about simply "liberating" neighboring Palestine. But mostly his boasting was ignored by the outside world – especially by Johnson, who was fully occupied with the Vietnam mess. But finally U.N. Secretary General U Thant felt it was time to address the matter – and in late May of 1967 traveled to Egypt to see if he could get Nassar to back down a bit on his anti-Israel posture. But to Nasser, this posture was so essential in his claim to be the Arab world's leader that there was no way he would ever back down.

Then Israel – tired of waiting around to see what Nasser was actually going to do – without any warning, on June the 5th suddenly struck a huge blow to Nasser's military operations. Nasser's air force, caught still positioned on the ground, was quickly destroyed by Israeli jets. This in turn left Nasser's completely surprised ground army without any aircover – as Israeli troops moved rapidly against them. In the matter of only a few days, the Israelis had once again rolled Nasser's troops all the way back to the Suez Canal.

Then most foolishly, Jordanian King Hussein and Syrian President Atassi decided to come to the aid of Nasser by attacking Israel ... only to have Israel turn its army in their direction ... and have the Arabs defeated on that front as well in only a matter of a few days. The Jordanian-administered eastern half of Palestine thus came under Israeli occupation ... as well as Syria's strategic Golan Heights.

And all of this was achieved in less than a week.

For America, this event was to produce strange developments. The Johnson Administration took an entirely neutral position on the matter ... despite the strange Israeli air attack on a clearly marked American research ship *Liberty* located in international waters north of the Sinai Peninsula ... killing 34 and wounding 171 crew members in the process. Ultimately Israel offered no good explanation for the attack ... and mostly America just let the issue pass – although Israel eventually offered financial compensation for the "mistake."

But oddest of all was the way Americans now swung themselves in full support of Israel against the Arab Palestinians ... much of this put into play by the strongly pro-Israeli American media. The Palestinians were now portrayed as villains ... especially their only defense team, the Palestinian Liberation Organization (PLO).

As for the Christian world of Palestine, that went completely (and probably purposely) unnoticed by the American press – and thus also the American citizenry – who actually knew virtually nothing about the ethnic dynamics of this issue. To Americans the matter was now quite simple: the good Israelis were always under attack by the bad Arabs. America should do what it could to always come to Israel's aid.

Sadly for Christian Palestinians, they found that under the new circumstances, it was simply easiest to give up their ancient position in Palestine and migrate to the Western world – leaving, for instance, Bethlehem and Nazareth mostly to incoming Muslim settlers ... thus dimming greatly the 2,000 year-old gospel light in this very holy land. And American Christians would have no idea whatsoever about the role they themselves played in supporting this development.

✳ ✳ ✳

1968 ... THE *ANNUS HORRIBILIS* (HORRIBLE YEAR)

Continuing crisis in America

The Vietnam Tet Offensive (January-February). At the end of January of 1968, America was shocked to wake up to the news that Viet Cong fighters had hit hard every American position across South Vietnam ... even the supposedly secure capital city Saigon. In fact they were able to break into the American embassy compound there and kill the marine guards ... something graphically displayed in the American TV evening news.

This threw patriotic Americans into confusion, for the event seemed to contradict so strongly Johnson's assurances that America was making great progress in the conduct of the war. Actually this was not at all untrue. Things were not going well for the Viet Cong. And their soldiers were growing exhausted ... something that the American public had no way of knowing. Thus this "Tet Offensive" (conducted during the Vietnamese Tet Lunar New Year holidays) was undertaken as a desperate measure as something as a last bold shot at the Americans ... in order to tire the Americans of the war before the Viet Cong themselves tired out.

And they succeeded – although it nearly destroyed the Viet Cong army in doing so. The event succeeded in getting the American press – totally unaware of the reality of the situation in Vietnam – to put before the American public the verdict that the Vietnam War was a total failure.

Johnson's announced retirement (March 31st). Johnson himself was exhausted from having to fight the Vietnam war not only abroad but also at home. Any effort to convince the American population at this point would have merely brought on larger protests (especially from the Boomer youth) that their government was lying ... and to be trusted in no matter at all. Indeed, so exhausted was Johnson that in concluding a televised speech at the end of March, he added something that was not on the written speech passed out beforehand to the American press: he would not be running for reelection as U.S. president in the upcoming November national elections. He was simply too tired to take on the challenge. Thus as for Vietnam – and his Great Society Programs – that would have to be the responsibility of others to deal with. Johnson was going home to Texas at the end of his term in the coming January.

Dr. King's assassination (April 4th). Less than a week later, America was hit by another shock: Dr. King had been shot and killed by James Earl Ray while King was in Memphis, Tennessee, to lead a local garbage workers' strike for better wages and working conditions. King's death not only deeply grieved Americans, it seemingly justified another – and quite extensive – Black plundering and torching of America's cities ... across the country. Even Washington DC was put to the torch – and had to impose an emergency afternoon curfew, its empty streets patrolled by National

Guardsmen ... an action lasting several days.

Student rebellion at Columbia University (April-May). But not to be left out of the action, at the end of April, a student protest led by Mark Rudd and his Students for a Democratic Society (SDS) organization broke out on the Columbia University campus in New York City. They were protesting the decision of the university's administration to build a gymnasium on undeveloped university land ... land that the university had been permitting local residents – mostly Black – to use for their own gardening purpose. To Rudd and the SDS, this decision simply to build there was another representation of the deep anti-Black racism that ran through White society ... and needed to be stopped. They planned (Maoist style) to shut down the university ... until the university acknowledged its sins and backed down on its plans.

But the SDS was not the only voice to be heard among Columbia's students. Some 2,000 other students (many simply hoping to graduate in May) – plus New York City police – took on the SDS occupiers of their campus buildings. It became a violent scene ... but was so strongly supported by a widening number of students (and outsiders) that the university was effectively shut down for the school year.

This event in turn inspired large numbers of American Boomer youth across the country to engage in their own rebellion against the fascism characteristic of the "American Establishment."

The sad Poor People's March on Washington (May-June). Dr. King, not at all happy about how the Black Panther Movement had taken over the civil rights movement he had so carefully started, had been slowly refocusing his activities less on the matter of racism and more and more on the matter of advancing the cause of America's poor ... Black or White. Thus he had planned a huge Poor-People's March on Washington to begin in May – participants drawn from the Black community's urban poor to the Appalachian Mountains' communities of poor Whites. They would occupy tents placed in the DC mall – like the 1932 Bonus Army ... but hopefully without the resistance from the DC police that the 1932 event provoked. The hope was to get Congress to take greater action in the interests of America's poor, White or Black. In fact the Sunday before he was assassinated, in his last sermon (preached to a crowd at the DC's National Cathedral) he made clear how action on behalf of the poor was so vital to the nation ... because it was providing a sad excuse for the kind of racism (implying both Black and White) that he found so tragic.

But with the racist bullet that killed Dr. King, it appeared that his new broader civil rights plan had been effectively terminated. But it was decided to go ahead with the March ... in part to honor Dr. King as much as to plead for Congressional action on behalf of the poor.

But the event, which took place from mid-May to the end of June proved to be mostly a sad display of what the loss of Dr. King had meant to the civil rights movement ... and to the deep resistance in Congress to any kind of Socialist programming demanded of the Federal government. Ultimately a spirit of tension, disappointment, and failure set in among the residents of "Resurrection City" (the mall's tent city) ... and participants began to withdraw. And the constant rains that fell that June – and the deep mud they lived with – did not help matters any. Ultimately the event shut down ... not sure that it had achieved any good purpose at all.

Bobby Kennedy is assassinated (June 5th). Partly, this demoralized spirit was inspired also by the assassination of yet another American leader ... Bobby Kennedy (JFK's brother) – the Democratic Party's most likely candidate for the coming November elections ... and the individual most likely to have been the next American President. He was shot exiting a political rally of his supporters by a young Palestinian-American angry about American support of Israel. But such vengeance served no one.

Once again, America was shocked to the extreme.

The crazy Democratic Party National Convention (August). Then when the Democratic Party gathered in Chicago to choose a presidential candidate, the event was accompanied by the mass assembly of young American protesters ... protesting the Vietnam war, protesting racism, protesting anything about America they could find grounds to protest. The behavior of the Chicago police sent by Mayor Richard Daley was even worse, attacking not only protesters but, in the surrounding mayhem, also delegates simply trying to attend the event. And a very loud, foul-mouthed Daley shouting at the speaker made the event even uglier.

All across America TV viewers were watching the appalling site. What was happening to America?

Nonetheless, the Democrats went on to choose Johnson's Vice President Hubert Humphrey as their presidential candidate. His rather scholarly personality was believed to be just the calming influence to get the country settled back down again.

The 1968 Presidential election (November). The Republican National Convention in Miami had been a much quieter affair, the Republicans once again choosing Nixon ... and bringing Maryland Governor Spiro Agnew on board as his Vice President, someone who had gained national attention when he came down hard on Black protesters and spared Baltimore and the rest of the state the agony inflicted by Black Power toughs following the King assassination.

But there was a third candidate running, White racist Alabama Governor George Wallace* – expected to cut deeply into the Democratic Party's "Solid South" support ... which is exactly what he did, giving Nixon 43.4 percent of the vote, Humphrey 42.7 percent and Wallace 13.5 percent, ruining the expectations of the Democrats for an easy win in the elections. But in any case, Nixon was able to get a strong majority in the electoral college vote (the one that actually counts), Nixon with 302 votes, Humphrey with 191 votes, and Wallace with 46 votes.

Political turmoil in West Europe

Student rebellion in West Germany. The Socialist German Students' Union (SDS) had been cut off from its sponsoring political party, the Social Democratic Party (SPD) of West Germany in 1961. Since 1954, when the West German Federal Government had joined NATO, the SPD had moved politically closer to the Center ... while the SDS moved even further to the Left (it was discovered years later that the student organization had been receiving considerable support from the East German Communist government).

In the mid-1960s, the SDS became inspired greatly by America's Black Panthers with their "burn baby, burn" mentality – plus the campus protests of America's Student for a Democratic Society (the American SDS). The German SDS mood of political protest thus deepened even further ... finding cause finally in June of 1967 to go beyond its broad "anti-Fascist" campaign – and protest specifically against the visit to Germany of the Iranian Shah. In the confrontation with the police over the matter, one person was killed.

Now the German SDS became even more radical ... especially the group headed by Rudi Dutschke – who took the lead in a number of protests in Germany against American imperialism in Vietnam ... coinciding with the huge anti-war protest march on the American Pentagon in October of 1967. The following year, returning from events developing in Czechoslovakia, he was nearly killed in an assassination attempt. After that (the end of the 1960s), the more radical elements of the SDS came under the leadership of Andreas Baader and Ulrike Meinhof ... forming a group that came to be known as the Red Army Faction – but also as the Baader-Meinhof Gang ... a group conducting bank robberies, bombings, assassinations, and shootouts with the police (especially intense during the 1970s).

––––––––––

*The world of American politics is truly amazing. When Wallace saw Blacks finally eligible to vote, as an ongoing governor of Alabama, he became a major supporter of Black economic and educational development ... and became well supported by Black voters!

The "Events of May" in France (1968).   Developments along a similar line began to unfold in France – but becoming more violent ... much more violent. These were protests by university students which broke out in Paris in May against academic bureaucracy, capitalism, the consumer culture, American imperialism in Vietnam ... or against most anything identified with the adult world.

The situation had been slowly building for a couple of months. But on May 2nd when the Sorbonne University was shut down, the situation became explosive. Four days later, some 20,000 students and teachers marched towards the Sorbonne to protest the closing ... and were met by Paris police. Things got very ugly at that point.   But the protest merely widened the next day and those following ... and by May 13th, some million protesters filled the streets of Paris.   Then they were joined by striking workers – although their cause was simply the demand for better working conditions.   Nonetheless, with both students and workers in full protest across France, it appeared that the country was facing something that looked like an actual civil war.

This in turn produced political turmoil at the highest level of French politics. The Socialists demanded the formation of a new government ... and at the end of May de Gaulle responded by slipping quietly out of Paris and heading to Germany "to avoid bloodshed." At the same time some half a million protesters, led by the workers' union (the CGT), marched through Paris ... calling for de Gaulle's resignation.

Finally a call from de Gaulle for new national elections, plus the rumor of government military and tanks forming around Paris, and then the march in Paris of some 800,000 of de Gaulle's supporters led the Communists to agree to the elections and the students to call off further protests.

Most surprisingly, the elections in June resulted in a huge Gaullist electoral victory ... and a huge reduction in size of the Communist and Socialist representation in the National Assembly.

There would be another student protest in Paris's Latin Quarter on the country's national holiday, Bastille Day (July 14th) – rather harshly put down by the Paris police. And that would bring the student's revolutionary mood pretty much to a close.[*]

The "Prague Spring" and the Czechoslovakian Crisis of 1968. A crisis arose in Czechoslovakia around this same time over economic reforms undertaken by the Czech leadership ... which succeeded in getting Czechoslovakia's Soviet masters extremely upset. Quite unsurprisingly, the Czech economy, which originally had been built on rather Western

---

[*]But such events went on to inspire John Lennon to write the song (and the Beatles' album) *Revolution* released in August of 1968.

capitalist standards, had not done well under Communism. But even more surprisingly, the Czech economy was doing even worse than the other nations in the Soviet Bloc. Thus it was that Czech Communist Party Leader Alexander Dubček decided to allow some degree of liberalization of the Czech economy in order to get it moving again. He termed the program "Socialism with a human face."

The problem with his program was that economic liberalization requires economic initiative to be transferred from state planners to society's citizens themselves ... entrepreneurs able freely to invest in ventures of their own – from farmers to auto manufacturers. In short, the true production community, large and small.

But such liberalization, once underway, does not stop merely with the realm of economics. Once there is a sense of the ability to act freely in the political atmosphere, it touches on all questions of life, private life as well as social life. And this was something that Kremlin officials back in Russia did not want to see develop. It was rather guaranteed to set things on a course that would be hard to continue to control from Moscow.

Soviet leader Leonid Brezhnev tried to get Dubček to step back from his program. Student protests in Poland in March of 1968 in support of action against "Stalinist" and "Zionist" revisionism (?) – which quickly spread across Poland – had required a swift police response to get things back under order. Brezhnev was in no mood to see "reform" take on a similar dangerous dynamic in Czechoslovakia. But Dubček made it clear that he was going to continue to move forward with his reforms.

This ultimately led Brezhnev to announce his "Brezhnev Doctrine'' – stating that Russia was forced to take action whenever "anti-social" forces threatened the world of Socialism. And because of events developing in Czechoslovakia, he was going to have to call on the members of the Warsaw Pact (the other East European countries under Soviet control) to take action to end this mutual threat.

So on the night of 20-21 August (1968) hundreds of thousands of soldiers and 1200 tanks of Russia, Bulgaria, Poland, and Hungary invaded Czechoslovakia ... totally surprising the Czechs. Dubček knew that it was pointless to resist and asked his people not to fight back ... though certainly he knew that the Czech hostility ran deep. Despite his plea, there were numerous – but small – instances of just such opposition across the country.

There was of course a huge international outcry over this Soviet bullying of Czechoslovakia. Even – and most surprisingly – Mao's China joined the voices of opposition to the Soviet move. Ultimately, America joined with some other nations in sponsoring a U.N. investigation into the event ... although little else was done about the matter. Johnson's America was so busy trying to keep up with events in Vietnam that it was totally unprepared – or was just unwilling – to do anything of any significance to help a people whose effort to find their own democratic freedom had just been undone by very direct Soviet action.

Consequently, lacking American diplomatic leadership, the Western world was forced to move on to other issues.

✳ ✳ ✳

CLOSING OUT THE 1960s

Nixon's America

Other than the ongoing Vietnam War, which had Nixon focused deeply, Nixon's first year in office was comparatively quiet.

The Apollo 11 Moon Landing. But there were a number of things that hit the news big his first year in office. A very exciting event was the Apollo 11 Moon Landing of American astronauts in mid-July (1969) ... something watched closely around the world. It was a huge plus for an America used to a news of negatives ... for it clearly put America way out front in the "space-race" with the Soviets (the Soviets saw it to be pointless to score merely a second-place position in the race to reach the moon ... and never themselves ever attempted such a moon landing).

Chappaquiddick. But that event was clouded a bit by the news that at very same time as the moon walk, the surviving male Kennedy (Teddy) had been involved in a tragedy when his car went off a small bridge onto the Chappaquiddick Island and the young lady that was with him died of either drowning or suffocation ... although Ted managed to get himself home safely. Being a Kennedy, the details of the event never came fully to light ... nor was Ted held to much account for the tragedy.

Woodstock. Then the next month (August), leaving the world of political protesting behind them, America's Boomer youth headed off to Woodstock, New York, for a massive three-day music festival – unrivaled before or since with the number of music superstars it involved ... or the size of the crowd (over 400,000) that gathered there.

The Manson murders. However, earlier that same month, America was shocked to hear about the mindless slaughter of pregnant Hollywood actress Sharon Tate and four others at her home ... and the following evening of a husband and wife murdered in a similar manner. Eventually the trail of evidence led to the hippie "family" of sleazy "spiritual guru" Charles Manson and a number of his devoted followers ... who killed simply for the joy of being able to do so (the trail of other murders – possibly 15 or 20 – seemingly led back to them as well). The trial the following year (June 1970) was quite naturally a national sensation – the size and pointlessness of the murders being so shocking to Middle Americans ... who were beginning to wonder if this ultimately was where the whole hippie movement, with its drugs and Boomer spiritual fantasy, was heading the nation.

De Gaulle's political fall

De Gaulle's determination to pursue an independent course for France in the realm of international politics continued to irritate America ... and other nations. In June of 1967, for a second time he vetoed Britain's effort to gain membership in the EEC. He would not back down on his opposition to Britain's joining the world of continental Europe ... a community that he believed strongly should be France-led.

That same year he provided support for the rebellion of Biafran tribesmen intent on withdrawing from the Britain-supported Federal Republic of Nigeria ... by doing so needlessly drawing out a civil war that Biafra was destined to lose and thereby increasing the casualty rate of the Biafrans considerably.

Also that same year he flew to Canada, supposedly there to help the country celebrate its centenary (Expo 67) ... but in fact there to speak boldly about the need for French-speaking Quebec to separate itself from the rest of English-speaking Canada. The Canadian government was furious ... and de Gaulle immediately returned to France without completing the scheduled visit.

The next year, he misinterpreted the huge gain his Gaullist party made in the 1968 elections, not understanding that this was not about him but about the conservative values his party represented – a natural reaction of French voters to the excesses of the French Leftists and their antics during the "events of May" (*les événements de mai*). Thus he decided to put some changes to the French constitution before the French voters in the form of a constitutional referendum ... calling for the decentralizing or concentrating of powers at a more regional level – and some other changes. None of it seemed supercritical ... except that de Gaulle threatened to resign if his proposals were not accepted – presuming this to be enough of a threat to get his proposals passed. After all, what was France without de Gaulle leading it! But when the referendum was held (27 April 1969), the results were only 47.6% in support, with 52.4% opposed. And as he threatened, he resigned the following day.

But France did not come to its knees begging him to return to power in order to save the nation. In fact, it moved forward quite easily without him under the former Gaullist Prime Minister (1962-1968) Georges Pompidou – now French President as of June 1969. Sadly, a very broken-hearted de Gaulle died the next year (November 1970).

Riots break out in Northern Ireland (August 1969)

In the late 1960s, Protestant-Catholic tensions were again building up in the largely-Protestant Northern Ireland ... still a part of Britain's United Kingdom – and still adamantly opposed to the idea of ever being joined to the very Catholic Irish Republic to the south. On the other hand, the Catholic minority in Northern Ireland considered itself discriminated against in every way possible ... and was demanding reforms along the lines of the civil rights efforts going on in America and elsewhere at the time. But Protestant Northern Ireland was just as tense over this matter – well aware that the militant IRA was still very focused on the idea of forcibly uniting Northern Ireland with the Irish Republic.

Thus when in August of 1969 – in the predominantly Catholic town of Derry – Catholics turned out to march for civil rights, Protestant militants also turned out to oppose them. The confrontation immediately turned violent ... and then made even worse when the (largely pro-Protestant) police moved into the matter. The chaos then spread to other parts of Northern Ireland, but most notably to the regional capital of Belfast ... where seven people were killed, hundreds wounded, and sections of the city burned out.

At this point, British Army units were sent to Northern Ireland to separate the warring factions ... soon themselves becoming targets of the angry militants, both Protestant and Catholic.

Things then settled down ... sort of. But tensions and occasional outbreaks of violence would continue to occur. In fact they would continue to do so over the many years to follow. Finally in 1998 was there some kind of agreement (the "Easter Accords") between the two parties to back off from this ongoing conflict ... although it was actually not until 2007 that the last of British troops were finally withdrawn from this testy situation.

✱ ✱ ✱

INTO THE 1970s

The European Economic Community begins its expansion

With Pompidou now President of France, the applications for admission to the EEC by Britain, Denmark, and Ireland finally moved forward without a French veto this time, being accepted in 1972 with actual membership effective as of 1 January 1973.* Norway, also scheduled to join at the same time, ultimately did not join – because the Norwegian citizens, in a national plebiscite held about the matter in late September of 1972, themselves rejected the entry, 46.5% voting yes, 53.5% voting no.

The American retreat from Vietnam

Clearly, Vietnam was the American all-consuming issue of those years. Because it was the biggest issue going into America's national elections in 1968, Johnson had cut back considerably the bombing of North Vietnam in the hopes of moving the Paris peace talks forward. However, not having succeeded in that political move, just prior to those elections he stopped the bombing altogether – in order to push South Vietnamese President Thieu to accept some of Johnson's peace proposals ... and to improve Humphrey's image going into the elections.

Actually, Nixon had secretly informed Thieu not to accept Johnson's proposals ... that although Nixon had promised American voters a full withdrawal of American troops from Vietnam, he would continue to give full support to South Vietnam by other means. Johnson knew about this Nixon proposal to Thieu (he had wiretapped both the South Vietnamese embassy and members of Nixon's staff) but dared not exploit the fact for fear that his wiretapping would be discovered. Also Humphrey was so certain of victory in the election that he did not bother to bring the matter up at the time. Indeed, the Democrats would later try to bring this matter forward as a serious violation of the Logan Act making it illegal for a civilian to get involved in diplomatic dynamics. But the effort did not go over well with much of the American populace, who understood Nixon's action to be a very logical move of someone headed for the presidency. Thus the matter was dropped.

But American politics at that point was intensely antagonistic ... political partisanship becoming vastly more important in the DC political game than national consensus-building.

But moving forward on the Vietnam issue was not going to be easy

----

*Greece had been admitted as an EEC associate member in 1961 but had its membership suspended in 1967 after a military coup established a Greek government run by a group of colonels. In 1962 Spain had tried to gain EEC membership, but was ultimately rejected in 1964 because the country was still under Franco's dictatorship. Greece would be restored to membership in 1981 and Spain and Portugal would be admitted in 1986 ... those countries no longer under dictatorial rule.

for Nixon. First of all, the South Vietnamese Army (ARVN) was going to need some considerable development. And North Vietnam needed to get the clear message that the withdrawal of American troops did not mean the end of American interest in Vietnam. Strong airpower protecting the South would remain in place. Consequently, at the same time that he announced the schedule for the withdrawal of American ground forces (to be completed fully just prior to the 1972 November national elections) he also upped the bombing of Communist positions.

But he needed to get the South as well as the North to understand the game plan. Convincing Thieu of his seriousness about the withdrawal was as difficult as convincing the North Vietnamese about the continuance of American commitment in the South.

To demonstrate his resolve to do things his way, in April of 1970, he sent a huge military force into neighboring Cambodia to shut down the Hồ Chí Minh Trail that had been used to bring vast amounts of supplies from the North to the Viet Cong operating in the South. Militarily, the Cambodian assault was a huge success.

The Kent State Tragedy (1970). But politically, it served as the cause for another huge anti-war protest in America, led here and there across the county in early May by the SDS. Tragically, at Kent State University in Ohio, the National Guard had been called out to protect the campus after the SDS had students burn down the ROTC (Reserve Officers' Training Corps) building on campus ... and an accidental firefight ended up with the National Guard killing four students and wounding nine other students.

The outrage over the Kent State killings quickly led to protests held at over 300 campuses across the country. But when the protests spread to New York City, "hard hat" workers came out in violent protest against the younger protesters ... and things got very ugly. And that divisive spirit showed itself again when Nixon was invited by Billy Graham to speak at a combined 4th of July celebration and campus crusade he was holding at the University of Tennessee ... and protesters tried to shout down his speech, only themselves to be shouted down by a wildly supportive audience! American battle lines were deepening.

Vietnam veterans against the war. Despite the fact that Nixon was pulling American troops out of Vietnam in a quite orderly fashion, this seemed not to soften the anti-war mood of young America. Thus in April of 1971 a protest against the war (and Nixon's refusal to simply quit Vietnam) led a huge number of Vietnam veterans to gather in DC to demonstrate their opposition to Nixon and his handling of the war.

At the same time, despite the fact that the Vietnam mess was a

Johnson byproduct, the Democratic Party was doing what it could to lay the Vietnam issue at the feet of Nixon in the hopes of undercutting his national popularity. Thus the rising moral voice of the Democratic Party, "Chappaquiddick Ted" Kennedy, invited a young Army Lieutenant, John Kerry, to Capitol Hill to testify before the Senate as to the horrible things his fellow soldiers were doing in Vietnam. He was very graphic about the atrocities that he had heard about (not actually witnessed) – making him the hero of the hour ... forming the foundations for his own eventual rise in national politics alongside Kennedy.   Trashing fellow Americans – even America itself – was now understood to be the correct way to demonstrate an individual's own "anti-fascist," thus saintly, moral character ... a common feature of "Liberal" American politics in those days (and largely since then) ... thanks to the rise of the Boomers – and the support and encouragement of their political mentors (such as Kennedy).

The Pentagon Papers. Adding to this mood was the publication in June of 1971 by *The New York Times* of secret documents that were part of a 1967 study commissioned by Johnson's Secretary of Defense, Robert McNamara, to give him details on how the Vietnam War actually got up and running. What the *Times* published, in what would come to be termed *The Pentagon Papers*, was very unflattering of the Johnson Administration ... and to some extent the Kennedy Administration before him. Truly shocking was Johnson's huge deception (not exactly unknown in DC) involved in getting Americans onboard with his desire to make Vietnam a testimony to his supposed diplomatic skills ... which sadly it did – for a while anyway.

But what should have shocked Americans as much was how Democratic Party politicians were able to transfer the blame for everything from Johnson on to Nixon. Nixon actually had no part whatsoever in the startup of the war – or anything else found in *The Pentagon Papers*! But instead of letting blame fall on Johnson for the Vietnam disaster, the lesson that the Democratic Party (and America's Liberal press) wanted Americans to come away with over all this was how dangerous it was to trust any "imperialist" in the White House – and most importantly, the imperialist occupying that position at that very time: Nixon.

Downgrading the Cold War with Russia and China.   Being the consummate practitioner of *Realpolitik* (Political Realism) Nixon, along with his Secretary of State Henry Kissinger, knew that they had to bring the major powers, Russia and China, into the game so that the American withdrawal from Vietnam did not turn into a Cold War catastrophe. Nixon had to make it worth Russia and China's while, because of America's scheduled withdrawal from Vietnam, not to slide into the picture as Vietnam's liberators.

Following a testing of the waters with China in the sending of an American table tennis team to China (April 1971), Nixon followed this up by sending Kissinger on a secret mission to China (July), then making a well-publicized visit with his wife to China in February of the next year (1972) ... where Nixon indicated that America was ready to end its isolationist stance with respect to China (obvious at that point) – even exchanging officials between themselves as something like ambassadors.

Unlike Johnson, the political Realist Nixon did not see the Communist world as a monolithic superpower bloc ... but instead merely as an array of nations who, most often, had only the label "Communist" identifying them – and little else by way of mutual national interest holding them together. Actually, Russia and China were very much competitors in the international power game. Thus Nixon intended to utilize their differences to strengthen the American position even more ... globally as well as in the Southeast Asian region.

Consequently, he and Kissinger then flew to Moscow in May of 1972 (only three months after Nixon's visit to China) to propose a stepping back or *détente* in the nuclear arms race, not only to ease East-West tensions, but to cut back on the sheer expense of the arms race. Brezhnev was quite pleased to receive the visit, plus the détente deal Nixon offered.

What he offered both Russia and China should have delighted the American Leftists the way it shocked the Right Wing of his Republican Party. Indeed, Americans in general tended to be highly favorable of this development. But the Democrats were in no way willing to acknowledge any kind of political success on Nixon's part.

At the same time, he had to make it clear to the North Vietnamese that he was deadly serious about his intent to keep South Vietnam from falling to the Communist regime of Hanoi. Thus when, after Nixon had reduced deeply America's troop presence in the South, and when in March of 1972 North Vietnam reacted by sending 120,000 of their troops South, Nixon ordered a massive bombing of both Hanoi and its harbor at Haiphong ... cutting off supplies coming into the North Vietnamese capital. This action, plus Nixon's recent diplomatic advances with both Russia and China, led China and Russia to lean heavily on North Vietnam to slow up its movement South.

Thus, by that same spring of 1972, Nixon had reduced the American troop presence in Vietnam to a mere 6,000 troops.   This too received no thanks from the anti-war Democrats.

Watergate

The 1972 American elections.   But the American people themselves showed their gratitude that November for the way Nixon brought the country out of the Vietnam mess – by giving him a resounding victory in the November elections. Nixon received 60.7% of the popular vote against his Democratic Party opponent George McGovern's mere 37.5%. And in the electoral college, all except Massachusetts and DC* voted for Nixon.

Yet at the same time in the Congressional side of the elections, although the Republicans gained 12 seats in the House of Representatives, the Democrats continued to hold on to their majority (242 Democrats to 192 Republicans). And in the Senate, the Democrats actually increased their majority (now 56 to 42) by acquiring two additional senate seats.

Thus a strongly Republican President, facing a strongly Democrat Congress, meant that America was not yet out of the political turmoil that descended on it in the mid-1960s.

Nixon under attack. And very stupidly, members of Nixon's reelection committee would give the Democrats the opportunity to get rid of the President they hated so much ... when they were caught by police in attempting to break into Democratic Party headquarters in the Watergate Apartment complex in DC. These individuals were tried and convicted for their crimes. But it was Nixon that the Democrats wanted to see behind bars.

He was not accused of ordering the break in. But the assumption was that certainly he would have done something (as would have any DC politician) to "correct" the very embarrassing situation his staffers created. So a Senate investigation committee was set up in February of 1973 by the saintly Ted Kennedy[†] to see what Congress could find that could incriminate the President ... which Nixon helped move along by firing special investigators appointed to look into the matter.

As 1973 rolled along, tensions got so high over the Watergate event that the well-publicized Congressional hearings replaced the afternoon soap

---

*The DC vote went 78% in favor of McGovern ... not surprising because since Johnson (and Roosevelt before him), the Democratic Party had come to identify itself with the idea that the country would be best run not from the Middle America "out there" in Georgia, or Kansas, or North Dakota – but instead from Washington, DC ... where supposedly America's real political brains were to be found! In the more recent national elections, the Democratic Party vote in DC has topped 90%! You might wonder why there are any Republicans at all in DC!

†For various reasons, however, it would be Sam Erwin, not Kennedy, who would chair the Senate Committee doing the investigation. One explanation offered was that having Kennedy head up this committee, a man who had high hopes of being the Democratic Party's Presidential nominee in the 1976 national election, might make the investigation look partisan! An unspoken explanation was that Kennedy's own moral credentials since the Chappaquiddick incident were hardly admirable.

operas as what Americans preferred to watch.

Trying to conduct foreign policy during the Watergate era.   As one last effort to convince both North and South Vietnam of Nixon's commitment to South Vietnam – and before a strongly Democratic Congress, which made it clear that they wanted full abandonment of Vietnam, was back in session – Nixon ordered the "Christmas bombing" again of Hanoi and Haiphong. This time both North and South Vietnamese representatives at the Paris talks finally signed the Paris Peace Accords (January 1973).

But in June of 1973, with the Watergate hearings going full blast, Congress felt itself fully empowered to pass the Case-Church Amendment – which stated that at the end of a two-month period, the President would no longer be allowed to provide any kind of military aid to Vietnam!

In short, in taking over American foreign policy in Vietnam, Congress undercut all the terms that had led to the Paris Peace Accord ... and left an open door for the North – still getting military aid from Russia – to resume its assault on the South.

Congress strips the President of his discretionary spending powers. Nixon had promised the American people in his run for the presidency that he would work hard to cut back on government spending. And this he proceeded to do, impounding or refusing to release funds for various spending programs put in place by the Democratic Congress. This irritated congressmen badly (including many Republicans) because they counted on being able to show local voters how much federal spending that they were able to direct back to the folks back home ("pork barreling"). And of course the powerful Washington bureaucracy was strongly opposed to Nixon's spending cuts. Thus now with Nixon on the defensive, Congress went after the president, enacting the 1974 Congressional Budget and Impoundment Control Act. This prohibited the president from undertaking any spending cuts without Congressional approval ... eliminating presidential budgetary powers that reached back to 1801, during Jefferson's presidency. And all this was done in the name of democratic anti-imperialism.

To ensure that the president was put under strict surveillance on this matter, Congress also set up the Congressional Budget Office ... not realizing they were also creating a government agency that would make very clear to spending critics exactly how much political pork barreling was actually going on in Congress. Oops!

The Arab-Israeli Yom Kippur or October War of 1973

While all of this anti-imperialist democracy was going on in America, tensions had been building in the Middle East between Israel and its Arab neighbors. Nothing had changed for the Arabs since the 1967 catastrophe ... including Arab anger over the postwar situation. Israel still controlled the Sinai Desert all the way up to the Suez Canal and West-Bank Palestine remained in Israeli hands – as well as Syria's Golan Heights.

In the meanwhile, Nasser had died in 1970, and was replaced by Anwar Sadat, who approached his Egyptian presidential duties not from the showy political stage that Nasser liked to play on, but quietly from his own version of Realpolitik. By 1972, he was cleverly putting together a plan that would indeed catch Israel off guard ... and, at least for a bit, throw Israel into retreat in the effort to regain lost Egyptian territory.

Egypt had long been gaining military support from Russia, helping enormously to modernize the Egyptian military ... although with the American détente, the Soviets were losing interest in this expensive involvement with Egypt. But in any case, without any warning or explanation, in July of 1972 Sadat simply ordered the 20,000 Russian advisors out of Egypt. He then, over the summer of 1973, began to conduct extensive military exercises – ones that always put Israel on alert ... although nothing further came from any of these episodes. At the same time Sadat had been sending out diplomatic missions to see if he could get some international help in getting the situation (as actually called for by a U.N. resolution ... though ignored by Israel) back to some kind of benefit to the Arab world. And secretly, he had been working with Syria's President Hafiz al-Assad and with the Arab-dominated oil cartel (OPEC) to get them to agree to cooperate in case of some kind of Egyptian action against Israel.

Then on October 6th of 1973, another of these exercises turned into the real thing ... when Sadat's troops crossed the Suez Canal and charged into the Sinai Desert, this time well protected by extensive Egyptian air power. Although this was timed to coincide with the Jewish holiday of Yom Kippur, in which the Israelis were supposedly focused elsewhere, the Israelis actually were not unprepared for the event. In fact some of the Israeli officers suspected something was afoot and wanted to strike first. But Israeli Prime Minister Golda Meir was adamant that the Israelis must not strike first, lest it cause them to lose the sympathy and support of the West, especially in America.

But the Egyptian attack proved to be much bigger and more effective than the Israelis had anticipated ... with the Egyptian army and air corps, aided by Surface-to-Air missiles (SAMs), quite able to match up with the Israeli equivalent. Both ground and air combat was therefore proving highly destructive to both sides.

At first the only field that Israel was able to move to its own advantage was against Syria in the Golan Heights. This they regained ... then headed to

Damascus, the Syrian capital. But the intervention of Iraqi troops blocked that move.

And as each side ran out of guns, tanks, and planes, the conflict eventually turned onto a matter of resupply, Egypt getting new supplies from Russia as of the 9th of October, and Nixon and Kissinger directing American supplies to Israel ... though with some of America's European allies refusing to cooperate in this move, delaying the American delivery until the 14th of October.

But when on the 19th of October Nixon asked Congress for $2.2 billion in aid for Israel, OPEC swung into action ... cutting back oil production and blocking all oil sales to America, Portugal, and the Netherlands (the European countries allowing America to use its airspace to run supplies to Israel).

Russia and America finally got the U.N. to come up with a ceasefire proposal on the 22nd of October. But with things on the ground finally going Israel's way, Israel ignored the ceasefire and even crossed the Suez Canal in order to surround an exhausted Egyptian army. Only when the Soviets threatened to intervene directly did the action come to something of a standstill (October 28th).

In the meantime, with OPEC production cut back even further, oil prices skyrocketed from $3 to over $11 per 42-gallon barrel. A huge international energy crisis thus exploded. Nixon tried to meet the challenge by opening American oil reserves – and reducing the speed limit on America's highways to 55 miles an hour – although this ultimately did little to address the energy crisis.

At the same time, OPEC members[*] now found themselves to be fantastically rich – creating a new political dynamic ... one which the Saudis handled wisely by making sure that the new wealth was distributed widely among its population.

But in the Shah's Iran, that wealth went largely to a few wealthy families ... bypassing the huge peasant population that was facing an enormous jump in the price of energy and fertilizer – with international food prices not moving up with those costs (American food production kept those prices fairly steady). The new dynamic was therefore making multitudes of Iranians actually poorer – much poorer. This would quickly translate into a huge political problem for the Shah ... one he seemed to not know how to address.

✳ ✳ ✳

———————————

[*]Neither Egypt or Syria were oil producers, and therefore suffered from the rise in oil prices ... like the non-Arab world!

WATERGATE FINISHES OFF THE NIXON PRESIDENCY …
AND HELPS BRING VIETNAM AND CAMBODIA TO DEADLY RUIN

Congress cuts off all support of South Vietnam. By early 1974, the energy crisis shaking the world also hit South Vietnam hard, the government unable to pay for fuel for its military. In May, Nixon asked Congress for supplemental funds to help Vietnam to get through the remaining time until it was up for renewed support under the new fiscal year only a month away (the end of June). But not only did Congress refuse this request, it also announced that America would be ending all further financial support of South Vietnam as of the end of 1976!

What in essence Congress was doing was inviting Russian-supported North Vietnam to undo whatever progress America – under Johnson – had undertaken to achieve, at the cost of hundreds of thousands of lives, both American and Vietnamese. This was to be a key move of Liberal America in its effort to end America's "imperialist" program … especially the part under the Nixon presidency.

But Nixon was the one who had brought the boys home … and had offered in its place economic support (plus air action if North Vietnam violated the Peace Accords). And since when did economic support to a struggling ally constitute imperialism? America had been doing this very effectively since the days of the Marshall Plan.

But political rhetoric rather than well-thought-through foreign policy was what this was all about. Politics was becoming a media event, not a well-planned and wisely-led government program.

Nixon's resignation, and Ford's assumption of the Presidency.   By early August of 1974, it was quite clear that a Democratic-Party-controlled House of Representatives was ready to impeach Nixon. And although the Senate would require a 2/3rds majority to convict, the Republicans – many going into elections that fall – were certain that any Congressional action was likely to hurt the Republicans deeply. Thus they pleaded with Nixon to resign. He agreed to do this.

Consequently on August 8th, Nixon appeared before the press to announce his resignation – and then flew off … to leave the presidency in the hands of his Vice President Gerald Ford.

But Gerald Ford was well liked on Capitol Hill. After all, it was Congress, not the American people, that elected him to the vice-presidency … when criminal charges were brought to Nixon's original vice president, Spiro Agnew, and Agnew was thus forced to resign.

But there were two problems that came with the Ford presidency. Congress, because it voted him into power, believed that it owned him. And secondly, Ford was a man of deep Christian integrity. He knew that the political Left was not finished in what it intended to do to Nixon now that he was a private citizen and subject to prison time. Thus Ford, after much prayer on the matter, came to the decision to issue Nixon a presidential pardon ... knowing the fury this would stir on the American Left. But America had other business it needed to attend to. And it was time to stop this attempt to lynch an American president.*

The horrible aftermath of Congress's "anti-imperialism." Tragically, it became quite apparent that the South Vietnamese government was not going to be able to stand up to the offensive orchestrated by the Soviet-supported North Vietnamese government when Congress announced its ending of all support of the South. Step by step the North advanced against the South ... until it was on the edge of full defeat (losing some 80,000 soldiers killed in the process). At this point (the end of April 1975) the decision was made to pull out all American personnel remaining in the South ... with terrorized Vietnamese trying to find a way themselves to make just such an escape.

The pictures of Americans fending off desperate Vietnamese as Americans made their own escape was truly humiliating. But there was nothing that the Ford Administration could do about a situation that was now directed from a "democratic" Congress ... and not the presidential office.

But the horror did not stop there. A huge number (perhaps a million) Vietnamese were carted off to Communist "re-education" camps ... where they suffered terribly, many dying in the process. Also South Vietnamese farms were "collectivized" Stalinist and Maoist style, which of course crippled the economy and brought on mass hunger.

But next door in Cambodia, the situation became even worse, when the shift in the regional power picture allowed the Communist Khmer Rouge to take over "neutral" Cambodia – and impose a Maoist-style regime in the country ... Maoist in the sense that these Communists hated urban society and were determined to convert all of Cambodia into some kind of rural paradise, or at least wipe out those elements of urban society unlikely to make such a conversion. Thus the residents of the capital city, Phnom Penh, were moved to work camps in the countryside – or were simply executed on the spot ... especially if they were suspected of being of the intellectual or Westernized variety of citizens.

------

*The American Left, which "forgave" (actually merely ignored) Ted Kennedy over the death of a young lady in his company, would never let up on Nixon – making sure that the history taught in American schools and universities would always present Nixon as the "evil president." Actually, Nixon would recover stature privately, and would be sought quietly by future presidents and public officials for his wise counsel.

Of course all of this collapsed the Cambodian economy, producing mass starvation – and further execution of individuals suspected of non-cooperation with the Khmer Rouge revolution. Thus were produced the "Killing Fields" of Cambodia – estimates running from 2 to 4 million Cambodians dying in the process, half by execution the other half by starvation.

The "boat people." By 1978-1979, millions of Vietnamese (and others) were trying desperately to escape the horror that had descended on their world, some heading overland in their effort to escape to Malaysia or Thailand but most simply taking boats and heading to the open sea in the hopes of being picked up by passing Western ships. Tragically, many died in the effort. But ultimately some 800,000 "boat people" were picked up ... and settled in America. Another quarter million were able to get to Europe or Britain's Commonwealth countries and to settle there.

Evaluating it all. Did Congress ever acknowledge its role in starting up this catastrophe with its abandonment of its South Vietnamese ally? The answer to that is a very clear "no." This was not a matter that Congress – or any of the American Left – wanted to bring up for discussion. So the whole tragedy was simply ignored by those now directing superpower America.

A spiritless American bi-centennial celebration (July 1976). Certainly a huge effort was undertaken to make the celebration of America's 200th year since the signing of its Declaration of Independence as grand an event as possible. But it was just too hard to wipe away the sentiment that something was deeply wrong with America. Yes, America had come a long, long way in its development over those 200 years. But the last decade had been confusing ... and at times just highly dispiriting.

Anyway, another national election was coming up that November, and the necessity of finding a leader to take America forward seemed more important that simply celebrating the past.

✳ ✳ ✳

**AMERICA MOVES FROM CHRISTIANITY TO SECULARISM
AS THE NATION'S MORAL-SPIRITUAL FOUNDATION**

America heads down the Secular road ... with the Supreme Court leading the way. The Constitution that the American Republic officially brought into being in the late 1700s spelled out a very limited government, one designed simply to keep the 13 now-independent American states joined together in a new Federal union ... and moving together (not in competition with each other) down the road of independence that they had maintained – even against British efforts to end that independence – at that point for a century and a half. The Constitution spells out no moral-religious conditions for its existence ... though it was well-testified at the time that American society itself was understood to stand on strong Christian moral-spiritual roots. Indeed, the First Amendment, demanded by America's leaders as a condition of acceptance of the Constitution, spells out very clearly that Congress was to make "no law respecting an establishment of religion or prohibiting its free exercise" ... the very first of the freedoms guaranteed in the First Amendment. America's religion belonged to the people ... not to Congress (meaning also, any Federal authority). And that's where things stood in America ... all the way up until the beginning of the 1960s.

As we have seen, the ACLU took it upon itself to go – not to Congress but to the Supreme Court – to begin its campaign to replace America's Christian moral-spiritual foundations with the "religious Humanism" (to quote the *Humanist Manifesto* of 1933) as the nation's moral-spiritual foundations. Of course the ACLU no longer called its religious ideology "religious Humanism," but posed itself as the voice of "science" rather than "religious superstition." In any case, according to the ACLU, God had no place in America's public life.

Thus in 1962 it got prayer in the nation's public schools shut down by the Supreme Court ... and in 1963 the reading of the Bible, a sacred document that had long formed the moral-spiritual instruction set that America was built on. And it got a "Progressive" (Democratic-Party-controlled) Congress and a naive Christian leadership to undercut any effort by way of a further amendment of the Constitution, an amendment seeking to make absolutely clear what the First Amendment meant by "no law ... prohibiting its free exercise" ... which is exactly what the ACLU succeeded in getting the Supreme Court to do: prohibiting – by the Supreme Court's own self-assumed law-making powers – religion's free exercise.

But the matter did not stop there. In 1971, the Supreme Court overturned the decision of a lower court that public funds used in Pennsylvania to pay for textbooks in Catholic schools did not violate the constitution, the Supreme Court instead deciding in the *Lemon v. Kurtzman* case that in fact this activity violated the Jeffersonian "separation of church and state" principle of the First Amendment. But the Court went further in specifying (the famous "Lemon test") that the government can act only when such action serves a purely "secular legislative purpose" ... in order to avoid "an excessive government entanglement with religion."

In short, a secular purpose rather than a Christian purpose was to guide American education. But Secularism is a worldview or religion like any other ... specifying the basic Truths that guide all existence – Truths that people believe in and live by as the fundamental principles of life. By the design of the American people themselves, Christianity used to play that role ... and led a Christian America forward over the centuries to rather grand success as a thriving democracy. But now – according to the authoritative ruling of the Supreme Court – only Secularism can play that role.

That action by the Supreme Court supporting Secular principles in opposition to Christian principles was therefore the equivalent of enacting a law "respecting an establishment of religion" (Secularism) ... as well as prohibiting the "free exercise" of America's long-standing religious traditions – both actions expressly forbidden by the Constitution, a Constitution that the Supreme Court was supposed to be upholding ... not amending or revising along political-ideological lines.

In short, the vital moral idea of a God who clearly had guided previous American generations – and most importantly its leadership – was now NOT to be taught – or even mentioned – to any rising American generation in its schooling.

Enjoying a great victory, but nervous that its support of "religious Humanism" in the 1930's *Humanist Manifesto*, would get it in trouble, Humanists were quick to authorize a *Humanist Manifesto II* in 1973 ... a new document that declared that its Humanist principles were secular and thus scientific – not religious.*

But this would not be the end of the momentum in which American "Progressives" would act to replace Christian religious principles with Secular-Humanist religious principles.

---

*However, the American Humanist Association's website with the banner phrase "Good without God" is a giveaway as to their strongly held religious beliefs.

CHAPTER TWENTY

PEACE

✳ ✳ ✳

CARTER'S "MORE MORAL" PRESIDENCY

The 1976 elections

The Republicans narrowly chose Ford to be their presidential candidate in the 1976 elections. Former Hollywood actor and two-term California governor (1967-1975) Ronald Reagan tried to get the Republican nomination ... but after a bitter contest with Ford, fell just slightly short of the goal.

On the other side of the contest, the Democrats might have wanted to put the Kennedy name into action ... but Chappaquiddick was still too closely associated with the Kennedy name. Instead they came up with a former single-term governor of Georgia (1971-1975), Jimmy Carter ... who went in short order from being virtually unknown nationally to the picture (shaped by the press) of an amazing political genius ... someone who promised to bring forward a more moral national political dynamic. This struck a responsive chord in America, a nation deeply hungry to put behind it an ugly political world it had been through over the last decade.

Interestingly, Carter made it a point that the Republican policy of Realpolitik, employed by Nixon and Ford – and Kissinger under both presidents – he was going to do away with ... because of its cynical, non-moral character.* He was also going to end America's program of working with dictators.

Anyway, Americans bought the Carter deal ... and voted 50.1% for Carter against Ford's 48% ... with the Electoral College voting 297 for Carter and 240 for Ford.

The surrender of the Panama Canal

---

*Yes ... but it was Realpolitik that moved Nixon to open relations with China and undertake détente with the Soviets ... plus find a way to get out of the Vietnam mess that former president Johnson started – and then simply gave up on.

Back in 1903, America bought the rights from the French to build a canal linking the Atlantic and Pacific ... which Colombia, claiming the narrow strip of land as its own, chose to block. As a result, America "helped" the Panamanian people secure their independence from Colombia ... and then have the Panamanians turn around and grant canal-building rights to America. From that point on the canal, built at American expense but largely by Panamanian workers, was considered American property ... in perpetuity.

But over the years, the Panamanians (and neighboring Hispanic nations) grew to resent the American ownership and military occupation of the Canal Zone ... a hostile sentiment that reached a flash point in early 1964, ultimately resulting in bloody violence – followed by the decision of the Panamanian government to break relations with the US.

Negotiations were soon undertaken to secure a treaty to increase the role of Panama in the affairs of the Canal ... resulting finally in 1967 in a treaty over the matter – which, however, failed ratification in the Panamanian parliament. The following year, a military coup led by Omar Torrijos not only changed the hands of Panama's government, it also led to the full rejection of the 1967 treaty.

Under Nixon, discussions were resumed in 1973 after Torrijos hosted a U.N. Security Council meeting in Panama to go over the issue. In 1974 the Kissinger-Tack Treaty was signed ... promising, at some future date yet to be decided on, to transfer ownership of the canal to Panama – under the condition, however, that America would continue to provide "security" at the canal.

But the full return of the canal to Panama became a high priority of the new Carter Administration. And within mere weeks of Carter taking office, negotiations concerning this exchange began ... completed that August (1977) with the signing of a new treaty – which was quickly ratified in a Panamanian referendum (96% approving) in October, and by the necessary 2/3rds in two Senatorial votes the following March and April (1978).

The actual terms of the transfer were that the Canal Zone was to be rather immediately done away with as such – that is, integrated into Panamanian sovereign territory – with the actual turnover of the canal to then take place in stages ... to be completed by the end of 1999.

Conservatives (mostly Republicans) were furious at the "giveaway" of such a strategic American naval asset ... pointing out that Carter also was yielding to the very kind of military dictator that he claimed he would avoid all diplomatic relations with! And why was Carter in such a hurry to do this? What exactly did America gain in this transaction? Would this make our Latin neighbors to the South love and respect America more? That seemed most unlikely.

But the fact was that the Conservatives had no means of stopping the exchange. It was a done deal.

Crisis in Iran ... and its impact on America and the world

One of Carter's initial concerns was Shah Mohammad Reza Pahlavi's Iranian government ... judged by Carter to be quite oppressive and needing reform if America was to continue to supply it with armaments (something he had attacked Ford for supporting). Indeed, Amnesty International reported that some 3,000 people were imprisoned in Iran simply for political reasons.

But the situation in Iran was very tricky. The political conditions there were certainly worsened by the fact that the Shah seemed unable to make the distinction between those who wanted the Shah overthrown and those who simply wanted to see some political reforms take place in Iran. But there were other problems troubling Iran ... big problems.

First of all, the Shah had lost a lot of his former popularity with Iran's huge agricultural community with 1) the huge inflation that hit the country as a result of the global energy crisis of the early 1970s, 2) the failure of agricultural prices to keep up with that inflation, and 3) the vast wealth from the huge increase in oil prices going only to a few select families rather than to Iranian society as a whole.

Then there was the matter of the large number of Western-educated Iranian youth with their engineering degrees from various Western universities ... jobless in Iran because the Iranian oil industry required very little of such expertise to conduct its operations. They were a very unhappy lot ... finding it easy to blame the Shah's government for their inability to find a place of prosperity back in their home country.

An additional factor in the Iranian dynamic was the enormous interest the Soviets had in political developments to the south of their empire – in Iran, Afghanistan and Pakistan ... the area that separated the Soviets from the strategic Persian Gulf and its entry into the Indian Ocean – through which a huge portion of the Western world's oil flowed. Consequently, a huge amount of political intrigue was undertaken by the Soviets to bring the area under Soviet mastery.

Helping shape this dynamic was the Afghan-Pakistani war undertaken by Mohammed Daoud Khan, who in 1973 overthrew the monarchy of his cousin Mohammed Zahir Shah and replaced it with a republic, which Daoud then ran as a personal dictatorship. Daoud's war with Pakistan interested the Soviets greatly, as Pakistan was a close American ally at the time and Daoud thus needed Soviet support to conduct his side of the contest. But Soviet support was cautious ... as the Soviets did not want to upset the Arab world by appearing to oppose Pakistan. And at the same time, the Soviets had an equal interest in seeing America's long-standing ally in the form of the Shah overthrown, or at least brought under Soviet authority.

But for the moment, the Soviets were most interested in supporting a large Communist political element in Afghanistan ... which however was itself divided into two opposing sub-groups, one in favor of overthrowing Daoud immediately and establishing a Communist regime there, the other rather willing to go more cautiously in the matter.

In any case, it was all a very, very tricky dynamic driving the politics of that part of the world.

Thankfully – with the help of some of his advisers (who were more understanding of the importance of practicing Realpolitik in the matter) – Carter came fairly quickly to understand that cutting off the Shah was definitely not the best policy to be undertaken.

But the Shah himself became a bit confused over the matter of exactly where Carter stood in Iranian-American relations ... initially releasing many of those imprisoned in the hopes of pleasing Carter. But then Carter surprised the Shah when on a visit to Asia at the end of 1977 Carter celebrated New Year's Eve with the Shah in Iran ... praising the Shah's Iran as "an island of stability in one of the more troubled areas of the world."

This then was interpreted by the Shah as permission to return his opponents to prison ... except that in attempting to do so, the Shah set off a firestorm of protests around the country, ones he seemed unable to control. Thus with the help of Iran's Muslim leaders – who had always detested the way the Shah had introduced Western ways into Iran – an anti-Shah movement began to spread across Iran during 1978. By the end of the summer these had virtually paralyzed Iran ... and merely grew worse as the end of the year approached.

But this was a development that Carter was blind to because he depended on the Shah's intelligence service to keep him informed about developments in Iran ... and negative information was not what the Iranian service wanted to pass on to Carter.

Then in mid-January, the Shah took the same move that he did back in 1953 ... simply leaving the country and going into exile – to wait out developments. But in early February, Iran's Muslim leader, the Ayatollah Ruhollah Khomeini, ended his exile in Paris and flew into Iran – received by cheering crowds as their liberator.

But the protesting Westernized Iranians had their own agenda they wanted to see put in place – and the two anti-Shah groups clashed. But in this contest, the Westernized Iranians were greatly outnumbered by the Muslim traditionalists in Iranian society ... and a crackdown on the Western voices began to silence those hoping to see a Western-style republic put in place.

And in all of this, America had no role to play whatsoever ... except as the enemy – the "evil Satan" – that helped unify the anti-Western movement taking over Iran.

But the shock to America (and the rest of the world) did not end there. With Iran in full commotion, the Iranian oil industry came to a halt ... creating an international oil shortage. And in response to this development, once again OPEC took advantage of the situation by tightening even further the world's oil supply – which quickly quadrupled oil prices ... and likewise drove up astronomically prices at the world's gas pumps ... if gasoline was even available at that point. Thus another global energy crisis was to hit the world in the late 1970s ... one that would last well into the early 1980s.

The Israeli-Palestinian peace: The Camp David Accords

Thankfully there were some positive developments in those days. A major victory for Carter was the agreement he was able to get Egypt and Israel to adopt, one which finally moved things forward diplomatically ... previously stalemated since the end of the 1973 Yom Kippur October War.

Carter had taken the initiative in his first year in office to visit Egypt, Jordan, Syria, and Israel ... to see if he could get some action to end that stalemate. But nothing much came of the effort.

Then Egyptian President Sadat took the initiative himself, flying to Israel in November (1977) to speak before the Israeli Knesset (parliament) about the possibilities of moving things forward. This was a daring move on Sadat's part, likely to alienate the rest of the Arab world – even if he succeeded ... which most people thought was not likely to happen anyway.

But Sadat's concerns were Egypt, suffering economic difficulties ... not the larger Arab world. Unlike Nasser, Sadat had no interest in playing the role as leader of the Arab world. He had Egypt to worry about. And he was hoping to recover lost Egyptian land opposite the Suez Canal in the Sinai Peninsula. At the same time, dealing only with Egypt – and not the larger and still quite hostile Arab world – seemed to be of some interest to Israeli Prime Minister Menachem Begin.

But efforts to actually come to some kind of agreement between Israel and Egypt seemed to lead nowhere ... prompting Carter to decide to host private bilateral talks between Sadat and Begin in America itself, at the Presidential retreat at Camp David. Thus it was that talks got started there on 5 September 1978.

However, early on it appeared that these talks were also leading nowhere ... determining Carter to come up with his own proposal and then to meet separately with Begin and Sadat – to see if some progress could not be made that way. However even with a lot of back and forth and constant revision of the Carter proposal, as the 12-day meeting was about to come to an end it still looked as if nothing was going to be accomplished.

And then on the last day, Begin came to an agreement with Sadat.* Some kind of process for Palestinian self-government in the West Bank and Gaza areas was to be put into operation; with the Sinai Peninsula being turned over to Egypt, the Israeli Knesset would be given the responsibility of deciding the fate of the Israeli settlements there; and additional peace agreements were to be pursued with Israel's other Arab neighbors.

And indeed, in the following March (1979) a formal treaty in line with the Camp David Accords went into effect, formally ending the state of war between Egypt and Israel – and beginning the withdrawal of Israeli troops from the Sinai Peninsula and the opening of the Suez Canal to use by Israel (it had been opened earlier in 1975 to other nations with the clearing of the Canal of the last of the mines left from the 1973 war).

But as a springboard for a similar end to the Arab-Israeli standoff this was not fated to be. Neighboring Jordan and Syria – as well as the larger Arab League – were in agreement with none of the terms of the Accords. In fact, the fellow Arab nations were so incensed by Sadat's agreement with Israel that they decided to terminate Egypt's membership in the Arab League. So in the end, little beyond the direct Egyptian-Israeli boundary settlement was accomplished ... except that Iraq's dictator Saddam Hussein felt that the door was opened for him – now that the Egyptian president was removed from his usual position as the leader of the Arab world – to take on that role himself.

Nonetheless, the Norwegians felt it right to extend to both Sadat and Begin the 1978 Nobel Peace prize for their efforts.

Tragically however, the Accords became the motivation for hardliners of the Egyptian Islamic Jihad to attempt to get rid of Sadat as Egyptian president ... which they accomplished in October of 1981 when he was assassinated while attending a military celebration. But his successor, General Hosni Mubarak, simply continued down the same road that Sadat had laid out.

❋ ❋ ❋

CHINA JOINS THE WORLD

Despite Nixon's opening of American relations with China, this would, for the time being, have little impact on how China went about its political business. That was a matter strictly up to Chairman Mao. But of course

---

*Neither Begin nor Sadat wanted to go home with nothing to show for the grand effort.

there were other political interests moving cautiously around Mao.

Lin Biao and the Gang of Four. General Lin Biao had indeed been able to bring the chaos created by Mao's young Red Guards under fair control. This cautiously pleased what was left of the Chinese "pragmatists" ... but alienated the radicals – most notably Mao's actress wife Jiang Qing (his fourth wife). But taking any kind of position of importance on any Chinese party matter was a very dangerous thing to do ... if you were not the Great Chairman himself.

What finally brought down General Lin, however, was not the rivalry going on between the pragmatists and the radicals ... but the fact that Lin took on too much personal authority in his response to the border conflict China was having with Soviet Russia in 1969. At first Mao reacted simply by elevating his close friend (a pragmatist however) Zhou Enlai to power as a personal advisor in order to counterbalance Lin's power. Then when Zhou promoted the Chinese opening to Nixon and the Americans (mid-1971), Lin's strong opposition to this move put Lin in deep trouble. Indeed, rumors (perhaps true) were that Lin was actually planning some kind of political coup. In any case, deciding in September of 1971 that it was simply time to avoid the consequences of a probable Chinese political loss, Lin apparently chose to flee to Russia ... only to have his plane mysteriously crash in the process. Lin would subsequently be condemned as a Chinese traitor.

Taking Lin's place now as the leading voice of the anti-Western radicals was Mao's wife, Jiang. She did not back down any in her political opposition to any opening to the West ... although as many as 1,000 Chinese officials (including military) were purged from the party for their probable support of Lin. But as a matter of overall importance, Mao tended to look more to Zhou than Jiang in the conduct of his affairs ... stirring the wrath of Jiang and some of her cohorts (the "Gang of Four").

Zhou and Mao die (1976).   Then when in 1972 Zhou found himself struggling with cancer, Mao decided to order the political rehabilitation of the formerly imprisoned pragmatist Deng Xiaoping ... in order to have him work with Zhou. But when in January of 1976 Zhou finally succumbed to the disease, Mao called on the "centrist" (cautiously neither radical nor pragmatist) Hua Guofeng to take Zhou's place.

However, Mao himself was struggling with his health ... and died that same September (1976). The next month, Jiang and the others of the "Gang of Four" were arrested and imprisoned.

The rise of Deng Xiaoping. At this point, Hua attempted to make himself into the apparent spiritual successor to Mao ... even though it was the pragmatist Deng who was now actually commanding the operations of the party from behind the scenes. And Deng's pragmatism would change dramatically the direction of Chinese politics – and economics – from that point forward.

Thus in 1977 the Cultural Revolution was declared to be officially over … and in 1978 Deng announced the startup of his Four Modernizations program, in which agriculture, industry, science and defense were to take on more of a Western look in their operation … with fourteen designated cities being open to foreign investment. Deng was intending to get the Chinese economy up and running (similar to the successful program that Taiwan had undertaken) by being active in the global market. And indeed, under Deng's reforms, the Chinese economy was quick to take off!

Politically, Deng would take for himself merely the position as chairman of the Central Military Commission … although everyone knew who was running the show. Hua would be removed from some of his positions … though certainly not removed from power altogether.

A Chinese-American détente. At the same time, Deng was quick to realize the international opportunities awaiting post-Maoist China. Carter himself had proved very helpful in this regard, sending his National Security Advisor Zbigniew Brzezinski to China in August of 1977 to discuss the possibility of improving US-China relations … American relations with Taiwan being one of the hurdles to be overcome. Negotiations that followed finally produced a full severance of American diplomatic ties with Taiwan … but under Deng's promise that America would be able to continue its commercial relations with Taiwan. This agreement in turn led Carter to invite Deng to visit America … which he did in late January-early February of 1979.

Carter and Deng had much to discuss … especially the matter of China wanting to invade Vietnam – at a time when the Soviets were Vietnam's major patron. But Deng affirmed that China was not afraid of this starting a war with Russia. This mounting problem was not something that pleased Carter. Otherwise, the visit was very positive (with even Nixon being invited to the White House – at Deng's insistence – to be part of the occasion).

The new China takes off. In 1980, Jiang and the other three members of the Gang of Four were finally put on trial, convicted of treason, but had the death penalty put aside in favor of life imprisonment. And the Maoist radical wing of the Party quickly disappeared.

And although the Party bureaucracy would still preside over Chinese programming, it was now the Chinese entrepreneurs who would actually take the lead in developing the Chinese economy … which then tended to grow annually by 10% almost every year thereafter! It was truly a Chinese miracle!

$$* \ * \ *$$

PROBLEMS IN AFGHANISTAN AND IRAN

Political instability in Afghanistan. In April of 1978, Russia's Afghan Communist clients made their move against Daoud's more or less internationally neutral government, assassinating Daoud and declaring the establishment of a new "Democratic Republic" under the Communist leader Nur Mohammad Taraki. Taraki in turn then moved strongly against the country's known intellectuals ... or anyone in Afghanistan harboring pro-West sentiments. But Taraki was just as cruel in eliminating those accused of just being conservative in political thinking – which was the actual moral-spiritual foundations of the country. Thus perhaps as many as 27,000 of Afghanistan's leaders (across a wide political spectrum) were arrested and executed in Afghan prisons over the next year and a half.

Unsurprisingly, all this inspired the outbreak of rebellions all across the country ... with much of the Afghan military joining the rebels. Adding to the turmoil, Carter – despite his earlier promise to conduct only "open diplomacy" – was secretly aiding the rebels financially.

Finally, a desperate Taraki called on the Soviets for direct assistance in putting down the uprisings. But the Soviets instead threw their support to Taraki's opposing Communist group, led by Hafizullah Amin ... who in turn had Taraki "removed" (assassinated) in October of 1979 and took control of the government. But Amin did not appear to be as dependent on the Soviets as they had hoped, and thus in December of that year the Soviets made their move to take direct control of Afghanistan. Amin was assassinated (KGB) ... and Babrak Karmal was put in his place as Afghan president. He in turn invited the Soviets to offer him full military assistance in bringing the country under control.

Soviet-American contention over Afghanistan. The Soviets were not fully aware of Carter's secret involvement in Afghanistan's dynamics at the time ... believing that Carter had only a minor interest in the area and therefore unlikely to have much of a reaction to a Soviet invasion of Afghanistan.

They were wrong. And it would bring an abrupt end to the Soviet-American discussions over the possibility of going even deeper into their prior Strategic Arms Limitation Talks (SALT). Earlier that year, in June of 1979, Carter and Soviet Premier Leonid Brezhnev had met in Vienna to sign a SALT II Agreement ... in the effort to update technological advances since the earlier (1972) SALT Agreement between Nixon and Brezhnev. Of particular interest in SALT was the matter of the MIRV missiles capable of carrying multiple nuclear warheads on a single rocket ... something that America had moved ahead of the Soviets on. Also, Brezhnev had been hoping the Vienna meeting would counterbalance some of the new China-America relationship going on at the time.

At the time, the Republicans in Congress were very upset that the limitation levels agreed on in the SALT II Agreement was merely voluntary ... which Carter certainly was willing to undertake – at a time in which many Americans still did not trust the Soviets on matters of "voluntary" self-restraint. Thus discussions in the Senate about ratifying the treaty dragged on ... until the December invasion of Afghanistan by the Soviets finally decided the matter.

At this point, even Carter was upset enough by the Soviet action in Afghanistan that he simply withdrew the treaty from further Senate consideration. SALT II was not completely dead. Carter would work to bring the MIRV issue under some kind of international understanding. But the treaty itself was dead.

The "more moral" Carter then followed up on his step-back from Soviet-American détente when he announced that American athletes would not be participating in the 1980 Moscow summer Olympics ... if the Soviets had not pulled out of Afghanistan by then. As threats go, there was little likelihood that the Soviets, at that point deeply committed militarily in Afghanistan, would be willing to perform such a retreat. Consequently, the only result of the Carter decision was that American athletes who had trained hard for the Olympics challenges would now not be able to compete.[*] And for Carter personally, it further worsened his image as he approached the 1980 national elections.

Catastrophe in Iran. But what really finished off Carter's chances for re-election were developments taking place in Iran – and the impact that had on the American economy and national morale.

When in October of 1979, Carter was considering the possibility of bringing the very sick Shah to America for cancer treatment ... the Iranian Muslim youth (the "Revolutionary Guard") became massively outraged. This then led them to attack the American Embassy in Tehran and take the American personnel there captive ... even displaying them blindfolded before a taunting crowd.

This so pleased the Iranians that the following month they easily approved a referendum establishing a new Islamic Republic. And these captured Americans would be held prisoner for the rest of Carter's term in office.

---

[*]The Soviets would then return the favor by boycotting the 1984 summer Olympics held in Los Angeles!

And this would be the case despite an attempt by Carter in April of 1980 to rescue these American captives. He planned (Operation Eagle Claw) to drop eight helicopters of Delta troops just outside of Tehran by night (Americans having first shut down Tehran's electrical grid) and have them taken by truck to the American embassy – where they could gather up the 52 American hostages held there and then fly them out of the country. But an unexpected sandstorm that developed in Southern Iran – which was supposed to be the launching site for the helicopter assault – produced both human and mechanical failure.[*]

In having to announce publicly the disaster in Iran, Carter's humiliation grew even worse – monumentally worse. Indeed, he suffered even further with the subsequent resignation of his Secretary of State Cyrus Vance, who had opposed the rescue attempt from the outset.

Carter's "Economic Czar" Volcker addresses the issue of inflation. But the shock to America (and the rest of the world) did not end there. With Iran in full commotion, the Iranian oil production dropped down to about a fourth of its normal production level … which, we have already noted, created an international oil shortage – and in general an international energy panic – one that would last well into the early 1980s.

Every economist understands how prices are determined by the iron law of supply and demand. When a shortage in the availability of something occurs – at a time when demand remains constant – prices are guaranteed to go up. This certainly was the case of energy costs … for people cannot simply cut back on their dependence on energy. And those offering energy for sale know full well that the price of the product they offer can be raised significantly in the face of a captive audience. Admittedly, Saudi Arabia increased its production somewhat in the face of the international energy shortage caused by the Iranian cutback … but not at the same rate as that cutback. And in the energy world it does not take much of a cutback (because of the inflexibility of demand) to drive prices sky high.

But there's another side to this law of supply and demand. Oversupply in the face of a world of demand that is slowing up will drop prices just as dramatically – such as what happens often in the housing industry when massive house-building gets well ahead of the actual number of people interested in buying new houses (oversupply), forcing builders to drop their prices dramatically in order to bring interested buyers forward.

So, farmers in the 1950s were paid to cut back farm production in

---

[*]Upon arrival to Iran, three helicopters went down in the sandstorm … and then eight American troops were killed following the decision to call off the assault – when another helicopter collided with one of the six C-130 transport planes that were supposed to carry the hostages out of Iran.

order to keep agricultural prices from falling away to the point where it cost more to produce the food than the food was able to be sold for on the open market. That's the policy of cutting back supply in the face of a shortage of demand … in order to maintain prices. That's what OPEC often does when too much energy production or "supply" is losing its pricing in the face of demand that has not risen any.

Likewise, to bring down prices … there are two avenues that can be taken. One is to simply increase supply … to a point that limited demand forces prices down in the face of this larger supply of goods (oil and gas in this case). Certainly OPEC could have done that in the face of this world shortage: simply up energy production (pump more oil and gas … done quite easily actually). But why would OPEC want to do that? OPEC members were getting rich – fantastically rich – from this supply-and-demand game.

The other route is to bring down demand. Higher prices should do that … especially in the face of production shortages. But again, people's energy needs are really not that adjustable.

But Carter's newly appointed Federal Reserve President Paul Volcker had another way of bringing down demand: just impoverish the economy to the point where people are simply required to live to lower – much lower – economic expectations. Therefore, a poorer society will be less demanding of goods … which should then bring down prices for available goods.

And he did this simply by increasing the cost of produced goods to such an extent that people simply could no longer afford to purchase them. To lure forth nervous or impoverished customers, in order to stay in business, producers would have to lower their prices. Thus voilà … inflation solved.

How was this 6'7" giant of a man able to do this? He simply jumped the already high Federal Discount Rate from 11% to 20% – by cutting back on the amount of Federal dollar reserves available to America's leading banks. In short, American banks – ones anyway that depended upon Federal credit dollars to be able then to turn around and offer loans to their own banking customers – had to "borrow" that money from the Fed at a 20% interest rate … requiring the banks in turn to have to offer their best or "prime" customers their own bank loans at a minimum of 22% or 23% annually – if the banks were to make any profit at all on the deal.

At first, this had the countering result of actually increasing, not decreasing, inflation. Interest rates charged by the financial industry to the industrial production sector are a key part of the costs that producers have to take into consideration in offering their products for sale. Thus if borrowed money becomes more expensive, then prices have to be raised in order to continue to make any kind of profit … even to make enough to pay the salaries and wages of the company's employees. Thus, by nearly doubling the Federal Discount Rate, Volcker actually worsened inflation.

Then too ... who would want to go to a bank and take out a loan at a 23% interest rate?

Mortgage rates for home purchasers, however, did not run quite as high ... as those rates are normally stretched out over a long period, usually 30 years of repayment. But even at a reduced rate of 16%, who still would want to buy a house and then pay back the loan at that high rate for the next 30 years? Thus new houses found themselves unsold ... at a time that builders were still required to repay those 20%+ bank loans they took out originally to build those homes. Soon bankruptcy was the only way out of total ruin for those unsuccessful home builders.

Likewise, car dealers were hit with the same problem ... that unless a customer was willing to pay cash for a car (few do) a car loan was almost as bad as a home mortgage. Thus the car business also dried up as purchasers decided to wait for rates to go down before they bought that new Chevy. Thus car dealerships across America also fell into bankruptcy.

But wait ... home builders and car dealers are key customers for banks. And if these customers go bankrupt, what was the bank itself supposed to do to keep itself in business? Banks now faced their own version of business failure.

And so – thanks to economic Czar Volcker – America fought inflation by making the nation poorer ... much, much poorer.

The Soviets break from the energy cartel. The Soviet economy was also finding itself in trouble at the time, though not for the same reason. In fact, Russia was a major oil exporter ... gaining a huge percentage of its international earnings from its oil and gas business. But the war it was conducting in Afghanistan was proving very costly ... while producing no visible rewards. Also there was increasing pressure from the Soviet citizenry to open to them the market for the consumer goods that other Europeans were able to afford.

But Russia was short in its holdings of the necessary international currencies such rising consumerism demanded (something of a "dollar shortage"). Thus the decision was made to offer its energy at a rate just under OPEC's rate ... in order to grab a larger share of the very lucrative global energy market.

Of course OPEC was in no mood to be left behind in the energy market ... and thus was forced to lower its prices a bit in order to keep its position there. But there is a huge margin in the cost-benefit gap in the energy world ... and the Soviets were thus easily able to come back with another price reduction. And so on. By 1982 ... something of a price war was going on.

And of course with much lower prices, this brought the world's energy crisis to an end. It was, after all, the energy issue that brought on the 1979-1982 global economic crisis in the first place. And with the lowering of energy costs, so too industrial producers were able to lower their prices ... making their products more attractive on the open market. Thus it was that America – and much of the rest of the world – regained economic momentum.

And too, huge pressure was also put on Volcker to reduce the Fed rate ... which – in the face of a threat to reduce the Fed's economic powers if he did not do so – he complied.

Thus it was that the global economy got itself back to some kind of normal.

Iraq attacks Iran (September 1980). Tensions had been building between Iran and its neighbor Iraq ever since the overthrow of the Shah's government.   Iraqi President Saddam Hussein was fearful of Shi'a Iran's exploitation of the Shi'a Muslim loyalties of some 60% of the Iraqi population ... at a time that Iraq was governed by a very secular Ba'athist* government, but one controlled basically by Sunni Muslims. At the same time, he was interested in regaining Arab lands ceded to Iran by hoping to exploit anti-Iranian (or anti-Persian) Arab cultural sentiments in those Iranian lands. And too, he was hoping by taking advantage of Iran's political chaos to be able to make Iraq the dominant power in the Persian Gulf region. Thus the full military assault on Iran.

At first – for a few months anyway – Saddam's troops were able to advance into the Arab region of Western Iran. But by December the Iranians were able to block any further Iraqi advances. Then the Iranians took to the counteroffensive ... and slowly regained the lost territory by the middle of 1982. But despite a U.N. resolution calling on all parties to halt their action, the Iranians then launched an attack into Iraq. This then for the next five years led to a vicious back and forth war – in which some of the latest weapons technologies were employed (including greatly outlawed chemical warfare) – which gained nothing for either side except a lot of death and destruction ... but supposedly great glory for those who had sacrificed their lives for the cause (a very intense sentiment in Shi'a Iran).

Then when in mid-1988 Iraq was able to launch a successful counterattack, the war simply ground to a halt. The Iran-Iraq War had become simply a gruesome stalemate.

✱ ✱ ✱

A WORLD OF "TOUGH"

*Ba'athist ... meaning renaissance or rebirth.

From Carter to Reagan

The 1980 elections.   The Democrats re-nominated Carter as their presidential candidate in the 1980 national elections ... despite some very strong opposition coming from Ted Kennedy. The Republicans offered Ronald Reagan as their candidate. In contrast to Carter's "peaceful" presentation, Reagan presented himself as a very tough individual, a true Cold Warrior who well understood the huge challenges facing America and the West ... and had every intention of taking on these challenges from a policy of power, not "niceness."

Volcker also played a key role in the election, dropping down considerably the Fed's discount rate, which immediately picked the economy back up considerably ... enough to take the strain off Carter and get him re-nominated. But oddly enough, Volcker then took the discount rate back up again soon thereafter ... throwing the American economy back into recession, helping immensely Reagan in the process.

Indeed, Reagan – in strong contrast to Volcker – said that he intended to deal with inflation not by crushing demand (Volcker) but instead by increasing supply.   Thus developed Reagan's "supply-side economics," something that he talked about constantly in his campaign.

And indeed the campaign went poorly for Carter and splendidly for Reagan ... Reagan with 489 electoral votes and Carter with only 49 electoral votes.   The popular vote went 50.7% for Reagan and 41% for Carter ... with a third-party candidate, the Republican Congressman John Anderson, running as an independent and gaining only 6.6% of the popular vote (no electoral votes).   Thus the Republican fear that Anderson would undercut Reagan deeply did not come to pass.[*]

The release of the American hostages in Iran. Then on inauguration day (20 January 1981) – just as Reagan was being sworn in as the new U.S. president – the American hostages were finally released and arrived in Germany ... on their way back to America. Americans wondered about the timing – for it seemed to have been set in order to humiliate Carter ... although it had been Carter that had actually negotiated the release. Many wondered if this had been done out of fear that the new, tough Reagan might do something drastic to Iran. Probably not ... though Americans would never know why the release took place at precisely the time it did.

An assassination attempt. But Reagan would be in office only a short time

---

[*]Anderson had hoped to build his candidacy on the support of the same people that four years earlier had supported George McGovern: the idealistic Boomers and their intellectualist mentors.

before he would be called on to demonstrate that toughness he represented. At the end of March, he was the object of an assassination attempt[*] by the madman John Hinckley, Jr. – which wounded Reagan and crippled badly his Press Secretary James Brady. But Reagan would retake from his Vice President George Bush his position (and his humor) as president only 12 days later. With his strong recovery, his popularity ratings hit nearly 75%!

The PATCO strike. Reagan would have another opportunity that August to demonstrate that same toughness when members of the Professional Air Traffic Controllers union (PATCO) went on strike … to which Reagan responded swiftly by firing the 11,000 strikers, cutting back flights to about 50%, and finding substitutes able to join the non-striking controllers to keep those flights moving. Once again, the nation was deeply impressed!

Thatcher and the Falklands War (April-June 1982)

The Argentine military dictatorship that had held power since 1976 (with frequent turnovers of command) was facing growing unpopularity at home because of the country's very poor economy – and the huge human rights violations involved in maintaining that dictatorship.   The generals thus decided that what the country needed was a good patriotic war.

Sitting 300 miles to the East of Argentina in the middle of the South Atlantic were the Falkland Islands … long-claimed by Argentina as its own territory – but also by Britain as a Crown Colony since 1841. The small population living there was by very strong instinct Anglo-British … not Hispanic.

But Britain by this point was no longer considered to be much of a global power anymore – at least in the eyes of the Argentine generals – and the decision was thus made by the military junta leader Leopoldo Galtieri to conduct at the beginning of April (1982) a large Argentine military assault on the Falkland Islands. It was expected that an easy victory in the matter could be achieved in a matter of days.

At first the Argentine military was quick to take control of the small capital city, Stanley. But the British Royal Navy was aware of something going in in the region – and had already been sending ships South in the Atlantic towards the Falklands. Then when news of the Argentine invasion reached Britain, Prime Minister Margaret Thatcher was quick to order a large British assault on the Argentine position – both on the islands and against

------

[*]Ford was also the object of an assassination attempt in September of 1975 by Sara Jane Moore. Actually, 17 days earlier, a Charles Manson follower, Lynette "Squeaky" Fromme, had also pointed a gun at Ford … and although the gun was otherwise loaded, there was actually no bullet in the chamber at the time.

the Argentine ships offshore. Thus a full Argentine-British war was on.

The rest of the world attempted to bring the crisis to an end through diplomacy ... with a U.N. resolution passing 10-1 (with Russia and China abstaining) calling for the withdrawal of the Argentine troops – to be followed by negotiations. At first America tried to work with both sides, but found neither the British nor the Argentines interested in compromise. Finally, Reagan simply decided to give full public support to Thatcher's Britain.

The consequent fighting over the next six weeks proved fierce, with the British not able to match the Argentines in terms of available aircraft. But when a British submarine sank the large Argentine battleship *General Belgrano* at the beginning of May, the bulk of the Argentine navy returned to port in Argentina. The British also lost ships, although not so disastrously ... and – under Thatcher's stiff resolve – the British navy held its position. Then British military units began their sweep across the Islands, with the Argentines forced into a most humiliating surrender. When Stanley found itself finally back in British hands in mid-June, the war was over.

The overall outcome of the war was the acclaim of Thatcher as the "Iron Lady" ... and the huge success of her Conservative Party in the national elections the next year. And it would draw Reagan and Thatcher closely together as strong allies. As for the Argentine military junta, the event backfired on it deeply. Galtieri was replaced by a more Liberal general, who would call for elections the following year ... resulting in the end of military governance and the return to Argentine democracy.

Nonetheless, despite the resumption of diplomatic relations between Britain and Argentina, there would be no agreement between the two as to whom exactly the Falkland Islands belonged!

Lebanon (1982-1984)

When in June of 1982, Begin's Israeli army suddenly attacked multi-ethnic Lebanon as supposedly a move against the Palestinian Liberation Organization (PLO) that had taken refuge there, the country fell into complete chaos. Consequently, Christians of all varieties and Muslims of all varieties fell into conflict with each other. The slaughter became so extensive that finally in August of 1982 the U.N. set up a Multinational Force (MNF) of troops from largely America, France and Italy (about 600-800 troops each) to be sent to Lebanon to evacuate PLO fighters from Lebanon ... and to separate the various factions.

But the violence did not abate, but merely grew worse ... especially when in mid-September Maronite Christian Arab allies of Israel (and supervised by Israeli Defense Minister Ariel Sharon) surrounded Palestinian refugee camps and began to kill the people found there. The world was horrified.

Consequently, America, France and Italy decided to increase substantially the number of their troops in order to regain some semblance of order … at least in central Lebanon (Syria had taken over much of the northern half of the country). And apparently the effort was working.

But the following April (1983) a suicide van loaded with explosives bombed the American Embassy in Beirut, killing 63 people, the first of many smaller attacks on American peacekeepers. Then in October two more truck bombs blew up the American and French barracks, killing 241 American and 58 French soldiers.[*]

At this point calls began to be heard in both America and France to "bring the boys home." Clearly the MNF was not able to restore Lebanon to a state of peace. But Reagan still wanted to hang tough in Lebanon. He had an obligation to fulfill.

But by February of 1984, Reagan was willing to acknowledge that his effort was not producing any progress … only the further loss of American life. Thus, admitting failure, he began pulling U.S. troops out of Lebanon.

But surprisingly, this admission of failure to achieve grand goals did not lessen the respect of the American people for their president. The ability of a leader to admit failure and pull back from a bad situation was actually considered by most as the measure of their leader's greatness. Normally, in the face of such failure, a terrible leader will want to dig ever deeper into a situation in the hope of yet somehow recovering his own sagging reputation – making the situation vastly worse … something seen way too often in history.

Grenada (October 1983)

Part of this Reagan picture, however, was shaped by an event elsewhere that took place at the same time as the military barracks bombing in Lebanon. A Marxist military coup had taken place in 1979 in the tiny Caribbean country of Granada, which in turn brought on considerable political chaos in the country. This then prompted neighboring countries and the former governor-general of the island to call on America to restore Granada to its constitutional order. And they found a receptive audience with Reagan, who was already concerned about what a Marxist regime – thus like Castro's Cuba, a Russian puppet – situated along the naval path to the Panama Canal might mean strategically to American naval power. After all, although Carter had set up the transfer of the Canal from American hands, the American navy still needed the Canal to connect its Atlantic and

---

[*]These suicide bombings were presumably conducted by Iran-backed Hezbollah operatives belonging to a group that called itself Islamic Jihad.

Pacific fleets. Also, with the shooting of civilians caught in the crossfire, the 600 American medical students studying in the country were an additional concern. Thus on 25 October (1983), Reagan sent American troops (joined by troops from six of the neighboring countries) to invade Grenada.

The action immediately brought on a huge outcry from the loud and highly angry "anti-imperialist" sector of American – and international – society. And the U.N. General Assembly voted a strong protest against the American action. However, the American success in overthrowing the Marxist regime came so quickly that it brought strong approval from the majority of the American public. And Reagan's disregard of the U.N. resolution only strengthened further his image as a president not easily swayed by world public opinion. And indeed, the world quickly got over its feelings about the matter. It had bigger things to focus on.

Reagan in trouble

Reagan's reelection (1984). The Democrats had little chance of gaining the White House, given Reagan's very high public approval ratings. But they did call on former Minnesota Senator and Carter's Vice President Walter Mondale to run as their candidate. Unsurprisingly, Reagan won 58.8 percent of the vote to Mondale's 40.6 percent and 525 Electoral College votes for Reagan to only 13 votes for Mondale. Reagan therefore expected to enjoy a very pleasant second term.

The Iran-Contra Affair. Then in November of 1986 a Lebanese newspaper article found its way to the American media ... about some kind of secret weapons sale to Iran made by officials high-up in the Reagan Administration – supposedly as part of an accompanying deal to gain the release of some American hostages held by the Iranian-backed Palestinian organization Hezbollah. The money received in the deal furthermore was also used secretly to fund a CIA-backed guerrilla group, the Contras," attempting to overthrow the Sandinista government of Nicaragua, a government with strong "Leftist" tendencies that made American officials very nervous. There were also rumors that drug money was also involved in the support of the Contras.

As far as the matter of paying for the release of those American hostages, this was in strong violation of the official stand against making just such payments – lest this simply encourage more hostage-taking for money. And as for the support of the Contras, this was in direct violation of a Boland Amendment passed by a Democratic-Party-controlled Congress designed to keep America out of the turmoil that was shaking Central America.

Indeed, at the time, Central America was suffering from deep unemployment ... which inspired Sandinista-supported guerrillas to try to overthrow the traditional neighboring regimes of Guatemala, Honduras and El Salvador. And in El Salvador the level of violence was running very high. Furthermore, with Cuba also supporting the Sandinista effort, American fears of indirect Soviet involvement in the region ran high. But this very fear was what inspired the Boland Amendment ... and at the same time the decision somewhere in the Reagan Administration to ignore the congressional ruling and insert American power into the dynamic ... in order to bring things back under more traditional control.

In response to the Congressional (and ultimately public) shock over these secret deals, the next month (December) Reagan himself set up a three-man commission under former Texas Senator John Tower to look into the matter. What the Tower Commission soon concluded (February 1987) was that the CIA should have made both the president and Congress aware of its activities – faulting Reagan for not following events closely within his own Administration.

Congress of course was looking for an outcome more damaging to the president than a simple chastisement for official failure. They wanted him impeached ... most tragically, impeachment somehow now being considered to be a very useful and quite normal political strategy in American politics! They thus formed their own commissions earlier in January – anticipating that the Tower Commission would fail to deliver the grounds they would need to impeach Reagan.

Thus from early May to early August (1987) the American public was treated to another well-broadcasted congressional investigation into what was now termed the "Iran-Contra Affair." But the best they could get from the matter was only Marine Colonel Ollie North being caught in a lie about the transfer of Contra funds ... something they could not act on because he had been extended immunity as part of his offering testimony in the matter. And the Senators ultimately proved to be unwilling to push Reagan on the matter – seeing nothing but trouble for the country (and themselves) in doing so.

Actually, Reagan (briefly) would suffer from a drop in his popularity. And, perhaps not surprisingly, Col. North would actually become something of a hero to American Conservatives.

THE COLLAPSE OF THE SOVIET EMPIRE

Gorbachev attempts to reform the Soviet system

The reason that Reagan's popularity ratings would soon climb again was because of his role in helping to shape developments going on in Eastern Europe ... within the Soviet Empire.

Economic, social and military problems in the Soviet Empire. Russia, once a major exporter of agricultural goods, had found that since the Soviet collectivization of Russian farms, agricultural production had dropped drastically ... to a point that Soviet Russia was dependent on agricultural imports to feed its people – an expense that burdened deeply Soviet finances. Then too, the emphasis of state financial support going to the Soviet military machine left very little for the world of the individual Russian consumer. Certainly at this point the average Russian citizen was well aware of the fact that in their supposed "workers' paradise" they were falling well beyond the worker's lifestyles in the capitalist West. Consequently, worker motivation in the Soviet system was in a state of rapid decline, worsened by the absenteeism and the alcoholism that afflicted the Soviet working world.

Briefly, the oil crisis that hit the world after the fall of the Shah in 1979 had boosted Soviet Russia's international earnings from its oil and gas exports ... but not to the extent that the Soviet leadership felt was necessary to pull the country out of its demoralized state. As already noted, they thus dropped their export pricings in order to gain a larger share of the international oil market ... only to have OPEC respond in kind – setting off a drop in oil pricings and thus earnings. This worsened deeply the social situation in Russia (as well as in the other oil exporting countries).

Then too there was the matter of the Soviet military intervention in Afghanistan ... in order to support a government willing to serve as a Soviet political puppet. This was undertaken in the early 1980s in the hope of producing a Soviet expansion that would put Russia at the top of a political pyramid controlling the vital Persian Gulf and its neighboring portion of the Indian Ocean – through which most of the Western world's oil supply had to pass.

But the vast majority of the Afghan population had proven to be most unwilling partners in this Soviet scheme and were fighting back – with considerable American support (money and weapons) ... and showing no signs of letting up in that opposition. And with these American-supplied weapons, the Afghan mujahedin were proving most able to shoot down Soviet planes and destroy Soviet tanks ... running up the Soviet cost in lost military supplies and men as well as finances that the Soviets could ill afford. Indeed, the Soviets were quickly discovering what it was that America took too long to figure out with its involvement in Vietnam, namely that the huge costs involved in intervening in a most unwilling country were in no way offset by any significant gains – economic, social or political ...

much less military.

The rapid turnover in Soviet leadership (1982-1985). Then too, there was the matter of the rapid change in Soviet leadership that followed upon the death of Brezhnev in late 1982. The Soviet KGB head Yuri Andropov replaced Brezhnev … in the hopes of stiffening the control of the Kremlin over Russian society. But he was of poor health – and died only a little over a year after having taken the position. But the person to follow him, Konstantin Chernenko, was of no better health … and he too died only a year later. Thus it was that in March of 1985 the Soviet leadership chose a younger – but also reform-minded – individual, Mikhail Gorbachev, to take over Soviet leadership. He seemed to be greatly energized by the ideas that he had in mind to introduce as new Soviet policy, something that he was certain would put energy back into Soviet society.

Reagan's "Star Wars program." This need to re-energize Soviet society was especially the case given the clear intention of American president Reagan to challenge the Soviet Empire in every way possible. Back in 1982 in a speech that Reagan had delivered before the British Parliament, he made it clear that he was dedicated to pushing the Soviet "Evil Empire" to the point of collapse. And Reagan quickly followed this up by putting the B1-Bomber program back into operation (after Carter had canceled it), then by arming NATO with American Pershing II missiles … and in 1983 announcing a Strategic Defense Initiative (SDI) that would develop laser-guided missiles able to knock down incoming Soviet missiles – effectively ending the Soviet nuclear deterrent.

　　Unsurprisingly, an "anti-imperialist" (Democratic-Party-controlled) Congress was most unwilling to support the expensive and supposedly unneeded SDI program. Senator Ted Kennedy had even mocked Reagan's program as being nothing more than "reckless Star Wars schemes" … offering a nickname for the program which Regan himself was willing to accept!

　　But as things turned out, the "Star Wars program" would not be needed … because the Soviet Empire itself had crumbled before even the end of the 1980s decade.

Gorbachev's reforms. In 1986 Gorbachev began to introduce his reforms, *glasnost* (a new openness in the society), *perestroika* (a restructuring of the economic system) and *demokratizatsiya* (democratization of the political system). His hope was that these reforms would put the Russian citizens back to work supporting the advancement of their society and its long-dreamed-of social revolution.

Indeed, these reforms were met with great enthusiasm ... in Russia itself, of course – but also in the countries of the East European Soviet Bloc. But what Gorbachev did not realize was that these reforms also set loose a revolution of its own ... a "revolution of rising expectations" in which these new steps into a world of greater political freedom would merely develop strongly the expectations for even greater freedom – well beyond what Gorbachev himself was ready to agree to.

Then too there was the back-and-forth in the relationship between Gorbachev and his most important rival, Reagan. In so many ways Reagan wanted to support Gorbachev in his reform efforts. The two men met together often to share ideas and hopes. But still, Reagan could be very challenging in this matter ... at one point standing in front of the wall in Berlin and telling Gorbachev (and the watching world): . . . if you truly want peace and liberalization, Mr. Gorbachev, open this gate! Mr. Gorbachev, tear down this wall!

Bush takes Reagan's place. But at this point, Reagan's eight years in office were coming to a close ... and his place was taken by his Vice President of those eight years, George H. W. Bush. It had been a fairly easy Bush victory in November (1988) over his Democratic Party rival, Massachusetts Governor Michael Dukakis ... Bush gaining 53.4 percent of the popular vote to Dukakis's 45.6 percent and 426 Electoral College votes to Dukakis's 111 votes.

And although Bush had little to do with what was about to develop within the Soviet Empire, those developments would become a big part of the larger political picture during the Bush years (January 1989 to January 1993).

The collapse of the Soviet Empire (1989)

Polish reforms get things moving (1989). Events that would finally bring down the Soviet Empire in Eastern Europe had their beginnings in Poland ... where demands for reform reached all the way back to the beginning of the 1980s. It started there with the creation in 1980 of a Polish worker's organization, "Solidarity" – under the skillful leadership of the worker-leader Lech Wałęsa – when workers' wages had fallen well behind the inflation set loose by the international oil crisis. Agreement by the Polish government to recognize this workers' movement opened the doors for wider demands for social reforms ... which once underway got harder and harder for the Polish Communist authorities to manage. Polish military action in 1981 led by General Wojciech Jaruzelski was called on ... as preferential to having the Soviet Russian military do the job of bringing things back under Communist control. But ultimately, Solidarity held together – with secret help from America ... and very open encouragement coming from the Vatican's Polish Pope John Paul.

Finally in 1989, discussions – plus Gorbachev's stand in favor of social reform – produced an agreement in April between Solidarity and the Jaruzelski Communist government for partially free parliamentary elections to be held in June. The results were a huge blow to the Communists. They of course got their preassigned 65% seating in the Sejm ... but Solidarity got all but one of the 100 Senate seats – all of which had been open to free competition. Nonetheless, based on their majority in the Sejm, the Communists were the ones to put together a government as of July.

But the Communists had experienced a huge blow in seeing how the free or popular vote swung so strongly in favor of the Solidarity candidates. Consequently in August, some of the Communist satellite parties making up the Communist majority in the Sejm decided to swing their support to Solidarity ... collapsing the Communist majority in the Sejm. Thus President Jaruzelski had to restructure the Polish government ... which marked a clear move of Poland past its Communist stage. Democracy of some sort had come to Poland. And Gorbachev seemed content to let things stand as such. It was clear that the Russians would not be intervening in the face of these kinds of reforms.

Hungarian reforms.   Things now began to unravel quickly for other countries in Communist Eastern Europe. Hungary had already begun to make some political and social reforms under the impetus of Gorbachev's lifting of the oppressive Soviet hand in East Europe. And in April of 1989 Hungary undertook its own Round Table talks along lines similar to those of Poland's. Then in May, Hungary began to dismantle the border fence facing Austria ... inviting not only Hungarians, but also floods of Germans (and Czechs) to make their way to the West through a fast-opening Hungary – throwing East Germany and Czechoslovakia into disorder. During this time, the Hungarian government also began to issue apologies for the way the Hungarian events of 1956 had wronged so many people. And in September a new government program was agreed on at the Round Table, with the Communist Party renaming itself in October as the Hungarian Socialist Party ... ready to compete in free elections for a new Hungarian Parliament (taking place in March of the following year, 1990). Again, Gorbachev did nothing to stop such developments.

Czechoslovakia's "Velvet Revolution."   Demonstrations were taking place everywhere across Eastern Europe – but had remained non-violent in Czechoslovakia ... until 17 November when police took on a peaceful student demonstration in Prague. This in turn merely made the demonstrations all the more dedicatedly anti-government in character. From 200,000, the protesters soon numbered 800,000 ... when finally on 24 November, the Communists simply resigned their government posts. Four days later came the announcement that the former Communist order would be dismantled. Then in mid-December a new, largely non-Communist cabinet was appointed. Elections in the new parliament were then held at the end of December, with former Czech reformer Alexander Dubček elected speaker of the parliament and reformist author/playwright Vaclav Havel elected president of Czechoslovakia. The following June (1990) national elections were held ... which simply ratified the various political changes that had recently taken place.

Communism's collapse in East Germany. Things proved to take a more violent path in East Germany. With some 30,000 East Germans rushing to the West through Hungary's open border, the East German Communist regime led by Erich Honecker closed the border to Hungary at the end of September. Then in early October he had to do the same with Czechoslovakia, when thousands of East Germans then headed there – because Czechoslovakia was seemingly headed toward reform. Meanwhile protesters were gathering in Leipzig, the event gathering numbers as it repeated itself every Monday in September (the Monday Demonstrations). By the first Monday in October, with protesters reaching 10,000 in number, Honecker had given orders to the Stasi (State Police) to simply shoot to kill the demonstrators.

Gorbachev paid a visit to Honecker in early October ... but made no headway in softening Honecker's resolve to suppress the protests. But Gorbachev did make it clear that Soviet troops stationed in East Germany were not there to protect Honecker's government. Honecker was to stand alone in his dealings with the German protesters. Finally the East German Communist Party had enough of Honecker ... and in mid-October deposed him as party head. But this did not appease the protesters, who on Monday October 23rd, now numbered around 300,000.

The decision was made at the beginning of November to reopen the border to Czechoslovakia ... again resulting in the flood of East Germans to Czechoslovakia – from which these Germans were then allowed without restriction to head to West Germany and freedom. At the same time some half a million Germans came to East Berlin to demand new freedoms in their country ... an event soon accompanied by the decision on November 9th of East German authorities to open the Berlin gates to West Berlin – the results there too being a flood of Germans out of East Germany. But having reached West Berlin they turned and began to attack the wall itself (joined by West Germans as well, of course). And by the beginning of December, the East German Communist Party (SED) was disintegrating ... leading to East Germany's own Round Table talks and the SED rebranding itself as simply a non-Marxist Socialist party. In mid-January of 1990, with a new "reformed" ex-Communist Hans Modrow taking over the government and with the Stasi's Berlin headquarters stormed by protesters, there was very little left of the old regime in East Germany. And indeed in elections held in March (1990) the Conservative Christian Democratic Union won handily and formed a new government under Lothar de Mazière. With that, talks got immediately underway about the reunification of the two Germanies.

Bulgaria. Bulgaria tended to follow the calmer line of Czechoslovakia in dealing with what was certainly becoming a new world for Communist Bulgaria. The Bulgarian Politburo in mid-November simply deposed the long-serving Todor Zhivkov as the nation's leader (who had been fervently opposed to Gorbachev's reform program), replacing him with former foreign minister Petar Mladenov ... and then freed up speech and assembly – taking considerable pressure off the government. A political coalition of reform parties then formed, demanding changes along Polish lines. In mid-December, the Communist Party announced its willingness to end its total control of national power and agreed to hold free national elections ... eventually taking place the next June (1990). Furthermore, the Communist Party took on a new identity as the Bulgarian Socialist Party ... and in those 1990 elections actually won the vote! Thus the political transition in Bulgaria was a very quiet one.

Romania. But the same cannot be said of Bulgaria's neighbor, Romania ... where things turned rather violent ... against the nation's previous leadership as well as to 1,000 Romanians who died in the chaos that developed! Rather than give over to the pressures for reform, Romania's long-standing dictator (since 1965) Nicolae Ceauşescu had himself re-elected in November ... indicating clearly that there was no way that he was going to follow the trend of the rest of the Warsaw Pact nations of East Europe. Things heated up considerably when just as he was leaving in mid-December for a trip to Iran, his security forces arrested the Hungarian Christian minister László Tőkés for his outspoken opposition to the Ceauşescu regime ... starting up serious rioting that lasted during his absence. Upon his return from Iran, Ceauşescu hoped to engineer his own public support in calling for a rally in demonstration of his regime. But the rally turned into a rally of opposition ... starting the spread of even more public opposition. Then when Ceauşescu ordered his security forces to fire on the opposition to bring it back under control, his security forces instead joined the protesters (22 December).

They then turned their tanks on his headquarters in an effort to capture Ceaușescu and his wife – who however escaped by means of a helicopter. But they were soon captured and then quickly tried and convicted of various crimes and immediately executed (Christmas Day, December 25th). Taking over the government at that point was Ion Iliescu, who announced elections to be held in the coming April (but actually held in May of 1990). Iliescu's National Salvation Front did exceptionally well in the elections.

But Romanian politics remained quite harsh ... when Iliescu called conservative coal miners and industrial workers to the Romanian capital, Bucharest, to counter student protests going on there soon after the elections. Then there were splits within the post-Communist leadership itself (mostly composed of former Communists however!) that produced continuing political confusion in Romania.

Albania. Albania had been under the very oppressive grip of the Communist dictator Enver Hoxha for over 40 years ... who finally died in 1985, still holding the country under that same grip. But his successor, Ramiz Alia, began to lighten gradually that very grip. Then with the events of late 1989 and early 1990 unfolding around it, Albania too opened up its society to the West. It then moved to hold elections a year later (March 1991) ... which however left former Communists still holding power. But economic conditions and general social expectations worked against the regime, forcing it to include non-Communists in a new coalition cabinet. But even then, it would be very, very hard for Albania to move from its long-standing Communist or Socialist mentality to the mechanics of a free market economy. This failure produced unrest that continued to mount during the rest of the 1990s. In fact, massive economic mismanagement (thanks in great part to the criminal gangs that now controlled much of the economy) sparked a crisis in 1997 ... which ended up with over 2,000 being killed in the chaos.

Yugoslavia. Yugoslavia was not really a nation, but instead a coalition of various nations – quite distinct from each other ... and often very hostile to each other. Yugoslavia however was not part of the now-collapsing Soviet Empire ... and had not been since Tito's departure from Stalin's Cominform in 1948. Thus what had been holding the country together was not the Soviet grip, as was the case elsewhere in Communist East Europe, but rather the hand by which Tito held the country together.

But his job was not easy ... especially since the rise of strong Croatian nationalist sentiments in the early 1970s. Tito had provided for some new degree of local autonomy as of the mid-1970s ... but this in no way quieted the growing nationalist sentiments tearing at Yugoslavia.

Then when Tito died in 1980 the divisive nationalist urge grew very strong ... especially among the Albanian-speaking majority in the province of Kosovo. Soon also Slovenia was pressing the Belgrade government for greater autonomy ... at the same time others were calling for the freeing up of Christian religious practice in Belgrade itself.

By 1989, the spirit impacting the rest of East Europe could also be felt most strongly in Yugoslavia, not only producing the rise of small non-Communist political organizations but also producing tensions between the Slovenian and Serbian Communist Party organizations. Then when both the Slovenians and Croatian Communists walked out of the Communist nationalist Congress in January of 1990 ... Communism found itself in deep trouble in Yugoslavia. Indeed, in regional elections held in Slovenia and Croatia, huge victories went to their nationalist (non-Communist) parties.

At this point both the Slovenians and the Croatians began to put into action plans to leave the Yugoslav Federation ... stirring up the wrath of large groups of Serbian minorities found in both regions. But this was not to stop the nationalist movement ... which produced huge voter turnouts favoring national independence (Slovenia, December 1990 and Croatia, May 1991). Serious trouble now began to brew.

The dissolution of the Soviet Union itself

Perhaps most unsurprisingly, the sight of various national groups in the East European Soviet Bloc being able to secure national independence from Moscow came quickly to have the same effect on the non-Russian minority republics making up the Soviet Union.

The first of these to go were the recently absorbed (a result of World War Two) Baltic republics, Estonia, Latvia, and Lithuania ... part of a "Singing Revolution" in which patriotic songs stirred a rising sense of nationalism – in step with the easing of Moscow's grip on things begun by Gorbachev. Finally, on 16 November 1988, Estonia declared itself to be a "sovereign nation" ... though still within the Soviet Union. Then, in follow-up to the departure from the Soviet Empire of the East Europeans in late 1989, Lithuania broke fully from the Soviet Union with its declaration of full independence on 11 March 1990. Estonia, Latvia and Georgia would follow Lithuania down the fully-independent path two months later. Soon other republics, importantly Ukraine, were at that point also deliberating full independence from Moscow. Then even Russia itself, under the leadership of Moscow's Mayor Boris Yeltsin, began to consider breaking from a failing Soviet Union and setting itself up simply as a member of a new Russian Federation.

Clearly, the Communist Party was losing control of the political situation in what, at this point, was a dissolving Soviet Union. The newly created

Soviet Parliament – in particular its Congress of People's Deputies – had not (as Gorbachev had hoped) brought new loyalties to the Soviet Union on the part of its various national groupings. The relaxed hand of the Kremlin had produced in fact quite the opposite.

Finally, Gorbachev's refusal to block these moves towards national sovereignty* so infuriated Soviet hardliners[†] that in mid-August of 1991 they attempted by way of a military coup to seize control ... and remove Gorbachev from power. They thus sent agents to arrest Gorbachev at his vacation estate (his *daca*) on 18 August ... but simply ended up detaining him there.

This then led Yeltsin immediately to turn the event into an opportunity to take Russia to full independence. Huge crowds of outraged Russians gathered in Moscow, with Yeltsin addressing them as their new Russian leader ... with the leaders of the attempted coup at that point self-secluded inside the Russian Parliament Building. A three-day standoff then resulted, with the coup leaders finally surrendering ... or being arrested in their attempt to flee Russia (22 August). On the same day, Gorbachev returned to Moscow. Then the purge of hardliners would begin.

Two days later Gorbachev resigned as head of the Communist Party ... and the Communist Party itself was suspended in its operations five days after that (29 August). Then in early November Yeltsin simply outlawed the Party in his newly independent Russia.

Thus for all practical purposes, the existence of the Soviet Union at this point was a mere fiction, with all the republics having declared their independence. In fact, in early December (1991) Yeltsin's Russia – now calling itself simply the Russian Federation – signed a treaty (the Belovezha Accords) with newly independent Ukraine and Belarus, declaring officially the end of the Soviet Union ... and creating a new Commonwealth of Independent States (the CIS) – offering each other mutual economic, political, and military support. Most of the other former Soviet republics would join (though over the years many would depart). Furthermore, on

---

*In fact, he stood behind a New Union Treaty which was about to be signed – which decentralized much of the Kremlin's authority by extending new powers to the Soviet Union's constituent republics. In a referendum held on March 1991 - with Estonia, Latvia, Lithuania, Armenia, Georgia and Moldova not participating however – some 78% of the remaining Soviet citizens voted in favor of the treaty ... renaming the USSR as a Union of Soviet "Sovereign" (not "Socialist") Republics. The republics Russia, Kazakhstan and Uzbekistan were about to sign this treaty when the coup occurred.

[†]Directors of the State Committee on the State of Emergency (the GKChP) formed in January of 1991. Actually, plans for just such a coup were first undertaken by the KGB as early as September of 1990. But they had to proceed cautiously ... until events in August of 1991 finally forced their hand.

24 December, the Soviet seat on the UN's Security Council was transferred to Yeltsin's new Russian Federation. Thus officially and internationally, the Soviet Union was no more.

Yeltsin tries to pick up the pieces

However, securing national independence – and knowing how to actually move forward successfully socially and economically with that independence – are two entirely different matters ... something that modern man has great difficulty understanding.

As we have already noted, in the late 1700s the French thought they could secure for themselves a new democracy on the same model that they had so recently observed in America when the colonies there simply declared independence from London's royal government. They failed to understand that the social habits necessary for such independence had been long established in the daily thinking and action of the American people themselves. Thus when the French attempted to create from scratch a similarly independent French democracy, they failed miserably ... in fact most brutally.

And in the mid-1800s Karl Marx fell into "enlightened" thinking along similar lines, believing that the newly rising class of industrial workers simply needed to revolt against their capitalist oppressors and thus establish a communal society ... one in which an oppressing "State" would not even be needed. Somehow members of his new Communist society would coexist in a state of pure brotherly love. Of course when Lenin and then Stalin attempted to put just such a Marxist society into operation, the event proved brutal in the extreme ... and took the extremely oppressive hand of Stalin to bring things back into some kind of social order.

Indeed, ever-tighter governmental control, not the withering away of the State, would always be needed when a people were abruptly pushed into a new social order ... one which they knew very little about or how to go about making it work beautifully on a purely "natural" basis.

And now Yeltsin was about to discover this same hard truth. Clearly the Russians knew nothing about self-government. Almost immediately Yeltsin's efforts to put in place an economic order based along quite Western lines proved most unworkable. The productivity of what was formerly a "planned" but now "free" economy declined overnight ... as voluntary employment became quite unreliable. And personal greed on the part of the economically ambitious – not economic service to the larger world – took over many Russian hearts. Consequently, a huge inflation hit the country ... as prices of products that simply were not readily available skyrocketed.

As a larger consequence, in the period between 1990 and 1995, the

Russian economy declined by 50% ... with much of the wealth that was actually available falling into fewer and fewer "entrepreneurial" hands. Consequently, life expectancy of the average Russian fell by 6 years in the 1991-1994 period ... as diminishing real wages, stress, alcoholism and poor nutrition hit Russian society hard – at a time that the Russian health care system also deteriorated.

National "freedom" had come to Yeltsin's Russia at a huge cost.

China heads off a similar challenge

Deng struggles to keep reform moving ahead. Certainly Deng's reforms in freeing up the government's control of the economy were helping to produce a huge boom in the Chinese economy. But inflation boomed right alongside the overall economic growth – benefiting some and hurting others – and producing much accompanying political and moral corruption ... which the Chinese Communist Party (CCP) was having a hard time controlling. At one point (1983), Party hardliners were able to use this situation to get the CCP to resume some of its former Maoist policies of clamping down on political thought and action. But Deng worked hard to put the nation back on the road of economic reform ... though he had to do so carefully to avoid new pushback from members of the older Maoist political community.

Then trouble erupted in 1986 when intellectuals and students, watching developments under Gorbachev's new perestroika and glasnost programs, began to be loud in their claims that Deng's reforms were not moving fast enough. This merely served to upset the political hardliners even more.

The protest movement at Tiananmen Square (1989). It was the huge movement to national freedom going on in Eastern Europe that once again stirred young Chinese to action ... thousands gathering in Beijing's huge Tiananmen Square to call for similar reforms in China. Soon they were joined by others, filling the square now with hundreds of thousands of permanently camped-out youthful protesters. And the protests began to spread to other Chinese cities as well. By early June there were perhaps as many as a million protesters occupying the Square.

The decision as to how to respond to this growing dynamic worked to split CCP leadership, hardliners calling for an end to the movement ... by military force if necessary. On the other hand, CCP General Secretary Zhao Ziyang tried to hold the line for continuing reform. But even Deng began to call for action against the protesters – fearing merely worsening chaos in letting them continue.

Thus it was that on the night of 3-4 June, the military was sent to clear the Square of all protesters ... resulting in a very ugly confrontation in which countless numbers of students were injured and even killed. And when the world awoke the next morning, it was to a Square filled only with Chinese tanks occupying the positions formerly held by the students. Further, Zhao was removed from power and placed under house arrest (where he would remain until his death 16 years later).

The Western world – that had been so supportive of the Deng reforms was appalled at the outcome. Congress reacted by voting to cut off all further military sales to China. But President Bush, who was at first quite critical of the Tiananmen events, soon backed off ... realizing that a harsh line against China merely served to strengthen instead the Chinese hardliners in their opposition to Deng's reforms. Instead, Bush tried quietly to show continuing support for the remaining Chinese instinct for reform.

Jiang Zemin. But Deng was careful to have Jiang Zemin, of the reformist wing of the Party, installed as Zhao's replacement as CCP General Secretary. And indeed, Jiang was able to get the reform movement put cautiously but effectively back in place in China ... even skillfully surviving a hardliner counteroffensive when the Soviet Union collapsed and hardliners became highly alarmed at the dangers this posed to the CCP.

That November (1989), Deng quietly retired ... and turned his huge responsibilities over to Jiang ... who himself was then able to hold the party's various leadership positions all the way up to the early 2000s (2002 and 2003). But Jiang's ability to take on all major political positions meant that the balance of power principle of dividing leading powers among several hands established by Deng found itself being put aside. Once again, the Chinese Communist Party and the Chinese State had come under the command of a single individual ... leaving a legacy not of Deng's variety but of Jiang's variety when Jiang finally retired in the early 2000s.

✳ ✳ ✳

EUROPE MOVES AHEAD

Expansion of the European Communities (1967-1986). In 1967, with the coming into effect of the Brussels Treaty, the authorities governing the "three pillars" of the European Communities (The European Coal and Steel Community, the European Economic Community, and the European Atomic Energy Community) merged their governing authorities into a single governing Council of European Communities. Then as of June 1979, the then-410 members of the European Parliament (governing those three communities) came to be directly elected by the citizens of the EC member nations ... which at that point included the 9 member nations: France,

Germany, Italy, the Netherlands, Belgium, Luxembourg, Denmark, Ireland, and Britain (the United Kingdom). Eventually Greece (1981), and Portugal and Spain (both in 1986) would be brought on as full members – after a lengthy period of consideration of each ... their admissions delayed because of various economic and political complications.

A big step forward towards true European unity was taken by the European Economic Community when in 1985, five of the ten members states signed the Schengen Agreement ... in which border checks were eliminated – allowing the free movement of citizens across those borders at any point (not just at checkpoints). The following year (1986) a symbolically significant development took place when the new European flag was put into official use ... and that same year signed an agreement (the Single European Act) calling for the creation of a single European market by the end of 1992.

The Maastricht Treaty ... and the new European Union (1992). Then the twelve member nations took a huge step forward in the European integration movement when they signed a treaty in Maastricht, Netherlands, a treaty that reshaped the European Communities organizations into a single European Union ... and at the same time set out a path leading toward shared European citizenship (the free movement of labor across European borders), a single European currency (ultimately the Euro), and a set of common foreign and security policies to be followed by the member nations. And the treaty represented a skillful compromise between those member nations skeptical of further unification and those who wanted to see even greater European unification.

In any case, the Maastricht Treaty, in reorganizing the older European Communities as the new European Union, laid the foundations for something resembling a European federation.

But it would take some skillful politicking to get this idea to be as gladly accepted by the European people themselves. In fact, in its first referendum on the matter, the Danish citizenry voted down the proposal ... requiring some negotiations on the matter and then a second referendum – when it was finally approved by 57% of the Danish voters. France too voted its approval only by a slim margin. And in Britain it took skillful political maneuvering for Prime Minister John Major to get parliamentary approval (Labor being fervently opposed ... as well as some of Major's Conservatives).

There were other factors complicating the move forward of the Maastricht Treaty. The obvious likelihood of German reunification now that the Berlin Wall had come down made France and Britain (and other Europeans) quite nervous, economically as well as politically. France, under President Mitterrand, insisted that it would approve the German expansion in the European Union only if the Germans gave up their strong mark –

and instead adopted the promised common currency. This French demand German Chancellor Helmut Kohl agreed to … actually opening wider the door to the adoption of just such a currency.   But on the other hand, the British were having difficulties maintaining the value of the British pound sterling according to a European Exchange Rate Mechanism (the ERM – one of the steps towards monetary union) … and simply withdrew from the ERM agreement, actually helping the pound regain its value – and helping the British economy and employment figures to improve dramatically.   This would not help create much enthusiasm in Britain for the idea of an all-European single currency (the British in fact would ultimately refuse to abandon the pound and adopt the euro as their national currency, the only European Union member nation to refuse to join the monetary union).

As far as the Maastricht provision for a set of common foreign and security policies, this had already been institutionalized somewhat since the early 1970s through formal agreements … and just through good diplomatic logic.   And, after all, there was NATO – which under American direction tended to give a high degree of unity to matters vital to European national interests.

At this point the EU was becoming something of a very formidable political, economic and social organization – compensating for the fact that European nations as individuals had lost the global pre-eminence that they once enjoyed … but now united, they constituted a new world power.

But it would be a quiet world power, focused mostly on just making European life itself as grand as possible – at little or no cost to the rest of the world. Europeans would be quite content to be just that: Europeans.

✱ ✱ ✱

AMERICA TAKES THE LEAD GLOBALLY

The Gulf War or "Desert Storm" (1990-1991).   With Egypt knocked out as the leading spokesman for the Arab world, Iraq finally had the opportunity to take over that privileged position.   Thus Iraq's Ba'athist military dictator (since 1979) Saddam Hussein had been pushing hard to establish himself as that Arab voice. But there were a number of problems facing him in that enterprise.

The biggest problem was that Iraq itself was not truly a nation – but instead a collection of various ethnic and religious groups … which had little love for each other. Indeed, the only reason for the existence of Iraq was that the British themselves drew up the design for the country when they carved up the Ottoman Empire at the end of World War Two … adding the oil-rich Kurdish (non-Arab) community in the North to the divided Arab world (mutually hostile Sunnis and Shi'ites) to the South – all for the sole purpose of giving British Petroleum control over this vast oil-rich region. The British even set up a "British-protected" Hashemite monarchy for Iraq – which did not much outlast the withdrawal of British influence in the region after World War Two.

In fact in 1958, Sunni Ba'athist officers in the Iraqi army overthrew the monarchy in a very bloody coup that year ... and with General Abd al-Karim Qasim in control, began the political contest with Nasser for leadership of the larger Arab world. Qasim of course had his own goals – and problems – at home to deal with. The Kurds in the north were fighting among themselves ... upsetting the Iraqi political scene greatly.   And it infuriated Qasim that the British had set oil-soaked Kuwait apart from Mesopotamia (ultimately "Iraq") in the British carve-up of Ottoman Turkey – because tiny Kuwait was more likely to remain under full British control. Qasim felt strongly that Kuwait belonged to Iraq.

But Qasim was himself overthrown (with British and American help) in 1963 ... because he had brought the Cold War to Iraq by siding closely with the Soviets. But the pro-Western regime that then came in place did not last long before it too (1968) was overthrown by another Ba'athist coup, the one that eventually brought Saddam to power.

But Saddam would find himself absorbed over the next eight years in a futile war with Iran – one that he had undertaken thinking he might lure the Arab minority living just inside Iran next to the Iraqi border to join his Iraq ... and bring their own oil lands into his country. But that part of the Arab world (including most of the huge Southeastern portion of Iraq) was Shi'ite – whereas the Ba'athist were Sunni in religious affiliation. And thus the Shi'ite Arabs in Iran seemed to prefer to stay with Shi'ite Iran than join Saddam's Sunni-controlled Iraq ... or at least that is how Iran played the matter. In any case, the long war led to nothing for Saddam ... except deep national debt.

At this point he looked to the matter of long interest to Iraq: Kuwait. Grabbing Kuwait would add enormously to Iraq oil income (the latter not always reliable because of the turmoil that often broke out in the oil lands of the Kurdish North). But grabbing Kuwait would likely bring some kind of a reaction from the oil-dependent Western world.

So ... Saddam (who had been heavily dependent on American support during his long war with Iran) inquired of the American ambassador at to what she thought would be the American reaction to such a move – and was given the answer that America had no interest in the boundary question with Kuwait ... and wanted to stay out of a dispute over Iraq's claim that somewhat now pro-Soviet Kuwait was slant drilling in an attempt to reach Iraqi oil reserves. Saddam thus took this as a "go-ahead" response on

America's part.

Consequently, in August of 1990, Saddam sent Iraqi troops into largely defenseless Kuwait in order to take over the country. This was supposed to make him a great Iraqi hero ... and a tough Arab leader.

But American President Bush had a very different view on the matter than his Iraqi ambassador ... and answered the cry of some of the rest of the Arab world in opposition to this takeover.   Saudi Arabia was particularly upset, fearing that Saddam's grab of defenseless Kuwait could prove to be merely the first step towards a takeover of an equally defenseless Saudi Arabia (which had never seen the need to possess a strong military).

Thus Bush told Saddam to get out of Kuwait. But at this point, this seemed to be an impossible request ... as his political reputation would be ruined by such a backdown.   So the matter dragged on as both sides, Iraq and a growing American-led coalition, tried to find a diplomatic solution to the problem. Finding none, finally in mid-January (1991) a massive aerial bombardment of the Iraqi forces occupying Kuwait got underway ... to which Saddam responded with his own scud missile attack on the 35-nation coalition assembled in Saudi Arabia (but also on Israel).

A month later (mid-February) the coalition was ready to move on Saddam's forces in Kuwait ... and in very short order threw those very troops out of the country ... with Iraqi troops setting fire to all the Kuwaiti oil wells in their retreat.* Then this same force followed his troops into Iraq ... but halted once it had become clear that Saddam had lost all further ability to conduct military operations.

But much criticism was aimed at Bush during all this ... at first by the Liberals in Congress for undertaking such an "imperialist" operation in the first place (protests which died away quickly when it became apparent how effective Bush's actions had been) ... and then by war hawks who were upset that Bush did not finish the job and just get rid of Saddam. Only later, when Bush's Secretary of Defense Dick Cheney (at that point out of Washington and serving as Halliburton's CEO) was being interviewed, he explained that Bush was well aware that to get involved in trying to reassemble a broken post-Saddam Iraq would come at a huge cost – with no obvious benefits to America. In fact, to do so would be the equivalent of falling into a "quagmire." Wise words ... soon forgotten by Cheney himself!

Bush out ... Clinton in

The next year (1992) was an election year in America – and Bush was having difficulty in his reelection bid with a sagging economy and a government

---

*But these were put out fairly quickly by Texan Red Adair's firefighters ... though not before a billion barrels of oil had been lost.

deficit - which Bush was trying to bring under control. Actually, the economy was rebounding as elections approached in November – something most American voters were not yet aware of. Taking advantage of this situation was billionaire Ross Perot, running quite strongly as an independent – claiming that he held all the answers to a rebounding economy. The race also included, of course, a Democratic Party candidate, the Arkansas governor Bill Clinton. Thus the American vote was spread widely in November, with Clinton getting 43%, Bush 37.5% and Perot 19%. But the electoral college vote was 370 for Clinton and 168 for Bush (none for Perot). Thus Bush was out and Clinton was in as the new American President as of January 1993.

Early in his career, Clinton was the youngest governor in the country ... an Idealistic Boomer, whose Idealism put him out of office after a single term ... but back in office when he put his Idealism aside and led the state the way he understood his people wanted to be led ... perhaps a result of his lessons in political Realism he would have learned in his Georgetown University years! He would need that same wisdom now as U.S. president – particularly being married to a rigorously Idealist Boomer wife, Hillary.

Realism replaces Boomer Idealism. At first it appeared that Clinton would again head down the Idealist path, attempting to bring the American nation under government healthcare programming – and opening the American military to homosexuality ... both programs which got blocked by the well-organized Republican Party opposition in Congress, led by hardliner Newt Gingrich (whom the Liberals would love to hate!). Gingrich had just conducted a major Republican Party takeover in Congress ... and Clinton realized that he would have to learn to work with this somehow (his wife Hillary unbending in this matter however).

As a realist, Clinton took on the matter of the growing national debt – but by increasing taxes rather than cutting back on government expenses (wanted by Newt's Republicans). But it certainly helped – not only slowing up the growth of that debt but actually reducing it somewhat ... the last time this would occur before America fell into the habit of running up massively the national debt in the regimes that followed (Bush, Jr., Obama, Trump, and now Biden)! Clinton also (to the distress of his Democratic Party) agreed with Gingrich to shift – at least in part – government "welfare" to instead government "workfare" – involving job training and job placement instead of just money transfers to welfare recipients. He also widened trade relations with neighboring Canada and Mexico – to the horror of Democratic-Party-supporting American Labor, which feared that this would lead to the loss of jobs to both countries. However, instead of losing jobs, this expanded the American economy considerably – and the number of American jobs that went with that expansion. And there was also the electronic communications revolution underway which also increased production greatly in America ... and in general in the West – as well as in China.

The Defense of Marriage Act (DOMA - 1996)

One issue that Clinton had to bow before, rather reluctantly, was the move by Republicans in 1996 to pass a bill that refused to recognize – thus offer federal benefits - to homosexual unions. Indeed, homosexuality was a longstanding Christian "no-no."

Boomer efforts in the 1970s to liberate American culture from such "authoritarian" standards went nowhere ... although it certainly engaged a lot of Christian denominations in the matter when a push was made by younger Americans (and their Liberal mentors) to recognize homosexual unions as legitimate American marriages. Such efforts came to nothing at the time – though every year from that point on, this issue would engage the Christian denominations in having to reconsider their stand on the matter at their national meetings.

Not much came of the effort until the mid-1980s when the AIDS virus ripped through the homosexual community like a plague ... and brought forward considerably Boomer sympathy – and the desire to take a stronger stand in support of AIDS "victims" (victims not of their own behavior, but victims of Middle America's lack of adequate homosexual sympathy and support). At this point the question of the place of homosexuals in Middle America became a crusading issue for the Boomer Left. But the Boomers had not yet replaced Vet America as the dominating force in American politics.

1989 was a big year for the homosexual community ... when Denmark moved to put homosexual unions on a par with male-female marriage; when New York's judiciary ruled that homosexual unions should enjoy the same rent-control protection as marriages; and when the California State Bar Association decided that homosexual unions should enjoy all the rights that California marriages enjoyed.

By the early 1990s, some of the Christian denominations were finding a growing number of pro-homosexual advocates gathering strength in the move to allow the conducting of homosexual marriages ... not yet advocating the ordaining of homosexuals as priests and pastors – but clearly with this in mind as well. And in 1993, the very Liberal Supreme Court of Hawaii undercut the state's right to refuse marriage rights to homosexuals.

This is what finally motivated the bill brought to Congress in 1996 as the Defense of Marriage Act. And with the Republicans in control of both houses of Congress, the bill passed easily. 343 Representatives in the House supported the measure, with only 65 opposed (only one Republican, the rest being Democrats); and 84 Senators supported the measure in the Senate – with the 14 opposing being Democrats (with 2 absentees). Two months later, Clinton signed the bill into law (Congress had the votes to override any vetoing of the bill anyway) … but made it clear that he did so under reluctance – though when he saw how popular the law was received in America he backtracked a bit and appeared to give full support to the concept. Indeed he would swing back and forth in support of the issue – or in backing away from such support – depending on how the political winds changed.

Europe moves forward

During those same 1990s,, much of the world found itself involved in a long, and thus rather unprecedented, period of economic growth … which made the world quite happy!

The European Union grows. In 1993 Europe put the Maastricht Treaty into full force, not only expanding the administrative unification of the European Community members but also ending the use of their national currencies (the German mark, the French franc, the Italian lira, etc.) in adopting the use of the new all-European currency, the euro. Then two years later (January 1995), seeing the tremendous advantages in doing so, Sweden, Finland and Austria became members of the European Union. Now there were fifteen European countries comprising this growing economic (and political) union.

The expansion of NATO (1999). In March of 1999, the Czech Republic, Hungary and Poland joined NATO. This of course extended NATO's reach deep into East Europe … upsetting Russia deeply. But a relatively helpless Russia had, at this point, little it could do about the matter.

China opens up to a new industrial dynamic. Meanwhile, off in the Far East, China continued to expand its economy rapidly – averaging an amazing 10% annual increase in China's gross national product (GNP) … with some bumps however along the way – bringing itself and the industrial world of the West into closer relationship. Definitely the Cold War was over!

But Russia struggles. Russia found itself now friendly to the West, with Russian leader Yeltsin and American President Clinton seeming to become quite the buddies!   But Russia was struggling economically … and socially. There was wealth to be made … but mostly in the hands of a small group of individuals with strong entrepreneurial instincts – not something native to the general Russian population. The rest of the Russians really struggled to find their way forward without the government there to take care of them every step of the way. Consequently, the net outcome of Russia's new social freedom was confusion, hunger ... and bitterness. But Yeltsin seemed to have no answer to this problem. Admittedly, Russia did not fall apart because of all this "freedom." But it was not doing well under it either.

Thus in April of 1993 Yeltsin put before his people a referendum based on a number of questions concerning the approval of his performance and the need for earlier elections ... and the probability of deep changes in the Russian Constitution. But with only 64% of the eligible population turning out for the referendum, the results were that his personal approval rating was 60% ... but his performance rating only 54% – and the call for early elections failed to gain a majority.

But that same September, Yeltsin moved ahead anyway to strengthen his presidential position against the powers of the Russian Parliament. He called for the dissolution of Parliament and the holding of new elections. But hardliner (basically Communist) members of parliament barricaded them inside the parliament building, refusing to be dismissed ... and called for Yeltsin's impeachment, also declaring Vice President Alexander Rutskoy to be the new acting president. At this point, things blew up in the streets of Moscow as protesters (who had not fared well economically under Yeltsin's liberal reforms) turned out to conduct a fiery anti-Yeltsin street contest. The police were called on to stop the action. But things only worsened day by day as negotiations (hosted by the Russian Orthodox Church) dragged on. When in early October protesters decided to storm the television center, they were met by police ... and countless numbers were killed in the clash. Then the military was called on to choose which side it was supporting ... which turned out to be Yeltsin. Thus tanks were brought out and turned on the parliament building, destroying the upper floors. But finally, quiet returned to the streets.

Generally at first the Russian people supported Yeltsin in his role in this "Second October Revolution" ... though that opinion about how that action was conducted would turn negative over the years as the Russian economy simply continued to stall ... despite Yeltsin's efforts to bring the Russian economy (and society in general) under his own tighter control.

Tragically, too many years under state-controlled Communism (and Tsarist autocracy before that) had not permitted the development among the Russian people of a mind-set able to self-develop under a new regime. Unlike the Chinese, who had never completely lost urban China's entrepreneurial instincts – even during the two decades of life under Maoism – the Russian people, having never really had the opportunity at any point in their history to develop much of an entrepreneurial spirit, simply did not know how to take care of themselves in an open economy ... once again giving witness to the fact that "democratic Idealists" (Rousseau, Marx, Wilson, and soon also Bush, Jr.) – who believe that democracy is naturally instinctive to any "politically free" individual – have no idea how democracy actually works.

Germany unites. Meanwhile, Germany moved to unite a somewhat unwilling East Germany with its Western Federal Republic (October 1990) ... subsequently finding that the East Germans had functioned too long under Socialism and also were having a hard time adjusting to West Germany's strongly entrepreneurial spirit ... much less seeing each other as fellow Germans. But time – and a lot of very costly West German investment – would slowly bring better social harmony within the now-united Germany. And a united Germany would also finally gain acceptance on the part of the Europeans (some of the British and French, for instance), long-nervous about German reunification.

Progress in East Europe. East Europe fared much better than Russia under its new freedoms ... economic growth registering itself generally across the former Soviet satellite countries.

Czechoslovakia splits. However, as of the end of 1992, Czechoslovakia split into two separate states, the Czech Republic (or Czechia) and Slovakia. The two societies had never been close, with the Czechs or Bohemians West-oriented and the Slovakians East-oriented. There was not only very little social connection between the two societies during their time of unity as Czechoslovakia (1919-1992) but little political connection as well ... especially as the capital city Prague seemed itself mostly just focused on matters in the Czech world. Slovakia's major city Bratislava also seemed to be of minor importance in the general scheme of things. Thus it was that in mid-1992 negotiations involving the departure of Slovakia were undertaken ... peacefully.

But Slovakia would find economic development very difficult to achieve on its own.

America is called on to take the lead in bringing world peace

"Black Hawk Down" (October 1993). The U.N. had been sending food donations to help a starving Somali population caught in the middle of an ongoing civil war ... only to have these contributions confiscated by the various warring groups in order to feed their own fighters. America was thus looked to in order to bring some protection to these food deliveries. Consequently, in October of 1993, Clinton ordered a land and helicopter assault on the most dangerous of the warlord groupings ... only to have two of his Black Hawk helicopters shot down and thus was forced to undertake a rescue operation in a country that was so terrorized by the warlords that locals were afraid to offer any assistance in the rescue operation. Consequently, Clinton simply got his men out ... and ordered an end to any further American assistance in Somalia. He was sorry about the suffering of the Somali civilian population. But he was unwilling to continue an operation that had virtually no chance of success.

And Americans were deeply appreciative of Clinton's wisdom in this matter ... similar to their reaction to Reagan's Lebanon pullout.

The Oslo Accords (1993 and 1995). Secret talks between the Israeli government and the Palestinian Liberation Organization (PLO) resulted in the Palestinian recognition of the right of Israel to exist and the Israeli recognition of the PLO as the Palestinian spokesman ... with an agreement (founded heavily on Carter's earlier Camp David accord between Israel and Egypt) to continue the talks over the next five years – to finally put the earlier U.N. resolutions 242 into force. This would create a recognized Palestinian state in the West Bank region. In September of 1993, Clinton hosted in D.C. the formal signing of this "Oslo Accord" (the first of two such "Oslo Accords) – and then did what he could to support the fulfillment of this agreement. Unfortunately, the Israeli Prime Minister Yitzak Rabin, who had signed this agreement – and then a follow-up agreement (the Taba Agreement of September 1995) – was assassinated in November of 1995 by an angry young Israeli hardliner ... throwing the process back into chaos.

Restoring Haiti's "democracy" (September 1994). In 1994, Haiti's military overthrew the country's first truly democratically-elected president (1991), former Catholic priest Jean Bertrand Aristide ... plunging the country into confusion and economic catastrophe. Inevitably, masses of Haitians tried to escape the horrible conditions that fell on Haiti – by finding anything that would float ... hopefully bringing them to safety as refugees in America. But vastly overloaded, most of these boats sank somewhere along the way. The situation was deeply tragic.

Once again, the U.N. asked Clinton to step in to end the chaos. But still stinging from the Somali disaster, Clinton at first hesitated to get involved. But sensing that – unlike the Somali situation – he had the support of the Haitian population, he finally decided to take on the challenge. First he sent strong American representatives – former president Clinton, Gulf war General Colin Powell, and Senator Nunn to Haiti to inform the Haitian military junta that if they did not restore Aristide to power, then Clinton would be obligated to send U.S. troops to Haiti to do the job themselves.

At first the junta thought Clinton was bluffing. But in September of

1994, as U.S. ships carrying some 20,000 82nd Airborne Division troops drew closer to Haiti, the junta realized that they were in deep trouble ... and backed down, agreeing to turn the country over to Aristide the following month. And thus with these American troops in position in Haiti, the transfer was carried out peacefully. Then the American troops were soon pulled out. And Clinton indeed looked to be the leader that the world was hoping him to be.*

Ethnic cleansing in Rwanda (1994). In 1994 the world was shocked to see in Rwanda the wholesale slaughter of Tutsi tribesmen (perhaps as many as a million losing their lives) by members of the Hutu tribe. Again, the U.N. called for American (and other) assistance to end this East African horror. But Clinton was unwilling to budge – seeing in this an exact replica of the Somali situation. Thus there was no way he was going to jump into the Rwandan pit. Clinton took a lot of harsh criticism from American Liberals for this decision.   However, Americans in general seemed quite appreciative of his decision to stay out of the Rwandan mess.

Bosnia (1995).   Meanwhile, the situation in the former Yugoslavia was becoming increasingly ugly. The departure of Croatia and Slovenia from the Yugoslavian Federation in late 1990 and early 1991 did not end the breakup of former Yugoslavia. The Serbs, who had served as the Yugoslavian political centerpiece – and were found scattered in smaller Serbian communities all around the region – were very angry at how they had become minoritized in Croatia and Slovenia.

Then in March of 1992, Bosnia-Herzegovina also declared independence ... except here the Serbian minority was quite large, some 31 percent of the population. The Serbian government under Slobodan Milošević therefore was in no mood to see that sizable portion of their Serbian world disappear into an independent Bosnia – where an additional 44 percent were Muslim (thanks to the former Turkish hold over the land there) and 17 percent Croat (plus 8 percent of other ethnic backgrounds).

Consequently, Milošević immediately (April 1992) sent his military forces into Bosnia, where they were joined by local Serbian fighters – in an effort to send the Muslim portion of the population in flight out of the area ... so that Bosnia would be incorporated into a Greater Serbia. Of course the non-Serbs fought back ... with both Serbs and non-Serbs attacking each

---

*Of course it was not long before Haitian politics took on a familiar look ... even under Aristide ... and by 2004 Haiti had again fallen into a state of civil war. Aristide was then "rescued" by U.S. forces that flew him out of Haiti ... and into exile in South Africa. He would eventually (in 2011) return to Haiti ... only to find all kind of legal impediments preventing him and his party from a fair representation in the country's National Assembly.

other, slaughtering the population here and there that had not already fled. Bosnia thus turned into a horrifying death zone … and the beautiful Bosnian city, Sarajevo – which had hosted the 1984 Olympic winter games – was turned into a ghastly bombed-out city, whose streets were dangerous to even enter.

Other Europeans – and the U.N. – condemned the fighting … although there was little they could do about the matter. So they called on Clinton to intervene. At first Clinton was hesitant to do anything more than stop any military sales to the Serbs. Clinton was in no hurry to get in the middle of another mess.

But to see such slaughter going on in the center of Europe was too much to stomach (for instance, in 1995 some 8,000 men and boys were killed by Serbian troops in the town of Srebrenica). Thus Clinton finally agreed to use NATO airpower to hit Serbian positions poised to attack Bosnian Muslim towns and villages. And the Croatians also joined the action … to protect fellow Croats in the Bosnian north. Even the Serbian capital Belgrade was hit in order to demonstrate NATO resolve.

Finally, with a quarter of a million dead from the war (and another million homeless), an exhausted Serbia was willing to sit down and negotiate an armistice, resulting in the Dayton Accords (signed in December of 1995 in Dayton, Ohio) by the political leaders of the NATO powers as well as the Serbian and Bosnian leadership. And a 60,000-troop monitoring force (one-third American) was put in place in Bosnia to oversee the withdrawal of Serbian forces – and just in general secure the peace agreement. Bosnia was then subdivided formally into various ethnic areas … and when all parties appeared ready to accept the outcome, the monitoring force was gradually reduced in size.

But all this demonstrated the importance of having superpower America willing to serve in the role as international peacekeeper … for there was no other force at hand so able to perform the task it did. And Clinton came away – again, looking very presidential.

Kosovo (1999).   But in March of 1999, upon the final withdrawal of the international peacekeeping forces stationed in the area, violence in former Yugoslavia once again exploded … this time in the southern region of Kosovo. Here part of the population was Albanian in language and Muslim in religion … quite different from the Slavic language and Orthodox faith of the Serbian communities scattered here and there around the region. Once again the violence erupted when Serbian President Milošević began an effort to remove the non-Serbian people from what the Serbs considered to be part of their national territory … except that the Albanian Kosovars (92 percent of the population) vastly outnumbered the Serbs (only 4 percent) in the region. But Milošević was determined to attempt this "ethnic cleansing" nonetheless.

And thus he soon had over a million Kosovars in flight from their homes and into neighboring countries as refugees. As for the rest of the Kosovars, his troops were determined simply to slaughter. And of course Kosovar militants were no less eager to do the same thing to the Serbs living in Kosovo.

But this time it was Clinton who took the lead in the matter, by calling on NATO to intervene ... beginning (late March) attacks once again from the air on Serbian troops and military sites in order to get the Serbs to back off from their attacks on the Kosovar population The hope was that Milošević would quickly realize that he was outmatched. But instead, Milošević simply dug in deeper. Then the Serbian capital Belgrade was extensively bombed (very unfortunately doing damage to the Chinese Embassy and killing three individuals in the process... oops!).

Once again, Milošević finally (mid-June) had to admit defeat ... and agree to back his troops out of the Kosovo region – and offer no opposition to the stationing of 50,000 NATO troops there (including 7,000 Americans) as peacekeepers. But this time, Milošević himself had to pay the penalty for his actions. He was arrested as a war criminal and put in a Dutch prison ... where subsequently he died during his long trial.

And – to show Kosovar appreciation – a huge statue of Clinton now (since 2009) stands just off the Bill Clinton Boulevard in Kosovo's capital city, Pristina!

Mounting problems with the world of Islam

The first Muslim bombing of the World Trade Center (February 1993). But America had its own version of such international bloodying when it itself became the object of attack at the World Trade Center in New York City. An explosives-filled van parked in the parking garage of the North Tower of the World Trade Center exploded ... destroying six stories of this towering New York structure. Six people were killed and over a thousand others injured ... though the situation would have been far worse had the van been parked closer to one of the supporting walls of the tower. For clearly the intention of the bombers was to collapse the entire building in such a way that it would then also fall against the other twin tower ... bringing both of them down – and the death of tens of thousands of individuals working there.

Enough physical evidence was found that enabled investigators to discover that behind this action was a group of local Muslim fanatics, trained and supported by a Pakistani-based group that went by the name of al-

Qaeda (or al-Qa'ida – meaning "foundation") under the direction of Khalid Sheikh Mohammed ... but the action itself being actually conducted by his nephew Ramzi Yousef – and fellow supporters based in a couple of local mosques, one in Jersey City and one in Brooklyn. The individuals involved in the action would soon be tracked down and arrested ... except one who escaped to Iraq – but was arrested and imprisoned there.

The FBI tried to connect the al-Qaeda organization with Saddam Hussein. But ultimately, they could come up with no evidence linking the two. But it certainly put al-Qaeda on the FBI's watch list.

The Afghan Taliban. Afghanistan was always just a huge region of different ethnic groups ... once held together through a broad alliance of local tribal and religious leaders with the Afghan Shah. When he was overthrown in 1973 by his cousin who claimed to be setting up an Afghan Republic in doing so ... the alliance broke down and Afghanistan found itself caught in contests, very bloody in many cases, for control of this or that part of the country. The Soviets had hoped to use this opportunity to put their own "protection" over some kind of pro-Soviet government operating out of Afghanistan's capital Kabul since 1978 ... even sending Soviet troops into Afghanistan to shore up the pro-Soviet puppet government in 1979. But this government had little power beyond the capital city itself ... and was easily subject to political undermining by Afghan tribal leaders – supported quietly by American financial and weapons assistance. Finally, with the Soviet pullout from Afghanistan in 1989 – and the collapse of the Soviet system itself that soon followed – the Afghanistan system collapsed ... opening the way for the creation in 1992 of the Islamic State of Afghanistan. But this only intensified the inter-tribal and inter-religious fighting gripping the country. Tens of thousands (probably even hundreds of thousands) of Afghans died as a result of all this political turmoil.

The strongest group in the country – making up about 40 percent of the population are the Pashtun ... occupying the southern and southeastern parts of the country – as well as a good part of northern Pakistan. They are the ones usually governing the country. The Pashtun are an ultra-conservative Sunni Muslim people – that have long looked down on the Tajiks (30 percent of the population) and Uzbeks (10 percent of the population) in the northern parts of the country. And they despise deeply the Hazaras (not quite 10 percent) living in the mountainous center of the country.

In the midst of all this conflict, a small group of mostly Pashtun Sunni hardliners, who called themselves the "Taliban" (from the Arabic word for "student"), formed in the Pashtun region of Northern Pakistan around the teachings of an Islamic fundamentalist teacher, Muhammad Omar. For various reasons, this Taliban group also found itself strongly supported by elements in the Pakistani intelligence service.

In 1994 members of the Taliban crossed into Afghanistan and quickly set themselves up in Kandahar ...from which they brutally organized much of the rest of the Pashtun community into a fighting force. And in 1996 – with strong support from both Pakistan and Saudi Arabia – they were able to march their troops on Kabul and force the government there to flee to the north.

But many Afghans, in order to escape the brutality of the Taliban, followed the former government north ... where finally there was established a "Northern Alliance" under the former Afghan Defense Minister Ahmed Shah Massoud. By 2001, over a million Afghanis had fled to the north ... where Massoud was able to establish something of a stable and fairly open society there.

In all this, America took no action. But the country wondered why its supposed allies Saudi Arabia and especially supposedly-modernizing Pakistan would be supportive of the Taliban regime. In the very near future, this would become a very high priority matter to America ... especially as al-Qaeda was allowed to set up military training camps in Taliban-controlled Afghanistan.

Al-Qaeda bombs the American embassies in Tanzania and Kenya (August 1998). Then, without any prior notice or any explanation, suicide bombers ripped apart the American embassies in Dar es Salaam (Tanzania) and Nairobi (Kenya), killing 212 people in the process and wounding hundreds more. The American CIA was quick to detect this as the hand of al-Qaeda ... or more particularly its Egyptian branch, Egyptian Islamic Jihad.

A furious Clinton immediately responded with guided missile strikes on al-Qaeda's Afghan training camps (the al-Qaeda camps in Pakistan, however, were definitely off limits to a similar American response!). But also he targeted a supposed chemical weapons factory in Sudan – although it turned out that he was wrong about what it was that this factory was actually manufacturing (pharmaceuticals mostly)!

Saddam Hussein's Iraq. Meanwhile, tensions were growing over Saddam Hussein's activities in Iraq. Actually, problems developing with Saddam Hussein's Iraq during those days originally had little to do with the issue of Islam – though that would soon develop as a matter of critical importance to Iraq ... when American action in Iraq would soon throw the country into a vicious civil war among the country's Sunnis, Shi'ites and Kurds.

Since the forced removal of Iraqi troops from neighboring Kuwait in 1991, a very close watch had been put on Saddam ... out of a concern about how he would try to restore his "strongman" reputation in the region. Great was the concern that he would violate the post-Gulf-War agreements forbidding the use – or even development – of chemical or biological weapons. But added to that was a growing concern that he might even try to develop nuclear weaponry.* In short, a growing concern was that Saddam might be secretly developing "weapons of mass destruction" (WMDs).

Thus it was that in October of 1998, Clinton extended financial aid to Saddam's political opponents in Iraq ... and then in December – along with the British – conducted airstrikes against Iraq. But though justified as addressing the issue of Iraqi WMDs, actually it was military sites – not industrial development sites – that were struck. Certainly another motive was simply that of crippling or even bringing Saddam's regime down altogether.

Actually, the airstrike did not go over well with much of the international community ... especially the Arab world – but also Russia, China and even France. Even some Americans claimed that this was only a Clinton distraction from the scandal that was sweeping America at the time, one concerning Clinton's just-discovered affair with a young White House intern. But it is more likely that what motivated this action was a growing concern among the Washington leadership (and the British as well) that the Muslim world was becoming increasingly threatening to the Western world ... and that Saddam was possibly supporting this development. Thus a show of force seemed to be necessary to back down any such ambitions potentially arising in that threatening world.

Time would soon tell who had this right.

---

*Actually, Israel had already addressed that issue when in June of 1981, the Israeli air force conducted a surprise airstrike against Iraq's nuclear reactor located near Baghdad.

CHAPTER TWENTY-ONE

THE TROUBLED 21st CENTURY

* * *

9/11 AND IRAQ

Bush Jr. takes command in America

The American elections (2000). Clinton had finished out his second presidential term and thus the Democratic Party turned to his Vice President Al Gore to be their 2000 presidential candidate. On the other side of the aisle, the Republicans chose the son of the former President Bush (for our purposes in this narrative identified simply as George Bush, Jr.) to be their candidate. Both were moderate centrists, close in age (both being early Baby Boomers ... like Clinton), of similar backgrounds and upbringing. Unsurprisingly, therefore, the election was fairly respectable ... until the very end when the vote was so close that recounts were ordered, in particular in Florida where the vote was very close, and the state whose electoral vote would decide the close election. Ultimately the decision went in favor of Bush, Jr. – and Gore graciously accepted his loss.

Bush, Jr. had been governor of Texas, the only individual to have actually been reelected to that position up to that point. He considered himself a "compassionate conservative" ... which in good Boomer fashion meant almost anything he wanted it to mean. But indeed, he was focused on upgrading the status of America's Black and Hispanic minorities ... especially in the realm of early education.

9/11. In fact, he was in a Florida classroom publicizing his "No Child Left Behind" program ... when on the early morning of September 11th, 2001, he was abruptly informed that a major tragedy had just hit. An airplane had just crashed into the North Tower of the New York World Trade Center. And soon another plane did the same to the South Tower, confirming the suspicion that this was not just some horrible aerial accident. Then a third plane hit the Pentagon building in D.C. And a fourth plane was found to have been brought down in rural Pennsylvania by some of its passengers when news reached them of what had just happened ... and they realized that the Arab pirates who had just taken over their plane were heading it also to D.C. – with the most probably intention of hitting either the White House or the Capitol Building.

All in all, the actions of these suicide pirates ended up killing some 2,800 people (office workers, firemen and police called to the sites, airplane passengers, and others) and wounding many more ... in fact wounding deeply the heart of America – as well as the hearts of other nations who also lost nationals in the event ... or simply felt a deep hurt for what they knew their fellow Americans had just gone through. However, many in the Muslim world were shockingly a strong exception to this spirit of sympathy – for they saw the event as something to be celebrated.

And once again, it took very little time to figure out who the actual culprits were: local members of al-Qaeda – some 24 of them (five each to a plane, except one who was missing).

The "Bush Doctrine." Very quickly a number of countries (most notably Britain, but also fellow NATO members ... and others) indicated a willingness to join with America in going after the al-Qaeda groups training in Afghanistan. Bush thus informed the Taliban that if they did not surrender the al-Qaeda operatives to America, America and its allies would be forced to do the job themselves. But the Taliban refused to cooperate.

But instead of simply setting up a strike team ready to go quickly after the al-Qaeda trainees, Bush decided to expand matters considerably with his "Bush Doctrine" aimed more broadly at any authority, any government, openly supporting such behavior as al-Qaeda's ... any society allowing the tyranny of such Muslim fanaticism to exist in its territory. Such a country was destined to find itself in direct conflict with America.

How exactly Bush planned to enforce his Bush Doctrine remained something of a mystery. As for Afghanistan, that was fairly clear. Bush and America's allies were intending to invade Afghanistan and "liberate " that country from Taliban-backed fanaticism. But what about nuclear armed, and supposedly American-allied Pakistan? Pakistan made it very clear that it too was not going to simply turn al-Qaeda operatives over to America. Did Bush intend to invade Pakistan as well? And al-Qaeda operatives were to be found all around the Middle East, such as the Egyptian group that made the first attempt on the Twin Towers in 1993. Was Bush going to take on the entire Arab World ... which seemed to be in fair sympathy with al-Qaeda's goals of crippling Western society? In any case, it quickly became clear that Bush had not carefully thought through his Bush Doctrine. But now he was going to have to put some meat on his boast to be this tough guy president ... with grand plans to straighten out the world.

At first, the CIA prepared itself for immediate action against al-Qaeda, by mobilizing operatives and by paying local Afghan tribal lords to get them to help their operatives find and bring down al-Qaeda leader Osama bin Laden. But then when in early October Bush amplified the operation to the remaking of the whole of Afghanistan, the matter was turned over to the Defense Department – which would then need some time to get itself ready for a massive military operation against Taliban Afghanistan.

The Afghan "conquest"

However, working in favor of Bush's goal was the Northern Alliance. It had just lost its leader (assassinated) Massoud just two days prior to 9/11 – probably in anticipation by al-Qaeda or the Taliban of how the Western reaction to what they had planned for 9/11 might play out. But the Northern Alliance did not fall apart and, with the help of American (and NATO) firepower, was able to take control in the northern city of Mazar-i-Sharif in early November and then use its airport to bring in military supplies and even food for its troops and people. Then they marched on Kabul, and quickly sent the Taliban into flight.

Thus it all seemed to be over so quickly, so grandly. Celebrations were held in Kabul – and around the Western world. Laura Bush, the president's wife, even addressed the nation with a speech rejoicing how such freedom was greatly received by the Afghans ... and especially by its women, freed from Taliban oppression.

Of course the Taliban had not capitulated ... but instead had simply retreated to a more defensible position in the Tora Bora Mountains ... and were also able to hold their position at the southern city of Kandahar in the heart of Pashtun territory ... which would then become their new headquarters. Thus the Afghan war was hardly over.

In any case, American and NATO troops (and other smaller support troops) were able to take position in the non-Pashtun lands of central and northern Afghanistan ... and install in Kabul's Presidential Palace a new Afghan president, Hamid Karzai. But exactly how much authority Karzai would exercise outside of Kabul itself depended on two factors ... not necessarily connected: the ability of Western forces to secure militarily various areas of the country, and the ability of Karzai to enter into some kind of political relationship with the various tribal chiefs located around the country ... at least in the North – outside of Taliban-Pashtun territory.

Efforts would be made to roll back the Taliban from their position in the south of the country. But these efforts would come to little ... except the loss of life. And it became clear that the Western troops would have to remain in place for the foreseeable future in order to protect the part of Afghanistan that was "free." Thus a very expensive settling in became part of the grand Afghan outcome.

Bush decides to take on Saddam's Iraq

For reasons known only to Bush, Jr., he soon decided that the world would be a much better place if Saddam Hussein would simply disappear. The only problem was that he found he had no good excuse for undertaking such a move. At first he tried to use his Bush Doctrine, claiming that Saddam had to go because of his support of al-Qaeda. But he had no actual evidence of such a connection ... and he found that convincing the world otherwise was going nowhere. Then he went back to the old weapons-of-mass-destruction (WMDs) accusation leveled against Saddam. But coming up with evidence for this proved to be more confusing than confirming. And as time went along, he found his NATO partners not interested in supporting him ... except for the British Prime Minister Tony Blair – who had long cultivated a very close relationship with both Presidents Clinton and Bush, Jr. ... and who seemed ready to go with Bush on this matter. Sadly in doing so it would eventually turn out to be Blair's political downfall.

Not even Bush's cabinet was in one accord on this move against Saddam. The CIA chief, George Tenet, Secretary of State (and former military man) Colin Powell, and National Security Advisor Condeleezza Rice were very hesitant about going after Saddam. Where was the evidence that would justify such an aggressive action as taking down the leader of a foreign country? But Secretary of Defense Donald Rumsfeld was all for such a military action. He was eager to show what his new "professional military" was capable of accomplishing. And Bush's closest advisor, his Vice President Dick Cheney, was willing to overlook his 1994 assurance to the press that going after Saddam would be to fall into a quagmire ... because it was very clear that Bush had his heart set on the matter. Thus Cheney chose to support the President rather than warn him of what clearly were the huge problems that would surely come their way in undertaking this action.

Backing up his assurance that all would go well with the Iraqi program, Rumsfeld assured Bush that he had a perfect candidate to assume power in Iraq once Saddam was out of the way, Ahmed Chalabi. Chalabi hated Saddam intensely (Saddam was Sunni, Chalabi was Shi'ite) and would do everything he could to undo Saddam and his political legacy. Chalabi had a Ph.D. in mathematics ... and was a full Westerner (or so his loyalties were supposed to run) – having lived in the West since 1956. But that very fact should have raised serious doubts about his strong political foundations in a post-Saddam Iraq. Powell's State Department was certain that Chalabi had absolutely no standing in Iraq. And the CIA even considered the thought that he might actually be a Shi'ite agent working for Iran. But Bush was not interested in what the CIA or the State Department had to say on this matter.

In any case, in September of 2002, Bush went before the United Nations to lay his case for Saddam's violation of Iraq's WMD prohibition ... but came away only with the decision of the Security Council in November to undertake renewed inspections in Iraq in the search for such WMDs. This was not what Bush wanted. But for the moment he settled with that agreement.

Then he went before Congress to get backing for his plans ... claiming that Rumsfeld's Pentagon had come up with conclusive evidence that Saddam was developing nuclear weapons. Supposedly Niger had sold Saddam yellow cake uranium – vital to such weapons development (the whole affair would later prove to have been untrue). At first the CIA would not give a similar backing on the matter to Bush. But then Tenet simply caved to pressure and offered additional "evidence" sought by Bush, certifying that aluminum tubes had been discovered in Iraq, ones certainly designed to be used as centrifuges in enriching uranium. Finally, on the basis of this "evidence," Congress finally supported Bush's program.[*]

Meanwhile, Bush's frustration with the U.N. WMDs search mounted ... as the search came up with no evidence of any such development. Thus Bush used his one last card to play in sending in February of 2003 the highly respected Powell to the U.N., armed with photos, charts, etc. "proving" conclusively that such WMDs in fact did exist in Iraq. But even this seemed not to move the opinions of America's allies – except, again, Blair's Britain. Then when an American resolution calling for the execution of the "serious consequences" part of the earlier agreement with Saddam looked as if it was going to run into the stiff opposition of France, Germany, and Russia, Bush simply withdrew his proposal. It was clear that he was going to get no backing from the U.N. (or NATO as well).

"Shock and Awe" (March 2003). Bush was now ready to move on his own (with Blair's British cooperation) – based on Rumsfeld's assurances that things would move as swiftly in Iraq as they had in Afghanistan. They would quickly knock out the Saddam government and then let Chalabi and

---

[*]In the House: 297 in support (215 Republicans and 81 Democrats) and 133 opposed (6 Republicans, 126 Democrats and 1 Independent). In the Senate: 77 in support (48 Republicans and 29 Democrats) and 23 against (only 1 Republican, 21 Democrats and 1 Independent). Notably, those in support were Democratic Senators Biden, Clinton and Schumer ... who would later come to regret their decision.

his supporters immediately form a new ruling team ... so that America could then back out of Iraq before a stunned international community would even know what just hit them!

The first part of Rumsfeld's assurances proved to be right – in that a massive aerial bombardment of Baghdad* sent Saddam fleeing ... thus immediately collapsing his Ba'athist government. But the second part of Rumsfeld's assurance was not even close to having any real weight to it. Very quickly it was revealed that Chalabi had no support group ready to take control in Iraq. In fact, he was a quite unknown figure in that country.

Consequently, America now had a "quagmire" to deal with.

From very bad to catastrophic. With their dictator gone and Iraq now presumably a free country, the Iraqis poured into the streets to celebrate their liberation. But liberation also meant the disappearance of a regime of law and order, which reflected itself in the rash of thefts ... such as ancient items taken from the Iraqi Museum. But American military commanders were quick to call on elements of the Iraqi army to help get things back in order on the streets. Worse, long-standing Sunni and Shi'ite hatreds now sparked religious reprisals, first by the Shi'ites against Sunnis, the Shi'ites glad to be out from under Sunni control enforced by Saddam's Ba'athist Party. Then the Sunnis responded in kind ... and thus Iraq found itself in a state of civil war.

Then in early May Bush sent to Iraq a new U.S. Administrator, Jerry Bremer – a Rumsfeld appointee ... who had the intention of bringing Iraq under his own personal mastery. Despite the warnings of the previous Administrator not to do this, Bremer issued Order No. 1 .... calling for the "deBaathification" of Iraq. Since no professional positions were open to Iraqis unless they became members of the Ba'athist Party, Bremer's Order No 1 removed every teacher, doctor, civil engineer, civil servant, etc. from their jobs ... leaving the country without any kind of local leadership or even professional service. Then a week later he disregarded military advice and issued Order No. 2 ... calling on all Iraqi military to surrender their guns to American authorities. This these men were most unwilling to do ... with the result that, on his very own, Bremer turned a huge number of experienced Iraqi soldiers into bitterly anti-American fighters.

Within a few days the first attacks on the occupying American soldiers began. And thus, General Franks and all the top military command – in complete disgust over the way Bremer was handling matters in Iraq – chose to "retire" ... leaving command in the hands of an inexperienced one-star American general.

---

*The American attack produced a very graphic picture of Baghdad in flames ... and thus the label "shock and awe" came to be assigned to the event.

Also, the Shi'ites found themselves under a young leader, Muqtada al-Sadr, who – instead of being grateful for the way the Americans had freed their community from Sunni dominance – chose to turn his "Mahdi Army" on the occupying troops (British as well as Americans) in order to demonstrate his own personal coming-to-glory as the Shi'ite community's new leader. And in this he was getting considerable support from the bitterly anti-American Shi'ite Iran next door.

And the Kurds in the north saw this as an opportunity to pull out of Iraq and set up their own independent Kurdish nation... a move destined to plunge the Kurdish region into its own war, as Kurdish leaders fought among themselves to take control. But it also infuriated America's ally Turkey – where a huge Kurdish section of Turkey now looked to the possibility of breaking away from Turkey in order to join the Kurdish development.

What a catastrophe this all turned out to be. And tragically it was entirely predictable ... for Iraq was always destined to be a "quagmire, as Cheney himself knew beforehand. America now had a very expensive war on multiple fronts in the region to contend with ... with nothing really to gain from it all.*

A small bit of good news was that finally in June of 2004 Bremer was able to announce the formation of a provisional Iraqi government and an interim constitution. And Rumsfeld also announced that his troops would now pursue a "small footprint" strategy of serving mostly as trainers of Iraqi troops ... who would then take over as soon as possible America's policing role in the country. This was supposed to be part of his original idea that America would quickly depart once Saddam was overthrown (he was actually found and arrested the previous December). But this would not turn out to be the case, despite Rumsfeld's efforts to bring things to a satisfactory resolution. And he would find it necessary to depart from this strategy in order to hit hard local opposition – as in Sunni Fallujah or constantly against al-Sadr's Shi'ite Mahdi Army – and then return to base.

But the "good news" was enough to get Bush reelected to a second term as president.

Things drag on. The following year (October 2005) a national election was

---

*In December of 2004, an incredibly ill-informed President Bush presented Bremer America's highest civilian honor, the Medal of Freedom, stating: "For fourteen months Jerry Bremer worked day and night in difficult and dangerous conditions to stabilize the country, to help its people rebuild and to establish a political process that would lead to justice and liberty." However, at this point Iraq was hardly "stabilized" nor experiencing justice and liberty – due mostly to Bremer's massive political ineptitude. Bremer, however, blamed the very obvious Iraqi catastrophe on the inadequate American military support he was expected to work with. Working with the Iraqis themselves was way beyond Bremer's understanding or abilities.

held for the new Provisional Government ... with the outraged Sunnis mostly boycotting the election. The Shi'ites now controlled Iraq ... enraging the Sunnis even more. Thus the elections failed to bring democratic harmony ("Iraqi Freedom" as Bush entitled the whole enterprise) to Iraq ... but only a deepening of the civil war.

Things only worsened in 2006, with the blowing up of one of Shi'ite Islam's holiest mosques, the al-Askari or Golden Dome Mosque in Samarra ... bringing al-Sadr and his Shi'ite death squads out to kill Sunnis ... including their clerics. Then when the announcement was made of a partial American and British withdrawal, al-Sadr boasted this development as his forces kicking out the imperialist invaders.

And for Bush's Republican Party, things were looking grim as the November elections approached. The results were that the Democrats now became the majority party in the House and the Republicans were reduced to a mere tie with the Democrats in the Senate ... but with two independent Senators tending to vote with the Democrats. Then a day after the elections, Bush announced that Rumsfeld would be replaced by CIA director Robert Gates. The Republicans were upset that this had not been done before the elections ... when it might have made the Republican Party loss much smaller.

The 2007 "troop surge." At the beginning of the new year (2007) a desperate Bush announced that he was stopping the troop drawdown in Iraq and was in fact sending an additional 20,000 troops to Iraq to hit Iraqi insurgents hard and retake the villages lost to them. He was also relaxing the anti-Ba'athist policy and diverting Iraqi funding in the direction of new reconstruction and jobs in Iraq. Democrats in Congress were outraged and supported a resolution (non-binding however) disapproving Bush's "troop surge." Nonetheless, the surge worked, villages were retaken and even al-Sadr had become more cooperative. And by the end of the year the level of violence in Iraq had subsided considerably. Finally, in the last months of his presidency (late 2008), he announced the beginning of a new round of troop withdrawals from Iraq.

Blair resigns as British Prime Minister (2007). Sadly for Blair, his alliance with Bush in this Iraqi affair proved to be his undoing. In 1987, when he became British Prime Minister, he was the youngest of the 20th century prime ministers, and the leader of the Labour Party in the largest electoral victory in the party's history. His popularity continued as he introduced a number of widely popular and rather "centrist" social reforms ... and his foreign policy moves such as his intervention in Kosovo and Sierra Leone were also widely appreciated. Thus he led his party in 2001 to a massive victory in the national elections of that year.

But his popularity would begin to drop with his involvement in the Iraqi mess. Thus he was reelected in 2005, but by a substantially reduced margin ... but even then gaining the support he did because at the time his country was still doing very well economically. The next year (2006), now suffering very low performance ratings, he announced that he would be stepping down within a year ... and did so the following June. Sad.

✳ ✳ ✳

ECONOMIC PROBLEMS DURING THE BUSH PRESIDENCY

Growing income inequality in America. Similar to the late 1800s, America was beginning to register a huge and ever-widening gap between the richest and the poorest in America. The relative income equality of the 1940s, 1950s, and 1960s had – since the 1970s – been changing to one in which a greedy few vastly outdistanced the economic growth of those of a lower social status.

For instance, in the twenty-five-year period of 1979 to 2004, the lowest fifth of American income earners had advanced by only 6 percent ... not even close to keeping up with the inflation rate hitting the country. In short, they had become even poorer. The next fifth advanced by 17 percent, the middle fifth by 21 percent, and the next highest fifth by 29 percent ... closer to the inflation rate. In short, they had made no real gains economically – although, even at that, they lived fairly well. But the top fifth had advanced during that period by 69 percent ... and of that group, the top 1 percent had advanced by 176 percent.

Indeed, in a study done by the *New York Times*, during the year 2005, the national income figure increased by 9 percent ... although that growth had benefited only the top 10 percent of American income earners. In fact, the top 1 percent registered a growth of 14 percent. The lower 90 percent actually registered a slight dip in real wealth. Worse, the top 0.1 percent of the population (some 300,000 individuals) made the same total income as the bottom 50 percent or 150 million Americans. Their incomes were 440 times the average income of that lower half ... twice the disparity that existed in 1980.

Thus, the horrible income spread of the late 1800s, had returned to America. But unlike the reforming urge of the Teddy Roosevelt and Howard Taft presidencies at the beginning of the 1900s, no one in Washington seemed to be willing to do anything about this matter.

Certainly part of this was due to the change in the character of the American economy itself as it moved from heavy industry to the world of high-tech industry ... with the low-tech jobs now going "offshore" (Africa, Asia, Latin America).   A high school education typical of the lower realm of American society no longer serviced the needs of America's new industrial order. An expensive college education (growing ever more expensive with each passing year) would be required – putting a lot of Americans in deep debt just to keep up with the shift in the working world.

A culture of greed. In turn this was causing Americans to lose sight of the need for more economic discipline – both individually and nationally. Thus Americans – in order to keep up a fairly fancy lifestyle – found themselves in mounting debt ... especially with the introduction of the charge and debit cards.

But actually, a culture of greed was impacting even more the professional world (lawyers, doctors, corporate presidents, etc.) – where salaries were climbing annually at a rapid rate way beyond any real improvement in the services they actually provided American society. They simply were getting very rich ... because that was now considered their "entitlement" ... in a society that now tended to look at every matter not as one of duty or obligation but instead as one of entitlement.

The huge American trade imbalance.   Part of the fancier American lifestyle was that Americans were "helping" the world's economy by buying more of what foreign manufacturers provided than what America itself sold to those same people abroad. In short, America was experiencing a huge and ever-growing deficit in the balance of trade.

America was able to do this because the dollar was still very strong ... constituting about 60 percent of the world's hard-currency reserves. In short, America was able to sustain this imbalance in the flow of material wealth (industrial goods and services) in favor of America ... because of the strength of the dollar.

The government's own economic failings. The war in Iraq had been very expensive ... and had earned America nothing economically in return. As a result, the war – plus America's growing love of government programs to compensate for the increasingly hard economic times many Americans were going through – ran the public debt way up ... doubling the size of that debt during the eight years of the Bush presidency: from $5 trillion to $10 trillion. True, the figures describing the country's income had increased – but much of that simply due to inflation – so that the percentage of that national income owed by the government only went from 57 percent to 70 percent. But still that was a real shift in the government's economic position. But in any case, it meant that in 2008, every tax-paying American now shared about $60 thousand of that debt ... an impossible figure to sustain (but which would grow even worse over the coming years!)

Of course, debt means that someone or some institution has extended some kind of "loan" to the indebted party. Indeed, about half of that debt was being covered by America's own Social Security Trust Fund ... once a fairly independent source of investment for America's retirees – but now in the full grip of the American government. Consequently, there was no longer any real material wealth supporting the Trust Fund ... only government IOUs. Most tragically, it had become simply another version of the 1920s Ponzi Scheme, where the fund had no real wealth to distribute to investors ... except out of the money coming in from new investors – which was then distributed to prior participants as fake "payouts" supposedly coming from the investment program itself (from earnings from real economic ventures). Indeed, there was actually nothing there of real substance ... except the game itself.

It could be wondered why anyone beyond a government-controlled income source would ever be interested in purchasing shares of that debt. True, many Americans continued to buy government bonds ... the traditional way that the government covered its debts (as, for instance in both World War One and World War Two). But looking at the fact that the government might actually have to start paying off the federal debt – had it actually done so, it would have taken all the government spending that was not already committed to a number of ongoing programs.

Thus the Federal Reserve decided to go in a direction opposite that which Volcker took when he raised the interest rate to 20 percent – killing off a lot of American business in the process. Instead, the Federal Reserve kept dropping the interest rate paid on the debt that others were holding, to a point where the government was willing to pay off that debt at a rate less than 1 percent! In short, those who would want to "invest" their life savings in purchasing the bonds that originally financed that debt would now find themselves putting their money in a program that paid itself back at a rate lower than the annual inflation rate. In short, they would be throwing their money away in purchasing government bonds.

So why then was it that China and Japan chose to continue to fill the role of financier behind the American debt, each country coming to hold about 20 percent of that debt? Unsurprisingly, this was not exactly done out of a spirit of kindness ... but for simple economic reasons. Americans were key purchasers of the industrial production of both countries ... and any American economic retreat would have damaged greatly their own industries. Besides, for China, holding such economic leverage over America played well in its growing interest in replacing America as the world's major superpower.

The financial catastrophe of 2008. But ultimately it was this culture of greed at home in America that nearly toppled the American economy in the last days of the Bush II Administration. It had to do with the huge American housing market. The debt-addicted American world found that the home-construction industry was not keeping up with a growing demand of debt-consumed Americans (huge college loans, for instance) to move anyway on the American dream of home ownership. But there was also a bit of urgency driving this dream ... as the price of housing had virtually doubled in the recent years and thus panicked purchasers felt that it was necessary to take on the home-owning challenge before the housing market got even worse for them.

No one is able to purchase an expensive home on the basis of a cash payment ... but instead is going to have to enlist the services of a bank willing to extend to a purchaser a loan (mortgage) – usually 30 years in duration as a payback matter – to cover the cost of the home. Of course banks are supposedly not stupid ... and are supposed to look closely at the financial situation of a potential mortgage purchaser – to make certain that the purchaser is in the position economically to repay that loan on a steady basis.

But at this point, the financial world seemed more interested in running up its business numbers (a matter of corporate prestige) than going at the matter with its traditional wisdom. A big part of this was that mortgage banks would have found their businesses slowing up greatly – because a serious consideration of the financial position of these already over-extended debtors would have lost them a lot of business. Relatively speaking it was harder and harder to find customers not already fully loaded up with debt – hardly in a position to take on more.

Thus these huge banking organizations began to extend "subprime" mortgages to "subprime" purchasers ... a very foolish thing to do. But at first this all seemed to go very well. Banks found themselves in business running at high speed.

Then the bottom fell out of the dreamy enterprise. Contractors raced to get into the highly lucrative housing market ... producing a housing boom of enormous magnitude. In fact the building boom was so great that soon recently-constructed houses were sitting there waiting for a purchaser. Some got sold, many did not. So, the contractors did what the market demanded: they lowered the prices of their finished home – until (like the oil market of the early 1980s) they found themselves in competition to corner the market with ever-lower-priced homes.

But recent mortgage buyers were now finding that their mortgages were running at a higher rate than the cost of new housing – inviting many of them to sell in order to purchase a cheaper home. But this merely put even more houses on the over-saturated housing market. Many therefore simply "bankrupted" themselves to get out of the mortgage obligation altogether.

Now the banks found themselves in trouble as panic hit the mortgage industry. And Wall Street was watching events closely, quickly losing confidence in a number of major banking corporations ... and began to sell, sell, sell. At this point the two largest mortgage companies Fannie Mae (the Federal National Mortgage Association) and Freddie Mac (the Federal Home Loan Mortgage Corporation) - not really federally owned companies, but federally backed – found themselves facing bankruptcy (their stock had lost 90 percent of its value by August of 2008). But so too were the huge mortgage corporations Bear Stearns and Lehman Brothers. Ultimately, Congress decided to bail out Fannie Mae and Freddie Mac ($100 billion of taxpayers' money) ... slowing up – but not stopping completely – the panic. The huge financial firm J.P. Morgan was able to buy and thus save Bear Stearns ... but Lehman Brothers could find no backing and simply collapsed. Likewise, Washington Mutual, America's largest savings and loan bank also collapsed. And America's largest insurance company, AIG (American International Group) nearly did so ... its stock dropping from $70 a share down to $1.25 a share. It was saved only when the Federal Reserve stepped in and offered AIG an $85 billion bailout – increased the following year of Obama's first year in the White House to $180 billion. In short, the U.S. government found itself owning 80 percent of this huge insurance company. And AIG would then have to start selling off its subsidiaries in order to begin repayment of that huge debt.

TARP. Indeed, Bush took economic control, getting Congress to authorize a $700 billion TARP (Troubled Assets Relief Program) to purchase parts or the whole of troubled American financial corporations ... in order to calm the Wall Street panic that was ripping American corporations apart.

But even at that, now the American automobile industry found itself in the same panic mode. Not only were houses now sitting unsold, so were cars facing the same problem: people were too frightened to take up a car loan. Thus the American "Big Three" (Ford, General Motors and Chrysler) were finding themselves in deep trouble at the same time as the housing market. In 2008, although the production capacity of the Big Three was 17 million cars a year, that year they produced only 10 million cars – a drop in their production rate by 45 percent of what it had been in 2007. Thus the labor force had to be cut back, worsening the unemployment picture ... and the solvency of the Big Three themselves unable to come even close to meeting their operational costs. Here too, Congress had to step in to save these major American corporations from total destruction – even though both General Motors and Chrysler were forced to declare bankruptcy ... in order to begin some kind of a rebuilding program.

Secularism pushes Christianity into further retreat

Middle America was also finding itself facing a huge loss in another area of its traditional social world: the federal courts forcing an even deeper retreat of America from its Christian social-cultural legacy ... actively substituting Secularism as America's moral-spiritual underpinning. The Boomers were now the leaders of the adult world and – with the help of the ACLU – as dedicated as ever to seeing the Christian cultural roots of their parents (and, for that matter, nearly all Americans before them) dug up and replaced by fully Secular social-moral foundations.

One particular individual would bring case after case to court – trying through different challenges to erase the Christian legacy from the public scene. Most notable was his *Newdow v. U.S. Congress* (2000-2004) case in which he tried to get the "under God" portion removed from the U.S. Pledge of Allegiance. He got a bit ahead of himself and, though he got the ever-Liberal 9th Circuit Court (covering Hawaii and the American West) to support him, he failed when the case advanced to the Supreme Court ... though he would bring more cases to court in pressing forward (2005-2010).

Things proved to be more successful for the American Left when the ACLU jumped into a case, *Kitzmiller v. Dover Area School District* (2005) when parents were outraged that a paragraph had been issued by the school board of Dover, Pennsylvania, to teachers to be read at the beginning of the 2004 school year – stating that students might want to explore the book *Of Pandas and People* ... as a way of discovering that there were other explanations of Evolution than Darwin's. District Court Judge John Jones helped determine the outcome of the hearings by the way he called (or didn't call) specific individuals to speak on the matter. Thus not only did the decision go against the school board about this paragraph, Jones imposed a $1 million fine on the school board for "the breathtaking inanity of the Board's decision" (Jones' own words). Jones (and the ACLU) made it clear that "science" not "religion" were the only matters to involve themselves in the education of America's youth. The impoverished (and soon outvoted) Board carried the matter no further forward. Jones's decision thus stood as a ruling across the country. But also, he didn't get the Supreme Court appointment that he seemed to be angling for.

Once again, the federal courts were telling Americans what it was – and was not – that they were to rest their worldview, their faith in life, on. Such matters were to be purely Material or Secular. Christianity, the worldview that had carried America forward through countless generations, was now forbidden in America's public life, especially in the training of rising American generations ... thanks to the ACLU – and those clever lawyers in black robes.

✳ ✳ ✳

OBAMA BRINGS DEEP "CHANGE" TO AMERICA

Obama and the Democrats take charge.

There was little likelihood that the Republican presidential candidate, John McCain had any chance at all in the November elections that year (2008) – despite Senator McCain's personal greatness as an American patriot (refused to betray his America during his 6-year captivity as a North Vietnamese prisoner of war) of a long line of American servicemen (his father and grandfather were U.S. Admirals) and years of service in both the Navy (since 1958) and in Congress (since 1982). The Democrats thus played not on his service record but instead on his age (he was 72 at the time) and his Vice President, the "beauty-king bimbo" Sarah Palin, Alaska governor ... and though very pretty, hardly a bimbo. But they didn't need to go that low. The Republicans were destined anyway to a lashing from an American electorate – angry at the Republican White House that got them engaged in Iraq ... and – fairly or not – blaming it for the country's near economic collapse ... right at the very time of the elections.

Thus, most unsurprisingly, eight years of Bush-conceived military disaster and economic nonsense produced a huge anti-Republican Party reaction in the national elections of 2008, one that brought to power the first of America's next generation, the Gen-Xer Barack Obama.

In so many ways, Obama was the typical Gen-Xer – in that his Boomer upbringing had left him deeply confused about his own personal identity ... what exactly that identity was and what he was to do with it in finally finding it. Nothing certain was laid out for him – in accordance with the Boomer view of his parental generation, that their Gen-X offspring were "free" to explore their personal identities on their own.   With Obama being bi-racial with a White Hippie Mother and an absentee African father, Obama had a lot of hunting to do. Ultimately, in this process he finally decided that he was Black ... despite the fact that it was a White mother and White grandparents most responsible for his upbringing.

And without any doubt, it was his "Blackness" that inspired Black TV celebrity Oprah Winfrey to push Obama to take up the personal goal of the American presidency ... and then to help considerably in pushing

Obama past Hillary Clinton's highly-developed political machine to gain the Democratic Party's presidential nomination.

And he was able to do this despite his lack of much political experience or deep political rootedness in Washington politics. This was because in this new age of constant (24/7) barrage of entertaining news and media social hype – complements of not only the TV, but also the computer and the smartphone – the media (such as Winfrey's widely-viewed daytime show) would be the platform from which American leaders would now be selected. All the media needed to do was to shape and ultimately control the political narrative. And that is exactly what the media now lived for.

But such public image-making did not answer deeply the question as to where Obama's personal loyalties actually were located. He was known in his very brief service in the U.S. Senate (less than two years) to be on the far Left politically in his legislative action. Now as an ideologically Leftist national leader, what part of America would he support ... and what part would he find himself opposing? Obama would be the president of what people exactly? Would his self-defined "Blackness" shape deeply the "Change" he promised that he was devoted to bringing to America? Where would he leave Middle America in all this "Change"?

Thus with little national political experience behind him other than his not quite three years of service in the U.S. Senate, Obama was soundly victorious over McCain – Obama with 52.9 percent of the popular vote to McCain's 45.7 percent ... and with an Obama 365 electoral vote to McCain's 173 votes.   And along with that, the Democrats increased their majority in the House to 257 seats versus the Republicans' 178 seats. And they now held a majority in the Senate, 57 seats to the Republicans' 41 seats. America was now headed down a very Leftist-Liberal road (Obama was considered to be on the very far Left of even the Democratic Party) – particularly since during his campaign he had made so much of the word "change" as his key theme (though the details remained vague).

The world also knew what was in store for America, with the very Liberal Norwegian Nobel Committee nominating Obama in February for the 2009 Peace Prize (which he would in fact receive later that year) – when Obama had been in the White House less than two weeks ... and had done nothing notable to bring such important attention. But it wasn't what he had done that got him that position. It was what, at that point, he represented socially and culturally.

The Liberal world loved him. The Conservative world watched in wonderment to see what would be unfolding under Obama's presidency dedicated to "change" – backed up by a solid Democratic Party majority in Congress.

Homosexuality and the marriage issue

One of the first matters to undergo deep change was the long-lingering matter of who or what exactly qualified as "marriage" in America. That would be a matter not of Congress to decide – it had already done so in 1996 – but of the Supreme Court to decide ... Obama, and by now everyone else, realizing that it was the Supreme Court, not Congress, that was America's supreme legislative authority.

When in 2008 California voters narrowly passed Proposition 8 banning same-sex marriages, both the homosexual community and the California courts (which had previously declared such a ban unconstitutional) swung into action. Back and forth went the case of *Kristin M. Perry v. Arnold Schwarzenegger* in the California courts – then joined by the Federal Ninth Circuit Court ... in which Proposition 8 was declared unconstitutional on both a California and a Federal basis.

Coming to office in 2009, Obama was quick in his move to take action on the homosexual issue – with his 2009 Hate Crimes Prevention Act ... categorizing as a hate crime any act motivated by a person's hatred of homosexuality. Thus according to the law, homophobia (a dislike for the homosexual lifestyle) was the moral problem, not sodomy. Indeed, intense punishment under the law against homophobia was put in place to make absolutely sure that everyone understood the shift in the moral picture. And with this legislation, the definition of a hate crime would soon move beyond action, now to even just comments made by anyone still intent on vocally demonstrating opposition to homosexuality. An unkind comment about the practice of sodomy could now cost a person his or her job, and probably worse if a plaintiff wanted to pursue the issue even further. Thus it was that homosexuality now enjoyed full legal support, and harsh punishment for anyone not in agreement with this new position.

Also, Obama, through his Attorney General Eric Holder, made it very clear in a letter to Congress (February 2011) that his Administration would no longer enforce the Defense of Marriage Act (DOMA) – despite Obama's inauguration vows promising to see that the laws of Congress were faithfully executed. Being deeply dedicated to bringing "change" to America, Obama felt that he had the right to be politically (ideologically) selective in this matter.

The Supreme Court takes the lead in the matter. But Obama's biggest impact on America's moral foundations would take place because of his two Supreme Court appointments ... giving the Supreme Court a much more Leftist orientation. In his May 2009 appointment of the childless and unmarried Sonia Sotomayor, of Puerto Rican origins, he was actually merely replacing one Progressivist or Liberal justice with another ... although Sotomayor's Liberalism was even further to the Left than that of the David Souter she was replacing.*

Then the following May (2010), Obama made yet another Supreme Court appointment, a strongly Liberal Elena Kagan, replacing the somewhat Liberal John Paul Stevens. It is important to note that Kagan was actually another childless and unmarried female, was Dean of Harvard's Law School ... and well-known for her strongly Liberal views on matters. At Harvard, she had forcefully opposed the military's appearing on Harvard campus for recruiting purposes because of its "don't ask; don't tell" policy concerning homosexuals and their behavior in the military. And she was Jewish, the third such individual at that point making up the nine-member Supreme Court.

But ultimately the decision came as a matter of where the "swing" justice Anthony Kennedy stood on the matter. And with respect to the issue of homosexuality, he was a strong supporter of full homosexual equality in American society.

And thus it was that the Supreme Court took on DOMA, Congress's key legislative piece concerning this matter of marriage. First was the 2013 decision in the *United States v. Windsor* case, ending one of the DOMA provisions ... soon followed by the 2015 decision in the *Obergefell v. Hodges* case, simply striking down all of DOMA.

And there was virtually nothing that the people's representatives in Congress, supposedly America's supreme legislative body, could do about these Supreme Court decisions. The reality was increasingly clear that the Supreme Court, even by the slimmest of margins (the decision of only five justices needed), was America's Supreme Legislature as well as Supreme Court ... deciding for America what exactly its foundational laws were to be.

The pro-homosexual social forces go on the attack. Even before the final 2015 *Obergefell v. Hodges* Supreme Court decision, the homosexual community was on a crusade to bring down any who dared to oppose, even object to, the idea of homosexual marriage ... when in 2013 owners of an Oregon bakery told one of their regular customers that when it came to baking her and her partner a wedding cake, they could not do so on the grounds of their own religious principles, and invited the two to go elsewhere to have that cake made. But the lesbian couple were not ones to have their rights violated ... and brought a lawsuit against the bakery. Then

----

*Previously, as a 2nd Circuit Court justice, she became well-known for her rather colorful political comments ... such as the one in 2001 in which she stated: "I would hope that a wise Latina woman with the richness of her experiences would more often than not reach a better conclusion than a white male who hasn't lived that life."

when the story hit Facebook and the internet, protesters began to gather outside the bakers' shop ... forcing the couple to have to close their bakery and try to work out of their home. But that was not enough to satisfy the crusaders ... who were thrilled to hear that an Oregon administrative court had imposed a $135,000 fine on the bakers. And efforts of the bakers to appeal their case, *Klein v. Oregon Bureau of Labor and Industries*, in Oregon's higher courts led them nowhere. The ruin of both the bakery and the personal finances of the bakers themselves was considered to be just punishment on behalf of a couple "deeply hurt" by the failure of the bakers to be willing to make them that wedding cake.

The message was thus loud and clear. Those who still (after centuries of such a standard) wanted to stay with those standards – insisting that marriage was/is intended to be between a man and a woman, principally to provide the care and nurture of a rising generation – that if they did so, they could expect severe punishment to come their way.

This marked a huge shift in the American social-moral scene ... one, since its founding, the nation had built its power upon – not on high-ranking and very select, and thus small, group of ruling officials, but on the grass roots foundations of millions of strong American families. But now the courts (and the president) made it quite clear that marriage was no longer about such social service. It was about meeting the sexual desires of individuals, whatever direction those might go. After all, wasn't this what "freedom" was all about ... not having to answer to any higher authority than your own personal inclinations?

As it turned out (and Obama himself commented in 2008 on how the breakdown of the American family had hurt deeply the Black community)[*] this action on behalf of personal "freedom" and personal "rights" would do enormous damage to all sorts of areas of American society.

Black-White relations turn ugly

Obama knew this problem personally, his African father and his White mother having separated soon after Obama was born in Hawaii in 1961. He would see his father only once after that – a half-hour visit with his father when Obama was 10. He would grow up having difficulty deciding whether he was Black or White ... although he finally found while a student at Columbia

---

[*]In one of his less ideological moments – Obama commented (on Father's Day of 2008, when first running for the presidency), "Children who grow up without a father are five times more likely to live in poverty and commit crime; nine times more likely to drop out of schools, and 20 times more likely to end up in prison. They are more likely to have behavioral problems, or run away from home or become teenage parents themselves. And the foundations of our community are weaker because of it."

University in New York City that he more easily identified himself as Black – finding the Black churches he attended in nearby Harlem to be a much better fit for him than the surrounding White world. That identity would then grow as it led him this way and that in his early professional years ... first as a Harvard Law student and then as a summer intern (1989) at a Chicago law firm – where he met Michelle Robinson ... and married her in 1992 in a ceremony led by the Black preacher, Jeremiah Wright, who became to Obama something like the father he had never known growing up.[*]

As eventually a Chicago lawyer himself, he became involved in a number of various community service organizations ... and taught constitutional law as a lecturer at the University of Chicago Law School. In 1995, he took the time to publish an autobiography, *Dreams of My Father*, about the challenge of growing up bi-racial. The next year (1996) he was elected to finish out a term as Illinois State Senator, then reelected in 1998 and 2002. And in 2004 he became a national figure, delivering a keynote address at the Democratic Party National Convention ... at the same time running for the U.S. Senate ... against a Republican who had to step down over a sex scandal that summer just before the election – giving Obama an easy ride into Congress in January of 2005 as Illinois' new senator.

It did not take long for Oprah Winfrey – at the very top of both CNN's and Time's list of the world's most powerful women – to find deep interest in Obama ... and suggest at several interviews with him that he should run as U.S. President. Why not? It was about time America had a Black president.

And thus it was decided that he would indeed run ... on the platform of bringing deep "change" to America. And obviously that had deep racial implications.

Thus elected President in the 2008 elections, not only was Obama quick to support the homosexual community, he was just as quick to jump into matters when race was understood to be at the heart of things.

The Trayvon Martin – George Zimmerman tragedy (2012). When a young Black, Trayvon Martin was shot and killed in a struggle with White (Hispanic) neighborhood watch volunteer George Zimmerman in early 2012, the incident quickly became a national issue, with the Black community furious over the event and demanding that Zimmerman be charged for murder ... before the details of the event were even known. And that included Obama, who intervened to demand action – and commented that

---

[*]Despite Obama and his family having found themselves under the pastoral leadership of Jeremiah Wright for nearly two decades, when in running for the presidency in 2008 the media caught parts of a highly racist sermon preached by Wright (not likely his first ... just the first time it hit the national media), Obama abruptly and completely cut Wright out of his life.

if he had a son, he would have looked like Trayvon.

During the trial, it was revealed that Martin was shot only when Zimmerman found himself on the ground and Martin on top of him, pounding away at Zimmerman for over 40 seconds. Ultimately Zimmerman, under the "Stand Your Ground Law" was found innocent of the charges. Needless to say, this was not the verdict that the Black community demanded ... and birthed the "Black Lives Matter" movement.

The Ferguson Missouri incident (2014). But even more explosive was the event in Ferguson Missouri that erupted in August of 2014 when a local police officer, Darren Wilson, shot and killed a young Black, Michael Brown. A very false portrayal of the event was issued by another Black, who was with Brown at the event, and who claimed that Brown had raised his hands and requested "don't shoot" when stopped by Wilson – but was shot in the back by Wilson anyway. This then set the Blacks off over a ten-day period on a rampage of plunder and torching of American neighborhoods – chanting the now-famous words "hands up, don't shoot." Even White youth (such as at the nearby St. Louis University) turned out in huge numbers, demanding Wilson be brought to justice – and demanding also an end to all injustice and poverty afflicting America ... that this event represented.

And Obama quickly (only several days after the shooting) made it clear that the Department of Justice was not going to simply let the local authorities sweep this matter under the rug – Obama indicating that he was fairly certain this would be how the matter would be handled locally because of the racism that runs through America – and sent Attorney General Holder to Missouri to do his own investigation.

Eventually other witnesses at the scene gave a very different account of the event, describing Brown as having charged Wilson when he was shot – and he was definitely not shot in the back trying to step back from the confrontation. Finally, try as he might, after a long investigation (lasting until March of the following year) Holder had to admit that the Justice Department could find no basis for bringing charges against Wilson. But, being Black himself, Holder could not resist the temptation to spell out how he felt the same agonies that America's minorities surely felt in such a White America. In short, instead of supporting the racial reconciliation that the nation needed, he merely invited American minorities to continue to register their deep animosities to the way America was structured. Like Obama, he was indicating that America needed change – deep change.[*]

---

[*]All of this despite statistics put out around that time by a government report which cited 2011 figures showing that that murder was the No. 1 killer of Black males of the age 15-34, running at 40 percent of the deaths in that age range (compared to 3.8 percent for White males of that same age) – nearly all of that Black on Black killings. However, the report also pointed out that more Whites

Refusing to stand at the playing of the National Anthem. Thus it was also that Obama just had to come out at the beginning of the 2016 football season to support the mostly Black players who – at game time – refused to stand in respect during the playing of the National Anthem ... instead kneeling in protest against American racism – especially against the racial oppression conducted by the police. Obama expressed his own concern about the racism afflicting America – and the importance of making a show of our opposition to this evil ... leaving it to the listener to decide whose racist evil he was referring to ... racism on the part of both Whites and Blacks – or just White racism?

**The Federal Judiciary removes restrictions against
big money's involvement in national and local elections.**

On the other hand, and also very harmful to Middle America, it would be the Conservatives on the Supreme Court (including Kennedy in this case) that would take American politics off in yet another direction. In a 5-4 decision in the *Citizens United v. Federal Election Commission* case (2010), the Supreme Court overruled an earlier 1990 decision (*Austin v. Michigan Chamber of Commerce*) that upheld restrictions against election spending by corporations ... claiming in the *Citizens United* decision that such restrictions, such as contained in the 2002 Bipartisan Campaign Reform Act, violated the First Amendment's freedom of speech clause. Supporting the decision were Kennedy, Alito, Scalia, Roberts, and Thomas (in part). Dissenting in the decision (in most parts) were Stevens, Ginsburg, Breyer, and Sotomayor. This was definitely not a popular decision with the American citizenry ... but stood nonetheless.

Also in 2010, a decision of the nine-member U.S. Court of Appeals for the District of Columbia decided unanimously in the *SpeechNow.org v. the Federal Election Commission* case – as a follow-up to the *Citizens United* case – to strike down as unconstitutional limitations on funding for groups or programs involved in electoral campaigns ... although restrictions against direct contributions to individual candidates supposedly still held. This decision helped immensely to open the way for the growth of the huge

---

than Blacks are killed by police, almost on a 2 to 1 ratio, although Whites make up five times the number of Blacks, so therefore the percentage figure for Blacks is higher. Nonetheless this does not conform well to the highly inflated claim that Blacks are subject to some especially high rate of killing by cops. Indeed, very tragically, blaming the police for the chaos that rocks Black neighborhoods is a horrible distraction from the real causes, which are: little moral training in manhood by missing fathers, poor educational motivation, high unemployment, and gang membership as the only option that many young Blacks find as their path to manhood. All of this serves to create a very violent environment in which both police and civilians are expected to function in a civilized fashion.

Super PACs (political action committees) – massive funding organizations created to shape national and local election outcomes.

Such organizations were, however, required to register and report their activity publicly. But such requirements hardly slowed up the Super PACs as unique shapers of electoral outcomes. That was, after all, the purpose of their very existence.

As a consequence of these court rulings, money would now speak more loudly that the vote of the ordinary citizen in deciding political contests.

✳ ✳ ✳

OBAMA AND THE WORLD

Obama's "New Beginning" challenge to the Arab world. Actually, Obama tried to appear more centrist … and seemingly more interested in America's position internationally than in playing a role in the midst of America's ongoing cultural wars. He focused particularly on the Middle East – trying to "change" Arab perceptions of America. In June of 2009 he went to Cairo to deliver an address inviting a more respectful dialogue between Christians and Muslims. Obama was strongly Christian, but had also lived at length in his youth in Muslim Indonesia … and cited that fact as part of his desire to win Muslim hearts back to America.

Iraq. He also announced early on that America would be drawing down even more troops from Iraq than had Bush during his last days in office. All American troops were now scheduled to be out of Iraq by 2011. He would do so … but then – at Iraq's request – have to return troops to Iraq in 2014 due to new problems arising in the region.

With (or even because of) the American troop drawdown, things in Iraq stalled politically – as the various groups and their representatives in the Iraqi Assembly went for months after an election in March of 2010, unable to design a ruling coalition for the country. Ayad Allawi's Iraqiya Party had the largest representation in the Assembly (90 seats) … though far from a majority. Allawi was a Shi'ite "moderate" – willing to bring Sunnis into a ruling coalition. Undoubtedly, he was the candidate the West was hoping would be able to get things under control and moving forward in Iraq. But the incumbent Shi'ite hardliner Nouri al-Maliki and his Islamic Dawa Party (with 89 seats) was insistent that any coalition had to have al-Maliki remain in place as prime minister. Finally in December, 9 months since the election, Allawi's party took the pressure to join in coalition with al-Malaki, with al-Malaki remaining prime minister.

Indeed, with the American pullout, things quickly got "back to normal"

... when in October of 2012, Iraqi Vice President al-Hashemi, escaped to Turkey in anticipation of his being sentenced to death for the crime (quite false) of inciting most of the violence that still shook Iraq. Actually, his real crime was that he was Sunni ... and the al-Maliki government was dead-set against the Sunni's having any significant voice in the governance of Iraq. The only real outcome of all this was that the sentence stirred the deep anger (and accompanying violence) of Iraq's Sunni community, both Arab and Kurd. But it also served to worsen Iraq's relations with its Sunni neighbors, Saudi Arabia, Qatar and Turkey. But, of course, it all played to the delight of Shi'ite Iran. And so things "progressed" in that part of the Middle East.

Afghanistan. But seeing the situation in Afghanistan worsen, soon after taking office as president, Obama announced that America would not be pulling its troops of out Afghanistan, but instead, would follow the successful program in Iraq – of conducting a "surge" of American troops (17,000 more) in Afghanistan.

But the Taliban simply pulled back (mostly back into Pakistan) to wait to see how long this "surge" was going to last. Thus there was no immediate serious "progress" that the American troops surge was able to accomplish. There was no way – with Pakistan (which America would not or even could not touch) willing to offer sanctuary to the Taliban – that America was going to be able to destroy or even cripple the Taliban. And indeed, America-backed Afghan president Karzai began to negotiate with the Taliban ... even suggesting that America do the same. Any kind of peace and stability in Afghanistan was going to have to respect Taliban power in some form or other.

But Obama's response that December was to announce the deployment of yet another 30,000 soldiers to Afghanistan. But most strangely, he also announced that he would then, the following July (2010), begin troop withdrawals from Afghanistan. This of course confused deeply the Karzai government. It also gave the Taliban even more reason to simply wait out Obama – until the Americans drew their numbers back down ... once again allowing the Taliban to regain lost territory – and then some. None of this American "strategy" therefore made any sense.

Osama bin Laden is finally killed (May 2011). On the night of May 7th, a Navy SEAL team was dropped by two Black Hawk helicopters into a compound in Pakistan at Abbottabad (near the Pakistani Military Academy) where Osama bin Laden was living ... and carried out his execution – and then took his body to be buried in the Arabian Sea.

While the West cheered the outcome, the Arab world largely did not.

And the Pakistanis were most upset ... especially over this matter of who was – and who was not – even aware of bin Laden's presence in Abbottabad ... and why the Pakistani authorities were so blindsided by this American action undertaken in their country.

But in any case, something that should have been done ten years earlier – rather than making Afghanistan and then Iraq the very unrewarding object of American democracy crusades – was finally carried out. The action unnerved the Arab world. But it would get past that event faster than it would dealing with the "democratic" legacies that Bush II (and to some extent Obama) tried most foolishly to impose on the Muslim world.

The "Arab Spring" (also 2011)

Meanwhile there were other events shaking deeply the Arab world. Revolts of Arab youth were shaking the foundations of several of the major Arab nations.

Tunisia.   It all started in Tunisia in mid-December of 2010, when a street vendor set himself ablaze ... in protest against the rising inflation, unemployment and general disillusionment of the Tunisians with respect to the Ben Ali government. The action quickly sparked more street protests – spread quickly through the means of the internet – by the Tunisian youth.

Sensing that he had lost all political standing, Ben Ali fled to Saudi Arabia in February (2012). And his government stepped down ... to make way for an interim government.

But all the Tunisian storm and fury soon spread to other Arab countries.

Egypt. In Egypt, thousands of youth gathered in Cairo's Tahrir Square in late January to begin their own protests against the Mubarak government ... for a variety of political and economic reasons. Here too, the Egyptian leadership folded – when Mubarak simply stepped down in mid-February ... placing a military junta in charge of the country. But this hardly satisfied the Tahrir Square assembly, which now was camped out there in rather permanent demonstration on behalf of the demand for food, jobs – and of course more personal freedom, as well as punishment for Egypt's former leaders.

Into the early summer the protests continued ... with conflicts between the protesters and Egyptian police growing more violent. Meanwhile the demands for the death penalty for Mubarak became a central theme ... at a time that Mubarak found himself actually quite ill. In August Mubarak was brought to trial ... and finally in June of the following year (2012) he and his sons were found guilty of corruption ... though they were soon acquitted on technical matters.

At the same time, presidential elections were held (two rounds, one in May and one in June of 2012), with the recently appointed Prime Minister Ahmed Shafik – representing the modernist or secular viewpoint (and the Egyptian military) – gaining 48.3 percent of the vote and Mohammed Morsi - representing a strongly traditionalist Muslim viewpoint (and the Muslim Brotherhood) – gaining 51.7 percent of the vote. Thus Morsi became Egypt's new president at the end of June. Realizing what was then likely to follow, Shafik flew to the United Arab Emirates – in order to avoid arrest. Indeed, in August, Morsi put out an order for Shafik's detention for questioning on "corruption" charges should he attempt to return to Egypt. So things went for "now democratic" Egypt.

But with Morsi's Muslim Brotherhood now trying to "change" Egypt, Morsi was finding himself facing a lot of pushback … especially after he took on whatever powers necessary to "protect the revolution." By June of 2013 tens of millions of Egyptians had taken to the streets across Egypt to protest the policies of Morsi … and the chaos that was tearing Egypt apart.

This was the cue for the Egyptian military to step in (also June of 2013), place Egypt's Defense Minister General Abdel Fattah el-Sisi in charge, and arrest Morsi. Now it was the turn of the Muslim Brotherhood to stage protests around the country. But so did the pro-Sisi supporters. Little by little, the military gained the upper hand … and the Muslim Brotherhood was forced to back down at the same rate. Something resembling peace and order finally descended on Egypt.

Most interesting, American President Obama was initially very upset about this overthrow of Egyptian "democracy" … although he then softened up a bit on the matter when he came to understand Morsi's massive unpopularity in an Egypt that did not want to be turned back into a rigorously Muslim society. Nonetheless, he still registered his ire about the military taking over in Egypt by ending all further sales of military equipment (such as the F-16 fighter jet) to Egypt. What he exactly hoped to achieve by such "punishment" was not clear. But it all certainly worked to the benefit of France … and Putin's Russia – glad to step in to service the Egyptian military's strategic needs.

In 2014, a new round of Egyptian elections was held – boycotted by the Muslim Brotherhood – resulting in Sisi's election to the presidency by a 96 percent vote – for a four-year term (until 2018; but reelected that same year) … a period in which Egypt made fair economic and social progress … unlike other parts of the Middle East.

Libya. Muammar Gaddafi's Libya was also hit very hard by the spirit of revolt sweeping the Middle East. Gaddafi had led the military overthrow of the Idris monarchy in 1969 ... and had been taking Libya on a very strange, and quite wandering journey ever since. Thanks to the vast oil wealth that flowed to Libya, the Libyans had been quite tolerant of Gaddafi's erratic rule. But as oil prices rose and fell, so did Gaddafi's ability to keep his people happy and in line with him. Besides his own peculiar behavior (he would swing back and forth in trying to become the Arab world's leader, then Africa's leader, and even something of a Third World philosopher), the cultural division between the two North African societies or cultures that had been thrown together by the Italians in creating their unified Libyan colony in 1934 had failed to make a truly "Libyan" society. Tripolitania in the West and Cyrenaica in the East were quite different in their reaction to Gaddafi's secularist tendencies ... Tripolitania tending to be rather supportive and Cyrenaica tending to be quite hostile to such modernizing tendencies. Thus Gaddafi could be quite heavy-handed in dealing with the dedicated opposition of Muslim Fundamentalists ... numerous in the Cyrenaica East.

Obama disliked Gaddafi because of his heavy-handed ways ... not realizing that should the Muslim Fundamentalist take control (there really was no group standing at the center between the strongly modernists and the strongly traditionalists) they would turn out to be just as heavy-handed. Obama's dream of somehow helping to set up the conditions for democracy to come to Libya would most certainly turn out disastrously.

And Obama (and the Liberal West) would have just such an opportunity to bring Libya to bloody chaos when the Arab Spring hit Libya ... due greatly to the drop in global oil prices – and therefore Gaddafi's ability to finance his governmental system.

Here the spreading world of Arab protest had little to do with anyone demanding "democracy" ... but instead a deep clash between Libyan modernism – heavily dependent on military support – and widely popular in the West ... and Libyan traditionalism – heavily dependent on Islamic fundamentalist or "jihadist" support – and widely popular in the East.

In any case, when violent protests broke out in Libya, in March (2011) the U.N. Security Council decided to get in on the act by passing a resolution 10-0 – with abstentions from Russia, China, India, Germany, and Brazil ... not a good start politically – calling for U.N. intervention in the growing civil war in Libya in order to "protect" the civilian population from Gaddafi's oppressive policies. And to provide this protection, France and Britain would take actual military action against Gaddafi (thus supporting the Muslim traditionalists in this conflict) ... with America providing supply and intelligence to France and Britain (and also knocking out Libyan air defense installations) ... though no ground troops. However, he did not get Congress's permission to engage in any of this, violating the 1973 War Powers Act, which upset many members of Congress when he claimed he did not need such Congressional authorization because American troops were not directly involved (except of course in the bombings and missiles sent against Gaddafi's forces!). NATO would then be called on to take over the bombing campaign in Libya ... helping the anti-Gaddafi rebels regain territory that they had lost in the first stages of the conflict.

This covering of the Western effort with moral justification, was furthered in June with the International Criminal Court issuing an arrest warrant against Gaddafi for committing crimes against his people.

In September a National Transition Council was set up in anticipation of the ultimate success of the effort to depose Gaddafi ... and was quickly recognized by the U.N. as Libya's legal representative.

Thus it was that the anti-Gaddafi forces – aided heavily by French, British and American involvement – drove the Gaddafi forces into retreat ... until they were able to seize and murder Gaddafi on the spot that October. Libya was now free! Fighting would continue ... though without its leader, it was destined to go nowhere. And some of the anti-Gaddafi militias refused to disarm ... keeping the situation very strained.

America would soon receive just reward for its contribution to the Libyan campaign, when in September of the following year (2012) Muslim militia (Ansar al-Sharia) killed the American Ambassador Christopher Stevens and two CIA contractors and wounded ten others. Interestingly, these Muslim jihadists were part of the group that America and the West had worked so hard to bring to victory in this civil war.

At first, American Secretary of State Hillary Clinton claimed that this tragedy resulted as a spontaneous act inspired by an anti-Muslim movie coming out about that time ... covering up the fact that this had obviously been a long-building operation – one which Ambassador Stevens was well aware of and had made repeated requests for enhanced security – which had simply been ignored. When the truth finally came out (a Congressional hearing in 2015), it would prove to be a major embarrassment to the Obama Administration. But it would be Hillary that would have to take the fall for the blunder. She would resign (in part also to prepare for her own run for the presidency in 2016) and Obama would replace her with former (but unsuccessful) 2004 Democratic Party presidential candidate John Kerry.

Syria. The "Arab Spring" would come to Syria as well ... although it would not hit until mid-March, when inspired young protesters filled the streets of Damascus, demanding various political "reforms" ... in line with the general mood that was challenging Tunisian and Egyptian leadership at that same time. The critical problem was that "reforms" meant very different things to very different groups joining the protest, some wanting more "modernization" along economic and secular cultural lines. Others wanted a move to more traditionalist Muslim cultural lines ... although the issue of Sunni versus Shi'ite lines divided these Muslim traditionalists bitterly. And another major problem was that Syrian society itself was a messy mixture of various ethnic groups, each with its own ethnic goals: Arab Sunni, Shiite, Alawi, Druze, Sufi, and Salafi Muslims ... plus Kurdish (non-Arab) Muslims, Arab Orthodox and Catholic Christians, and numerous tribal groups. Also the economy had been hit hard by a recent drought, Israel had been attacking savagely various Palestinian refugee groups that had fled to Syria, and thousands of Iraqis had escaped to Syria to avoid the American-initiated civil war tearing Iraq apart. Socially, Syria was a mess.

The only thing holding the country together (typical of fiercely multi-ethnic societies) was the strong hand of the young Syrian President Bashar al-Assad – a Alawi Muslim ... not one of the mainstream Muslim groups – and actually a strong Secularist of the "modernist" camp. As was typical of the way the Arab Spring was turning increasingly violent the longer the "reform" action continued, it soon moved from reform to civil war ... as "reformers" came to demand that Assad step down – only to be countered in the streets by huge numbers of Assad supporters insistent that the protesters back down.

Unsurprisingly, as the chaos worsened over the summer, the hand of Assad grew tougher ... until it had the West once again demanding that Assad go lightly in his effort to put down the rebellion (at that point he was even using chemical weapons). What might come to be the political outcome in Syria should he have given in to the rising demands of the West clearly was given no thought ... or else the Westerners were incredibly misinformed about how political dynamics worked outside of their own "polite" societies.

In August, Obama issued a threat to Assad that America would react strongly if he crossed a "red line" by continuing to use unacceptably repressive weapons – particularly the chemical weapons. But Assad chose to ignore the threat ... which then forced Obama to demonstrate what he meant by "react strongly." But it was quickly apparent that Obama had no such intent or capability to "react strongly." It was most embarrassing.

At this point Russian President Putin came forward by offering to mediate in the matter. But it also became quickly apparent that his real intentions were simply to draw Assad away from his former close relationship with the West ... and into his own Russian political orbit. And that is indeed what happened – as a result of the West's (most notably Obama's) diplomatic failure.

The worsening of the situation. In any case Assad managed to stay in relative command of a collapsing Syrian society ... despite the efforts at this point of Obama and the West to bring Assad down. In fact, America –

in concert with Saudi Arabia – began secretly to ship military items (even tanks) to a group of anti-Assad militants (the "Free Syrian Army") supporting the Syrian National Coalition ... recently formed by various groups outside of Syria – for various reasons. For Obama, supposedly this group would bring true "democracy" to Syria. To Saudi Arabia (and others) the purpose was to undercut the Shi'ites (Assad's Alawi were sort of a Shi'ite faction) and bring Syria under Sunni Islam.

In any case, it would not be this Coalition that would advance the Sunni Muslim cause but rather individual Muslim jihadists who gathered in war-torn Syria to put in place their jihadist dream of a restored Islamic caliphate (Islam's traditional society headed by a "caliph" or "successor" to Muhammad). They organized themselves around a political organization known in the West as the Islamic State of Iraq and Syria or ISIS[*] ... taking control of a huge amount of territory in chaotic Syria and a bitterly resentful Iraq ... Sunnis angry that Americans had turned their formerly Sunni Ba'athist government over to the Shi'ites. Indeed, in 2014, ISIS was able to put in place that very caliphate, under Abu Bakr al-Baghdadi.

And at this point ISIS was drawing fired-up young Sunni Muslims to the region to join the great jihad ... butchering in the most graphic ways (recorded on camera and displayed to the world via the internet) any one they deemed opposed to their mission and blowing up Shi'ite mosques. They even (beginning in June of 2015) blew up the formerly well-preserved 2000-year-old Roman town of Palmyra – that too displayed proudly on the internet as another great Sunni achievement ... along with all the captured Syrian soldiers, medical personnel – and men, women and children of the town – also butchered in typical jihadist style. By the end of 2015, ISIS held within its territorial control some ten million people, under the command of some 30,000 jihadists.

The spread of the disaster. Not to be left out of all the excitement, the youthful spirit of reform even spread to the West itself, with young protesters taking to the streets of Athens in June of 2011 – to take on violently the police sent to disperse the growing mob that had gathered there to protest against various Greek injustices. And in England, in August of that year, minority youth took up the cause ... to plunder, then torch, various neighborhoods of London – and then other British towns as well – their purpose being ...? And by that October, Italian youth had joined the fun, torching sections of Rome in protest against "economic injustice."

---

[*]ISIS's roots reached back to 1999 when the Salafi Jihadist Abu Musab al-Zarqawi founded a jihadist organization designed to collapse the Western political-social-cultural order ... which would go on to support bin Laden's al-Qaeda organization ... and other similar jihadist groups – culminating in ISIS.

Nor were young (and some older) Americans going to pass up this opportunity to protest against American "economic injustice" ... citing an older attack opposing the 2008-2009 Washington bailout of failing American corporations - that is, attacking the "too big to fail" mentality behind the rescue of American capitalism – as they moved to "Occupy Wall Street." For two months (mid-September to mid-November) they settled themselves into the heart of the Wall Street neighborhood, protesting economic inequality, greed, income inequality, and whatever other sins they detected in the way America worked economically and socially.   Having tolerated this event long enough, finally on the night of November 15th, New York police forced the protesters to shut down their encampment and move on. Attempts would later be made to start the process back up again. But these failed to take hold. Whatever Occupy Wall Street was designed for seemed ultimately to have virtually no impact on American society ... other than to have given the news something to keep themselves busy reporting.

The truly tragic part of all this – of the Arab Spring – however, is what it did to Syria (and parts of Iraq). The decision of the larger world to get involved in the Syrian social breakdown turned matters there much worse – far, far worse. As a result of the civil war – and of the takeover by ISIS – huge parts of Syria became totally devastated (its cities in deep ruin) and humanly uninhabitable. As a result, millions of Syrians found it necessary to flee the violence and economic collapse hitting them. But where were they to go? But by early 2018, some 5½ million Syrians had escaped to very dismal refugee camps in Lebanon, Jordan, Turkey and Iraq.   But others were able to get to Europe, where Greece, Italy, France, Germany and others took them in.   Indeed, Germany alone took in over a million refugees ... including some from Iraq and Afghanistan.

Lessons not learned.   Once again, the West's (particularly America's) devotion to the crusade to spread democracy to the rest of the world (by force if necessary) succeeded only in making a social crisis far, far worse than it should have been. Rather than helping a leader of a country maintain some degree of control over the instinctive love of youth to take to the streets to improve a world they are just getting to know (and thus know very little about it at that point), the West chose the side of the protesters ... seeing in such fired-up behavior the roots of the personal freedom that they have long supposed – since the time of Rousseau back in the French world of the 1700s – is the underlying foundation of democracy. The failure of the French Revolution in the late 1700s should have made it quite clear to these dreaming Idealists why it is that this type of thinking is virtually guaranteed to produce nothing but social disaster.

It is easy to wonder what the International Criminal Court – had it existed at the time – would have tried to do about Lincoln committing "crimes" against his people – which they accused Gaddafi of doing – when in 1861 Lincoln sent his troops against American Southerners intent on preserving slavery by breaking from the American Union. Thus too, under these "higher" moral terms of the ICC – and Western Liberalism in general – Washington should never have been allowed to put down either Shay's Rebellion in 1786 or the Whiskey Rebellion in 1791. Instead, the new American union should have been allowed to go down the "natural" democratic route ... one guaranteed to collapse into social chaos an otherwise long-standing (since the early 1600s), self-created and self-disciplining America – an amazing society that so many Americans had just died in the recent war with England to preserve and protect.

Apparently, under democracy, a society has no right to use its disciplining forces to stop a bloody rebellion from destroying it.

But this is exactly the reason that America's Founding Fathers, in putting together an American Constitution in 1787, were dedicated to founding a Republic ... not a Democracy. They were very clear on this matter because unlike today, they knew their own Western history very well ... and they understood completely the verdict of Aristotle about good and bad government. They understood that a good society is built not on the particular form of government, whether by one, a few, or the many – but instead on the strength of the moral foundations holding that society together ... and guiding its government in keeping it moving ahead on exactly those foundations. They knew from the Roman philosopher-politician Cicero what happens to a society when it decides to "upgrade" those foundations on the basis of some new sense of higher enlightenment on the part of supposedly well-meaning individuals or groups, an "upgrading" that throws the whole moral-legal basis of that society into confusion ... and ultimately bloody tyranny.

In short, you don't mess with a community's structure. True, there are issues – political, economic, and social – that constantly need to be addressed. But you don't throw the moral-legal structure itself into confusion with "revolutionary" changes ... especially those that are built simply on the whims of an ambitious leadership or on the fiery impulses of a people. Political tyranny is guaranteed to be the end product of such a dynamic ... and never a new society now enjoying greater peace and prosperity.

This is the reason that the Founding Fathers chose to bring the former colonies, but now independent states, together in a Federal Union as a Republic ... and not as a Democracy. They understood that a Republic is a society built on a strong foundation of Law ... not on the ever-changing (and usually very selfish) human desires of this or that group or party of the demos (the people) ... typical of a democracy. They were fully aware of the way democracy is easily led by ambitious people-charmers or "Sophists" to do very short-sighted, solely self-interested, and thus socially self-destructive things.

True, they would give voice to the people themselves in the House of Representatives. But the rest of the Federation was built on much narrower political entitlements expected to give a necessary conservative voice to American governance: respected members of the Senate chosen by the governors or assemblies of each member state, the President chosen by an Electoral College whose members were also chosen by the officials of each member state, and Federal judges appointed by the President and confirmed by the Senate.

Of course these limitations would irritate greatly the rising voices at the beginning of the 20th century (Woodrow Wilson and his Democratic Party in particular) in favor of pure democracy ... who felt it imperative to change what they could of those limitations on purely popular government found in the Constitution.

Thus also began the grand effort to "make the world safe for democracy" ... involving an America jumping into an unprecedentedly bloody war – done so on behalf of such "democracy," which if successful, President Wilson assured the American nation would make this horrible war "the war to end all wars." What blind idiocy ... but an idiocy that refused to go away.

Thus by this time – as America and the West took up the challenges of the newly rising 21st century – the wisdom of the Founding Fathers had been long-forgotten in America (now clearly leading the West with its new version of "political wisdom") ... by Bush Jr., who presumed that he was going to bring democratic freedom to both Afghanistan and Iraq – and then by Obama, who planned to do the same in other parts of the Muslim Middle East. Intense suffering on the part of millions would be the only result of such cruel stupidity.

✳ ✳ ✳

ISSUES ELSEWHERE IN THE WORLD

Russia and Ukraine

Russia had been under the direction of Vladimir Putin since the beginning of the 21st century ... in one way or another. He was a former KGB officer (16 years with the KGB), then a politician who eventually (1996) joined Yeltsin's Administration as head of the new Federal Security Service (taking up the role of the former KGB), then briefly Russian prime minister (mid-1999 to mid-2000), and then acting Russian president when Yeltsin resigned. That fall he was elected Russian president, then reelected four years later.

But the Russian constitution allowed only two consecutive presidential terms ... so in 2008 Putin had one of his cabinet ministers, Dmitry Medvedev, run as president under his own authorization – with the understanding that Putin would then be appointed as prime minister.   From this position, the highly ambitious Putin could continue to run Russia – in conjunction with Medvedev of course. That arrangement would last during Medvedev's four years as president. At that point (2012), Putin then could run again as president (he won easily) – and Medvedev could serve as prime minister. This was thus jokingly termed a "tandemocracy" – or government run by two officials in tandem with each other! The actual fact was however that Putin was the new Stalin, Khrushchev, Brezhnev – possessing full authority to run Russia personally. That was, after all, the Russian political tradition since the time of the tsars.

Meanwhile, next door in Ukraine, the situation was quite confusing. The problem was that Ukraine is not wholly Ukrainian in language but a mix, with Russian-speaking Ukrainians becoming a greater portion of the population in eastern Ukraine ... with the easternmost provinces (or oblasts) of Luhansk and Donetsk being fully Russian-speaking. Likewise, the Crimean Peninsula, complements of the expulsion by Stalin of the Turkic peoples previously living there, was now completely Russian ethnically. Originally part of Soviet Russia, Crimea was attached to Ukraine in 1954 as some kind of Ukrainian gift by the post-Stalinist leadership.

Then with the process of trying to get all the various ethnic communities of the Soviet Union to become one Soviet-wise – meaning all Russian speaking - considerable efforts were made not only in the Stalinist era but also in the one that followed to make Ukraine (and others) fully Russian-speaking. Thus education of the rising generations was supposed to be only in Russian. Likewise business and every other public activity. But of course many of the Ukrainians fought back to keep their Ukrainian language and culture. So these dynamics - and tensions - were still there when the Soviet Union dissolved in 1991 and Ukraine found itself fully independent as a presidential republic.

Independent Ukraine's prime minister, Leonid Kuchma, was able to defeat Ukraine's first president, Leonid Kravchuk in 1994, ... on the basis of a promise to promote the further industrialization of Ukraine in very pro-market ways. Actually, his way turned out to be quite corrupt ... leading the press to attack him ... which he answered by shutting down any opposing voices. Despite all that, he was reelected in 1999 and served until 2005.

During Kuchma's second term, his prime minister Viktor Yuschenko and deputy prime minister Yulia Tymoshenko took on the leaders (Ukrainian "oligarchs") of the coal mining and natural gas industries (although

Tymoshenko herself was majorly wealthy as a gas industry executive!) ... causing the Ukrainian Communist Party (still in full operation) to join with groups representing the oligarchs to have Yuschenko voted out of office in 2001. Kuchma then replaced him with the very pro-Russian – and Russian-speaking - Viktor Yanukovych. But Yuschenko, joined by Tymoshenko, worked to rebuild their own support team.

As the 2004 election campaign got underway, Yanukovych accused Yuschenko of being a Nazi (a favorite piece of slander to throw at a political opponent) – which was far from true. Further, Yuschenko was poisoned and badly disfigured – but survived.

But even more significantly occurred the "Orange Revolution" ... (November 2004 to the final round of the elections in January of 2005). The first round in the voting in November was reported to have been conducted so corruptly – in favor of Yanukovych – that masses of protesters, inspired by Orange leader Tymoshenko, took to the streets in anger ... wearing orange-clothing symbolic of their stand. Actually, a lot of what inspired the matter was that Yuschenko came across as "one of the people" – the Ukrainian-speaking people. Yanukovich was viewed as simply the tool of the corrupt Kuchma – and way too Russian to the tastes of fervent Ukrainian nationalists.

In any case, as a result of the runoff elections (January 2005), Yuschenko became Ukrainian president and Tymoshenko became Ukraine's prime minister. But her position at the top of the energy issue made her an easy political target – in Russia as well as Ukraine, as it turned out. Charges of corruption both in Russia and Ukraine were brought against her. And then Yuschenko turned against her ... and forced her to resign (that same December). But she was able to rally sufficient political support for her bloc to take a huge number of seats in the 2006 parliamentary elections ... and thus Yuschenko called her back to power as prime minister in 2007 – serving in that position until 2010.

She ran (and barely lost) the presidential race against a returned Yanukovych in 2010 ... and then was imprisoned because of a criminal case brought against her (likely inspired by Yanukovych) ... although another massive uprising of the Ukrainian people in 2014 would result in her release from three years of imprisonment ... and the downfall of the Yanukovych government.

This February 2014 uprising, termed the "Revolution of Dignity," was again mostly about Ukrainian nationalism versus Russian cultural "intrusion" into Ukrainian society. In this, both Tymoshenko and Yanukovych served symbolically the Ukrainian and Russian sides. The event actually got going in November of 2013 when Yanukovych decided not to sign a trade agreement with the European Union – as directed by the Ukrainian Rada (Parliament)

– but instead to enter into a closer economic relationship with Russia. This is what started the calls for Yanukovych's resignation. By the following February, a huge encampment of youthful protesters had gathered at a square (*maidan*) in central Kyiv (thus the Maidan or Euromaidan Uprising). When police were sent to clear the square, over a hundred protesters and 13 police officers were killed in the 5-day confrontation.

The end result (21 February) was that Yanukovych agreed to set up an interim unity government, undertake constitutional reforms, and hold early elections. But when police retreated from the scene, Yanukovych chose to take himself to Moscow. And the next day the Rada voted overwhelmingly to remove Yanukovych from office.

But this was not the only result. Yanukovych claimed that the Rada had conducted an illegal coup … and called on Russia for help. This was then the signal for pro-Russian groups in the eastern provinces to take local control – even declaring full independence (such as in Donetsk and Luhansk) … which they would then hold from that point on. Thus, Ukrainian sovereignty in its eastern oblasts was mostly a fiction from that point on … despite how the international community chose to view matters.

Even more brazenly, this gave Putin (with enthusiastic support from the Russian Diet) the opportunity to march masked and unmarked soldiers (the "little green men") into Crimea (February and March of 2014) and grab the Russian-Ukrainian joint naval base – and end the Ukrainian part of the naval partnership. Crimea was now fully a Russian oblast … though it still had to be reached by land via sections of territory still held by Ukraine. Solving that deeply annoying problem for Russia would come later.

And what did the Western world's American leader do in response to this bold power grab by Putin? Actually Obama had already sensed that Putin was about to do something to take advantage of Ukraine's problems … and in a 90-minute phone call to Putin, warned him not to make a move on Ukraine, or "serious consequences" would result. Obviously, Putin was not impressed – seeing Obama as a man of high principle … and weak action (the two often go together!) and thus made his move on Ukraine anyway.

Ultimately, Obama's "serious consequences" were for Obama to work out with the European Union arrangements to place degrees of energy-trade reductions against Russia – Russia's chief international income earner.

Ultimately, all this achieved was to put Obama on high moral ground … at considerable expense to America's European allies - who were (and still are) deeply dependent on Russian gas and oil supplies. As was clear to all, America, still being energy-independent at the time, put these "consequences" into effect at no cost to America itself. In fact, feelings of irritation were easily aroused because the cutback in Russian energy clearly increased prices and thus the profitability of the American energy export sector!

Xi's China

BRICS is a grouping of Brazil, Russia, India and China formed in 2009 – to which South Africa was joined in 2010 to make this grouping come to be termed BRICS. Together, these five countries contain 42% of the world's population ... seeking a similar figure in terms of the world's wealth – basically in competition with the G7 bloc of Canada, France, Germany, Italy, Japan, Great Britain and America – this latter group containing only 10% of the world's population but over half of the world's wealth. The European Union (EU) serves also as something of an associate G7 member ... making the group essentially the economic (and somewhat political) voice of the "West."

It is the understood goal of BRICS to replace the West as the dominating force in world affairs, politically, economically, socially and culturally. It is a curious matter for them to hold the goal of mutual global dominance by 2050 – given the often-bitter rivalry between India and China ... and occasionally China and Russia. But having the West as a mutual opponent serves to keep such unity in place ... at least to some extent.

One of the items they wanted to put in place was a New Development Bank – to rival the West-dominated and long-standing International Monetary Fund (IMF). The purpose was to steady their own fluctuating currency markets and create reserves for their own economic development. However, China already takes care of itself in this matter – but offered to take the lead in funding the bank ... in order to take the lead in BRICS itself. The goal was also to attract more countries to their side of the East-West competition ... by being able to extend development monies to these other countries – something that China was already very busy doing.

Indeed, as of the beginning of 2024, Iran, Ethiopia, Saudi Arabia, Egypt, Argentina and the United Arab Emirates joined BRICS – making it what ... BRICSIESEAU? Some 35 other countries have also indicated a desire to join the organization. This does not bode well for the dollar-dependent Western industrial world ... which is of course the purpose of the BRICS venture in the first place.

From Deng to Xi. All of this is in keeping with China's express goal of making itself the sole global superpower by the middle of the 21st century. Tragically, Deng Xiaoping's effort to shape Chinese leadership into a collective matter in order to prevent any further Mao-like concentration of power in a single hand did not outlast Deng's stepping down from Chinese leadership at the end of the 1980s.

Behind him came Jiang Zemin, who began the process of acquiring full power as China's leader. He began his move to power in 1989 by taking position as the General Secretary of the Chinese Communist Party ... as well as the vital Central Military Commission – Deng's only formal office. Then in 1993, he took office as the country's president as well – thus holding personally the reins to both party and civil government. Thus when he stepped down from his various offices in 2002-2005 (the last to leave being the Central Military Commission) such autocratic power had once again become the style of Chinese leadership.

This understanding of the Chinese leader's role was then passed on to the younger Hu Jintao, who also came to soon hold all three positions – until he stepped down from those various offices in 2012 and 2013. And he would be followed – in all three vital offices – by the very ambitious Xi Jinping. Xi was actually groomed for that position all the way back in 2007-2008, when Hu made him China's second in command in both the party and civil governments.

Xi's social-economic policy. Once in full power in 2013, Xi tightened his grip over Chinese life even more than his predecessors. He interned into rather Mao-like "reeducation" (concentration) camps some one million Turkic-Muslim Uyghurs in the Xinjiang province ... in order to make way for the takeover of the region by Han ("true") Chinese. He tightened censorship of the Chinese" wired" (internet) generation – and took up much of Mao's style to develop a "cult of personality" ... the usual way of gaining popularity as the people's "tyrant" (the leader who does the thinking for the people). Thus he also made himself the leader of the National Security Commission ... responsible for maintaining Chinese "law and order" – thus full control of Chinese society at all levels of its existence.

But his ambition was not only to lock down China under his grip ... but to bring the world under that same grip. And he would first use the growing power of the Chinese economy and its highly disciplined (and obedient) workforce to begin the process ... before moving to more ambitious diplomatic and then military means.

Actually, the economic move was made well before Xi arrived on the scene ... starting out with the West's encouragement of China to go down the international corporate trade route ... but allowing the Chinese exemptions to the IMF's currency regulation requirements. In other words, the Chinese were able to print enough currency (renminbi or yuan) that it would make Chinese products incredibly cheaper than goods produced in the West. The government was even allowed to subsidize Chinese industry in its covering production costs to ensure that Chinese products not only sold well abroad, but would be able to corner the market for a number of goods. As a consequence, the Chinese economy began to show such growth since 1990, that it doubled the value of the Chinese economy every seven years!

Chinese profitability became so great that the Chinese government made itself available to America to help cover its rapidly mounting national debt – considered at first to be a very generous act ... until it began to dawn on Americans that China was actually purchasing economic leverage on American government operations in a very subtle way.

In fact, everything that China did was very subtle ... sort of like the ancient Chinese board game of "Go" – the object of which is to be able to place stones on the 19x19-block checkerboard so as to surround and confine the opponent. This is why the Chinese agreed to form the close economic relationship of BRICS in 2009-2010.

Thus the Chinese not only put themselves in a position at home to dominate the market, under Xi's new leadership, they then also began to "assist" other countries here and there – with their 2013 Belt and Road initiative (also known as China's "New Silk Road" Initiative) – by using their huge dollar reserves to invest and take leadership in various sectors of the economies of these largely Third World countries (but also most of the countries of East Europe) ... especially in the realm of the mining and production of very strategic raw materials.* And they were playing the same games with not only America's position abroad but also with that of America's European allies.

Of course complaints were made to China at the point that it was clear that Chinese benefits first extended to China – when it was struggling to get moving down the industrial road – no longer were fair now that China was the world's second largest national economy (after America). And the American and European economies and rising unemployment in their workforces were clearly taking a hit from the Chinese economic policy.† But Obama quickly learned that the Chinese would not budge from their pivotal position – when Obama's negotiators came back empty-handed from talks with the Chinese. Why should China give up anything ... when America and the West had nothing to offer in exchange?

---

*The number of countries brought into this Chinese game would come soon to be more than 150 countries ... with 75 percent of the world's population and over half of the world's production capacity.

†Obama's Democratic Party would also be hit hard by these sad economic developments in the 2010 Congressional elections – which led to a Republican takeover of the House – and a gain of seven seats in the Senate (though not yet a Republican majority) ... as well as large Republican gains in the states' and cities' elections.

Xi takes charge of the South China Sea. Actually, Chinese ambitions in the South China Sea – which extends south from China, passing the Philippines in the East and Vietnam in the West and reaching all the way south to Malaysia and Indonesia – had already begun (cautiously) even before Xi arrived on the scene. Even Jiang, back in 2000, commented about the necessity of a great power to possess a strong maritime presence ... and by 2006 was using "law enforcement ships" to police the South China Sea. Then Hu's 2008 comment about the country's need for self-defense was followed up the next year with the publication of the nine-dash lines map, claiming historic rights to the Exclusive Economic Zone (EEZ) which reached down and across the South China Sea ... to just a few miles off the shores of the other countries surrounding that sea.

The Philippines and Japan had already come to strong disagreement with China over China's territorial claims – and the way they were handled in the matter of oil exploration and fishing rights in those waters – when in 2009 Malaysia and Vietnam submitted to the U.N. their own claims to those waters. And in 2010, Obama stated (via his Secretary of State Hillary Clinton) that America had a very strong interest in seeing the "open access to Asia's maritime commons" (the open high seas) maintained – at a time at which Chinese-Americans relations were reaching a very low point.

Then in 2011, the Spratly Islands to the West of the Philippines became a hot issue when Chinese naval ships forced a Philippine ship to leave the area ... at a time when the Vietnamese were growing increasingly irate at the harassment by Chinese ships of Vietnamese ships doing exploratory work in what it claimed were Vietnam's offshore oil fields.

The following year (2012), Obama announced a "Pivot to Asia" strategy, attempting to shift American foreign policy away from the Middle East (a disaster at that point) and direct it more to East Asia. This pleased Australia, Vietnam, Japan, Korea, etc. It upset even more Xi – who read this as an American effort to impose itself into what China considered the region that it was supposed to "lead" (willingly or not on the part of its neighbors). However, Obama indicated that this new policy was as much directed to the bettering of American-Chinese relations as it was with the relations with its other Asian "partners." Xi did not buy this explanation at all.

That was also the year that China launched its first aircraft carrier.

In 2013, the Philippines challenged China before the U.N. Permanent Court of Arbitration for violating the U.N. Convention on the Law of the Sea (UNCLOS). But China simply refused to submit itself to arbitration – claiming that the U.N.-appointed tribunal lacked jurisdiction in the matter. Thus a 2016 verdict in favor of the Philippines was simply ignored by China.

While all this was going on, China began to dredge some reefs in the Spratly Islands, creating an island – on which they could then build an airstrip and naval and military facilities ... clearly to put muscle behind their territorial claim to the entire South China Sea. By 2016, work there was completed.

And what was Obama's response in his Pivot to Asia? As Xi expected, Obama was a man of words – and little else. Why hadn't Obama ordered the dredging of his own island ... to put some kind of muscle behind the rightful claim that this was "high seas" – vital to the economies of all surrounding nations – and not the exclusive territorial possession of China. Thus like the game of *Go*, this was a big China win – and an equally big loss by America and the West ... from which there would be no opportunity for a comeback.

Iran

Although very conservative Muslims had taken control of Iran with the fall of the Shah in 1979, there remained in Iran a large portion of the population that was quite "modern" and pro-West ... even though supportive of the country's new Islamic Republic. Tragically, during the first years of the new Islamic Republic under presidency of the Muslim cleric Ayatollah Ali Khamenei (1981-1989) – and the overall direction of the country by the Supreme Leader Ayatollah Ruhollah Khomeini – the treatment of such pro-Westerners was quite harsh ... with thousands (the actual figure unknown) of Iranians being killed by the decisions of the revolutionary courts, controlled by the Revolutionary Guards.

When Khomeini died in 1989, Khamenei took his position as Supreme Leader – although the country actually moved to a more "modernist" position with Akbar Hashemi Rafsanjani becoming Iran's president. Then in 1997 Rafsanjani was followed in office by the cleric Mohammad Khatami – who basically continued Iran's democratic reforms ... irritating the Islamic conservatives in the process. And in 2005, with Rafsanjani eligible to run again as president, he found himself up against the arch-conservative Tehran mayor Mahmoud Ahmadinejad. The elections that year went strongly in favor of Ahmadinejad – 61.7 percent to Rafsanjani's 35.9 percent. Thus it was that Iran turned back to being again a very militant Shi'ite Muslim Republic ... very hostile to the West – and America in particular.

When elections took place then in 2009, Iran exploded into violence when Ayatollah Khamenei came could strongly for Ahmadinejad – who again won with a resounding 62.6 percent of the vote against the centrist Mir Hossein Mousavi with 33.7 percent – and some 14 million unused ballots were discovered (along with other voting irregularities). Anti-Ahmadinejad protesters took to the streets (the Green Movement), only to be opposed by Ahmadinejad supporters – and the situation turned very ugly. Interestingly, America and the West stood with the protesters in their view of the integrity of the election, whereas Asian (including China), African, and Latin American countries supported Ahmadinejad. In any case, Ahmadinejad was soon able to bring things back under control ... and continue to move the country down the very conservative Shi'ite Muslim road.

But there was another issue that drew the West into great concern about developments in Iran. Ahmadinejad had been pressing forward the matter of nuclear development in Iran – finding the U.N. in opposition because this development violated a number of international agreements. Ahmadinejad protested that Iran's nuclear development was strictly for low-level atomic energy production ... not for military purposes. But with Iran sitting on top of one of the world's largest oil and gas reserves, the need for nuclear energy made little economic sense. Furthermore, it was known that Iran was working hard to develop its missile technology. America and the West were very unhappy. But there was little they could do.

Then with the election in 2013 of the cleric – but a modernist reformer – Hassan Rouhani as Iranian president, Iran moved to improve relations with the West. The huge issue that had to be dealt with was Iran's nuclear program. Negotiations between Iran and the U.N. Security Council members, plus Germany, thus got underway over this matter ... resulting in the 2015 Joint Comprehensive Plan of Action (JCPOA). Under this plan, Iran agreed to undo much of its nuclear program and allow inspectors to inspect its nuclear sites to confirm that they were in conformity with the agreement – Iran in return having its oil markets again open to the West and having banking assets abroad that had been previously seized now released in stages.

Obama and his secretary of state Kerry assured America that this was the best way to keep Iran (at least for the foreseeable future) from developing nuclear weapons. Others however, and most notably Israel, were very unconvinced that Iran would not find some way to continue weapons development out of sight of the inspectors. And the Iranian further development of its missile technology was of enormous concern to Israel – especially given the many statements that Iran liked to make about bringing the West to its knees. But JCPOA would be accepted by Washington – at least as long as Obama remained as America's president.

The European Union

The Treaty of Nice (2001-2003). In 2001, European Union member-states signed a treaty at Nice, to provide for changes in the EU's legal basis so as to be able to include newly-independent nations of the former Soviet bloc ... and other countries as well seeking association with the EU.

Agreement on the terms of this treaty did not come easily (reminiscent of the problems between America's larger and smaller states when they assembled to draw up a new constitution in 1787) ... as France wanted equally-weighted voting in the Council ... and Germany, with a much larger population, felt that representation should vary according to the size of the member country – with its reunification Germany now being the largest of the EU members. The results were the compromise of a "double majority" – both a majority of the member states as well as a majority of the EU population to be represented in a "yes" vote on matters.

Also troubles arose when a unanimous consent of all member states was necessary for the ratification of the Treaty ... and Ireland, when the Treaty was put to a popular referendum, with a very low voter turnout, at first failed to approve the Treaty. Many of the Irish, who were of a mind to stay neutral in the world's various international contentions, were afraid of turning its foreign policy over to an international authority. After much debate on the matter, a year later a second referendum was held and the Irish finally approved the Treaty.

In any case, this opened the door for the entry of new members into the EU ... with Poland, Hungary, the Czech Republic, Slovakia, Slovenia, Estonia, Latvia, and Lithuania joining in 2004 – along with Cyprus and Malta. And then Bulgaria and Romania followed in 2007. Thus at this point, EU membership stood at 28 countries. Only Switzerland and Norway, plus Albania and several of the former Yugoslavian regions of the Balkans, found themselves out of this much-expanded European "West."

The Treaty of Lisbon (2007-2009). In 2007, members of the European Union signed a treaty in Lisbon that made some significant developments in the legal character of the EU. Step by step, Europe had been moving toward an all-European government system that resembled the governments of most of the member states. However, an earlier effort in 2005 to create a stronger constitution had failed, when French and Dutch voters rejected constitutional revisions put before them for ratification.

But the 2007 treaty was accepted – again only after two attempts at passage in Ireland with a "no" in 2008 and then finally a "yes" in 2009.

The treaty provided for the continuance of the European Council - made up of the leaders (usually the prime ministers) of the various member countries, whose task has long been to give the EU its general direction and to make policy decisions for the union. The treaty likewise continued to assign the Council the duty of appointing and overseeing the European Commission – the "Cabinet" or committee that had the responsibility of managing the day to day operations of the EU ... including its rather hefty bureaucracy.

Where the Treaty of Lisbon beefed matters up was in making the

European Parliament, whose members were directly elected by the citizens of the members states, something of a co-equal legislative branch alongside the Council – requiring the two bodies to work together in supporting or vetoing decisions of the European Commission, in determining the EU budget, and in shaping the EU's foreign policy … although the Council still carried greater weight than the Parliament in foreign policy matters. Likewise, the Treaty created the offices of President, to lead the Council, and a High Representative of the Union for Foreign Affairs, something like an EU Foreign Minister.

THE BRIEF TRUMP ERA

Donald Trump

The 2016 elections. The Democrats put forward as their presidential candidate Hillary Clinton … clearly moving down the Progressivist or post-traditionalist road in doing so – and expecting a dazzling electoral victory in the 2016 presidential elections in doing so.   But weren't they shocked when the person who represented most vividly the traits that Progressivist America deplored won the election. How did this happen?

Apparently there were still a "basketful of deplorables" out there, conservative voters as Hillary herself termed them … unable to see the moral picture clearly. And thus they voted for the highly ego-centric and theatrical (thus true Boomer) Donald Trump. But the reaction was immediate. Not only in America but across the world masses of people (mostly youth … and women dressed in pink) turned out in huge numbers to declare that Trump was "not my president."

Impeach, impeach, impeach. And immediately action was taken up by Congressional Democrats to find grounds to impeach Trump as quickly as possible. And they found documents (paid for by the Hillary election campaign) that supposedly connected Trump with some kind of Russian conspiracy to have him rather than Hillary elected as US President. And surely these offered the legal means to impeach Trump.

However, an investigating committee they assembled did not come up with the results they wanted – after a two-year effort to find something by which to bring Trump down. So they tried again, basing their second impeachment effort on the way Trump held off American payments to Ukraine until Ukrainian corruption could be cleaned up a bit … implicating Democratic leader Joe Biden's son in the corruption matter. But the

Democrats backed down when they realized bringing Joe's son Hunter into the discussion would hurt rather than help their impeachment effort. So they simply switched to Trump's impeachment on the basis of his refusal to honor subpoenas demanding his appearance in front of the Democratic-controlled Congressional committee pursuing the impeachment possibilities.

Tragically, all this pointed out how deeply America was divided. There seemed to be no middle ground between Republican Party "conservatives" and Democratic Party "progressives" splitting the country into two hostile communities. And the media was no help in the matter, slanting the "news" – again, mostly just deeply ideologized social commentary – on the one hand in support of the "Trumpian" Republicans (mostly Fox News) and, on the other hand, in support of Trump's dedicated opponents (mostly all the other national media).

Trump's flamboyant personality. And Trump was no help in the matter. He had no professional experience in public office ... and seemed totally unaware of the niceties required to make a contentious political engagement not go up in flames. Indeed, besides being a very wealthy, very successful, urban construction magnate, he was a host for years of a widely-watched TV program ... one that delighted in bring in contestants and then cutting them down ("you're fired") in some kind of competition for larger service in the community. Trump used that same TV flare to undercut his fellow Republican contestants in the 2016 race for the Republican Party presidential candidacy. He termed his election opponent "Crooked Hillary." But even before that, in the Republican primaries he termed his opponents "Little Marco" (Senator Marco Rubio) or "Lyin' Ted" (Senator Ted Cruz). About Florida governor Jeb Bush (another son of Bush, Sr.)

> *Jeb failed as Jeb! He gave up and enlisted Mommy and his brother (who got us into the quicksand of Iraq). Spent $120 million. Weak no chance!*

He even went after former Republican presidential candidate – and well-recognized war hero and national patriot John McCain:

> *. . . not a war hero, he's a war hero because he was captured. I like people that weren't captured.*

In this he would foolishly make dedicated opponents of the McCain organization. But Trump seemed not to care.

Trump simply had no idea of how to build support among any except those willing to follow him slavishly. He had his wild supporters of course. He built a huge Trump following around his "Make America Great Again" (MAGA) theme. But he seemed unable or just unwilling to bring the all-important political "center" to his support. That would require compromise. And he was just not interested in such political niceties. Theatrics seemed to be the only strategy (if you can call it a strategy) that he was willing to employ to get things done. But in this, he was fairly correct in understanding how political fortunes were made. It was critical to keep the media focused on you as a political candidate … hopefully positively. But any attention, even negative, served higher political purposes at this point in the American culture.

He used those theatrics a bit in his effort to develop a Trump "foreign policy" … although what that exactly amounted to was never very clear. He seemed to repulse most of his European allies. Germany's longstanding Chancellor Angela Merkel clearly disliked Trump … although she did her best to keep Germany on excellent working terms with its American ally. And neither Russia's Putin nor China's Xi seemed to have much regard for Trump. And whatever new relationship he thought he was building by way of his visits with North Korea's Kim Jung-Un seemed to go nowhere.

The Coronavirus disease 2019 (COVID-19)

Covid-19's global impact (2020-2021). An outbreak of the Coronavirus in Wuhan China in December of 2019 soon spread to the rest of the world in early 2020. When first Italy and Spain were hit particularly hard, they underwent a "lockdown" – keeping people in their homes, allowing them out only for such "essential services" as food shopping. Soon the idea was taken up by other countries … and by the different states in America. Restaurants, schools, churches, were shut down by governmental order … and the streets became deserted. But even then, by March, both Italy and America had overtaken China in the number of deaths reported from the virus.

Due to the similarity to previous Coronavirus outbreaks – the SARS virus (severe acute respiratory syndrome) in 2002-2004 and the MERS virus (Middle East respiratory syndrome) in 2012-2015 – vaccines to fight the virus were finally brought to production … notably first in America, then Britain (early spring of 2021) and by mid-2021 the Euro area and Canada.

According to the best estimates, these vaccines ultimately saved the lives of anywhere from 15 to 20 million deaths globally. But even then, as of October 2021, it was reported that some five million people globally had died from the virus. Hardest hit – in terms of population percentages –

tended to be Latin American and East European societies.*

The reopening of that closed-off existence was very gradual – crashing the economies of the world's societies as work came to a halt during those days of lockdown. America's economy declined by 9 percent in the second quarter of 2020. But for other industrial societies, the figures were worse: In the same quarter, Britain's economy declined by 21.4 percent; in the larger Euro area the figure was 12.4 percent, Canada 12.4 Percent, and Mexico 19 percent. Needless to say, the economic decline was at least as bad, if not worse – though precise figures are hard to come by – in the Third World.

However ... China actually benefited greatly economically from all this, pulling out of its Covid-induced economic downturn very quickly ... thanks to its government's infrastructure spending. In fact, because of the huge demand for Chinese goods still being produced while the rest of the world remained in its economic shutdown stage, China's economic growth reached nearly 30 percent in 2020! But this then allowed the Chinese government to slow its economic support for its industry in 2021, slowing the country's economic growth somewhat.

At the same time, massive inflation hit the world as markets reopened ... and prices skyrocketed for the small amount of production available for sale at that point.

The political outfall in America

Congress gets in on the act. In early March, Trump authorized $8.3 billion in emergency funding for hospital care and medical research. But by mid-March it was very apparent that this hardly addressed the depth of the crisis – and thus Trump requested of Congress $1.2 trillion ... not only for medical support but also to help keep struggling businesses alive. But Congress's House Majority Party (Democrat) leader Nancy Pelosi responded with a call for $2.5 trillion instead ... which included funding for Democratic Party goals of educational programming, environmental support, and other items – items that had nothing to do with the virus outbreak. Furthermore, her program involved a cutback in support for the deeply suffering American business world. But she was going to hold the Coronavirus spending hostage until she got Trump and the Republicans to move things in her direction. Finally she got the Republicans to accept a $2.2 trillion spending bill ... which included a $1200 or $2400 grant to every American household (depending on single or double adult status) ... for whatever reasons. All of this added

____

*For America, that number was 827,000 deaths. Globally the 5 million count probably is rather low, as Third World countries did not collect data adequately. In fact, it is speculated that in India alone, over 4 million people may have died of the virus.

enormously to the country's national debt.

Black Lives Matter. But there were other repercussions from the way the virus hit the American nation. In May of 2020, a Black man, George Floyd, was taken down by a White cop, Derek Chauvin, and held to the ground by keeping his knee on Floyd's neck, with an already somewhat sick Floyd protesting that he couldn't breathe. Consequently, Floyd died. All of this was caught on camera ... and shown across all the media, Facebook and YouTube as well as the national media. Black protests were immediate and extensive ... conducted under the theme "Black Lives Matter." But this also turned into the occasion for more Black plunder and torching of American cities across the country.

Antifa. But this soon inspired young, mostly White "Anti-Fascist" (or "Antifa") protesters to join the protests – the pandemic restrictions helping immensely to inspire an Antifa attack on the "Fascist" American police ... called out to bring widespread rioting back under some degree of control. Indeed, it soon appeared that Antifa believed that it was conducting some kind of revolution against all social authority – especially when in June, Antifa youth were allowed to take control of downtown Seattle and turn six city blocks into their police-free "Capitol Hill Autonomous Zone" ... defended by fully-armed youth.

"Defund the police." At the same time, a number of big-city mayors (Liberal Democrats) joined the furor by announcing that they would be helping to "defund the police" ... transferring police funding to more worthy social causes. At this point "defund the police" had become a key piece in the "political correctness" followed closely by aspiring young politicians (and some of the older ones as well). But this would leave America's urban police underfunded and soon understaffed, as police retired in massive numbers in response to this new social mood. Unsurprisingly, the crime rate in America climbed rapidly as a follow-up.

The American immigration crisis

The massive movement of people – mostly across the Mexican-American border – is not a new thing ... with as many as 1.5 million+ apprehended at that border in the year 2000, a drop in 2003 to 900 thousand, a rise to 1.2 million in 2005, then a drop in 2011 to around 400 thousand. Originally these were mostly Mexicans seeking refuge in America. But by 2014, about half of these illegal entrants were non-Mexican, principally from the three Central American or "Northern Triangle" countries of Guatemala, Honduras and El Salvador. And by 2014, this number included a massive increase in the number of "unaccompanied minors" crossing the border ... thanks largely to a 2008 law offering protections for just such minors – played up by smugglers to increase their businesses.

During his electoral campaign in 2016, Trump promised that he was going to build a huge fence across the border with Mexico ... and make Mexico cover its costs. There was no way that this was going to happen. But Trump did what he could in coming to office in doing some building – or more often, rebuilding – of that wall ... some 450 miles of construction – which Mexico did not pay for! But the overall length of the border is 1,954 miles ... offering illegals plenty of opportunity to find their way into America through the more remote (and more dangerous) routes.

And Trump attempted to block all unregistered entry into America ... requiring migrants claiming asylum rights to register at the border – and remain in Mexico until they could be processed for entry. As a consequence, by 2019, there were well over a million individuals waiting in Mexico for their cases to be heard.

But with the global Coronavirus outbreak, the rate of illegal immigration across that southern border skyrocketed ... and there was actually very little that Trump could do to stop that huge influx.

Venezuela

In 1999, Venezuela underwent something of a Cuban-like social revolution, installing a "popular" dictatorship under Hugo Chavez, in which Chavez planned to use Venezuela's massive oil earnings to bring Venezuela under full Socialism. In 2013, Chavez died, and his place was taken by Nicolás Maduro – who basically continued the Chavez program – including its strong dislike of America.

But international oil pricing had dropped considerably in those years ... leaving the Venezuelan government no longer able to offer the rewards of Socialism to its people. In the meantime, huge numbers (about 4 million or 12 percent of the population) of the more entrepreneurial middle-class Venezuelans had simply abandoned their homeland ... as the country sank rapidly into national poverty.

Trump's response to all this was try to bring down the Maduro government in 2017, by ending oil imports from Venezuela* - as well as American food and medicine exports to Venezuela. And in 2018, America and the West did what it could to support the more politically centrist Juan Guaidó in his run for Venezuelan president that year. But that election was marked by much confusion and corruption ... plus the full support of Maduro

---

*Anyway, America really did not need Venezuelan oil as it was basically oil-self-sufficient by this point, thanks to American shale-oil production.

by the Venezuelan military. In any case, the Venezuelan National Assembly (and the West) concluded in 2019 that Guaidó was the person they would recognize as "interim president."

But the political reality was that Maduro considered himself properly elected to a second term as Venezuelan president ... and had China, Russia, Cuba, Iran and even Syria and Bolivia strongly supporting that claim – in an attempt to block all further American and Western influence in Venezuela ... and to replace that with Chinese, Russian, etc. influence not only in Venezuela but also in the broader Central and South American world.

China

Meanwhile, Xi Jinping moved to make his personal rule even tighter over China, getting the Chinese National People's Congress in March of 2018 to vote (2,964 to 2!) to end the Chinese constitution's two-term limit on the presidency ... that had been put in place when Deng Xiaoping brought China out of its terrible Maoist legacy in the late 1970s/early 1980s. The presumption supposedly was that putting China under ever-tighter presidential rule would guarantee the continuing move of China toward a similar ever-tighter global domination.

And the world of technology factored majorly in advancing China's international program. With the help of a lot of Chinese government subsidies, China's electronics communications industries have been able to capture much of the world market by being able to offer cheaper products – often just copies of Western technological development ... in complete disregard of the World Trade Organization's international patent rights. Thus China's telecommunications giant Huawei was able to move into a position of dominance in the new 5G telecommunications sector ... as well as China's Alibaba and Tencent, who have achieved monopolistic status in China, move to a position of dominance abroad by buying out foreign companies.

Trump tried to head off this Chinese move in March of 2018 by imposing tariffs amounting to $250 billion in Chinese goods coming into America ... in order to bring Chinese pricing closer to American products. But then China retaliated with a $100 billion tariff against American goods – although the balance of trade between the two countries was already heavily in favor of China. To try to work out a compromise between the two countries, Xi and Trump met at a G-20* summit in Japan in June of 2019 ... though little

---

*The G-20 (Group of 20) constitutes an international forum of the world's major industrial powers (including the European Union and the new African Union), formed in 1999 to work out international economic problems at the time. It meets at least annually to take on such questions as international trade and finance, but also climate change and sustainable social development ... or any other issue of timely global socio-economic importance.

was actually accomplished. But at least other Western countries moved down the same trail as Trump, to end the dumping of Chinese goods into their economies – or having the Chinese subsidized companies buy their European companies.

Nonetheless, as a sign of China's rising global status, in April of 2019 40 countries gathered in Beijing to celebrate the achievements of China's "Belt and Road Initiative" – started up in 2013 to integrate the world's economies with China's economy. Attending were not only Xi's new partner Putin, but also leaders of African and Middle Eastern nations. Even leaders from America's traditional partners Italy, Spain, Greece, Turkey and its new partners Poland, the Czech Republic, and Hungary – as well as America's Latin American friends Chile and Argentina – were in attendance. Even Switzerland left its long-standing neutral position in order to attend the event.

Russia

Clearly China and Russia had put aside their historic differences (border disputes in Central Asia) and had come together … for the single purpose of undercutting American international leadership – and the Western world looking to America for such leadership. Thus Russia's "President-for-Life" Putin was quick to join China in swinging to the support of any country finding itself in some form of contention with America or the West. And stupid moves by American leaders simplified that task greatly, as in the way Obama opened the door for Russia to come to the aid of Assad's Syria … and then Iran when Trump rejected Obama's treaty with Iran that had opened up Iranian oil sales to the West and Venezuela when Trump went up against Maduro.

And to further cement the Chinese-Russian connection, Xi and Putin worked together to develop China's Maritime Silk Road connecting China's economy more closely with Europe by means of a direct trade route across the now open waters of the Arctic above Russia's northern Siberia. At the same time the two countries tied their economies more closely together by means of a Russian pipeline sending much-needed natural gas to China … and extensive cooperation in the development of the new 5G technology – and other modern infrastructure development. Then too, Russia's natural gas pipeline to Europe – and Germany's dependence on that Russian gas supply to run its own economy – was designed to put Russia in a very strong economic position in the Western economies, once so very dependent on American leadership.

And all of this made the Russians more than glad to have Putin continue to govern their world. The 1990s experiment in democracy had been rather disastrous. And thus they were pleased to have Putin take the responsibility of self-government out of their hands and place that responsibility solely in his own hands. That was a political pattern more understandable to the Russians.

Indeed, in a poll taken by the Levada Center* in 2019, it was revealed that 70 percent of the Russians believed that Stalin played a completely or relatively positive role in the life of the country! In short, the clear majority of the Russian people wanted no further part of whatever it was that America or the European West had to offer as political Idealism (its "democracy").

The world of Islam

One of the great tragedies involving American leadership was the inability of its executive officers to understand the very complex cultural underlay of the various "nations" of the Middle East. These Middle Eastern states were societies highly divided by strongly opposing religious subcommunities – plus a huge division in their societies over this matter of what to do about the intruding Western cultural challenge. Bush and Obama somehow simply supposed that the Middle East was waiting anxiously to bring Western style democracy to their societies ... not realizing that this matter was already throwing Middle Eastern societies into horrible turmoil. While certainly there were those hoping for just such cultural change to come their way, this small group of Middle Easterners were more than offset by an even bigger group of Middle Easterners very, very hostile to the West and its ways. Thus 9/11. Thus Iran's "Death to the Great Satan America." Thus ISIS and the new Muslim Caliphate in the war-torn zone of Western Iraq and Eastern Syria. Thus even the long-time American NATO ally Turkey, taking on a more traditional Muslim look.

We have already noted that Obama finally made the shift away from trying to overthrow Muslim dictatorships ... by at least attempting to improve relations with the Ayatollah's Iran. But with Trump coming to the White House, that nuclear-development agreement was put aside – Trump being quite certain that any country whose motto was "Death to America" was not one to be trusted ... particularly with Iran also drawing ever-closer to America's major international opponents, China and Russia. Trump was certain that continuing to appease Iran with this or that diplomatic reward was not likely to back Iran away from its sense that in alliance with China and Russia, Iran had a much bigger game to play internationally.

At the same time, Trump was of the mindset that it was time to back America out of its very expensive involvement in Middle Eastern affairs ... at least in terms of American ground troops stationed here and there in

____

*FP Morning Brief (*Foreign Policy*), January 12, 2021.

the effort to support or oppose this or that regime. Thus it was that he made the decision to withdraw American troops from Syria ... and then begin negotiations in anticipation of a similar American withdrawal from Afghanistan. In this he was willing to work with even the Afghan Taliban and Afghanistan's various tribal leaders ... for a scheduled withdrawal as of May 2021 (Trump presuming that he would be reelected to a second term as U.S. president at that point).

By this, Trump did not mean the withdrawal of American national interest in the Middle East ... only a change in strategy. Indeed, in anticipation of his Syrian withdrawal, Trump ordered a brief but highly effective step up of an American air and ground offensive directed at the Islamic Caliphate ... and brought the Caliphate to collapse with a massive American bombing in January of 2019.   This did not end the Islamic spirit of jihadism. But it weakened it considerably with this demonstration of American resolve.

Trump then worked to strengthen the American position in the Persian Gulf region ... by beefing up America's naval presence there (and irritating the Iranians majorly), by selling arms to Saudi Arabia, and by leading Arab states of the region (Bahrain and the United Arab Emirates) to come to new diplomatic agreements with Israel ... strong diplomatic moves that were largely ignored by the mostly very Liberal American press – which was in no mood to acknowledge any Trump political or diplomatic achievement.

The chaotic American 2020 national elections

The Republicans again chose Trump and Vice President Mike Pence to be their candidates for the 2020 presidential race. And the Democrats chose the former Vice President and veteran DC politician Joe Biden to represent them in that race ... an amazing choice considering the fact that Biden was only two years short of his 80th birthday. Biden then announced that he would be selecting a "woman of color" to be his running mate ... a category rather than a particular individual being of greatest interest to him. He finally ended up selecting Kamala Harris, a U.S. Senator from California since 2017 and California Attorney General prior to that (2011-2017).

Tragically, the pandemic would add to the very unusual way that the election was conducted. From the selection of the candidates to the actual voting, actual physical participation was greatly handicapped by the new public participation restrictions. Thus the conventions of both parties were conducted mostly through online participation ... and the vote itself in November was done heavily by means of mail-in ballots.

But that in itself would become a matter of great political debate ... as the Republicans complained that mail-in voting easily led to fraud (no way to check to see who actually sent in the ballot or what actually happened to the ballots once sent out). The Democrats took the position that this made voting much easier – and more just … especially since it was well-known that the voters who did not bother to come out to vote at the local polling stations tended to be Democrats.

Ultimately, over 81 million votes went to Biden and over 74 million votes went to Trump. This was the largest number ever of votes cast in an American presidential election, with both candidates (even Trump) receiving more votes than any previous candidate. But Trump would not follow the long-standing tradition of graciously accepting the electoral verdict … but immediately went to a counterattack, claiming (without any specific evidence) that Biden had won the election strictly through voter fraud. And he would not back down from that position, even after Trump's Attorney General William Barr announced that an extensive FBI investigation into the matter found no evidence supporting the idea that Biden had won through widespread fraud. But still, Trump would not let up but did what he could to throw enough state elections into question (most notably in Georgia, Michigan, Nevada and Pennsylvania) in his effort to get the electoral vote to go in his favor. Nonetheless, on December 14th the Electoral College was called on to decide the vote … confirming Biden as the winner of the national election.

Then when on January 6th, Congress convened to give official authorization to the election and its results, Trump simultaneously called for a gathering in front of the White House … where he continued to complain about the fraudulent nature of the election – and then directed this massive crowd to head over to Capitol Hill to protest the election. This they did … in the process going crazy with their protest spirit, even invading the Capital Building itself – and sending the assembled legislators scrambling for safety. In all this mayhem, a female Trump supporter was shot and killed, several protesters died (presumably from medical emergencies), and numerous officers were hurt badly, one dying from his wounds, before they could be cleared out. Many of the participants would later be identified and arrested for what was clearly a federal crime.

Once again, demands for the impeachment of Trump resulted (the third such effort) … and indeed on the 13th of the month the House successfully voted exactly that. But the 2/3rds requirement in the Senate for an actual conviction failed, with 57 Senators (including 7 Republicans) voting to convict and 43 Senators (all Republicans) voting to acquit.

And Inauguration Day (January 20th) then followed … with Trump refusing to participate in the formal installation of the new president.

But private-citizen Trump would not simply slip off into quiet presidential retirement … for he himself had added considerably to the resolve of his political adversaries (enemies actually at this point) to put him behind bars as a common criminal.

✳ ✳ ✳

THE BIDEN ERA

The new president, Joe Biden, was pre-Boomer, that is, something of a "Silent" ... one of those individuals born just before or during World War Two and deeply committed to some higher cause shaped by forces larger than simply their own imagination. Biden was/is a "loyalist" not untypical of most Silents – a loyalist especially to the Democratic Party of which he has been a longtime member. He was elected to the U.S. Senate representing the tiny state of Delaware when he was only 30, served numerous terms, becoming even the lead Democrat of the Senate Foreign Relations Committee and, as a Democrat, running for the office of President a couple of times before becoming Obama's running mate and thus Vice President in 2008. Then finally – after four years out of the electoral office business (2016-2020) – he became America's President.

Given the fact that America itself seemed to have lost sight of exactly what it was that all Americans should stand for (and not just against), it is not surprising that Biden's "loyalism" found its natural place in a much narrower context than that of the American national interest. Indeed, was there even anyone with a sense of what that higher national interest truly should be at that point? As Biden took office, political interests seemed to register themselves almost solely along the lines of one or another of the narrower political interests dividing the country.

Briefly, very briefly, a flicker of hope arose when Biden pledged in his inauguration speech that he planned to be the president of all Americans, not just those who voted for him. But sadly, that same afternoon he entered his new presidential offices and issued 17 executive orders ... each one of them in support of the ideological agenda of his Democratic Party – most of them largely designed to undo whatever Trump had achieved during his four years in office. No conferences were held across party lines to bring a larger American grouping on board; no discussion, no explanation was offered. Biden simply jumped to the task of putting into full operation his party's political agenda ... because as president, he supposedly had the power to do so.

Thus it was that he made good on his campaign promise that he would halt further construction of a wall along America's southern border ... instead offering open borders to refugees seeking asylum in America. He ordered the halt of the construction of the Canada to America oil pipeline, despite the fact that this would also end petroleum self-sufficiency in North America ... because it contributed to the larger, and certainly very problematic, climate change impacting the world. And he soon made it clear that his Washington bureaucracy existed in order to take care of a younger generation not able to be brought to a better world simply through the efforts of family and local authorities.

The flood of immigrants into America.   Not surprisingly, all this became the signal for a flooding of the southern border by masses of people attempting to get into America – legally or illegally.   Within two years, that number exploded in size.   It was announced that as of the end of September, 2023, The U.S. Customs and Border Protection announced that some 3 million people had crossed the border during the previous fiscal year ... 142,000 have done so illegally simply during the month of September.   It was also reported that some 425,000 "unaccompanied children"* had been let into the country since Biden took office.

Of course, all of this was changing the ethnic-cultural character of the country ... as fully intended by the Democrats.   In 1965, under Johnson's Immigration Act, some 9.6 million foreign-born individuals were living in America ... some 5 percent of the population.   By the year 2000, there were over 30 million immigrants living in America - one-third of whom arrived in the 1990s.   And by 2020, that number reached approximately 50 million individuals, most of them (77%) legally ... the rest in the country as "undocumented" residents.

Mass migration elsewhere.   By the way, America was not the only country receiving this massive wave of immigrants.   As of the year 2020, Germany had 15.8 million international migrants living there (most coming from East Europe), Saudi Arabia 13.5 million (heavily from India), Russia 11.6 million, Britain 9.4 million, the United Arab Emirates 8.7 million (also heavily from India), France 8.5 million, Canada 8 million, Australia 7.7 million, and Spain 6.8 million.   Europe alone accounted for 86.7 million of those migrants.†   Contributing to this outflow were India, with 17.9 million having left the country, Mexico with 11.2 million having left their homeland, Russia with 10.8 million leaving, China with 10.5 million, and Syria with 8.5 million having done so.

Global warming and the energy question

Meanwhile, global warming has become an ever-growing concern ... as the

____

*The DACA program (Deferred Action for Childhood Arrivals) – originated by Obama back in 2012, terminated by Trump, and resumed by Biden in October of 2022.

†"Key facts about recent trends in global migration," Pew Research Center, December 16, 2022.

world's average surface temperature has increased by 1.1 degrees Celsius (nearly 2 degrees Fahrenheit) in comparison to the 1850-1900 pre-industrial average temperatures. Even that small of a shift has produced a growing number of heat waves, wildfires, droughts, flooding and huge storms. And this is expected to increase in the next century by as much as 4 degrees Celsius (over 7 degrees Fahrenheit). And despite the 2015 Climate Accord in which 189 countries agreed to reduce carbon dioxide emissions (the biggest single source of the problem), CO2 emission has actually continued to increase.

But this raises another question. Hydrocarbons (oil and gas) are the biggest cause of global warming ... but they are also the providers of much of the vast amount of energy needed to run a modern society. Nuclear energy plus renewable energy sources such as solar and wind are wonderful alternatives to hydrocarbon energy in providing the electricity that runs most homes, towns and businesses. And the transportation industry (cars and trucks) is attempting to switch to battery-powered engines (for cars at least). But that development has a long way to go.

The huge run-up of the American government's "national debt"

All of this social-political programming issuing from DC has been undertaken at the taxpayers' – or rather future taxpayers' – expense ... consequently rapidly running up the federal debt to astronomic heights ... hitting 34 trillion dollars as of the end of 2023 ... one trillion of that amount added in merely the last few months of 2023. Wow ... in just under a quarter-century of American leadership, the federal government has been allowed to run the debt up almost seven-fold ... from five to thirty-four trillion dollars! And all of this taking place as massive inflation has rocked the nation ... making material needs (such as gasoline for the car and food for the table) now extremely expensive for the average American ... whose income growth has fallen well below the national inflation rate over that time period. In other words, the average American has become much poorer in comparison to the rising costs of food, fuel, housing, education, etc. – across the board.

In the meantime, financing the Federal debt became once again prohibitive ... and doable only by more Federal borrowing in order to pay off the interest obligations accrued in its previous borrowing! It was another one of the Federal government's own Ponzi schemes (like social security) ... holding off bankruptcy by appearing to have means to continue payments by funds that just aren't there. Borrowing beyond its means of effective repayment – by any organization – simply to keep itself in operation is not production. It's stagecraft.

The abandonment of Afghanistan

First of all, it must be noted that Trump, not Biden, was the one who initiated the idea of a full termination of American involvement in Afghanistan, when in February of 2020 Trump negotiated an American pullout with the Taliban, scheduled for May 1st of 2021 – Trump presuming to be reelected in the coming November elections and thus able to preside over this event.

Bush Jr.'s decision in 2001 to send the U.S. military into Afghanistan after al Qaeda – and then resorting to pro-Western nation-building in that country when nothing came of the anti-al-Qaeda effort – was a terrible idea ... on a number of fronts. Billions of dollars would have to be devoted to curbing the Taliban's power ... and building some kind of pro-Western political system in Afghanistan to counter the Taliban. And once the program was put in place, it would take years, even generations, of ongoing American support to lay the cultural groundwork that would give this nation-building effort some degree of sustainability. After all, American troops are still in Germany, Japan, South Korea, Kosovo ... serving just such a purpose: protecting the social groundwork laid out by an America that in the mid-20th-century took up major responsibilities as one of the world's global superpowers.

In short, nation-building is a huge responsibility that should never be undertaken on the basis of a mere political whim. And pulling out abruptly for a mere short-term political gain can have only one result: social catastrophe.

What seems to have inspired Trump to undertake this pullout was that Americans had tired deeply of the country's involvement in an Afghanistan that seemed to have no further relevance to American politics.

But worse, Trump seemed to have believed that the Taliban would of its own hold to the various conditions (support of an orderly American pullout and certain personal freedoms for the Afghans even after the American departure) of the agreement – and thus began to pull American troops out of Afghanistan, with only 2500 still left in the country as of the end of his presidency ... and even those still on schedule for a final pullout in May.

In coming to office as president, Biden took up the same policy ... although there were advisors who warned him of the dangers of a full pullout. But Biden assured even the press, which now was awakened to the potential problems involved in a full pullout, that he expected the Taliban to respect the terms of the agreement. However, he simply would not face up to the fact that with the removal of the American troops, America would have no means to enforce the terms of that agreement. So, just a few months into his presidency (April), he announced a full American pullout, to be completed by the end of the coming August.

With this announcement, political morale of the pro-American Afghan social-political system began to collapse. Indeed, the speed of the Taliban takeover of regions, towns and villages apparently surprised even the Taliban. And as the end-of-August deadline approached, the country's capital, Kabul, resembled the scene of Saigon when in the mid-1970s Congress terminated American support of the South Vietnamese society and government. It was a horrible scene of people grabbing onto airplanes as they began their takeoff from the country.

However, by the end of the month thousands of people, locals as well as American citizens, were brought out of the country. Yet shamefully, with the last American soldier pulled out, large amounts of military equipment remained left behind (supposedly dismantled ... but also quite able to be repaired by clever hands). And by no means were all the people who would certainly be hunted down by the Taliban airlifted out of the country ... likely including some Americans still remaining in the country. All in all, it was a grand American disaster.

And China had to be loving to watch America sneak off from a serious global responsibility ... quick to bring notice to the rest of the world that it would be wise not to put trust in America's promise of great-power protection. And indeed, America was not looking at all like a great power at that point.

Did the president(s) of the United States not understand any of this dynamic? What did they think they were achieving from this tactical retreat? Was there some hidden strategic advantage to be gained that would compensate for the obvious political loss from this move? If so, it would remain a mystery.

And again ... China had to be loving all of this!

Russia attacks Ukraine

Russian dictator Putin had long been alarmed about Ukraine's desire to link itself more closely to the West ... in 2008 even requesting membership in NATO (but not accepted by the West). As far as Putin was concerned, Ukraine really had no right anyway to exist as an independent nation. Besides, the eastern part of Ukraine was inhabited by Russian-speaking rather than Ukrainian-speaking citizens ... some 20 percent of the Ukrainian population. Thus Putin was a big supporter of the Russian-speaking separatists that in 2014 took over government buildings in the Donbas region (principally in the Donetsk and Luhansk oblasts) to bring the region to independence. But the Ukrainian government refused to recognize their program ... and sent troops into the region to reaffirm Ukrainian control there. Despite Russia covertly sending tanks and troops to aid the separatists, Ukraine was ultimately fairly successful in its operation ... although the conflict continued on a small basis thereafter.

But by 2017, the war was ramping back up again ... with tens of thousands of Russian troops and their equipment in the region assisting the separatist, who were still at it ... trying to secure independence. Then supposedly in 2019, both sides seemed to have come to an agreement to back off on the conflict. But the conflict continued nonetheless ... at least on a small scale.

Then in February of 2022, with Russian troops massed at the Ukrainian border – both in Russia but also in Belarus – Russian troops suddenly poured into Ukraine. Putin explained that he was sending his "peacekeeping" troops into Ukraine in order to demilitarize and "de-nazify" Ukraine. At the same time, Russia also hit hard by way of missile attack Ukraine's capital of Kyiv, as well as numerous sites around Ukraine.

The reaction of the world was fairly immediate. The U.N. General Assembly (not the Security Council because of a likely Russian veto) passed a resolution the following month (March) demanding that Russia immediately withdraw from Ukraine. This call was also backed up by the International Court of Justice. And the Council of Europe simply removed Russia from its membership. Economic sanctions were also placed on Russia by various countries ... by America and Canada, by the European Community in general, and by numerous corporations in the West. But most Third World countries – dependent on Russian trade – did not ... as well as Europe's Serbia and NATO partner Turkey. And most notably, neither did China or India.

But most surprising was Ukraine's ability not to collapse under the Russian assault ... but to fight back boldly – thanks to the leadership the country had under its president, Volodymyr Zelensky. The fact that Zelensky was formerly a TV actor, comedian, and producer before becoming the country's president in 2019 surprised everyone ... when he proved that he was also a most capable political leader. He was elected to office by a massive 73 percent of the vote in the second round of the 2019 national election ... based on his strong anti-establishment and anti-corruption campaign. And being of Russian rather than Ukrainian cultural background, he had hoped to end the Russian-Ukrainian cultural division tearing at the country.

But in any case, he refused to stand down in the face of the Russian aggression, and visiting the fronts in the north and east often, he personally inspired his troops to stand ... ultimately causing the Russians to have to pull back from their position in the north of Ukraine (they had almost reached Kyiv) ... and then in early 2023 undertaking a painfully slow but morally effective counteroffensive against well-dug-in Russian troops in the east.

Putin nonetheless found his Russian position fairly secure in his holdings in the two Russian-speaking oblasts. But this had come at a horrible cost, not only to the Ukrainians but also to his own troops. As of mid-2023, it was estimated that around 10 thousand Ukrainian civilians had been killed* and 18 thousand wounded. Additionally, 16 million Ukrainians had been forced to flee their homes ... half of those even leaving the country as refugees ... creating a massive refugee crisis not seen in Europe since the end of World War Two. As for troops, it is estimated that as of the same time period, some 70 thousand Ukrainian troops had been killed and another 100 thousand wounded. On the Russian side, it was estimated that nearly 90 thousand were killed and 170 to 180 thousand wounded.

Most tragically, as of this writing, neither side – Russia or Ukraine – is able to come to agreeable peace terms ... the outcome so strategically significant to both people. Thus some kind of compromise on the matter is currently nowhere in sight.

Meanwhile in March of 2023, the International Criminal Court issued a warrant for the arrest of Putin ... a warrant, however, not likely to be observed outside of the world of NATO and the West.

Israel and Hamas go at each other

Another surprise attack alarmed the world when in early October of 2023, without any warning, the Palestinian political organization Hamas, chose a Jewish holiday to send battalions of its militants from Palestine's Gaza district into southern Israel ... killing some 1,400 civilians and wounding many more – and capturing numerous other Israelis as hostages, dragged back into Gaza for political purposes. They even sent sophisticated missiles to hit Tel Aviv and other cities. All of this was well photographed for cruel political purposes.

What Hamas's purpose was ultimately all about seems a dark mystery. Certainly Israel was going to strike back ... and in a very big way. And that is exactly what proceeded to unfold ... with infuriated Israeli troops hitting Gaza neighborhoods (homes, schools, markets, hospitals and all) in reaction to the Hamas attack ... and killing countless Palestinian civilians in the process. Israel also shut off all food shipments that it could into Gaza. Thus thousands of Palestinians soon found themselves starving ... despite the effort of various international agencies to send some degree of food relief into the region from Egypt in the south.

America and the West announced that certainly they were opposed

---

*This figure did not include an estimated 25 thousand civilians killed in the battle of Mariupol ... uncertifiable because the Russians were reported to have brought cremation equipment to clean up the human carnage caused by their assault on this most strategic city (along the corridor from Russia to its naval base in the Crimea).

to Hamas ... but also to Israeli occupation of Gaza. Biden even flew to Israel to discuss some kind of path to peace with Israeli Prime Minister Benjamin Netanyahu. But Netanyahu certainly seemed totally committed to destroying Hamas ... even though that would likely mean the closing down of yet another Palestinian region (Gaza) ... as the Israelis have done since the massive Jewish arrival there from Europe after World War Two. And once again, the surrounding Arab world would have to take these Palestinian refugees in ... based for the most part in quite inhospitable refugee camps.

Was this what Hamas wanted? Or was there a larger purpose in all of this ... perhaps setting the entire Arab world off in opposition to not only Israel but the generally Israel-supporting West? Was Iran behind this "distraction"? What about Russia ... and China?

Most ironically, what Hamas did was to restore the political popularity of Netanyahu in Israel ... at a time when his rankings were sinking fast. In effect, Hamas now made him the Israeli "man of the hour." Netanyahu could not have planned a better political comeback than what Hamas had provided him!

So far, the dynamic also makes America and the West appear simply less and less effective as the world's "referees" ... something that the world looked to with the close of the Cold War in the 1990s – but wasted away since then by less-than-effective American diplomacy in the face of the various social crises that have hit the world since 9/11.

Is this then all that this is about ... to make it clear that the days of the dominance of the West – Europe, previous to the disaster of the two twentieth century world wars ... and now America, since then – have lost their clout? Is this a call for the world to look elsewhere for some great power or powers to take control of international developments?

Only time will tell.

CHAPTER TWENTY-TWO

THE LESSONS OF HISTORY

* * *

A SOCIETY AS A MORAL STRUCTURE

A society is basically just a moral structure designed to defend and promote a particular people

The study of social dynamics is not a new thing. Since man himself set out to find answers to why his social world was shaped and acted the way it did, he actually has been asking the great moral question: is this the way society is supposed to work?

And there is an amazing amount of speculation on this matter – debates on the subject that reach even back into very ancient times. The Greeks left a rich literature to their descendants in dealing with this very issue. Socrates, Plato and Aristotle spent a huge amount of energy trying to answer this question.

Aristotle's insights. Aristotle studied carefully a wide variety of societies existing either currently or historically (thus employing true social science) and came up simply with a very astute observation: the "good society," as opposed to the "bad society," was distinguished not by the number of people involved in governing that society, whether a government of one, the few, or the many. The good society was characterized by the moral character of those, whether one, few or many, called to govern the society.

The Jewish Biblical record. The Jews of the Bible too had their way of addressing the same issue, using the power of historical narrative – the Biblical account about the many centuries of existence of their leaders and their people – to highlight the good and the bad of their own social behavior. In virtually every instance the good was identified with Israel's ability to stay on course with God's instructions, through following God's unchanging Word (the same Word that put the universe into existence), but also his ad-hoc counsel given to those in a leadership position, usually one or another of the Hebrew judges or prophets. However, when the Israelites wandered from this Godly social-moral counsel and discipline, and proceeded to "walk in their own counsel" (which they would do repeatedly), they would fall into trouble … until God, out of simply the grace of his ever-faithful heart, would come to rescue them from their self-inflicted moral folly.

Toynbee's insights into why societies fail. More recently, the British historian Arnold Toynbee, in his twelve-volume *A Study of History** – taking nearly thirty years, 1934-1961, to complete – examined 28 civilizations in order to see what made them strong or weak, rising or falling. What he noted was the inability of a society to stay on course with the moral foundations that originally brought it into existence and growth, instead – over time – wandering from that moral course because, in the face of new, rising challenges, a closed and detached elite group of leaders tried to follow unrealistic or utopian (but always self-evidently rational, even if socially suicidal) alternate courses that they themselves dreamed up. In doing so, these social elite would foolishly abandon their society's precious, well-tested traditional moral legacy – instead of carefully (thus wisely) drawing on that same legacy in creative ways in order to meet the new challenges of life as they arose.

A society is a spirit of things, not a thing in itself

It is important to note that the self-understood purpose of a community – and the rules that guide the members of that community in fulfilling that social purpose – will vary widely from society to society … from East to West, from ancient times to the present.

That is because a society is not a "thing" like a tree, or a mountain, or an apple, or a squirrel, a pair of scissors or a shovel … an object that exists in some clearly definable material form. Instead a society is simply a compelling idea of things, a unifying sense of purpose, a social spirit found in a particular people's hearts, a spirit designed to help that people deal with the challenges they face as a community. It is a set of values held in the human heart that lead people to live cooperatively rather than competitively … seeking the larger good rather than mere selfish gain, wanting to live in harmony with the world rather than in contest or battle with the surrounding world.

Unfortunately, "modern" Westerners have come typically to see a

---

*Toynbee, Arnold. *A Study of History*, Vol. 1: Abridgement of Volumes I-VI; Vol 2: Abridgement of Volumes VII-X. New York: Oxford University Press, 1946 (Vol. 1, renewed in 1974) and 1957 (Vol 2, renewed in 1985).

society as one founded on particular – and somewhat predictable –patterns or social rules in life ... objective patterns found "out there" in the natural world – whether mathematical, material, social, or psychological. Westerners believe that these objective patterns can be studied and understood by the careful observer in such a way that events can not only be anticipated but even be directed or controlled by the "enlightened" individual (the philosopher or scientist ... but also the "awakened" religious individual). Indeed, this "modern" understanding or appreciation of life seems to be a totally self-evident Truth to many Westerners ... especially to those of a more "intellectualist" nature.

Hindu-Buddhist views on such matters

But in fact, such an understanding of social life and its dynamics is not so self-evident to everyone. For instance, the basic orderliness of life is not so self-evident to many Hindus and Buddhists. For most Hindus, karma – not basic order – is at the heart of life. To the Hindu way of thinking, we do not inhabit a world which operates in an orderly fashion in accordance with some kind of benign transcendent will or all-encompassing set of natural laws. Rather, according to the Hindu view of things, life is a complex array of individual lives that come together as a larger whole through the mysterious outworking of the consequences (karma) of personal deeds committed in our previous lifetimes. We all as individuals live out our separate but interconnected lives in order to atone for the deeds of earlier lifetimes. Until karma is fully satisfied, we as individuals are destined to go on living, dying and being reborn in an endless cycle, with no hope of escaping the iron grip of karma. To a Hindu, this is the ultimate reality of life – a reality before which all other judgments about life must bow.

For Buddhists, whose faith grew up within this basic Hindu world-view, life is itself merely an illusion. When we try to make it real and work for us, life only produces suffering – lifetime after lifetime. Wisdom demands that we find release (nirvana) from this endless cycle. This is achieved only by becoming aware of the illusory quality of life – and stilling our passions for the life of illusions. When we achieve such emotional detachment, then we have broken the hold of suffering and the eternal sentence of rebirths. We have achieved nirvana.

So, indeed, the Western sense of the basic order to life is a very special cultural achievement. It comes naturally to us only because it is all-pervasive within our culture. It inhabits our thoughts about all matters. It drives us to try to solve life's problems – to look for solutions to everything, rather than to throw up our hands in resignation. It has made us "progressive" and ever-reforming. It has made us devoted; it has made us scientific. It has made us "modern."

The dangers of social-moral Idealism

But this "objective" Western view of things has its own problems. Most unfortunate has been the tendency in the modern West of "progressive" social-political reformers – ones found in public office, in academia, in the press, even in the field of entertainment, etc. – to want to put in place of flawed social orders their own versions of supposedly more progressive social orders ... "utopias"* of one form or another. Such utopias or ideal social orders are presented as the sum of well-designed (designed, of course, by these Idealists) legal structures, laws, political offices, civil and social institutions, that direct the behavior of the members of a society. To them, a good society is a matter purely of good laws and proper political structuring.   It is all very mechanical, all very personality-neutral in its operation.

This ideal society or utopia proposed by these Idealist-reformers is supposed to work very effectively based on their Humanist belief that it is not man's unrestrained self-serving instincts that create the problems that bring crisis to a society ... but instead simply the social confusion caused by improperly designed social orders. These Idealists or Humanists believe that you only have to reform – or better yet rebuild from the ground up – an entirely new social order. Then the members of that social order will most naturally or automatically take their places in the new social scheme ... because they too will see its vastly better qualities. That certainly was the intent of the designers of the 1933 *Humanist Manifesto*.

However ... as we have seen in ample detail, Plato failed at constructing just such a perfect society in Syracuse ... nearly costing him his life. John Locke's "Grand Model" for the Carolina colony proved to be fairly useless in the face of the various "realities" settlers to that colony came to face. Maximilien Robespierre turned into a murderous butcher in trying to enforce his Jacobin dream for Revolutionary France. Karl Marx would provide the perfect ideal of a society that would live entirely freely and communally according to his program of "scientific socialism" (Communism) ... which produced merely the unprecedentedly brutal tyrannies of Stalin's Russia and Mao's China. Woodrow Wilson would lead American boys off to a "Great War" ... in order to kill a lot of German boys – so that global democracy and

---

*The word "utopia" comes from the Greek, meaning literally "nowhere." It was brought into popular usage through Thomas More's work of that same name *Utopia*, published in 1516. The book is actually political satire ... not intellectualist Idealism.   Utopia is a hypothetical Socialist society – which ambiguously can be understood idealistically to be a very good society ... or be seen cynically as a very bad social form!

a world of perpetual peace could finally be founded. Lyndon Johnson sent hundreds of thousands of America boys off to Vietnam ... to kill Vietnamese Communists ... so that democracy could be put in place in Vietnam. In both Wilson's and Johnson's cases, in doing so, they ended up merely killing hundreds of thousands of people – with no "democracy" resulting from the effort. Bush Junior did the same in Afghanistan and Iraq – as did Obama in Libya and Syria – with the same gruesome results.

No matter the historical record, such Humanist Idealism never seems to slow up or go away. Humanists never bother to learn that trying to impose utopian plans on societies that have a foundational social-moral order very different from that of the Idealist dreamers has always been destined to produce only social disaster: horrible political breakdown and the death of hundreds of thousands of people – even millions – and ultimately, after the grand experiment has once again failed miserably, the necessity of imposing some kind of brutal political regime over that society in order to bring it back to liveable conditions.

In short, beautiful social plans do not automatically make for beautiful social results. But this is a hard reality almost impossible to get the world of intellectual and bureaucratic social planners to understand.

So then ... what does it take to improve a less-than-perfect society?

FINDING A HIGHER SOCIAL PURPOSE

At the heart of all social morality is a strong sense of purpose that directs a society as it takes on the many challenges that life offers. Humans cannot thrive on this planet without serving some larger sense of purpose. "Growing up" for a child is exactly that of discovering a larger sense of purpose for their own existence. They must see themselves as "born" to live to this or that larger purpose – by some deeper instinct to take up the role one day as mothers and fathers of their own offspring. But they will also see themselves called to serve even larger calls to purpose: as a farmer, a plumber, a teacher, an architect ... but also as a service worker in their community, as a worker among the poor, as a soldier sent off to defend their society, as an elected public official.

Without such a higher sense of purpose, life loses its meaning. And the results of such a loss can be cruel and even deadly to someone.

But a society must itself also live to its own sense of purpose, or it too will fall into spiritual ruin. After all, it is a society's sense of purpose that creates the moral structure that defines for its various members their particular roles in the mutual social effort that their society exemplifies.

Indeed, it is usually some part of that larger social sense of purpose that then directs a society's social members in their own personal quest for purpose in life. All of this works together: the social and personal sense of purpose ... and the moral life it calls for.

Unfortunately, social purpose and personal purpose are not self-evident in the way the reality of physical things are self-evident. Again ... social purpose or social morality is a matter of the spirit, not of some material or physical reality. And that spirit can be one of great goodness ... but sadly also one of great evil. And it is not always that easy to see which of these two categories a powerful sense of purpose is directing life toward. That requires perspective – the element of time – before the goodness or evil will reveal themselves ... by way of the social outcomes a society (or a person) experiences.

That is why a careful study of history – and not just immediate "enlightenment" – helps a person or a people find that perspective ... well before more distant outcomes are able to reveal themselves. Most tragically, the more common failure to take a larger view of things – the tendency to want to simply jump into an exciting, even "revolutionary," social project – is famous for its very tragic results.

The cruelty of the nationalist impulse that drove the West in the 20th century. World War One (the "Great War") was a horrible example of moral abandon ... that served only to undercut deeply Europe's leading position in world affairs. Nobody was a winner of that horrible adventure. Actually, this nightmare would not go away – and would become even the cause for yet another round at such suicidal madness, World War Two.

A big part of the problem was that "nationalism" was a fairly new social norm in Europe, born largely out of the reaction of fellow Europeans to Napoleon's French-driven wars in the early 1800s. For as long as anyone could remember, prior to that, all social boundaries and social identities were fixed by the family fortunes of the various European dynasties. And these mostly had little to do with the "national" or linguistic character of the different social groups that these monarchs reigned over.

But the reaction to the sweeping success of Napoleon's fired-up French commoner troops against the European monarchs' mercenary troops finally drove the monarchs to mobilize what they could of the nationalist or linguistic impulses of their various subjects ... to come back at the French on equally "nationalistic" terms.

But at first, these monarchs had no interest in taking nationalist matters any further than this. But they had stirred up a hornets' nest of nationalist sentiments – the latter shaped greatly by the Romantic stories (in their own language), music and dance popular among the common people. This was a new force that would not be quieted down easily.

However, Germany's Chancellor Bismarck intended fully to use just such nationalist sentiment to build a new German society. In this he proved to be awesomely successful. This in turn forced other European monarchs to move in this same direction ... to identify their thrones with the nationalist impulses of their subject people – that had things so stirred up by the later 1800s.

But this was a new moral force with no larger political or moral interests beyond the full glorification of the nation ... in opposition to other nations undergoing the same impulse. And thus the Great War ... Germans killing French because they were French, English killing Germans because they were simply Germans – and for no other apparent reason. A huge moral tragedy.

But despite the ugliness of the Great War, it would be the nationalist impulses of Hitler and Mussolini leading them once again to try to achieve national greatness for their respective societies. And naturally they would do so by trying to bring down neighboring societies. But most unsurprisingly, this served only to cripple all of Europe's Western societies (including their own) ... and succeeded only in bringing to a close Western Europe's former place of leadership in the global scheme of things. Only Russia, way to the East, and America, way to the West, came out of that venture as strong powers.

And Japan was nearly destroyed in its own fired-up nationalist venture.

Better examples of excellent social purpose

America's examples. With the collapse of the Soviet Empire in the 1980s and even the Soviet Union itself at the beginning of the 1990s, America found itself as the world's sole superpower ... looked to by the rest of the world to be something of a policeman on the international beat. And America wisely (its leaders in fact the source of that wisdom) chose to see America's sense of purpose exactly along those lines: not to dominate or impose new social orders according to American political-social principles ... but simply to intervene to protect societies when they fell into civil disorder over this or that bitter social-moral breakdown.

Thus Bush Sr. – in close alliance with a number of other powers in the region – made a move to expel Saddam Hussein from his occupation of Kuwait ... but then, once having quickly succeeded in this venture, refused to take the matter further. When he was criticized for not having finished the job by overthrowing Saddam himself, his Defense Secretary Cheney later explained that the President and his staff had known quite well that to overthrow Saddam Hussein – and thus being forced to take on the task of "democratizing" a post-Saddam Iraq – would have been a bad idea and would have led to a "quagmire."* Interestingly, Cheney as Bush Jr's Vice President would then a mere ten years later help the younger Bush decide that the Iraqi quagmire at that point was not really a problem. Thus wisdom was replaced by folly.

Bush Sr's successor Clinton, continued the elder Bush's wise program ... answering the call of the United Nations to help protect its food program undertaken in a civil-war-torn Somalia. But Clinton wisely withdrew such American involvement when it became clear that American troops would get no support from a terrorized Somali population. Clinton also refused to step into the horrible tribal war in Burundi when he realized that the problem was much bigger and deeper than anything America could handle with any degree of success. But he did take action quickly and successfully in bringing Haiti's democratically-elected but militarily-deposed president back to power ... understanding the wide support in Haiti itself he had in this undertaking. Most interestingly, he did not – at first – get that same support from fellow Idealists at home in America. And Clinton – in close cooperation with NATO allies – answered the call to end the genocide in Bosnia ... simply forcing Serbia out of the Bosnia. Successful in this enterprise, he resisted the temptation to then go on to try to restructure either Bosnian or Serbian society. And Clinton was again called on to perform the same task in Kosovo when a similar crisis shifted to that part of the region. He chose to act swiftly ... but with carefully designed restraint. And the success of it all was well understood and appreciated by everyone (the Serbians not so much!) ... Americans as well as Europeans and U.N. officials. These were examples of excellent leadership.

Europe's example. Not surprisingly, in the second half of the 20th century, Europeans decided that it was time to build their identities on something larger than just their nationalist or linguistic sentiments ... to unite as a New Europe – one in which the borders separating the various member-states of a new political union would come down, politically, economically, and socially. A new moral foundation was to be built in place of the failed nationalist foundations ... one which recognized a European society of peaceful and fully cooperative social instincts. They would not achieve this union in a single dramatic step, but would build that new moral base slowly, step by step, as part of a long process starting up in the 1950s ... an expansion still going on today. And Western Europe (now expanded into Eastern Europe) has prospered greatly in this regard.

––––––––––––––––––

*That explanation was offered to the press in 1994, a year after Cheney was out of office ... and at the time when he was CEO of the huge oil and gas corporation Halliburton.

Some other basic principles of the "better way"

Knowing when to act. YA society certainly cannot exist only as a very passive entity. It also needs to know when it is seriously time to put to use its political, economic and social assets ... to address a dangerous challenge – lest it get pushed aside by an aggressive competitor. Sadly a war-wearied Chamberlain failed to understand this and simply kept trying to find ways to "appease" Hitler rather than stand up to him – making it much easier for Hitler to move against Germany's neighbor Czechoslovakia ... and ultimately Poland.

Churchill finally came to the rescue of a disheartened Britain by inspiring the moral nerve his fellow Brits needed to stand up to horrible German aggression – rather than cave in to the Germans like the French. And this not only saved Churchill's Britain from Nazi tyranny ... it made Britain available as the vital launch pad for the larger Western counterattack against Hitler's Nazi tyranny

The importance of alliances. That sense of purpose must most wisely work cooperatively with the social interests of other societies ... in order to share – not foolishly waste – social assets. Again, Bush Sr. and Clinton made it a major point to work with other countries – most normally America's NATO partners, but with others as well – in undertaking America's huge responsibilities. America did not undertake these projects as a matter of singular American interest.

Unfortunately, Bush Jr. lacked that wisdom, and ended up finding that his desire to knock out Saddam Hussein – and finish his father's "unfinished work" in Iraq – was almost a solo task. Nearly all of America's traditional allies were however wise enough to see very good reason NOT to involve themselves in Bush Jr's personal project. Unfortunately, Britain's Prime Minister Tony Blair was the major exception, and agreed to work with Bush in the Iraqi invasion ... ultimately costing him the loss of what was up until then his very popular British political leadership.

✳ ✳ ✳

MORALITY IS NOT INSTINCTIVE – BUT MUST BE TAUGHT

In general, most people are quite aware of the fact that the social rules that guide their social lives need to be carefully taught to rising generations ... or the very shape and existence of their community will not long endure.

As Ignatius of Loyola, founder of the Jesuit Christian Order put the matter so bluntly back in the 1500s, "Give me a child till he is seven years old, and I will show you the man." Children's rational world has merely begun to take shape. Depending on how the adult world is being presented to them (or not), a new generation will most surely form itself with its own ideas and understandings of how the world is supposed to work, and what a person's particular place in that drama is supposed to be. Not only did the Jesuits understand this vital principle, but so more recently did Hitler, with his massive youth organization, Hitler Jugend (Hitler Youth), created in 1926, whose purpose was to turn young Germans into proper Nazis. So also did Mao understand this is moving to build his Cultural Revolution of the mid-1960s almost entirely on China's youth.

But everyone understands this at some level ... especially attentive parents. Failure to discipline a rising generation to the social rules that guided their own social development will lead to grand social failure.

Male and female social roles. Thus it has been in history that in all societies much care was always given to the social-moral development of rising generations ... especially to this matter of the development of male and female character. Most interestingly however, girls became women more automatically – and quite early on – in preparation for the eventuality of becoming pregnant and having children to nurse. At the same time, men were expected to protect their wives and children during this very vulnerable period for women and children ... and at the same time find ways to meet the financial needs of the family. This was a pretty standard picture across the world – and across all periods of history ... although that pattern seems to be under strong social-moral challenge today.

The vital role of the father as male instructor. Traditionally, a young man rather automatically trained and then took up the work and profession of his father. But with the development of modern society, that inherited pattern became less and less the determinative matter. Occupational choices were much more widely available ... especially in urban society. Since the onset of modern times, men – in order to avoid the alternative of having to take up the brutal job as a common industrial laborer – therefore took up special technical training to prepare them for this wider set of possible occupations. Now more recently, women have tended to hold off on the marriage-childbearing routine ... and joined the men in this same technical enterprise.

Learning to work together as a team. Also, learning to work as a team was always a vital part of bringing a youth successfully to manhood ... and the broader social responsibilities traditionally awaiting him as an adult. He would be needed to stand in defense not only of his family, but of the larger social order ... to the point even of death in its defense if need be.

Here, failure to undergo this kind of disciplined development (usually because of an absentee or brutal father) would rather automatically bring very antisocial behavior on the part of a young man ... and ultimately the likelihood of prison. But an alternative was once also used – of letting a socially deviant youth choose military service rather than prison (prison, anyway, famous for teaching even worse social habits!). That was actually a wise choice – because it offered the social-moral discipline that was lacking in the young man's earlier development.

Little wonder too that the young men who served in the military have tended to be much more supportive of the idea of the necessary social order – "patriotism" as we know it. We saw this strongly present in the Vet generation – both American and European – a generation which served sacrificially in World War Two.

Participation in sports was another, less drastic, way for a young man to achieve this same path of social-moral discipline as he approached manhood. Sports taught the importance to young men of "fair play" or "good sportsmanship." A "win" in sports was actually dishonorable if it was not achieved in accordance with the rules of the game. But sadly, sports today is considered merely a game, something for pleasure. Thus the original social purpose for sports is greatly missing.

The focus on gender equality. But now the matter of male/female social growth has undergone some very "innovative" developments in the last half-century. The idea of distinct male and female social roles has been downplayed ... in the attempt to make their roles not only equal but in fact the same.

Indeed, according to "progressive" minds, not giving any particular focus on male development will now result in less toxic manhood. Tragically this type of thinking has produced some very ugly social results.[*]

"Gender studies" exists widely as a collegiate studies program ... but one focused almost entirely on female development – especially professional development – in order to promote women's social standing in a formerly male-led world. Men apparently don't need such special attention.

Also, in 2019 the name "Boy Scouts of America" was simply renamed BSA to indicate that it does not focus only on male training ... but now includes female units inside the organization. The two sexual units within

---

[*]Enlightened Humanists have not yet figured out why the prison population of men involves so many times over the number of women sent to prison. An October 2023 Federal Bureau of Prisons report lists men as comprising 93.2% of the American prison population, women 6.8%. Men find it much harder to find a "natural" – that is, uninstructed – place in the adult world than do women.

BSA have not yet been completely intermixed ... although given the trend of recent gender attitudes, this will likely develop in the near future. Girl Scouts however continues to exist as an organization devoted to female training.

The ranks of the military (all the way to the top) have been opened to women also on an equal basis ... although it has not yet been determined whether or not fighting women will bond with fighting men – the way the latter have historically bonded with each other in battle.

Racial equality. Racial equality makes great sense in a democratic society. But that equality must be earned ... not be merely assigned.

Yes ... we humans have a natural suspicion about those who do not look like us. But a well-demonstrated period of proper social performance by these suspect groups can easily get a society moved past that prejudice.

Every non-White-Anglo-Saxon-Protestant (non-WASP) group arriving in America went through this same tough period of testing ... as to whether or not they would "fit in" to the pre-existing social order. It was not easy. Ugly things happened. But attitude adjustments occurred as these immigrant groups "proved" themselves.

The situation for Blacks has been much more dragged out. On the one hand, Black musicians and athletes long ago "proved" themselves ... and were thus accepted, even well honored. But for the rest of the Black world, the acceptance has been painfully slow.

Unsurprisingly, the tendency of Liberal officials to want to "assign" equality to Blacks in other areas of social life has not been very successful.

But there are a growing number of Blacks in a widening realm of social activity who – like the Polish, Italians, Greeks, etc. – have proved themselves and have earned high respect in society.   And many of these individuals are much opposed to the idea that Black equality will ever be achieved by official assignment ... seeing in such efforts a tendency to create ever-deeper suspicion within the White community that Black achievement has been assigned – rather than earned. This is very humiliating to those deserving of the honors they have rightly earned.

Once again, the efforts of the "enlightened ones" to impose social-moral standards on others seldom works out as planned.

Religious "equality." As for religious equality ... modern society is confusing itself in supposing that science and religion are two separate social entities ... science now supposedly being the higher order and religion being a lower (even unnecessary) order. However ... both science and religion are simply different versions of what is properly called a "worldview." Worldviews – including both science and religion – are simply the way a society and its people understand the dynamics of life. And worldviews vary widely from society to society and from time period to time period.

Modern science ("natural philosophy" as it was termed at the time) started out in the 1600s as a Christian enterprise ... Christians eagerly investigating the "natural" world around them – as testimony to the glory of the Creator God. God's perfect hand was displayed beautifully in every aspect of the structure and action of the surrounding physical world that they were discovering in their research work.

A huge problem arose however when the secular-material aspect of this rising sense of natural philosophy looked back at the "truths" of Scripture ... ancient events, dates, heroes, etc. To the increasingly secular mindset of rising generations of natural philosophers or "scientists" (since the early 1800s), these appeared to be no more than myth.

And indeed, in one sense they were correct. Scripture deeply involves ancient myth. But being of the mindset that they were, these "modern" minds were completely blind to the way Truth – powerful Truth about life and its ways – has long been conveyed through "myth." To the secular mind, nothing can be "True" unless it can demonstrate its truthfulness the way they expect to find Truth in the surrounding physical or material world.

Of course such a "scientific" approach has never done well in discovering the great truths of human life and its processes ... individually and socially. This is because human life is not a material entity. It is not something that can be found standing "out there" like a physical object. It is not a "thing" that can be brought into their science laboratories to have experiments conducted on social behavior. You just can't do that with a society ... any society. Thus the techniques of modern science have no ways to measure and thus manage social-moral truth.

Ultimately, modern "science" – unable to prove or disprove what it is that makes for social Truth – simply dismisses the ancient Truths of Scripture (and other historical sources) as mere superstition, mere religion, mere lie. Worse, they presume that man would live better with no such binding "myth" holding back a more "natural" or religious-free human development ... whatever that might be.

And that "natural" (unstructured, undisciplined) moral development produced by the Secularist's cynical attitudes about these matters is increasingly producing the most tragic personal and social results ... not just moral confusion, but identity confusion and ultimately political-social confusion ... and its consequent cruelty.

This is because their new secular "laws" of science are just mere speculation ... backed up by their own rigid religious tenets, their own religious doctrines ... derived from their own Materialist worldview. Theirs is the greater lie than what they accuse Scripture of being.

And most tragically, they show no sign of learning from the disastrous results of their efforts … any more than the similarly enlightened ones of the past (Robespierre, Marx, Wilson, etc.) – or their devoted followers – learned any significant social or personal lessons from the huge disasters their theories produced.

✳ ✳ ✳

ULTIMATELY … THE VITAL ROLE OF MORAL LEADERSHIP

Besides being highly ambitious, the leader of a society must exemplify the very best of that society's moral system

To anyone who has looked seriously at how human history has worked over the countless generations of human life on this planet, it is always very clear how a single individual can shape the character and operation of society.

History is full of such examples. Chinese history, for instance, is really the study of personal dynasties, ones that have arisen out of a period of confusion when the Chinese society is torn apart by warring warlords, until one of these warlords is able to establish ascendancy over the others, and thus begin a new dynasty, and a new period of peace and social development.

The Hebrew Bible is really a story of ancient Hebrew patriarchs and prophets, Abraham, Moses, Joshua, David, Nathan, Elijah, Elisha, etc., and the huge impact they personally had on the shaping of the Hebrew nation.

Western history is filled with the stories of how such individuals as Alexander the Great, Julius Caesar, Constantine, Charlemagne, Luther, Calvin, Louis XIV, etc., had a huge impact on the defining of the social order of their days.

More recently we have also seen how Washington, Napoleon, Lincoln, Lenin, Hitler, Stalin, Gandhi, Churchill, Mao, Johnson (LBJ) shaped our world – in ways good or bad – in their days.

Inspirers or dominators? It most certainly takes a special personal type to lead a society … someone who has a higher goal in life than the average person. There really is no way to produce such a leader, although leadership itself can be cultivated and developed. Leaders are just born with more aggressive personalities. There can be all sorts of explanations for this. But the fact is, they are just different.

Quite obviously also, there can be a vast difference between a good leader … and a bad leader. The good leader – especially *the great leader* – typically is one who is able to *inspire* the rest of society in its activities. *The bad leader* – especially the dangerous leader or tyrant – will find it necessary to *dominate and intimidate* others in order to get them to work under his leadership.

Thus Alexander the Great and Stalin went at leadership very differently ... Alexander inspiring his troops and Stalin intimidating the Russians into total submission. Thus Washington could inspire Americans during its "revolution" ... leading these American commoners all the way to the unprecedented success of actually defeating a huge royal army of a king sent to bring them under his tyrannical control. On the other hand – and most tragically – Robespierre could keep his French "revolution" moving ahead only through murderous intimidation of much of the rest of the French leadership ... ultimately producing disastrous results for France.

But even "inspired" leadership can be dangerous. Hitler was brought to power as Germany's Chancellor in 1933. But what happened next to Germany had little to do with the mechanics of the German Weimar Republic or the office of Chancellor. In fact, that German constitutional order was quickly put aside – with the German people themselves being fully supportive of Hitler – in order to build a German Third Reich or Empire around the very person of their Führer (Leader) Hitler. For better or worse (in this case horribly worse) the German nation redefined itself around the personality of this single individual.

Mao went at leadership inspiring China's peasants, but at the same time dominating and intimidating – actually terrorizing – its urban population. Failing at this misadventure, he then turned to inspiring (actually brainwashing) a rising generation of Chinese youth to follow him most devotedly in attacking that older, more urban, more traditional sector of Chinese society that he detested so much.

Thus, as can be seen in the above examples, there must be a strong sense of moral boundaries operative in the leader himself, or horrible things can result ... for power is very corrupting of human behavior if it is allowed to go unchecked. We are reminded of Lord Acton's famous statement: "Power corrupts ... absolute power corrupts absolutely."*

The divine hand in the shaping of effective leadership. We cannot emphasize enough the fact that those who have had the greatest influence

---

*The actual quote from a letter he wrote to Anglican bishop Creighton in 1887 reads: "Power tends to corrupt and absolute power corrupts absolutely. Great men are almost always bad men, even when they exercise influence and not authority; still more when you superadd the tendency of the certainty of corruption by authority." Although Acton was an active Catholic, he was strongly opposed to his Church's move to declare the infallibility of the pope (1870) ... seeing no way that the office itself offered such sanctification to anyone – and in fact historically tended to produce quite the opposite.

on society, on history itself, were not bureaucratic *fonctionnaires*,* but instead dynamic individuals of great charismatic character, able to inspire others – many others – to follow them step by step as they led ... even if the path they were taking the people down was highly dangerous.

And the word charismatic is key here. Charisma is an old Greek word χάρισμα (*khárisma*) implying a special anointing, a heavenly or divine grace placed upon a person, such as makes that person unusually gifted as a leader. That divine grace as a gifting comes not from another person or social institution or material or physical property. It has long been understood as coming from above, above as in Heaven, the gods, or God himself ... but possibly also from evil or satanic elements as well, if care is not taken in measuring or judging by ancient spiritual standards the voice of such a non-worldly or supernatural source.

The Chinese, for instance, have understood for thousands of years this phenomenon in the form of what they called since ancient times the *Tianming* (Mandate of Heaven). Chinese Emperors gained the necessary respect and support from the Chinese nation in being able to demonstrate the many ways that Heaven (*Tian*) had smiled on their rule. Visible social success indicated clearly the approval and support of Heaven. But the downside of that same idea was that when floods, famines, diseases or enemy raiders attacked Chinese society, that same respect and support among the people would melt away. To the people this was a clear sign that the *Tian* had obviously withdrawn that special favor that Chinese society depended on so greatly. And this change in political climate would be the signal to Chinese warlords to put forth their candidacy as the new Emperor. And a violent round of civil war (often lasting centuries) would result, until it was clear that Heaven had once again made its choice: a victor, a *Tianzi* (Son of Heaven) would finally emerge to take charge of China.

But other examples abound. Alexander the Great believed that he was actually the son of a God (or at least that's how he presented himself to the society that supported him) and went to the Siwa Oasis in the middle of the Libyan Desert to have the Ammonite priests there attest to this fact.

Likewise, David was anointed at a very early age by Samuel as God's chosen leader of Israel, and David was willing to wait through very troubled times, even passing up opportunities to launch his own career, as he waited for God (and only God) to bring his kingship into being.

So also the Roman imperial candidate Constantine was vitally aware of God's appointment of him as future Emperor, moving against a much larger enemy candidate under the sign God had given him to conquer with: the Chi-Rho sign of Jesus the Christ.

─────────────

*French for those who govern from their chairs behind desks in governmental office buildings.

And closer to home, we know that both Washington and Lincoln were men of immense Christian faith, drawing on that faith to keep them moving forward during very dark times, when others would have quit.

Of course there have been rulers who have operated apart from just such a sense of divine appointment. But lacking such higher "legitimacy" they are driven to rule by force, often by sheer terror inflicted on a subject people – as paranoia and fear of losing their position (never really quite "legitimate" in the eyes of the people) drives them forward. Certainly Stalin and Mao fit this description. And the manner and ultimately durability of the societies that they ruled over attest to the problems that soon enough develop for a society when it lacks a "higher" hand supporting it.

To be sure, such a "higher hand" is historically defined in different ways, with different versions of Heaven, different versions of God. Or are they all that different?

What we humans can understand about the Realm of God can come only through human interpretation, and thus is going to come to us through different cultural versions. But they all point to the same higher source of power, one existing above all human capability itself.

Christianity itself is built entirely on that understanding, not just through the life, death and Resurrection of Jesus but through the empowerment of the Holy Spirit (and in the case of the Apostle Paul, a post-resurrection encounter with Jesus himself), God's very hand in getting Jesus's early followers up and running as a powerful people.

One thing also is clear about these key historical examples: Heaven's call on them to the task of leadership was always quite real to the leaders themselves.

Skeptics. Others, such as intellectuals, who operate only from their self-conceived world of pure reason (thus needing no God beyond their own personal intelligence), will mock those who put forward the claim of divine calling. Why not? No such calling ever came to them – and never will come to them, as long as they put huge material boundaries around their personal sense of reality.

As the opening chapters of the Bible put things, such scoffers have chosen to do what Adam and Eve did in cutting themselves off from God and his counsel (and provision). They have eaten from the Tree of the Knowledge of Good and Evil – so as to be themselves like God … as the Deceiver himself beguiled them into believing would be the grand result of this act of disobedience to God. Such individuals can scoff all they want. But they will never find the social significance that they so greatly crave in trying to be so reasonable.

Why is this connection with the higher power of Heaven or God thus so important to social leadership? Leaders are not your average person. Your average person naturally wants to fit in, be an integral part of society. There is absolutely nothing wrong with those instincts. A strong society depends on exactly that very instinct being found widely among its people.

But leaders (at whatever level of society, all the way from the royal or imperial palaces down to moms and dads at the family dinner tables) – in any circumstance in which they assume the responsibilities of leadership – must answer to a different voice than that of the immediately approving world around them. Kings, emperors and presidents – as well as just "commoner" parents – push ahead because they see in their respective worlds of great moral (and loving/caring) responsibility – whether to the many or the few under their care – something higher or more noble, something not yet attained, something that not even the society they are dealing with can yet see or understand. And by answering to that higher vision, that higher calling placed on their hearts, they do not pull back from a social responsibility simply because the society they are supervising – from independent-minded little children to jealous political rivals – does not see things their way. Yet equally importantly, it is an accompanying responsibility of theirs to help those in their care to see and understand as much of this same vision as possible … in particular what then is required of them in order that they become useful contributors to their own societies.

Thus it is that true leaders (and not just those occupying high political office) are designed to draw others forward to a higher task, even when the society itself is afraid or confused … especially when it is afraid or confused. Leaders must lead the people to a higher call, a call that those under their care do not yet see or understand, yet one that is vital to the survival and growth of that society. Leaders must lead.

George Washington. A truly amazing leader was General – then President - Washington. Here was someone who was able to inspire thousands of young men to fight off a much larger invading force of experienced British troops … and then when the fight was over, unlike so many who have attained such prominence in their leadership, step into retirement as a simple farmer. There were efforts by very unhappy officers to put him in charge of a postwar America – because the Continental Congress was not (actually, could not) deliver on the promises of financial rewards for those who had served very sacrificially in this fight to preserve American independence. But Washington himself moved boldly to dismantle this plan … realizing how such a political move would undo every good thing their previous efforts had achieved.

He would a few years later be called on to preside at the 1787 gathering of the representatives of the various states in their effort to draft a new

Constitution. Through that hot summer, Washington was largely a silent presence ... but one whose mere glance could still all uncivil conversation – and keep the delegates moving forward.

It was always clear that Washington was the only one qualified to lead this new Federal Union. But exactly how he would operate, and in what capacity he would do so, was a seriously debated matter. As a "president" there was absolutely no precedent to know what that would entail. Nothing like this new American Republic had ever existed before.

Most everyone expected that he would simply become something like every other Western leader: a king (thus George I of America!). But here too, Washington knew that he was to lead – not dominate or control – the new Republic ... lead long enough anyway to help the new Republic get on its feet so as to be able to move forward into a brave new world. He had absolutely no interest in making himself an American monarch.

In short, Washington always answered to a higher sense of his role in life than simply dominating everyone else. Actually, he intended to return to his farm after a single four-year term of service as the country's first president. However, he reluctantly agreed to serve a second term ... but only on the basis of the pleas of most everyone that he continue in the role he had assumed. It was working out beautifully for the new Republic.

But he refused to serve a third term ... establishing by his own example the principle that a person should hold no such presidential power in the Republic for more than two terms – a principle violated by Roosevelt when he went for a third and then fourth term ... leading Congress to initiate the 22nd Amendment in 1951 making the two-term principal a fully constitutional matter. Again ... a key limit on power established by Washington.

Better than most, he understood the vital importance of high moral principle – rather than human ambition – leading the country ... at all levels of society. Thus in his farewell address delivered in 1796 as he was stepping down from the presidency, he offered his country a number of key principles that had guided him through his days ... in the hopes that the country would itself continue to operate under those same insights.

First of all, he was very aware of the dangers of political sectionalism (the American North, South and West with their political differences) destroying the unity of the country. It was very important for Americans to understand the higher call placed on their new Federal Union or Republic ... for it served as a model offered to the rest of the world of a society governed by its people ... not by some particular social group.

He also warned about the dangers of readily changing the constitutional foundations on which the Republic rested ... especially the way political powers were carefully separated by a checks and balances system that required the full cooperation among its leading offices in order to avoid the dangers of despotism. He stressed the importance of proven precedent rather than political ambition being the basis on which adjustments are made to the political process. He states specifically:

> *If in the opinion of the people the distribution or modification of the constitutional powers be in any particular wrong, let it be corrected by an amendment in the way which the Constitution designates. But let there be no change by usurpation; for though this, in one instance, may be the instrument of good, it is the customary weapon by which free governments are destroyed. The precedent must always greatly overbalance in permanent evil any partial or transient benefit which the use can at any time yield.*

He then went on to describe the key role that religion and morality should play in keeping any society on such a positive course:

> *Of all the dispositions and habits which lead to political prosperity, religion and morality are indispensable supports. In vain would that man claim the tribute of patriotism who should labor to subvert these great pillars of human happiness, these firmest props of the duties of men and citizens. The mere politician, equally with the pious man, ought to respect and to cherish them. A volume could not trace all their connections with private and public felicity. Let it simply be asked where is the security for property, for reputation, for life, if the sense of religious obligation desert the oaths, which are the instruments of investigation in courts of justice? And let us with caution indulge the supposition that morality can be maintained without religion. Whatever may be conceded to the influence of refined education on minds of peculiar structure, reason and experience both forbid us to expect that national morality can prevail in exclusion of religious principle.*

These were the words of a wise leader … not just the rationalizations of a very ambitious political actor anxious to take command in order to increase his own sense of political importance. Washington's example would offer the country a restraining sense of moral purpose, one that would help the country through various crises, crises that mere political ambition would have turned into massive political catastrophes – as the French Revolution had just amply demonstrated.

Abraham Lincoln. As another example, there was Lincoln, who was so brave as to actually undertake the crushing responsibility of breaking the intention of the Southern states to abandon and thus cripple the American Union. Presidents before him had seen the difficulty of trying to keep the Union together in the face of this horrible question of slavery, and had simply looked the other way, kicking the can of slavery down the road for someone else after them to deal with.

But Lincoln, in assuming the American Presidency, understood that the burden of leading the Union through this deadly challenge was his, by literally Divine appointment. And to God, and God alone, did he increasingly look for comfort and support as he put the nation through this terrible crisis – in order to finally get this matter settled once and for all.

Keeping people with him tested every ounce of Lincoln's personal strength as a leader. Yes, he had his supporters. Great leaders do. But he had also a huge number of whiners who complained about how all this killing of America's young men was way beyond the nation's ability to sustain. They were ready to quit, to let the South be on its way with its slaves and all, and leave what was left of America to get on with things as best it could. Even on his home front, with his wife, he faced the constant demand to "give it up" so that the Lincoln family could just get things back to normal. But "normal" was not an option for America, and Lincoln knew this. God himself had called America to greater things than just letting matters go. America, after all, was a covenant nation, commissioned by God to give hope to the world by setting before the world the living, breathing human example of how the little people of the world no longer needed to live in bondage to the powerful of this world. America had to live on as a light to the world showing the way to something we call true democracy.

As Lincoln himself put the matter at the memorial service for those tens of thousands of young men who had died in this horrible 3-day battle on the fields of Gettysburg, Pennsylvania:

> *It is rather for us to be here dedicated to the great task remaining before us – that from these honored dead we take increased devotion to that cause for which they gave the last full measure of devotion – that we here highly resolve that these dead shall not have died in vain – that this nation, under God, shall have a new birth of freedom – and that government of the people, by the people, for the people, shall not perish from the earth.*

It is little wonder that for generations after this speech in 1863, it and the opening lines of America's 1776 Declaration of Independence would be the most memorized words in American history. Lincoln, leading this nation, under God, was determined that this country would not quit in the face of the horrible sacrifice required of those answering the noble call that God himself had placed on the American nation.

And thus America answered its president's reminder of this high calling with a huge "yes! Yes, we will so commit ourselves and our sacred honor to this most noble, this Divine, cause."

Winston Churchill. Look at how Churchill stiffened the resolve of a British people, under deep attack by the Nazi Luftwaffe, to stay the course – to never give up, to fight until victory was theirs. This was the follow-up to the poor leadership of Chamberlain, whose lack of political wisdom undercut those German military officers who were about to make a move to bring down the Hitlerian regime ... a regime obviously (not so obvious to a blind Chamberlain however) drawing Germany ever closer to another ruinous war. Just as the French folded under the lack of decisive leadership when Hitler turned against the French, it looked as if Chamberlain was very likely to "come to terms" with Hitler himself.   That would have put Britain under the same domination that the French then found themselves. Thankfully under his replacement Churchill, that simply was not going to happen. Under Churchill's call, his inspiring leadership, the British would continue to fight ... no matter how dark the circumstances seemed to be. Now that was true leadership.

Inspiring leadership. More recently we have seen this under Ukrainian President Volodymyr Zelensky ... a man not only willing to fight, but one able to inspire the Ukrainians themselves to fight ... against a much larger Russian army. Thus Putin's plans to take Ukraine – the way he earlier so easily took the naval base at Crimea – have failed ... and will likely continue to fail. This kind of Ukrainian leadership was most unexpected by Putin, expecting instead of the Ukrainians another weak response to Russian aggression ... such also as that which he encountered from the American "superpower" president Obama in Putin's takeover of Crimea ... one similar to the response of Obama to the Chinese taking claim to the entire South China Sea. Bold talk ... and no significant action.

In short, leadership is supremely critical in determining how an entire society will go at challenges placed before it. Weak leadership leads to a weak social response. Strong leadership leads to a strong social response.

That is what inspired leadership achieves. This is not what ordinary office-holders do. The latter simply follow plans and programs placed before them. Leaders however inspire others to take action, to take up the hard, even sacrificial, work together so that their society may move forward. It is after all, the effort of the masses of "little people," not the fancy ideas of bureaucratic social planners, that bring societies their grand successes.

The same holds true in shaping ordinary individuals

At the same time, it is very important to emphasize how it was that, in America's foundational stages, the Puritans were very aware that God's hand was there also to guide everyone, including New England's ordinary individuals, in doing those ordinary things that human life ultimately depends on. That was the whole point of the Puritan experiment in America. At a time when European kings were defending their positions against a rising middle class, the kings claiming special divine appointment, the Puritans answered back that the same God is just as much interested in and supportive of the "little people" – as clearly was Jesus in his time. They claimed that what God truly wanted to see come to pass was a people who lived and worked together in harmony as equals before God ... and each other. And thus the democracy concept was brought front and central in the Puritan experiment. It provided a powerful moral legacy for a new America, one that carried the nation forward for nearly four centuries.

Throughout the Christian West, this social dynamic has normally found its foundation in the home. Family goals and social discipline – but ultimately the way the family looked above to God – developed repeatedly among the rising generations because of the moral-spiritual leadership that the parents provided their children. Parents were/are the rising generation's first encounter with inspiring leadership. Children develop social instincts and social trust at a very early age, because of the leadership their parents provide.

From there, such social inspiration was/is cultivated further through inspiring classroom teachers and inspiring pastors. The high quality of the classroom, and the high quality of the pulpit, was also key to American democratic success.

That social pattern must never be replaced by the domination, even dictatorship, of the distant "enlightened ones" found in bureaucratic offices or seated behind high judicial benches – or even in front of TV cameras offering 24-hour wisdom or comments on how they believe life should take shape in America – willing to assume, even to take away, such local responsibility from the community's families, schools and churches or synagogues. In America, those in such high social position were long-expected to be there to inspire such grass roots development of the American family, school and church/synagogue – not replace it.

CHRISTIANITY AS THE FOUNDATION OF WESTERN CIVILIZATION

The British political leader, but also the author of volumes of Western history, Winston Churchill, referred to Western Civilization as "Christian Civilization." And rightly so. The Christian worldview officially shaped the European (and later, American) Western world since the early 300s, over 1700 years ago (but beginning its influence well before even then). Christianity was central to the understanding of what society was all about, what its purpose was, and how life was to be moved forward to higher things. Until 50 years ago this same Christian understanding about life was also the mainstay of the American idea, giving the country three and a half centuries of national vision and social purpose during its development from a European backwater to its position at the head of the Christian world as its primary defender. Christianity was a central element in America's rise to its status as the world's sole Superpower.

The recent decline of Christianity's moral-spiritual role

Meanwhile, as a slow but gathering process occurring over the last half-century, all of that cultural-spiritual dynamic has been pushed aside step by step by federal judicial decree, in the effort to replace the Christian legacy with Secular Humanism. The results of that substitution both at home and abroad have been dramatically much less than excellent.

The 2018 and 2019 Pew Reports. On May 29, 2018 the Pew Research Center released a report on the status of Christianity in fifteen Western European countries,[*] and on October 17, 2019, the Pew Research Center released a similar report on Christianity in America.[†] Both reports clearly demonstrated how deeply that Christian character of America and the West has declined.

In Europe, 64% of the population identified themselves as Christians … although only 18% were actually church-attending Christians and 46% were rated as "non-practicing Christians." Those rated as religiously unaffiliated were 24% of the population, with 4% "other." The highest of church-attending countries were Italy (40%), Portugal (35%), Ireland (34%), Austria (28%), Switzerland (27%), Germany 22%), and Spain (21%). Lowest were Sweden and Finland (9% … although 68% of the Finns considered themselves to be non-practicing Christians), Belgium and Denmark (10%), Norway (14%) and the Netherlands (15%). Both France and Britain were rated at 18%.

———————————

[*]https://www.pewresearch.org/religion/2018/05/29/being-christian-in-western-europe/

[†]https://www.pewforum.org/2019/10/17/in-u-s-decline-of-christianity-continues-at-rapid-pace/

The largest number of religiously unaffiliated were found in the Netherlands (48%), Norway (43%), Sweden (42%), Belgium (38%), and Spain and Denmark (30%).

The American study found that only 65% of Americans still described themselves as Christians, down 12 percent over the previous ten years. At the same time, those that claimed no religious affiliation (from atheists to simply "nothing in particular") rose to 26% of the population, up from 17% in 2009. In short, the American and European statistics overall were quite similar.

The Pew study went even deeper in the American study, looking at actual trends in the Christian dynamic in the country. Thus the study found that the age of the Americans being surveyed was even more skewed against Christianity. Of the oldest group, the Silents, the decline in Christian affiliation was only 2 percent; for the Boomers it was 6%; and Gen-X 8 percent. But the percentage drop among the Millennials (born in the 1981-1996 period) was a huge 16 percent. This left 84% of the older Silents still standing in 2019 as Christians – whereas only 49% of the Millennials still identified themselves as Christians. That is a terrible indicator as to where America is headed in the future morally and spiritually as a nation.

Not surprisingly also, political party affiliation made a big difference. For those that identified themselves politically as Republican, or leaned in that direction, the ten-year decline was 7 percent. But the Democrats marked a 17 percent decline in Christian identity. As a consequence, in 2019, 79 percent of the Republicans still identified themselves as Christians, whereas the figure stood at 55% for the Democrats. That is a very significant political difference, pointing further to the likely moral and spiritual direction in which the country is headed, depending upon which of the two political parties is in power in Washington.

Christianity and society. Christianity at its heart (as set forth by Jesus himself) was about Godly empowerment of the individual, in the face of life's many and often quite difficult challenges. Christianity supported human life with the understanding that, with simple faith in God alone, these challenges could be met and conquered by even the least socially significant of individuals – because God himself offered his powerful support to those who simply trusted him as their Heavenly Father. God was not interested in a person's social status, as societies tend to be and do.

Christianity also demonstrated clearly (during the worst of times of Roman persecution) that individual strengthening through Divine empowerment also worked awesomely well in producing the right structuring for social as well as personal life. In fact, it was the witness of the Christians in their immense personal and social strength that impressed a morally decadent Rome to begin to look to Christianity as the solution to the decay that infected Roman life in every imaginable social area possible.

Admittedly, Christianity has been used as a civic formula for autocracy. But that was never its original nature. And from time to time reforms have swept the Christian world in order to bring the people back to the original character of the Christian faith … as Jesus himself clearly laid it out. The Protestant Reformation of the 1500s and 1600s, during which English Puritanism was founded, was just such an early example – and a critical social foundation for New England and all it stood for. Also, the Great Awakenings were key to keeping Christianity on course in the face of the natural instinct of man to want to displace Divine guidance and support with personal autonomy: the ever-present temptation to want to play God himself.

Europe looks to America. For the past 70 years, since the end of World War Two, Europe has looked to America to play the leading role in defending Western civilization – allowing Europeans to look after their own material development in the meantime. As they lost their leading position in world events, so also they lost interest in the moral-spiritual order that once had made Europe itself the center of global affairs. They were content to live to some kind of grand material, but not grand spiritual, purpose. As philosophers ranging from Aristotle to Toynbee have observed, such moral-spiritual decline was an indication of Europe's overall political-social decline as well.

America's own self-imposed decline. But America too now finds itself headed down the same moral-spiritual road as Europe. Worse, many American leaders themselves have called on Americans to take a strong stand against the supposed tyranny of Middle America. These post-modern crusaders feel the need to attack a traditional America still possessing the strong and well-tested and well-proven Christian social standards that for generations America has faithfully lived by.

But what do they actually stand for? We know what they stand against. But a society cannot survive simply on the basis of its people being against its very social-moral existence. Where is the unifying idea that will pull America together, and Western civilization with it? Who today is offering strong moral guidance to our great Western or Christian civilization?

In all of this, America seems to be asleep at the wheel, its leading political voices in Washington more intent in playing the game of crippling each other, as if Washington politics were merely a TV game show for wannabe celebrities. True leadership that would bring everyone togther at a higher moral-spiritual level seems to be in short supply.

The critical need for another "Great Awakening." We have arrived at the same point in which if our civilization is to be saved from its own self-inflicted folly, we are going to need another Divine intervention. Or else the days of American global leadership, as well as the modern Western or Christian Civilization's social-moral-spiritual leadership in the world's development, are over.

China can hardly wait for this to happen!

✳ ✳ ✳

**A CALL TO RENEW THE COVENANT WITH GOD
EXTENDED TO US THROUGH JESUS CHRIST**

So ... at this point it is of critical importance that America finds its way back to the original Covenant with God, similar to the one presented by Moses as the Hebrews were about to enter the Promised Land, and exactly the same one that Winthrop referred to in delivering his famous sermon, "City on a Hill," as the Puritans were about to depart in their ships in order to begin their great Christian experiment in America:

> *. . .   Thus stands the cause between God and us. We are entered into covenant with Him for this work. We have taken out a commission.*
>
> *. . .   if we shall neglect the observation of these articles, [and] embrace this present world and prosecute our carnal intentions, seeking great things for ourselves and our posterity, the Lord will surely break out in wrath against us, and be revenged of such a people, and make us know the price of the breach of such a covenant.*
>
> *. . .   Now the only way to avoid this shipwreck [of God's wrath], and to provide for our posterity, is to follow the counsel of Micah, to do justly, to love mercy, to walk humbly with our God. For this end, we must be knit together, in this work, as one man. We must entertain each other in brotherly affection. We must be willing to abridge ourselves of our superfluities, for the supply of others' necessities. We must delight in each other; make others' conditions our own; rejoice together, mourn together, labor and suffer together, always having before our eyes our commission and community in the work, as members of the same body.*
>
> *. . .   Beloved, there is now set before us life and death, good and evil, in that we are commanded this day to love the Lord our God, and to love one another, to walk in his ways and to keep his*

Commandments and his ordinance and his laws, and the articles of our Covenant with Him, that we may live and be multiplied, and that the Lord our God may bless us in the land whither we go to possess it.

But if our hearts shall turn away, so that we will not obey, but shall be seduced, and worship other Gods, our pleasure and profits, and serve them; it is propounded unto us this day, we shall surely perish out of the good land whither we pass over this vast sea to possess it.

Therefore let us choose life, that we and our seed may live, by obeying His voice and cleaving to Him, for He is our life and our prosperity.

Maranatha ("may our Lord come"). We are way beyond the possibility of human self-help. As a fully-confused and wandering Fourth-Generation people, our help at this point can come only from the intervention of God. And so we pray that God might come and free us from our self-inflicted folly.

But we might also add: "However, dear Lord, please do not make it hurt too much." The Great Depression of the 1930s cured us of our 1920s silliness. The toughness required of human life during the Depression got America smart real fast, and prepared the country for the enormous task of fighting both the German and the Japanese Empires at the same time. Thankfully God had intervened in order to toughen up America, or a still-silly America would have failed horribly to meet successfully the challenge of a war placed before it in 1941.

But today we have over a half-century of silliness to get over, not just ten years, as was the case following the Roaring Twenties. Thus it might take much more "toughening up" of our character than even another ten-year Great Depression to get us back to being a First-Generation people, a people once again able to take on the huge challenges that await us. We are saddled with an enormous national debt and a Secular-Socialist moral-spiritual dependency we have fallen under at home, and we face the amazing inability to focus on, or even understand, much less answer, the monumental challenges to America rising abroad.

But we are hoping that God will honor the Covenant that our ancestors once signed onto, for themselves and for the future generations to come after them. That is our fondest hope. It is, in fact, our only hope.

Maranatha!

INDEX